i TOEFL iBT® READING

New Edition

LinguaForum

New Edition TOEFL iBT® i Reading

Contents Development	LinguaForum
Project Director	Issac Kim
Project Managers	Selene Joo, Sharon SB Cho, Sue Lee
Project Assistants	Will Winchester, Chris Newton
Main Author	Craig Michael Smith
Authors	Mark West, Josephine Chung, Duvu Kim, James Kapper, Diane Gardener, Noah Williams
Proofreaders	Kyle Wilson, Aidan Hammond, Jamie Marr, Susan Kim, Paul Lee
Editing & Design	Design Yeon, Hyun Jung Cho
Audio Recording	109Sound
Publisher	Gil Ho Lee

Tel 02)590-6900 **Fax** 02)590-6901
ISBN 978-89-286-3729-4 [13740] **Price** ₩18,000

TIME Education Co. Ltd
5F Peugeot Biz Tower, 310, Gwangnaru-ro, Seongdong-gu, Seoul, 04799, Republic of KOREA

Copyright © 2017 by LinguaForum

No unauthorized photocopying

All rights reserved. No part of this book may be reproduced or transmitted in any form or by any means, electronic or mechanical, including photocopying, recording, or any other information storage and retrieval system without the written permission of the publisher.

Printed in the Republic of Korea

New Edition
iTOEFL iBT® READING

LinguaForum

Contents

i Reading Structure	6
TOEFL iBT	8
TOEFL iBT Reading	9
Study Plan	10
Diagnostic Test	12

PART A. Question Types

Chapter 01	**Vocabulary**	28
Chapter 02	**Reference**	36
Chapter 03	**Sentence Simplification**	44
Chapter 04	**Factual Information & Negative Fact**	54
Chapter 05	**Inference**	62
Chapter 06	**Rhetorical Purpose**	70
Chapter 07	**Sentence Insertion**	78
Chapter 08	**Prose Summary**	86
Chapter 09	**Fill in a Table**	98

New Edition **TOEFL iBT i Reading**

PART B. Approaching Themes

Chapter 10 **Humanities I** 112

Chapter 11 **Humanities II** 128

Chapter 12 **Life Science I** 144

Chapter 13 **Life Science II** 160

Chapter 14 **Physical Science** 176

Chapter 15 **Social Science** 192

Actual Test 1 210
Actual Test 2 222

Answer Key & Explanations A2 ~ A166

i Reading Structure

Diagnostic Test

실제 시험의 구성 및 난이도로 제작된 Diagnostic Test를 통하여 자신의 실력을 스스로 점검할 수 있도록 하였으며, 이 결과에 따라 수준에 맞는 학습을 진행할 수 있도록 하였다.

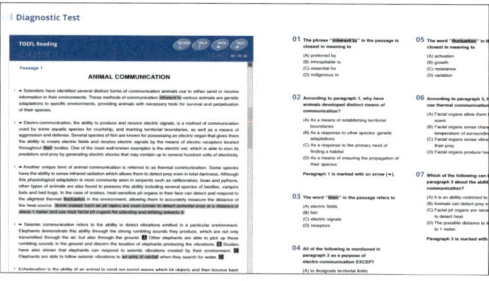

PART A _ Question Types

Keys to Solution
각 문제 유형의 문제 풀이 전략을 상세하게 학습할 수 있다.

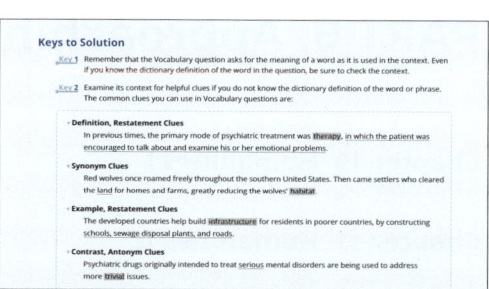

Sample Question
예시 문제를 통해 문제 풀이 전략을 구체적으로 활용해 보고 연습할 수 있다.

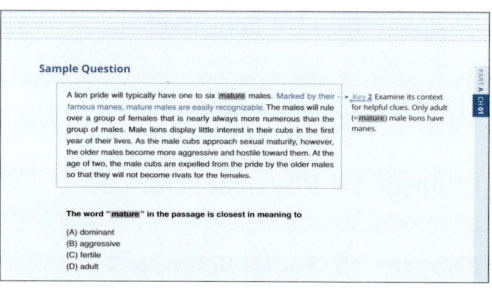

Basic Drill
각 문제 유형에 필요한 기초 스킬을 익히고 난 후, 단문 길이의 지문 및 문제를 통해 각 문제 유형을 집중적으로 연습할 수 있다.

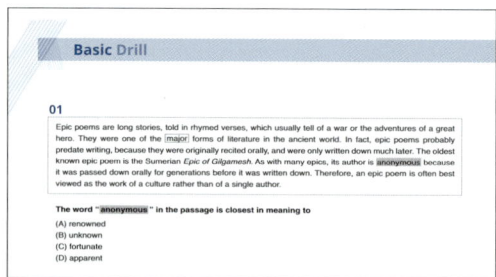

Reading Practice
실제 TOEFL iBT에서 출제되는 다양한 주제의 독해 지문들을 통해 본격적으로 독해 연습을 해 볼 수 있다.

PART B _ Approaching Themes

Reading Preview

Chapter에 수록된 지문을 학습하기에 앞서, 각 지문의 주제에 대한 배경지식을 관련 사진과 함께 제시하여, 타 시험에 비해 수준이 높은 TOEFL 지문 주제들에 대한 배경지식을 쉽게 이해할 수 있도록 하였다.

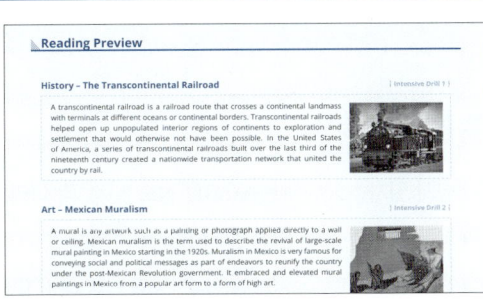

Intensive Drill

실제 TOEFL iBT에서 출제되는 주제별로 구성된 다양한 지문을 통해 충분히 독해 연습을 할 수 있도록 하였다. 각 Chapter에 3개의 세트가 수록되어 있다.

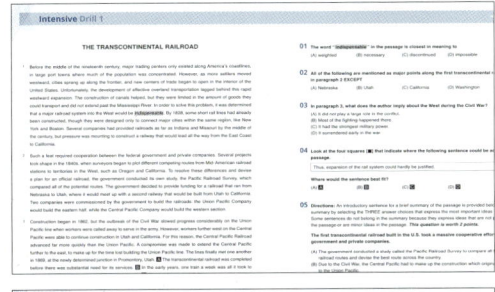

Mini Test

Intensive Drill보다 난이도가 높은 지문을 통해 여러 가지 문제 유형을 골고루 접하고 TOEFL iBT를 학습할 기회를 마련하였다. 각 Chapter에 2개의 세트가 수록되어 있다.

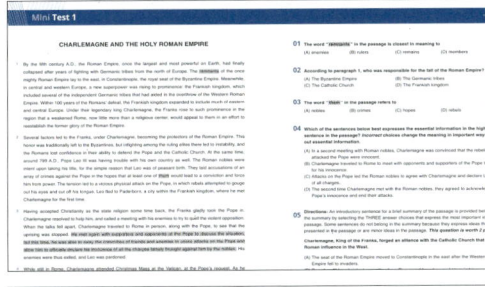

iBT Practice

실제 TOEFL iBT에서 자주 출제되는 주제의 지문을 실전과 동일한 길이와 문제로 구성하여, 실전 감각을 키울 수 있도록 하였다.

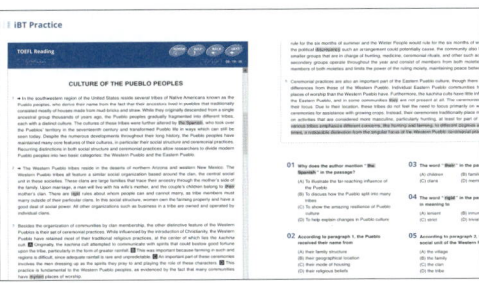

Actual Test

2회분의 Actual Test를 수록하여, 실전에서의 자신의 예상 점수를 가늠해 보고 실전 적응력을 높일 수 있도록 하였다.

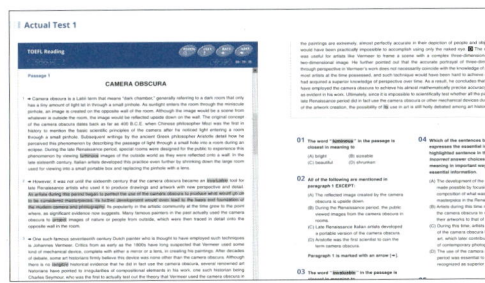

TOEFL iBT

New Edition TOEFL iBT i Reading

TOEFL iBT 시험은 대학 수준의 영어를 사용하고 이해할 수 있는 능력을 측정한다. 그리고 학술적 주제의 과제를 수행하는 데 듣기, 읽기, 말하기 및 쓰기 실력을 얼마나 잘 결합하는지를 평가한다.

■ 한국 내 응시

- **실시 일자**: 1년에 50회 정도 실시, 각 나라와 지역별로 시험일에 차이가 있음
- **시험 장소**: ETS Test Center
- **접수 방법**: 인터넷 접수: 시험일로부터 최소 7일전 인터넷으로 등록 (www.ets.org/toefl)
  전화 접수: 시험일로부터 최소 7일전 전화로 등록
- **응시료**: $185(USD)
- **지불 형식**: 신용/직불카드 – American Express®, Discover®, JCB®, MasterCard®, VISA®
  전자 수표(e-수표) 또는 PayPal® 계정
- **유효 신분증**: 여권 (유효기간, 서명 확인 필수), 주민등록증, 운전면허증, 군인신분증
- **소요 시간**: 약 4시간 30분 소요
- **성적 확인**: 시험일로부터 약 10일 후에 온라인상에서 확인 가능
  성적표 유효기간: 2년

■ 시험 영역

영역	제한 시간	지문 및 문항 수	과제
Reading	60~80분	3~4개 지문 - 지문당 12~14문항 (총 36~56문항)	대학 교재 글을 읽고 질문에 답하기
Listening	60~90분	2~3개 대화 - 대화당 5문항 4~6개 강의 - 강의당 6문항 (총 34~51문항)	강의, 교실 토론 및 대화를 듣고 질문에 답하기
휴식	10분		
Speaking	20분	독립형 2개 통합형 4개	익숙한 주제에 대한 의견을 표현하기, 읽기와 듣기 과제를 바탕으로 말하기
Writing	55분	통합형 1개 독립형 1개	읽기 및 듣기 과제를 바탕으로 글쓰기, 특정 주제에 대한 글쓰기

TOEFL iBT Reading

New Edition **TOEFL iBT i Reading**

■ Reading 구성

3개 혹은 4개의 지문으로 구성되며, 각 지문당 12~14 문제가 출제된다. 지문당 길이는 약 700단어 이다.

■ 화면 구성

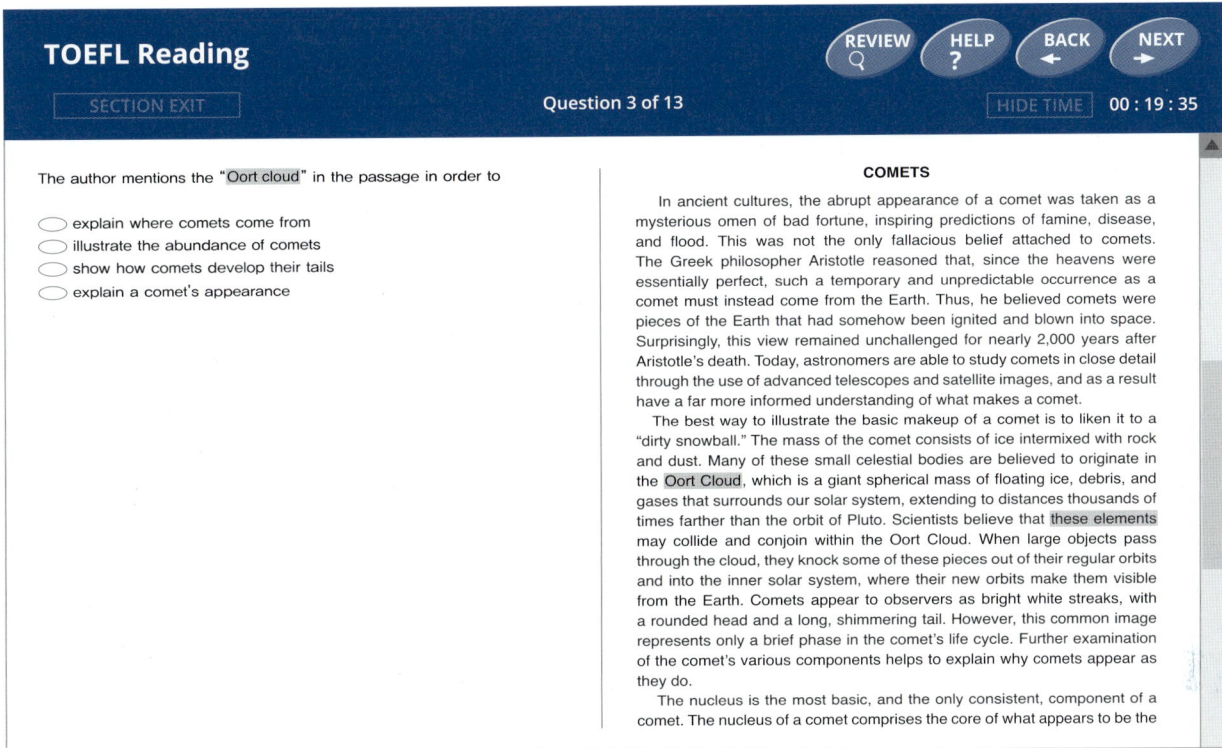

■ 문제 유형: 총 9가지 유형의 문제 출제

Vocabulary	지문 속 표현과 가장 유사한 의미의 어휘를 묻는 유형
Reference	지시어가 가리키는 대상을 묻는 유형
Sentence Simplification	주어진 문장의 핵심 정보를 가장 정확하게 재구성한 문장을 묻는 유형
Factual Information & Negative Fact	지문의 세부 정보를 묻는 유형
Inference	지문 속 정보로 가능한 추론을 묻는 유형
Rhetorical Purpose	필자의 수사학적 의도를 묻는 유형
Sentence Insertion	주어진 문장을 지문에 삽입하기에 가장 적절한 위치를 묻는 유형
Prose Summary	지문 요약을 위해 주요 내용을 묻는 유형
Fill in a Table	지문 속 정보가 해당되는 각 범주를 묻는 유형

Study Plan

■ 나에게 맞는 Study Plan 고르는 방법

방법 1
Diagnostic Test(p.12) 점수 결과에 따라 본인에게 맞는 Study Plan 사용
- 맞은 개수 28개 이상 ➡ **4-Week Study Plan**
- 맞은 개수 27개 이하 ➡ **6-Week Study Plan**

방법 2
본인에게 해당하는 항목을 골라 체크(✓)한 후, 체크 개수에 따른 Study Plan 사용
- ☐ 토플 시험을 본 적이 있다.
- ☐ 토플 점수가 80점 이상이다.
- ☐ 토플 문제 유형에 대한 지식이 있다.
- ☐ 지문의 주제를 찾을 수 있다.
- ☐ 문단끼리의 관계를 파악할 수 있다.
- ☐ 토플 Reading 문제집 한 권을 끝낸 경험이 있다.

- 체크 4개 이상 ➡ **4-Week Study Plan**
- 체크 3개 이하 ➡ **6-Week Study Plan**

■ Study Plan 100% 활용하기

4 Week Study Plan
문제 유형에 따른 문제 풀이 전략을 빠르게 파악하고 연습한 후, 실전 대비용 지문들과 실전 모의고사(Actual Test)를 통해 독해 실력을 탄탄하게 다질 수 있다. 문제 유형에 대한 기본 지식이 있는 학생들을 위한 한 달 속성 과정이다.

6 Week Study Plan
하루에 문제 유형 하나씩 학습하며 유형에 따른 문제 풀이 방법을 탄탄히 익힌다. 그 후, 짧은 지문(Intensive Drill) → 중간 지문(Mini Test) → 긴 지문(iBT Practice) 순으로 단계적인 학습을 거쳐 실전에 대한 부담감을 줄이고, 차근차근히 대비해 갈 수 있도록 구성된 과정이다.

1. Study Plan에 제시된 학습 분량을 공부한다. 최대한 Study Plan을 지키고 미루지 않도록 한다.
2. 링구아포럼 홈페이지(www.linguaforum.com)에서 제공하는 단어장과 단어테스트를 활용하여 학습한 지문의 어휘를 공부한다.
3. 정해진 학습 분량을 공부한 후, 해설집을 통해 틀린 문제의 문제 유형과 정답 관련 문장을 분석하여 오답 노트를 작성한다.
4. 학습 분량이 없는 요일을 활용하여, 한 주 동안 작성한 오답 노트를 복습한다. 자주 틀리는 문제 유형을 파악하고 PART A(Ch. 01~09)에서 관련 유형을 찾아 복습한다.
5. PART B(Ch. 10~15) 학습 시, 목차를 통해 관심 있는 배경지식 분야를 우선으로 학습할 수도 있다.

4-Week Study Plan

WEEK 1	Day 1	Day 2	Day 3	Day 4	Day 5
	Diagnostic Test	Ch. 01-02	Ch. 03-04	Ch. 05-06	Ch. 07-08

WEEK 2	Day 6	Day 7	Day 8	Day 9	Day 10
	Ch. 09	Ch. 10 Intensive Drill	Ch. 10 Mini Test & iBT Practice	Ch. 11 Intensive Drill	Ch. 11 Mini Test & iBT Practice

WEEK 3	Day 11	Day 12	Day 13	Day 14	Day 15
	Ch. 12 Intensive Drill	Ch. 12 Mini Test & iBT Practice	Ch. 13 Intensive Drill	Ch. 13 Mini Test & iBT Practice	Ch. 14 Intensive Drill

WEEK 4	Day 16	Day 17	Day 18	Day 19	Day 20
	Ch. 14 Mini Test & iBT Practice	Ch. 15 Intensive Drill	Ch. 15 Mini Test & iBT Practice	Actual Test 1	Actual Test 2

6-Week Study Plan

WEEK 1	Day 1	Day 2	Day 3	Day 4	Day 5
	Diagnostic Test	Ch. 01	Ch. 02	Ch. 03	Ch. 04

WEEK 2	Day 6	Day 7	Day 8	Day 9	Day 10
	Ch. 05	Ch. 06	Ch. 07	Ch. 08	Ch. 09

WEEK 3	Day 11	Day 12	Day 13	Day 14	Day 15
	Ch. 10 Intensive Drill	Ch. 10 Mini Test	Ch. 10 iBT Practice	Ch. 11 Intensive Drill	Ch. 11 Mini Test

WEEK 4	Day 16	Day 17	Day 18	Day 19	Day 20
	Ch. 11 iBT Practice	Ch. 12 Intensive Drill	Ch. 12 Mini Test	Ch. 12 iBT Practice	Ch. 13 Intensive Drill

WEEK 5	Day 21	Day 22	Day 23	Day 24	Day 25
	Ch. 13 Mini Test	Ch. 13 iBT Practice	Ch. 14 Intensive Drill	Ch. 14 Mini Test	Ch. 14 iBT Practice

WEEK 6	Day 26	Day 27	Day 28	Day 29	Day 30
	Ch. 15 Intensive Drill	Ch. 15 Mini Test	Ch. 15 iBT Practice	Actual Test 1	Actual Test 2

* 링구아포럼 홈페이지(www.linguaforum.com)에서 제공하는 단어장과 단어테스트를 이용하여 어휘 실력을 향상시킬 수 있습니다.

TOEFL iBT i Reading   www.linguaforum.com

Diagnostic Test

Diagnostic Test

Passage 1

ANIMAL COMMUNICATION

1 → Scientists have identified several distinct forms of communication animals use to either send or receive information in their environments. These methods of communication inherent to various animals are genetic adaptations to specific environments, providing animals with necessary tools for survival and perpetuation of their species.

2 → Electro-communication, the ability to produce and receive electric signals, is a method of communication used by some aquatic species for courtship, and marking territorial boundaries, as well as a means of aggression and defense. Several species of fish are known for possessing an electric organ that gives them the ability to create electric fields and receive electric signals by the means of electro receptors located throughout their bodies. One of the most well-known examples is the electric eel, which is able to stun its predators and prey by generating electric shocks that may contain up to several hundred volts of electricity.

3 → Another unique form of animal communication is referred to as thermal communication. Some species have the ability to sense infrared radiation which allows them to detect prey even in total darkness. Although this physiological adaptation is most commonly seen in serpents such as rattlesnakes, boas and pythons, other types of animals are also found to possess this ability including several species of beetles, vampire bats and bed bugs. In the case of snakes, heat-sensitive pit organs in their face can detect and respond to the slightest thermal fluctuation in the environment, allowing them to accurately measure the distance of the heat source. Some snakes such as pit vipers are even known to detect potential prey at a distance of about 1 meter and use their facial pit organs for orienting and striking towards it.

4 → Seismic communication refers to the ability to detect vibrations emitted in a particular environment. Elephants demonstrate this ability through the strong rumbling sounds they produce, which are not only transmitted through the air, but also through the ground. **A** Other elephants are able to pick up these rumbling sounds in the ground and discern the location of elephants producing the vibrations. **B** Studies have also shown that elephants can respond to seismic vibrations created by their environment. **C** Elephants are able to follow seismic vibrations to an area of rainfall when they search for water. **D**

5 Echolocation is the ability of an animal to send out sound waves which hit objects and then bounce back as vibrations to the animal. Consequently, these allow animals to identify where objects are located in their surroundings. Bats, toothed-whales and dolphins have all shown the ability to use echolocation. In the case of dolphins, they produce high-frequency clicks to echolocate objects nearby. In addition to determining the shape and size of an object, this ability allows dolphins to determine the speed, distance, direction of travel and even some basic facts about the internal structure of objects in the water around them. This information is critical for dolphins to find food and navigate in dark or murky waters.

01 The phrase "inherent to" in the passage is closest in meaning to

(A) preferred by
(B) inhospitable to
(C) essential for
(D) indigenous to

02 According to paragraph 1, why have animals developed distinct means of communication?

(A) As a means of establishing territorial boundaries
(B) As a response to other species' genetic adaptations
(C) As a response to the primary need of finding a habitat
(D) As a means of ensuring the propagation of their species

Paragraph 1 is marked with an arrow [➡].

03 The word "their" in the passage refers to

(A) electric fields
(B) fish
(C) electric signals
(D) receptors

04 All of the following is mentioned in paragraph 2 as a purpose of electro-communication EXCEPT

(A) to designate territorial limits
(B) to identify the location of prey
(C) to acquire a mate
(D) to attack predators

Paragraph 2 is marked with an arrow [➡].

05 The word "fluctuation" in the passage is closest in meaning to

(A) activation
(B) growth
(C) resistance
(D) variation

06 According to paragraph 3, how do snakes use thermal communication to locate prey?

(A) Facial organs allow them to detect a prey's scent.
(B) Facial organs sense changes in temperature of surrounding environments.
(C) Facial organs sense vibrations given off by their prey.
(D) Facial organs produce heat to locate prey.

07 Which of the following can be inferred from paragraph 3 about the ability to use thermal communication?

(A) It is an ability restricted to reptile species.
(B) Animals can detect prey even if blind.
(C) Facial pit organs are necessary for reptiles to detect heat.
(D) The possible distance to locate prey is up to 1 meter.

Paragraph 3 is marked with an arrow [➡].

08 Which of the sentences below best expresses the essential information in the highlighted sentence in the passage? *Incorrect* answer choices change the meaning in important ways or leave out essential information.

(A) Certain snakes can sense their prey roughly a meter away and use their facial organs to determine its location and attack it.
(B) Some snakes are able to sense the prey's location, regardless of the distance, with their facial pit organs.
(C) Determining the location of their prey is an easy job for some snakes even with prey up to one meter away from them.
(D) The use of the snake's facial pit organs is essential in determining the location of prey and catching it.

09 According to paragraph 4, how do elephants use seismic communication to locate other elephants?

(A) By detecting seismic vibrations transmitted through the water
(B) By following rainfall patterns in their environment
(C) By emitting loud rumbling cries audible to other elephants
(D) By reading rumbling sounds sent through the ground

Paragraph 4 is marked with an arrow [→].

10 Why does the author mention "an area of rainfall" in the passage?

(A) To illustrate different methods of detecting the source of rain
(B) To show how elephants use seismic vibrations from the environment for survival
(C) To emphasize the importance of rain in the elephant's survival
(D) To explain the reason why the elephants inhabit near the water source

11 The word "these" in the passage refers to

(A) animals
(B) sound waves
(C) vibrations
(D) objects

12 All of the following are mentioned in paragraph 5 as types of information acquired by echolocation EXCEPT

(A) amount of heat emitted by an object
(B) location of an object
(C) shape and size of an object
(D) internal components of an object

Paragraph 5 is marked with an arrow [→].

13 Look at the four squares [■] that indicate where the following sentence could be added to the passage.

> For example, some African elephants are able to sense underground vibrations generated by thunder during distant thunderstorms.

Where would the sentence best fit?

Click on a square [■] to add the sentence to the passage.

(A) A   (B) B   (C) C   (D) D

14 **Directions:** An introductory sentence for a brief summary of the passage is provided below. Complete the summary by selecting the THREE answer choices that express the most important ideas in the passage. Some sentences do not belong in the summary because they express ideas that are not presented in the passage or are minor ideas in the passage. ***This question is worth 2 points.***

Drag your answer choices to the spaces where they belong. To remove an answer choice, click on it. To review the passage, click **View Text**.

Several animal species have developed unique forms of communication.
-
-
-

Answer Choices	
(A) Different species of animals use different methods of communication.	(D) Methods of animal communication is vital for their survival.
(B) The primary purpose of animal communication is attack and defense.	(E) Animals' means of communication is determined by their environment.
(C) One application of animal communication is detecting prey's location.	(F) The use of communication among animals is continually evolving.

THE ORIGIN OF LANGUAGE

1 **A** Several theories have been proposed to explain why human language has evolved into the complex mechanism as it is today. **B** Although linguistic experts do not have sufficient evidence to pinpoint the exact date language came into existence, current research suggests that it first evolved around 350,000 to 150,000 years ago. **C** Some of the earliest theories put forth include humans' mimicking animal noises, which later developed into words. **D** Another theory is that nonverbal emotional vocalizations, such as gasping in surprise or screaming out in pain, gradually evolved into more specific forms of communication. In the past century, however, the debate among linguistic scientists is comprised of two main theories to explain the origin of language, namely the Continuity Theory and the Discontinuity Theory.

2 → The Continuity Theory of language evolution argues that language must have developed over time, beginning with humans' earliest ancestors, with various aspects of language developing at different stages until it resembled present speech. Supporters of this theory have made a correlation of humans' ability for abstract and complex thought and expression to Darwin's theory of evolution. This builds on the idea that language exhibits so much complexity that one cannot imagine it simply appearing from nothing. The most significant argument asserted by continuity theorists is that human language evolved from an innate ability within us and that without this innate linguistic device, we would never have developed the capacity to speak.

3 To prove their belief that language developed from our primate ancestor's innate ability for language, the proponents of the Continuity Theory point out experiments in which various kinds of non-spoken languages were taught over extended periods of time to primates. In accordance with the researchers' claim that even though the primates do not speak in the wild, they have a mind inherently capable of learning language, primates were able to learn how to communicate different kinds of situations, primarily with the researchers, but also with fellow primates and their offspring by means of sign language. Furthermore, although no primates have been able to learn any spoken language, they have demonstrated a degree of language capacity by using random symbols to denote physical objects.

4 → On the other hand, the Discontinuity Theory suggests that language must have appeared suddenly within humankind's history. Supporters of this theory postulate this may have come about due to a genetic mutation in humans, which was subsequently passed on through their ancestors, eventually turning into an inherent ability.

5 → In order to support this theory, several linguists conducted research which revealed that the gene essential to the development of language and speech is significantly different in humans compared to other primates. They assert that the amino-acid composition of the gene changed rapidly at roughly the same time humans began to develop the ability to speak. They also discovered and claimed that this gene functions and looks different in humans and primates, meaning that the human brain is wired for language use, while the primate's brain is not. Despite their strong claims about a genetic mutation creating the capacity for speech in humans, the specific event, if any, that could have caused such a genetic mutation is still not known.

15 The word "it" in the passage refers to

(A) evidence
(B) date
(C) language
(D) mechanism

16 The word "mimicking" in the passage is closest in meaning to

(A) emitting
(B) imitating
(C) repeating
(D) chanting

17 Why does the author mention "nonverbal emotional vocalizations" in the passage?

(A) To show one of the arguments regarding the origin of human language
(B) To differentiate the use of communication between humans and animals
(C) To compare the evolution of communication between humans and animals
(D) To elucidate the first incident of nonverbal human vocalization in history

18 According to paragraph 2, what do supporters of the Continuity Theory believe about language evolution?

(A) Not all humans have the ability to acquire linguistic skills.
(B) Language use in human suddenly appeared at a certain stage of evolution.
(C) Humans have developed their specific language ability over a short time.
(D) Humans possess an inborn ability to use language.

Paragraph 2 is marked with an arrow [➜].

19 Why does the author mention "sign language" in the passage?

(A) To highlight the importance of non-spoken language among primates
(B) To assert humans' various communicative tools
(C) To demonstrate that primates also have a linguistic device
(D) To illustrate the complexity of the primates' ability to communicate

20 The word "random" in the passage is closest in meaning to

(A) original
(B) explicit
(C) unsystematic
(D) crude

21 The word "which" in the passage refers to

(A) Discontinuity Theory
(B) language
(C) inherent ability
(D) genetic mutation

22 According to paragraph 4, what do supporters of the Discontinuity Theory believe about human's acquisition of language?

(A) It is a result of a genetic mutation in humans.
(B) It is a result of a recessive gene in humans.
(C) It is a result of a learned behavior in humans.
(D) It is a result of a ceaseless effort in humans.

Paragraph 4 is marked with an arrow [➜].

23 The passage supports all of the following statements about the Discontinuity Theory EXCEPT:

(A) Only the human brain is wired for language use, not the primate brain.
(B) The ability to use language is an inheritable ability.
(C) A sudden mutation occurred as a result of environmental adaptation.
(D) Language appeared suddenly in the evolution of human.

24 Which of the sentences below best expresses the essential information in the highlighted sentence in the passage? *Incorrect* answer choices change the meaning in important ways or leave out essential information.

(A) Supporters of the Discontinuity Theory carried out significant research about the nature of the human language gene.
(B) The gene necessary for language in humans has been shown by supporters of the Discontinuity Theory to be different from primates'.
(C) Researchers still argue over whether the genetic makeup for the language is different between humans and primates.
(D) Researchers are still not ready to prove why the language gene in humans is different from primates'.

25 Which of the following can be inferred from paragraph 5 about the Discontinuity Theory?

(A) The existence of amino acid guarantees language use in a species.
(B) Supporters of the theory are unconcerned about the cause of the genetic mutation.
(C) The evolutions of humans and primates are not correlated.
(D) Humans are genetically predisposed to language while primates are not.

Paragraph 5 is marked with an arrow [→].

26 Look at the four squares [■] that indicate where the following sentence could be added to the passage.

> This is roughly the same time when modern Homo sapiens appeared.

Where would the sentence best fit?

Click on a square [■] to add the sentence to the passage.

(A) A (B) B (C) C (D) D

27 **Directions:** Select the appropriate sentences from the answer choices and match them to the type of theory to which they relate. TWO of the answer choices will NOT be used. ***This question is worth 3 points.***

Drag your answer choices to the spaces where they belong. To remove an answer choice, click on it. To review the passage, click on **View Text**.

Answer Choices	Continuity Theory
(A) Language developed at different stages over a period of time. (B) Primates are able to use complex language as humans do. (C) Primates have been shown to demonstrate inherent language abilities.	• • •
(D) Language appeared suddenly in the course of human history.	**Discontinuity Theory**
(E) The ability for language can be taught in a lab. (F) Language evolved from an innate human ability. (G) Language was caused by a genetic mutation.	• •

THE CODE OF HAMMURABI

1   One of the first known records of a penal code was established by Hammurabi more than 3,000 years ago. Hammurabi, who reigned from 1792 to 1750 B.C., expanded the city-state of Babylon along the Euphrates River to unite all of Mesopotamia, an area in what is now modern-day Iraq. Hammurabi is best known for the creation of a new code of Babylonian law, referred to as the Code of Hammurabi. This code is a series of 282 laws and standards which instituted rules for a variety of social issues, as well as laying down fines and punishments for infractions of the code.

2   ➡ As one of the earliest surviving codes of law ever recorded in history, it was inscribed on a stele, which was a massive, black, finger-shaped, stone pillar. These were erected as a monument, usually for funerary or commemorative purposes. At the top of it there is a carving that depicts Hammurabi receiving the laws from the Babylonian gods. It proclaims that the gods chose Hammurabi to bring the laws to his people, in much the same way Moses was instructed in the Bible to bring the Ten Commandments to his people. During Hammurabi's reign, the code was installed in a public place, although researchers assert the fact that very few people would have actually been literate at that time.

3   ➡ The laws established by Hammurabi cover a wide array of social spheres, ranging from administrative law to family law. Laws were also prevalent in the making of contracts, payments, liability, property, employment-related issues and military service. **A** Hammurabi made sure that each offense described in the code had a very specific accompanying punishment. **B** The punishments, which were beatings, fines, exile and execution, tended to be extremely harsh compared to modern judiciary standards and often resulted in death and physical disfigurement. **C** The punishments often followed the philosophy of "an eye for an eye, a tooth for a tooth." **D** These rather brutal and barbaric practices were meant to instill fear inside the Babylonian people so they would not ever consider breaking the law.

4   ➡ Different standards of justice, however, were set forth for each of the three classes of Babylonian society: those with property, freedmen and slaves. For instance, if a doctor killed a rich patient his hand would be cut off, but if he killed a slave, he was only required to pay a sum of money as a fine.

5   ➡ The legacy of Hammurabi's code still has very significant implications today. He is regarded as the man who created the earliest legal code which sought humanitarian application of law and due to this reputation as one of the pioneering lawgivers, Hammurabi's depiction can even be found in several U.S. government buildings, most notably the U.S. Supreme Court building as Hammurabi is featured on the marble bas relief of historic lawgivers on the south wall of the courtroom.

28 The word "expanded" in the passage is closest in meaning to

(A) enlarged
(B) curtailed
(C) conquered
(D) reformed

29 The word "it" in the passage refers to

(A) funerary
(B) stele
(C) pillar
(D) code of law

30 The word "depicts" in the passage is closest in meaning to

(A) commemorates
(B) worships
(C) portrays
(D) degrades

31 According to paragraph 2, who chose Hammurabi to give the laws to the Babylonians?

(A) Moses
(B) Mesopotamians
(C) The public
(D) Babylonian gods

Paragraph 2 is marked with an arrow [➜].

32 Why does the author mention "the Bible" in the passage?

(A) To show similarity in creation between the Code of Hammurabi and the Ten Commandments
(B) To give more weight to the importance of the Code of Hammurabi in comparison to the Bible
(C) To underline the god's role in both the cases of Hammurabi and Moses
(D) To contrast two different historical figures' achievements

33 Which of the following can be inferred from paragraph 2 about the code of Hammurabi?

(A) It was disclosed to the public on a special occasion.
(B) It could be read by few people.
(C) It was installed in most public places.
(D) It stated Hammurabi was a god.

Paragraph 2 is marked with an arrow [➜].

34 The word "cover" in the passage is closest in meaning to

(A) affect
(B) include
(C) reassess
(D) criticize

35 Based on the information in paragraph 3, which of the following is NOT mentioned as a punishment in Hammurabi's code?

(A) Exile
(B) Execution
(C) Fine
(D) Imprisonment

Paragraph 3 is marked with an arrow [→].

36 Which of the sentences below best expresses the essential information in the highlighted sentence in the passage? *Incorrect* answer choices change the meaning in important ways or leave out essential information.

(A) It is still believed that the barbaric codes are the reasons for low crime rates in Babylon.
(B) The purpose of the harsh punishments was to prevent Babylonians from committing a crime.
(C) The fear of cruel punishment effectively lowered the crime rates among the Babylonians.
(D) Because of the harsh punishments, no Babylonians were willing to plot against Hammurabi.

37 The word "he" in the passage refers to

(A) patient
(B) slave
(C) freedman
(D) doctor

38 In paragraph 4, all of the following are mentioned as classes in Babylonian society EXCEPT

(A) slaves
(B) property owners
(C) women
(D) freedmen

Paragraph 4 is marked with an arrow [→].

39 Which of the following can be inferred from paragraph 5 about Hammurabi?

(A) His code is still in use today.
(B) Hammurabi is still honored today.
(C) Hammurabi failed to make his city, Babylon, prosper.
(D) The judicial system in the U.S. reflects his code.

Paragraph 5 is marked with an arrow [→].

40 Look at the four squares [■] that indicate where the following sentence could be added to the passage.

> An example of this philosophy is if a man harms another man, then he too should be harmed.

Where would the sentence best fit?

Click on a square [■] to add the sentence to the passage.

(A) A   (B) B   (C) C   (D) D

41 Directions: An introductory sentence for a brief summary of the passage is provided below. Complete the summary by selecting the THREE answer choices that express the most important ideas in the passage. Some sentences do not belong in the summary because they express ideas that are not presented in the passage or are minor ideas in the passage. ***This question is worth 2 points.***

The first known record of a penal code is the Code of Hammurabi.
•
•
•

Answer Choices	
(A) Hammurabi expanded his empire along the Euphrates River to Mesopotamia.	(D) The pillar of the Code of Hammurabi was erected as a monument.
(B) The depiction on the stele says the code was passed from the Babylonian gods to Hammurabi.	(E) The Code of Hammurabi is very cruel and specific to crime.
(C) The punishments of the Code of Hammurabi often included death and physical disfigurement.	(F) Hammurabi's achievement of creating the first legal code is still highly regarded.

TOEFL iBT i Reading   www.linguaforum.com

PART A
Question Types

Chapter 01   Vocabulary
Chapter 02   Reference
Chapter 03   Sentence Simplification
Chapter 04   Factual Information & Negative Fact
Chapter 05   Inference
Chapter 06   Rhetorical Purpose
Chapter 07   Sentence Insertion
Chapter 08   Prose Summary
Chapter 09   Fill in a Table

Chapter 01　Vocabulary

Vocabulary questions ask you to find the synonym of a word or phrase given in the passage. In order to answer these questions, you need to understand the context or the situation of the passage. If you cannot find the perfect synonym, you need to find the vocabulary word choice with the most similar meaning to the given word or phrase. There are 3-5 Vocabulary questions for each passage. This question is worth 1 point.

How the Question is Worded

☐ The word/phrase "_____" in the passage is closest in meaning to

Keys to Solution

Key 1　Remember that the Vocabulary question asks for the meaning of a word as it is used in the context. Even if you know the dictionary definition of the word in the question, be sure to check the context.

Key 2　Examine its context for helpful clues if you do not know the dictionary definition of the word or phrase. The common clues you can use in Vocabulary questions are:

> **+ Definition, Restatement Clues**
> In previous times, the primary mode of psychiatric treatment was therapy, in which the patient was encouraged to talk about and examine his or her emotional problems.
>
> **+ Synonym Clues**
> Red wolves once roamed freely throughout the southern United States. Then came settlers who cleared the land for homes and farms, greatly reducing the wolves' habitat.
>
> **+ Example, Restatement Clues**
> The developed countries help build infrastructure for residents in poorer countries, by constructing schools, sewage disposal plants, and roads.
>
> **+ Contrast, Antonym Clues**
> Psychiatric drugs originally intended to treat serious mental disorders are being used to address more trivial issues.
>
> **+ Inference Clues**
> The program was canceled after the reporters were found guilty of unethically using a number of methods to get their information.

Sample Question

> A lion pride will typically have one to six **mature** males. Marked by their famous manes, mature males are easily recognizable. The males will rule over a group of females that is nearly always more numerous than the group of males. Male lions display little interest in their cubs in the first year of their lives. As the male cubs approach sexual maturity, however, the older males become more aggressive and hostile toward them. At the age of two, the male cubs are expelled from the pride by the older males so that they will not become rivals for the females.

Key 2 Examine its context for helpful clues. Only adult (= mature) male lions have manes.

The word "mature" in the passage is closest in meaning to

(A) dominant
(B) aggressive
(C) fertile
(D) adult

Answer & Explanations

Answer Book p. A2

(D)
Find the helpful clues from the supportive sentences near the target vocabulary. You can find an inference clue in the following sentence: "Marked by their famous manes, mature males are easily recognizable." You can infer the meaning of the word mature is "grown-up" or "adult" because only adult male lions have manes.

Basic Drill

01

Epic poems are long stories, told in rhymed verses, which usually tell of a war or the adventures of a great hero. They were one of the major forms of literature in the ancient world. In fact, epic poems probably predate writing, because they were originally recited orally, and were only written down much later. The oldest known epic poem is the Sumerian *Epic of Gilgamesh*. As with many epics, its author is anonymous because it was passed down orally for generations before it was written down. Therefore, an epic poem is often best viewed as the work of a culture rather than of a single author.

The word "anonymous" in the passage is closest in meaning to

(A) renowned
(B) unknown
(C) fortunate
(D) apparent

02

Rocks can essentially be classified into three types according to how they are formed. Sedimentary rock, such as limestone, is formed from small particles that have worn away. As these particles pile up, the pressure compacts them to form solid layers. A second type, metamorphic rock, refers to rock that has changed its chemical and physical composition due to intense heat and pressure. Marble and slate are common examples of metamorphic rock. The third type is igneous rock, which is formed through an exothermic reaction, the loss of heat. A common example is basalt, which is formed when molten lava cools.

The phrase "worn away" in the passage is closest in meaning to

(A) eroded
(B) compressed
(C) stuck together
(D) heated up

Vocab Quiz

The word ☐ in the passage is closest in meaning to

01 major	☐ negligible	☐ main	☐ varied
02 common	☐ unique	☐ notable	☐ typical

03

Until about 1100 AD, Dorset culture was widespread throughout most of the Canadian Arctic and the west coast of Greenland. Over the next 300 or so years, however, the culture shrank and eventually disappeared. Theories for its disappearance vary. The predominant theory involves the Thule people, the ancestors of modern-day Inuit, who began to migrate east around 1200 AD. The Thule possessed more advanced weapons, such as bows and arrows, and were better hunters compared to the Dorset. It is also thought that the Thule may have carried diseases which the Dorset were susceptible to. Anthropologists believe these two factors contributed to the decline of Dorset culture.

The phrase " susceptible to " in the passage is closest in meaning to

(A) conducive to
(B) immune to
(C) responsible for
(D) vulnerable to

04

The New England and middle colonies were at a relative disadvantage with regard to their lack of staples to exchange for English finished goods, but the abundance of their own shipping and mercantile enterprises worked in their favor. This was not to the liking of the British, who wished to ensure their own dominance in shipping and their importance as the sole lifeline to the colonies. After 1660, the English government raised prohibitive duties against certain major colonial exports. This hit the New York and New England colonies especially hard, and resulted in an unfavorable trade balance.

The word " unfavorable " in the passage is closest in meaning to

(A) promising
(B) encouraging
(C) adverse
(D) inevitable

Vocab Quiz

The word ☐ in the passage is closest in meaning to

03 shrank	☐ dwindled	☐ changed	☐ thrived
04 lack	☐ deficiency	☐ quality	☐ richness

Basic Drill

05

Since it was first diagnosed in 1981, AIDS has steadily spread into an epidemic across the United States. There are approximately one million Americans, or 0.06 percent of the total population, currently living with HIV, the viral precursor to full-blown AIDS. Those infections are unevenly distributed throughout society, however. African-Americans make up nearly 50 percent of all cases of HIV, despite the fact that they account for only 13 percent of the population. The statistics for African-American women are particularly grim, with African-Americans making up 72 percent of all female virus carriers. Infection rates among Latin-Americans, the other major minority group in America, are similarly lopsided.

The word "distributed" in the passage is closest in meaning to

(A) treated
(B) weighed
(C) prevented
(D) disseminated

Vocab Quiz

The word ☐ in the passage is closest in meaning to

05 steadily   ☐ continuously   ☐ soon   ☐ quickly

06

One of the most famous architects in history, Frank Lloyd Wright is remembered for his emphasizing the dictum, "Form follows function." That motto is the basis of "functionalism," which gave rise to Wright's own design for the Guggenheim Museum in New York City. One of the world's most famous art museums, the Guggenheim Museum is built around a great helical gallery several stories in height. The gallery comprises a broad ramp along which works of art are displayed. Thus, the building's form — a structure built around a broad, helical ramp — complements its function, which is to display a large number of exhibits within a limited space and in an easily accessible setting.

The word "comprises" in the passage is closest in meaning to

(A) distinguishes
(B) consists of
(C) individuates
(D) puts emphasis on

Vocab Quiz

The word ☐ in the passage is closest in meaning to

| 06 complements | ☐ embodies | ☐ intensifies | ☐ supplements |

AGE OF THE EARTH

1. Calculating the age of the Earth has been a problem that philosophers, scientists, and historians have been tackling for ages. Before the advent of modern-day radiometric dating, pinpointing the age of the Earth was open to great interpretation.

2. Though many had put an age to the Earth, the first to employ a scientific approach was Lord Kelvin in the nineteenth century. His estimate of 100 million years was based on his calculations of heat transfer within the Earth and from the Sun to the Earth. However, the mathematical model he developed did not include nuclear fusion, which creates the heat in the Sun, or plate tectonics — scientific discoveries that were not made until much later. Nevertheless, though his estimate was incorrect, it is recognized as one of the first to employ the scientific method in determining the age of the Earth.

3. In 1899, Irish physicist John Joly proposed using the salinity of the world's oceans to calculate the age of the ocean, and by extension, the age of the Earth. Theorizing that the salt in the ocean must have come from the erosion of the land into the sea, he proposed that the ocean's age could be calculated by knowing the amount of salt that is added each year. Using this approach, Joly calculated the age of the world's oceans to be between 80 to 100 million years. Though accepted as the most compelling idea at first, his approach was soon criticized for being inaccurate. However, his idea of measuring elements of matter on the Earth drove him and other scientists to consider new possibilities.

4. With the discovery of radiation in 1896, scientists began to devise ever more accurate means of measurement. In 1913, British geologist Arthur Holmes developed a method to measure the age of minerals using radiometric dating. His initial estimates put the Earth's age at around 1.6 billion years. Yet as he refined his method, his estimate of the Earth's age continued to grow.

5. Since Holmes' discovery, scientists have developed and refined the technique of radiometric dating to a great degree. Today, radiometric dating has put the age of the Earth to be 4.56 billion years. But this is still much younger than the universe, which is estimated to have come into being 13.7 billion years ago.

|Vocabulary|

01 The word "Nevertheless" in the passage is closest in meaning to

(A) Otherwise
(B) However
(C) Finally
(D) Consequently

|Vocabulary|

02 The word "proposed" in the passage is closest in meaning to

(A) suggested
(B) objected to
(C) persisted in
(D) finished

|Vocabulary|

03 The phrase "most compelling" in the passage is closest in meaning to

(A) most dangerous
(B) easiest
(C) strongest
(D) most unexpected

|Reference|

04 The word "this" in the passage refers to

(A) Holmes' discovery
(B) radiometric dating
(C) age of the Earth
(D) universe

|Factual Information|

05 According to the passage, which of the following is true of John Joly?

(A) He developed the theory of radiometric dating.
(B) He was the first to use the scientific method in calculating the age of the Earth.
(C) He failed to include nuclear fusion in his theory.
(D) He calculated the ocean's age to determine the age of the Earth.

Chapter 02   Reference

In English, instead of repeating the same nouns or noun phrases, we use reference words. This helps the passage to be read more easily and to flow more smoothly. Reference questions test your ability to figure out what the pronouns, noun phrases, or other reference words refer to in the passage. There are 0-2 Reference questions for each passage. This question is worth 1 point.

How the Question is Worded

☐ The word/phrase "_____" in the passage refers to

Keys to Solution

Key 1 Carefully read the sentence that contains the pronoun and check the surrounding text for the referent.

Key 2 Substitute the answer choice you chose in place of the pronoun to see if the sentence preserves its original meaning. The correct referent will be the only logical replacement for the pronoun.

Key 3 The common referent types you can find in Reference questions are:

> + **Personal Pronouns: it, its, they, their, them, etc.**
>   Jazz is a mixture of many different kinds of music. It is a combination of the music of West Africa, the work songs the slaves sang, and religious music.
>
> + **Demonstrative Pronouns: this, that, these, those, etc.**
>   Some architects have taken great steps to design buildings that include trees, parks or gardens. These can be incorporated either in the building's vicinity or more directly into the building's design.
>
> + **Demonstrative Adjectives: this, that, these, those, etc. (+ term, problem, condition, etc.)**
>   A centenarian is a person who has lived longer than the age of 100 years. This term has also been used interchangeably with longevity, since global life expectancies are generally less than 100 years.
>
> + **Indefinite Pronouns: some, others, one, another, etc.**
>   Simply put, energy cannot be created or destroyed. Energy may change forms, or it may be transferred from one object to another, but there is always the same amount of total energy.
>
> + **Relative Pronouns: who, which, that, etc.**
>   Nylon had many advantages: it was tough and stiff, it tended to keep its shape, and moisture could not soak into it, which discouraged the growth of bacteria.

Sample Question

> When people collect in an area to settle down, the area of their settlement can be distinguished based on various criteria. One of the main factors that distinguish the area of their settlement is their population. It creates a settlement hierarchy which sorts human settlements by the size of them. For instance, a hamlet describes a tiny population of less than 100 people. Several hamlets could form a community, having essential service facilities such as hospitals or schools. This community is called a village. A town contains several villages, with a population ranging from at least 1,000 to 20,000 at most.

Key 1 Carefully read the sentence that contains them and check the surrounding text for the referent.

The word "them" in the passage refers to

(A) service facilities
(B) people
(C) factors
(D) settlements

Key 2 Substitute the answer choice you chose in place of the pronoun to see if the sentence preserves its original meaning.

Answer & Explanations   Answer Book p. A8

(D)
According to the previous sentence, "the size of them" means "their(the settlements') population."
Therefore, the word them refers to "settlements."

Basic Drill

01

The first law of thermodynamics is one of the most fundamental laws of the physical world. The first part of the first law of thermodynamics states that energy must be conserved at all times, which is known as the law of conservation of energy. Simply put, energy cannot be created or destroyed. Energy may change forms, or it may be transferred from one object to another, but there is always the same amount of total energy. An important concept in understanding this is the concept of a closed system. A closed system is a set of objects that are not influenced by anything outside of that system. Within a closed system, energy cannot be created or destroyed, but energy may be added to or taken out of a closed system.

The word "this" in the passage refers to

(A) closed system
(B) amount of total energy
(C) law of the thermodynamics
(D) law of conservation of energy

02

The most important scientific tools for astronomers are telescopes. This is demonstrated by the fact that the first major discoveries about the solar system, those of Galileo, accompanied the invention of the telescope. As telescopes have increased in power over the centuries, they have allowed astronomers to make more and more discoveries about the nature of the universe. The first telescopes used glass lenses to focus their light, but most modern telescopes now use mirrors as their major light amplifiers. In a lens telescope, the light must pass through the lens, so the lens must be entirely perfect. But in a mirror telescope, the light simply bounces off the mirror. This means that only the surface of the mirror must be perfect, making it much easier to manufacture large mirrors.

The word "they" in the passage refers to

(A) discoveries
(B) scientific tools
(C) telescopes
(D) centuries

Vocab Quiz

The word ☐ in the passage is closest in meaning to

01 fundamental ☐ sophisticated ☐ difficult ☐ basic
02 nature ☐ detail ☐ attribute ☐ mystery

03

The túngara frog, an indigenous amphibian in Central America, is well known for its distinctive breeding behavior. In order to seduce females, male frogs produce two types of mating calls distinguished by their complexity: a basic one and a complex one. The former one merely consists of a whine, which is sufficient to bring in a female. However, as more complex mating calls can attract more females, males conspicuously add chucks to the whine calls. While making these whine-chuck calls in shallow pools on the forest floor, male túngara frogs leave ripples on the water surface. Although these efforts are much more efficient in grasping the attention of females, male frogs also make themselves vulnerable by leaving physical traces that can draw the unwanted attention of predators.

The word " themselves " in the passage refers to

(A) male frogs
(B) females
(C) calls
(D) predators

04

It is reasonable to suppose that speech was a gradual outgrowth of the system of communication used by our pre-human ancestors — calls, gestures, or a combination of the two. In order for human speech to arise from these systems, however, they first had to undergo significant development. Each ape call is mutually exclusive; one call cannot convey two ideas at the same time. For example, there may be one vocalization that means "food" and another that means "danger." If a chimp notices a ripe banana, but at the same time spots a leopard waiting to pounce, it can send only one of those messages to its fellows, because a call system lacks a way of combining the messages "food" and "danger." Speech, on the other hand, permits such combinations.

The word " another " in the passage refers to

(A) vocalization
(B) food
(C) chimp
(D) danger

Vocab Quiz

The word ☐ in the passage is closest in meaning to

03 indigenous	☐ endangered	☐ notorious	☐ native
04 permits	☐ allows	☐ refines	☐ excels

Basic Drill

05

From the very start, the culture of the American colonies was significantly different from its English mother culture. Many of what are seen as "American values" were present from the time of the first colonies. A good example would be the importance that American culture places on independence and individuality. These values played a large role in the shaping of America in a number of aspects.

The first would be the reformation of religion among the early settlers. It is well known that the first settlers were largely motivated by their desire for religious freedom in their choice to come over. Specifically, they felt that church officials in England held too much power over the members of the church by enforcing strict religious obedience. The early settlers practiced a form of Christianity that taught that it was the individual's responsibility to develop his or her own understanding of religion, and rejected the way of the Anglican Church in England, where only priests could interpret the Bible.

The sense of individuality and independence did not just extend to its impact on the religious life in Americans. It also laid the foundation for American democracy as people began to question a person's right to rule another. Instead of following the repressive laws of Britain, America developed its own balance between liberty and equality and eventually adopted the Constitution of the United States of America in 1788, the world's first formal blueprint for a modern democracy.

The phrase "The first" in the passage refers to

(A) value
(B) aspect
(C) independence
(D) role

Vocab Quiz

The word ☐ in the passage is closest in meaning to

05 impact   ☐ influence   ☐ cause   ☐ grip

06

Eratosthenes, one of the fathers of Greek geometry, was most interested in devising a system of latitude and longitude for navigation. Such a system would allow merchants to find their location accurately at sea. In order to do this, however, Eratosthenes first needed to know the distance around the Earth. At the time, this was impossible to measure through direct observation.

So instead, Eratosthenes resorted to the rules of geometry to solve the problem. As a young man, he had noticed that at noon on the longest day of the summer, the sun did not cast a shadow in his hometown of Cyrene. This meant that the sun was directly overhead. Later, when he studied in Alexandria, he noticed that the sun did in fact cast a shadow at noon on the longest day of the summer. Using a pole and string, he measured the angle of the shadow, which was about 7 degrees. From this, Eratosthenes knew that the distance from Cyrene to Alexandria was also 7 degrees of the Earth's 360-degree circumference, or about 2 percent of the total distance around the Earth. Eratosthenes came up with a figure of 47,000 kilometers as the distance around the Earth. The true distance is 40,008 kilometers. The inaccuracy in his number comes from the fact that he could not accurately measure the distance between the two cities.

The phrase "the problem" in the passage refers to

(A) the inability to develop a reliable navigation system
(B) the inability to find practical uses for geometry
(C) the inability to directly measure the distance around the Earth
(D) the inability to chart accurate locations at sea

Vocab Quiz

The phrase ☐ in the passage is closest in meaning to

06 resorted to   ☐ supported   ☐ misled   ☐ turned to

Reading Practice

ECONOMIES OF THE TANG AND SONG DYNASTIES

1   The economies of the Chinese Tang and Song Dynasties flourished for more than 600 years from the seventh century to the late thirteenth century. The population of China began to explode during this time, fueling advancements in technology, as well as an economic revolution. During the Tang Dynasty (618-907 C.E.) the government paid much attention to the development of agriculture and irrigation, which in turn led to greater efficiency in agricultural production for trading with neighboring countries. This dynasty also saw significant growth in the handicraft industry, most notably with silk, as well as pottery, paper-making, and ship-building.

2   The Song Dynasty (960-1276 C.E.) further expanded these industrial developments and realized that huge sums of money were to be made by increasing the trade of these products. As a result, they established numerous markets along the borders of their Northern neighbors and pushed forward with massive sea trade routes, primarily with their Korean and Japanese neighbors, but also with regions located as far away as Eastern Africa. In exchange for items such as copper coins, silk, porcelain, spices, tea, and printed books, the Song Dynasty received silver and animals such as horses, camels, and sheep.

3   However, as trade in the Tang and Song Dynasties increased exponentially, merchants were faced with the problem of cumbersome modes of currency. For hundreds of years, bronze or copper coins had been used as the basic unit of currency in China, each coin having a hole in the middle to allow large amounts of coins to be strung together for larger transactions. Unfortunately, as these were extremely heavy to carry, Chinese merchants from the Tang Dynasty eventually developed the idea of producing the world's first paper currency to mitigate the burden of carrying around large bunches of coins. As this new currency form began to take precedence, deposit shops were set up in the kingdom, where merchants were able to acquire receipts of deposit certificates for money or goods they left in these shops. Authorities in the early Song period permitted a select few shops a monopoly on the issuing of deposit certificates, but by the twelfth century, the government took charge of the deposit system and produced the world's first government-issued paper money.

| Vocabulary |

01 The word "flourished" in the passage is closest in meaning to

(A) thrived
(B) shrank
(C) rebounded
(D) revolutionized

| Sentence Simplification |

02 Which of the sentences below best expresses the essential information in the highlighted sentence in the passage? *Incorrect* answer choices change the meaning in important ways or leave out essential information.

(A) Although they already had markets in Northern countries, the majority of their income came from the huge sea trade routes created with their Japanese and Korean neighbors.
(B) Ultimately, they chose to increase trade with their Northern neighbors, because they had difficulty expanding their sea trade routes with Japan, Korea, and several East African countries.
(C) Consequently, in addition to creating sea trade routes with neighbors both close and far away, markets were set up for trade with their Northern neighbors.
(D) The expansion of sea trade routes to Japan, Korea, and Africa was the result of a decrease in the trade of goods and products along the Northern border.

| Vocabulary |

03 The word "cumbersome" in the passage is closest in meaning to

(A) innovative
(B) burdensome
(C) rampant
(D) inferior

| Reference |

04 The word "they" in the passage refers to

(A) receipts
(B) merchants
(C) authorities
(D) deposit certificates

| Factual Information |

05 According to paragraph 3, how did Chinese merchants solve the problem of carrying around large amounts of money?

(A) By forcing the government to develop a new currency
(B) By trading in smaller amounts with neighboring countries
(C) By establishing a new value for their currency
(D) By creating a new, lighter form of their currency

Chapter 03 Sentence Simplification

Sentence Simplification questions ask you to find the best restatement of key information from long and complex sentences. To answer these questions, you will need not only a firm grasp of English grammar, but also the ability to restate information without changing its meaning. There is 0-1 Sentence Simplification question for each passage. This question is worth 1 point.

How the Question is Worded

☐ Which of the sentences below best expresses the essential information in the highlighted sentence in the passage? *Incorrect* answer choices change the meaning in important ways or leave out essential information.

Keys to Solution

Key 1 Divide the highlighted sentence into meaningful parts to grasp its correct meaning.

Key 2 Identify key ideas and eliminate unimportant information. Information that provides examples or equivalent ideas, such as appositive phrases, is unimportant information.

Key 3 Decide which answer choice best paraphrases only the key information from the original sentence. You need to understand how key ideas relate to one another.

Key 4 Eliminate answer choices if they
- leave out important pieces of information
- contain information that is not mentioned in the original sentence
- confuse the relationship between the ideas
- generally alter the meaning of the original sentence

Sample Question

Hummingbirds are a unique family of bird species. Found only in the Western Hemisphere, hummingbirds are the smallest birds in the world, with some species being as small as 6 centimeters and weighing as little as 5 grams. Like most small animals, hummingbirds lead extremely active lives. They visit hundreds of flowers daily to eat nectar, a sweet liquid inside certain flowers, at a rate of nearly twice their bodyweight, but they also catch insects and spiders now and then to satisfy their nutritional needs, as nectar is a poor source of nutrients.

Which of the sentences below best expresses the essential information in the highlighted sentence in the passage? *Incorrect* **answer choices change the meaning in important ways or leave out essential information.**

(A) Hummingbirds visit flowers every day, as they need to consume twice of their bodyweight in sweet liquid to meet their nutritional needs.
(B) Hummingbirds sometimes prey on insects and spiders for nutrients in addition to drinking nectar from flowers every day.
(C) Hummingbirds are in a constant search for nectar and insects, as they need to consume twice the amount of their own bodyweight daily.
(D) The essential nutrients hummingbirds need can be fulfilled by either consuming nectar or consuming insects and spiders.

▶ **Key 1 & 2** Divide the highlighted sentence into meaningful parts. Then identify key ideas and eliminate unimportant information.

① They visit ~~hundreds of~~ flowers daily to eat nectar, ~~a sweet liquid inside certain flowers, at a rate of nearly twice their bodyweight,~~ ② but they also catch insects and spiders now and then to satisfy their nutritional needs, ③ ~~as nectar is a poor source of nutrients~~.

▶ **Key 4** Eliminate answer choices if they:
- leave out important pieces of information → (A)
- contain information that is not mentioned in the original sentence → (C)
- generally alter the meaning of the original sentence → (D)

Answer & Explanations

Answer Book p. A14

(B)

(B) best summarizes the key idea of the highlighted sentence without changing its meaning.

Basic Drill

01

Setting tax policy is a crucial responsibility of the government, as such policies not only ensure the funding of government programs, but also have a significant impact on the economy in general. A good example of this comes from the early 1980s, when America was faced with a serious recession. The government made significant cuts in the tax rates for companies, but not for regular citizens, even though regular citizens had little money at the time. The logic behind this was that cutting individual taxes would not help, because it would only increase the amount of money consumers can spend without fixing the problems in supply. By cutting taxes for companies, the government allowed those companies to use the tax money they saved to increase their supply.

Which of the sentences below best expresses the essential information in the highlighted sentence in the passage? *Incorrect* **answer choices change the meaning in important ways or leave out essential information.**

(A) Cutting taxes would not help because it would only increase the amount of money consumers had.
(B) Cutting individual taxes would be meaningless because it would increase consumers' money but not supply.
(C) Cutting individual taxes would not fix problems in supply but only save consumer's money.
(D) Cutting individual taxes would not increase consumer spending or fix problems in supply.

Vocab Quiz

The word ☐ in the passage is closest in meaning to

01 crucial ☐ important ☐ optional ☐ trivial

02

It has long been known that communities often choose courses of action that are either very damaging or even fatal to the community. For example, the society that lived on Easter Island practiced extensive logging, even though eventual deforestation of their island led to the destruction of their society. Today, many countries around the world continue to pollute the environment, despite well-documented evidence that such pollution may make human life much more difficult or even impossible in the future. Such self-destructive behavior is explained by game theory, which states that every decision maker acts in his or her own self-interest, maximizing their own benefit, and the welfare of others is secondary. In such situations, individual interests often conflict with the interests of the group as a whole.

Which of the sentences below best expresses the essential information in the highlighted sentence in the passage? *Incorrect* **answer choices change the meaning in important ways or leave out essential information.**

(A) Today, many nations continue to pollute the environment for lack of well-documented evidence regarding the effects.
(B) Many nations that pollute the environment are not well aware of their actions, and thus continue to do so.
(C) Even though many nations know the future consequences of their actions, they continue to pollute the environment.
(D) It is well documented that many nations pollute the environment despite the fact that this will make life impossible in the future.

Vocab Quiz

The word ☐ in the passage is closest in meaning to

02 extensive   ☐ impractical   ☐ spontaneous   ☐ massive

Basic Drill

03

Cave paintings of the early Magdalenian period differed from those of the previous Aurignacian period. Whereas Aurignacian painters made use of the natural shape of the rock for modeling, and used sophisticated color pallets to make polychrome images, artists of the early Magdalenian period created flat drawings that consisted merely of black outlines with no detail or color. Another difference was that early Magdalenians abandoned the larger compositions favored by Aurignacian artists in favor of solitary figures. However, their style gradually developed over time until the late Magdalenian artists surpassed their Aurignacian predecessors in the creation of more sophisticated designs with beautifully rendered details.

Which of the sentences below best expresses the essential information in the highlighted sentence in the passage? *Incorrect* **answer choices change the meaning in important ways or leave out essential information.**

(A) Magdalenian artists created colorful models of their subjects in rock, whereas Aurignacian artists preferred to create simple black drawings.
(B) Magdalenian artists did not have the means to create detailed polychrome images with depth and volume as Aurignacian painters did.
(C) The early Magdalenian artists made flat drawings with relatively simple techniques compared to Aurignacian artists' techniques.
(D) The cave painting of the early Magdalenian period was very dull even though sophisticated modeling and coloring techniques were used.

Vocab Quiz

The word ☐ in the passage is closest in meaning to

03 solitary   ☐ various   ☐ isolated   ☐ sensual

PART A Question Types

04

Psychopharmacology, the study of how mood-altering drugs affect mood, sensation, thinking, and behavior, is a rapidly growing field of medicine. While the use of psychiatric drugs has been in existence for over 50 years, improvements in the understanding of brain chemistry and the consequent discovery of new drug types have greatly expanded their use over time, and there are now drugs available for the treatment of nearly every major form of psychiatric disorder. This has undeniably led to the improvement of innumerable lives, but many are now voicing concerns over the expanded use of drugs in treating the mentally ill and any unforeseen adverse medical and social consequences.

Which of the sentences below best expresses the essential information in the highlighted sentence in the passage? *Incorrect* **answer choices change the meaning in important ways or leave out essential information.**

(A) Although psychiatric drugs are not new and have existed for over 50 years, improvements in brain chemistry have only recently allowed them to be used to treat most mental illnesses.
(B) Discoveries relating to brain chemistry and the resulting development of new drugs have greatly expanded the use of psychiatric drugs to include treatment of most mental illnesses.
(C) Lots of discoveries in the understanding of brain chemistry and new drug types were made in the last 50 years, but there are still more to be discovered to treat all major forms of psychiatric disorders.
(D) While psychiatric drugs have existed for over 50 years, the inventions of new drugs now allow doctors to treat nearly every form of mental illness.

Vocab Quiz

The word ☐ in the passage is closest in meaning to

04 innumerable   ☐ hopeless   ☐ successive   ☐ countless

Basic Drill

05

The Earth has layers that were formed during a process known as planetary differentiation, which took place when the Earth was approximately 500 million years old. The young planet was heated up by impacts during its accretion, as well as by the decay of radioactive isotopes, and existed in a primarily liquid state, which allowed heavier material to sink to the center of the planet and lighter material to rise, resulting in the formation of a core, mantle, crust, and gaseous atmosphere.

Since then, the outer crust has cooled enough to support life, but the inner layers of the planet still remain hot. Approximately 90 percent of the heat in the interior of the planet is generated by the decay of radioactive elements in the mantle. The remaining 10 percent is heat left over from planetary formation or a result from the pressure generated deep within the planet. The temperature of the Earth's inner core is approximately 7,000 degrees Celsius, more than three times the melting temperature of the iron it is made of; yet the inner core is solid because of the great pressure exerted on it. Above the inner core is the outer core, also made of iron, which exists in a liquid state at a cooler temperature of approximately 3,000 degrees Celsius. The mantle, which rests above the outer core and drives the process of plate tectonics, largely consists of molten olivine, which is viscous but not liquid.

Which of the sentences below best expresses the essential information in the highlighted sentence in the passage? *Incorrect* answer choices change the meaning in important ways or leave out essential information.

(A) The inner core of the Earth is composed of molten iron because of its high temperature and great pressure.
(B) The pressure applied to the inner core of the Earth keeps it in a solid state despite its high temperature.
(C) Due to the combination of high temperature and high pressure, the inner core of the Earth can exist in a solid state.
(D) The condition of the Earth's inner core varies depending on its temperature and the pressure exerted on it.

Vocab Quiz

The word ☐ in the passage is closest in meaning to

05 primarily   ☐ mostly   ☐ fully   ☐ relatively

06

The idea that language determines our thoughts, or at least influences them, is known as linguistic determinism. The theory was first presented in the West by Wilhelm von Humbolt, a famous German linguist of the nineteenth century. His ideas were later expanded upon by Franz Boas, who, through his study of various languages around the world, came to realize how complete and total the differences between those various languages could be. This gave rise to the belief that if languages were so radically different, then the thoughts allowed by those languages must be quite different as well. The assumption was that in order to think something, a person had to be able to say it.

The concepts of linguistic determinism were most clearly focused in the work of Edward Sapir and his protégé Benjamin Whorf. Although Sapir and Whorf never developed an explicit theory of linguistic determinism, the ideas expressed in their numerous writings have come to be known as the Sapir-Whorf hypothesis. The Sapir-Whorf hypothesis is a less rigid theory of linguistic determinism than the previous theories of the German linguists. Whereas earlier linguists had claimed that thoughts are impossible without language and are therefore controlled by language, Sapir and Whorf claimed that thoughts were merely influenced by language, which gave rise to competing theories of strong and weak linguistic determinism.

Which of the sentences below best expresses the essential information in the highlighted sentence in the passage? *Incorrect* **answer choices change the meaning in important ways or leave out essential information.**

(A) While earlier linguists felt that it would be impossible to control our thoughts without language, Sapir and Whorf were not influenced by these ideas.
(B) Sapir and Whorf supported the theory of strong linguistic determinism, which means thoughts are strongly connected to language.
(C) Earlier linguists had claimed that thoughts and language were always connected, but Sapir and Whorf argued that this connection was not that significant.
(D) Although earlier linguists had claimed that thoughts could only exist through language, Sapir and Whorf argued that language only helped to shape our thoughts.

Vocab Quiz

The word ☐ in the passage is closest in meaning to

06 previous   ☐ other   ☐ subsequent   ☐ earlier

Reading Practice

SOLAR ACTIVITY

1   Like Earth, the Sun has several different forms of visible activity, or weather. But unlike Earth, the Sun's weather is created by forces deep within the Sun rather than in its atmosphere. The Sun is made of electrically charged particles, which create a strong magnetic field around the Sun. Because the Sun rotates slightly faster at its equator than it does at its poles, its magnetic field slowly gets pulled out of balance. A helpful analogy is to think of the Sun's magnetic field as a giant rubber band. As the Sun rotates, the rubber band slowly twists, becoming tighter and tighter.

2   As the magnetic field of the Sun gets twisted, resulting in an imbalance of the magnetic field in one part of the Sun, it becomes stronger in one area and gives the Sun its first form of weather by preventing heat from rising up from the center of the Sun to this particular area of the surface. The result is a sunspot which is cooler than the rest of the surface. Because they are cooler than the rest of the sun, these sunspots appear to be darker. These dark spots can be several times the size of Earth, and astronomers have been observing them for hundreds of years. Sunspots appear to follow an 11-year cycle of activity. Although no one has been able to adequately explain the causes for this cycle as of yet, it seems that the height of the cycle represents the time of greatest imbalance in the Sun's magnetic field, resulting in more sunspots.

3   Eventually, the magnetic field around a sunspot will become so twisted that it will snap. All the energy that has been stored in the twists of the magnetic field will be released in this one moment. The result is a huge jump in temperature called a solar flare. In as little as ten seconds, the temperature will rise to as much as 20 million degrees, up from about 1 million. Solar flares also release huge amounts of radiation, primarily in the form of X-rays, into space. When this radiation reaches the Earth, it can damage satellites and affect weather patterns.

Answer Book p. A18

|Sentence Simplification|

01 **Which of the sentences below best expresses the essential information in the highlighted sentence in the passage?** *Incorrect* **answer choices change the meaning in important ways or leave out essential information.**

(A) The magnetic field of the Sun gets stronger in one section as it gets twisted, and this magnetic field results in a first form of weather on the Sun.
(B) The stronger magnetic field in a specific area of the Sun's surface causes the twisted magnetic field and a large temperature difference on the Sun.
(C) When the magnetic field of the Sun gets twisted and concentrated in one part of the Sun's surface, it prevents the transference of heat.
(D) The imbalance in the magnetic field on the specific area of the Sun's surface determines whether the magnetic field will be twisted or not.

|Vocabulary|

02 **The word " result " in the passage is closest in meaning to**

(A) reason
(B) condition
(C) origin
(D) consequence

|Vocabulary|

03 **The word " adequately " in the passage is closest in meaning to**

(A) sufficiently
(B) scientifically
(C) logically
(D) perfectly

|Reference|

04 **The word " it " in the passage refers to**

(A) sunspot
(B) magnetic field
(C) energy
(D) radiation

|Negative Fact|

05 **All of the following are true of solar flares EXCEPT:**

(A) They are the final result of the imbalances in the Sun's magnetic field.
(B) They result in a rapid increase in the surface temperature of the Sun.
(C) They have little effect on the Earth because of their distance.
(D) They discharge large amounts of radiation into space.

Chapter **03** Sentence Simplification 53

Chapter 04 Factual Information & Negative Fact

Factual Information questions ask you to choose an answer that is correct according to the passage. Negative Fact questions ask you to choose an answer that is untrue according to the passage or contains information not mentioned in the passage. There are 3-6 Factual Information questions and 0-2 Negative Fact questions for each passage. Each question is worth 1 point.

How the Question is Worded

Factual Information
- ☐ According to paragraph #, which of the following is true of ~?
- ☐ According to paragraph #, what/how/why ~?
- ☐ In paragraph #, the author states that
- ☐ Select the TWO answer choices that are ~. To receive/earn credit, you must select TWO answers.

Negative Fact
- ☐ According to paragraph #, which of the following is NOT true of ~?
- ☐ All of the following are mentioned in paragraph # EXCEPT:

Keys to Solution

Factual Information

Key 1 Identify the key words in the question, and scan the passage for them or corresponding ideas. Then carefully read the related information.

Key 2 The correct answer is a restatement of particular information from the passage. Therefore, while the wording may be different, similar ideas should be apparent.

Key 3 Eliminate the false answer choices that contain
- information that is contradicted by the passage or not mentioned in the passage
- information that is stated in the passage but is irrelevant to the question

Negative Fact

Key 1 Identify the key words in the question, and scan the passage for them or corresponding ideas. Then carefully read the related information.

Key 2 As with Factual Information questions, the correct answer will be paraphrased. It is important to recognize corresponding ideas.

Key 3 Identify correct statements of information one by one, and you will eventually find the incorrect one.

Key 4 Choose the answer choice that contains
- information that is contradicted by the passage or not mentioned in the passage
- information that is stated in the passage but is irrelevant to the question

Sample Question

As psychologists have long argued over whether personality or situation is more influential to a person's behavior, the theory of interactionism was proposed to resolve the debate. Interactionists argue that personality traits and situations interact to influence one's behavior, and each variable has an influence on how powerful the other variable is in predicting behavior. For example, some situations, like army boot camp, are where people are not allowed to express their individual personalities. These situations are called "strong situations," in which the situations have a very strong likelihood of accurately predicting behavior. On the contrary, "weak situations," such as relaxing alone, allow more freedom for personal expression, so one's personality will be a strong predictor of behavior. Likewise, each personality trait can be gauged for how well its presence can predict behavior. For instance, for those who are highly independent, their personality is a strong predictor of behavior, while for those who are more self-conscious, the situation may be a stronger predictor of behavior.

[01] **Key 1** Identify the key words (strong situations) in the question, and scan the passage for them.

| Factual Information |

01 According to the passage, which of the following is true of strong situations?

(A) Both the personality and the situation are strong predictors of behavior.
(B) They are not likely to allow for the expression of unique personalities.
(C) One's personality is the main factor that determines the behavior.
(D) Highly independent people can easily overcome such situations.

[01] **Key 3** Eliminate the false answer choices.
(A) & (C) contain information that is not mentioned in the passage.
(D) contains information that is stated in the passage but is irrelevant to the question.

| Negative Fact |

02 All of the following are mentioned in the passage EXCEPT:

(A) Personality traits will be strong in predicting behavior in weak situations.
(B) Each personality trait has a different impact in predicting behaviors.
(C) Both the situation and personality traits will influence an individual's behavior.
(D) Very self-conscious people will not be affected by strong situations.

[02] **Key 3** Identify correct statements of information one by one.
→ (A), (B), and (C)

[02] **Key 4** Choose the answer choice that contains information that is contradicted by the passage.

Answer & Explanations

Answer Book p. A20

01 - (B)
According to the passage, people are not allowed to express their individual personalities in strong situations.

02 - (D)
According to the passage, the situation may be a stronger predictor of behavior for those who are very self-conscious.

Basic Drill

01

One may find it intriguing that even prehistoric cave paintings could last intact for over 40,000 years and still show off their vivid colors. The Native Americans used inorganic pigments to color their drawings with materials such as grinded clays and minerals. The color of inorganic pigments varied from red to dark brown, but the extracted pigments were qualitatively undifferentiated. During the Renaissance, master painters threw their souls into finding rich and lustrous colors for their masterpieces. One of their arduous methods of preparing pigments was using plant material. Squashed blackberries could create dazzling purple, and the extract of blueberries with a slight hint of vinegar could create a lovely elusive blue. The artists were keen to produce fresh pigments from plants, as they could be easily discolored or denatured.

According to the passage, the author states that painters in the Renaissance used pigments from plants because

(A) the pigments from clays and muds were low in quality
(B) it was easier to extract pigments from plants than from earth minerals
(C) they wanted more diverse and rich pigments for their paintings
(D) the pigments from other material besides plants could easily be ruined

02

Acid rain is rain that has unusually high levels of acid in it, and is a result of air pollution. When fossil fuels are burned, they release chemicals containing sulfur and nitrogen into the air. Once in the air, these chemicals combine with water vapor to form sulfuric and nitric acids, which then return to Earth when it rains. Since it is the result of burning fossil fuels, acid rain presents the greatest problem to industrial nations that rely heavily on coal as a source of energy. However, more advanced nations, such as the United States and many parts of Western Europe, have developed technology that reduces the amount of sulfur and nitrogen released from their power plants. They are therefore at least partially able to control their acid rain problems.

According to the passage, advanced nations are less susceptible to acid rain because

(A) they consume less energy compared to developing nations
(B) they have the technology for cleaner energy production
(C) they have the technology to separate the acid from the rain
(D) they have stricter environmental laws on burning fossil fuels

Vocab Quiz

The word ☐ in the passage is closest in meaning to

| 01 arduous | ☐ distinctive | ☐ strenuous | ☐ common |
| 02 released | ☐ caused | ☐ blended | ☐ emitted |

03

Modernism was probably the most influential intellectual and artistic movement of the twentieth century. Modernism is difficult to define because it has many aspects, but it is essentially the complete rejection of the artistic values of the previous centuries. Artists like Pablo Picasso discarded traditional attitudes toward perspective and realism, and created highly fragmented and abstract works. Similarly, many writers left traditional structures of writing. T. S. Eliot dispensed with structure and organization in his poetry to create free verse, which followed none of the established poetic rules. In the sphere of music, composers began to experiment with new sounds, focusing on the destruction of harmony rather than the creation of it.

According to the passage, what is a common characteristic in all forms of modernism?

(A) The denial of traditional values in art
(B) The integration of different perspectives
(C) The pursuit of realism
(D) The segmentation of existing structure

04

To the naked eye, planets and stars may appear to be similar. However, unlike stars, which are very hot and shine with their own light, planets are much cooler and do not shine on their own. The light one can see from a planet is actually reflected sunlight, as some of the light is reflected back into space when the Sun's light hits a planet. Planets maintain the same orbit, century after century, through a fragile balance of speed and gravity. As the planets orbit around the Sun, their circular motion tends to push them outwards. However, that outward push is exactly balanced by the Sun's gravity, which pulls the planets towards the Sun. This balance keeps the planets in their assigned orbits.

All of the following are true of planets EXCEPT:

(A) They give off their own light.
(B) They travel in fixed orbits.
(C) They are affected by the Sun's gravity.
(D) Their light is merely reflected sunlight.

Vocab Quiz

The word ☐ in the passage is closest in meaning to

03 discarded	☐ pursued	☐ abandoned	☐ proposed
04 fragile	☐ delicate	☐ ideal	☐ fixed

Basic Drill

05

During the advent of the Industrial Revolution, widespread social acceptance of child labor meant that children made up a large percentage of those who moved from the farm to the factory. In 1833, nearly two-thirds of the factory workers in Leeds, a major industrial center in England, were under the age of 15. England was hardly the only nation where children formed a majority of the factory workforce. As the Industrial Revolution spread throughout Europe and the United States, so did this new form of child labor. Child labor in Industrial Revolution factories, however, quickly proved to be far less benign than child labor on the homestead. With no legal safeguards, children working in the factories of this time were little more than the property of indifferent factory owners. It was typical for a child to work more than ten hours a day under miserable conditions for 30 to 40 percent of the wages for an adult. Furthermore, children were subjected to harsh punishments when they failed to keep pace with older workers. Children were routinely whipped, dunked in cold water, and subjected to other inhumane punishments when they failed to meet their work quotas. Children who tried to run away to escape such treatment were occasionally chained to their work stations.

All of the following are mentioned in the passage as hardships for child laborers during the Industrial Revolution EXCEPT

(A) long working hours
(B) lower wages compared to those of adult workers
(C) extremely cruel punishments
(D) arbitrary and unjustified firings

Vocab Quiz

The word ☐ in the passage is closest in meaning to

05 widespread   ☐ changing   ☐ prevalent   ☐ passive

06

Map making, or cartography, is an activity of vital importance for human civilization. Maps improve the speed and safety of travel, allow civilizations to set the boundaries of their territories, and occasionally by their absence inspire further exploration of the world. The first known maps date back to around 7,000 B.C. The earliest maps are maps of cities and may have been used by city planners. World maps at this time were next to useless. Early civilizations knew very little about the wider world around them. Long-distance travel was extremely difficult, and so the world maps of early civilizations were based largely on the map makers' religious beliefs.

The first civilization to take a scientific approach to map making was the ancient Greeks. The ancient Greeks, incidentally, were also the first to have an accurate view of the shape of the world. This knowledge was a crucial element in the Greek system of map making. It was the Greeks who first developed the system of latitude and longitude that we still use on maps today. Understanding that the world is a sphere allowed the Greeks to divide their maps according to a 360-degree system. This turned the world into a grid, on which they could precisely describe any location. While the Greek system of map making was a good one, Greek maps were still quite faulty because they had no accurate means of measuring distance at the time.

According to the passage, which of the following is NOT true of map making?

(A) Due to their use of latitude and longitude, Greek maps are still highly accurate.
(B) The development of map making resulted in faster and safer travel.
(C) Maps were originally used as city maps by city planners.
(D) Greek maps were developed based on a 360-degree system.

Vocab Quiz

The word ☐ in the passage is closest in meaning to

06 approach   ☐ evidence   ☐ evaluation   ☐ method

Reading Practice

THE ROBBER BARONS

1   As an economic system, capitalism assumes that open markets and free competition are always of benefit to the customer. The idea is that in order to compete in an open market, a company must offer higher-quality products at a lower cost than its competitors. The result of this competition is that the consumer gets the best possible product at the lowest possible cost. Another assumption of capitalism is that governments must refrain from regulating or interfering in the business practices of companies because this prevents free competition. The problem, however, is that this system relies on companies operating in an honest and ethical manner, which is not always the case.

2   In the nineteenth century, America was still a developing nation in many ways. Although the Industrial Revolution was rapidly transforming much of the nation, the United States was still a rustic, backward nation when compared with the great nations of Europe. Much of the country's territory was undeveloped and lacked even basic infrastructures, such as usable roads and electricity. Therefore, the focus of the United States during this period was on development, and the men driving this development were the robber barons.

3   The robber barons were not actual nobility, but rather were the leading businessmen of the time. They owned the factories, shipyards, and railway companies that built the infrastructure America lacked, and these entrepreneurial activities helped them accumulate great wealth. The robber barons got their name from the fact that many of the business practices they engaged in were unethical and sometimes even criminal. Willing to do whatever was necessary to ensure their dominance in business, the robber barons used ruthless practices and unscrupulous approaches to their business, such as bribing officials, threatening competitors, taking advantage of their employees, and caring little for the environmental impacts of their industries. In creating their vast business empires, the robber barons routinely engaged in anti-competitive business practices to destroy their competitors, which resulted in a powerful monopoly that gave them the power to regulate the supply and price of commodities, in contrast to the original intention of capitalism. Without the threat of real competition, helpless consumers had no choice but to pay the unreasonable prices set by the robber barons.

|Factual Information|

01 Select the TWO answer choices that are true about capitalism. To receive credit, you must select TWO answers.

(A) To serve its intended function, it requires companies to run in an ethical manner.
(B) The competition it creates ensures lower prices and higher-quality products.
(C) It prevents the government from interfering in business.
(D) It increases the level of competition among customers for high-quality products.

|Reference|

02 The phrase "this system" in the passage refers to

(A) open market
(B) capitalism
(C) free competition
(D) problem

|Factual Information|

03 According to paragraph 2, what difficulty did America face in the nineteenth century?

(A) It lacked effective forms of business management.
(B) It lacked the workforce to become a developed nation.
(C) It could not deal with the rapid transformations of the Industrial Revolution.
(D) Large portions of its territory were far less developed than those of Europe.

|Vocabulary|

04 The word "accumulate" in the passage is closest in meaning to

(A) consume
(B) invest
(C) amass
(D) share

|Sentence Simplication|

05 Which of the sentences below best expresses the essential information in the highlighted sentence in the passage? *Incorrect* answer choices change the meaning in important ways or leave out essential information.

(A) The robber barons used a number of dishonest methods regularly to monopolize industries.
(B) The robber barons often used unethical business practice because they were dominant in their fields.
(C) The robber barons were eager to change the original purpose of capitalism to control the market.
(D) The robber barons were willing to do anything in order to create their own business empires.

Chapter 05 Inference

Inference questions test your ability to understand information that is only implied, not directly stated in the passage. Inferences can be made by using a set of facts directly stated in the passage to draw logical conclusions. There are 1-3 Inference questions for each passage. This question is worth 1 point.

How the Question is Worded

- According to paragraph #, what can be inferred about ~?
- Which of the following can be inferred from the passage about ~?
- It can be inferred from paragraph # that
- In paragraph #, what does the author imply about ~?
- The author of the passage implies that
- Which of the following can be concluded from the passage?

Keys to Solution

Key 1 Find the key words in the question and scan the passage for them or corresponding ideas. Then carefully read and understand the related information.

Key 2 Have a thorough understanding of the passage and do not look for answer clues outside of the passage, such as from personal experiences, beliefs, or values. Everything you need to answer the question is provided in the passage.

Key 3 Eliminate false answer choices that contain
- information that is contradicted by the passage
- information that is not mentioned in the passage

Key 4 Familiarize yourself with various types of Inference questions, and use different strategies depending on the question.

> + Some Inference questions are based on a single statement, or connections between several statements in the same part of the passage. In this case, find the correct answer through a close reading by paying attention to specific details.
>
> + Some Inference questions ask you to find a conclusion that is implied throughout an entire paragraph, or several paragraphs. In this case, find the relationship between the major ideas by having a thorough understanding of the whole passage.
>
> + Some Inference questions may ask you to predict a possible outcome by applying rules, laws, or principles discussed in the passage. In this case, have a correct understanding of the basic principles.

Sample Question

> Midden analysis is the analysis of the discarded artifacts of ancient civilizations. What people throw away can tell archaeologists a great deal about a culture. Animal bones and vegetable remains can provide important clues about the diet of ancient peoples. Discarded tools tell us of their occupations. Broken pottery, scraps of clothing, and other personal objects can tell us of their lifestyles. Furthermore, midden analysis can often tell us a great deal about the habitat in which a people lived. Chemical analysis of plant matter, for example, provides information regarding temperatures, average rainfall, and other climatic information about the time period.

Key 2 Have a thorough understanding of the passage. Climatic information about the time period can be gained by chemical analysis of plant matter.

It can be inferred from the passage that

(A) midden analysis is only functional in certain climates
(B) climate affects the chemical composition of plants
(C) abandoned tools are good clues for ancient eating habits
(D) remains are generally layered according to temperature changes

Key 3 Eliminate false answer choices.
(A), (C), and (D) contain information that is not mentioned in the passage.

Answer & Explanations Answer Book p. A26

(B)
You can find the fact that chemical composition in plant matter tells us information about the climate during the period when the plant lived. You can infer from this fact that climate has an effect on the chemical composition of plants.

Basic Drill

01

Core sampling is an essential tool for scientists wishing to investigate the fundamental data of the Earth in biological, chemical, and geological aspects. In core sampling, a hollow drill is used to drill into the substance of the Earth, for example, sediment or rock. The material contained in the hollow section of the drill can then be brought up and studied. Core sampling can be conducted in any areas with any material where the Earth is stable enough to form layers. A good example would be the ocean floor. On the ocean floor, there is almost no activity to disturb the layering process, such as waves or human activity. Therefore, sediment builds up in progressive layers, with each layer being older than the one on top of it. The sedimentation on the seafloor helps scientists to understand the climate pattern over time, since the seafloor mirrors changes in the Earth's climate.

Based on the information from the passage, what can be inferred about core sampling?

(A) It is a relatively new technique in geology.
(B) It is not very useful near human population centers.
(C) It was first developed for deep-sea exploration.
(D) It can be performed even in cases of mixed sediment.

02

Redox reactions involve the transfer of electrons between two chemical species as a result of the differences in the electronegativities of two chemicals. Electronegativity is a chemical attribute which describes the ability to draw electrons from other chemicals. Chemicals that have the ability to take electrons from other chemicals are said to be highly electronegative, while those that tend to lose electrons easily are said to be electropositive. A common example of a redox reaction would be the formation of rust. Rust forms when iron, a highly electropositive metal, comes into contact with water. When this happens, iron loses electrons to the oxygen atoms in water. The oxygen atoms and the iron are then bound together to form a new chemical compound called iron oxide, or rust. The formation of rust happens more quickly in salt water because salt water is more electrically conductive than regular water and thus allows the electrons to move from the iron atoms to the oxygen atoms more easily.

According to the passage, what does the author imply about oxygen?

(A) It is necessary for all redox reactions.
(B) It is present in higher concentrations in salt water.
(C) It is an electronegative chemical.
(D) It is only able to bind with iron.

Vocab Quiz

The word ☐ in the passage is closest in meaning to

01 mirrors	☐ reflects	☐ causes	☐ influences
02 attribute	☐ term	☐ property	☐ status

03

Opera is an extended art form where singers and musicians perform a dramatic work combining text and musical score in a theatrical setting, called an opera house. The first composition considered opera, *Dafne*, was developed in the Italian city of Florence during the 1590s. At the time, a group of humanists, musicians, poets, and intellectuals known as the Camerata were interested in injecting storytelling into music, as they were inspired by the belief that the great tragic plays of ancient Greece had been sung rather than simply acted. Another motivation may have been the desire of the composers to find an alternative to the production of music for the Church, which they found rigid, conventional, and oppressive. This is supported by the selection of material for the opera. Early composers took their material from the mythologies of ancient Rome and Greece, which were full of plots, betrayals, and love affairs. From the very beginning, the sobriety of the Church had little place in opera.

It can be inferred from the passage that early operas

(A) were always performed in Greece
(B) rarely, if ever, dealt with religious topics
(C) placed more importance on creativity than quality
(D) were only written by composers

04

Both temperature and salinity affect the density of water. In turn, density affects the ability of a substance to float. Less-dense substances will rise above denser substances, which can be seen with oil and water. Sea water is not perfectly clear, as sunlight only penetrates through the first few hundred feet of sea water and, as a result, all of the sun's heat is absorbed by the upper surface layer of sea water. Wave action mixes this upper-level water together fairly evenly, and so the temperature remains relatively uniform. Beyond the reach of sunlight and wave action, however, the temperature of the ocean drops rapidly by more than 20 degrees Celsius after a few hundred feet, and then continues to drop at a far slower rate. The rapid temperature change results in two layers of water with very different densities, surface water and deep water, separated by the thin layer called thermocline. Nearly 90 percent of the world's water is below the thermocline, but the vast majority of sea life lives above it.

Which of the following can be inferred from the passage about deep water?

(A) It is easily affected by the amount of sunlight it gets.
(B) It has a higher density compared to the other layers.
(C) It provides adequate conditions for marine life.
(D) It is only a small fraction of the Earth's water.

Vocab Quiz

The word ☐ in the passage is closest in meaning to

03 alternative	☐ opponent	☐ substitute	☐ explanation
04 fairly	☐ reasonably	☐ absolutely	☐ partially

Basic Drill

05

The custom of paying a bride price before marriage is still a well-established part of many African cultures. In paying a bride price, the family of the groom must provide payment to the family of the bride before the marriage is allowed. The bride price can vary greatly from culture to culture in Africa. In the Zulu and Swazi tribes of southern Africa, the bride price often takes the form of cattle. The actual payment of money sometimes takes place, but payment in goods is more frequent. The amount paid in a bride price can also vary. In modern times, the bride price is usually quite small, and its value is mainly symbolic. However, the bride price can still be quite high, especially among prominent or highly traditional families.

There are a number of justifications used to explain the payment of a bride price. The first is that the bride price represents an acknowledgement of the expense the bride's family has gone to in order to raise her and bring her up as a suitable bride for the groom. It also represents payment for the loss of a family member, since the bride will officially become a member of her husband's family and will leave her own. On a deeper level, the bride price represents payment for the fact that the bride will bring children into the family of the groom, thereby increasing the wealth of the family. This concept is reinforced by the fact that the bride price must often be returned if the bride fails to bear children.

In paragraph 2, what does the author imply about African families?

(A) They place great importance on childbirth.
(B) They never see their daughters after marriage.
(C) They pay the bride price on the day of the wedding.
(D) They make a great effort to raise their daughters for a higher bride price.

Vocab Quiz

The word ☐ in the passage is closest in meaning to

05 suitable   ☐ proper   ☐ youthful   ☐ radiant

06

From the thirteenth to the fifteenth century, the wool trade was the foundation of the British economy. The British held a monopoly on the finest grade of wool that was being produced in Europe at the time. However, relatively little of the wool the island produced was actually spun into yarn to produce cloth. Rather, the bulk of the raw wool was shipped across the channel to Flanders, where the best weavers produced very high-quality cloth. It is true that wool was produced elsewhere, but it was often of such poor quality and roughness that it could not compete with the quality that came from England.

Because the export of raw wool was extremely lucrative, the trade became the target of the British Crown, who sought to control it and, by extension, profit from it. Customs and taxes were levied on wool exports to mainland Europe. Because the King was so closely tied to the Church of England at this time in history, many of these profits made their way back to the Church. Consequently, the Church also took a vested interest in the wool trade and the potential profits that could be reaped from it.

Despite the high demand for British wool and the involvement of the Crown and the Church, England remained solely focused on the production and export of raw wool. Refinement of the wool into higher-value cloth was done almost exclusively in Flanders, which imported the raw wool and shipped the cloth back to England at a profit. English manufacturers only began to focus on producing high-grade cloth in the eighteenth century with the arrival of the Industrial Revolution and the large-scale mechanization of weaving and production.

In paragraph 3, what does the author imply about production of cloth during the Industrial Revolution?

(A) The export of raw wool still remained the main focus of the Crown.
(B) Technological advances allowed for woolen cloth production in England.
(C) Flanders soon lost its status as a producer of the finest woolen cloth.
(D) The Church took a renewed interest in taxing exports of raw and refined wool.

Vocab Quiz

The word ☐ in the passage is closest in meaning to

06 potential ☐ tremendous ☐ consecutive ☐ prospective

Reading Practice

THE EVOLUTION OF HUMAN SOCIETY

1   Anthropologists consider the evolution of human society to involve four social revolutions: hunter-gatherer, agrarian, industrial, and post-industrial. The first two of these are considered to have had a profound influence on each other, despite being quite different in nature.

2   A hunter-gatherer society is perhaps the earliest form of human groups. They lived by hunting, fishing, and gathering wild sources of food. Because they had to follow the animals and the seasons, they led a nomadic life. This lifestyle dictated many aspects of their society and culture. Hunter-gatherer societies were typically small groups of people, numbering between 20 to 30 for small groups, and up to 150 for larger ones. Consequently, many of their possessions were small, portable, and sourced directly from the animals they hunted or their surrounding natural environment. The clothing they wore was made from animal skins and hides, and their tools were from scavenged wood or stone. In most cases, their shelters were portable or semi-permanent, allowing them to readily follow their food sources with the seasons and migration patterns. Labor was typically divided along gender lines, with men usually responsible for hunting while women most of the gathering. This distinction was not exclusive, though, as many aspects of daily life were shared between men and women. Childcare, for instance, was typically a cooperative affair, where a child would be cared for by the community to a large degree, rather than exclusively by its mother.

3   Because of the permanent nature of its food source and higher level of productivity, agrarian societies were able to support a much denser population base, with the result that many aspects of culture, economy, and society evolved in ways markedly different from the nomadic hunter-gatherers. As a result of the excess food which could be stored and sold later at a profit, complex economies evolved to manage and grow the surpluses. Consequently, agrarian societies heralded the development of permanent dwellings, community spaces, and utilities such as roads and running water, as well as the evolution of more complex governing structures.

4   In short, the emergence of agrarian societies established the foundation for many aspects of our modern culture today. Our systems of governance, transportation, and communication all had their early start in an agrarian society. Agrarian societies were also the foundation for the move toward industrial technology and our modern society.

|Negative Fact|

01 **According to paragraph 2, which of the following is NOT true of hunter-gatherer societies?**

(A) Children were raised cooperatively by the group.
(B) They tended to be nomadic and followed the seasons and the animals.
(C) Their dwellings were large enough to house many people.
(D) Their tools were developed from materials at hand.

|Inference|

02 **Based on the information in paragraph 2, what can be inferred about hunter-gatherer societies?**

(A) The development of permanent shelters was key to food security.
(B) Animal hides and skins were often used as the base currency in these societies.
(C) One's social position in the group was decided by his or her material possessions.
(D) Their primitive tools and shelters were a direct result of their nomadic life.

|Sentence Simplification|

03 **Which of the sentences below best expresses the essential information in the highlighted sentence in the passage?** *Incorrect* **answer choices change the meaning in important ways or leave out essential information.**

(A) Large populations, by their nature, exemplify the many differences between agrarian societies and hunter-gatherer societies.
(B) Different cultural, economic, and social features between agrarian societies and nomadic societies caused differences in population density and productivity of food.
(C) In contrast to hunter-gatherer societies, the culture and economy of agrarian societies developed separately and independently of each other because of its food surplus.
(D) Food surplus and high productivity in agrarian societies led to a bigger population and resulted in distinctions in many aspects from hunter-gatherer societies.

|Inference|

04 **Which of the following can be inferred from paragraph 3 about agrarian society?**

(A) Agrarian society met the prerequisite to become a complex society.
(B) A denser population could only be sustained by agrarian society.
(C) Excess food in agrarian societies boosted trade with other societies.
(D) Agrarians were better educated than members of hunter-gatherer societies.

|Vocabulary|

05 **The word "emergence" in the passage is closest in meaning to**

(A) capability
(B) advent
(C) structure
(D) progression

Chapter 06   Rhetorical Purpose

Rhetorical Purpose questions ask you to determine why the author states a certain word, phrase, or paragraph in the passage, or what type of organizing ideas the author uses to explain the particular information. Sometimes you will be asked to identify how a paragraph is organized or how a paragraph relates to another. There are 1-2 Rhetorical Purpose questions for each passage. This question is worth 1 point.

How the Question is Worded

- Why does the author mention "~" in paragraph #?
- The author mentions "~" in paragraph # in order to
- In paragraph #, the author explains ~ by
- Which of the following best describes the way paragraph # is organized?
- What is the relationship between paragraph # and # in the passage?
- What is the purpose of paragraph # in the overall discussion?

Keys to Solution

Key 1 Locate the section of the passage that contains the word or phrase from the question and see what role that particular information plays in relation to the paragraph. In case of the questions asking how a paragraph is organized or how a paragraph relates to another, see what role the paragraph plays in relation to the entire passage.

Key 2 Familiarize yourself with the various ways of organizing ideas in a passage and expressions frequently used in answer choices:

• Explanation	To explain, To describe, To discuss
• Exemplification	To give an example of, To illustrate, To exemplify
• Classification	To classify, To list
• Comparison / Contrast	To compare / To contrast
• Support / Refutation	To support / To contradict, To criticize, To refute
• Emphasis	To emphasize, To highlight
• Substantiation	To demonstrate, To show, To give a reason for, To give evidence of
• Opinion	To suggest, To present, To propose, To argue

Sample Question

> Changes in environment and evolution are completely intertwined and cannot be considered separate matters, since environmental changes present new challenges that a species must adapt to or it may face extinction. Instances illustrating this fact are numerous. Dramatic climatic changes 64 million years ago led to the extinction of the dinosaurs and the flourish of mammals. Also, rapid changes in the African climate led early hominids to develop bigger and more complex brains to deal with unpredictable weather, which would become the base of modern human beings. The introduction of antibiotics in medicine has led the evolution of antibiotic-resistant strains of bacteria. These are just a few of the ways in which environmental changes help drive evolution.

Key 1 Locate the section of the passage that contains "antibiotics" and see what role it plays in relation to the passage.

Why does the author discuss "antibiotics" in the passage?

(A) To point out a wide range of uses for antibiotics
(B) To give an example of environmental changes that an organism has adapted to
(C) To discuss how the creation of medicine can sometimes endanger human health
(D) To show that the effects of evolution are not always positive

---

Answer & Explanations Answer Book p. A32

(B)
The main idea is that the organism inevitably has to adapt to environmental changes. The passage supports its main idea by listing a number of examples illustrating ways organisms adapt to the challenges caused by environmental changes, and antibiotics are one such example.

Basic Drill

01

The Earth's magnetic field is roughly in line with its axis of rotation, and in some places extends for tens of thousands of miles beyond the Earth. The magnetic field of the Earth, however, is not entirely stable, since it is generated by a geodynamo, the kinetic energy derived from the Earth's liquid core. The Earth's magnetic field has undergone a large number of major shifts and reversals throughout the history of the Earth. Any number of factors can lead to local or temporary disturbances in the magnetic field. Firstly, according to the Earth's geologic record, its magnetic field flips on average about once every 200,000 years. Also, its pattern of declination has shown westward drifting features for more than 400 years. In addition, the overall strength of the Earth's magnetic field weakens and causes greater instability when a newly generated field lines up in the opposite direction of an existing magnetic field, or when a new field continues to grow.

In the passage, the author explains the Earth's magnetic field by

(A) contrasting it with the magnetic field of another planet
(B) giving examples of factors that contribute to its instability
(C) explaining the role of the Earth's liquid core in making it unstable
(D) mentioning various theories of what causes its instability

02

The Nile is the longest river in the world, flowing from Lake Victoria of Uganda to the Mediterranean Sea. It is considered a primary water source to a number of countries in Africa. Even in ancient times, the Nile had such a crucial role in the lives of Egyptians that many believed the great civilization of Ancient Egypt was indebted to the Nile. Although the inundation of the Nile was a great threat to the Egyptians, as the overflowing water often ravaged communities near its banks, the Egyptians relied on the regular occurrence of inundation in their agricultural practices by using a calendar. The water level of the river would rise from June to September, depositing a layer of mineral-rich soil on the river's banks. As the inundation receded in October, farmers plowed and planted crops to well-watered and fertile soil called silt. Egyptians' unique farming practices using the Nile allowed them to devote more time and resources to cultural, technological, and artistic pursuits.

The author mentions " calendar " in the passage in order to

(A) demonstrate the advancements of ancient Egyptian civilization
(B) compare the calendar system of Egypt to those of other cultures
(C) indicate the essential reason why Egyptians created their own calendar
(D) explain how Egyptians anticipated the cycles of river inundation

Vocab Quiz

The word ☐ in the passage is closest in meaning to

01 roughly	☐ figuratively	☐ precisely	☐ approximately
02 primary	☐ fundamental	☐ subsidiary	☐ absolute

03

In his experiment conducted in 1928, Griffith used two types of bacteria: type III-S (smooth) and type II-R (rough). The former type of bacteria had a capsule that protected itself from the host's immune system, resulting in the death of the host, while the latter lacked the capsule and was killed by the host's immune system. During the experiment, Griffith discovered that once bacteria from III-S were killed by heat, they were no longer lethal. In the following stage of the observation, Griffith injected a combination of heat-killed III-S and live II-R into mice. Surprisingly, this mixture of nonlethal bacteria became virulent and killed the mice. Griffith concluded that some part of dead III-S somehow transferred to the II-R and allowed the II-R to create a protective coat, eventually killing the host. Today, we know the transformed information that survived the heating process is called DNA and that it can be transferred through a process known as transformation.

In the passage, the author explains transformation by

(A) describing an unexpected result in Griffith's experiment
(B) contrasting several types of bacteria found in mice
(C) analyzing the processes used in Griffith's experiment
(D) highlighting the importance of protective capsules in the immune system

04

Cultivation theory, first developed by sociologist George Gebner in the 1960s, attempts to explain the effects that mass media have on the attitudes of the public. In its simplest form, cultivation theory says that mass media, such as television and radio, help to form our view of the world. Our understanding of how the world works and our feelings about the world are heavily influenced by mass media. This is important because what is shown as reality in mass media is often quite different from what actually happens in the real world. For example, if a person watches a great number of police dramas on TV, that person might believe that police are frequently involved in gun battles with criminals. However, in real life, most police go through their entire careers without ever firing their weapons. This is just one example of how mass media can give the public an inaccurate view of reality.

The author mentions " police dramas " in the passage in order to

(A) suggest a cause for the violence in society
(B) illustrate how mass media creates erroneous views of reality
(C) explain the negative effects of violent TV shows
(D) argue that people should not watch such TV shows

Vocab Quiz

The word ☐ in the passage is closest in meaning to

03 mixture	☐ substance	☐ modification	☐ combination
04 entire	☐ mundane	☐ whole	☐ strenuous

Chapter 06 Rhetorical Purpose

Basic Drill

05

The end of the American Civil War was supposed to bring freedom to African-American slaves, and for a while it did. After the war, the Southern states were controlled by the Northern army via a military government. During this time, African-Americans enjoyed relatively equal treatment in the South. As the Southern states were slowly readmitted into the Union and the Northern army withdrew, however, many of the freedoms that African-Americans had gained were again taken from them.

The first attack on African-American freedoms came in the election of 1876. White Southerners used violence and intimidation to keep African-Americans from voting in this election. The result was a Southern government that was entirely white and inimical to African-Americans. Southern states quickly passed a number of laws intended to keep African-Americans from enjoying the freedoms they had won. Informally known as the Jim Crow laws, these laws basically separated whites and African-Americans in the South. African-Americans were prohibited from eating in the same restaurants, going to the same schools, and even using the same water fountains as whites.

The most damaging laws to African-Americans, however, were the voting laws. The Southern states passed laws requiring literacy tests and a special voting tax for all voters. While some African-Americans could pass the literacy test, few could afford to pay the voting tax. These two laws were very effective in limiting the political power of African-Americans. In 1900, Alabama had 181,000 African-Americans who were old enough to vote, yet only 3,000 were actually registered to do so. The voting laws ensured that African-Americans had no voice in government and no effective way to fight against their unfair treatment.

In paragraph 3, why does the author give details about African-American voters in Alabama?

(A) To suggest that the Jim Crow laws were most severe in Alabama
(B) To show the effectiveness of the voting laws in excluding African-American voters
(C) To indicate that while African-Americans had large numbers, they lacked political organization
(D) To better illustrate the small proportion of the African-American population that could read and write

Vocab Quiz

The word ☐ in the passage is closest in meaning to

05 inimical   ☐ cooperative   ☐ hostile   ☐ indifferent

06

Establishing the dates for found artifacts is one of the principal jobs of archaeologists. Modern archaeologists have a number of highly accurate scientific methods to determine the date of an artifact, but in the early days of archaeology, this was mainly done through guesswork. The first attempt to develop an organized system for dating artifacts came in 1820, when Christian Thomsen, a Danish archaeologist, suggested his three-age system. The basis of Thomsen's dating system was the examination of tools found at an archaeological site. According to Thomsen, all early cultures had progressed from first using stone tools to bronze tools and finally to iron tools. Thus, if bronze tools were found at a site, an archaeologist could say with certainty that the site came after the Stone Age but before the Iron Age. Analyzing the sophistication with which tools were made could help further determine a more detailed time period for a site.

Thomsen's dating system, however, had a number of problems. First, while his system was helpful for dating sites within the same culture, it was not very effective in dating sites from multiple cultures. Different civilizations adopted bronze and iron technology at different times, and one culture may have still been in the Bronze Age while another culture had already progressed to the Iron Age. Furthermore, some civilizations never adopted these technologies, or they skipped steps. The peoples of the Sahara, for example, went directly from using stone tools to iron tools, skipping the Bronze Age entirely. Another example would be the Maya civilization in Central America, which never progressed beyond stone tools.

What is the purpose of paragraph 2 in the overall discussion?

(A) It compares the three-age system to a newly developed dating system.
(B) It provides examples suggesting that the three-age system was flawed.
(C) It explains the procedure of using the three-age system in detail.
(D) It suggests alternative methods of determining the date of an artifact.

Vocab Quiz

The word ☐ in the passage is closest in meaning to

06 principal ☐ chief ☐ supplementary ☐ trivial

Reading Practice

METAMORPHOSIS IN THE ANIMAL KINGDOM

1 Metamorphosis refers to a biological process where an animal goes through a sudden, drastic change in its physiology. Generally, animals that undergo metamorphosis begin in a larvae state and then transform into a physiologically different adult state, each state exhibiting dramatically different characteristics. This change in form is largely due in part to either a change in the functions carried out by a particular species or a change in the species' lifestyle and environment.

2 Environment plays a crucial role in the metamorphosis of animals that are born in water but later need to prepare themselves physiologically for a terrestrial life. In other words, their bodies need to change to adapt to a life on land. Salamanders demonstrate an example of this need to adapt to a life on land, as a large majority of salamanders will lose their tail fin and external gills, originally used for swimming, which are replaced with a new layer of skin more suitable for land. **A** In the case of tadpoles and frogs, tadpoles lose their tails, which are replaced by limbs, allowing adult frogs to easily move around on more solid surfaces. **B** An interesting feature of the tadpole's metamorphosis results from its diet. **C** As it loses its strong teeth, necessary for the consumption of pond plants, the adult frog ends up developing strong tongue muscles to accommodate a change to a more carnivorous diet. **D**

3 The majority of insects also go through some form of metamorphosis, although their changes can be classified into ametabolous, hemimetabolous, and holometabolous stages. Ametabolous insects, like the mayfly, have no larvae stage and undergo an immediate transformation to adult stage. Hemimetabolous insects, such as the grasshopper, go through a gradual transformation into adult state. Lastly, holometabolous insects, such as the caterpillar and butterfly, undergo a complete physiological transformation from larvae to adult state.

4 When amphibians evolved for life on land, they still kept a connection to their original aquatic environments. On the other hand, reptiles, which were the first vertebrates, or animals with a backbone, were some of the first species to settle on land and therefore did not develop a radical physiological need to adapt to a terrestrial environment. Some reptiles do undergo small changes, such as a snake shedding its skin, but these changes are extremely gradual. In addition, while some reptiles do spend time in aquatic environments, they are generally born on land and do not go through severe physiological changes that occur in species that undergo metamorphosis.

Answer Book p. A36

|Factual Information|

01 In paragraph 2, the author states that

(A) salamanders metamorphose to adapt to an environment different from where they were born
(B) frogs retain the same diet as when they were tadpoles
(C) tadpoles' carnivorous diet facilitates their metamorphosis
(D) salamanders are able to modify their physiology based on their environment

|Rhetorical Purpose|

02 What is the relationship between paragraphs 1 and 2 in the passage?

(A) Paragraph 2 offers additional evidence for the theory explained in paragraph 1.
(B) Paragraph 1 presents an outline of the topics that are discussed in paragraph 2.
(C) Paragraph 2 summarizes the findings presented in paragraph 1.
(D) Paragraph 1 introduces a controversial topic that is argued in paragraph 2.

|Rhetorical Purpose|

03 The author mentions "caterpillar and butterfly" in the passage as an example of which of the following?

(A) Immediate metamorphosis to an adult stage
(B) No physical transformation to an adult stage
(C) Complete physiological metamorphose to an adult stage
(D) Gradual transformation to an adult stage

|Inference|

04 Which of the following can be concluded from the passage?

(A) Holometabolous insects are considered to be more evolved than ametabolous insects.
(B) Reptiles probably undergo metamorphosis in extreme conditions in order to survive.
(C) Species without the need to adapt to a new environment have less need for metamorphosis.
(D) Species that undergo a greater range of metamorphosis have a higher chance of survival.

|Sentence Insertion|

05 Look at the four squares [■] that indicate where the following sentence could be added to the passage.

> In a similar vein, the transition of its eyes from the side to the front of its head also allows it to locate and catch prey more easily.

Where would the sentence best fit?

(A) A   (B) B   (C) C   (D) D

Chapter 07   Sentence Insertion

Sentence Insertion questions ask you to determine the most logical place where a given sentence should be put. Reading passages in the TOEFL iBT are written coherently and have a logical flow, with or without the insertion sentence. Do not waste time looking for spots where the sentence will clear up an illogical or incoherent transition. Instead, look for places where it simply provides additional relevant information. There is 1 Sentence Insertion question for each passage, and it is always the next-to-last question. This question is worth 1 point.

How the Question is Worded

☐ Look at the four squares [■] that indicate where the following sentence could be added to the passage.

> [You will see an insertion sentence.]

Where would the sentence best fit?

> Click on a square [■] to add the sentence to the passage.

Keys to Solution

Key 1   Search for any reference words such as pronouns and pro-forms in the insertion sentence and look for such referents in surrounding sentences. Reference words provide hints for the correct location because they refer to previously mentioned nouns and ideas. Commonly used reference words are *it, they, this, these, the former, some*, etc.

Key 2   Search for any transitional words or phrases in the insertion sentence. Such transitions indicate the function of the insertion sentence, like explaining a sequence or providing an example.

+ **The common clues you can use in Sentence Insertion questions are:**

• Additional Explanation	in addition, furthermore, moreover, also, as well, besides
• Comparison	similarly, likewise
• Contrast	but, however, in contrast, on the other hand, on the contrary
• Cause and Consequence	due to, because of, therefore, consequently, as a result, thus, hence, in conclusion
• Example	for example, for instance

Key 3   Double-check the passage after inserting the given sentence to make sure that the passage makes sense with the insertion sentence. If the flow is illogical or unnatural, find another place to put the insertion sentence.

Sample Question

Coral reefs, often called "rainforests of the sea," are some of the most diverse ecosystems on Earth. Although coral reefs add up to less than half a percent of the ocean floor, more than a quarter of all marine species spend part of their lives in the reefs. **A** Relying on them for food and shelter, these species live in symbiosis with the reefs. **B** Unfortunately, due to overfishing and coastal waste water, the ecosystem has been interrupted and this has resulted in endangerment to the coral reefs. **C** The disrupted balance has induced a higher level of algae, which threatens the reefs by decreasing the coral growth rate. **D**

> **Key 1** Search for any reference words in the insertion sentence and look for such referents in surrounding sentences. "this mutualism" is the reference word of "symbiosis with the reefs."

Look at the four squares [■] that indicate where the following sentence could be added to the passage.

Therefore, keeping this mutualism under control is crucial in maintaining a healthy marine ecosystem.

> **Key 2** Search for any transitional words or phrases in the insertion sentence. According to the transitional word "Therefore" you can infer that the insertion sentence is stating the consequence of the previous sentence.

Where would the sentence best fit?

(A) **A**
(B) **B**
(C) **C**
(D) **D**

Answer & Explanations

Answer Book p. A38

(B)

According to the reference word "this mutualism" and the transitional word "Therefore" in the insertion sentence, you can presume that the insertion sentence should be added after description of some species' mutualistic relationship. **B** is the correct place because the previous sentence is describing the symbiosis between coral reefs and marine species.

Basic Drill

01

Stoicism is the study of the unified account of the world through three main approaches: logic, monistic physics, and naturalistic ethics, with the most emphasis on the latter, which focused on the divine principle of pervading nature. The stoic philosophers believed that generative, divine principles of the universe can ultimately reveal the essential reasons for and virtues of human life. They believed that human beings are part of nature and also possess ultimate knowledge within themselves. Ultimate knowledge relates to qualities that form human personalities and comprise human life. **A** It emphasizes the core, or so-called cardinal virtues: wisdom, courage, self-control, and justice. **B** The stoic philosophers viewed these virtues as ways of mapping the main areas of human experience and expertise. **C** They believed, when taken together, these virtues are essential to leading a full human life because the correct exercise of any one virtue depends on possessing and exercising the others as well. **D**

Choose the correct square [■] where the given sentence should be added.

But among all virtues, why these four?

(A) A   (B) B   (C) C   (D) D

02

Although the works of James Fenimore Cooper are considered to be of low literary quality by modern standards and quite unlike what people think of as classics, Cooper's novels have an important place in the history of American literature for a number of reasons. First, the hero of his novels, Natty Bumppo, served as a prototype for later heroes in American fiction. More than 150 years later, one can still see Bumppo's qualities of rugged individualism mirrored in the modern action heroes of books and films. Secondly, Cooper's novels awakened a hunger for truly American novels. Before Cooper's time, American readers had generally looked to European authors as the source of much of their literature. These novels naturally dealt with European issues rather than American ones. **A** After the success of Cooper's novels, however, Americans were no longer content with this situation. **B** They began to demand novels that took place in American settings and dealt with American issues. **C** Therefore, Cooper's novels were influential in promoting the growth of American literature in general. **D**

Choose the correct square [■] where the given sentence should be added.

In short, they wanted novels for Americans, written by Americans.

(A) A   (B) B   (C) C   (D) D

Vocab Quiz

The word ☐ in the passage is closest in meaning to

01 reveal	☐ unveil	☐ reform	☐ refine
02 prototype	☐ duplicate	☐ model	☐ motivation

03

The ideas of Charles Darwin had significant effects well beyond the areas of biology and ecology. The basic premise of Darwin's ideas — the concept that organisms must adapt or face extinction — made its way into the social theories of the nineteenth century as well. Social Darwinism, the adaptation of Darwin's ideas to human societies, was the dominant social philosophy of the nineteenth century. In its basic form, Social Darwinism claimed that the same forces which cause the evolution of organisms caused the evolution of societies as well. **A** According to this view, it was natural that societies which were better adapted to the pressures of the era would advance and oppress those which were not so well adapted. **B** Social Darwinist groups had different perspectives about the precise mechanism that enables the theory. **C** However, the most common opinion was that the competition between individuals in laissez-faire capitalism served as this mechanism, where it was considered natural and proper to exploit the weak to benefit the strong. **D**

Choose the correct square [■] where the given sentence should be added.

In other words, the rise and fall of the societies were determined by the law of survival of the fittest.

(A) A   (B) B   (C) C   (D) D

04

The forest canopy is defined as the upper reaches of the forest. It is composed of large, slow-growth trees, which rise high above the forest floor and then spread their branches over a wide area. **A** Examples of canopy trees include pines, oaks, and redwoods. **B** The uppermost layer of the canopy is sometimes 120 feet off the forest floor, which can soar 20 to 100 feet above the next-tallest trees. **C** They rise as a straight column of wood for many feet and then, at their tops, branch out and spread in a heavy layer of leaves. **D** The billions of leaves of the canopy act as solar panels and convert sunlight to energy through photosynthesis. In fact, canopy trees have such a monopoly on sunlight in the forest that they are responsible for nearly 90 percent of all photosynthesis that occurs, so they support the majority of the production of fruits, seeds, and flowers.

Choose the correct square [■] where the given sentence should be added.

Due to this formation, canopy trees are able to absorb the greatest amount of sunlight.

(A) A   (B) B   (C) C   (D) D

Vocab Quiz

The word ☐ in the passage is closest in meaning to

03 precise	☐ hidden	☐ underlying	☐ exact
04 spread	☐ shield	☐ extend	☐ support

Basic Drill

05

Direct democracy, sometimes called pure democracy, is a form of democracy where the power of decision making lies directly with the public. It is usually contrasted with a representative democracy, where the general public votes for representatives, who then make laws on the public's behalf. In a direct democracy, the public chooses its leaders, votes on its laws, and is actively involved in the major decisions of society. The power of a direct democracy is based on three tenets: the power of initiative, the power of referendum, and the power of recall. **[A]** The power of initiative is the power to raise issues that should be voted on. **[B]** In a direct democracy, any citizen can, in theory, suggest a new law or policy. **[C]** In practice, issues are usually raised through petitions. **[D]** The power of referendum is simply the power to approve or reject initiatives through a direct vote. In this way, citizens in a direct democracy are actively involved in creating their own laws. Initiatives and referendums together dramatically reduce the direct costs, time, and effort spent on government decisions. The final tenet of a direct democracy is the power of recall. Under the power of recall, the public has the right to remove government officials it is unhappy with. This means that the leaders of the nation are directly accountable to the public, since they can basically be removed from office at any time. Proponents of direct democracy believe these aspects have positive net social benefits and limit the influence of numerically small but politically powerful pressure groups.

Choose the correct square [■] where the given sentence should be added.

If a citizen can get a certain number of signatures for his or her idea, that person can force the society to vote on the idea.

(A) A   (B) B   (C) C   (D) D

Vocab Quiz

The word ☐ in the passage is closest in meaning to

05 tenet   ☐ principle   ☐ phase   ☐ outcome

06

White's law, named after the famous anthropologist Leslie White, is a theory which attempts to explain how the availability of energy affects the speed of advancement in a civilization. **A** The basic assumption of White's law is that out of the three major aspects of civilization — technological, sociological, and ideological — the technological aspect plays the greatest role in driving the evolution of a civilization. **B** White thought that the intent of all technology is to help people overcome the challenges of survival. **C** Farming technology provides us with greater amounts of food, and housing technology provides us with shelter. **D** Since all technology requires some form of energy to operate, greater amounts of energy should allow us to use greater amounts of technology, which in turn should allow society to advance. The same would be true of more efficient energy usage. If technology is created to use less energy, that should have the same basic effect as increasing the total amount of energy available.

White distinguished five different stages in the evolution of civilization, according to the different forms of energy used to power technology. In the first stage, energy is provided by our own muscles and humans must do all of their own work. In the second stage of development, humans begin to use animals to power their technology, as a farmer does when he uses a horse to pull his plow. The third stage occurs when humans begin to use plants as a source of power. This stage can be identified by a huge increase in the efficiency of farming. In the fourth stage, humans begin to rely on natural resources such as coal and oil as their primary sources of energy. In the final stage, nuclear power is utilized to provide energy.

Choose the correct square [■] where the given sentence should be added.

White's law basically states that civilization evolves as the amount of energy harnessed per person is increased, or as the efficiency of energy usage is increased.

(A) **A**   (B) **B**   (C) **C**   (D) **D**

Vocab Quiz

The word ☐ in the passage is closest in meaning to

06 intent   ☐ value   ☐ virtue   ☐ purpose

Reading Practice

ATMOSPHERIC CIRCULATION

1   Much of the world's weather is determined by two atmospheric cells: the Hadley cell and the Polar cell. Cells are atmospheric cycles that are driven by thermal energy. As the sun heats the air near the surface of the earth, the air begins to rise. At a certain point, however, this air encounters a barrier and cannot rise any further. As new air is heated and begins to rise, the warm air near this barrier is pushed sideways, since it cannot move vertically anymore. As it moves, it begins to lose its heat, until it once again begins to sink towards the earth, pushing the cooler air below it sideways and forming a circular movement of air, which is called a cell.

2   The Hadley cell begins about 5 degrees north or south of the equator, where the sun's heating effect is the strongest. The high temperatures near the equator allow the air to pick up tremendous amounts of moisture from the oceans before it begins to rise. The energy contained in the warm, moist air causes violent thunderstorms, which transport that energy high into the atmosphere. As the warm, moist air begins its horizontal movement, it begins to lose energy in the form of heat. By the time it reaches a latitude of about 30 degrees north or south, it has lost enough heat energy to once again sink towards the earth. In the last part of the cycle, the air flows back towards the equator to begin the cycle again. An important effect of this is that the Hadley cell creates the strong trade winds that early sailors used to cross the seas.

3   **A** The Polar cell begins at much higher latitudes, where the air is considerably cooler and drier. **B** At about 60 degrees north or south, the air still has enough heat to drive a cell cycle. **C** As the air rises, it encounters a similar barrier and begins to move laterally instead of vertically. **D** By the time it reaches the North or South Pole, it has lost nearly all of its heat and sinks back down to the earth. The major difference is that the air was never warm enough to pick up much moisture, so this part of the cycle involves much less water loss than it does in the Hadley cell. The major effect of the Polar cell on weather is that it creates a jet stream, the strong eastern wind pattern that controls much of the weather at northern and southern latitudes.

| Rhetorical Purpose |

01 Why does the author mention "trade winds"?

(A) To discuss the discovery of the Hadley cell
(B) To illustrate the dangers of thunderstorms in the Hadley cell
(C) To explain the weather effects created by the Hadley cell
(D) To accentuate the importance of the Hadley cell in the history of trade

| Reference |

02 The word "it" in the passage refers to

(A) heat
(B) air
(C) barrier
(D) cycle

| Rhetorical Purpose |

03 How does the author explain the movement of air in the Hadley cell and the Polar cell?

(A) By discussing the role of heat in the movement of the air
(B) By clarifying how each cell influences the other
(C) By contrasting the direction of movement within each cell
(D) By explaining how weather can disrupt the normal movement in each cell

| Inference |

04 Which of the following can be inferred from the passage about the movement of air?

(A) Air near the equator moves faster than air near the Poles.
(B) Cool air tends to sink below warm air.
(C) The loss of moisture tends to slow the movement of air.
(D) The movement of air is influenced by changes in weather patterns.

| Sentence Insertion |

05 Look at the four squares [■] that indicate where the following sentence could be added to the passage.

> Although these atmospheric conditions are somewhat different, the mechanics that drive the Polar cell are the same as those for the Hadley cell.

Where would the sentence best fit?

(A) A   (B) B   (C) C   (D) D

Chapter 08 Prose Summary

Prose Summary questions ask you to recognize and summarize major ideas within the passage. You will see an introductory sentence and six statements. You must select three statements that, along with the introductory sentence, create a complete and coherent summary of the passage. When a Prose Summary question does not appear as the last question, a Fill in a Table question (See Chapter 09) will appear instead. You will receive the full 2 points by selecting all three of the correct statements for the summary, 1 point by selecting two and 0 point by selecting one or none.

How the Question is Worded

☐ **Directions:** An introductory sentence for a brief summary of the passage is provided below. Complete the summary by selecting the THREE answer choices that express the most important ideas in the passage. Some sentences do not belong in the summary because they express ideas that are not presented in the passage or are minor ideas in the passage. **This question is worth 2 points.**

Drag your answer choices to the spaces where they belong. To remove an answer choice, click on it. To review the passage, click on **View Text**.

(Introductory sentence)
-
-
-

Answer Choices	
(A)	(D)
(B)	(E)
(C)	(F)

Keys to Solution

Key 1 Read the introductory sentence provided in the question. The introductory sentence directly states the main idea of the passage, so select statements that directly relate to the introductory sentence.

Key 2 Match the main idea of each paragraph with answer choices before you answer the question. The answers for the Prose Summary question are mostly the main points of each paragraph.

Key 3 Take notes on major facts and details as you read the passage; exclude minor ideas.

Key 4 Eliminate answer choices if they
- are not mentioned in the passage or if they directly contradict information in the passage
- are only minor details in the passage

Sample Question

Numerous studies were undertaken to determine the exact nature of the risk windfarms pose to avian populations, particularly birds and bats. As a whole, bird and bat fatalities differ greatly among facilities and regions, but were in the range of 4 to 14 per wind turbine per year.

Most birds killed by wind turbines were song birds. Since most of these birds migrate at night at altitudes far above wind turbines, it is believed that the majority of these deaths take place during take-off and landing, at resting areas near wind turbine sites. Regarding bats, one of the primary causes of death is direct collision with the turbine blades or poles. Another main cause of death is barotrauma, an injury normally caused by changes in atmospheric pressure, which in the case of bats results from spinning turbine blades.

In response to this growing problem, extensive monitoring has been added at numerous wind turbine sites, and researchers and operators have come up with several options for minimizing or mitigating mortality of birds and bats. Some of these examples are using lighting or noise generators to repel them, ceasing operation during periods that could increase mortality rates, and adopting newer turbine designs in areas with lower avian populations. Fortunately, it was reported that these endeavors to reduce the mortality rates in avian populations are bringing about encouraging results in some regions.

Directions: An introductory sentence for a brief summary of the passage is provided below. Complete the summary by selecting the THREE answer choices that express the most important ideas in the passage. Some sentences do not belong in the summary because they express ideas that are not presented in the passage or are minor ideas in the passage. *This question is worth 2 points.*

Wind farms pose some hazard to birds and bats.

-
-
-

Answer Choices

(A) Migrating song birds are among the greatest casualties in avian populations caused by wind turbines.	(D) Many studies regarding the risk of wind turbines to birds and bats have yet to find a solution.
(B) Birds flying at night and at high altitudes are at greater risk of mortality from wind turbines.	(E) The various efforts to cut the fatality rates among birds and bats are showing positive outcomes.
(C) Facilities and regions are the biggest variables in bird and bat fatalities from wind turbines.	(F) Direct collision with the wind turbines and barotrauma are the two major causes of death among bats.

Answer & Explanations

Answer Book p. A44

(A), (E), (F)

(A), (E) and (F) summarize paragraph 2 and 3.
(B) and (D) are not accurate information. (C) is not mentioned.

Basic Drill

01

THE DARK AGE OF GREECE

Many civilizations undergo a series of high points and low points during their history. Among early civilizations, we call the low points "dark ages" because civilizations often fell apart to such a point that it is hard to get an accurate picture of their history during these periods. During a dark age, a civilization may not have produced monuments, statues, or other objects which we use to learn about early civilizations.

One of the most significant dark ages was the dark age of Greece, which lasted from about 1100 BC to 900 BC. Prior to that time, Greece had a highly advanced society called the Mycenaean civilization. The Mycenaeans were a trading civilization, and they did much to spread their culture across the eastern Mediterranean. In fact, the Mycenaean civilization was so important that when it collapsed in the twelfth century BC, most other civilizations in the region collapsed as well. The next 200 years are like a blank page to historians, and thus we know very little about this period. One major reason for this is that writing basically stopped. The collapse of the Mycenaeans brought an end to writing in the area, and thus an end to the written records historians rely on.

The little that we know about this period has been learned from archaeology. It seems that civilization became much less advanced. The pottery from this period is much simpler and less artistic. This suggests that there was a lack of wealthy people to buy higher-quality products. Another interesting point is that most of the large cities of earlier time periods appear to have been abandoned in favor of much smaller settlements. This would suggest a large decrease in population, possibly due to a widespread lack of food and consequent starvation.

Sometime around 800 BC, the Greeks began to emerge from this dark age, most likely due to the influence of other civilizations. They had lost their early writing system, but began to use the writing system of the Phoenicians. They began constructing larger cities and trading with their neighbors again. Over the next 300 years, their civilization continued to rise, and their dark age was left behind.

Directions: An introductory sentence for a brief summary of the passage is provided below. Complete the summary by selecting the THREE answer choices that express the most important ideas in the passage. Some sentences do not belong in the summary because they express ideas that are not presented in the passage or are minor ideas in the passage. **This question is worth 2 points.**

The dark age of Greece was a period of collapse in civilization which lasted from 1100 BC to 900 BC.
•
•
•

Answer Choices	
(A) The Mycenaean civilization, a highly advanced Greek society, had a great influence on the eastern Mediterranean region.	(D) The dark age of Greece seems to have been characterized by less-advanced civilization and significant drops in population.
(B) The dark age of Greece, starting with the collapse of the Mycenaean civilization, included most of the civilizations in the eastern Mediterranean.	(E) Many pieces of evidence suggest that there was a huge increase in population during the dark age of Greece.
(C) Despite the loss of writing and the end of large-scale construction, historians were able to gain information about the dark age of Greece.	(F) The Greeks were able to emerge from their dark age with the aid of other civilizations such as the Phoenicians.

Vocab Quiz

The word ☐ in the passage is closest in meaning to

01-1 accurate   ☐ exact   ☐ general   ☐ estimated
01-2 period   ☐ culture   ☐ cycle   ☐ time

Basic Drill

02

EARTH'S ENERGY BUDGET

The Earth has three major naturally occurring energy sources: solar radiation, tidal energy caused by the moon's gravitational pull on the oceans, and internal heating caused mostly by the radioactive decay of metals deep inside the Earth. Of these three sources, solar radiation accounts for 99.97 percent of all the energy available on Earth. In fact, the amount of energy contributed by tidal action and internal heating is less than the annual fluctuation in solar radiation. The total amount of incoming energy and the amount of energy either used or emitted into space are roughly equal. This balance is called the energy budget.

Of all the solar energy that reaches the Earth, 6 percent is reflected back into space by the upper atmosphere. Another 20 percent is reflected by the tops of clouds, and 4 percent is reflected from the surface. This means that 30 percent of all the solar energy reaching the Earth immediately escapes back into space. Of the remaining 70 percent, 19 percent is absorbed into the atmosphere — 3 percent by clouds and 16 percent by atmospheric gases and dust. That means that 51 percent of all solar energy is absorbed by ground sources.

The 70 percent of the solar energy that is absorbed by the Earth must also eventually be released into space, or the temperature of the Earth would continuously rise. This energy is released through indirect radiation. All ground heat is eventually radiated back into the atmosphere, where it eventually escapes into space. Indirect ground radiation occurs through three processes. The surface radiates 21 percent of the solar energy it absorbs directly as heat. Another 23 percent is transferred back into the atmosphere through the evaporation of surface water. The remaining 7 percent is lost as the ground heats the air near its surface.

This complex balance of incoming and outgoing energy is controlled by a number of factors. One such factor is the reflectivity of different surface materials. For example, ice reflects about 35 percent of solar energy, while forests only reflect 5 percent. Therefore, environmental changes, such as the melting of glaciers and deforestation, can affect the Earth's energy budget. In addition, gases in the atmosphere, especially carbon dioxide, play an important role in the absorption of solar energy, so changes in their levels affect the energy budget as well.

Directions: An introductory sentence for a brief summary of the passage is provided below. Complete the summary by selecting the THREE answer choices that express the most important ideas in the passage. Some sentences do not belong in the summary because they express ideas that are not presented in the passage or are minor ideas in the passage. **This question is worth 2 points.**

The energy budget is the balance of the input and output of energy from the Earth.
•
•
•

Answer Choices	
(A) All solar energy must be transferred back into space either by immediate reflection or indirect radiation to maintain the energy budget.	(D) Environmental changes which affect the reflectivity of ground surfaces or the absorption ability of the atmosphere can greatly affect the energy budget.
(B) Although other sources contribute minor amounts to the total energy input of the Earth, most energy comes from the Sun.	(E) Clouds play an important role in reflecting and absorbing solar energy, and are vital to the energy budget.
(C) Only 70 percent of all solar energy is absorbed by the Earth's atmosphere and surface levels.	(F) Solar energy absorbed by ground surfaces can be radiated back into space through three atmospheric processes.

Vocab Quiz

The word ☐ in the passage is closest in meaning to

02-1 eventually   ☐ continually   ☐ subsequently   ☐ ultimately
02-2 especially   ☐ notably   ☐ rarely   ☐ generally

Basic Drill

03

WORKING MEMORY

The development of the first computers in the 1960s had an important influence on psychology. As computers became more advanced and began to "think" in more complex ways, psychologists began to make comparisons between the workings of computers and the human brain. Many of these comparisons have turned out to be wrong or inaccurate; the human brain is quite different from a computer. But the comparison between human memory and computer memory has stood up to rigorous testing.

A computer has two forms of memory. While its hard drive stores all the information in the computer over long periods of time, its RAM, or Random Access Memory, stores the files that the computer needs to use at the present time. Once the computer stops using a file, it is "forgotten" by its RAM and returned to the hard drive. The human brain works in a similar way. Psychologists call our "hard drive" long-term memory, and our "RAM" working memory.

Working memory serves a number of functions. This is where new information is stored before it is processed into long-term memory. Working memory also allows us to call up information from our long-term memory when we need to use it. For example, a person's address is stored in his or her long-term memory, but it is called up to working memory when that person fills out an envelope at the post office. Working memory also allows us to integrate old information with new information. If a person studied sociology several years ago, all that information would be in their long-term memory. If that same person takes a new sociology class, some of that old information will be called up to working memory, so connections can be made between the new and the old information.

With so many important jobs to do, working memory plays a vital role in our intelligence. Just as a computer's performance is partially limited by its RAM capacity (computers with too little RAM cannot run larger, more complex programs), so is our ability to process and handle information partially determined by our working memory. A person who can store more pieces of information in working memory can work with more information at one time. That person can also make a greater number of connections between new and old information. Therefore, a higher capacity for working memory boosts human mental performance just as more RAM does for a computer.

Directions: An introductory sentence for a brief summary of the passage is provided below. Complete the summary by selecting the THREE answer choices that express the most important ideas in the passage. Some sentences do not belong in the summary because they express ideas that are not presented in the passage or are minor ideas in the passage. **This question is worth 2 points.**

> **Psychologists have found a strong resemblance between the structures of computer memory and human memory.**
>
> -
> -
> -

Answer Choices	
(A) A computer's RAM capacity determines the computer's ability to handle information effectively.	(D) Working memory is essential when a person studies new subjects or reviews old subjects.
(B) A computer's hard drive is comparable to a human's long-term memory, as its RAM is to a human's working memory.	(E) Working memory has a strong relation to intelligence because of its role in processing information.
(C) Working memory is what is used to store new information and handle existing information.	(F) Making connections between different pieces of information is the most important function of working memory.

Vocab Quiz

The word ☐ in the passage is closest in meaning to

03-1 rigorous   ☐ numerous   ☐ precise   ☐ fundamental
03-2 boosts   ☐ increases   ☐ disturbs   ☐ affects

Basic Drill

04

OSMOREGULATION

Different from terrestrial mammals, marine mammals must constantly maintain and regulate the concentration and volume of their internal body fluid, as water and electrolytes constantly cross back and forth through their body walls. This active maintenance and regulation of internal water and electrolyte concentration is referred to as osmoregulation. To maintain a constant internal fluid balance with little deviation, the amount of water and electrolytes entering the animal must be equal to that going out. For instance, if a dolphin takes in a great amount of water and electrolytes, it must be able to excrete an equal amount through breathing, feces and urine, or milk during lactation. On the other hand, when a seal is fasting, it needs to have the capability to endure the absence of food and water by having a unique mechanism to reduce water loss and produce water from its metabolism.

Marine mammals take in water and electrolytes through the ingestion of food and water. Compared to land mammals, the diet of marine mammals consists of a far greater amount of water, up to 80 percent of what they ingest. Due to this, most marine mammals do not ingest seawater, although they have the capacity to do so. The ratio of water to electrolytes can differ according to the type of an organism consumed; the electrolyte content of a vertebrate food source is usually one third that of the seawater, while an invertebrate is essentially the same as the surrounding seawater. As such, an organism's diet has a significant impact on the degree to which it must actively manage its electrolyte intake. In addition, animals can also produce water as a by-product of metabolism, which is called metabolic water production. Likewise, the amount of metabolic water varies according to their diets.

There are several methods marine mammals use to control their output of water and electrolytes. The methods to get rid of the surplus water in their internal fluid are excretion and evaporation. Water is evaporated through the skin and lungs. No electrolytes are lost in the process of evaporation because marine mammals lack sweat glands, which would allow salt to pass through to the surface of the skin. However, by excreting water through urine or feces, both water and electrolytes can be removed from the body. Because salt, comprising a large portion of electrolytes, must be excreted by the kidney, marine mammals have developed a specialized kidney that can accommodate the high volume of water and electrolytes that must be processed. This specialized kidney regulates the internal fluid balance by controlling the concentration of the urine.

Directions: An introductory sentence for a brief summary of the passage is provided below. Complete the summary by selecting the THREE answer choices that express the most important ideas in the passage. Some sentences do not belong in the summary because they express ideas that are not presented in the passage or are minor ideas in the passage. **This question is worth 2 points.**

Marine mammals employ unique methods to regulate their body fluid balance.
•
•
•

Answer Choices	
(A) Marine mammals can absorb water and electrolytes by ingesting food and water, and yield water through metabolism.	(D) Marine mammals have the ability to maintain and regulate their internal body fluid balance, called osmoregulation.
(B) Both dolphins and seals are typical examples of marine mammals' adaptation to saline environments.	(E) Excretion and evaporation are the typical methods marine mammals use to control their output of water and electrolytes.
(C) Marine mammals developed special sweat glands and kidneys to control the output of electrolytes.	(F) The electrolyte content ratio differs by prey, as invertebrates have three times more electrolytes than vertebrates do.

Vocab Quiz

The word ▢ in the passage is closest in meaning to

04-1 endure   ☐ counteract   ☐ complement   ☐ survive
04-2 surplus   ☐ excess   ☐ worthless   ☐ residual

Reading Practice

THE IMPACT OF GLOBAL WARMING ON OCEAN TEMPERATURES

1   Most researchers agree that the recent global warming trend is due to greenhouse gases humans have put into the atmosphere. Over the past few decades, there has been an intense scientific debate over whether global warming would affect the oscillations between El Niño and La Niña. El Niño is characterized by unusually warm ocean temperatures in the Equatorial Pacific, as opposed to La Niña, which is characterized by unusually cold ocean temperatures in the Equatorial Pacific. For the past several millennia, the Pacific Ocean has alternated between these two states in an irregular, though basically balanced oscillation. Some theorize that if the oscillation stops, the Earth will go through a continuous El Niño-like state which could warm the Earth very quickly.

2   Ordinarily the cool surface layer of the eastern Pacific Ocean acts as a water-cooled radiator and removes heat from the tropical atmosphere by carrying it hundreds of meters below the surface. The ocean currents act as the coolant that absorbs atmospheric heat, but in an El Niño year, both the shallow and deep waters are too hot to diffuse the atmospheric heat, causing a warming and strange weather patterns. Although El Niño events are too short to have lasting effects nowadays, some climate scientists question the tropical Pacific's ability to cool the atmosphere under growing global warming effects. However, recent studies into the ancient climate of the Eocene Epoch indicate that the tropical Pacific may actually be more resilient to global warming than the current climate theory claims.

3   **A** Some of the researchers hypothesized that the Eocene Epoch would be the best period to compare with if a continuous El Niño-like state had ever existed. **B** Contrary to most beliefs that the Pacific Ocean consists of two layers with shallows absorbing heat and depths carrying it away, it has been proven that the tropical eastern Pacific also has a third layer wedged between the two. **C** Because this third layer historically remained cool and acted as a barrier between the warmer shallow and depth water, Eocene tropics were not much different than they are today. **D** This finding was further supported by other studies which used sediment records of ancient lakebeds in present-day Wyoming and Germany. These sediment records demonstrated that El Niño events occurred with identical regularity in the Eocene Epoch's climate computer model, indicating that there was no continuous El Niño state, even though the climate was significantly warmer.

|Reference|

01 The word "it" in the passage refers to

(A) atmosphere   (B) radiator   (C) surface   (D) heat

|Vocabulary|

02 The word "ancient" in the passage is closest in meaning to

(A) humid   (B) inconsistent   (C) prehistoric   (D) unchanging

|Rhetorical Purpose|

03 In paragraph 3, why does the author give details about "sediment records"?

(A) To prove the geological similarity between Wyoming and Germany
(B) To explain the role of the third layer of the tropical Pacific during Eocene Epoch
(C) To illustrate how Eocene tropics were able to maintain their warm climate
(D) To support the theory that a continuous El Niño-like state is unlikely to happen

|Sentence Insertion|

04 Look at the four squares [■] that indicate where the following sentence could be added to the passage.

> Based on this hypothesis, they simulated the computer model of a "hothouses" climate in the Eocene Epoch to see the tropical Pacific's role under a continuous El Niño-like state.

Where would the sentence best fit?

(A) **A**   (B) **B**   (C) **C**   (D) **D**

|Prose Summary|

05 **Directions:** An introductory sentence for a brief summary of the passage is provided below. Complete the summary by selecting the THREE answer choices that express the most important ideas in the passage. Some sentences do not belong in the summary because they express ideas that are not presented in the passage or are minor ideas in the passage. ***This question is worth 2 points.***

There has been controversial debate over whether global warming may cause a significant impact on the Earth's temperatures.

(A) The climate of the Eocene Epoch has been studied to find out the role of the tropical Pacific under a continuous El Niño-like state.
(B) Sediment records of ancient lakebeds showed an inconsistent El Niño cycle with the Eocene Epoch's climate model.
(C) There is much evidence supporting the fact that greenhouse gases caused by humans are the main cause of global warming.
(D) Some researchers believe global warming will disenable the tropical Pacific's role of cooling the tropical atmosphere and lead to a continuous El Niño-like state.
(E) During a La Niña year, the role of the tropical Pacific is crucial, as it cools the significantly warm climate.
(F) Some evidence suggests there will not be an El Niño-like state in the future because the Pacific Ocean will remove the heat from the tropical atmosphere.

Chapter 09   Fill in a Table

Fill in a Table questions ask you to categorize specific facts in the passage. These questions present a chart with two or three categories, and you must place five or seven statements in their appropriate categories.

There will be two more extra sentences in the answer choices that do not fit into either category. When a Fill in a Table question does not appear as the last question, a Summary question(See Chapter 08) will appear instead. Summary questions have a higher chance of appearing compared to Fill in a Table questions.

Three Point Question		Four Point Question	
Correct Answers	Points	Correct Answers	Points
5	3 points	7	4 points
4	2 points	6	3 points
3	1 point	5	2 points
0-2	0 point	4	1 point
		0-3	0 point

How the Question is Worded

☐ **Directions:** Select the appropriate phrases from the answer choices and match them to the category to which they relate. TWO of the answer choices will NOT be used. ***This question is worth 3 points.***

Drag your answer choices to the spaces where they belong. To remove an answer choice, click on it. To review the passage, click on **View Text**.	
Answer Choices	**Category 1**
(A) (B) (C) (D) (E) (F) (G)	• • •
	Category 2
	• •

Keys to Solution

Key 1   Check the categories from the Fill in a Table question before reading the passage and take notes of details regarding each category as you read the passage.

Key 2   Remember that several answer choices will paraphrase ideas from the passages. Make sure you recognize similar ideas that are worded differently.

Key 3   Eliminate the answer choices that
- directly contradict the passage or are not mentioned in the passage
- do not belong to any of the categories

Sample Question

One of the central ideas behind the United States government is the separation of powers. All powers of the central government are divided among three co-equal departments — the executive, the legislative, and the judiciary. The idea of dividing the powers of the government in this way was to ensure that no one body could take control and override the will of the people. For the founding fathers of the United States, protecting America from tyranny was one of the most important goals.

The executive branch is headed by the President of the United States. Today, the President's power has grown substantially from what it was when America was first founded. For example, America's first President had only four Cabinet departments — State, Treasury, War, and Justice. Today, there are 15 departments.

The legislative branch of government is the Congress. This is the part of government responsible for making the laws of the land. The American Congress is divided into two parts — the House of Representatives and the Senate. The House of Representatives has 435 members who are elected on the basis of state population. The Senate has 100 members, two per state regardless of state size. Together, these two bodies balance the will of the majority with the needs of individual states.

The judicial branch of the United States government is the Supreme Court. There are nine members of the Supreme Court, including the Chief Justice. The Supreme Court is the only one of the three branches whose members are not directly elected. Instead, the President nominates a person to the court and the Senate confirms the nomination. Once appointed, Supreme Court justices can serve for life.

Directions: Select the appropriate phrases from the answer choices and match them to the type of department to which they relate. TWO of the answer choices will NOT be used. **This question is worth 3 points.**

Answer Choices	The Executive
(A) Comprised of 12 members (B) Led by the President of the United States (C) Run by justices authorized by the President and the Senate (D) Headed by the Congress (E) Establishes the laws (F) Decides the number of its members according to the size of states (G) Consists of the House of Representatives and the Senate	• •
	The Legislative
	• •
	The Judiciary
	•

Answer & Explanations   Answer Book p. A52

[The Executive – (B), (E)], [The Legislative – (D), (G)], [The Judiciary – (C)]
The executive is headed by the President, and has grown in power compared to when America was first founded. The legislative establishes the laws, and consists of two parts: the House of Representatives and the Senate. The judiciary is the only branch whose members are chosen by the President and the Senate.

Basic Drill

01

THE BONE RECORD OF HUMAN ANCESTORS

Archaeologists and anthropologists interested in tracing the evolution of the human species must rely largely on what is commonly called the bone record. The bone record is the collection of fossilized bones gathered from different sites. By dating these bones and placing them in chronological order, scientists can trace both the evolution and movement of the human species.

The oldest bones in the bone record belong to a species named *Australopithecus*. *Australopithecus* first emerged about 4.4 million years ago, and is the first human ancestor to definitively diverge from ape species. The primary distinction between apes and *Australopithecus* is that *Australopithecus* was a fully bipedal creature; it walked in an upright manner on two feet. While some apes are able to stand upright, they can only do so for short periods of time. Nevertheless, the brain of *Australopithecus* was only about 35 percent of the size of a modern human's, and its intelligence was probably not much higher than a chimpanzee's. *Australopithecus* was also much smaller than modern humans. Typical heights for the species were about 1.2 to 1.4 meters, with males being significantly larger than females. *Australopithecus* did not make tools, but it did use rocks and sticks to reach for food, to crush nuts, and for other purposes. Because of its small size and lack of weapons for defense, *Australopithecus* was a common prey for lions and other predators of western and southern Africa where it lived.

The bones of *Australopithecus* began to disappear from the bone record around 1.8 million years ago, when the species was quickly replaced by the more advanced *Homo erectus*. *Homo erectus* was a much more "human" species. It stood at around 1.75 meters, about the same height as the average modern human. Its brain was about 75 percent of the size of a modern human's, and this larger brain size allowed it to fashion a number of stone tools and weapons. With its larger size and new weapons, *Homo erectus* quickly went from being hunted to being the hunter. *Homo erectus* was a far more successful species than *Australopithecus*, and spread from Africa into southern Europe and Asia. *Homo erectus* still was not fully human, however. The structure of its vocal cords suggests that it was incapable of forming speech and was limited to grunts and growls for communication.

Directions: Select the appropriate phrases from the answer choices and match them to the species of human ancestor to which they relate. TWO of the answer choices will NOT be used. **This question is worth 3 points.**

Answer Choices	Australopithecus
(A) Roughly the same size as modern humans (B) Able to make its own tools (C) Intelligence similar to chimpanzees (D) Defenseless against predators (E) Entirely a meat eater (F) More similar to humans (G) Able to stand upright only for a short time	• •
	Homo Erectus
	• • •

Vocab Quiz

The word ☐ in the passage is closest in meaning to

01-1 sites   ☐ locations   ☐ structures   ☐ timelines

01-2 replaced   ☐ conquered   ☐ abated   ☐ supplanted

Basic Drill

02

THE SPLIT OF THE CHRISTIAN CHURCH

The division of the Christian Church has its roots in the division of the Roman Empire. The Christians in the Latin-speaking Western Empire slowly began to drift apart from the Greek-speaking Christians of the Eastern Empire. While the gaps between these two groups steadily grew over the next 700 years, they were still technically members of the same Christian faith. In 1054, however, the Christian Church was irrevocably split into the Western Catholic Church and the Eastern Orthodox Church.

The causes for this split were innumerable. Certainly, the language barrier between the two churches played a major role, but there were other, more decisive factors in the breakup of the Christian Church. The power of the Pope was one such issue. The early Christian Church was ruled by five prelates, or church fathers. These prelates were stationed in the five most-prominent cities of the Roman world, with the Roman prelate receiving the most honor. In the early church, while the Roman prelate had been entitled to a greater amount of the respect, all five prelates wielded the same amount of power within the church. As the divisions between eastern and western Christians grew, the Roman prelate began to claim authority over his four eastern colleagues. The eastern prelates rejected the supremacy of the Roman Pope, and this was the first major source of tension within the church.

The other factor leading to the Great Schism of 1054 was the more complex issue of religious belief. Since the earliest days of the church, people had debated the exact nature of Christ. Was Christ a man, or was he a god? If he was a god, was he the equal of his father, or was he a lesser god? To solve such difficult questions, the Christians had developed a complex concept called the Trinity. The idea of the Trinity maintained that the three divine beings mentioned in the Bible — the Father, the Son(Christ), and the Holy Spirit — were in fact different facets of the same god. They were at once divided and the same. The Western Church, under the guidance of the Pope, had explicitly stated this to be true. The Eastern prelates, however, were not as vocal on the matter. They preferred to leave their beliefs unstated. These differences ultimately led to the split of the Christian Church in 1054.

Directions: Select the appropriate phrases from the answer choices and match them to the group of Christians to which they relate. TWO of the answer choices will NOT be used. **This question is worth 3 points.**

Answer Choices	Western Church
(A) Wanted equality among the prelates	•
(B) Accepted the Bible as the only authority	•
(C) Spoke Latin	**Eastern Church**
(D) Did not officially advocate the concept of the Trinity	•
(E) Did not acknowledge the power of the Pope	•
(F) Supported the concept of the Trinity	•
(G) Actively pushed for a split in the church	

Vocab Quiz

The word ☐ in the passage is closest in meaning to

02-1 innumerable ☐ controversial ☐ unveiled ☐ countless

02-2 facets ☐ aspects ☐ descriptions ☐ origins

Basic Drill

03

CELLULOSE DIGESTION IN TERMITES

Cellulose, the world's most abundant carbohydrate, is an endless string of 3,000 or more sugar molecules. Although it is a very common substance on the Earth, most organisms lack the ability to digest cellulose and have difficulty ingesting it as an energy source. Grazing mammals, such as cows and goats, are able to digest cellulose directly, but in a time-consuming way. Termites, one of the smallest orders of insects, receive their nutrition from cellulose with help of certain microorganisms. Termites use two distinct feeding strategies to assimilate cellulose indirectly depending on their degree of evolution.

Primitive termites digest cellulose by means of tiny one-celled animals in their digestive tract. These one-celled microorganisms, called protozoa, do the actual work of breaking down the cellulose. Termites swallow grass, leaves, and branches that are delivered to the fermentation chamber, where protozoa reside and do the work. These tiny workers then break the cellulose down into sugar and enable their host to take in the sugar as an energy source. Since termites and protozoa are two different organisms, the culture of cellulose digesters is passed along through a special process from one generation to the next. Initially, newly hatched termites lack these microorganisms for their cellulose digestion. Therefore, adults secrete a special liquid, rich in digesters, for young termites to feed on, thereby allowing young termites to obtain protozoa. When treated with antibiotics or an anti-protozoan solution, the protozoa in their digestive system will die and the termites will slowly starve to death, unable to digest cellulose into absorbable sugar molecules.

More-advanced termite species practice a different type of feeding strategy. Unlike their primitive brethren, advanced termites break down cellulose outside their body. Without going through a time-consuming fermentation chamber process, these species are more nimble and efficient in comparison. In order to digest cellulose in the air, advanced termites live in symbiosis with fungi, the only organism able to break down cellulose in the presence of oxygen. Termites gather grass, twigs and other woody materials by chewing up and delivering them to their nest. In the nest, the chewed-up wood is piled up in a small ventilated chamber called a comb. The termites then place spores of a special fungus called *Termitomyces* on the comb, and as the spores grow on the comb, they convert the cellulose from woody pulp into sugars and nitrogen for termites to intake. Needless to say, termites and their micro-digesters rely on each other for survival.

Directions: Select the appropriate phrases from the answer choices and match them to the species of termite to which they relate. TWO of the answer choices will NOT be used. **This question is worth 3 points.**

Answer Choices	Advanced Termites
(A) Break down cellulose in the gut	•
(B) Born with digesters	•
(C) Pass on the microorganisms via secretion	•
(D) Consume what fungi have digested	**Primitive Termites**
(E) Digest cellulose in a more time-efficient way	•
(F) Can digest cellulose directly	•
(G) Pile up vegetation in the nest	

Vocab Quiz

The word ☐ in the passage is closest in meaning to

03-1 string ☐ cluster ☐ variety ☐ series

03-2 convert ☐ transform ☐ break ☐ push

Basic Drill

04

ASSOCIATIVE AND IMITATIVE LEARNING

Most animal species are capable of at least some level of learning. Animal learning mechanisms appear in large part to be quite similar to the learning mechanisms of human infants. While explicit instruction is nearly impossible, most animals are capable of learning through association and imitation.

Associative learning is the most widely known form of animal learning. In associative learning, the animal begins to associate a particular action with a particular outcome. The most famous example of this is that of Pavlov's dogs. In Pavlov's famous experiment, his dogs began to associate the ringing of a bell with the result of being fed. In time, they began to get excited merely by the ringing of the bell, even if they were not fed. This kind of learning is common in the wild. For example, a bear that breaks into a beehive to get the honey may receive many painful stings. If this happens several times, the bear may begin to associate beehives with pain and begin to avoid them. Another example comes from the island of Koshima, where Japanese scientists were studying macaques, a species of monkey. The scientists left potatoes on the beach for the monkeys each morning. Eventually the monkeys began to associate the action of going to the beach, which they did not do before, with the finding of food. Now the macaques on Koshima walk down to the beach each morning.

Another type of learning common in animals is imitative learning. Unlike associative learning, imitative learning does not rely on the animal's past experiences. Imitative learning may occur simply by watching others. After the macaques on Koshima learned to walk to the beach for food, they saw one macaque washing her potatoes in the ocean before eating them. Slowly the other macaques began to imitate her behavior, and now all the macaques on the island wash their potatoes before eating them. The macaques have also developed a taste for salt and even dip their potatoes into the water between bites. The macaques also picked up a number of new behaviors from imitating individuals in their species. The macaques now go down to the beach to splash and swim in the ocean on especially hot days. They were not rewarded for this behavior by the scientists, so they could not have possibly learned this through associative learning. The only explanation is that they saw one of their members splashing in the water and learned from her example that splashing in the water helps cool their bodies down. Thus, imitative learning is thought to be an important mechanism in the development of new behaviors in a species.

Answer Book p. A53

Directions: Select the appropriate phrases from the answer choices and match them to the type of learning to which they relate. TWO of the answer choices will NOT be used. *This question is worth 3 points.*

Answer Choices	Associative Learning
(A) Can be seen in most animals (B) Formed by repeated experience	• •
(C) Helps develop new behaviors	**Imitative Learning**
(D) Based on the connection between distinct actions and outcomes (E) Relies on others to display behavior	• •
(F) The rarest type of learning for animals	**Both**
(G) Learns through human	•

Vocab Quiz

The word ☐ in the passage is closest in meaning to

04-1 particular   ☐ specific   ☐ separate   ☐ general
04-2 merely   ☐ exclusively   ☐ simply   ☐ completely

Reading Practice

TIKOPIA AND EASTER ISLAND SOCIETIES

1 The challenges faced by the Easter Island and Tikopia societies were some of the most extreme that have confronted any society in the history of human civilization. Located on small, isolated islands, as both societies were, nearly every social pressure, from resource allocation to population control, was exacerbated by their isolation. Yet despite facing similar environmental pressures, the Tikopia have survived for nearly 3,000 years, while the Easter Island society completely failed in the late 1500s. The answer to the different fates of these two societies lies primarily in their management of resources.

2 While Tikopia society has a very high population density, its total population is small enough that all members of the society know each other personally. The Tikopia have a powerful sense of the common good of their society, and all decisions are considered with respect to how they will affect the society as a whole. In addition, the Tikopia have long understood that their island simply cannot support a larger population, and important cultural taboos were designed to ensure population stability. The Tikopia feel it is immoral to have large families, and thus practice extensive family planning, even resorting to infanticide in earlier times.

3 **A** The Tikopia also have strict rules designed to prevent the overexploitation of their limited resources. **B** If a person wishes to catch or eat fish, he or she must first seek the permission of the chief so as to prevent the depletion of fish stocks. **C** In addition, the trees on the island all produce edible fruit and have been cultured in such a way to replicate the natural tree cover of the rainforest, creating an extremely efficient and environmentally friendly agricultural system. **D**

4 Easter Island society, in contrast, is a lesson in overexploitation, poor resource planning, and negligent environmental practices that eventually doomed the society. Easter Island society was a typical Polynesian culture in that it had an elite, royal class of chiefs who lived far above the conditions of the rest of society. Enormous amounts of manpower went into meeting the needs of the chiefs, and first among those needs was the construction of moai, the giant stone heads for which Easter Island is now famous. Moai were built essentially as a form of competition between rival chiefs, with larger moai signifying greater power. Monument construction required cutting down large numbers of trees to transport and lift the huge stone blocks. Trees were also heavily harvested for the construction of canoes and for use as firewood. The result was massive deforestation. By 1500, the large palms used in canoe and monument construction were gone, and so these activities stopped. Within another 100 years, the island had been completely deforested, and the islanders were reduced to using grasses and leaves for their cooking fires. Deforestation also led to massive soil erosion, which reduced crop yields as well as migrating bird species, eliminating an important source of protein. Without the food resources to feed the population, Easter Island society collapsed.

Answer Book p. A57

|Vocabulary|

01 The word "exacerbated" in the passage is closest in meaning to

(A) represented   (B) caused   (C) worsened   (D) handled

|Inference|

02 Based on the information in paragraph 4, what can be inferred about Easter Island society?

(A) Its population growth was unprecedented in island societies.
(B) There was a huge economic and political gap between the general public and chiefs.
(C) Most aspects of life were tightly controlled.
(D) The construction of the moai was its only cultural achievement.

|Rhetorical Purpose|

03 The author mentions "moai" in the passage in order to

(A) discuss the greatest achievements of Easter Island society
(B) provide an example of the poor resource decisions made by Easter Island society
(C) illustrate the intense rivalry between the Tikopia and Easter Island societies
(D) discuss the construction methods of the Easter Islanders

|Sentence Insertion|

04 Look at the four squares [■] that indicate where the following sentence could be added to the passage.

> In fact, this system is so advanced and environmentally sound that modern day ecologists are trying to replicate it in other parts of the world.

Where would the sentence best fit?

(A) A   (B) B   (C) C   (D) D

|Fill in a Table|

05 Directions: Select the appropriate phrases from the answer choices and match them to the society to which they relate. TWO of the answer choices will NOT be used. ***This question is worth 3 points.***

Answer Choices	Tikopia
(A) Geographically isolated	•
(B) Highly hierarchical society	•
(C) Strictly controlled use of all available resources	**Easter Island**
(D) Placed emphasis on the common good	•
(E) Had a greater number of resources	•
(F) Made little use of existing resources	**Both**
(G) Manpower and resources put to uses not essential for survival	•

Chapter 09 Fill in a Table   109

TOEFL iBT i Reading   www.linguaforum.com

PART B
Approaching Themes

Chapter 10 Humanities I
Chapter 11 Humanities II
Chapter 12 Life Science I
Chapter 13 Life Science II
Chapter 14 Physical Science
Chapter 15 Social Science

Chapter 10 Humanities I

☐ **Humanities**
  A study of how people process and document the human experience

☐ **Related fields**
  History, Art, Literature, Religion, Music, Philosophy, Linguistics, Languages, etc.

Reading Preview

History – The Transcontinental Railroad

| Intensive Drill 1 |

A transcontinental railroad is a railroad route that crosses a continental landmass with terminals at different oceans or continental borders. Transcontinental railroads helped open up unpopulated interior regions of continents to exploration and settlement that would otherwise not have been possible. In the United States of America, a series of transcontinental railroads built over the last third of the nineteenth century created a nationwide transportation network that united the country by rail.

Art – Mexican Muralism

| Intensive Drill 2 |

A mural is any artwork such as a painting or photograph applied directly to a wall or ceiling. Mexican muralism is the term used to describe the revival of large-scale mural painting in Mexico starting in the 1920s. Muralism in Mexico is very famous for conveying social and political messages as part of endeavors to reunify the country under the post-Mexican Revolution government. It embraced and elevated mural paintings in Mexico from a popular art form to a form of high art.

Music – Figured Bass in Baroque Music

| Intensive Drill 3 |

Figured bass, also known as thoroughbass and basso continuo, is a type of shorthand notation in which musical figures are written below the notes of the bass part to indicate the chords to be played. It arose in the early seventeenth century in Italy and soon became widespread during the Baroque period to the extent that this era is sometimes referred to as the age of basso continuo.

History - Charlemagne and the Holy Roman Empire

| Mini Test 1 |

Charlemagne, also known as Charles the Great, was King of the Franks. He united most of Western Europe during the early Middle Ages and laid the foundations for modern France, Germany, and the Low Countries. In 800, he became the first Holy Roman Emperor, the first recognized emperor in Western Europe since the fall of the Western Roman Empire. In addition, the recognition from the Pope granted him divine legitimacy in the eyes of his contemporaries.

The Holy Roman Empire was a feudal monarchy that covered a large portion of Europe, centering around Germany, from 962 to 1806. It was established by the coronation of the Frankish king Charlemagne as Roman emperor by Pope Leo III on Christmas Day in the year 800, and ended with the renunciation of the Roman imperial title by Francis II in 1806.

Archaeology – The Ancient City of Petra

| Mini Test 2 |

Petra is a historical and archaeological city in southern Jordan. The city is famous for its rock-cut architecture and water conduit system. Another name for Petra is the Rose City, due to the color of the stone out of which it is carved. It was the capital of the Nabataean kingdom beginning around the sixth century BC, and was absorbed into the Roman Empire in AD 106. Excavations and studies of the site are still ongoing.

Anthropology – Culture of the Pueblo Peoples

| iBT Practice |

The Pueblo Indians, situated in the Southwestern United States, are one of the oldest cultures in the United States. They are believed to be the descendants of three major cultures, specifically the Mogollon, Hohokam, and Anasazi, with their history tracing back approximately 7,000 years. Despite their prosperity, the Ancient Puebloans' way of life declined in the 1300s, probably due to drought and intertribal warfare, and they migrated south, primarily into New Mexico and Arizona, becoming what is known today as the Pueblo people.

Intensive Drill 1

THE TRANSCONTINENTAL RAILROAD

1   Before the middle of the nineteenth century, major trading centers only existed along America's coastlines, in large port towns where much of the population was concentrated. However, as more settlers moved westward, cities sprang up along the frontier, and new centers of trade began to open in the interior of the United States. Unfortunately, the development of effective overland transportation lagged behind this rapid westward expansion. The construction of canals helped, but they were limited in the amount of goods they could transport and did not extend past the Mississippi River. In order to solve this problem, it was determined that a major railroad system into the West would be indispensable. By 1828, some short rail lines had already been constructed, though they were designed only to connect major cities within the same region, like New York and Boston. Several companies had provided railroads as far as Indiana and Missouri by the middle of the century, but pressure was mounting to construct a railway that would lead all the way from the East Coast to California.

2   Such a feat required cooperation between the federal government and private companies. Several projects took shape in the 1840s, when surveyors began to plot different competing routes from Mid-American railroad stations to territories in the West, such as Oregon and California. To resolve these differences and devise a plan for an official railroad, the government conducted its own study, the Pacific Railroad Survey, which compared all of the potential routes. The government decided to provide funding for a railroad that ran from Nebraska to Utah, where it would meet up with a second railway that would be built from Utah to California. Two companies were commissioned by the government to build the railroads: the Union Pacific Company would build the eastern half, while the Central Pacific Company would build the western section.

3   Construction began in 1862, but the outbreak of the Civil War slowed progress considerably on the Union Pacific line when workers were called away to serve in the army. However, workers further west on the Central Pacific were able to continue construction in Utah and California. For this reason, the Central Pacific Railroad advanced far more quickly than the Union Pacific. A compromise was made to extend the Central Pacific further to the east, to make up for the time lost building the Union Pacific line. The lines finally met one another in 1869, at the newly determined junction in Promontory, Utah. **A** The transcontinental railroad was completed before there was substantial need for its services. **B** In the early years, one train a week was all it took to deliver all the supplies needed by settlers in the West. **C** However, as settlements in the West expanded, so did the railroad. By the 1880s, new rail lines ran the entire length of the West Coast, from Washington state in the north to Los Angeles in the south. **D**

Answer Book p. A60

01 The word "indispensable" in the passage is closest in meaning to

(A) weighted   (B) necessary   (C) discontinued   (D) impossible

02 All of the following are mentioned as major points along the first transcontinental railroad in paragraph 2 EXCEPT

(A) Nebraska   (B) Utah   (C) California   (D) Washington

03 In paragraph 3, what does the author imply about the West during the Civil War?

(A) It did not play a large role in the conflict.
(B) Most of the fighting happened there.
(C) It had the strongest military power.
(D) It surrendered early in the war.

04 Look at the four squares [■] that indicate where the following sentence could be added to the passage.

> Thus, expansion of the rail system could hardly be justified.

Where would the sentence best fit?

(A) A   (B) B   (C) C   (D) D

05 **Directions:** An introductory sentence for a brief summary of the passage is provided below. Complete the summary by selecting the THREE answer choices that express the most important ideas in the passage. Some sentences do not belong in the summary because they express ideas that are not presented in the passage or are minor ideas in the passage. *This question is worth 2 points.*

The first transcontinental railroad built in the U.S. took a massive cooperative effort between the government and private companies.

(A) The government conducted a study called the Pacific Railroad Survey to compare all the potential railroad routes and devise the best route across the country.
(B) Due to the Civil War, the Central Pacific had to make up the construction which originally belonged to the Union Pacific.
(C) The government commissioned two companies, the Union Pacific and Central Pacific, to build the two major sections of the railroad.
(D) Although the transcontinental railroad was completed in 1869, it was much later when the railroad proved its worth, due to slow population growth in many western regions.
(E) Early railroads were so short that they only served to connect major cities on the eastern seaboard, such as Boston and New York.
(F) Before the transcontinental railroad was built, goods were transported mainly through canals which extended past the Mississippi River.

Intensive Drill 2

MEXICAN MURALISM

1. The Mexican mural movement came out of the aftermath of the Mexican Revolution, which took place from 1910 to 1920. The Mexican government at that time began to fund large-scale wall paintings in civic buildings and structures, with the objective of creating a historical narrative and identity for the general public, of which most were poor and illiterate. The government felt that through the creation of massive, public murals, a new kind of Mexican sentiment embodying the cultural values of Mexico would instill a greater sense of pride and sentiment in the general population. One of the main concerns of the government was to unify the population under one ideology, thereby encouraging artists to produce works that would educate and benefit the masses.

2. Many artists at the time seized the opportunity to produce these artworks, claiming that muralism would be an art of social and political discourse. In other words, they saw it as a creative opportunity to blend art and politics together, which was a quite radical idea at the time. Although many of the artists commissioned to produce murals had different ideologies, styles, and personalities, their desire to use art as a means for social revolution is evident in their works.

3. Three artists grew in prominence out of the movement and are widely recognized for their innovative and influential art pieces today. The first of these artists, David Siqueiros, is considered to have been the most innovative. His artworks are characterized by bold lines and brushstrokes that stood out prominently, as well as their tendency to use overly exaggerated perspectives. His goal in mural painting was to create a new type of mural that incorporated modern technology. In order to carry out his vision and break from traditional forms of painting, he would spray, pour, drip, or splatter paint onto his murals.

4. Diego Rivera was also a significant artist of the Mexican mural movement, but unlike Siqueiros, he favored a more traditional style of painting. His artworks incorporated bright, vibrant colors, with a heavy emphasis placed on oranges, reds, and earthy browns. The most prevalent scenes he created were market scenes that were reminiscent of Mexico's historically indigenous cultures. He firmly believed that Mexicans needed to be imbued with a new vision of life, and he tried to instill Mexicans with a strong sense of pride in their cultural heritage.

5. The last artist, Jose Clemente Orozco, took an entirely different approach from Siqueiros and Rivera in creating murals. He focused more on depictions of human suffering and the atrocities that had become common during the Mexican Revolution. His objective in portraying the horrors of war was to provide what he felt was an honest portrayal of Mexico's heritage. Despite producing some artistically astounding murals, his work was heavily criticized by both the government and art critics for failure to capture the essence of providing the Mexican people with a new sense of cultural pride and identity.

Answer Book p. A62

01 According to paragraph 2, which of following is true of Mexican murals?

(A) Artists in Mexico drew upon each other's similar artistic styles when painting.
(B) A merging of art and politics was widely accepted at the time.
(C) Artists' motives for murals were both politically and socially driven.
(D) Artists were assigned to create murals with an identical ideology.

02 The phrase "his vision" in the passage refers to

(A) enlightening the poor and illiterate with his wall paintings
(B) synthesizing traditional and modern styles together
(C) adopting bold lines and brushstrokes in his paintings
(D) creating wall paintings using modern technology

03 The author mentions "the horrors of war" in the passage as an example of which of the following?

(A) depictions of the Mexican Revolution
(B) wall paintings expressing hostility to Mexico's heritage
(C) artwork with emphasis on extremely exaggerated perspectives
(D) murals representing the government's desire to foster cultural values of Mexico

04 According to the passage, which of the following is NOT true of murals in Mexico?

(A) They were used to provide a historical narrative and identity for Mexicans.
(B) They were meant to inspire a great sense of pride and sentiment in Mexicans.
(C) Artists viewed them as a means to express abstract concepts.
(D) They were viewed as a tool for social revolution by artists.

05 **Directions:** An introductory sentence for a brief summary of the passage is provided below. Complete the summary by selecting the THREE answer choices that express the most important ideas in the passage. Some sentences do not belong in the summary because they express ideas that are not presented in the passage or are minor ideas in the passage. *This question is worth 2 points.*

The Mexican government in the 1920s commissioned artists to produce wall paintings as a means to unify the Mexican people.

(A) Art critics heavily criticized Orozco's works for depicting the horrors of war.
(B) Siqueiros' work was heavily influenced by his relationships with women.
(C) Siqueiros produced original murals inspired by modern technology.
(D) Orozco's works focused on atrocities from the Mexican Revolution.
(E) Rivera favored the use of earth tones in his murals.
(F) Rivera's works generally depicted scenes of indigenous Mexicans.

Intensive Drill 3

FIGURED BASS IN BAROQUE MUSIC

1   As the Baroque Period of music came into prominence during the time from 1600 to 1750 A.D., composers wanted to move away from the somber, simplistic musical styles of the preceding Medieval Period and instead produce music that was richer in melody and rhythm. The music of the Medieval Period was almost exclusively composed for religious purposes, primarily church masses. Due to the solemn, venerable mood of the mass in churches, composers had little room for any kind of musical variation or experimentation. In addition, music during the Medieval Period predominantly consisted of chants and madrigals that used the human voice as its principal musical instrument. Although harpsichords and organs were sometimes used for musical accompaniment, their overall musical presence was generally subdued.

2   **A** However, by the 1600s, Baroque composers began to write music not only for religious services, but also wrote secular compositions for royalty and the general public, who started to favor more lively and intricate styles of music. **B** As Baroque music began to break with strictly religious music and experiment increasingly with musical creativity, elaborate musical compositions became the dominant style. **C** These compositions were rich in new rhythmic structures, introducing more complex melodies and other forms of musical ornamentation that created a heightened sense of dynamism and energy. **D**

3   One of the most popular compositional techniques to emerge in this new brand of musical composition was figured bass, sometimes referred to as thoroughbass, which was essentially a form of musical shorthand written into the bass line of the music score. Composers used figured bass to provide musical accompaniment to their compositions by incorporating instruments such as the harpsichord and a predecessor to the modern guitar. The orchestra would play the composed music as it was, note-by-note, while the figured bass would be roughly sketched out. The figured bass provided a framework for these instruments to play the bass line of the musical composition by giving them basic chords to follow. However, unlike the uniform musical arrangements characteristic of the Medieval Period, these accompanying instruments were given greater creative freedom to improvise on these chords. This is of particular importance, since improvisation was a common feature in Baroque music and reflected the musical ideals of the composers at that time.

4   Although these accompanists were required to follow and observe the underlying rhythmic and harmonic structure of the compositions, the development of figured bass musical shorthand provided just enough information for the accompanist to improvise these melodies and rhythms. Baroque composers generally conceded that writing out every note for these accompanists would restrict the freedom of well-trained accompanists, as well as prevent them from fully demonstrating the extent of their ability. Therefore, in order to better showcase these accompanists' skills, composers used figured bass to write compositions with more complex harmonies, contrasting musical themes, and innovative melodies and sequences of chords, which gave rise to a new form of musical variance unfathomed in the Medieval Period.

01 In paragraph 1, what does the author imply about Medieval music?

(A) Medieval music was popular among nobles in Europe.
(B) Medieval music was generally not composed for the public.
(C) Medieval music evolved various elaborate styles used in church masses.
(D) Medieval music gradually introduced new kinds of rhythms.

02 The phrase "break with" in the passage is closest in meaning to

(A) deal with (B) favor
(C) separate from (D) resemble

03 In paragraph 4, the author states that

(A) figured bass notation allowed accompanists to show their talent
(B) baroque composers wrote out every note for each musician
(C) complex and innovative musical structures developed from Medieval styles
(D) figured bass was a form of musical shorthand for all musicians in the orchestra

04 Look at the four squares [■] that indicate where the following sentence could be added to the passage.

> Especially chamber music, one of the more complicated forms of music developed at that time, was among their most beloved.

Where would the sentence best fit?

(A) A (B) B (C) C (D) D

05 **Directions:** Select the appropriate phrases from the answer choices and match them to the period of music to which they relate. TWO of the answer choices will NOT be used. *This question is worth 3 points.*

Answer Choices	Baroque Music
(A) Greater improvisation (B) Strict musical style with little variation (C) In need of large numbers of musicians (D) Complex, intricate musical styles and structures (E) Musicians able to demonstrate their talent and skills (F) Music for nobility, deeply religious (G) Human voice as the principal instrument	• • •
	Medieval Music
	• •

Mini Test 1

CHARLEMAGNE AND THE HOLY ROMAN EMPIRE

1   By the fifth century A.D., the Roman Empire, once the largest and most powerful on Earth, had finally collapsed after years of fighting with Germanic tribes from the north of Europe. The remnants of the once mighty Roman Empire lay to the east, in Constantinople, the royal seat of the Byzantine Empire. Meanwhile, in central and western Europe, a new superpower was rising to prominence: the Frankish kingdom, which included several of the independent Germanic tribes that had aided in the overthrow of the Western Roman Empire. Within 100 years of the Romans' defeat, the Frankish kingdom expanded to include much of eastern and central Europe. Under their legendary king Charlemagne, the Franks rose to such prominence in the region that a weakened Rome, now little more than a religious center, would appeal to them in an effort to reestablish the former glory of the Roman Empire.

2   Several factors led to the Franks, under Charlemagne, becoming the protectors of the Roman Empire. This honor was traditionally left to the Byzantines, but infighting among the ruling elites there led to instability, and the Romans lost confidence in their ability to defend the Pope and the Catholic Church. At the same time, around 799 A.D., Pope Leo III was having trouble with his own country as well. The Roman nobles were intent upon taking his title, for the simple reason that Leo was of peasant birth. They laid accusations of an array of crimes against the Pope in the hopes that at least one of them would lead to a conviction and force him from power. The tension led to a vicious physical attack on the Pope, in which rebels attempted to gouge out his eyes and cut off his tongue. Leo fled to Paderborn, a city within the Frankish kingdom, where he met Charlemagne for the first time.

3   Having accepted Christianity as the state religion some time back, the Franks gladly took the Pope in. Charlemagne resolved to help him, and called a meeting with his enemies to try to quell the violent opposition. When the talks fell apart, Charlemagne traveled to Rome in person, along with the Pope, to see that the uprising was stopped. He met again with supporters and opponents of the Pope to discuss the situation, but this time, he was able to sway the committee of friends and enemies to cease attacks on the Pope and allow him to officially declare his innocence of all the charges falsely brought against him by the nobles. His enemies were thus exiled, and Leo was pardoned.

4   While still in Rome, Charlemagne attended Christmas Mass at the Vatican, at the Pope's request. As he knelt down to pray, the Pope placed a crown on his head, officially making him Emperor of the Romans. For the Pope, the act served to thank Charlemagne for his defense and to increase the influence of the Catholic Church across the vast Frankish territory. Charlemagne, meanwhile, seized upon the opportunity to renew the Roman Empire under the rule of the Franks. This did not become official until two centuries later, when a portion of the Frankish lands was renamed the Holy Roman Empire, an institution that would persist for nearly a thousand years.

Answer Book p. A66

01 The word " remnants " in the passage is closest in meaning to

(A) enemies (B) rulers (C) remains (D) members

02 According to paragraph 1, who was responsible for the fall of the Roman Empire?

(A) The Byzantine Empire
(B) The Germanic tribes
(C) The Catholic Church
(D) The Frankish kingdom

03 The word " them " in the passage refers to

(A) nobles (B) crimes (C) hopes (D) rebels

04 Which of the sentences below best expresses the essential information in the highlighted sentence in the passage? *Incorrect* choices change the meaning in important ways or leave out essential information.

(A) In a second meeting with Roman nobles, Charlemagne was convinced that the rebels who attacked the Pope were innocent.
(B) Charlemagne traveled to Rome to meet with opponents and supporters of the Pope to argue for his innocence.
(C) Attacks on the Pope led the Roman nobles to agree with Charlemagne and declare Leo III innocent of all charges.
(D) The second time Charlemagne met with the Roman nobles, they agreed to acknowledge the Pope's innocence and end their attacks.

05 **Directions:** An introductory sentence for a brief summary of the passage is provided below. Complete the summary by selecting the THREE answer choices that express the most important ideas in the passage. Some sentences do not belong in the summary because they express ideas that are not presented in the passage or are minor ideas in the passage. *This question is worth 2 points.*

Charlemagne, King of the Franks, forged an alliance with the Catholic Church that expanded Roman influence in the West.

(A) The seat of the Roman Empire moved to Constantinople in the east after the Western Roman Empire fell to invaders.
(B) Pope Leo III faced violent opposition from Roman nobles who sought to ruin his name and strip him of his position.
(C) The Frankish kingdom formed out of an alliance between several German tribes and grew to be a powerful force in Europe.
(D) Charlemagne was able to influence the nobles to stop their rebellion against the Pope, bringing peace to Rome again.
(E) The Byzantine Empire had grown unstable due to fighting between members of the government.
(F) The Pope made Charlemagne the Emperor of the Roman Empire to thank him and expand the influence of the Catholic Church across the Frankish Kingdom.

Mini Test 2

THE ANCIENT CITY OF PETRA

1 One of the most amazing relics of the ancient world is Petra, an archaeological site in the country of Jordan. Petra is an ancient city that was literally carved out of the walls of a mountain in a style known as rock-cut architecture. The city was founded in 100 BC by a group of Arab peoples called the Nabataeans, who made it the capital city of their kingdom. In ancient times, Petra was a major center of trade in the Middle East, as it lay at the intersection of several different trade routes. **A** Petra also rose to prominence because of its water supply, which made the desert city habitable. **B** The city sits in a low-lying valley among several large mountains, along the route of several mountain streams. **C** The Nabataeans, however, constructed dams and special channels that could divert the water either away from the city or into special holding tanks, where it was stored to be used in times of drought. **D** The fact that Petra had a constant store of water made the city even more popular with passing traders, as they could buy some of the city's water when it had become scarce elsewhere during the dry seasons.

2 The city had the advantage of being a natural fortress, as it was surrounded on all sides by high mountains. The main entrance to the city, called the *siq*, was its main point of defense. The *siq* was a long chasm that cut through the giant sandstone cliffs. It was created by a fault in the mountain which had been slowly worn away by water over the years. It was only a few meters wide but stretched for nearly a mile, with towering cliff walls on each side. Visitors had to navigate this long corridor in order to reach the city. The end of the narrow *siq* opened into the city's most spectacular ruin, called the treasury. The facade of the treasury was heavily influenced by Greek architecture, with stately columns and sculptures decorating the outward facing wall. The city was also home to several ancient tombs, which have since allowed archaeologists to trace the history of this site according to the style in which these tombs were built — most reflected the early Nabataean style, while others were influenced by later inhabitants such as the Romans and Muslims.

3 Despite the defenses and riches of the city, the Nabataeans were unable to defend Petra against Roman attacks, and it fell to the Empire in 106 AD, having been under Nabataean rule for just over 200 years. Under Roman rule, the city continued to prosper for a time, as evidenced by the Roman additions to the city's original architecture. But when major trade routes began to shift in the fifth century, the city saw a decline in commerce, and it slowly fell into ruin. Islamic forces invaded Petra and took control of the city a hundred years later, and what remained of Nabataean culture quickly disappeared. The city remained largely unknown to the modern Western world until Swiss explorer Johann Burckhardt was shown the ruins by local Bedouins on an 1812 expedition, and reported back to his colleagues in Europe. In 1985, the United Nations named it a World Heritage Site, and it was later also named one of the New Seven Wonders of the World.

01 The word "divert" in the passage is closest in meaning to

(A) redirect   (B) capture   (C) circulate   (D) release

02 The phrase "this site" in the passage refers to

(A) treasury   (B) ruin   (C) *siq*   (D) city

03 According to paragraph 3, what was the first major cause of Petra's decline in commerce?

(A) The defeat of the Nabataeans
(B) Changes to major trade routes
(C) Its discovery by Westerners
(D) Damage from natural disasters

04 Look at the four squares [■] that indicate where the following sentence could be added to the passage.

> Unfortunately, this also makes it a frequent victim of floods.

Where would the sentence best fit?

(A) A   (B) B   (C) C   (D) D

05 **Directions:** An introductory sentence for a brief summary of the passage is provided below. Complete the summary by selecting the THREE answer choices that express the most important ideas in the passage. Some sentences do not belong in the summary because they express ideas that are not presented in the passage or are minor ideas in the passage. **This question is worth 2 points.**

The ancient city of Petra, a bustling center of trade in ancient times, is now a treasured archaeological site.

(A) Petra lay at the intersection of many different routes used by traders and had plenty of water resources, which contributed to its growth.
(B) Tombs built in several different styles have helped archaeologists date parts of the site according to which peoples inhabited the city.
(C) Petra is characterized by being a natural fortress with the aid of the main entrance, called the *siq*, and having ruins such as the treasury and some ancient tombs.
(D) Petra, which had been ruled by several different peoples, was rediscovered in the nineteenth century and has been named as a World Heritage site.
(E) Water bodies in Petra provided Nabataeans with necessary water, but were responsible for many floods.
(F) A Swiss explorer, Johann Burckhardt, discovered Petra with the help of local Bedouins and later made efforts to get the site to be named a World Heritage Site.

CULTURE OF THE PUEBLO PEOPLES

1 → In the southwestern region of the United States reside several tribes of Native Americans known as the Pueblo peoples, who derive their name from the fact that their ancestors lived in pueblos that traditionally consisted mostly of houses made from mud-bricks and straw. While they originally descended from a single ancestral group thousands of years ago, the Pueblo peoples gradually fragmented into different tribes, each with a distinct culture. The cultures of these tribes were further altered by the Spanish, who took over the Pueblos' territory in the seventeenth century and transformed Pueblo life in ways which can still be seen today. Despite the numerous developments throughout their long history, the Pueblo peoples have maintained many core features of their cultures, in particular their social structure and ceremonial practices. Recurring distinctions in both social structure and ceremonial practices allow researchers to divide modern Pueblo peoples into two basic categories: the Western Pueblo and the Eastern Pueblo.

2 → The Western Pueblo tribes reside in the deserts of northern Arizona and western New Mexico. The Western Pueblo tribes all feature a similar social organization based around the clan, the central social unit in these societies. These clans are large families that trace their ancestry through the mother's side of the family. Upon marriage, a man will live with his wife's mother, and the couple's children belong to their mother's clan. There are rigid rules about whom people can and cannot marry, as tribe members must marry outside of their particular clans. In this social structure, women own the farming property and have a good deal of social power. All other organizations such as business in a tribe are owned and operated by individual clans.

3 Besides the organization of communities by clan membership, the other distinctive feature of the Western Pueblos is their set of ceremonial practices. While influenced by the introduction of Christianity, the Western Pueblo have retained most of their traditional religious practices, at the center of which lies the *kachina* cult. **A** Originally, the *kachina* cult attempted to communicate with spirits that could bestow good fortune upon the tribe, particularly in the form of greater rainfall. **B** This was important because farming in such arid regions is difficult, since adequate rainfall is rare and unpredictable. **C** An important part of these ceremonies involves the men dressing up as the spirits they pray to and playing the role of these characters. **D** This practice is fundamental to the Western Pueblo peoples, as evidenced by the fact that many communities have myriad places of worship.

4 → The Eastern Pueblo, who are primarily located in the valley along the Rio Grande River in New Mexico, have different social structures and ceremonial practices from their western counterparts. First, the Eastern Pueblo do not strictly adhere to a clan system, so clans do not play as critical a social role as they do in the Western Pueblo society. Lineage is usually traced along both the mother's and father's families, with members from both groups living among an extended family. Second, most Eastern Pueblos are divided into two moieties, or central social groups: the Summer People and the Winter People. These terms come from a traditional method of sharing power in the Eastern Pueblo societies: the Summer People would

rule for the six months of summer and the Winter People would rule for the six months of winter. To offset the political discrepancy such an arrangement could potentially cause, the community also has numerous smaller groups that are in charge of hunting, medicine, ceremonial rituals, and other such activities. These secondary groups operate throughout the year and consist of members from both moieties. This unites members of both moieties and limits the power of the ruling moiety, maintaining peace between the two.

5   Ceremonial practices are also an important part of the Eastern Pueblo culture, though there are significant differences from those of the Western Pueblo. Individual Eastern Pueblo communities have far fewer places of worship than the Western Pueblo have. Furthermore, the *kachina* cults have little influence among the Eastern Pueblo, and in some communities they are not present at all. The ceremonies also differ in their focus. Due to their location, these tribes do not feel the need to focus primarily on weather-centric ceremonies for assistance with growing crops. Instead, their ceremonies traditionally place more emphasis on activities that are considered more masculine, particularly hunting, at least for part of the year. The various tribes emphasize different concerns, like hunting and farming, to different degrees and at different times, a noticeable distinction from the singular focus of the Western Pueblo ceremonial practices.

01 Why does the author mention " the Spanish " in the passage?

(A) To illustrate the far-reaching influence of the Pueblo
(B) To discuss how the Pueblo split into many tribes
(C) To show the amazing resilience of Pueblo culture
(D) To help explain changes in Pueblo culture

02 According to paragraph 1, the Pueblo received their name from

(A) their family structure
(B) their geographical location
(C) their mode of housing
(D) their religious beliefs

Paragraph 1 is marked with an arrow [➡].

03 The word " their " in the passage refers to

(A) children   (B) families
(C) clans   (D) members

04 The word " rigid " in the passage is closest in meaning to

(A) lenient   (B) innumerable
(C) strict   (D) trivial

05 According to paragraph 2, the basic social unit of the Western Pueblo is

(A) the village
(B) the family
(C) the clan
(D) the tribe

Paragraph 2 is marked with an arrow [➡].

06 The word "myriad" in the passage is closest in meaning to

(A) isolated
(B) huge
(C) numerous
(D) magnificent

07 The word "critical" in the passage is closest in meaning to

(A) static
(B) important
(C) active
(D) trivial

08 The word "discrepancy" in the passage is closest in meaning to

(A) autocracy
(B) cooperation
(C) influence
(D) inconsistency

09 According to paragraph 4, in the Eastern Pueblo society, all of the following duties are performed by specially chosen groups EXCEPT

(A) rituals
(B) farming
(C) medicine
(D) hunting

Paragraph 4 is marked with an arrow [→].

10 The word "they" in the passage refers to

(A) ceremonies
(B) *kachina* cults
(C) communities
(D) places of worship

11 Which of the sentences below best expresses the essential information in the highlighted sentence in the passage? *Incorrect* answer choices change the meaning in important ways or leave out essential information.

(A) The Eastern Pueblo practice religious ceremonies to invoke the help of spirits to different extents and at different times.
(B) The religious ceremonies of the Eastern Pueblo have a singular focus, which distinguishes them from the Western Pueblo.
(C) The Eastern Pueblo, unlike the Western, use religious ceremonies for a variety of occasions, depending on the specific need and time.
(D) The religious ceremonies of the Western Pueblo only occur in times of great need, which is quite contrary to the Eastern Pueblo.

12 Look at the four squares [■] that indicate where the following sentence could be added to the passage.

> The activities of the cult are an attempt to mitigate this and bring some level of stability.

Where would the sentence best fit?

Click on a square [■] to add the sentence to the passage.

(A) A
(B) B
(C) C
(D) D

13 Directions: Select the appropriate phrases from the answer choices and match them to the group of Pueblo peoples to which they relate. TWO of the answer choices will NOT be used. ***This question is worth 4 points.***

Drag your answer choices to the spaces where they belong. To remove an answer choice, click on it. To review the passage, click **View Text**.

Answer Choices	Eastern Pueblos
(A) Live in a region where rainfall is often sparse and hard to predict (B) Should marry members from different clans (C) Divided into two groups that take turns ruling the tribe (D) Women own farms and have a great deal of social influence (E) Only allow marriages within the same clan (F) Trace ancestry through both the mother and the father (G) Ask the spirits for good fortune through religious ceremonies (H) Include communities that contain many places of worship (I) Tribal members compete to gain political dominance	• •
	Western Pueblos
	• • • •
	Both
	•

Chapter 11   Humanities II

☐ **Humanities**
　A study of how people process and document the human experience

☐ **Related fields**
　History, Art, Literature, Religion, Music, Philosophy, Linguistics, Languages, etc.

Reading Preview

History – The Salon of Paris

| Intensive Drill 1 |

The Salon was the official art exhibition of the French Academy of Fine Arts *(Academie des Beaux-Arts)* in Paris. First held in 1667, its name stems from its location at the *Salon Carré* in the Louvre. For almost 150 years, from 1740 to 1890, the Salon was the most prestigious annual or biannual art event in the world. However, as many artists found it to be a bureaucratic and conservative organization, several groups broke away from the Salon.

Art – Art Restoration and Conservation

| Intensive Drill 2 |

Art restoration denotes the repair or renovation of artworks that have sustained damage or decay. This includes all actions directly applied to a work of art to prevent further damage. These actions are only carried out when a work of art has lost part of its significance or function based on the respect for the original artwork.

Art conservation denotes the maintenance and preservation of works of art and their protection from future damage and deterioration. This includes preventive conservation and remedial conservation. All measures and actions should respect the significance and the physical properties of the artwork.

Theater – Theater Acting and Film Acting

| Intensive Drill 3 |

Theater is a collaborative form of fine art that uses live performers, typically actors, to present the experience of a real or imagined event before a live audience in a specific place, often a stage. The term is now broadly used to include performances of plays and musical theater.

Film is a series of still images which, when shown on a screen, creates the illusion of moving images. The name "film" originates from the fact that photographic film has historically been the medium for recording and displaying motion pictures. The word "cinema" is often used to refer to its industry or the art of filmmaking itself.

Literature – The *Iliad* and The *Odyssey*

| Mini Test 1 |

The *Iliad* is an ancient Greek epic poem which tells of the battles and events during the weeks of a quarrel between King Agamemnon and the Warrior Achiles in the midst of the Trojan War, the ten-year siege of the city of Troy by a coalition of Greek states. Along with the *Odyssey*, it is considered to be one of the oldest extant works of Western literature.

The *Odyssey* is an ancient Greek epic poem which is a sequel to the *Illiad*. It mainly depicts the Greek hero Odysseus and his journey home after the fall of Troy. The poem is fundamental to the modern Western canon.

Craft – Pottery of the Hopi Indians

| Mini Test 2 |

The Hopi are a Native American tribe who primarily reside on the Hopi Reservation in northeastern Arizona. The Hopi were skilled artisans and had a special gift for making intricately woven rugs and pottery. In fact, Hopi pottery is among the most recognizable of all the pottery-making tribes, with its vivid colors and distinct hieroglyphics. The pottery is still used in the everyday and ceremonial life of the Hopi.

Art History – Dada

| iBT Practice |

Dada or Dadaism was an art movement that began in Zurich, Switzerland in 1916. The roots of Dada arose as a reaction to World War I and the nationalism that many thought had led to the war. Influenced by other avant-garde movements such as Cubism, Futurism, Constructivism, and Expressionism, its output was wildly diverse, ranging from performance art to poetry, photography, sculpture, and painting. Dada's aesthetic was marked by its mockery of materialistic and nationalistic attitudes and proved a powerful influence on artists in many cities.

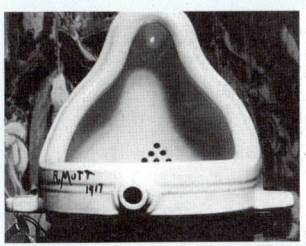

Intensive Drill 1

THE SALON OF PARIS

1   Today, Paris is well known for its contributions to new and daring art movements. However, early attempts at experimental art in the city actually faced strong opposition from the government, which favored art that was of a more classical, academic nature. Until the late nineteenth century, the art world of Paris revolved around the *Salon de Paris*, a regular exhibition of painting and sculpture by the French government. If an artist had any hopes of becoming a great success, it was mandatory that he or she be accepted to the Paris Salon, as this was the only great form of exposure available at the time. In addition, its influence on French painting, artistic style in particular, painterly conventions, and the reputation of artist was enormous.

2   The Salon of Paris was first opened as a way of exhibiting work from the city's premier art academy in 1667, and was not initially available to the public. This changed over the years as the exhibition grew to greater prominence, but even after it opened to the public and art from outside the school became more frequently accepted, the Salon maintained a reputation for art that reflected only the conventional styles taught in art schools. Beginning in 1725, the Salon was held in the prestigious Louvre Palace, and in 1748 the Salon adopted a system in which prominent teachers from the art academy judged the works and awarded medals to the best. The judges were extremely selective in what art was to be included in the exhibition, and their tastes were very conservative in nature. Many rising artists who found themselves being rejected year after year complained to the authorities, who moved to establish the *Salon des Refuses*, or the "Salon of Rejects," in which they allowed some of the art rejected by the Salon to be shown.

3   However, by the late nineteenth century, this measure was not enough to satisfy artists of new and emerging styles. **A** In response to the conservative Salon, a small group of artists was allowed to organize its own yearly exhibition in 1884, featuring works from all styles, called the *Salon des Indépendants*. **B** The values of the new exhibition were very different from those of the official Salon. **C** First of all, the system of judges was abandoned, and the public was allowed to judge works of art based on their own values rather than the opinions of academics. **D** In addition, no work of art was rejected, and all submissions found a place on the exhibition grounds. This free-thinking approach gave much-needed exposure to France's rising artists, many of whom represented the very future of modern art. For instance, the works of now-legendary painters such as Henri Matisse, Georges Braque, and Vincent Van Gogh made some of their first appearances here.

Answer Book p. A74

01 The word "mandatory" in the passage is closest in meaning to

(A) important
(B) usual
(C) compulsory
(D) logical

02 In paragraph 1, why does the author give details about modern Paris's reputation for experimental art?

(A) To express admiration for a few great artists who worked in Paris
(B) To explain why Paris is an important city to artists of all styles
(C) To introduce a surprising contradiction to the city's reputation
(D) To pose a question about the state of experimental art in France

03 According to paragraph 2, what led authorities to establish of the *Salon des Refusés*?

(A) Artists complained that their works were too often rejected.
(B) The government wanted to exploit the rejected artists.
(C) The judges were only accepting one style of art.
(D) The public demanded that the artists' work be shown.

04 Look at the four squares [■] that indicate where the following sentence could be added to the passage.

> The people who established this new exhibition were members of the Impressionist movement, whose work was especially disliked by the Salon.

Where would the sentence best fit?

(A) A   (B) B   (C) C   (D) D

05 **Directions:** Select the appropriate phrases from the answer choices and match them to the salon to which they relate. TWO of the answer choices will NOT be used. ***This question is worth 3 points.***

Answer Choices	Salon de Paris
(A) Judged works by famous art teachers	•
(B) Only featured previously rejected works	•
(C) Left judgement to the public, not academics	•
(D) Was at one time closed to the general public	
(E) Was seen as the only way to gain attention as an artist	**Salon des Indepéndants**
(F) Never turned down a serious submission	•
(G) Accepted only experimental works of art	•

Chapter **11** Humanities II   131

Intensive Drill 2

ART RESTORATION AND CONSERVATION

1   Great masterpieces of art are destined to live forever as a beloved part of our cultural heritage. However, works of art are inherently fragile. Paint may chip or flake off over the years; canvases may bend or warp. For this reason, experts are continually making efforts to restore and conserve great works of art so that they may survive in perpetuity.

2   Conservation and restoration have a long history in the art world, but until the nineteenth century, most of the work had been done by isolated individuals, and involved simply cleaning or touching up pieces of art for themselves or other collectors. The methods used were often only temporarily effective, and sometimes caused long-term damage to the "restored" pieces. For example, it was not uncommon to apply varnish to a painting to serve as a protective coating. However, these conservators unknowingly used inferior materials that, in just a few years' time, would yellow and peel. In addition, early conservators used paints that had no more permanent value than the originals, and sometimes even less. Thus, paintings had to be restored quite frequently. With each restoration, the paintings lost more and more of their original integrity and sustained more long-term damage.

3   During the nineteenth century, however, renowned scientists like Louis Pasteur and Michael Faraday began to study the effects of the environment on works of art, and their findings served to inform museum curators about the best ways to maintain their precious art collections. In 1888, Friedrich Rathgen became the first chemist to be employed directly by a museum, the Royal Museum of Berlin, thus officially transforming the practice of art conservation into a profession. Shortly after World War I, the British Museum hired chemist Harold Plenderleith to restore paintings that had suffered damage while hidden from enemies in the London Underground. These chemists and others identified and created pigments that would keep their color longer. They also discovered that ultraviolet radiation, such as that from the sun, had a profound effect on the brilliance of the paint. In response to this, museum curators placed their most sensitive paintings in display areas with a minimum of sunlight to keep them from fading.

4   Today, art conservators are careful not to alter a work of art in any way that is not absolutely necessary to its survival. They normally practice one of two methods: interventive conservation and preventive conservation. Interventive conservation is similar to the restoration techniques of old, in that the conservator actually interacts with a work of art directly in order to clean it or to remedy some flaw. Even the most advanced interventive techniques can cause damage to artwork, so ample justification is required before a conservator can undertake such a process. More common is preventive conservation, in which measures are taken to prevent any future damage to a work of art. This involves simply protecting the art from environmental factors that can contribute to decay, so that little or no interventive work will be needed in the future.

01 According to paragraph 2, all of the following were problems in early restoration efforts EXCEPT

(A) using poor-quality paints
(B) applying harmful varnishes
(C) removing paintings from sunlight
(D) restoring paintings often

02 According to paragraph 2, what can be inferred about early art conservators?

(A) They did not have enough knowledge necessary for restoring art.
(B) They were amateurs who were new to art.
(C) They sought to improve upon the art instead of just restoring it.
(D) They used paint that was of high quality.

03 Which of the sentences below best expresses the essential information in the highlighted sentence in the passage? *Incorrect* answer choices change the meaning in important ways or leave out essential information.

(A) The effects of the environment on works of art were not fully understood until they were researched by museum curators in the nineteenth century.
(B) Museums began to change the way they protected their art collections from environmental damage after hiring chemists to perform research.
(C) Scientists of the nineteenth century determined that the wrong environment can damage works of art, and they urged museum curators to consider their research.
(D) Research by famous scientists in the nineteenth century influenced the way museum curators protected their art collections from environmental damage.

04 The phrase "such a process" in the passage refers to

(A) protecting art from environmental factors
(B) ample justification
(C) preventive conservation
(D) interventive conservation

05 **Directions:** An introductory sentence for a brief summary of the passage is provided below. Complete the summary by selecting the THREE answer choices that express the most important ideas in the passage. Some sentences do not belong in the summary because they express ideas that are not presented in the passage or are minor ideas in the passage. *This question is worth 2 points.*

Continuous efforts to restore and conserve great artwork are ongoing by experts.

(A) For hundreds of years, art conservators used damaging techniques and materials of poor quality to restore works of art.
(B) In the struggle to preserve precious artworks, museums began to recognize the skills of chemists in the process of conservation.
(C) Art conservation is a complex practice that involves several different disciplines, from art history to chemistry.
(D) Museum curators shield paintings from exposure to ultraviolet radiation, which can greatly diminish a work's quality.
(E) Scientific research was instrumental in determining which paints were of the best quality in regard to the endurance of the pigments.
(F) Modern art conservators use both interventive and preventive conservation methods, but try not to make any unnecessary modification to artwork.

Intensive Drill 3

THEATER ACTING AND FILM ACTING

1. Though live performance on a stage and performing on screen are both considered part of the dramatic arts, there are several fundamental differences between them. The first difference comes from scripts. In stage acting, the audience is often very familiar with the performance materials even before they see the acting. Because theater by its nature is repetitive and familiar to the audience, the audience is expected to know the plot of the story. The script, which is written by the playwright, is sacrosanct in stage acting. Neither errors nor deviations from it are tolerated by actors or audiences alike. In this way, the performance aims to be as truthful a representation of the playwright's words as possible. In filmmaking, on the other hand, the audience has not seen the script before watching the film. Therefore they have no expectation that the actors or directors are following a script with great fidelity. It is not uncommon, in fact, for the script for a film to be written or rewritten on the fly. The audience is unaware of this and only ever sees one version, which they consider to be the faithful version.

2. Similar expectations hold true for how characters are portrayed in theater as compared to film. In theater, the characters, their roles, mannerisms, tone of voice, intents, and even costume are more or less well defined. The audience arrives at the theater with a preconceived notion of what a given character looks and sounds like. Likewise, one actor's performance of a character will be compared and critiqued with another's. In film, the characters are defined by the actors and directors. When casting a part, directors look for a person who fits the world they are trying to create. The job of the film actor is to imbue the role with personality and presence that convinces the audience the character is a real person.

3. Another difference between stage and film acting comes from the physical location where they are performed. On a stage, actors must convey their acting even to audience members in the back row. **A** This means that the performances should be "larger than life"; louder voices and more dramatic and defined movements are required. **B** All this is necessary for the audience to engage with the actors and the material while seated in the theater, particularly if they are seated at some distance from the performers. **C** In film, on the other hand, actors behave more naturally, speaking in a normal volume and moving and gesturing in a natural way. **D** Technical elements such as lighting, sound, camera angles, and musical score add additional impact to the acting.

4. Stage acting happens in real time without any editing. The actors work intensely to capture and maintain the audience's attention. The live performance creates a strong, intimate connection between the actors and the audience, something that a film cannot do to the same degree. This is the reason some people say that live performances leave a stronger lasting impression on their audience.

Answer Book p. A78

01 All of the following are mentioned in paragraph 1 EXCPET:

(A) The audience has few preconceived notions of stage acting.
(B) Both stage acting and filmmaking are considered dramatic arts.
(C) The scripts in stage acting are considered sacrosanct and not altered.
(D) Audiences are allowed to see only the final version of films.

02 According to paragraph 2, which of the following is true of film acting?

(A) Actors must follow how a character was portrayed previously.
(B) Directors choose actors to match audiences' expectations of the role.
(C) Characters are subject to comparison with previously acted roles.
(D) Actors and directors together portray the characters to suit the plot.

03 How does paragraph 2 relate to the earlier discussion of audience expectations in different performance settings?

(A) It explains why audiences have different expectations for different performance settings.
(B) It describes a new type of performance setting where both merits of different settings are combined.
(C) It contrasts the degree of tolerance for changes to original contexts in different performance types.
(D) It illustrates another example of what audiences expect from different performance settings.

04 Look at the four squares [■] that indicate where the following sentence could be added to the passage.

> This is why actors often remark that they feed off the energy of the audience, something that film actors cannot experience directly.

Where would the sentence best fit?

(A) A   (B) B   (C) C   (D) D

05 **Directions:** An introductory sentence for a brief summary of the passage is provided below. Complete the summary by selecting the THREE answer choices that express the most important ideas in the passage. Some sentences do not belong in the summary because they express ideas that are not presented in the passage or are minor ideas in the passage. *This question is worth 2 points.*

The way film and live theater differ creates different experiences for the audience.

(A) Filmed performance's well-knit plot provides a more immersive experience than stage acting does.
(B) The script should not be changed in stage acting, while it can be altered on a whim in film.
(C) A character can be modified in film, but in theater it is not subject to change.
(D) Film uses more technical effects to leave stronger impressions on audiences, compared to stage acting.
(E) Actors in film act naturally while the actors on stage perform with more exaggeration.
(F) Scripts for a film cannot be revised while scripts for theater can be modified.

Chapter 11 Humanities II   135

Mini Test 1

THE *ILIAD* AND THE *ODYSSEY*

1   The Greek poet Homer is widely held to be the earliest and most important Greek writer. His works were written at a turning pointing in Greek history when verse was turning from an oral tradition to written words. At the same time, Greek society was developing and changing, and ideas of social organization, economics, philosophy, and politics were emerging and evolving. Many of these ideas went on to form important and defining elements upon which Western civilization developed. Consequently, Homer's works not only mirrored the ideas of his contemporaries, but also went on to greatly influence Western literature.

2   Nothing definitive is known of Homer the man; indeed, there is much conjecture as to whether he really existed. Numerous scholars have shown that except for the works the *Iliad* and the *Odyssey*, other works attributed to him may have been written by anonymous writers. It was not uncommon for writers to attribute epic poems to being "of Homer," further obscuring the issue. Furthermore, the stories bear many similarities to popular oral poems and stories, so that some scholars argue that his poems were merely amalgamations of numerous oral stories. What is roundly accepted, though, is that the *Iliad* and the *Odyssey* share many stylistic similarities, enough that they appear to be written by the same author.

3   For the Greeks, Homer's works the *Iliad* and the *Odyssey* highlighted and celebrated how they had become the dominant power in the Mediterranean region. The former is essentially a story of military dominance. It tells of the Mycenaean victory at Troy, which was a battle for control of a valuable sea passage. Many of the characters in the *Iliad* choose military glory over family life, willingly sacrificing the chance to live a long life with those they love. The *Odyssey*, on the other hand, focuses more on characteristics and attributes that Greeks should aspire to. One of the most important values in the *Odyssey* is loyalty, as Odysseus's devotion to his family, his country, and his god is unwavering. This value stands out continuously during the course of the book by describing the faithful wife waiting patiently for years for her husband to return, and the hero who acts courageously and honorably for his country. It also described in great detail the gods and how they behaved, in effect setting the template for how we understand Greek mythology today.

4   In this way, Homer's epic poems became a template for the further stories of Greece's rise to power in the region. Homer's work was written as Greek civilization was emerging, and thus his writings capture many of the ideas and beliefs that would come to be defining elements of Western civilization. We see in his writings examples of the common good outweighing the power of the individual, the obligations that men have to their leaders, and obligations that women and men have to each other. The stories are, in a sense, morality tales that show how one should behave in the new civilization the Greeks were forging. Homer's writings have also gone on to influence countless forms of western literature, from *Don Quiote* to recent films such as *O Brother Where Art Thou?*

01 The word "definitive" in the passage is closest in meaning to

(A) tremendous
(B) impressive
(C) detailed
(D) decisive

02 The phrase "The former" in the passage refers to

(A) The *Iliad*
(B) The Mediterranean region
(C) The *Odyssey*
(D) Homer

03 It can be inferred from paragraph 4 that

(A) it was common for Greeks to find Homer's writings opposing popularly held views in society
(B) Homer's stories are considered old-fashioned because of their restricted focus on moral values
(C) the moral beliefs in Homer's stories corresponded to contemporary moral standards
(D) few contemporary critics still recognize the significance of Homer's writing

04 Select the TWO answer choices that are true about the *Iliad* and the *Odyssey*.
To receive credit, you must select TWO answers.

(A) The *Iliad* and the *Odyssey* became the guideline for further stories of Greece's dominance.
(B) Scholars dispute whether Homer wrote both the *Iliad* and the *Odyssey* at the same time.
(C) There is sufficient evidence showing that the *Iliad* and the *Odyssey* are written by multiple authors.
(D) Greeks saw the *Iliad* and the *Odyssey* as symbols of Greece's domination in the Mediterranean region.

05 **Directions:** Select the appropriate phrases from the answer choices and match them to the Homer's poems. TWO of the answer choices will NOT be used. ***This question is worth 3 points.***

Answer Choices	The *Iliad*
(A) Describes details of gods	•
(B) Emphasizes value of loyalty	•
(C) Values wisdom over strength	**The *Odyssey***
(D) Portrays the civilization of Greece	
(E) Underlines the ideal values in Greece	•
(F) Emphasizes military honor over family	•
(G) Illustrates a story of military victory	•

Mini Test 2

POTTERY OF THE HOPI INDIANS

1   The pottery of the Hopi Indian tribe of southwestern America is among the most vibrant Native American traditions. The Hopi and their neighboring tribes began making pottery over 2,000 years ago, and the traditional process of pottery making has changed very little since then. The potter, almost always a woman in Hopi culture, first must obtain the clay that is needed to make the pot. Clay is traditionally gathered near the home, simply by digging small pits in the ground. Larger mines do exist, and many of them are kept secret from outsiders by members of the tribe, as clay is often seen as an almost sacred material. Traditional prayers are offered up to the spirits when the clay is taken from the earth. The clay must be conditioned for several days before it is ready to be used, and the women do this by grinding the hard substance into a fine powder and soaking it in water until it is soft and flexible.

2   After this step is completed, the clay can be molded into the shape of the pot. Most often, the pot is carefully molded by hand, using small amounts of water to keep the clay soft and smooth throughout the process. Another popular method, most often used for much larger objects, is to use long coils of clay that can be stacked. A base is made from a flat piece of clay, and the pot is literally built from the ground up by stacking the coils on top of one another. Once molded, the pot is left to dry for a short time before the potter returns to polish it. Polishing involves the use of a small, wet pebble, which is scraped up and down the sides of the pot at a rapid pace. This ensures that there are no imperfections such as air bubbles in the clay, which can ruin the pot when it goes into the firing stage.

3   Designs for the pot are often in the form of pictures or shapes that are scratched into the clay surface with a special tool. This process is known as scraffito, and it must be done very carefully, because marks that are too shallow may not show up after firing, while marks that are too deep risk breaking the inner surface, which can cause the pot to shatter when heated. Traditional designs often feature the Avanyul, a feathered serpent from Hopi folklore, and several other symbols that have a personal, spiritual significance to the potter, such as wolves or waterfowl. Painting is not uncommon either, and is traditionally done with a piece of a yucca plant that has been chewed at one end to form a brush.

4   Finally, the pot is placed in a shallow pit to be fired. **A** Placed on a bed of large broken pottery shards, the pot is then covered further with more shards. **B** The whole arrangement is then covered with a mound of dried cow or sheep feces, and wood is used to set the feces ablaze. **C** The potter recites a traditional prayer for good luck in completing her work of art, as any number of things can go wrong during the firing. **D** A gust of wind, for instance, can blow ashes or feces onto the pot which may stick to the clay, ruining the design of the pot and the many days of work that went into shaping it. After several hours of cooking, the pot is hardened and ready for use.

Answer Book p. A82

01 The word "them" in the passage refers to

(A) small pits   (B) mines   (C) members   (D) outsiders

02 The word "flexible" in the passage is closest in meaning to

(A) pliable   (B) fragile   (C) dense   (D) heavy

03 Which of the sentences below best expresses the essential information in the highlighted sentence in the passage? *Incorrect* answer choices change the meaning in important ways or leave out essential information.

(A) Since designs cut too deep can damage the pot and designs cut too shallow will likely not show after firing, scraffito must be performed delicately.
(B) Decorating a pot with scraffito must be done carefully so as not to cause the pot to break when it goes into the oven.
(C) Because designs that do not penetrate enough of the clay often disappear when the pot is fired, scraffito must be etched deeply into the surface.
(D) Since scraffito is a risky practice that can accidentally destroy a pot, it is considered by most an unnecessary step in the process.

04 Look at the four squares [■] that indicate where the following sentence could be added to the passage.

The space between the pieces allows air to pass into the furnace and feed the flames.

Where would the sentence best fit?

(A) **A**   (B) **B**   (C) **C**   (D) **D**

05 Directions: An introductory sentence for a brief summary of the passage is provided below. Complete the summary by selecting the THREE answer choices that express the most important ideas in the passage. Some sentences do not belong in the summary because they express ideas that are not presented in the passage or are minor ideas in the passage. **This question is worth 2 points.**

Hopi Indians' long and intensive process for making traditional pottery is much the same as it has been for hundreds of years.

(A) After the clay is properly conditioned, it is molded by hand, or built up as long strips of clay.
(B) In traditional Hopi society, women are the ones who most often make pottery, though the opportunity extends to males and females alike.
(C) Potters add patterns onto the surface of the pottery by carving or painting pictures.
(D) If a pot is to be painted, it generally features images of animals that have some spiritual significance to the artist.
(E) Tiny imperfections in the surface of the clay can cause the pot to burst when it is fired in the oven.
(F) In the final stage, the pot is covered in pottery shards and animal feces, and set ablaze until it hardens into a usable state.

DADA

1 ➡ The course of Western art forever changed after World War I. The brutality and violence of the war affected an entire generation of young poets, writers, painters, and other artists. They were disappointed that Western ideals like peace and democracy had not prevented such violence. The outrage felt by these artists gave rise to the most subversive art movement the world had ever seen. Its practitioners called it Dada, and it stood for everything that art was not; it was, in a sense, "anti-art." Instead of pleasing the tastes of viewers, Dada artists sought to shock and offend them. Dadaists sought to challenge people's traditional beliefs by challenging the ways in which they viewed art. Dada artists wanted not only to change the art world, but to change the beliefs and attitudes of the people as well. Throughout its short history, Dada spread to several cities around the world, taking on a new and unique form wherever it appeared.

2 Dada was begun by a small group of artists in Zurich, Switzerland. Switzerland was neutral in the war, and it was a refuge for people from nearby warring countries such as Germany and Austria. Artists moved to Switzerland both to escape the war and to protest it. The movement centered on a local nightclub called the Cabaret Voltaire, where performance art was the main attraction. In one early performance, poet Hugo Ball read three pieces of experimental poetry while bouncing around the stage in a costume made of cardboard cylinders and a pair of cardboard wings. In short, the performance was completely absurd, and audiences left the club both shocked and confused at such disregard for their own pleasure. This, of course, was Ball's intention. Similar performances at the Cabaret included many important artists who would later go on to achieve great fame. One of them was Max Ernst, who, with the help of fellow artists, established a Dada group in Cologne, Germany shortly after the war.

3 ➡ **A** From Zurich, some members of the original Dada group moved to New York City to join an already thriving community of Dada artists there. **B** The atmosphere in New York was much different from that of Zurich and Cologne. **C** New York artists practiced what was perhaps the most playful form of Dada to date. **D** Whereas cynicism played a major role in European Dada, irony and humor were important to the New York scene. The basic goals, however, remained the same: the creation of anti-art that challenged the beliefs of mainstream society. French artist Marcel Duchamp created one of the best-known artworks here, a sculpture called *Fountain*, which featured an overturned bathroom urinal. Audiences reacted with disgust to the piece, and the work was almost universally reviled by the mainstream art community. However, it did spark a great deal of lively debate, as the artist had hoped it would.

4 Artists in Paris had been closely following the work of various Dada groups around the world, but a real movement of Dada did not begin in Paris until 1920, when several of the movement's original members moved there. For many years prior to this, the city had held a stronger reputation for its literature than for its art. However, once an array of artists began pouring into the city, Dada succeeded in Paris more than in any other city. Writers such as Andre Breton took up the cause of the Dadaists and published essays on the Dada philosophy. French painter Jean Crotti held the first exhibition of Dada paintings at the Society

of Independent Artists. Composer Erik Satie collaborated with Pablo Picasso and others to create one of the most bizarre and scandalous ballets of the time. Whereas most ballets include graceful dancing and beautiful music, Satie and Picasso's ballet featured Cubist-style sets, an orchestra of noisemaking instruments, and costumes so large and awkward that few of the dancers could move with ease. Despite the wide array of art produced in Paris, the Dada movement began to go out of style in 1922, and by 1924 it had all but disappeared. Though Dada may be gone, the lasting influence of Dada can still be found in modern styles of music such as punk rock, and it is also alive and well in many modern art films.

Glossary

Cubist: early twentieth-century avant-garde style of art

---

01 The word " they " in the passage refers to

(A) artists
(B) beliefs
(C) people
(D) Dadaists

02 The word " its " in the passage refers to

(A) Dada
(B) art world
(C) form
(D) history

03 According to paragraph 1, what can be inferred about the effects of World War I on artists?

(A) It resulted in the deaths of many famous artists.
(B) It caused artists to lose faith in their societies.
(C) It restricted artists' freedom of expression.
(D) It became more difficult to earn a living in art.

Paragraph 1 is marked with an arrow [➡].

04 The word " refuge " in the passage is closest in meaning to

(A) route
(B) chapel
(C) shelter
(D) journey

05 The word "absurd " in the passage is closest in meaning to

(A) juvenile
(B) brutal
(C) vulgar
(D) preposterous

06 The word " This " in the passage refers to

(A) The contradiction of Ball's performance
(B) The audience's reaction to Ball's performance
(C) The achievement of great fame by performers
(D) The beginning of a new art movement

07 According to paragraph 3, how was the Dada scene in New York City different from other cities?

(A) It was more lighthearted than other versions.
(B) It attracted more of the world's attention.
(C) Its artists were more famous than most others.
(D) It marked the end of the movement.

Paragraph 3 is marked with an arrow [➡].

08 The word " collaborated " in the passage is closest in meaning to

(A) competed
(B) communicated
(C) disagreed
(D) cooperated

09 Which of the sentences below best expresses the essential information in the highlighted sentence in the passage? *Incorrect* answer choices change the meaning in important ways or leave out essential information.

(A) Satie and Picasso added a taste of Cubist-style to the original graceful ballet dancing and music.
(B) Although Satie and Picasso tried experimental alterations to authentic ballet, the audience was indifferent to Cubist-style ballet.
(C) Contrary to the delicate classic ballets, Satie and Picasso's Cubist-style ballet was composed of atypical settings.
(D) Satie and Picasso's endeavor to add Cubism to traditional ballets is considered one of the most innovative approaches.

10 According to the passage, which of the following is NOT true of Dada?

(A) It involved a wide scope of art ranging from literature and fine art to ballet.
(B) It opposed mainstream belief systems and traditional forms of art.
(C) Dada artists did not cater to the tastes of audiences.
(D) Dada first emerged in France and spread to other cities.

11 All of the following are mentioned in the passage as Dadaist art work EXCEPT

(A) sculpture
(B) fashion
(C) painting
(D) poetry

12 Look at the four squares [■] that indicate where the following sentence could be added to the passage.

> These artists were less burdened by the violence in Europe, and the result was this relatively carefree attitude.

Where would the sentence best fit?

Click on a square [■] to add the sentence to the passage.

(A) A (B) B (C) C (D) D

13 Directions: An introductory sentence for a brief summary of the passage is provided below. Complete the summary by selecting the THREE answer choices that express the most important ideas in the passage. Some sentences do not belong in the summary because they express ideas that are not presented in the passage or are minor ideas in the passage. **This question is worth 2 points.**

Drag your answer choices to the spaces where they belong. To remove an answer choice, click on it. To review the passage, click **View Text**.

Dada was a worldwide artistic movement that attempted to shake traditional notions of art and society.
-
-
-

Answer Choices	
(A) World War I inspired artists from Paris, Zurich, and even New York to show pride in their countries by making art that was more patriotic.	(D) Dada reached its climax in Paris, where artists collaborated to put on a bizarre Dada ballet.
(B) A group of artists created the subversive art movement Dada in Zurich, and they shocked audiences with nonsensical performances.	(E) Switzerland was neutral during the war, making Zurich the ideal city for an artistic movement to begin in.
(C) While European Dada movements featured seriousness and cynicism, American Dada had unique characteristics such as irony and humor.	(F) Dada succeeded the most in Paris compared to other cities, as Jean Crotti, a French painter, held the first exhibition of Dada painting.

Chapter 12 Life Science I

- **Life Science**
  A scientific study of all types of living organisms such as microorganisms, plants, animals, and human beings
- **Related fields**
  Microbiology, Botany, Entomology, Marine biology, Zoology, Physiology, etc.

Reading Preview

Physiology – Sleep Deprivation
| Intensive Drill 1 |

Sleep deprivation is the condition of not having enough sleep. It often goes undiagnosed because few people know much about sleep disorders and most consider them unimportant. Prolonged wakefulness can be due to acute total sleep deprivation (SD) or to chronic partial sleep restriction. A chronic sleep-restricted state can cause fatigue, daytime sleepiness, clumsiness, and weight loss or weight gain. It adversely affects the brain and cognitive functions as well.

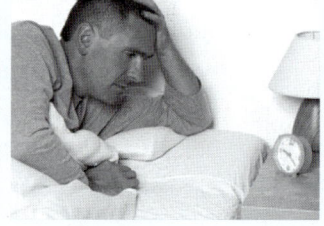

Microbiology– Viruses and Bacteria
| Intensive Drill 2 |

Viruses are small infectious agents that replicate only inside the living cells of other organisms. Viruses can infect all types of life forms, from animals and plants to microorganisms, including bacteria and archaea.

Bacteria are single-celled microbes. Typically a few micrometers in length, they can be found most everywhere. Bacteria also live in symbiotic and parasitic relationships with plants and animals.

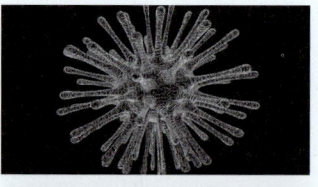

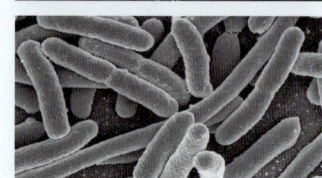

Marine Biology – Feeding Mechanisms of Marine Organisms

| Intensive Drill 3 |

Over 70 percent of the Earth is covered by water more than a mile deep. The ocean is the largest habitat on Earth and has an abundance of life forms. It consists of different layers according to depth and these layers, or zones, have their own characteristics. Marine organisms developed distinct feeding strategies according to the zones they live in, as every organism has to evolve and develop mechanisms in response to the different types of food in their habitats.

Botany – Colonization of Plant Life on Earth

| Mini Test 1 |

Although some plants still remain dependent on an aquatic environment, it is widely believed that the evolution of land plants occurred through the gradual development of ancestral aquatic green algae over millions of years. To adapt to the less-hydrating land environment, land plants have developed new physical structures and reproductive mechanisms.

Microbiology – Cell Structure

| Mini Test 2 |

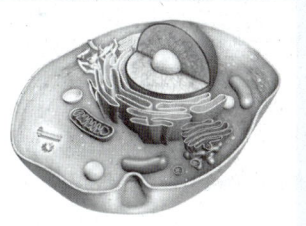

A cell is the smallest structural, functional, and biological unit of all living organisms on our planet earth. As a fundamental unit of life, it is a small compartment that holds the biological equipment necessary to keep an organism alive and successful. It shares many common mechanisms across different classes of organisms such as microorganisms, plants, and animals. Between these classes there are also key differences in cell architecture.

Physiology – Circadian Rhythm

| iBT Practice |

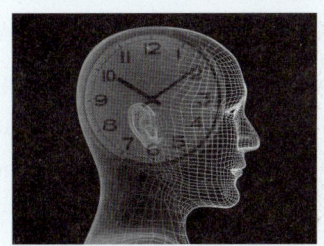

A circadian rhythm is any biological process that shows an endogenous, entrainable oscillation in a roughly 24-hour cycle. These 24-hour rhythms are driven by an internal body clock, and they have been observed in plants, animals, fungi, and cyanobacteria. In a strict sense, circadian rhythms are endogenously developed, although they can be modulated by external cues such as sunlight and temperature. It is important in determining the sleeping and feeding patterns of all animals, including humans.

Intensive Drill 1

SLEEP DEPRIVATION

1   Sleep is an essential part of our mental and physical health, so a lack of adequate sleep can be physically and mentally detrimental to our health. Physically speaking, our body needs sleep to recover and rejuvenate. Because our body releases human growth hormone, HGH, when it is sleeping, this enables our body to maintain healthy muscle mass, thicker skin, and stronger bones. However, poor sleep habits reduce the amount of HGH that is released, which has an effect on the physical health and strength of muscles, skin, and bones. In addition, with little sleep, our body is typically under greater amounts of stress and releases the stress hormone cortisol, which in excess amounts can start to break down collagen, the critical protein in our skin that keeps it elastic.

2   In addition, lack of sleep has been correlated with an increase in appetite and cravings for certain high-fat and high-carbohydrate foods. There is a link between sleep and the peptides that regulate appetite, and when the amount of sleep is reduced, the levels and effectiveness of the peptides are altered detrimentally. Research shows that people who get less than six hours of sleep a night are 30 percent more likely to be overweight. The increased chance to become overweight also raises the risk of problems with our cardiovascular system. Because sleep has a vital role in our body's ability to repair our blood vessels and heart, its deprivation can lead to higher risk of chronic health problems such as high blood pressure, heart disease, and strokes.

3   Above all, the most obvious effect poor sleep has is on our cognitive abilities. Poor sleep affects our everyday life with impaired alertness, concentration, reasoning, and problem solving. It gets in the way of our decision-making process and stifles creativity too. Obviously, this has the greatest impact on students. It has been shown that students with minor sleep deprivation tend to receive lower grades compared to students who get sufficient sleep. Also, studies have shown that a lack of sleep and poor-quality sleep actually lead to an increase in accidents on the job. Factory workers reported a greater frequency of accidents, and drivers operating cars and heavy machinery under the effects of little sleep have been shown to have the same reaction times as drunk drivers.

4   **A** Likewise, lack of sleep makes it harder to recall and assimilate past knowledge with new knowledge and experiences, while sufficient sleep helps to consolidate memories. **B** In particular, sleep-deprived people are particularly poor at recognizing and assessing how their lack of sleep is affecting them physically and emotionally. **C** This is particularly concerning for people who work in professions such as judges, airline pilots, or doctors, where they must constantly assess their ability to perform their tasks safely and accurately. **D**

Answer Book p. A88

01 The word "reduces" in the passage is closest in meaning to

(A) boosts
(B) diminishes
(C) alters
(D) blocks

02 All of the following are mentioned in paragraph 1 EXCEPT:

(A) Our body is under great stress when it lacks enough sleep.
(B) Excessive amounts of cortisol destroy collagen.
(C) Collagen reinforces the strength of muscles, skin, and bones.
(D) Sleep deprivation decreases the level of HGH that is released.

03 It can be inferred from paragraph 3 that

(A) sufficient sleep is essential to succeed at both work and school
(B) students with better grades are good at managing their time
(C) sleep deprivation leads to shorter life expectancy
(D) the level of sleep deprivation is determined by occupational groups

04 Look at the four squares [■] that indicate where the following sentence could be added to the passage.

> Sleep deprivation can also affect how we interpret events and the world around us.

Where would the sentence best fit?

(A) A (B) B (C) C (D) D

05 **Directions:** An introductory sentence for a brief summary of the passage is provided below. Complete the summary by selecting the THREE answer choices that express the most important ideas in the passage. Some sentences do not belong in the summary because they express ideas that are not presented in the passage or are minor ideas in the passage. *This question is worth 2 points.*

Sleep deprivation can cause significant physical and mental damage to our body and mind.

(A) Poor sleep impairs collagen production for concentration, reasoning, and problem solving.
(B) Lack of sleep reduces the level of HGH and releases the stress hormone cortisol.
(C) Sleep deprivation increases appetite due to impaired peptide regulation and causes weight gain.
(D) The negative impact of sleep deprivation is most critical in students, as it can lead to low grades.
(E) Both critical cognitive functions and memory consolidation are impaired when sleep is deprived.
(F) People who are undergoing sleep deprivation overlook its adverse effects.

Intensive Drill 2

VIRUSES AND BACTERIA

1   Bacteria and viruses are often spoken of in similar terms, especially in regard to their ability to cause disease. However, beyond this common trait, the two differ in a number of important ways. For instance, bacteria are living organisms, and as such can survive independently of other living things. Viruses, on the other hand, are inactive unless they find their way into a living host, at which time they are able to grow and reproduce.

2   One major difference between bacteria and viruses is their composition. Bacteria are the simplest forms of life on Earth, but are rather complex in their makeup when compared to viruses. Like any cell, a bacterium is surrounded by a protective wall, or membrane, that holds its contents together. Inside the membrane is a bundle of DNA that carries the bacterium's genetic information. Viruses are similar in that they also contain genes in the form of either DNA or RNA, though in far smaller quantities. In viruses, however, these materials are contained not in a cell membrane, but in a thinner outer coating of proteins.

3   Bacteria and viruses also differ greatly in their methods of reproduction. Again, it is the bacterium's status as a single-celled living organism that sets it apart from the virus. Bacteria reproduce asexually through cell division. Once they grow to a certain size, the DNA inside splits into two identical structures called progeny cells, and slowly the cell breaks apart, with one group of DNA in each new cell. Reproduction of bacteria is limited, however, by the nutrients available in the environment. Viruses, on the other hand, cannot reproduce until they have latched onto a host. After a virus attaches itself to a host cell, the virus works its way into the cell through the membrane. As the virus's protein shell dissolves, the genetic information in the virus is released into the cell where it can reproduce and spread. Viruses will continue to reproduce rapidly until the host's resources have been completely used up, at which time they will simply look for a new host.

4   **A** Diseases caused by viruses range from the common cold to HIV, and can be either temporary and relatively harmless or life-long and potentially deadly. **B** While there is no real cure for viral diseases, vaccines and antiviral drugs can help. **C** Vaccines introduce a very small portion of the virus into the body, so that if a person does come in contact with the virus, he or she is already immune to its effects. **D** Antiviral drugs have only come into being in the last 20 years or so, and they work by halting the reproduction of the virus rather than killing it. Bacterial infections are far easier to treat; antibiotic drugs work with the immune system to quickly kill most infections.

Answer Book p. A90

01 The word "its" in the passage refers to

(A) cell (B) bacterium (C) membrane (D) make-up

02 Which of the sentences below best expresses the essential information in the highlighted sentence in the passage? *Incorrect* answer choices change the meaning in important ways or leave out essential information.

(A) As the cell grows larger, it splits into two separate identical cells, each with the same genetic material as the original cell.
(B) When the cell splits in two, it grows large enough so that its DNA can replicate and create a new cell.
(C) DNA is replicated within the cell, at which point the cell grows larger and eventually splits into two different cells.
(D) Cells reproduce by dividing themselves into two separate corresponding cells with different genetic material.

03 According to paragraph 3, what can be inferred about the reproduction of viruses?

(A) It always reproduces the same number of viruses.
(B) It occurs through the division of a single cell.
(C) It can go on indefinitely if there is a live host.
(D) It can occur outside a host cell.

04 Look at the four squares [■] that indicate where the following sentence could be added to the passage.

> Most types of bacteria are beneficial to humans, and not all viruses carry disease, but both can be harmful when they disrupt the normal functions of the human body.

Where would the sentence best fit?

(A) A (B) B (C) C (D) D

05 **Directions:** Select the appropriate phrases from the answer choices and match them to the type of microorganism to which they relate. TWO of the answer choices will NOT be used. *This question is worth 3 points.*

Answer Choices	Viruses
(A) Cannot reproduce outside of a host	•
(B) Can be cured by antibiotic drugs	•
(C) Contain bundles of DNA at their center	**Bacteria**
(D) Single-celled organisms that can live independently	•
(E) Reproduce by inserting its genetic information into a cell	•
(F) Lack an outer coating to protect genetic material	**Both**
(G) Do not disrupt functions of the human body	•

Intensive Drill 3

FEEDING MECHANISMS OF MARINE ORGANISMS

1   The oceans are vast and cover two-thirds of the Earth's surface. They are organized into various layers based on depth and the amount of light received from the Sun. Each layer consists of a different mixture of marine species that are adapted to its light levels, pressures, and temperatures. One such adaptation can be found in the feeding behavior of ocean creatures. Marine organisms adopt various types of distinctive features and feeding mechanisms that acclimate to the environment in different zones of the ocean.

2   Filter-feeding is one of the most common feeding strategies in aquatic habitats where sunlight penetrates the water. This layer of ocean, also known as the sunlight zone, contains plentiful but tiny organisms that are suspended in water such as plankton and krill, providing the foundation of the marine food chain. Filter-feeding is a method in which animals take in mouthfuls of water, filter out undesirable parts through structures that act as sieves, and swallow the food left in their mouths. Filter feeders range from small creatures like sponges to enormous mammals like blue whales. Each has its own specialized equipment for filter-feeding. For example, immobile organisms like sponges have a water current system made of chambers and canals for water to flow through them. The system pumps in water, filters the food from the water, then expels the water out. Baleen whales, instead of teeth, have fringe-like hair called baleen that traps prey and forces out water. Basking sharks and whale sharks have bristle-like gill rakers that strain food as they swim through the water with their mouths open.

3   Unlike the sunlight zone, the deep sea or midnight zone lacks sunlight and is as dark as night. Deep-sea organisms living in this layer of ocean have evolved different types of feeding mechanisms for survival. Due to the absence of photosynthesis, food is scarce and hard to find in deep-sea regions. As a result, deep-sea creatures have developed physical features to ensure that captured prey has little chance of escape. Some have extremely long fang-like teeth that point inward to trap prey up in their mouths. Furthermore, many have large mouths, huge hinged jaws, and bulky and expandable stomachs to capture and process large quantities food at once. Deep-sea creatures do not expend much energy for swimming in search of food. Instead, they either sit and wait for prey or attract prey using clever adaptations such as lures. Anglerfish have a long fin sprouting from middle of their heads, like a fishing rod. By wiggling their fins, anglerfish draw prey close enough for them to ingest as whole. Some anglerfish even emit light at the edge of their fins to seduce more quarries.

Answer Book p. A92

01 The phrase "its" in the passage refers to

(A) mixture
(B) Sun
(C) layer
(D) depth

02 According to paragraph 1, how are the layers of the ocean distinguished?

(A) By the feeding behaviors of marine animals
(B) By the color of the water
(C) By the amount of penetrating light
(D) By the temperature of the water

03 The word "scarce" in the passage is closest in meaning to

(A) rare
(B) invisible
(C) unique
(D) insignificant

04 In paragraph 3, why does the author give details about "physical features"?

(A) To explain how marine creatures adapted themselves to the deep sea
(B) To rebut the idea that different ocean zones affect the appearance of marine animals
(C) To describe how deep-sea creatures manage to avoid predators
(D) To give interesting facts about how deep-sea animals digest food

05 **Directions:** An introductory sentence for a brief summary of the passage is provided below. Complete the summary by selecting the THREE answer choices that express the most important ideas in the passage. Some sentences do not belong in the summary because they express ideas that are not presented in the passage or are minor ideas in the passage. *This question is worth 2 points.*

Marine animals have specialized characteristics used for their feeding mechanisms.

(A) The ocean has several layers according to their depth and amount of sunlight they receive, which influence the traits of marine animals.
(B) In the sunlight zone, large numbers of plankton are present in the water due to the penetrating sunlight.
(C) In the midnight zone, marine animals have evolved to hunt efficiently without needing to consume much energy.
(D) Two most common marine feeding habits in the deep-sea level are filter-feeding and luring.
(E) Many marine creatures in the sunlight zone use their distinctive body parts as water filters when consuming food.
(F) Sharks evolved to have distinct physical features which let them to take down their prey in a very short time.

COLONIZATION OF PLANT LIFE ON EARTH

1. Millions of plant species are present across the globe, but like all life on earth, they originated in the ocean and gradually made their way to land. The first organisms to settle on land more than a billion years ago are called cyanobacteria. Since these organisms are able to photosynthesize sunlight, they released huge amounts of oxygen into the atmosphere, easing the migration of other plant forms from the ocean to land. There were several reasons that settling on land was beneficial to plants.

2. First, plants were able to photosynthesize sunlight easier, as the passage of sunlight to plants on land is more direct than to plants in water. In addition, the greater presence of carbon dioxide in the atmosphere than in the ocean facilitated the process of transforming carbon dioxide into oxygen. Lastly, the earth's soil was deeply rich in mineral nutrients, which were not as plentiful in the ocean. However, the plants also encountered several obstacles to survival as they made the switch from life in the ocean to life on land. Because plants were used to living in a constantly moist, aquatic environment, they needed to make sure that they did not dry out as they settled on land. Moreover, they had little gravitational support on land and needed to adapt to this environmental change.

3. One of the most significant organisms to help plant life make the transition from water to land was soil fungi, and plants and soil fungi ended up forming a mutual relationship with each other. The soil fungi provided the plants with essential nutrients that helped the plants to grow and spread, and in return, the fungi received the carbon dioxide processed from the plants, which they stored in the soil.

4. Plants also underwent dramatic physiological changes as they accustomed themselves to an environment with less water. While the original algae ancestors of plants had fairly simple bodies, plants needed to develop new structures to live on land, such as roots, leaves, and vascular tissue. The development of these physiological structures was crucial, as plants needed a way to transport water and nutrients through their bodies. Consequently, the first plants to grow on land were quite small and needed to grow in environments close to water. However, over time plants grew larger and deeper roots, which provided them with a more stable foundation to stand upright, thereby solving the gravitational problem. More importantly, roots allowed the plants to access nutrients and water in the soil, which traveled through newly developed vascular tissue, resulting in plants growing faster and taller. Leaves also evolved to capture larger amounts of sunlight, which aided in plants' developmental process.

5. As plants grew stronger and ubiquitously spread across the globe, they had a very significant ecological impact on the planet. Whereas carbon dioxide levels in the atmosphere were originally very high, the amount of oxygen released into the air greatly increased and allowed for other life forms to thrive. The larger amount of oxygen in the atmosphere also contributed to an increase in wildfires that are essential for plant species to produce seeds, grow, and reproduce.

01 According to paragraph 3, which of the following is true of soil fungi?

(A) Soil fungi and plant life developed an indispensable relationship with each other for survival.
(B) Soil fungi absorb essential nutrients from the plant life.
(C) Soil fungi was responsible for an increase in carbon dioxide in the atmosphere.
(D) Soil fungi initially struggled to survive as plants move to land.

02 Which of the sentences below best expresses the essential information in the highlighted sentence in the passage? *Incorrect* answer choices change the meaning in important ways or leave out essential information.

(A) As plants colonized land, they formed a mutual relationship with soil fungi, receiving essential nutrients to grow.
(B) The relationship between plants and soil fungi was unidirectional, as only plants benefited from fungi.
(C) Plants receive essential nutrients from soil fungi and provide carbon dioxide to them in exchange.
(D) Plants gave essential nutrients for fungi to live and the fungi aided plants by emitting carbon dioxide in return.

03 The word " Consequently " in the passage is closest in meaning to

(A) Likewise   (B) Meanwhile   (C) Furthermore   (D) Thus

04 In paragraph 5, what does the author imply about plants?

(A) Plants were rapidly able to reduce high levels of carbon dioxide in the atmosphere.
(B) Without the colonization of plants, it might have been more difficult for other life forms to evolve.
(C) Wildfires can play a large role in preventing the colonization of plant life.
(D) Higher levels of carbon dioxide in the atmosphere had a detrimental effect on plant colonization.

05 **Directions:** An introductory sentence for a brief summary of the passage is provided below. Complete the summary by selecting the THREE answer choices that express the most important ideas in the passage. Some sentences do not belong in the summary because they express ideas that are not presented in the passage or are minor ideas in the passage. *This question is worth 2 points.*

Cyanobacteria's settlement on land made the environment easier for other plant forms to migrate to land.

(A) An increase in gravity on land allowed plants to grow taller and develop deeper roots to stand upright.
(B) Plants colonized the land by storing carbon dioxide from the atmosphere in their vascular structures.
(C) Despite some obstacles, a number of plant species migrated to land from the ocean to live a more beneficial life.
(D) To adapt to the environmental change on land, plants created a mutual relationship with another species, developed new structures, or improved their body structures.
(E) The roots of plants not only provided a stable gravitational support but also supplied nutrients and water from the soil.
(F) Plants' successful prosperity across the globe also made it easier for other life forms to thrive on the earth.

Mini Test 2

CELL STRUCTURE

1   Cells are often called the building blocks of life, as they are the smallest functional unit of all life on Earth. Some life forms, like bacteria, consist of only one cell, while the human body is estimated to contain over 100 trillion cells. While every cell is a mostly autonomous unit, cells can also join with one another or work in cooperation to make up extremely complex forms of life. Cells vary in size and shape across different living organisms, depending upon their function or the organism in which they are found, but all are composed of the same basic parts.

2   Every cell has a protective covering that holds together its many parts and prevents interference from outside forces. This is called the cell membrane, and may be thought of as the skin of the cell. **A** The cell membrane is selectively permeable — this means that it can choose to let some materials pass through it and to block others. **B** Attached to the cell membrane is the cytoskeleton, a rigid structure that helps the cell maintain its shape. **C** Like a human skeleton, the cytoskeleton forms a defensive grid-like pattern around the cell that holds the membrane in place and protects the internal components of the cell. **D** The cytoskeleton may serve other purposes as well: it may contain what are called flagella, small hairs that help the cell move through external liquid.

3   Inside the cell membrane is a fluid called cytoplasm, which surrounds and cushions all of the internal cell parts. Located within the cytoplasm are organelles, small parts of the cell that serve specific functions to promote the cell's well-being. What organs are to the human body, organelles are to the cell. Of the several existing organelles, one of the most significant is the mitochondrion. Mitochondria are often called the power plants of the cell, as they produce the energy needed by the cell. They do this by taking various nutrients from the cytoplasm, which they use as their "fuel," and mix them with oxygen in a process called cellular respiration. The result is the creation of another substance, called ATP, which provides the cell with ample energy to survive by regulating its internal metabolism.

4   The most important part of the cell as a whole is the nucleus, or the control center of the cell. Safe within the nucleus is the genetic information that determines every characteristic and trait of that cell. The nucleus is constructed much like a smaller cell within a larger cell. It is protected by a double-layered membrane that separates the material inside from the cytoplasm floating around it. It also has its own type of skeleton, called a nuclear lamina, which gives support to the structure of the nucleus. The nucleus transmits genetic information through pores in the membrane to other parts of the cell about the formation, maintenance, and reproduction of the cell as a whole. When the cell reproduces, it is this important DNA that determines how all future cells will look and function.

Answer Book p. A96

01 The word "autonomous" in the passage is closest in meaning to

(A) cohesive (B) independent (C) significant (D) subordinate

02 According to paragraph 2, all of the following are true of the cytoskeleton EXCEPT:

(A) It helps the cell keep its shape.
(B) It is attached to the cell membrane.
(C) It has pores that allow nutrients to enter.
(D) It protects the cell from internal damage.

03 Why does the author mention "power plants" in the passage?

(A) To explain the significance of organelles
(B) To illustrate the function of mitochondria
(C) To show how much energy a cell requires
(D) To prove that cells are self-sufficient

04 Look at the four squares [■] that indicate where the following sentence could be added to the passage.

> In this way, the cell is able to absorb the nutrients it needs without letting in unnecessary or harmful elements.

Where would the sentence best fit?

(A) A (B) B (C) C (D) D

05 **Directions:** An introductory sentence for a brief summary of the passage is provided below. Complete the summary by selecting the THREE answer choices that express the most important ideas in the passage. Some sentences do not belong in the summary because they express ideas that are not presented in the passage or are minor ideas in the passage. *The question is worth 2 points.*

Although cells vary in their size and shape, they are made up of the same basic parts which ensure the health and well-being of the cell.

(A) Inside the membrane are several organelles, one of which, mitochondria, converts oxygen and other nutrients into energy.
(B) The cell derives its shape from the cytoskeleton, which forms a rigid grid-like pattern of support beneath the cell wall.
(C) The outermost parts of the cell are the cell membrane and cytoskeleton, which selectively let necessary substances in and maintain its shape, respectively.
(D) Tiny hairs called flagella that protrude from the cell membrane can be used by the cell to move through liquid surroundings.
(E) The nucleus controls other parts of the cell and is composed of a bundle of DNA and other materials that communicate with the various parts.
(F) The nuclear lamina lines the inner walls of the nuclear membrane and protects the material inside.

Chapter 12 Life Science I 155

CIRCADIAN RHYTHM

1   The health and well-being of humans, animals, and even plants are largely dependent on natural biological rhythms that help regulate bodily functions and optimize an organism's ability to carry out vital tasks. Most organisms are subject to what is called a circadian rhythm, a roughly 24-hour cycle that is divided into periods of sleep and wakefulness. The circadian rhythm has a far-reaching influence on the daily lives of organisms, regulating physical activity, chemical processes, and behavior. Although circadian rhythms are generated internally, they are heavily influenced by environmental cues, most notably the difference between day and night. However, circumstances do arise in which organisms lack the ability to pick up on such cues, or the cues are altogether absent. In such cases, circadian rhythms are regulated almost entirely by an "internal clock" that informs an organism's biological processes. For the most part, though, circadian rhythms are uniform and predictable across a vast range of species.

2 ➡ The circadian rhythm is controlled by a part of the brain called the hypothalamus, which acts as a clearing house for internal and external cues, collecting and interpreting them to ultimately determine one's sleep patterns. Sleep is induced naturally by a chemical called melatonin, and melatonin production is directly associated with activity in the hypothalamus. The retina of the eye contains special cells that, when activated by light, send signals to the hypothalamus that tell it that surroundings are lit. The hypothalamus sends this information on to the pineal gland, also in the brain, which either produces or inhibits the production of melatonin, depending on the information it receives. If the retina detects light, then the pineal gland halts production of melatonin, and as the hormone cycles out of the brain, wakefulness follows. The wavelength of the light detected determines how much melatonin should be produced. The opposite is true when night falls; the lack of light stimulates the pineal gland to produce more melatonin in preparation for the organism's coming sleep. Some other preparations include lowering body temperature and blood pressure.

3 ➡ Humans and other animals follow this basic model most of the time, but under unusual circumstances, this is not always possible. In the extreme northern and southern parts of the world, where the sun does not set for months at a time, the environmental cues that would generally control the circadian rhythm are not always present. Studies have produced mixed results in regard to how Arctic animals respond to sustained sunlight. Reindeer will display no consistent circadian rhythm for several months out of the year. This is called a free-running rhythm and is regulated only by the animal's awareness of its needs, like those for food and sleep. When the day-night cycle does resume, the reindeer return to a regular circadian rhythm. In another study, squirrels in Alaska were found to follow a strict circadian rhythm year round, despite constant sunlight or darkness. The reason for this is unknown, except that perhaps the sun's position relative to the horizon is enough of a cue to maintain a cycle.

4   While some organisms can successfully maintain a free-running rhythm, it can be harmful for humans to do so. Not getting sufficient sleep at regular intervals can cause hormones in the brain to become unbalanced. If a deficiency of sleep continues for long enough, it may even result in mental illness. By ignoring the

circadian rhythm, one's waking and sleeping schedule becomes out of sync with the biological processes that occur during regular sleep, in which muscles regenerate, memories are stored, and a number of other important processes are carried out. Missing out on any one of these processes can have serious negative physical effects like muscle loss and even heart failure. Sometimes a person's circadian rhythm can become inconsistent when he or she travels a long distance across many time zones. **A** This is commonly called "jet lag," since it mostly applies to air travel. **B** While the body is still accustomed to the rhythms it established at the place of departure, it is suddenly faced with new environmental cues. **C** This can result in irregular sleep patterns, fatigue, and mental exhaustion. **D**

01 The word "range" in the passage is closest in meaning to

(A) majority
(B) society
(C) spectrum
(D) number

02 The word "inhibits" in the passage is closest in meaning to

(A) balances
(B) constrains
(C) stimulates
(D) delays

03 The word "it" in the passage refers to

(A) hypothalamus
(B) melatonin
(C) brain
(D) pineal gland

04 According to paragraph 2, the amount of melatonin produced is determined by

(A) the signals sent out by the hypothalamus
(B) the length of time the body has been asleep
(C) the wavelength of the light detected by the eye
(D) the level of hormones in the brain

Paragraph 2 is marked with an arrow [➡].

05 According to paragraph 2, all of the following are mentioned as preparations for sleep EXCEPT

(A) lower body temperature
(B) an increase in melatonin
(C) decreased mental alertness
(D) a change in blood pressure

Paragraph 2 is marked with an arrow [➡].

06 Which of the sentences below best expresses the essential information in the highlighted sentence in the passage? *Incorrect* answer choices change the meaning in important ways or leave out essential information.

(A) In the Polar Regions, daylight can be scarce for long periods, even for a month, affecting environmental cues.
(B) Environmental cues are subtler in extreme northern regions with more sunlight, compared to extreme southern regions.
(C) At extreme latitudes, environmental cues that usually act to regulate circadian rhythms are limited.
(D) Months of prolonged daylight can make it difficult to perceive existing environmental cues at low latitudes regions.

07 The word " sustained " in the passage is closest in meaning to

(A) continued
(B) intense
(C) sudden
(D) weakened

08 Why does the author mention " Reindeer " in the passage?

(A) To show how some animals manage their irregular rhythms
(B) To explain why some animals cannot develop a circadian rhythm
(C) To give an example of an animal that has a strict circadian rhythm
(D) To come to a conclusion about different animals' circadian rhythms

09 According to paragraph 3, scientists theorize that the circadian rhythm of Alaskan squirrels could be regulated by

(A) the rising and setting of the sun
(B) basic needs like hunger or exhaustion
(C) the position of the sun relative to the horizon
(D) prolonged sunlight or darkness for several months

Paragraph 3 is marked with an arrow [➡].

10 The word " sufficient " in the passage is closest in meaning to

(A) comfortable
(B) light
(C) deep
(D) enough

11 Look at the four squares [■] that indicate where the following sentence could be added to the passage.

> Over time, however, the human body can adapt to the new cues if effort is taken to follow them.

Where would the sentence best fit?

Click on a square [■] to add the sentence to the passage.

(A) A   (B) B   (C) C   (D) D

12

Directions: An introductory sentence for a brief summary of the passage is provided below. Complete the summary by selecting the THREE answer choices that express the most important ideas in the passage. Some sentences do not belong in the summary because they express ideas that are not presented in the passage or are minor ideas in the passage. ***This question is worth 2 points.***

Drag your answer choices to the spaces where they belong. To remove an answer choice, click on it. To review the passage, click **View Text**.

The restorative cycle of sleep and wakefulness known as the circadian rhythm helps regulate biological processes.
-
-
-

Answer Choices

(A) In the absence of obvious environmental cues like night and day, some animals show abnormal behaviors.	(D) The circadian rhythm is so important to maintaining good health that ignoring it can seriously affect human health.
(B) The circadian rhythm is regulated by a complex network of cells, glands, and hormones within the brain.	(E) Some animals successfully adjust their circadian rhythm for a limited period when daytime lasts for months.
(C) The cues that help establish the circadian rhythm most often come from an organism's internal clock.	(F) Humans' circadian rhythm can be interrupted when traveling across several time zones, causing fatigue and disorientation.

Chapter 13 Life Science II

- **Life Science**
  A scientific study of all types of living organisms such as microorganisms, plants, animals, and human beings
- **Related fields**
  Microbiology, Botany, Entomology, Marine biology, Zoology, Physiology, etc.

Reading Preview

Zoology – Parental Care of Birds and Crocodiles
| Intensive Drill 1 |

The name archosaur is derived from ancient Greek, meaning "ruling reptile." The archosaurs were the direct ancestors of the dinosaurs and they have great significance in the history of life on land, because they were the common ancestor of crocodiles and birds. As descendents of the same ancestor, birds and crocodiles have several anatomical structures and behavioral characteristics in common.

Zoology – Precocial and Altricial Species
| Intensive Drill 2 |

Precocial species
Precocial refers to a pattern of growth and development in organisms which are relatively mature and mobile from the moment of birth or hatching. Familiar examples of precocial mammals are most ungulates, the guinea pig, and most species of hare.

Altricial species
Altricial refers to a pattern of growth and development in organisms which are incapable of moving around on their own soon after hatching or being born. Many mammals, including humans, are characterized as altricial organisms.

Botany – Kudzu

| Intensive Drill 3 |

Kudzu, also called as Japanese arrowroot, is a deciduous woody vine that may reach 35 to 100 feet in length. It occurs along field edges and near riparian areas. This invasive vine colonizes by prolific growth along the ground and into tree canopies. It has its origin in Japan and southern parts of China, and was introduced into the United States in the late 1800s for erosion control and as livestock forage.

Entomology – Honeybee Communication

| Mini Test 1 |

Honeybees appear to have their center of origin in South and Southeast Asia, and can be found on every continent on earth except for Antarctica. Like some other bee species, honeybees are social and live in colonies numbering in the thousands. Three types of adult honeybees reside in every colony: the queen, male drones, and infertile female workers. In addition to five senses, honeybees have additional communication aids at their disposal, specifically chemical and choreographic.

Botany – Seeds and Spores

| Mini Test 2 |

Seeds
A seed is a structure that contains a young plant inside a protective outer covering. The formation of the seed is part of the process of reproduction in seed plants. Three important parts of seeds are the embryo, stored food source, and seed coat.

Spores
A spore is a single-celled reproductive unit of non-flowering plants, bacteria, fungi, and algae. They undergo an asexual form of reproduction; the plant or fungus does not need to mate with another to form new particles.

Botany – Carnivorous Plants

| iBT Practice |

Carnivorous plants are defined as plants that attract, catch, digest, and absorb the body juices of animal prey. Carnivorous plants have adapted to grow in regions with large amounts of light where the soil is either thin or poor in nutrients, especially nitrogen. The major types of carnivorous plants are sundews, pitcher plants, butterworts, bladderworts, and the unique Venus flytrap. More than 150 different types of insects have been identified as victims of these plants.

Intensive Drill 1

PARENTAL CARE OF BIRDS AND CROCODILES

1   Both birds and crocodiles, modern descendants of the archosaur, still share several physiological and behavioral traits. Anatomically speaking, they have evolved similar four-chambered hearts, as well as a one-way passage of air through their lungs. However, their behavioral similarities, especially in relation to fostering their offspring in nests, deserve particular attention, as both adult crocodiles and birds spend time nurturing their young to various degrees. One of the biggest questions still debated among researchers is whether or not these similarities in parental care between birds and crocodiles evolved independently or as the result of a common ancestor. Recent fossil evidence dated about 200 million years ago suggests that common ancestors, such as non-avian dinosaurs and pterosaurs, also provided extended care for their young in nests.

2   In the case of modern-day crocodiles, females still watch over their eggs in their nest, using their own urine as a means to moisten their nest and keep the eggs warm. Because the temperature of the eggs during their incubation period is a determining factor in the sex of the baby, the female crocodile meticulously regulates the temperature of her nest. As soon as the babies hatch from their eggs, the mother carries her newborn babies to shallow water, where they gradually accustom themselves to moving in the water and hunting for prey. At first, the young spend a lot of time around their mother, feeding off of bits of food that fall down from the mother's mouth. This process of newborn acquisition of food from the mother's mouth is moderately akin to the process of regurgitation that adult birds use to feed their young. However, after several weeks of intense care provided by their mother, sometimes up to two months, the young crocodiles are finally able to function independently and leave the nesting site.

3   In the case of adult birds taking care of their young, although parental care patterns vary greatly from species to species, they all still retain some inherently common traits. One of the most notable nurturing traits shared among bird species is that both the male and female parents contribute to varying degrees in raising their young. In many cases, the father will leave the nest to gather food, whereby he will regurgitate his food findings to the mother, who will then in turn pass some of the food from her mouth to the children's mouths. During the period when the young birds grow from helpless beings to adults, the mother continuously broods her young, guarding them and keeping them warm, and also protects them from predators and any environmental factors that could lead to their death. Despite some bird species being able to leave their nests a few weeks after birth, most young birds need their parents' care for a longer period of time before they are able to leave the nest.

01 The phrase "akin to" in the passage is closest in meaning to

(A) related with (B) opposite to (C) compared to (D) similar to

02 According to paragraph 2, which of the following is NOT true of female crocodiles?

(A) They control the temperature of their eggs.
(B) They expect male crocodiles to provide food for their young.
(C) They assist the newborns in getting used to moving in water.
(D) They allow newborns to feed on food from their mouths.

03 In paragraph 3, the author explains parental care patterns of birds by

(A) comparing the nurturing styles of different species
(B) detailing the roles each parent plays in raising their families
(C) illustrating the importance of the father's gathering of food
(D) describing the roles of each parent in protecting their young from predators

04 Which of the sentences below best expresses the essential information in the highlighted sentence in the passage? *Incorrect* answer choices change the meaning in important ways or leave out essential information.

(A) Because young birds grow up with continuous care from their parents, they are more likely to become helpless even when they are all grown up.
(B) Birds are known for their extreme parental care as mothers continuously protect their young and keep them warm.
(C) Mother birds make the most effort to protect themselves from possible dangers from environmental factors and predators.
(D) While young birds grow into adults, the mothers constantly look after their young and defend them from possible threats.

05 **Directions:** Select the appropriate phrases from the answer choices and match them to the species of animal to which they relate. TWO of the answer choices will NOT be used. ***This question is worth 3 points.***

Answer Choices	Crocodiles
(A) Encourage babies to hunt for prey in shallow water (B) Defend their young against predators (C) Teach babies to gather food (D) Regulate the temperature of eggs for sex determination (E) Encourage babies to leave the nest after birth (F) Feed babies by regurgitation (G) Raise the young with parental care from both sexes	• •
	Birds
	• • •

Intensive Drill 2

PRECOCIAL AND ALTRICIAL SPECIES

1   Most animals, when they are born, require a great deal of care from one or more of their parents before they are fit enough to survive on their own. Others, however, are ready from a very early point in their development to leave the nest and fend for themselves. These two broad groups of animals can be characterized as either precocial or altricial. Precocial refers to animals that require little care after birth, while altricial refers to those that rely on their parents for a longer period. The characteristics of each group can vary widely depending on the type of animal in question, and it can sometimes be difficult to distinguish one from the other.

2   Precocial animals have a much longer gestation period than altricial animals. For this reason, they are more fully developed when they are finally born. Animals can present precocial habits across a broad spectrum, and nowhere in nature is this better exemplified than in birds. **A** The young of most precocial bird species are born with well-developed skeletons, feathers, and an excellent sense of sight. **B** Some species of birds have young that are ready to leave the nest within 24 hours of hatching, and may be called superprecocial because of this amazing ability. **C** Less precocial chicks still require some care; for instance, some are born without the ability to regulate their body temperature, and must rely on the mother to their warmth for a short period of time until they are able to regulate it themselves. **D** There are also some mammals, such as deer and goats, which are precocial to a certain degree, though they number far fewer than birds.

3   The other group of animals, those said to be altricial, require a great deal more care before they become independent. This group comprises most mammal species. Altricial young are often born without a number of basic survival traits, such as a coat of fur or fully open eyes. For this reason, they must be allowed some time to develop before they can be expected to survive without direct care from the mother. Humans are included among altricial species, and require one of the longest periods of care of any species. Other mammals, such as giraffes, display much shorter periods. It is believed by many scientists that this is due to their large size as adults. The young can gestate for a longer period within a larger adult, one result of which is that the young mammal is larger and more developed when it leaves the womb. In comparison to humans, giraffes have a gestation period of 15 months, whereas the gestation period for humans is only 9.

Answer Book p. A104

01 According to paragraph 2, what makes an animal superprecocial?

(A) It has a well developed skeleton at birth.
(B) It is born with the traits it needs for survival.
(C) It can leave its mother almost immediately.
(D) It requires fully developed eyesight.

02 The phrase "This group" in the passage refers to

(A) mammal species
(B) humans
(C) altricial species
(D) precocial species

03 In the passage, what can be inferred about the distinction between altricial and precocial habits?

(A) It is not always clear because habits vary greatly.
(B) It is prominent among animals of the same species.
(C) Precocial species are relatively large in size, while altricial species are mostly small.
(D) Altricial species are considered more evolved than precocial species.

04 Look at the four squares [■] that indicate where the following sentence could be added to the passage.

Another such species can actually dig its way out of the nest after hatching and leave immediately.

Where would the sentence best fit?

(A) **A**   (B) **B**   (C) **C**   (D) **D**

05 **Directions:** Select the appropriate phrases from the answer choices and match them to the type of animal to which they relate. TWO of the answer choices will NOT be used. ***This question is worth 3 points.***

Answer Choices	Altricial
(A) Include most mammals (B) May leave mothers within hours of birth (C) Can vary within a species (D) Has a well-developed skeleton at birth (E) Associated only with egg-laying species (F) Mostly exemplified in birds (G) Requires a relatively long period of care	• •
	Precocial
	• • •

Chapter 13 Life Science II 165

KUDZU

1 The American Southeast is famous for its beautiful rural areas that are home to a wide array of flora, including several species of trees and flowering plants. One particular plant that became dominant in this region within the past century is kudzu. Kudzu is a distinctive plant, immediately recognizable by its hairy vines, big leaves, and purple flowers blooming from long stems. Kudzu is not native to the United States, though; its origins can actually be traced to East Asia, particularly China and Japan, where its starchy roots were often eaten and its stems were used to produce fiber for ropes. However, since its introduction into the American Southeast, it has spread out over most of the area and become a threat that must be constantly and closely watched.

2 Kudzu first became popular among people in the United States during the 1880s. The pleasant appearance of the plant, as well as its rapid growth, made it an attractive provider of shade in the warm, sunny climate of the Southeast. Fifty years later, beginning in the 1930s, farmers found other uses for kudzu. Due to its high protein content, it served as a convenient food source for livestock, and its deep roots helped anchor soil in order to prevent erosion. It became so popular that people would grow millions of seeds at a time and planted kudzu almost anywhere that they could, particularly in Alabama, Georgia, North Carolina, Virginia, and other such southeastern states.

3 However, such avid promotion of kudzu proved to have harmful consequences. Kudzu's quick rate of growth — up to a foot a day — soon became a major problem. It grew over open fields, up the trunks of trees, along sides of highways, and anywhere else, quickly overtaking land, vegetation, and infrastructure. By the 1950s, kudzu was hated by most farmers as an invasive plant species that could not be contained, and the U.S. government subsequently removed its status as an acceptable cover crop. Studies have shown that kudzu has cost agricultural and lumber industries several millions of dollars each year. The primary threat it poses is by blocking out sunlight other plants need, thus interfering with crop and timber production.

4 Fortunately, there are a few ways to counteract kudzu's spread. The most effective way of removing, or at least controlling, an infestation is the removal of the plant's root crown. These are knobs of plant tissue at the top of the root. By closely cutting this knob away from the root system, people can slow down the plant's growth. The leftover root system, which runs very deep, is then normally treated with herbicide. While this helps control the spread, it cannot stop it. Another proposed method would include using natural agents like bacteria or animals to destroy the plant, but currently this is not feasible, and kudzu remains a prevalent pest.

Answer Book p. A105

01 Which of the sentences below best expresses the essential information in the highlighted sentence in the passage? *Incorrect* answer choices change the meaning in important ways or leave out essential information.

(A) Originally from East Asia, Kudzu was used there as food and a source for making tools.
(B) Originally from China and Japan, Kudzu is often used in the United States to produce various fibers.
(C) Kudzu was used in the United States to produce starchy foods and fibers for tools in contrast to countries in East Asia.
(D) While Kudzu was regarded as an ornamental plant in the United States, it was highly utilized in East Asian countries.

02 According to paragraph 2, kudzu was popular in the U.S. for all of the following reasons EXCEPT:

(A) It helped preserve soil.
(B) It did not grow quickly.
(C) It was a pretty decoration.
(D) It was useful in feeding cattle.

03 The word "avid" in the passage is closest in meaning to

(A) cautious   (B) eager   (C) brief   (D) rare

04 In paragraph 3, why does the author mention the U.S. government's decision and studies on kudzu?

(A) To point out the desirable environment necessary for kudzu to grow
(B) To compare the popularity of kudzu in the U.S. with that in other countries
(C) To explain how kudzu has become widespread throughout the U.S.
(D) To give evidence that damage caused by kudzu is very serious

05 **Directions:** An introductory sentence for a brief summary of the passage is provided below. Complete the summary by selecting the THREE answer choices that express the most important ideas in the passage. Some sentences do not belong in the summary because they express ideas that are not presented in the passage or are minor ideas in the passage. *This question is worth 2 points.*

While it was a popular plant in America during the 1880s, kudzu is now considered an invasive species and requires constant effort to manage.

(A) A great amount of Kudzu was planted mostly due to its attractive appearance, with large leaves, purple flower blooms, and long vines.
(B) At first, Americans used kudzu for a variety of agricultural and decorative purposes.
(C) Kudzu has a shallow root system that makes it easy to dig up and kill, preventing infestations.
(D) The most effective way of killing Kudzu is removing the root's upper part and poisoning the roots.
(E) After its introduction, kudzu quickly grew out over a large area, harming land, plants, and infrastructure.
(F) Kudzu was first introduced from Asia to America in the nineteenth century and still remains a beloved plant.

Mini Test 1

HONEYBEE COMMUNICATION

1   Honeybees are very social creatures, as they live together in large hives that are divided into a highly structured hierarchy. Honeybees function as a collective unit: they depend on each other to build, defend, and sustain their hives. Thus, they have various methods of communicating with each other, including releasing various scents and dancing. Extensive research has shown that the purpose of their dance is twofold: to inform other members of the colonies of the location of nectar that bees use to make honey, their primary staple, and to recruit other bees to retrieve this nectar. In spite of numerous theories about the particular significance of the modes of communication used, researchers generally agree that there are essentially three: dance, sounds emitted during dance, and the distribution of odors from the food source.

2   The most immediate mode of communication that honeybees use is dance. These movements have been noticed by observers since the ancient days of Aristotle, but their exact purpose was not discovered until after the mid-twentieth century. An audience of honeybees from a hive must watch the dance closely and catch every detail in order to understand the message correctly. The dancer provides crucial information through various movements. Some of these movements include the rotation of the bee's tail a certain number of times and positioning its body at specific angles, and they are incorporated into two possible dances. The round dance is used to indicate food sources that are nearby, and the more complicated waggle dance indicates the location of food sources that are further away. This particular dance indicates the exact direction in which a food source is located and how far away it is.

3   In addition to the dance itself, different sounds are made by the dancer and detected through the antennae of honeybees. Ultimately, both visual movement and sound are necessary to relay the information properly. Moreover, the specific sounds must be made correctly to create a successful dance. **A** Experiments with bees that had artificially clipped wings or mutated, shorter wings showed that they produced a higher vibration when dancing, and as a result they could not recruit members from the colony to seek out the food source. **B** By comparing the dances of various other species of bees and the conditions in which these dances are performed, researchers now believe sounds are an adaptation to dancing in locations with little light. **C** The sounds supposedly help the audience bees follow the dancer's movements in these environments, but this is still speculative. **D**

4   The use of odor is another important mode of communication, though its usefulness in finding food is highly debated among researchers. Some have suggested that picking up these odors, instead of dancing, is the primary method bees use to find available food sources, but most believe that it plays a secondary role. The scent of certain flowers, nectar, and other properties of the food source rubs off on the scout as it searches for food. As the scout dances, the audience will pick up on this scent. This action is supposed to help them detect the exact location of the food source, as they can trace the smell to the spot.

Answer Book p. A107

01 The word "provides" in the passage is closest in meaning to

(A) supplies   (B) distorts   (C) withholds   (D) receives

02 According to paragraph 2, the waggle dance tells the audience

(A) only that food is nearby
(B) the distance and direction of the food
(C) the quality of the food
(D) the exact location of the food

03 According to paragraph 3, why were bees with shorter wings unable to transmit effective messages?

(A) They were not able to get enough of the food's scent on their wings.
(B) They made lower vibrational sound when dancing.
(C) They produced the incorrect sounds when they danced.
(D) They could not turn their bodies quickly enough when dancing.

04 Look at the four squares [■] that indicate where the following sentence could be added to the passage.

> Another theory is that certain sounds inform the audience that the food source is of a particularly desirable quality.

Where would the sentence best fit?

(A) **A**   (B) **B**   (C) **C**   (D) **D**

05 **Directions:** An introductory sentence for a brief summary of the passage is provided below. Complete the summary by selecting the THREE answer choices that express the most important ideas in the passage. Some sentences do not belong in the summary because they express ideas that are not presented in the passage or are minor ideas in the passage. *This question is worth 2 points.*

In the process of providing information regarding food sources, honeybees must utilize a number of modes of communication.

(A) Aristotle was the first person to realize that the dance of honeybees was done in an attempt to collect nectar for the hive.
(B) A honeybee provides other bees with the smell of the nectar so that the others can find the exact food source.
(C) Honeybees with antennae that are shorter than the average size cannot detect the sounds needed in order to understand the waggle dance.
(D) The sounds that honeybees make with their wings play a significant role in helping audience members decipher the message of the dance.
(E) The use of mutated bees has been crucial in determining the exact movements that honeybees make in their various dances.
(F) Honeybees use two different dances as the primary method of telling other members of their hives where food sources are located.

Chapter 13 Life Science II   169

Mini Test 2

SEEDS AND SPORES

1 There are several ways to categorize the many types of plants on Earth, but when it comes to reproduction, plants can generally be divided into two basic categories: those which reproduce by means of seeds, and those which reproduce through the use of spores. Though they serve the same basic functions, the differences between these two reproductive units and the methods of reproduction they represent are many.

2 The more familiar of the two categories is the seed-bearing plant. Seeds are basically small, enclosed units that contain an embryo of the parent plant. The embryo, an undeveloped version of the parent plant, is the most important component, as it can eventually grow into a new plant. All seeds feature certain protective structures to ensure the health of the embryo. For instance, it is usually protected by an outer covering known as a seed coat, a layer of material that helps both to retain moisture in the seed and to keep it from becoming damaged by environmental factors. Seeds also contain a source of food for the embryo to feed on as it develops. This food is usually a combination of oils, starches, and proteins, which occupies the space between the embryo and the seed coat.

3 Seeds are considered the end stage in the process of reproduction in seed plants, having been preceded by other familiar processes such as pollination and flowering. All that remains is for the seeds to be spread, which may be accomplished with the help of wind, water, or even animals. Seed plants are the most advanced form of plant in evolutionary terms. For this reason, they often dominate their respective ecological niches, like forests and grasslands. Those few plants that still reproduce entirely asexually — without a partner — represent the most basic form. Between them lies an intermediate stage in the evolution of plants: the spore plant.

4 Spores are much simpler in their makeup than seeds, and are a common reproductive unit of bacteria and fungi in addition to plants. One of the key differences between seeds and spores is that spores do not have the same support mechanisms, such as stored food resources or defensive coverings. So spores from plants are less able to survive in unfavorable conditions for long periods of time before growing into a full plant. As a rule, spores are released in large numbers as a way of giving them a better chance of growing to maturity.

5 Despite their many shortcomings, spores do have some advantages over seeds. Spores are extremely light compared to seeds, and can thus be dispersed more easily and over greater distances, even by light breezes. The most common type of spore plant is the fern, which releases spores from the underside of its leaves. Some species of fern may be said to bridge the evolutionary gap between spore-producing plants and seed-producing plants. The presence of ferns dates back over 300 million years, and over the course of their long evolution, some have evolved into seed-bearing plants.

Answer Book p. A109

01 Which of the sentences below best expresses the essential information in the highlighted sentence in the passage? *Incorrect* answer choices change the meaning in important ways or leave out essential information.

(A) Moisture is retained in the seed by the embryo, which lies inside the protective covering of the seed coat.
(B) An outer covering called a seed coat provides the embryo with moisture so that it can protect itself from potential damage.
(C) The embryo is protected from damage by moisture within the seed, which the seed coat keeps from drying out.
(D) The seed coat protects the embryo from drying out and from becoming damaged by outside forces.

02 In paragraph 2, what is true of seed plants?

(A) Seeds provide nutrients for the embryo.
(B) A seed coat contains genetic information required for the new plant.
(C) Not all of them have protective features for the embryo.
(D) The food for the embryo is located on the surface of the seed coat.

03 The phrase "this reason" in the passage refers to

(A) the spreading of seeds with the help of wind, water, and animals
(B) the idea that seed plants are the most advanced type of plants
(C) the presence of a food source for the embryo within the seed
(D) the assertion that seeds are the end stage in the process of reproduction

04 According to paragraph 4, spores are vulnerable because

(A) they cannot spread over a very large area
(B) they are attractive to predators on the ground
(C) they lack a food source and a means of protection
(D) they cannot take root within the ground

05 Directions: Select the appropriate phrases from the answer choices and match them to the type of plants. TWO of the answer choices will NOT be used. *This question is worth 3 points.*

Answer Choices	Seed Plants
(A) Vulnerable to predators (B) Contain a protective outer covering (C) Released in very large numbers (D) Restricted to green plants only (E) Considered the most advanced plant form (F) Less likely to survive in a hostile environment (G) Can be spread over great distances due to weight	• •
	Spore Plants
	• • •

Chapter **13** Life Science II 171

iBT Practice

CARNIVOROUS PLANTS

1 ➡ All plants rely on nutrients taken from the soil in order to survive. However, in areas where the soil does not contain enough vital nutrients, some plants have adapted to supplement their diets from another source: living organisms. Though they are few in number, carnivorous plants are nonetheless fascinating beings whose "diets" range from one-celled organisms to insects in order to survive. They are commonly found in marshlands. Carnivorous plants feature one of several types of "traps" to capture prey, which they consume to make up for nutrients that may be missing from the soil.

2 ➡ The most well-known of these plants are the snap traps, which includes the Venus flytrap. Snap traps are easily identified by their leaves, which are separated into two lobes that have the ability to fold together. These carnivorous plants capture prey through mechanisms that are not unlike the common household mousetrap. Inside the lobes, the surface is covered with tiny hairs that are sensitive to movement. When the plant's prey brushes against the hairs, it triggers a closing mechanism that rapidly brings the two lobes together, trapping the prey securely inside. The speed at which the traps respond is unheard of for most plant life: the time between triggering the hairs and snapping shut is less than a second. As the prey struggles inside the trap, it only triggers more hairs, causing the leaves to tighten their grip. The plant then secretes liquid chemicals from special glands into the trap to dissolve the prey and absorb all of its nutrients. Besides the Venus flytrap, only one other type of snap trap exists today, referred to as the waterwheel plant. The two share a common ancestor and differ only in a few ways. For instance, the waterwheel is an aquatic plant, while the flytrap is exclusively terrestrial. In addition, the flytrap feeds primarily on arthropods like spiders, while the waterwheel lives off of simple invertebrates, like certain types of plankton.

3 ➡ Pitfall traps are among the most strangely beautiful types of carnivorous plants, though they may also be the most primitive. They function much more simply than snap traps, though the wide variety of pitfall traps, also known as pitcher plants, means that some are more complex than others. The simplest type of this carnivorous plant is best exemplified by the sun pitcher plant. It consists of tall leaves that roll into a tubular shape. The mouth of the leaf, and the opening of the trap are wider than the rest of the body. The sun pitcher plant simply waits for unsuspecting prey to slip down the sides of the tube, where digestive enzymes wait in a small pool to drown and ingest it. More complex forms of pitfall traps use basically the same mechanism for killing and eating their prey, but the actual trap can be far more elaborate. The cobra plant features a large, vacant bulb at its tip with small transparent dots that let sunshine in. When insects, mostly ants, crawl into the bulb, they struggle to escape through these "false exits," but eventually they tire themselves out and fall down the tube into the digestive chamber, where they are dissolved by the plant's digestive enzymes.

4 ➡ A third type of carnivorous plant uses flypaper traps to capture its prey. **A** This plant is extremely numerous and varies greatly in appearance from species to species. **B** Their leaves contain glands that release a sticky type of mucus which can be used to trap insects that unknowingly land on them. **C** One

type of flypaper trap is the butterwort plant. The butterwort has broad, bright green leaves that are grouped closely together. Flying insects are attracted to the butterwort because the thin layer of mucus on its leaves has the semblance of dew, making the plant look like it is covered in water droplets. When the insect lands, the leaves release more of this sticky substance, which further traps the insect. Another type of flypaper trap is the cape sundew, which has an appearance quite unlike its distant cousin the butterwort. The leaves of the cape sundew are long and thin, like tentacles. Tiny hairs run up and down the length of the tentacles, each containing a large drop of mucus. As with the butterwort, insects are attracted to the cape sundew, expecting to find water, but instead become trapped in the mucus. The tendrils then curl up, enclosing the insect in a tight coil that aids in digestion.

Glossary

lobe: A rounded part of something, for example one of the rounded sections along the edges of some leaves

arthropod: Any invertebrate of the phylum arthropoda, having jointed limbs, a segmented body, and an exoskeleton made of chitin

---

01 The word "capture" in the passage is closest in meaning to

(A) monitor
(B) catch
(C) digest
(D) lure

02 According to paragraph 1, carnivorous plants get nutrients from living organisms because

(A) they have to develop immunities against harmful insects
(B) they cannot get necessary nutrients from the soil they live in
(C) they need to protect themselves from harmful chemicals from the soil
(D) marshlands are the place where organisms high in protein are abundant

Paragraph 1 is marked with an arrow [→].

03 Why does the author mention a "mousetrap" in the passage?

(A) To explain on the weaknesses of the snap trap
(B) To better illustrate how the snap trap functions
(C) To emphasize the strength of the snap trap's leaves
(D) To contrast the flytrap with other snap traps

04 According to paragraph 2, what is NOT true of snap traps?

(A) They catch their prey by closing their lobes.
(B) They consume their prey by dissolving it with chemicals.
(C) They are mostly terrestrial plants.
(D) Their tiny hairs sense the presence of prey.

Paragraph 2 is marked with an arrow [→].

05 According to paragraph 2, what can be inferred about the snap trap?

(A) Once it catches its prey, there is little chance that the prey can escape.
(B) It mostly feeds on insects that are very large and high in nutrients.
(C) There are various species of snap traps which differ by hunting mechanism.
(D) Snap traps are on the verge of extinction due to the destruction of their habitat.

Paragraph 2 is marked with an arrow [→].

06 The word " ingest " in the passage is closest in meaning to

(A) ensnare   (B) utilize
(C) poison   (D) consume

07 The word " elaborate " in the passage is closest in meaning to

(A) primitive (B) deep
(C) acidic   (D) complex

08 Which of the sentences below best expresses the essential information in the highlighted sentence in the passage? *Incorrect* answer choices change the meaning in important ways or leave out essential information.

(A) The cobra plant captures its prey by luring it into a bulb which produces digestive chemicals.
(B) The bulb of the cobra plant tires insects by fooling them with false exits, at which point they fall into the digestive chamber.
(C) Insects become trapped inside the bulb of the cobra plant because bright colors attract them to the plant's "stomach."
(D) When ants crawl into the cobra plant's bulb, it quickly closes the exit and traps them in its digestive chamber.

09 According to paragraph 3, what is true of the pitfall trap?

(A) It uses mechanisms for killing its prey that are similar to the snap trap's.
(B) It is filled with digestive substances.
(C) It is not as colorful as other carnivorous plants.
(D) It is the most advanced form among all carnivorous plants.

Paragraph 3 is marked with an arrow [→].

10 The word " them " in the passage refers to

(A) insects   (B) leaves
(C) glands   (D) species

11 The word " semblance " in the passage is closest in meaning to

(A) merit   (B) composition
(C) appearance (D) nature

12 According to paragraph 4, flypaper traps attract insects looking for

(A) food
(B) shelter
(C) water
(D) mates

Paragraph 4 is marked with an arrow [→].

13 Look at the four squares [■] that indicate where the following sentence could be added to the passage.

> However, all of them share the same basic trapping mechanism.

Where would the sentence best fit?

Click on a square [■] to add the sentence to the passage.

(A) A   (B) B   (C) C   (D) D

14 Directions: An introductory sentence for a brief summary of the passage is provided below. Complete the summary by selecting the THREE answer choices that express the most important ideas in the passage. Some sentences do not belong in the summary because they express ideas that are not presented in the passage or are minor ideas in the passage. *This question is worth 2 points.*

Drag your answer choices to the spaces where they belong. To remove an answer choice, click on it. To review the passage, click **View Text**.

There are many species of carnivorous plants, all of which have their own unique methods for catching prey.
-
-
-

Answer Choices	
(A) The waterwheel plant and the Venus flytrap are the only two existing species of snap trap plants.	(D) Carnivorous plants are most commonly found in areas that do not provide all the essential nutrients for plant life.
(B) The most primitive carnivorous plants are designed to let insects trap themselves.	(E) Some carnivorous plants aggressively capture their prey using reflexes triggered by sensitive hairs.
(C) Some carnivorous plants use sticky mucus to attract insects which then get stuck on the leaves.	(F) A few carnivorous plants cannot thrive in terrestrial environments, and thus are only found in water.

Chapter 14 Physical Science

- **Physical Science**
  An area of science that deals with materials that are not alive and the ways in which nonliving things work
- **Related fields**
  Physics, Astronomy, Chemistry, Earth Science, Environmental Science, Geography, Geology, etc.

Reading Preview

Physics – Isaac Newton | Intensive Drill 1 |

Sir Isaac Newton was an English physicist and mathematician who was instrumental in the scientific revolution of the seventeenth century. In optics, he laid the foundation for modern physical optics by discovering the composition of white light. In mechanics, his three laws of motion, the basic principles of modern physics, resulted in the formulation of the law of universal gravitation. In mathematics, he was the original discoverer of the infinitesimal calculus.

Chemistry – Organic and Inorganic Chemistry | Intensive Drill 2 |

Organic Chemistry
Organic chemistry is a subdiscipline of chemistry involving the scientific study of the structure, properties, and reactions of organic compounds and organic materials. Though it was originally limited to compounds produced by living organisms, it has broadened to include manmade substances.

Inorganic Chemistry
Inorganic chemistry is a subdiscipline of chemistry involving the scientific study of the synthesis, formation, and properties of inorganic compounds and inorganic materials. It is based on inanimate substances found in nature as minerals. The scope of inorganic chemistry was shaped by the earlier field of organic chemistry in the mid-eighteenth century.

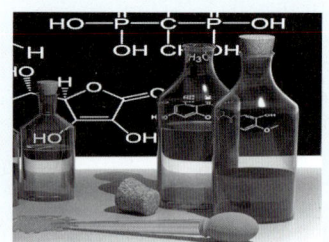

Geography – Mountain and Continental Glaciers

| Intensive Drill 3 |

Mountain Glaciers
Mountain glaciers, also called as alpine glaciers, develop in high mountainous regions. They often increase in size and begin to flow out of ice fields that span several peaks or even a mountain range. The largest mountain glaciers are found in Arctic Canada, Alaska, the Andes in South America, and the Himalayas in Asia.

Continental Glaciers
Continental glaciers, also called ice sheet glaciers, are continuous masses of ice and are much bigger in size compared to mountain glaciers. They have horizontal formation, accumulating hundreds of meters in thickness. They can be found in regions near the earth's north or south poles.

Physics – Nuclear Power

| Mini Test 1 |

Nuclear power is generated using Uranium, which is a metal mined in various parts of the world. It produces around 11 percent of the world's energy needs, and produces huge amounts of energy from small amounts of fuel, without the pollution that results from burning fossil fuels. The first large-scale nuclear power station opened at Calder Hall in Cumbria, England, in 1956.

Geology – Volcano Monitoring

| Mini Test 2 |

Volcanic eruption happens when lava and gas are discharged from a volcanic vent. Its hot liquid lava can drastically alter the geography of a region and its volcanic rock fragments can be hazardous. Volcano monitoring is the research of what happens in a volcano and when new magma rises in the volcano. It is essential in assessing the threats and associated risks a volcano poses.

Astronomy – Comets

| iBT Practice |

Comets are small, fragile, irregularly shaped bodies composed of a mixture of nonvolatile minerals and frozen gases. Their name "comet" comes from the Latin word *cometa* which means "long-haired." Although most of the smaller objects in our Solar System represent very recent discoveries, comets have been observed since ancient times because they are the only small bodies in the Solar System that can be seen with the naked eye. The earliest known record of a comet sighting was made by a Chinese astrologer in 1059 B.C.

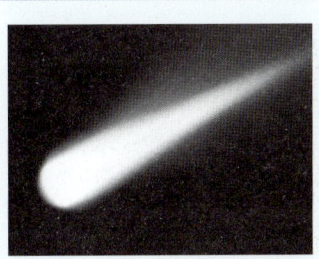

Intensive Drill 1

ISAAC NEWTON

1   One of the most influential figures in modern history was Isaac Newton, a British scholar whose work led to breakthroughs in many different sciences, including mathematics, astronomy, biology, and chemistry. Surprisingly, for a man with such a brilliant mind, Newton performed below average in his school years. He was admitted to the prestigious Trinity College, but neglected classes to work on his own private studies. When the school closed because of an outbreak of the plague, Newton finally had the time he needed to develop his many theories in math and science. It is often said that Newton made some of his most important discoveries within the year that followed, which is why it is called his *annus mirabilis*, or "year of miracles." His discoveries were later recorded in his famous book *Philosophiae Naturalis Principia Mathematica*, often referred to as simply the *Principia*, widely considered the most important work of science in history.

2   The highlight of Newton's book was his three laws of motion. The first law explained the force of inertia, stating that an object will remain either still or moving at a constant speed and direction until acted upon by another force. For example, a satellite moving through space will continue to move at a constant speed and direction unless it encounters an obstacle that alters its speed and direction.

3   According to the second law, acceleration is produced when a force acts on a mass; hence, the greater the mass, the greater the amount of force is needed to move it. It proposes a direct relationship between force, mass, and acceleration, and a way to calculate the force acting on an object by multiplying the object's mass by the rate at which its speed changes. In the third law, Newton states that every time a force acts on an object, that object also exerts an equal force in return. Take, for example, a man pushing a large rock up a hill: the man exerts force on the rock to move it, while the rock exerts an equal amount of force on the man's muscles.

4   These three simple rules laid the groundwork for another of Newton's most famous theories, that of gravitation, which also appears in the *Principia*. Newton theorized that each body with mass attracts other bodies with mass, the attraction being stronger for greater masses and at shorter distances. This attraction is of course the force of gravity, and it is an illustration of his third law of motion, that every force creates an opposite and equal force. **A** Newton applied this theory to an important problem of his day: why the planets move in circular orbits. **B** The moon orbits the Earth, he theorized, because it is held there by Earth's gravity. **C** However, the force exerted back onto the Earth by the moon keeps it at a distance. **D**

01 The word " breakthroughs " in the passage is closest in meaning to

(A) confusions (B) developments (C) reforms (D) foundations

02 Why does the author mention a " satellite " in the passage?

(A) To show what types of objects are affected by his laws of motion
(B) To illustrate how inertia determines the behavior of objects in motion
(C) To explain how the force of inertia differs among objects
(D) To emphasize that his laws of motion are universal throughout nature

03 According to paragraph 4, all of the following are true of gravity EXCEPT:

(A) It is stronger in objects with greater mass.
(B) It explains why planets move in circular orbits.
(C) It is a force exerted by all objects with mass.
(D) It functions according to Newton's second law.

04 Look at the four squares [■] that indicate where the following sentence could be added to the passage.

> Newton combined gravitation with his laws of motion to find the solution.

Where would the sentence best fit?

(A) A (B) B (C) C (D) D

05 **Directions:** An introductory sentence for a brief summary of the passage is provided below. Complete the summary by selecting the THREE answer choices that express the most important ideas in the passage. Some sentences do not belong in the summary because they express ideas that are not presented in the passage or are minor ideas in the passage. *This question is worth 2 points.*

Isaac Newton is one of history's most influential scientists, and his work laid the foundation for the study of basic principles of physics.

(A) Newton studied all manner of sciences besides physics, especially math, and is also famous for the invention of calculus.
(B) Newton had enough time for research during his break from college and soon published his theories in his *Principia*.
(C) Despite his later success as a scientist and teacher, Newton was a below-average student in college.
(D) The most famous of Newton's theories are the three laws of motion, which explain how objects move in relation to the forces that act on them.
(E) Newton used the laws of motion to arrive at his theory of gravity, which helped him explain the motion of planets.
(F) Newton's laws of motion are not sophisticated enough to explain the motion of atoms and other microscopic phenomena.

Intensive Drill 2

ORGANIC AND INORGANIC CHEMISTRY

1   The field of chemistry is a complex one involving many sub-disciplines and applications. However, at its simplest, the study of chemistry can be divided into two main groups according to the structure of the chemicals being studied: organic chemistry and inorganic chemistry. Organic compounds contain a carbon compound in its structure and other elements such as hydrogen, oxygen, and nitrogen are attached to this carbon backbone. Carbon is an extremely versatile atom with the potential to form many kinds of bonds with a myriad of atoms. In addition, carbon is one of the few elements that can bond with itself to form straight chains, branched chains, rings, and other shapes. Organic compounds are also formed from a relatively small number of elements, but due to the nature of carbon, these elements are able to be combined in an almost unlimited number of combinations. Consequently, living things have taken advantage of the flexibility of carbon and possess it in the chemical structures of their DNA, lipids, and fatty acids, as well as proteins and enzymes, which are the foundations for cellular processes within organisms.

2   Opposite organic chemistry, inorganic chemistry is concerned with molecules that do not contain the carbon compound. There are countless compounds and numerous amounts of applications that fall under the realm of inorganic. Contrary to organic compounds' biological nature, inorganic compounds have a geologically-based nature and are associated with the nonliving portion of the world. Not all, but most inorganic compounds contain metal, and because of this characteristic, inorganic compounds tend to conduct electricity, which organic compounds are not capable of. In terms of complexity, they are less complex in their structure, hence less stable than organic compounds.

3   The applications for both types of chemistry are wide-ranging and often overlap. Organic chemistry is a highly creative science field in which chemists create new molecules and explore the properties of existing compound, and is a foundation of biochemistry, biotechnology, and medicine, since they play such a critical role in life processes. It has a vital role in economic growth and is essential to a diverse range of industries including rubber, plastics, fuel, pharmaceutical, and agrichemical industries. Meanwhile, inorganic chemistry is a highly practical science and useful for specific purposes due to the thermal-stability of high melting points and electrical conductivity properties. Usually inorganic chemistry focuses on how inorganic elements can be modified, separated, or used in products. As such, inorganic chemistry is a key element of environmental science, particularly the recovery and prevention of pollution. Microchip industries, fibers, and mining are also areas where inorganic chemistry plays an important role.

01 The word " versatile " in the passage is closest in meaning to

(A) adaptable
(B) productive
(C) advantageous
(D) comprehensive

02 Which of the sentences below best expresses the essential information in the highlighted sentence in the passage? *Incorrect* answer choices change the meaning in important ways or leave out essential information.

(A) Therefore, adopting the chemical configuration of carbon is essential in the cellular processes of every organism.
(B) Hence, having a flexible carbonic genetic makeup is considered to be the best advantage living things can have.
(C) As a result, living beings utilize carbon's adaptability in their chemical makeup of various biological compositions.
(D) Thus, DNA, lipids, fatty acids, proteins, and enzymes in every living organism have carbon in their chemical configuration.

03 The word " realm " in the passage is closest in meaning to

(A) border
(B) outcome
(C) facet
(D) sphere

04 The author mentions " metal " in the passage in order to

(A) highlight a shared characteristic in organic and inorganic compounds
(B) illustrate an example of inorganic compounds' use
(C) describe the nature of inorganic compounds
(D) point out inorganic compounds' electrical conductivity

05 **Directions:** Select the appropriate phrases from the answer choices and match them to the field of chemistry to which they relate. TWO of the answer choices will NOT be used. *This question is worth 3 points.*

Answer Choices	Organic Chemistry
(A) More advanced than the other field (B) Has carbon in its compound (C) Tends to have a mineral nature (D) Has elements attached to its hydrogen backbone (E) Can have almost infinite combinations of elements (F) Mainly associated with living organisms (G) Has a vital role in environmental science	• • •
	Inorganic Chemistry
	• •

Intensive Drill 3

MOUNTAIN AND CONTINENTAL GLACIERS

1   Glaciers can be roughly divided into two very different types: mountain glaciers and continental glaciers. The most well-known type of glacier is the mountain variety, also called an alpine glacier. Mountain glaciers form when valleys become filled with ice after years of continuous freezing snow, which condenses into ice and slowly begins its descent down the valley slope. The shape taken by mountain glaciers is largely determined by the topography of the area in which they form, and in general they are longer than they are wide, due to their gradual momentum in one fairly specific direction. The shape generally conforms to the rocky passes that they fill as they flow toward lower elevations. One exception to this is a type of mountain glacier called a piedmont glacier, which forms at the bottom of a mountain or valley. Because it flows outward rather than in a single direction, it can have more of a circular shape than other mountain glaciers. Because mountain glaciers exist in subarctic climates, they are affected by the elements in ways that continental glaciers are not, sometimes even putting them in danger of collapse. For example, rainfall can melt small portions of mountain glaciers, forming icy streams of water that can, over long periods of time, carve elaborate ice caves ever deeper into the glacier.

2   Continental glaciers are quite different. As their name suggests, they are massive in size and far more expansive. Today, the only continental glaciers in existence are the ice sheets of the Arctic and Antarctic regions. These continental glaciers formed over millions of years, as layer after layer of snow fell to the Earth and became compacted into one thick sheet of ice weighing millions of tons. The bedrock of the continent of Antarctica is almost completely covered in glacier ice, with only a few isolated mountain ranges penetrating the thick ice sheet. In some areas, the ice is so plentiful that it extends beyond the edge of the continent and into the ocean, forming what are known as ice shelves. On the Antarctic mainland, the ice can reach depths of over a mile. The effect of such a thick, heavy layer of ice is that it depresses the actual land mass so that most of it is below sea level. The pressure exerted on the deepest layers of the ice sheet by the denser and heavier upper layers causes some of this deeper ice to melt, creating a slippery layer of ice and water below the ice sheet. Unlike mountain glaciers, continental glaciers do not flow in any consistent manner, but gravity may cause portions of the continental glacier to slide along the fine bottom layer of ice down any slopes.

01 Which of the sentences below best expresses the essential information in the highlighted sentence in the passage? *Incorrect* answer choices change the meaning in important ways or leave out essential information.

(A) Mountain glaciers are formed by valleys and mountains, which give them the long and wide shape that allows them to travel downhill.
(B) The topography of an area determines the direction in which the mountain glacier will flow as it travels with a steady momentum.
(C) The movement of mountain glaciers in one specific direction causes them to become wider than they are long.
(D) Mountain glaciers take the shape of the surrounding area through which they travel, and mostly in a long and narrow form.

02 According to paragraph 1, what can be inferred about ice caves?

(A) They will fill with ice when the water in them freezes.
(B) They are elaborate structures formed over long periods.
(C) They can weaken a glacier until parts of it cave in.
(D) They form rivers of glacier water that can run for miles.

03 The word "it" in the passage refers to

(A) layer of ice   (B) effect   (C) mass   (D) level

04 According to paragraph 2, when are ice shelves created?

(A) When a glacier collapses due to long-term erosion
(B) When an ice sheet extends beyond the land
(C) When pieces of the glacier break off into the ocean
(D) When an ice sheet becomes too heavy to support

05 **Directions:** Select the appropriate phrases from the answer choices and match them to the type of glacier to which they relate. TWO of the answer choices will NOT be used. *This question is worth 3 points.*

Answer Choices	Mountain Glacier
(A) Shaped by the path along which it flows	•
(B) Created as valleys at high elevation continuously fill with snow	•
(C) Exposed to more of nature's elements	•
(D) Shrinking at a faster rate due to climate change	**Continental Glacier**
(E) Heavy enough to force the land mass on which it sits below sea level	•
(F) Home to a greater diversity of wildlife	•
(G) Flows in an irregular fashion	

Mini Test 1

NUCLEAR POWER

1. Nuclear power is the subject of much controversy around the world. Despite the fact that it is a clean and efficient source of electricity, it comes with some very serious risks. Today, there are over 400 nuclear power plants in operation worldwide, and countries like France get as much as 77 percent of their energy from this source. Few people fully understand the mechanism that drives this energy source. In many ways, it is similar to more traditional sources such as coal-fired power plants. Both nuclear and coal-fired plants rely on pressurized steam to drive electric generators. The controversy surrounding nuclear power stems from how this steam is produced — the process of nuclear fission.

2. The term nuclear fission refers simply to the splitting of an atom. It occurs regularly in nature, albeit much more slowly than in power plants, and is the reason we call certain elements "radioactive." In the case of power plants, the substance that is used is uranium-235, which is unique among the different types of uranium in that it can undergo induced fission — nuclear fission that is created by human intervention under artificial conditions. An atom of uranium-235 releases a great deal of energy when it absorbs a neutron from outside itself. In less than a second, the neutron creates unstable conditions within the atom that cause a very sudden reaction. When the atom bursts apart, energy is released and heat is created. In the presence of other uranium-235 atoms, the particles released by the first instance of fission cause fission in the surrounding atoms, creating a chain reaction that results in the release of massive amounts of energy.

3. However, this is not the same energy that is used to power homes and businesses. The purpose of fission reactions is simply to create heat. This is used to heat a store of water to its boiling point so that it rapidly evaporates, letting off steam. The steam is the real source of the power, since, like the water in a hydroelectric dam, the force of its movement sets in motion a series of electric generators that ultimately produce the plant's energy. After the electricity is produced, the steam goes through a cooling phase and is released into the atmosphere by way of giant concrete towers. The steam released from these cooling towers does not contain harmful radiation, as the water never comes into contact with the radioactive materials in the plant.

4. **A** Admittedly, nuclear power faces a big problem when it comes to the disposal of the spent uranium. **B** Once the element is no longer useful for production, it must be thrown away or stored somewhere, and though its radioactivity is diminished through use in the plant, it is still a dangerous and deadly substance. **C** Improperly stored uranium can contaminate the ground and the water supply around it, posing a serious threat to public health. **D** For this reason, radioactive waste is stored in secure facilities under the strict supervision of experts, where it is allowed to cool and decay without threatening the environment. As the number of nuclear power plants grows, and the waste they produce increases, storing nuclear waste becomes a serious problem with nuclear power.

01 The word "it" in the passage refers to

(A) fission
(B) energy
(C) atom
(D) reaction

02 The word "diminished" in the passage is closest in meaning to

(A) released
(B) reduced
(C) strengthened
(D) changed

03 According to the passage, all of the following are true of nuclear power EXCEPT:

(A) Steam is released into the atmosphere by cooling towers.
(B) Creating nuclear power produces nuclear waste.
(C) Nuclear fission is used to create steam.
(D) Waste from the process is stored in the ground until it cools.

04 Look at the four squares [■] that indicate where the following sentence could be added to the passage.

> Only after tens of thousands of years of natural decay will the uranium reach levels that are safe again.

Where would the sentence best fit?

(A) A
(B) B
(C) C
(D) D

05 **Directions:** An introductory sentence for a brief summary of the passage is provided below. Complete the summary by selecting the THREE answer choices that express the most important ideas in the passage. Some sentences do not belong in the summary because they express ideas that are not presented in the passage or are minor ideas in the passage. ***The question is worth 2 points.***

Electricity can be created from nuclear power, and the process comes with some dangers.

(A) Nuclear power plants induce fission in uranium by introducing a neutron that destabilizes the uranium atom until it breaks apart.
(B) The electric generators in a nuclear power plant are driven by steam, created by the rapid heating of water through nuclear fission.
(C) Although nuclear power is popular throughout much of Europe, it is still seen as controversial in other places, like the United States.
(D) Nuclear waste from power plants can remain a danger to the public for hundreds of years, and so it must be stored in special facilities.
(E) A special kind of uranium, uranium-235, is required in nuclear power plants because it is an especially unstable isotope.
(F) A process is used to cool the steam produced by power plants before it is released into the atmosphere.

VOLCANO MONITORING

1   One of the most reliable and frequently employed methods of monitoring volcanoes and predicting eruptions is through the measurement of local seismic disruptions. This is because impending volcanic eruptions frequently lead off with minor earthquakes. As magma rises in the volcano, it must squeeze through a constricted chamber or series of chambers while under great pressure. The force will crack some of the rock or force rocks with pre-existing cracks to convulse, setting off tremors of varying frequencies. This seismic activity is relatively weak and occurs roughly ten kilometers beneath the volcano. In order to detect such weak quakes, scientists must set up a network of seismometers around the volcano in order to catch the slightest fluctuations in seismic activity that are usually a prelude to a volcanic eruption. About four to eight seismometers are placed about twenty kilometers from one of the vents, and several more are placed on the volcano itself. All of these have to be close in order to catch the quakes, as a seismometer being placed too far away could not detect subtle shifts in seismic activity. Fortunately, this method has been used so extensively that it is quite advanced, and scientists are experienced in detecting crucial seismic activity quickly, accurately, and in real time.

2   While seismic monitoring is the most widely used and trusted method of monitoring volcanoes, there are other technologies that allow scientists to observe landscape deformation, which usually accompanies volcanic activity. **A** In addition to causing quakes, the increased magma flow will also make the volcano swell and alter the surrounding landscape, particularly its evenness and elevation, though these changes are too slight to be noticed with the naked eye. **B** Scientists use a variety of tools to observe such changes. **C** In particular, scientists use Global Positioning System (GPS) satellites to study a very detailed map of the earth's surface, though GPS is not primarily used to study volcanoes. **D** Additionally, scientists have Interferometric Synthetic Aperture Radar (InSAR) satellites. These satellites use radar to map out changes in the landscape and the development of deformations very accurately, detecting possible volcanic activity.

3   In addition to the deformations in the ground caused by volcanic activity, scientists can measure chemical gaseous emissions. Gauging the emission of certain gases like sulfur dioxide and carbon dioxide is helpful. As magma rises to the surface, it will give off greater amounts of these two gases, so increased amounts around a volcanic area would be a good indication of increased activity. While it is possible to monitor such activity at a safe distance via satellite, weather can interfere with accurate readings. Therefore, the direct sampling of these emissions by people is a more accurate method, though this means having to get near an active vent to retrieve the samples. This is difficult because acidic gases like sulfur dioxide easily dissolve in bodies of water, skewing precise measurements. Carbon dioxide is less likely to vanish in such a manner, though, so it could be more helpful in predicting volcanic activity.

Answer Book p. A123

01 **According to paragraph 1, why must scientists use a network of seismometers around volcanoes?**

(A) The earthquakes that occur are not very strong.
(B) They must be ready to replace damaged instruments.
(C) It predicts the exact intensity of the next volcano eruption.
(D) They are not certain where tremors will occur.

02 **Which of the sentences below best expresses the essential information in the highlighted sentence in the passage?** *Incorrect* **answer choices change the meaning in important ways or leave out essential information.**

(A) Before a volcanic eruption, the land elevation and evenness around the region become distorted, but this is hard to see.
(B) The increased magma flow transforms neighboring areas in ways that are hard to detect, as well as causing quakes.
(C) The earthquakes change the evenness and elevation of surrounding areas and cause the volcanic magma to swell.
(D) The increased swelling of a volcano that is about to erupt is due to the earthquakes that shift the land elevation.

03 **The word " Gauging " in the passage is closest in meaning to**

(A) Preventing
(B) Absorbing
(C) Measuring
(D) Discovering

04 **According to paragraph 3, why are gaseous emissions from magma directly sampled?**

(A) Accurate readings of emissions can be hindered by bad weather.
(B) It is impossible to read gas emissions using satellites.
(C) It is the simplest method to sample the gas from magma.
(D) Sampling of gases absorbed in the bodies of water is required.

05 **Look at the four squares [■] that indicate where the following sentence could be added to the passage.**

> One major tool is the satellite.

Where would the sentence best fit?

(A) A   (B) B   (C) C   (D) D

iBT Practice

COMETS

1 ➡ In ancient cultures, the abrupt appearance of a comet was taken as a mysterious omen of bad fortune, inspiring predictions of famine, disease, and flood. This was not the only fallacious belief attached to comets. The Greek philosopher Aristotle reasoned that, since the heavens were essentially perfect, such a temporary and unpredictable occurrence as a comet must instead come from the Earth. Thus, he believed comets were pieces of the Earth that had somehow been ignited and blown into space. Surprisingly, this view remained unchallenged for nearly 2,000 years after Aristotle's death. Today, astronomers are able to study comets in close detail through the use of advanced telescopes and satellite images, and as a result have a far more informed understanding of what makes a comet.

2 The best way to illustrate the basic makeup of a comet is to liken it to a "dirty snowball." The mass of the comet consists of ice intermixed with rock and dust. Many of these small celestial bodies are believed to originate in the Oort Cloud, which is a giant spherical mass of floating ice, debris, and gases that surrounds our solar system, extending to distances thousands of times farther than the orbit of Pluto. Scientists believe that these elements may collide and conjoin within the Oort Cloud. When large objects pass through the cloud, they knock some of these pieces out of their regular orbits and into the inner solar system, where their new orbits make them visible from the Earth. Comets appear to observers as bright white streaks, with a rounded head and a long, shimmering tail. However, this common image represents only a brief phase in the comet's life cycle. Further examination of the comet's various components helps to explain why comets appear as they do.

3 ➡ The nucleus is the most basic, and the only consistent, component of a comet. The nucleus of a comet comprises the core of what appears to be the comet's head, and consists of a densely packed mixture of mostly ice and rock. The nucleus of a comet can measure anywhere from 100 meters to 30 miles in diameter, but most average about 10 miles across. The nuclei of comets are some of the darkest bodies in the heavens; they only reflect about 4 percent of the sunlight that shines on them. The intense darkness of the nucleus is generally attributed to an accretion of rock and dust on the surface that covers the ice trapped within. Offsetting this darkness only slightly is the thick shroud of dust and debris that surrounds the nucleus bound by its gravitational pull, but even though this covering reflects more light than the surface of the nucleus, it still does not account for the bright appearance of comets in the sky.

4 ➡ What produces the bright image that is visible to humans, sometimes even with the naked eye, is the other two major components of comets, the coma and tail. It should be noted that these two phenomena are relatively rare during the entire lifespan of a comet, and only occur under special conditions. The coma is a nebulous cloud of gases and dust particles that forms a giant gaseous ball around the nucleus. This formation is much larger than the nucleus, however, measuring tens of thousands of times its size. A coma cannot form around the comet until it passes into the inner solar system, where it is exposed to the heat of the sun. When this happens, the ice inside the comet turns to vapor through a process called sublimation,

and is then ejected from the comet through holes in the surface of the nucleus. This highly reflective water vapor forms a temporary atmosphere around the comet that shines brightly when exposed to the sun's rays. In addition to the sun's heat, the comet is also subject to solar winds and radiation pressure. **A** For this reason, portions of the coma are forced away from the comet, leaving a trail in the sky that is known as the comet's tail. **B** Contrary to popular belief, the direction in which the tail points is not related to the comet's forward momentum. **C** As the comet revolves around the sun, the tail is continually changing directions in relation to its position to the solar winds and other forces. **D**

01 The word " abrupt " in the passage is closest in meaning to

(A) luminous
(B) periodic
(C) sudden
(D) continuous

02 According to paragraph 1, Aristotle theorized that comets were

(A) bad omens of natural disasters
(B) pieces of Earth that exploded into space
(C) heavenly bodies far away from Earth
(D) mixed fragments of Earth and heaven

Paragraph 1 is marked with an arrow [➡].

03 The author mentions the " Oort Cloud " in the passage in order to

(A) explain where comets come from
(B) illustrate the abundance of comets
(C) show how comets develop their tails
(D) explain a comet's appearance

04 The phrase " these elements " in the passage refers to

(A) rock and dust
(B) ice, debris, and gases
(C) celestial bodies
(D) objects

05 The word " they " in the passage refers to

(A) bodies
(B) comets
(C) nuclei
(D) heavens

06 The word " accretion " in the passage is closest in meaning to

(A) accumulation
(B) blend
(C) formation
(D) decay

07 Which of the sentences below best expresses the essential information in the highlighted sentence in the passage? *Incorrect* answer choices change the meaning in important ways or leave out essential nformation.

(A) The nucleus is surrounded by a cloud of dust and debris that absorbs light and darkens its usually bright appearance.
(B) A shroud of dust and debris may partially account for the comet's brightness, though it is still slightly darker than the nucleus it surrounds.
(C) The thick cloud of dust and debris surrounding the comet reflects more light than the nucleus, but not enough to fully explain its brightness.
(D) Light that is reflected by the nucleus is absorbed by a shroud of dust and debris, which may account for its brightness.

08 According to paragraph 3, the nuclei of comets are very dark because

(A) they are composed mostly of rock and ice
(B) they are much farther away than they appear
(C) they are coated with a layer of dust and rock
(D) they are surrounded by gases that do not reflect light

Paragraph 3 is marked with an arrow [➜].

09 The word " revolves " in the passage is closest in meaning to

(A) arises
(B) rotates
(C) explodes
(D) stays

10 According to paragraph 4, it can be inferred that sublimation is the process by which

(A) a liquid turns into a solid
(B) a solid turns into a gas
(C) a gas turns into a liquid
(D) a liquid turns into a gas

Paragraph 4 is marked with an arrow [➜].

11 According to paragraph 4, which of the following is true of comets?

(A) The majority are formed in the inner solar system.
(B) Their tail indicates the comet's direction of travel.
(C) The coma is many times larger than the nucleus.
(D) They shine when their reflective surface is exposed to the sun.

Paragraph 4 is marked with an arrow [➜].

12 Look at the four squares [■] that indicate where the following sentence could be added to the passage.

> Instead, the tail always points away from the sun.

Where would the sentence best fit?

Click on a square [■] to add the sentence to the passage.

(A) **A**   (B) **B**   (C) **C**   (D) **D**

13 Directions: An introductory sentence for a brief summary of the passage is provided below. Complete the summary by selecting the THREE answer choices that express the most important ideas in the passage. Some sentences do not belong in the summary because they express ideas that are not presented in the passage or are minor ideas in the passage. **This question is worth 2 points.**

Drag your answer choices to the spaces where they belong. To remove an answer choice, click on it. To review the passage, click **View Text**.

The appearance of a comet is best understood by considering its three basic components: the nucleus, the coma, and the tail.
-
-
-

Answer Choices

(A) The coma is created when the heat of the sun causes the ice within the comet to release highly reflective gases.	(D) Comets are forced out of the solar system when large objects knock them from their orbits at the outer edge of the solar system.
(B) A tail of dust and gases can stretch for 1 astronomical unit, or 150 million kilometers, behind the average comet.	(E) The pressure exerted on a comet by solar winds forces the dust and gases of the comet backward into what appears as a tail.
(C) Because the nucleus is several thousand times smaller than the coma around it, it is not directly visible with the naked eye.	(F) The only permanent part of a comet that exists throughout its lifespan is the nucleus, a dark and dense collection of rock and dust covering the ice.

Chapter 15 Social Science

- **Social Science**
  A branch of science that deals with the institutions and functioning of human society and the interpersonal relationships of individuals as members of society
- **Related fields**
  Archaeology, Anthropology, Psychology, Economics, Sociology, Political Science, etc.

Reading Preview

Sociology – Thomas Malthus and Population Control | Intensive Drill 1 |

Thomas Malthus was a British demographer and political economist, best known for his highly influential views on population growth. In 1798, he published a lengthy pamphlet criticizing the views of the Utopians, who believed that life could and would definitely improve for humans on earth, and gained prominence as a result. With his significant insight on population and demographics, he is regarded as the founder of modern demography.

Anthropology – Social Acculturation | Intensive Drill 2 |

Acculturation is the process of cultural and psychological change that results from the contact of two or more cultures. Started in the 1880s, this field of study has become a significant focus of social science. Though acculturation encompasses a bidirectional process of change, most researches have focused on the adjustment and adaptations of minorities in response to their contact with the dominant majority.

Architecture – Renaissance Architecture

| Intensive Drill 3 |

Renaissance architecture is the architecture of the period between the early fourteenth and early seventeenth centuries in different regions of Europe. It is characterized by its emphasis on symmetry, proportion, and geometry, which can be commonly seen in classical ruins of Greece and Rome. Stylistically, it followed Gothic architecture and was succeeded by Baroque architecture.

Economics – Slums of the Industrial Revolution

| Mini Test 1 |

The Industrial Revolution was the transition to new manufacturing processes in the eighteenth and nineteenth centuries. Prior to the Industrial Revolution, manufacturing was often done in small scale via manpower. This period is marked with a shift in production to using machinery, factories, and mass production. Though the Industrial Revolution brought higher standards of living for the middle and upper classes, the working class had to go through inhumane living conditions.

Psychology – Memory

| Mini Test 2 |

Memory is the term given to the process involved in the encoding, storing, and retrieving of information. It is both a result of and an influence on perception, attention, and learning. It is essential to all our lives, as we cannot operate in the present, learn new materials, or think about the future without it. The first study of human memory was conducted by Aristotle at least 2,000 years ago.

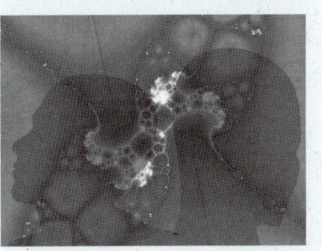

Economics – Adam Smith and *The Wealth of Nations*

| iBT Practice |

Adam Smith was a Scottish social philosopher, political economist, and a key figure in the Scottish Enlightenment. He wrote what is considered the bible of capitalism, *An Inquiry into the Nature and Causes of the Wealth of Nations*, generally referred to by its shortened title *The Wealth of Nations*. In this book, Smith mainly analyzed the relationship between work and the production of a nation's wealth, and described what he considered to be the appropriate roles of government.

Intensive Drill 1

THOMAS MALTHUS AND POPULATION CONTROL

1   Thomas Malthus was a nineteenth-century British scholar who did influential work in the field of demography, the mathematical study of populations. His most famous work, *An Essay on the Principles of Population*, has influenced countless scientists since its first publication. In this essay, Malthus argued that population growth would always exceed man's ability to produce enough food and other goods to support the population. He believed that population would always grow to the farthest limits of subsistence, but ruinous forces such as war or famine would keep it from growing any farther. Malthus argued that this phenomenon was responsible for the high rate of poverty during his time, since a limited food supply had to continually provide for a growing population. If population were in line with production, however, then society as a whole would experience greater well-being.

2   To this end, Malthus argued for population control as a means of righting the balance between population growth and food supply. In *An Essay on the Principles of Population*, he stated that natural forms of population control often worked, to a degree. Human vice, or moral weakness, whether in the form of violent crime or life-threatening habits such as alcoholism, would often be enough to do the unpleasant job of keeping the population from growing beyond the point of subsistence. However, if this failed, then the consequences would become far worse. Widespread famine, deadly diseases, and even plagues would then step in to decrease the population. The conditions of overpopulation and the spread of poverty and poor living conditions would be such that these forces would occur quite naturally. Malthus went so far as to argue that the Black Death of the Middle Ages was a plague brought on by an unsafe surge in the European population.

3   To an extent, Malthus believed that these tragedies could be avoided if humans were to conduct their own sort of population control. He had a number of suggestions for how societies could control their populations to avoid famine or plague. One of them was the teaching of moral restraint in regard to sexual activity. In his day, it was believed that producing many children made a nation strong, and that it should be allowed to go on unchecked. Malthus argued that having many children had quite the opposite effect, and believed that the people, especially poor people, should be conditioned to avoid most relationships that might lead to having children. In addition, Malthus did not rule out the possibility of controlled breeding among people. He proposed the idea that the most healthy and intelligent people be allowed to breed with few limits, while strict limits should be placed on the poor and less fit. In this way, the population could be managed and a stronger breed of people could be created that were less likely to drain society of its resources.

01 The word "ruinous" in the passage is closest in meaning to

(A) dangerous   (B) strong   (C) internal   (D) destructive

02 According to paragraph 2, why would population not surpass subsistence levels?

(A) It would only then be limited by available resources.
(B) It would begin to decrease after it reaches its peak.
(C) It would eventually be kept in check by natural forces.
(D) It would create a large population of poor people.

03 Why does the author mention the "Black Death" in the passage?

(A) To illustrate one of the deadly consequences of poor living conditions
(B) To explain the basic premise of Malthus's *An Essay on the Principles of Population*
(C) To show that unchecked population growth always leads to natural disasters
(D) To give an example of how Malthus thought nature could control overpopulation

04 Which of the sentences below best expresses the essential information in the highlighted sentence in the passage? *Incorrect* answer choices change the meaning in important ways or leave out essential information.

(A) Malthus claimed that breeding without limits should be discouraged, especially among the poor, as it will have a negative effect on a nation.
(B) Malthus believed that by discouraging breeding among the poor, it would be possible to strengthen the nation.
(C) Malthus supported the idea that the breeding should be restrained among all classes regardless of their financial condition.
(D) Malthus was in agreement with the social policies of his day that promoted national strength through breeding.

05 Directions: An introductory sentence for a brief summary of the passage is provided below. Complete the summary by selecting the THREE answer choices that express the most important ideas in the passage. Some sentences do not belong in the summary because they express ideas that are not presented in the passage or are minor ideas in the passage. **This question is worth 2 points.**

Thomas Malthus believed that unchecked population growth would lead to disaster, and some controls were necessary.

(A) Unhealthy living conditions such as those suffered by the poor were breeding grounds for diseases.
(B) The basis of Malthus's theory was the idea that human populations will always grow to the farthest limits of the food supply, endangering society.
(C) Malthus's work encouraged leaders to change their attitudes toward human reproduction.
(D) Malthus posited that nature had its own means of controlling population but that these means were not always effective.
(E) To ensure the well-being of society, Malthus argued, it is necessary to control population growth through artificial means, including controlled breeding.
(F) Famine and plague are the most prevalent examples of natural forms of population control.

Intensive Drill 2

SOCIAL ACCULTURATION

1 Social acculturation is the process through which immigrants or minority groups adapt and eventually integrate into the larger or dominant culture of their society. The standard model for social acculturation was first proposed by Kalvero Oberg in 1954. Oberg described social acculturation as a four-step process: euphoria, frustration, negotiation, and assimilation. The euphoric stage typically only lasts for several weeks. In this stage, nearly everything about the new culture is seen in a positive light. The euphoria that people often feel in this stage is strongly related to a sense of novelty. New experiences are often greeted with enthusiasm, and the first few weeks in a new culture are typically nothing but a string of novel experiences.

2 Once the initial period of novelty has worn off, immigrants often experience a period of frustration. Immigrants must relearn most of the skills that are needed in everyday life. Language is obviously the greatest part of this process, but even in situations where the immigrant is fluent in the new language, a learning curve still exists. Immigrants are typically unaware of, or at least not totally familiar with, the cultural practices of their new society. They may lack knowledge that is considered common sense in the new culture, and this can make even simple tasks, such as going to the doctor, more difficult. Individuals in this stage often express their frustration by finding fault with the society around them and treating their mother culture with feelings of nostalgia. They may be reluctant or unwilling to take part in the new culture and may seek to close themselves off from it as much as possible.

3 The phase of frustration can vary greatly for different people because they all have very different personalities. Indeed, some never progress beyond this stage. Eventually, however, most people enter the stage of negotiation, in which they learn to adapt and deal with the problems that they experience in the new society. Slowly, they become more familiar with the culture and more proficient at social tasks. There may be some temporary slippage back into the frustration stage when they are confronted with a particularly challenging social situation, but for the most part, immigrants tend to continue to make forward progress once they have entered this stage.

4 In the final phase, assimilation, the immigrants become fully integrated into their new culture, to the point where they can be seen as regular members of that society. Assimilation can take an extremely long time, and may not even occur in the lifetime of first-generation immigrants. In many cases it is only the children of immigrants, who are born in the new culture, who can be said to have truly assimilated.

01 The word "novel" in the passage is closest in meaning to

(A) familiar
(B) favorable
(C) unusual
(D) exciting

02 In paragraph 2, all of the following are mentioned as effects of the stage of frustration EXCEPT

(A) a withdrawal from society
(B) criticism of one's new society
(C) nostalgic memories of one's former culture
(D) a refusal to perform even simple chores

03 The word "some" in the passage refers to

(A) problems
(B) people
(C) personalities
(D) tasks

04 According to paragraph 4, the stage of assimilation often only occurs after

(A) immigrants have completely mastered the new language
(B) young immigrants spent their adolescent periods in the new culture
(C) a second generation is born in the new culture
(D) immigrants have made the decision to interact with the new culture

05 **Directions:** An introductory sentence for a brief summary of the passage is provided below. Complete the summary by selecting the THREE answer choices that express the most important ideas in the passage. Some sentences do not belong in the summary because they express ideas that are not presented in the passage or are minor ideas in the passage. *This question is worth 2 points.*

Kalvero Oberg proposed the standard model for social acculturation, which is the process through which immigrants adapt to a new culture.

(A) During the process of social acculturation, immigrants progress through various stages in which they may feel positively or negatively towards the new culture.
(B) The process of social acculturation was first developed by Kalvero Oberg in 1954 to help immigrants assimilate into new cultures.
(C) Though not everyone experiences the process of social acculturation at the same rate, people usually experience the same general stages.
(D) In the first stage of social acculturation, immigrants are often impressed by the novelty of the new culture.
(E) Many immigrants never reach the final stages of social acculturation, and return to their mother cultures out of discouragement.
(F) Immigrants need to overcome the challenges of living in an unfamiliar environment until they fully assimilate to the new culture.

Intensive Drill 3

RENAISSANCE ARCHITECTURE

1   The period of European history known as the Renaissance was marked by a renewed interest in learning and the arts. Having just emerged from the Middle Ages, a time during which the Catholic church largely suppressed the pursuit of science and art, artists and thinkers who were disappointed with the failings of their own culture turned to a culture predating their own for inspiration. Ancient Rome became the model for bold new intellectuals who wished to revitalize their weakened culture. One of the earliest and most pronounced examples of Renaissance principles can be found in the architecture of the period. Drawing inspiration from the ruins of ancient Rome, architects reinvented the European skyline, constructing cathedrals and castles that featured a marked departure from the styles of the previous medieval period.

2   The two dominant styles of medieval architecture produced massive, hulking buildings that were more threatening than beautiful. The Romanesque style was often fortress-like in design, with its lack of decoration and use of hard lines. The Gothic style, on the other hand, was far more ornamental, with statuettes of various saints and demons adorning the exterior, and steep, pointed spires that reached to heights unprecedented in medieval construction. However, even the Gothic style inspired far more dread than it did artistic appreciation. In contrast to both styles, Renaissance architecture was a lively celebration of the art form, in turns both majestic and lighthearted, that gladly disposed of the dreary conventions of the past.

3   The birthplace of Renaissance architecture was the city of Florence, Italy, in the early fifteenth century. Here, an architect by the name of Filippo Brunelleschi started a new artistic trend with his work on the city's main cathedral. Though the cathedral itself was built in the Gothic style more common to the Middle Ages, Brunelleschi designed its giant dome based on that of the Pantheon of ancient Rome. He had studied the structure at great length and admired the style in which it was built for its orderly and symmetrical appearance. These same characteristics showed up in his design for the church of San Lorenzo, a strict geometrical design which featured Roman columns and archways. Throughout his career, Brunelleschi relied on these basic principles in his work as an architect, initiating a new style based on classical guidelines that would quickly become popular throughout Europe.

4   Perhaps the second most influential architect of the Renaissance was Donato Bramante, whose work is typical of what is called High Renaissance architecture. The High Renaissance period took place during the late fifteenth and early sixteenth centuries, and is characterized by an almost universal mastery of classical forms by architects from all over Italy. Often cited as a near-perfect piece of High Renaissance architecture, Bramante's *Tempietto* was built on the supposed place where St. Peter was killed in ancient times, and is thus the most sacred site in Rome. The small, round monument was built in explicit imitation of ancient Roman temples. Bramante later participated in the design and construction of the giant dome atop St. Peter's Basilica at the Vatican, a monumental achievement in Renaissance design for which he is best known today.

Answer Book p. A133

01 According to paragraph 1, what caused Renaissance thinkers to look to ancient Rome for inspiration?

(A) They recognized Rome as being the world's greatest empire.
(B) They wanted to bring art and education back to their culture.
(C) They wished to achieve the same status as the ancient Romans.
(D) They idealized the bold intellectuals from ancient Rome.

02 The word "threatening" in the passage is closest in meaning to

(A) inspiring
(B) attractive
(C) intimidating
(D) significant

03 In paragraph 2, why does the author give details about "the Romanesque style" and "the Gothic style"?

(A) To show that the Renaissance style had a major impact on the Romanesque and Gothic styles
(B) To emphasize that Renaissance architecture is the most advanced style
(C) To give a clearer picture of how Renaissance architecture is different from previous styles
(D) To explain detailed information about the Romanesque and Gothic styles

04 The phrase "the structure" in the passage refers to

(A) cathedral
(B) Pantheon
(C) dome
(D) church

05 Directions: An introductory sentence for a brief summary of the passage is provided below. Complete the summary by selecting the THREE answer choices that express the most important ideas in the passage. Some sentences do not belong in the summary because they express ideas that are not presented in the passage or are minor ideas in the passage. *This question is worth 2 points.*

The Renaissance period saw the introduction of numerous elements of ancient Roman architecture into European culture that forever changed the art of architecture.

(A) Thanks to the intellectuals of the time, philosophy and the arts enjoyed a renewed vitality during the Renaissance period.
(B) Several Renaissance buildings have their origins in Florence and were built by Brunelleschi, who studied roman ruins at length.
(C) The High Renaissance period is marked by a very explicit return to classic styles, the best example of which is the monument the *Tempietto* built by Bramante.
(D) The Renaissance style of architecture was wildly popular in Italy, but its influence did not spread much farther.
(E) The great achievement of the Gothic style was its use of tall, pointed spires that made cathedrals taller than any in history.
(F) In contrast to the dreary architecture of the Middle Ages, Renaissance architecture was often playful in its style.

Mini Test 1

SLUMS OF THE INDUSTRIAL REVOLUTION

1   During the Industrial Revolution, England's towns and villages were transformed over just a few decades into major industrial centers. Factories were built in towns such as Manchester and Birmingham due to their access to shipping routes, and these factories required a great deal of workers. These were often people whose former trades had been taken over by machines, leaving them out of work and desperate for income. While the upper-class factory owners lived in large houses outside the city, the workers generally lived together in filthy apartment houses at the city's center, near their places of work. Factory owners would often set up "company towns," sections of the city in which the apartment buildings, grocery stores, and schools were all owned by the factory owners. Whatever money the workers were able to earn was often paid right back to the factory owners in the form of rent and food bills.

2   Because of the massive influx of workers moving from the country into the industrial centers, tenements went up all over the industrial centers to house workers, but the residents there faced squalid living conditions. The houses were very small and were built side by side in very close quarters, making for dirty, crowded neighborhoods known as slums, which were characterized by high crime rates and poor living conditions. The neighborhoods would often have little better than open sewer systems. Several neighbors often had to share the same toilet facilities as well. The growth of such tenements was such that it put a special strain on the cities' water and sewage systems, so that it was not uncommon for sewage to be running into the streets and the yards of the tenement houses. Given these living conditions, it is not surprising that disease sprang up quickly in these areas due to sewage problems and contaminated water, and spread rapidly from one person to another due to the close proximity in which everyone lived. Large numbers of workers died from cholera and typhoid, which were spread through the bad water.

3   Conditions did slowly improve throughout the nineteenth century, as the government intervened and introduced several reforms. Parliament member Michael Thomas Sadler was a major supporter of workers' rights, and authored the Sadler Report in 1832 to show the government that factory owners were engaging in terrible abuse of workers, including women and children. In addition to reducing the average workday and limiting child labor, Sadler worked to ensure that factory owners provided their workers with decent living conditions, as well as education for their children. Further reforms limited the number of homes that could be built in a specific area. The Public Health Act of 1875 forced towns to pave and clean the roads, and a combination of gas lighting and new police forces improved the safety conditions on the streets. Closed, underground sewer systems were finally built, and all water was filtered for purity. New regulations also sought to help the poor and unemployed, providing soup kitchens for those who could not afford to feed themselves.

01 According to paragraph 1, many people came to work in factories because

(A) they did not receive a proper education
(B) their manpower was needed due to the Industrial Revolution
(C) they were not qualified for better jobs
(D) their jobs were lost to machine labor

02 The word "influx" in the sentence is closest in meaning to

(A) number (B) arrival (C) change (D) group

03 Which of the sentences below best expresses the essential information in the highlighted sentence in the passage? *Incorrect* answer choices change the meaning in important ways or leave out essential information.

(A) Poor sanitation and overcrowding in these areas inevitably led to the rise and rapid spread of diseases through the tenements and slums.
(B) Unsanitary living conditions allowed for diseases to spread quickly among those with poor sewage systems.
(C) Slums with sewage problems were major breeding grounds for diseases because people lived so closely to one another.
(D) It was not a coincidence that the poor hygiene in residential areas resulted in the wide spread of disease among the poor.

04 According to paragraph 2, what can be inferred about the living conditions in the industrial centers?

(A) The standards of living conditions were regulated by the government.
(B) Crime rates had been high long before the residential areas for workers were built.
(C) They worsened because towns could not handle the sudden population growth.
(D) They were already unfavorable to live in before the Industrial Revolution.

05 **Directions:** An introductory sentence for a brief summary of the passage is provided below. Complete the summary by selecting the THREE answer choices that express the most important ideas in the passage. Some sentences do not belong in the summary because they express ideas that are not presented in the passage or are minor ideas in the passage. *The question is worth 2 points.*

The Industrial Revolution caused a mass migration of workers into the cities, where for years living conditions were no better than in slums.

(A) Factory owners could afford to live in large houses outside the cities, while workers had to be close to the factories.
(B) Workers were housed in tenements — small apartment houses that were often crowded and dirty.
(C) Filthy living conditions in the slums contributed to high crime rates and the spread of deadly diseases.
(D) Reforms led by the government resulted in significant improvements in the lives of factory workers.
(E) Workers flocked to the cities despite having to live in slums because most industries were centralized there.
(F) Government regulations later required factory owners to provide children with an education.

Mini Test 2

MEMORY

1   In the past few decades, researchers have learned a great deal about how memory works, most notably that the process of creating memories can be separated into three stages or types: sensory memory, short-term memory, and long-term memory. The first of these three, sensory memory, is by far the most fleeting and insubstantial of the three stages. Sensory memory is different from what is usually thought of as memory, in that it refers to the ability to retain important information while ignoring everything else. In this way, it is closely related to attention and concentration. When one is focusing most of his or her attention on a specific task, for instance, any stimulus not related to that task is unlikely to be noticed, though it may superficially be perceived. This filter of sorts is very helpful in eliminating sounds or sights that may distract from the task at hand, thereby increasing one's ability to concentrate on what is most important at that moment.

2   When pertinent information is allowed into one's consciousness, however, it enters the domain of the short-term memory. Short-term memory has been shown to have a duration of just a few seconds to a few minutes, and is most useful in quickly recalling information most relevant to specific tasks, so for information to be successfully retrieved from short-term memory, it must be used within a very brief time period, or else the memory will decay. One example is reading a phone number from a phone book and then looking away to dial the number on a phone. **A** If a distraction comes in the middle of this process, it takes only seconds for the memory of the phone number to disappear. **B** One way that the effectiveness of short-term memory can be increased is by sorting information into small clusters. **C** In the example of the telephone number, a person who tries to remember the number in its entirety will more quickly forget it before dialing. **D** However, if this same person memorizes the number in groups of digits rather than as a whole, then the memory is likely to endure longer.

3   Long-term memory is much more complex, as it can retain many decades' worth of information. Long-term memories may be very old, such as the recollection of a childhood birthday party, or they may be recent, such as the top story on the morning news. This represents two distinct types of memories: episodic and semantic. Memories of events such as a party are called episodic memories, because they recall episodes from one's experience. Of course, there are also memories that are not connected to some specific time, place, or event. These are called semantic memories, and can include a wide variety of factual information, such as the rules of grammar or the lyrics to one's favorite song. Memories that are stored for the long term can be one or the other, and are often some mixture of the two as well. Distinctions between these two different types of memories serve as a kind of filing system that allows the brain to more easily recall individual memories.

Answer Book p. A137

01 The word "it" in the passage refers to

(A) task
(B) stimulus
(C) attention
(D) filter

02 According to paragraph 1, all of the following are true of sensory memory EXCEPT:

(A) It is helpful in filtering out information that is irrelevant.
(B) It is only temporary compared to long-term or short-term memory.
(C) It is often overwhelmed in the presence of too much stimulation.
(D) It improves concentration by ignoring most distractions.

03 Why does the author mention "telephone number" in the passage?

(A) To frame a discussion of how short-term memory helps with everyday tasks
(B) To show how repeating information can be helpful for memorization
(C) To give an example of a situation in which long-term memory is useful
(D) To explain the limits of short-term memory and how to improve it

04 Look at the four squares [■] that indicate where the following sentence could be added to the passage.

This involves breaking down large amounts of information into small parts that are easier to digest.

Where would the sentence best fit?

(A) A
(B) B
(C) C
(D) D

05 **Directions:** Select the appropriate phrases from the answer choices and match them to the type of memories to which they relate. TWO of the answer choices will NOT be used. *This question is worth 3 points.*

Answer Choices	Sensory Memory
(A) Can only be found in intellectuals	•
(B) Is related to attention and concentration	**Short-term Memory**
(C) Includes a recollection of old times	•
(D) Can be enhanced when information is processed in chunks	•
(E) Stores factual information	**Long-term Memory**
(F) Is the most evolved type of memory	•
(G) Only lasts for a brief period of time	•

Chapter 15 Social Science 203

iBT Practice

ADAM SMITH AND *THE WEALTH OF NATIONS*

1 ➜ In 1776, the same year America gained independence from the British, philosopher Adam Smith wrote a book that would earn him a permanent place in history, as well as the title "the father of modern economics." The book that made him such an esteemed figure was *The Wealth of Nations*, in which he outlined his theories on political economy — the ways in which human behavior, market factors, government regulations, and several other factors together drive business and commerce. Smith's work laid the foundation for the modern study of economics, most notably the classical school of economics, from which principles of capitalism and the free market economy originated. More than an economist, however, Smith had a keen interest in human nature, and it was his study of the interaction of human nature with social institutions that led to his groundbreaking work in economics.

2 ➜ At the age of 14, Smith began a long and intensive study of philosophy at the University of Glasgow in his home country of Scotland, later moving to Oxford. Upon graduating, he obtained his first job as a lecturer. It was through his lectures that he gained much positive attention from both his students and his contemporaries, eventually becoming a professor of moral philosophy back at the University of Glasgow. It was in this subject that he published his first book, *The Theory of Moral Sentiments*, which dealt mainly with his ideas about human nature. He believed human nature was an unchanging and universal characteristic of human beings that could be used to predict the behavior of people within societies. Smith wrote of how humans seemed to possess two different, seemingly conflicting tendencies: on one hand, they are passionate beings driven by self-preservation; on the other hand, they are rational beings with the ability to discriminate right from wrong. These two opposing forces seemed to regulate one another in human behavior, he said, since passionate, self-interested beings were still capable of establishing organized institutions for the betterment of all men.

3 The ideas put forth in *The Theory of Moral Sentiments* would lay the infrastructure for his study of political economy later on. In fact, it can be said that *The Wealth of Nations* was not its own separate economic treatise, but rather a continuation of the philosophical writings of his earlier work. Smith expanded on his idea of the duality of human nature to examine the workings of the ideal society in terms of its economy. According to his theory, the best society was one in which its participants were dependent upon one another to meet their economic needs. **A** Smith envisioned what he called a "system of perfect liberty," in which the market was left untouched by government institutions, and in which the terms of business were determined instead by "natural" forces. **B** Economic factors like supply and demand would serve as an "invisible hand" that could guide the markets toward prosperity without any need for government regulations. **C** This idea would later become known as laissez-faire capitalism. **D**

4 ➜ Under this condition, Smith argued, people can improve their own lot while also improving society. This is because the capitalist system exploits the duality of human nature, as discussed in his previous book. According to Smith's model, competition would become the factor that balances man's selfish tendencies

with his more rational ones. Because individual producers would be forced to compete with one another both for business and for good labor, prices would be determined by what consumers were willing and able to pay, and wages would be determined by how much workers are willing to sell their labor for, which would help commerce. The combined effect would create a healthy and robust economy driven both by consumers' freedom of choice and by producers' desire to outcompete other businesses to achieve unlimited wealth. In this way, self-interest could actually work for the good of society on the whole. Unfortunately, time proved Smith's theories somewhat idealistic, as fierce competition would lead to such villainy as the labor abuses of the Industrial Revolution just decades later. However, despite the introduction of certain government regulations, the basic tenets of Smith's philosophy still underpin the economic policies of most civilized nations today.

Glossary ✕

Laissez-faire: the doctrine that government should not interfere commercial affairs

---

01 The word "esteemed" in the passage is closest in meaning to

(A) talented (B) extraordinary
(C) respected (D) enduring

02 According to paragraph 1, Smith defined political economy as

(A) the measure of business and commerce in an economy
(B) the ways human nature can change social institutions
(C) the guiding of market activity by classical economic ideas
(D) the interaction between people, markets, and government

Paragraph 1 is marked with an arrow [➡].

03 The word "conflicting" in the passage is closest in meaning to

(A) fascinating (B) contradictory
(C) doubtful (D) practical

04 The word "discriminate" in the passage is closest in meaning to

(A) isolate (B) distinguish
(C) protect (D) exclude

05 In paragraph 2, the author states that

(A) Smith became famous after publishing his first work, *The Theory of Moral Sentiments*
(B) Smith believed human nature should not be used in predicting the public's behavior
(C) Smith asserted that humans have two tendencies that balance each other
(D) Smith changed his field of study from political economy to moral philosophy

Paragraph 2 is marked with an arrow [➡].

06 According to paragraph 2, Adam Smith saw humans as contradictory beings because

(A) they pursue self-interest and at the same time have moral discernment
(B) they seek freedom and at the same time try to establish social order
(C) they behave individually as well as collectively
(D) they want to achieve social equality and at the same time seek to climb the social ladder

Paragraph 2 is marked with an arrow [➡].

07 The word "infrastructure" in the passage is closest in meaning to

(A) foundation   (B) process
(C) regulation   (D) directive

08 The phrase "this condition" in the passage refers to

(A) the restrictions required for a healthy economy
(B) the tendency for the individual to act selfishly
(C) the idea that people have a double nature
(D) the market free of any intervention

09 Which of the sentences below best expresses the essential information in the highlighted sentence in the passage? *Incorrect* answer choices change the meaning in important ways or leave out essential information.

(A) Producers that compete for labor and business would set prices at whatever level would bring them the most profits.
(B) If businesses were forced to compete with one another, prices and wages would be determined by what consumers were able to demand.
(C) Competition between businesses would establish prices and wages that largely favor consumers and workers, which in turn would benefit commerce.
(D) Consumers set prices and wages for themselves because producers are intent upon competing with one another for business and labor.

10 Why does the author mention "labor abuses of the Industrial Revolution" in the passage?

(A) To suggest that Smith's ideas were open to misuse by immoral people
(B) To argue that Smith's idea is a realistic option in modern economics
(C) To illustrate inhumane aspects of the Industrial Revolution
(D) To show that market forces alone can prevent labor abuses

11 According to paragraph 4, what can be inferred about the economy envisioned by Smith?

(A) It is too dependent upon the government in order to function properly.
(B) It relies on human nature to improve society.
(C) It does not take extremely poor people into account.
(D) It has never been put into practice successfully.

Paragraph 4 is marked with an arrow [➡].

12 Look at the four squares [■] that indicate where the following sentence could be added to the passage.

> An example of this economic factor's impact on the market is producers and consumers working together to make sure goods were both bought and sold.

Where would the sentence best fit?

Click on a square [■] to add the sentence to the passage.

(A) **A**   (B) **B**   (C) **C**   (D) **D**

13 Directions: An introductory sentence for a brief summary of the passage is provided below. Complete the summary by selecting the THREE answer choices that express the most important ideas in the passage. Some sentences do not belong in the summary because they express ideas that are not presented in the passage or are minor ideas in the passage. **This question is worth 2 points.**

Drag your answer choices to the spaces where they belong. To remove an answer choice, click on it. To review the passage, click **View Text**.

In *The Wealth of Nations*, Adam Smith drew from his philosophy of human nature to describe the ideal economic system.
•
•
•

Answer Choices	
(A) Smith's interest in political economy led him to write *The Theory of Moral Sentiments*, which had a significant impact on his later works.	(D) Smith's theory is based on the idea that competition between producers would balance self-interest with reason, and benefit both consumers and producers.
(B) Smith described human nature as having two competing tendencies: one driven by passion and self-interest, and another by reason and sympathy.	(E) Smith's first book, *The Theory of Moral Sentiments*, laid the foundation for the well-known book that is still influential in economics, *The Wealth of Nations*.
(C) During Smith's travels across Europe, he was influenced by some of the continent's greatest political and economic theorists.	(F) The most prosperous society, Smith asserts, is one in which market factors are determined solely by the interaction of individual consumers and producers.

TOEFL iBT i Reading   www.linguaforum.com

Actual Test

Actual Test 1
Actual Test 2

Actual Test 1

Passage 1

CAMERA OBSCURA

1 → Camera obscura is a Latin term that means "dark chamber," generally referring to a dark room that only has a tiny amount of light let in through a small pinhole. As sunlight enters the room through the miniscule pinhole, an image is created on the opposite wall of the room. Although the image would be a scene from whatever is outside the room, the image would be reflected upside down on the wall. The original concept of the camera obscura dates back as far as 400 B.C.E. when Chinese philosopher Mozi was the first in history to mention the basic scientific principles of the camera after he noticed light entering a room through a small pinhole. Subsequent writings by the ancient Greek philosopher Aristotle detail how he perceived this phenomenon by describing the passage of light through a small hole into a room during an eclipse. During the late Renaissance period, special rooms were designed for the public to experience this phenomenon by viewing luminous images of the outside world as they were reflected onto a wall. In the late sixteenth century, Italian artists developed this practice even further by shrinking down the large room used for viewing into a small portable box and replacing the pinhole with a lens.

2 → However, it was not until the sixteenth century that the camera obscura became an invaluable tool for late Renaissance artists who used it to produce drawings and artwork with new perspective and detail. As artists during this period began to perfect the use of the camera obscura to produce what would go on to be considered masterpieces, its further development would even lead to the basis and foundation of the modern camera and photography. Its popularity in the artistic community at the time grew to the point where, as significant evidence now suggests. Many famous painters in the past actually used the camera obscura to project images of nature or people from outside, which were then traced in detail onto the opposite wall in the room.

3 → One such famous seventeenth century Dutch painter who is thought to have employed such techniques is Johannes Vermeer. Critics from as early as the 1800s have long suspected that Vermeer used some kind of mechanical device, complete with either a mirror or a lens, in creating his paintings. After decades of debate, some art historians firmly believe this device was none other than the camera obscura. Although there is no tangible historical evidence that he did in fact use the camera obscura, several renowned art historians have pointed to irregularities of compositional elements in his work, one such historian being Charles Seymour, who was the first to actually test out the theory that Vermeer used the camera obscura in his work. He did this by observing objects that commonly appear in Vermeer's paintings through the camera obscura, using similar lighting conditions to those of the paintings, and noticed that the resulting images were practically identical to the images in Vermeer's paintings.

4 → **A** However, the most prominent art historian to push forward the claim that artists like Vermeer used the camera obscura is David Hockney. **B** He postulated that artists, starting in the Renaissance period of the fifteenth century, traced optical images projected onto a wall and that these images would form the basis of the realistic qualities of paintings at that time. **C** Hockney's main critique of paintings from this period is that

the paintings are extremely, almost perfectly accurate in their depiction of people and objects, a feat that would have been practically impossible to accomplish using only the naked eye. **D** The camera obscura was useful for artists like Vermeer to frame a scene with a complex three-dimensional space into a two-dimensional image. He further pointed out that the accurate portrayal of three-dimensional space through perspective in Vermeer's work does not necessarily coincide with the knowledge of perspective that most artists at the time possessed, and such technique would have been hard to achieve even if Vermeer had acquired a superior knowledge of perspective over time. As a result, he concludes that Vermeer would have employed the camera obscura to achieve his almost mathematically precise accuracy in perspective, as evident in his work. Ultimately, since it is impossible to scientifically test whether all the paintings from the late Renaissance period did in fact use the camera obscura or other mechanical devices during the process of the artwork creation, the possibility of its use in art is still hotly debated among art historians today.

01 The word "luminous" in the passage is closest in meaning to

(A) bright
(B) sizeable
(C) beautiful
(D) shrunken

02 All of the following are mentioned in paragraph 1 EXCEPT:

(A) The reflected image created by the camera obscura is upside down.
(B) During the Renaissance period, the public viewed images from the camera obscura in rooms.
(C) Late Renaissance Italian artists developed a portable version of the camera obscura.
(D) Aristotle was the first scientist to coin the term camera obscura.

Paragraph 1 is marked with an arrow [→].

03 The word "invaluable" in the passage is closest in meaning to

(A) modern
(B) precious
(C) affordable
(D) valueless

04 Which of the sentences below best expresses the essential information in the highlighted sentence in the passage? *Incorrect* answer choices change the meaning in important ways or leave out essential information.

(A) The development of the modern camera was made possible by focusing on perfecting the composition of what was thought to be a masterpiece in the Renaissance.
(B) Artists during this time mastered the use of the camera obscura to raise the quality of their artworks to that of masterpieces.
(C) During this time, artists improved the use of the camera obscura for great works of art, which later contributed to the concepts of contemporary photography.
(D) The use of the camera obscura during this period was essential to create what were recognized as superior works of art.

05 The word "project" in the passage is closest in meaning to

(A) display
(B) paint
(C) describe
(D) narrate

06 The word "tangible" in the passage is closest in meaning to

(A) significant
(B) concrete
(C) arguable
(D) widespread

07 Paragraph 3 suggests which of the following about Vermeer and art historians?

(A) Charles Seymour proves the use of the camera obscura in Vermeer's painting.
(B) Art historians believe Vermeer's use of the camera obscura is responsible for his masterpieces.
(C) Art historians do not accept the theory put forth by Charles Seymour.
(D) There is not any accurate proof supporting Vermeer's use of the camera obscura.

Paragraph 3 is marked with an arrow [→].

08 The word "postulated" in the passage is closest in meaning to

(A) refuted
(B) admitted
(C) expected
(D) proposed

09 The word "its" in the passage refers to

(A) late Renaissance period
(B) camera obscura
(C) mechanical device
(D) artwork creation

10 According to paragraph 4, which of the following is true of Hockney's theory?

(A) The camera obscura was used only during the Renaissance period.
(B) It is impossible to produce realistically accurate artwork even with a use of the camera obscura.
(C) Renaissance artists relied on tracing optical images to produce realistic images.
(D) Vermeer was an expert at tracing optical images as projected on the wall.

Paragraph 4 is marked with an arrow [→].

11 How does paragraph 4 relate to the earlier discussion of art historians' claim about Vermeer?

(A) It explains the reason Vermeer used the camera obscura in his paintings.
(B) It provides another view in support of Vermeer's use of the camera obscura.
(C) It supports their claim by listing other artists who used the same techniques as Vermeer.
(D) It outlines various claims made by art historians.

Paragraph 4 is marked with an arrow [→].

12 Based on the information in paragraph 4, what can be inferred about Renaissance artists?

(A) The camera obscura aided them in depicting accurate perspective without a complete understanding of three dimensions.
(B) They studied advanced mathematical concepts to perfect their works.
(C) Only a few of them, like Vermeer, were celebrated for their advanced knowledge of perspective.
(D) They were criticized for their inaccuracy in depicting three-dimensional perspective.

Paragraph 4 is marked with an arrow [→].

13 Look at the four squares [■] that indicate where the following sentence could be added to the passage.

> He argued that it was the camera obscura that helped create those paintings.

Where would the sentence best fit?

Click on a square [■] to add the sentence to the passage.

(A) A (B) B (C) C (D) D

14 **Directions:** An introductory sentence for a brief summary of the passage is provided below. Complete the summary by selecting the THREE answer choices that express the most important ideas in the passage. Some sentences do not belong in the summary because they express ideas that are not presented in the passage or are minor ideas in the passage. ***This question is worth 2 points.***

Drag your answer choices to the spaces where they belong. To remove an answer choice, click on it. To review the passage, click on **View Text**.

The camera obscura is an optical device that led to photography and the photographic camera.

-
-
-

Answer Choices	
(A) Vermeer had advanced knowledge of mathematical perspective that he used in his paintings.	(D) Art historian Charles Seymour tested the theory that Vermeer used the camera obscura in his paintings.
(B) During the Renaissance period, artists developed and used the camera obscura to produce highly detailed works.	(E) The camera obscura was further developed by Italian artists for the public to be able to carry around smaller versions of it.
(C) Modern photography can be traced back to the Renaissance period's development of the camera obscura.	(F) Art historian David Hockney asserted that Vermeer used the camera obscura to achieve superior perspective in his work.

Passage 2

MARSUPIALS IN AUSTRALIA

1 ➔ Unique among mammals is the subclass known as metatheria, more commonly called marsupials. This group of mammals consists of animals such as the kangaroo and the opossum. Marsupials differ from other mammals in one essential way: unlike other mammals, their young do not fully develop inside the womb. Instead, they are born without being fully developed, and complete their development outside of the mother's body. They are able to do this partly because of a protective pouch that most adult marsupials possess. After being born, the tiny marsupials instinctively crawl into this pouch, where they safely feed and rest until fully grown. There are over 250 species of marsupials worldwide, but the vast majority of them inhabit the island continent of Australia, as well as surrounding islands such as New Zealand and New Guinea. The reasons for this uneven distribution are varied and complex.

2 ➔ Common marsupials like kangaroos and koala bears are readily associated with Australia, and factor prominently into Australian culture. It might seem perfectly logical that such a unique type of mammal would develop on an island, in total seclusion from other species, but surprisingly, marsupials did not originate in the South Pacific region. In fact, their journey to their final home in this region was a long and complicated one spanning many millions of years. The first known marsupials actually appeared in the Americas about 99 million years ago. Although the first fossil evidence was discovered in North America, it is more likely that South America was their place of origin, as a small number of marsupial species still inhabit this region. How marsupials reached Australia in such large numbers is still a debatable topic among scientists. To begin to answer this question, one must consider the geography of the planet as it looked millions of years ago, when marsupials were making their way to Australia.

3 ➔ At this time, the Earth was divided into two major supercontinents: Laurasia in the northern hemisphere and Gondwana in the southern. **A** Laurasia included what would later become North America and much of Asia. **B** Gondwana, on the other hand, was composed of what would become South America, Antarctica, India, and Africa. **C** Marsupials and other mammals evolved together on the same supercontinent, Gondwana. **D** Then, about 65 million years ago, as these supercontinents were slowly breaking apart, a giant piece of Antarctica separated from the mass to become the island of Australia.

4 Scientists believe that by the time this happened, several species of marsupials had already migrated to Australia by way of land connections that led them from their birthplace in the Americas, across Antarctica, and finally to the land mass that would become Australia. As the continent of Australia drifted northward from the supercontinent of Gondwana, these prehistoric marsupials became isolated and evolved into a vast array of different species. Today, about 200 different species of marsupials remain on the continent, greatly outnumbering native species of placental mammals. Why marsupials survived in such great numbers in Australia and not elsewhere is another topic of debate. Some scientists believe it was because Australia, due to its gradual movement toward ever-warmer climates, was spared some of the consequences of the severe climate change that occurred over the next several million years in most other parts of the

world. Therefore, its wildlife had a better chance of surviving the threat of extinction.

5 ➡ Despite the long separation of marsupials from most other mammals, the two groups still share a number of striking similarities. This is a prime example of convergent evolution, when two different species in comparable geographical locations adapt to their environments in similar ways. For example, the flying squirrel found in the West can be compared to the flying opossum of Australia. In each instance, the animal is one that is especially vulnerable to predators on the ground, and thus has a short lifespan in the wild because it is routinely preyed upon by snakes and other predators. In order to elude common predators on the ground, both animals developed a way to take advantage of their woodland environment to increase their safety. Each developed a webbing of skin between their front and hind limbs that allows them to glide through the air from tree to tree, decreasing the amount of time they spend on the ground. Though they are separated by thousands of miles, the similar living conditions caused the two animals to evolve the same defense mechanism.

15 The word "instinctively" in the passage is closest in meaning to

(A) regularly (B) effortlessly
(C) naturally (D) rapidly

16 According to paragraph 1, what can be inferred about marsupials?

(A) Their pouch is essential to the survival of their offspring.
(B) They can give birth to many offspring at a time.
(C) Every one of them has a pouch.
(D) They are spread evenly in Australia, New Zealand, and New Guinea.

Paragraph 1 is marked with an arrow [➡].

17 The phrase "this region" in the passage refers to

(A) South Pacific region
(B) Australia
(C) island
(D) Americas

18 The word "debatable" in the passage is closest in meaning to

(A) interesting (B) settled
(C) questionable (D) common

19 According to paragraph 2, the first fossils of prehistoric marsupials were discovered in

(A) Africa (B) Australia
(C) North America (D) South America

Paragraph 2 is marked with an arrow [➡].

20 According to paragraph 3, which of the following is NOT true of Gondwana?

(A) South America and Antarctica were a part of Gondwana.
(B) Gondwana was a part of a larger land mass, Laurasia.
(C) Modern-day Australia used to be a part of Gondwana.
(D) Marsupials lived on Gondwana long before it split apart.

Paragraph 3 is marked with an arrow [➡].

21 Why does the author discuss " supercontinents " in the passage?

(A) To show that the prehistoric world was a far different place
(B) To illustrate the broad range of prehistoric marsupials in Australia
(C) To discuss how marsupials and other mammals evolved together
(D) To explain how marsupials migrated to and became isolated in Australia

22 The word " migrated " in the passage is closest in meaning to

(A) spread (B) traveled
(C) fled (D) exiled

23 Which of the sentences below best expresses the essential information in the highlighted sentence in the passage? *Incorrect answer* **choices change the meaning in important ways or leave out essential information.**

(A) Scientists debate whether marsupials survived because Australia was more isolated than other regions or because it had a more favorable location.
(B) Marsupials are believed to have thrived in Australia because they were free of some of the hardship of severe climate change.
(C) Marsupials survived in great numbers in Australia because severe climate change drove competing mammals into extinction.
(D) Marsupials came to greatly outnumber other mammals in Australia because the island drifted away from Antarctica to areas with a colder climate.

24 The word " elude " in the passage is closest in meaning to

(A) scare (B) evade
(C) disrupt (D) manage

25 According to paragraph 5, convergent evolution occurs when

(A) species evolve in a way that is most appropriate to their environment
(B) species that live in isolation from other animals evolve similar sets of traits
(C) species that evolve alongside each other develop differently from other animals
(D) species in different places with similar environments evolve the same traits

Paragraph 5 is marked with an arrow [➡].

26 According to paragraph 5, what is one factor that guided the evolution of both flying squirrels and flying opossums?

(A) They were too easily preyed upon on the ground.
(B) Their main source of food was in trees.
(C) They were forced to adapt to climate change.
(D) Their woodland habitat was disappearing.

Paragraph 5 is marked with an arrow [➡].

27 Look at the four squares [■] that indicate where the following sentence could be added to the passage.

| These two giant land masses were combined forms of the seven continents we know today. |

Where would the sentence best fit?

Click on a square [■] to add the sentence to the passage.

(A) A (B) B (C) C (D) D

28 Directions: An introductory sentence for a brief summary of the passage is provided below. Complete the summary by selecting the THREE answer choices that express the most important ideas in the passage. Some sentences do not belong in the summary because they express ideas that are not presented in the passage or are minor ideas in the passage. ***This question is worth 2 points.***

Drag your answer choices to the spaces where they belong. To remove an answer choice, click on it. To review the passage, click on **View Text**.

Scientists still debate the origins of the marsupials' strong presence in Australia, but their isolation seems related to the separation of the supercontinent.

-
-
-

Answer Choices	
(A) Marsupials arrived in Australia by way of land connections between South America, Antarctica, and Australia as they evolved on Gondwana, one of the two supercontinents.	(D) No marsupials lived in Laurasia, which is why marsupials are not found in North America, formerly a part of Laurasia.
(B) For several millions of years, marsupials lived on the supercontinent Gondwana with other species.	(E) A few species of marsupials still live in South America, which once shared a supercontinent with Australia.
(C) After Gondwana divided into several land masses, Australia drifted toward warmer regions, which enabled marsupials to survive up until today.	(F) Though separate, some species of marsupials evolved to resemble mammals from other continents because they were exposed to similar environmental pressures.

COLONIAL AMERICAN FARMING

1 By the mid-seventeenth century, English colonial settlement in North America stretched from New England in the north to the Carolinas in the south. Early colonial American society was agricultural, with the vast majority of colonists making their living off their land in one form or another. However, considering the breadth of the geographic areas occupied by the colonists, it should not be surprising that the practice of agriculture took different forms in various colonies, and that these different agricultural practices led to the formation of distinct modes of living. This is particularly true when the southern colonies are compared to those of the north.

2 ➡ In the New England colonies, which can roughly be defined as stretching from what is now New York to Maine, agriculture was marginal at best, and farmers' lives involved tough and constant labor. The land was heavily wooded and rocky, so colonists first had to clear areas for planting, literally creating the fields they intended to farm. Most of this work had to be done by hand, as horses and oxen were perpetually in short supply. Even when the laborious task of preparing the fields for planting was completed, New England farmers could expect a sparse harvest. New England soil was poor, and the cold weather meant the growing season was brief. In short, farming in New England was a very humble occupation.

3 ➡ Because of the harsh conditions that prevailed, the most that Northern farmers could hope for was mere subsistence. Given the marginal nature of agriculture in the New England area, there was little sense in acquiring more land than was necessary to support one's family, and farms tended to be small family plots. The difficulties of New England farming also encouraged a high degree of cooperation among neighboring farmers, and it was common for them to trade with one another for necessary supplies, loan each other expensive or hard-to-find equipment such as plows and oxen, and pool their labor when large structures, such as barns, needed to be built. The result was a close-knit, egalitarian society in which the basic social unit was the small town or village.

4 Farmers in the southern colonies, especially those in Virginia and the Carolinas, faced a very different situation. In these areas, agriculture was easier and potentially far more profitable. The soil was rich and fertile, and the climate was much more conducive to farming. Furthermore, the difference in climate and soil composition made it possible to grow different kinds of crops than those grown in New England. Whereas New England farmers simply farmed to live, primarily growing staples such as corn and wheat which they needed to survive, farmers in the southern colonies focused predominately on cash crops such as tobacco, and later, cotton.

5 The difference was an immensely important one. **A** In growing crops for sale rather than for their own personal use, southern farmers had every inducement to acquire vast tracts of land, since more land for more crops would result in greater profits. **B** The commercial nature of southern farming meant that significant gaps in wealth quickly arose, with a small minority of successful farmers acquiring ever more

land and growing ever richer. **C** As a result, a plantation system arose in which a small southern aristocracy of wealthy farmers owned much of the best land, while poorer farmers had to make do with small plots in less-fertile areas. **D**

6 ➡ Moreover, the existence of large plantations meant that the southern population was more dispersed, and southern politics centered around counties covering large areas rather than the small towns and villages of New England. A further consequence of the focus on cash crops and the rise of the plantation system was that southern plantation owners were perpetually short of labor. Whereas New England farmers were able to tend to their relatively small fields using only the labor of their family members and occasionally relying on the help of their neighbors, this was entirely impractical on a southern plantation that might easily cover several hundred acres. It was for this reason that southern colonies made much greater use of slave labor than did farmers in New England.

Glossary

egalitarian: supporting or following ideas that all people are equal and should have the same rights and opportunities

---

29 The phrase "this work" in the passage refers to

(A) harvesting the crops
(B) working in the fields
(C) removing trees and rocks
(D) driving horses and oxen

30 The word "sparse" in the passage is closest in meaning to

(A) joyless
(B) abundant
(C) meager
(D) unripe

31 According to paragraph 2, all of the following created poor farming conditions in New England EXCEPT:

(A) The land was not suitable for farming.
(B) The cold weather made the growing season short.
(C) Access to horses and oxen was limited.
(D) The farmers in New England lacked a sufficient labor force.

Paragraph 2 is marked with an arrow [➡].

32 The word "harsh" in the passage is closest in meaning to

(A) unpredictable   (B) consistent
(C) favorable   (D) severe

33 The word "their" in the passage refers to

(A) farmers   (B) supplies
(C) barns   (D) oxen

34 According to paragraph 3, what was the basic social unit in New England society?

(A) family
(B) village
(C) farm
(D) state

Paragraph 3 is marked with an arrow [→].

35 The phrase "conducive to" in the passage is closest in meaning to

(A) necessary for
(B) favorable to
(C) accustomed to
(D) compliant with

36 The word "predominately" in the passage is closest in meaning to

(A) together
(B) slowly
(C) seriously
(D) primarily

37 The word "inducement" in the passage is closest in meaning to

(A) asset
(B) manner
(C) incentive
(D) merit

38 Which of the sentences below best expresses the essential information in the highlighted sentence in the passage? *Incorrect* answer choices change the meaning in important ways or leave out essential information.

(A) Southern farmers and New England farmers relied heavily on the work of others to keep their fields tended.
(B) Southern plantations were too large to be worked only by one's family and neighbors, as was the case in New England.
(C) New England owners tried to keep their plots small so that it was more practical to maintain their fields.
(D) Because they lacked nearby neighbors, southern plantation owners often could not tend their hundred-acres-sized fields.

39 According to paragraph 6, what effect did the plantation system have on government?

(A) It was localized to small villages and towns.
(B) It was run by those with the most land and money.
(C) It was not often enforced in the rural areas.
(D) It was broad and encompassed large counties.

Paragraph 6 is marked with an arrow [→].

40 According to the passage, what can be inferred about northern and southern farmers?

(A) Despite their best efforts, southern farmers could not succeed in growing staple crops.
(B) Unlike southern farmers, northern farmers were unlikely to become rich from farming.
(C) Northern and southern farmers both had many natural obstacles to overcome.
(D) Northern farmers received much financial aid from the government compared to southern farmers.

41 Look at the four squares [■] that indicate where the following sentence could be added to the passage.

> Southern society was thus more hierarchical than its New England counterpart.

Where would the sentence best fit?

Click on a square [■] to add the sentence to the passage.

(A) A   (B) B   (C) C   (D) D

42 **Directions:** Select the appropriate phrases from the answer choices and match them to the colonial society to which they relate. TWO of the answer choices will NOT be used. *This question is worth 3 points.*

Drag your answer choices to the spaces where they belong. To remove an answer choice, click on it. To review the passage, click on **View Text**.

Answer Choices	New England
(A) Farmed mostly for survival	•
(B) Created a relatively equal society	•
(C) Relied on saleable crops	•
(D) Farmed only for the wealthy	**The Southern Colonies**
(E) Sought more land for greater profits	•
(F) Banned the use of slaves	•
(G) Often helped by family and neighbors	

Actual Test 2

Passage 1

POST-EXCAVATION ANALYSIS

1 ➡ Although one of the main tasks of archaeology is to collect ancient artifacts to piece together how civilizations lived, the analysis and care of these artifacts, once collected, is also of importance. The method of studying objects that have been unearthed via archaeological excavation is referred to as post-excavation analysis. Often there is a need for a distinction between those who excavate artifacts and those who assess and analyze the materials that have been recovered from those sites. In effect, this post-excavation analysis is crucial for archaeologists to record not only discoveries made on site, but to also provide a record that will be available for future research. These records are important for archaeologists to refer to as they try to make objective inferences about their discoveries. Over the past few decades, the archaeological community has witnessed several considerable improvements in scientific technology, allowing archaeologists more accuracy when analyzing and dating objects. For the most part, the initial steps of this post-excavation analysis are carried out in general laboratories, while methods that call for more thorough precision take place in specialized labs. These methods have become indispensable for the analysis of inorganic materials that are collected, namely pottery, stone tools, and metals.

2 ➡ Pottery is of particular interest to archaeologists, since it provides clues as to how a civilization's economy and social infrastructure would have functioned, as pottery was used by almost everyone in a civilization. **A** It is considered an extremely valuable artifact, as it is able to withstand most environmental conditions and is therefore usually well preserved, even after hundreds of years. **B** There are several common systems and techniques that researchers use to classify pieces or shards of pottery. **C** For example, in order to classify pieces of pottery by color, researchers use a system called the Munsell color system. **D** This is important because under certain storage conditions, pottery can undergo secondary coloration. Researchers also make use of the Munsell color system to distinguish colors of the surface, outer layers, and the core of the shard, all of which can have their color affected by the environment over an extended period of time. As well as the Munsell color chart, researchers make use of petrology, which is the study of the characteristics of rocks that influence the degree of hardness and strength of the pottery material. By examining these characteristics with great scrutiny, researchers can provide a more precise location for the origin of the pottery.

3 ➡ The second most popular area of post-excavation analysis of inorganic remains is that of stone tools. For the vast majority of prehistoric sites, stone tools are a significant indicator of how early humans went about their daily lives. Although archaeologists are tasked with studying the physical qualities of finished tools, they must also direct a fair amount of focus on the rock material that prehistoric peoples used to craft their stone tools. By studying the surfaces of finished tools as well as rock material, archaeologists can make inferences as to how the tools were manufactured. Based on how the tools are manufactured, archaeologists can then classify the tools into specific categories according to their size, shape, usage, color, and material.

4 ➡ The third most common post-excavation method of analysis of inorganic material used by archaeologists

is the domain of metallurgical analysis. When metal objects are found, archaeologists first need to implement scrupulous cleaning methods to prevent them from further deteriorating, followed by refurbishing the metal artifact. The first method used to carry this out is called electrolysis, which is necessary for archaeologists to give the metal artifact preliminary treatment before undergoing more intense scrutiny. For example, if scientists discover a metal artifact underground, the artifact may have accumulated an encrustation of soil and sediment around it, which can erode the surface of the metal. After the metal artifact has been carefully and thoroughly cleaned, archaeologists can then study in detail its composition, as well as any evident peculiarities of its manufacturing. In certain situations, the metal artifact can be placed in a special kind of scanning electron microscope, which is useful for studying the details of the manufacture of such items like jewelry and weapons.

01 The word " thorough " in the passage is closest in meaning to

(A) critical
(B) complete
(C) organized
(D) extensive

02 According to paragraph 1, why is post-excavation analysis important?

(A) It facilitates the process of studying objects that have been unearthed.
(B) It provides crucial insight into the daily life and rituals of ancient civilizations.
(C) It allows them to record onsite discoveries and keep records for later research.
(D) It makes further improvements in the technology used in excavation.

Paragraph 1 is marked with an arrow [➡].

03 Why does the author mention " Munsell color system " in the passage?

(A) To show that classification according to color is not reliable
(B) To emphasize the need for detailed analysis of the physical properties of pottery
(C) To illustrate the difficulty of classifying pottery based on color
(D) To give an example of classification methods of pottery pieces

04 The phrase " As well as " in the passage is closest in meaning to

(A) Due to
(B) Similar to
(C) As for
(D) In addition to

05 The word " scrutiny " in the passage is closest in meaning to

(A) examination
(B) basis
(C) control
(D) deliberation

06 All of the following are mentioned in paragraph 2 EXCEPT:

(A) Characteristics of pottery are classified using the Munsell color system.
(B) Pottery is generally well preserved even after long periods of time.
(C) Pottery was used by upper-class citizens as a status symbol of wealth.
(D) Pottery discoveries indicate how a society's economy and infrastructure operated.

Paragraph 2 is marked with an arrow [➡].

07 Which of the sentences below best expresses the essential information in the highlighted sentence in the passage? *Incorrect* answer choices change the meaning in important ways or leave out essential information.

(A) Because the rock material of stone tools is the most important physical quality, archaeologists devote most of their time studying it.
(B) Archeologists have to focus on the rock material used to make stone tools, as well as the physical attributes of refined tools.
(C) Despite several physical qualities necessary for the study of stone tools, archaeologists prefer to focus on the study of rock material.
(D) Archaeologists spend a large amount of time studying rock material in order to understand the material's physical properties.

08 According to paragraph 3, which of the following is true of the post-excavation analysis of stone tools?

(A) Stone tools provide more information regarding prehistoric daily life than pottery does.
(B) Researchers make discoveries about early societies based on the rock material of stone tools.
(C) Analysis of stone tools is always a powerful indicator for every prehistoric site.
(D) Rock material is an indicating factor for the manufacturing of stone tools.

Paragraph 3 is marked with an arrow [➡].

09 The word " erode " in the passage is closest in meaning to

(A) break down   (B) wear away
(C) fortify   (D) mend

10 According to paragraph 4, what is necessary for archaeologists to do before analyzing metal objects?

(A) They must do a preliminary analysis of the excavated earth metal objects.
(B) They must employ cleaning techniques similar to those used in the analysis of stone tools.
(C) They must remove encrustation that builds up on the surface of unearthed metal objects.
(D) They must ensure that cleaning methods they employ do not further damage the objects.

Paragraph 4 is marked with an arrow [➡].

11 Which of the following best describes the way paragraph 4 is organized?

(A) A description of the steps necessary for analyzing metal objects
(B) A comparison of the methods employed for analyzing metal objects
(C) Reasons why archaeologists face several challenges in analyzing metal objects
(D) An analysis of the pros and cons of refurbishing metal objects

Paragraph 4 is marked with an arrow [➡].

12 Which of the following can be concluded from the passage?

(A) Conclusions drawn from post-excavation analysis are somewhat inaccurate and open for further discussion.
(B) Post-excavation analysis became a promising job due to its growing importance in archaeology.
(C) Insufficient technological resources are major obstacles for post-excavation analysis.
(D) Knowledge of ancient civilizations has increased due to post-excavation analysis and research.

13 **Look at the four squares [■] that indicate where the following sentence could be added to the passage.**

> This system provides extremely detailed information on the hue, lightness, and color purity of the soil the pottery pieces are found in.

Where would the sentence best fit?

Click on a square [■] to add the sentence to the passage.

(A) **A**　　　　(B) **B**　　　　(C) **C**　　　　(D) **D**

14 **Directions:** Select the appropriate phrases from the answer choices and match them to the category of artifacts to which they relate. TWO of the answer choices will NOT be used. ***This question is worth 3 points.***

Drag your answer choices to the spaces where they belong. To remove an answer choice, click on it. To review the passage, click on **View Text**.

Answer Choices	Pottery
(A) Use of electrolysis in cleaning objects (B) Studying rock material used in manufacturing process (C) Use of petrology for classification (D) Need for highly advanced devices for unearthing objects (E) Requiring color system for classification (F) Employing scanning devices for detailed study under certain conditions (G) Onsite implementation of object analysis	• •
	Stone Tools
	•
	Metal Artifacts
	• •

Passage 2

ICE AGE EXTINCTION EVENT

1   The end of the last Ice Age brought many dramatic changes to planet Earth. Among them was the sudden mass extinction of countless animal species throughout the world. Some well-known examples include the woolly mammoth, the saber-tooth tiger, and the giant sloth. Because of their enormous size, these animals are referred to as megafauna. Though a few species of megafauna survive today, like the elephant and the rhinoceros, most of them were wiped out during this Ice Age extinction event. The reasons for such a wide-ranging extinction of megafauna are still unclear to scientists. Two major theories have been proposed to explain it, though each theory has its limitations.

2   → One theory states that early humans had an active role in the extinction of megafauna through hunting. As the climate warmed and the ice sheets retreated, humans began migrating to new areas of the world, such as the Americas and the northern regions of Europe and Asia, which were previously uninhabited. Animals in these new lands were not adapted to living with humans, who were already proficient predators. Unaware of the threat humans posed, they did not know to flee them. They were also not equipped with the defenses they needed to avoid or fight off human attacks, and as a result these animals were hunted to extinction. Evidence supporting this theory comes from the fact that mass extinctions of megafauna occurred far more often in lands where human migrations took place, as opposed to areas where animals and humans evolved alongside one another. Very few surviving ancestors of megafauna remain in the Western Hemisphere, for example, whereas certain megafauna still exist in great numbers in Africa and South Asia, two regions where humans evolved alongside large mammals.

3   While the arrival of humans does coincide with the beginning of the extinction event, this does not constitute definitive proof for some scientists. These scientists claim that there is no evidence that any species of megafauna was regularly hunted by humans. The major exception to this is, of course, the woolly mammoth, the skeletons of which frequently display evidence of wounds inflicted by man-made weapons. Fossils from other megafauna have yet to yield such evidence, however, casting doubt on the idea that humans hunted megafauna to extinction. A further cause for skepticism is that some heavily hunted animals thrived during this period and even survive today. One example is the bison, an animal that is much hunted and whose ancestors have roamed the earth for tens of thousands of years. If the bison could be so heavily hunted and still survive this extinction event, some scientists reason that most megafauna should have survived human interference as well.

4   → **A** Besides the hunting theory, there is another prominent theory set forth to explain the Ice Age extinction event. **B** This one is concerned primarily with climate. **C** After all, it was a sharp rise in temperature that melted the frozen earth and brought about the end of the Ice Age. **D** Higher temperatures introduced several challenges to the prehistoric climate. Land that was once covered by forests became prairies and grasslands. This ecological change could have had any number of negative effects on megafauna. For one, it would have robbed some species of the shelter and safety provided by forests. In

the forest, giant mammals could obscure themselves from smaller but faster predators. Roaming the open grasslands, however, made them far more vulnerable to predators. The biggest impact of this change would have been the change in food supply. Higher temperatures led to irregular rainfall. As a result, only those plants well adapted to the new weather patterns survived. This further changed the kinds of plants that were available to megafauna. Different plants meant that many herbivores could not get their usual vital nutrients, and many suffered because of this.

5 ➡ However, this theory has a few problems of its own. One observation is that large herbivores had survived previous periods of climate change. Extinction events of this severity had not occurred during other periods of similar change. Other scientists argue that the transformation from woodlands to grasslands would have provided more food for giant herbivores, and should actually have aided in their survival. Some evidence even shows that grazing animals had a lower rate of extinction than animals with mixed diets. While neither theory holds up on its own, many scientists can agree that some combination of these two theories can probably explain the Ice Age extinction event.

15 Which of the sentences below best expresses the essential information in the highlighted sentence in the passage? *Incorrect answer* choices change the meaning in important ways or leave out essential information.

(A) A few species of megafauna survived in the Western Hemisphere, but did not fare as well in areas with an early human presence.
(B) More megafauna exist in areas where they evolved alongside humans than in areas to which humans later migrated.
(C) The migration of megafauna to the Western Hemisphere made them more vulnerable to extinction through human hunting.
(D) Having hunted megafauna to near extinction in Africa and Asia, early humans evolved alongside megafauna in the West.

16 According to paragraph 2, what prompted humans to inhabit new parts of the world?

(A) The worsening of climate conditions
(B) A growth in the population of megafauna
(C) A food shortage in their previous habitats
(D) The melting of ice due to milder temperatures

Paragraph 2 is marked with an arrow [➡].

17 According to paragraph 2, what can be inferred about megafauna that survived human attacks?

(A) They were so dangerous that humans had to avoid them.
(B) They evolved so that they could defend themselves from human attacks.
(C) Their population was so large that human attacks had little effect on their survival.
(D) Humans did not feel it was necessary to hunt them because they were not needed.

Paragraph 2 is marked with an arrow [➡].

18 The phrase "coincide with" in the passage is closest in meaning to

(A) have nothing to do with
(B) interfere with
(C) happen at the same time
(D) account for

19 The word "this" in the passage refers to

(A) the fact that most megafauna did not survive to the present
(B) the theory that megafauna were hunted into extinction
(C) the lack of direct evidence that megafauna were hunted by man
(D) the idea that megafauna were not accustomed to humans

20 Why does the author mention the "bison" in the passage?

(A) To give an example of one species that was hunted to near extinction
(B) To argue against the theory that hunting caused the extinction event
(C) To contradict the assertion that early humans hunted megafauna
(D) To support the theory that man caused the extinction of megafauna

21 The word "prominent" in the passage is closest in meaning to

(A) effective
(B) outstanding
(C) feasible
(D) conflicting

22 The word "challenges" in the passage is closest in meaning to

(A) advantages
(B) difficulties
(C) changes
(D) impacts

23 The word "obscure" in the passage is closest in meaning to

(A) control
(B) protect
(C) prevent
(D) hide

24 According to paragraph 4, scientists who support the climate theory believe all of the following to be consequences of higher temperatures EXCEPT

(A) the disappearance of woodlands
(B) the difference in patterns of rainfall
(C) the appearance of new megafauna
(D) the change in the native plant life

Paragraph 4 is marked with an arrow [→].

25 The word "transformation" in the passage is closest in meaning to

(A) advancement
(B) change
(C) destruction
(D) variety

26 According to paragraph 5, some scientists believe that the increase in grasslands

(A) impeded humans' ability to adapt to new environments
(B) could have provided more food for megafauna
(C) was responsible for the extinction of large herbivores
(D) may have increased the hunting of megafauna

Paragraph 5 is marked with an arrow [→].

27 Look at the four squares [■] that indicate where the following sentence could be added to the passage.

> The major catalyst in this theory is temperature.

Where would the sentence best fit?

Click on a square [■] to add the sentence to the passage.

(A) A (B) B (C) C (D) D

28 **Directions:** An introductory sentence for a brief summary of the passage is provided below. Complete the summary by selecting the THREE answer choices that express the most important ideas in the passage. Some sentences do not belong in the summary because they express ideas that are not presented in the passage or are minor ideas in the passage. ***This question is worth 2 points.***

Drag your answer choices to the spaces where they belong. To remove an answer choice, click on it. To review the passage, click on **View Text**.

There are two major theories that explain why megafauna became extinct as the last Ice Age ended.
•
•
•

Answer Choices	
(A) The reason why megafauna were wiped out had remained a mystery to scientists for a long time.	(D) Some scientists argue that ecological changes caused by rising temperatures were responsible for the extinction of megafauna.
(B) It is suggested that excessive hunting of megafauna by early humans resulted in their extinction.	(E) The two theories both have flaws, but a synthesis of the two may bring us closer to understanding the Ice Age extinction event.
(C) The Americas and northern Europe were not inhabited by humans or megafauna before the Ice Age ended.	(F) The bison is one example that shows megafauna can survive despite hunting by humans.

SHALE OIL AND OIL SANDS

1   Crude oil has become a fixture in modern lifestyles all over the world. Without it, there would be no fuel for cars, no asphalt for our roads or buildings, and no raw material from which to make the plastics and other oil that are essential to modern life. The world consumes over 80 million barrels of oil each day, and the number continues to grow. Unfortunately, oil is a limited resource, and although demand for this valuable resource rapidly increases, many experts claim that the world supply has already passed its summit and is on the decline. For this reason, petroleum companies are exploring new sources of crude oil, namely shale oil and oil sands.

2   ➡ Shale oil is produced from a substance known as oil shale, which is a type of rock that contains all the basic elements of petroleum. Oil shale consists mainly of kerogen, the decayed organic matter found in sedimentary rock that precedes the formation of crude oil. This substance can be extracted from the rock in which it is trapped and refined into a usable form of petroleum. Oil shale was used in prehistoric times as a source of fire, as the chemicals in it make it readily flammable. Even today, some countries still use unrefined oil shale as fuel for power plants. The most notable of these is Estonia, where domestic oil shale is a cheaper option than crude oil. The largest deposits of oil shale in the world can be found in the western United States, in an area known as the Green River basin. Along with giant deposits in Russia and Brazil, these reserves make up over 85 percent of the world's supply of oil shale.

3   ➡ In most parts of the world, however, oil shale is mined for the purpose of being processed into crude oil. Many people believe that shale oil may one day help to meet the world's growing demand for petroleum, and perhaps extend the world's supply of crude oil for a while. However, it has yet to overcome a few important drawbacks. Oil shale mining can be very destructive to the environment, as it involves clearing land of trees and digging up large amounts of earth to uncover the oil shale. Another obstacle is in processing the raw materials. The most common method of processing oil shale is by heating it in a vacuum, causing it to release kerogen in the form of a vapor, which can then be trapped and distilled, creating a kind of synthetic crude oil. All this additional processing takes time and comes at a cost. At present, the process of mining and refining oil shale is very expensive, more so than that of producing traditional crude oil. As refining technology becomes more advanced, it will be cheaper to produce oil from these rocks, hopefully making shale oil as widely used as traditional oil.

4   Another nontraditional source of petroleum is oil sands. Oil sands occur when crude oil bubbles to the surface of the earth and mixes with water, dirt, and various bacteria which, over time, work to break the oil down into a very thick tar-like substance. Its thickness is so great that it cannot flow unless strongly heated. However, its heavy, sticky nature makes it handy for paving roads as a component of asphalt. Today, the largest supply of oil sands can be found in Canada and Venezuela. Presently, oil sand reserves account for two-thirds of the world's entire supply of petroleum.

5 ➡ Today, the only nation with a large-scale, commercially exploited oil sands industry is Canada. Oil sands account for nearly half of Canada's total oil production; production is so great, in fact, that Canada has become the number one supplier of oil to the United States, surpassing even Middle Eastern oil-producing nations. **A** Because oil sands are too thick to flow like regular crude oil, they do not pool into the kind of pressurized wells from which traditional oil is often pumped. **B** However, wells can be artificially created by injecting hot steam into large reserves of oil sands, simultaneously heating and diluting them so that they flow more like crude oil. **C** Only then can the oil sands be extracted; and as with shale oil, this mining process can be quite expensive and use a great deal of energy. **D** Experts continue to look for cheaper and more efficient methods of mining and processing oil sands, as their abundance could have a major impact on the world's falling supply of oil in the near future.

Glossary

petroleum: an oil mixture of hydro carbons that can be extracted from layers of rock and used to produce fuel

---

29 The word "summit" in the passage is closest in meaning to

(A) nadir (B) peak
(C) average (D) limit

30 The phrase "This substance" in the passage refers to

(A) shale oil (B) kerogen
(C) petroleum (D) crude oil

31 The word "readily" in the passage is closest in meaning to

(A) effectively (B) slowly
(C) quickly (D) easily

32 According to paragraph 2, which of the following is NOT true of shale oil?

(A) It is created from organic matter.
(B) It can be used as a source of fire without refining it.
(C) It is not ready for practical use yet.
(D) The United States, Russia, and Brazil have large deposits of it.

Paragraph 2 is marked with an arrow [➡].

33 The word "synthetic" in the passage is closest in meaning to

(A) primitive (B) useful
(C) artificial (D) impractical

34 In paragraph 3, why does the author give details about oil shale mining process?

(A) To compare its mining process with that of crude oil
(B) To argue that oil shale is a cheaper option than crude oil
(C) To refute the argument that oil shale can be an alternative fuel source
(D) To show a problematic aspect of oil shale development

Paragraph 3 is marked with an arrow [➡].

35 According to paragraph 3, what can be inferred about processing shale oil?

(A) It comes from traditional practices.
(B) It is harmful to the environment.
(C) It is a very limited practice.
(D) It is too costly to be practical.

Paragraph 3 is marked with an arrow [➡].

36 Which of the sentences below best expresses the essential information in the highlighted sentence in the passage? *Incorrect* answer choices change the meaning in important ways or leave out essential information.

(A) When crude oil bubbles to the surface, it is transformed by bacteria and water into a thick substance called oil sands.
(B) Oil sands are a tar-like substance created by the exposure of surface oil deposits to water, dirt, and bacteria.
(C) Crude oil is the substance produced when oil sands bubble to the surface after years of mixing with water and dirt.
(D) Water, dirt, and bacteria mix with crude oil to create a tarry substance called oil sands that then bubbles to the surface.

37 The word "exploited" in the passage is closest in meaning to

(A) developed   (B) obtained
(C) altered   (D) stored

38 The word "simultaneously" in the passage is closest in meaning to

(A) extremely   (B) concurrently
(C) respectively   (D) in a timely manner

39 The word "their" in the passage refers to

(A) oil sands   (B) reserves
(C) methods   (D) experts

40 According to paragraph 5, why are shale oil and oil sands important?

(A) They provide cheaper energy for households.
(B) They can be made into cleaner fuels.
(C) They could compensate for decreasing oil supplies.
(D) They have the potential to be depleted soon.

Paragraph 5 is marked with an arrow [➡].

41 Look at the four squares [■] that indicate where the following sentence could be added to the passage.

> Adding to the expense is the cost of shipping oil sands, as they are too thick to flow through traditional pipelines.

Where would the sentence best fit?

Click on a square [■] to add the sentence to the passage.

(A) A   (B) B   (C) C   (D) D

42 Directions: Select the appropriate phrases from the answer choices and match them to the category of oil to which they relate. TWO of the answer choices will NOT be used. **This question is worth 4 points.**

Drag your answer choices to the spaces where they belong. To remove an answer choice, click on it. To review the passage, click on **View Text**.

Answer Choices	Shale Oil
(A) Expensive mining process	•
(B) About two-thirds of the world's oil supply	•

	Oil Sands
(C) Used for fire by prehistoric peoples	
(D) Large deposits in Venezuela	•
(E) A renewable resource, unlike petroleum	•
(F) Use of environmentally harmful mining techniques	•
(G) Traditionally used as a component of asphalt	•

	Both
(H) Potential to be a cleaner fuel than crude oil	
(I) Must be heavily processed because of thickness and stickiness	•

MEMO

MEMO

MEMO

New Edition
i TOEFL iBT® READING

Answer Key & Explanations

Diagnostic Test	A2
Part A Question Types	A2
Part B Approaching Themes	A60
Actual Test	A143

Diagnostic Test

Passage 1
01 (D) **02** (D) **03** (B) **04** (B) **05** (D) **06** (B) **07** (B) **08** (A) **09** (D) **10** (B) **11** (C) **12** (A)
13 (C) **14** (A), (D), (E)

Passage 2
15 (C) **16** (B) **17** (A) **18** (D) **19** (C) **20** (C) **21** (D) **22** (A) **23** (B) **24** (B) **25** (D) **26** (C)
27 [Continuity Theory – (A), (C), (F)], [Discontinuity Theory – (D), (G)]

Passage 3
28 (A) **29** (B) **30** (C) **31** (D) **32** (A) **33** (B) **34** (B) **35** (D) **36** (B) **37** (D) **38** (C) **39** (B)
40 (D) **41** (B), (E), (F)

PART A | Question Types

Chapter 01 Vocabulary

Sample Question
p.29

A lion pride will typically have one to six mature males. Marked by their famous manes, mature males are easily recognizable. The males will rule over a group of females that is nearly always more numerous than the group of males. Male lions display little interest in their cubs in the first year of their lives. As the male cubs approach sexual maturity, however, the older males become more aggressive and hostile toward them. At the age of two, the male cubs are expelled from the pride by the older males so that they will not become rivals for the females.	대체로 한 마리에서 여섯 마리의 성인 수컷 사자가 한 무리 안에 있다. 다 자란 수컷 사자는 유명한 갈기로 특징지어져 쉽게 알아볼 수 있다. 수컷 사자들은 거의 항상 수컷 집단보다 많은 암컷 집단을 거느리게 된다. 수컷 사자는 새끼가 태어난 첫해에는 새끼에게 관심을 보이지 않는다. 그러나 수컷 새끼 사자들이 성적으로 성숙한 시기가 되면 나이 든 수컷 사자들은 어린 수컷 사자들에게 더 공격적이고 적대적으로 된다. 두 살이 되면, 새끼 수컷 사자들은 암컷을 두고 라이벌 관계를 형성하지 않기 위해 나이 든 수컷 사자들에 의해 무리에서 방출된다.

지문의 mature 와 의미상 가장 가까운 것은?
(A) 지배적인
(B) 공격적인
(C) 가임의
(D) 성인의

어휘 | pride (사자의) 무리 **typically** 대체로 **mature** 다 자란, 성숙한 **marked by** ~로 특징지어지는, 표시되어 있는 **mane** 갈기 **numerous** 많은 **cub** (곰, 사자, 여우 등의) 새끼 **maturity** 성숙 **aggressive** 공격적인 **hostile** 적대적인 **expel** 방출하다, 추방하다

Basic Drill
p.30

01 (B) **02** (A) **03** (D) **04** (C) **05** (D) **06** (B)

Vocab Quiz **01** main **02** typical **03** dwindled **04** deficiency **05** continuously **06** supplements

01

Epic poems are long stories, told in rhymed verses, which usually tell of a war or the adventures of a great hero. They were one of the major forms of literature in the ancient world. In fact, epic poems probably predate writing, because they were originally recited orally, and were only written down much later. The oldest known epic poem is the Sumerian *Epic of Gilgamesh*. As with many epics, its author is anonymous because it was passed down orally for generations before it was written down. Therefore, an epic poem is often best viewed as the work of a culture rather than of a single author.

서사시는 운율이 있는 시로 된 긴 이야기로서, 주로 전쟁이나 위대한 영웅의 모험담을 들려준다. 서사시는 고대 세계에서 가장 주요한 문학 형태 중 하나였다. 사실, 서사시는 본래 구전으로 암송되었고 훨씬 후에 기록되었기 때문에 글보다 아마 앞서 있었을 것이다. 가장 오래된 것으로 알려진 서사시는 수메르의 『길가메시 서사시』이다. 많은 서사시가 그렇듯, 이것 역시 기록되기 이전에 여러 세대에 걸쳐 구전으로 전해 내려왔기 때문에 필자는 미상이다. 그러므로 서사시는 어떤 한 작가의 작품이라기보다는 한 문화의 창작물로 보는 경우가 많다.

지문의 anonymous 와 의미상 가장 가까운 것은?

(A) 유명한
(B) 알려지지 않은
(C) 운이 좋은
(D) 분명한

해설 | anonymous 의 의미는 서사시가 여러 세대에 걸쳐 구전으로 전해 내려 왔다는 사실로부터 unknown의 뜻을 가졌음을 알 수 있다.

어휘 | epic poem 서사시   **rhymed** 운율이 있는   **verse** 시, 시구   **predate** 앞서다   **orally** 구전으로, 입으로   **pass down** 전해오다

02

Rocks can essentially be classified into three types according to how they are formed. Sedimentary rock, such as limestone, is formed from small particles that have worn away. As these particles pile up, the pressure compacts them to form solid layers. A second type, metamorphic rock, refers to rock that has changed its chemical and physical composition due to intense heat and pressure. Marble and slate are common examples of metamorphic rock. The third type is igneous rock, which is formed through an exothermic reaction, the loss of heat. A common example is basalt, which is formed when molten lava cools.

기본적으로 암석은 형성되는 방법에 따라 세 가지로 분류될 수 있다. 석회암과 같은 퇴적암은 닳아진 작은 입자들로부터 형성된다. 이러한 입자들이 쌓임에 따라, 압력은 입자들이 단단한 층들을 형성하도록 압축한다. 두 번째 종류인 변성암은 뜨거운 열과 압력으로 인해 화학적 구성과 물리적 구성이 달라진 암석을 일컫는다. 대리석과 점판암은 변성암의 일반적인 예이다. 세 번째 종류는 화성암인데, 이것은 발열 반응을 통해 열을 잃어 형성된다. 흔한 예는 현무암인데, 이것은 녹은 용암이 식을 때 형성된다.

지문의 worn away 와 의미상 가장 가까운 것은?

(A) 침식된
(B) 압축된
(C) 뭉친
(D) 뜨거워진

해설 | worn away 는 '침식된, 차츰 닳은'이라는 의미이다.

어휘 | sedimentary rock 퇴적암   **limestone** 석회암, 석회석   **particle** 입자, 조각   **metamorphic rock** 변성암
refer to ~을 일컫다, ~을 언급하다   **marble** 대리석   **slate** 점판암   **igneous rock** 화성암   **exothermic** 발열의, 발열성의
basalt 현무암   **molten** 녹은   **lava** 용암

03

Until about 1100 AD, Dorset culture was widespread throughout most of the Canadian Arctic and the west coast of Greenland. Over the next 300 or so years, however, the culture shrank and eventually disappeared. Theories for its disappearance vary. The predominant theory involves the Thule people, the ancestors of modern-day Inuit, who began to migrate east around 1200 AD. The Thule possessed more advanced weapons, such as bows

서기 1100년 경까지 도셋 문화는 대부분의 캐나다 북극 지방과 그린란드의 서부 해안을 통해 널리 퍼졌다. 그러나 이후 300년 정도 동안, 이 문화는 위축되었고 마침내는 사라지고 말았다. 이 문화가 사라진 것에 대한 이론들은 다양하다. 가장 지배적인 이론은 서기 1200년경 동쪽으로 이주하기 시작한 지금의 이누이트 족의 선조인 툴레 인들과 관련 있다. 툴레 인들은 활과 화살 같은 더 발달한 무기들을 소유했으며, 도셋 인들에 비하면 더 훌륭한 사냥꾼들이었다. 또한, 툴레 인들은 도셋 인들이 취약했던 질병들을 가지고 있었을지도 모른다

and arrows, and were better hunters compared to the Dorset. It is also thought that the Thule may have carried diseases which the Dorset were susceptible to. Anthropologists believe these two factors contributed to the decline of Dorset culture.

고 추측된다. 인류학자들은 이러한 두 가지 요인이 도세트 문화의 쇠퇴를 가져왔다고 생각한다.

지문의 susceptible to 와 의미상 가장 가까운 것은?

(A) ~에 도움이 되는
(B) ~에 면역을 지닌
(C) ~에 책임이 있는
(D) ~에 피해를 당하기 쉬운

해설 | 도세트 문화의 쇠퇴를 가져왔다는 내용의 "… contributed to the decline of Dorset culture"에서 도세트 인들은 이 질병에 취약(피해를 당하기 쉬웠)했음을 알 수 있다.

어휘 | **widespread** 널리 퍼진　**predominant** 지배적인, 우세한　**ancestor** 선조, 조상　**migrate** 이주하다, 이동하다　**weapon** 무기　**bow** 활　**arrow** 화살　**anthropologist** 인류학자

04

The New England and middle colonies were at a relative disadvantage with regard to their lack of staples to exchange for English finished goods, but the abundance of their own shipping and mercantile enterprises worked in their favor. This was not to the liking of the British, who wished to ensure their own dominance in shipping and their importance as the sole lifeline to the colonies. After 1660, the English government raised prohibitive duties against certain major colonial exports. This hit the New York and New England colonies especially hard, and resulted in an unfavorable trade balance.

뉴잉글랜드와 중부 식민지들은 영국의 완제품들과 교환할 주요 산물들이 부족하다는 점에서 상대적으로 불리했지만, 자체 물류와 무역 회사들이 풍부하다는 점이 이점으로 작용했다. 해운업에서 우세한 위치를 유지하고 단 하나의 보급로로서 식민지에 미치는 영향력을 계속 행사하고자 했던 영국에게 이것은 마음에 들지 않는 것이었다. 1660년 이후, 영국 정부는 특정 식민지 주력 수출품들에 대해 금지적 관세를 높였다. 이것은 뉴욕과 뉴잉글랜드 식민지에 특히 타격을 입혔으며, 불리한 무역 수지를 낳았다.

지문의 unfavorable 과 의미상 가장 가까운 것은?

(A) 유망한
(B) 장려하는
(C) 불리한
(D) 불가피한

해설 | 영국이 뉴잉글랜드와 중부 식민지들의 주력 수출품들에 금지적 관세를 높임으로써 어떠한 무역 수지 결과를 낳았는지를 추측할 수 있다. 이 내용을 통해 unfavorable 은 '불리한'의 의미를 지녔음을 알 수 있다.

어휘 | **colony** 식민지　**staple** 주요 산물　**abundance** 풍부함　**dominance** 우세　**sole** 단 하나의　**lifeline** 보급로, 생명선　**prohibitive duty** 금지적 관세(수입 금지와 같은 효과를 올리기 위해 부과되는 고율의 관세)　**export** 수출품　**trade balance** 무역 수지

05

Since it was first diagnosed in 1981, AIDS has steadily spread into an epidemic across the United States. There are approximately one million Americans, or 0.06 percent of the total population, currently living with HIV, the viral precursor to full-blown AIDS. Those infections are unevenly distributed throughout society, however. African-Americans make up nearly 50 percent of all cases of HIV, despite the fact that they account for only 13 percent of the population. The statistics for African-American women are particularly grim, with African-Americans making up 72 percent of all female virus carriers. Infection rates among Latin-Americans, the other major minority group in America, are similarly lopsided.

에이즈는 1981년 처음 진단된 이후 지속적으로 미국에 전염병으로 퍼져 갔다. 전체 인구의 0.06%인 백만 가까이의 미국인들이 현재 완전히 진행된 에이즈의 바이러스 전조로 볼 수 있는 HIV를 가지고 살아간다. 하지만 이 감염은 불균등하게 분포되어 있다. 아프리카계 미국인들의 경우에는 전 인구의 13%만을 차지한다는 사실에도 불구하고 전체 HIV 감염자의 거의 50%를 차지한다. 아프리카계 미국인 여성에 대한 통계수치는 특히 암울한데, 아프리카계 미국인들이 전체 여성 보균자 중 72%를 차지하기 때문이다. 미국의 다른 주요 소수 민족인 라틴아메리카인들의 감염 비율도 마찬가지로 불균등하다.

지문의 distributed와 의미상 가장 가까운 것은?

(A) 치료된
(B) 평가된
(C) 예방된
(D) 퍼뜨려진

해설 | 동의어 단서를 찾을 수 있는 문제이다. 지문은 미국 내의 에이즈 감염에 대해 시사하고 있다. 이를 통해 distributed 는 첫 문장의 spread와 같은 의미를 지녔음을 알 수 있다.

어휘 | **diagnose** 진단하다　**steadily** 지속적으로　**epidemic** 전염병　**viral** 바이러스의　**precursor** 전조　**full-blown** (병이) 완전히 진행된, 만발한　**unevenly** 불균등하게　**distribute** 분포시키다　**grim** 암울한　**carrier** 보균자　**lopsided** 불균등한, 한쪽으로 치우친

06

One of the most famous architects in history, Frank Lloyd Wright is remembered for his emphasizing the dictum, "Form follows function." That motto is the basis of "functionalism," which gave rise to Wright's own design for the Guggenheim Museum in New York City. One of the world's most famous art museums, the Guggenheim Museum is built around a great helical gallery several stories in height. The gallery comprises a broad ramp along which works of art are displayed. Thus, the building's form — a structure built around a broad, helical ramp — complements its function, which is to display a large number of exhibits within a limited space and in an easily accessible setting.

역사상 가장 유명한 건축가 중 한 명인 Frank Lloyd Wright는 '형태는 기능을 따른다'라는 금언을 강조한 것으로 기억된다. 이 좌우명은 '기능주의'의 기반인데, 기능주의는 Wright 본인이 구상한 뉴욕의 구겐하임 미술관을 탄생시켰다. 세계에서 가장 유명한 미술관 중 하나인 구겐하임 미술관은 높이가 여러 층에 이르는 거대한 나선형의 화랑으로 지어졌다. 화랑은 예술 작품들이 전시된 것을 따라 있는 넓은 경사로로 구성되어 있다. 그래서 건물의 형태, 즉 넓은 나선형의 경사로로 건축된 구조는 제한된 공간 안에 많은 전시물을 전시하고 쉽게 접근할 수 있도록 그 기능을 보완한다.

지문의 comprises와 의미상 가장 가까운 것은?

(A) 구별한다
(B) ~로 구성된다
(C) 개성을 부여한다
(D) ~을 강조한다

해설 | comprises 의 의미는 이 건물이 나선형 경사로로 건축되어 있다는 뒤 문장을 통해 추측할 수 있다. 여기에서 comprises 는 '~로 구성되다'의 의미를 지녔음을 알 수 있다.

어휘 | **architect** 건축가　**dictum** 금언　**motto** 좌우명, 금언　**functionalism** 기능주의　**give rise to** ~을 탄생[발생]시키다　**helical** 나선형의　**ramp** 경사로　**complement** 보완하다　**accessible** 쉽게 접근할 수 있는

Reading Practice p.34

01 (B)　**02** (A)　**03** (C)　**04** (C)　**05** (D)

AGE OF THE EARTH

Calculating the age of the Earth has been a problem that philosophers, scientists, and historians have been tackling for ages. Before the advent of modern-day radiometric dating, pinpointing the age of the Earth was open to great interpretation.

Though many had put an age to the Earth, the first to employ a scientific approach was Lord Kelvin in the nineteenth century. His estimate of 100 million years was based on his calculations of heat transfer within the Earth and from the Sun to the Earth. However, the mathematical model he developed did not include nuclear fusion, which creates the heat in the Sun, or plate tectonics — scientific discoveries that were not made until much later. Nevertheless, Q01 though his estimate was incorrect, it is recognized as one of the first to employ the scientific method in determining the age of the Earth.

지구의 나이

지구의 나이를 계산하는 것은 철학자, 과학자, 그리고 역사학자들이 오랫동안 씨름해왔던 문제였다. 현대의 방사성 연대 측정법이 도래하기 이전에, 지구의 나이를 특정하는 것에 대해서는 다양한 해석이 있었다.

많은 이들이 지구의 나이를 추측했지만, 첫 번째로 과학적인 접근법을 사용한 사람은 19세기의 Kelvin 경이었다. 1억 년이라는 그의 추정치는 지구 내부와 태양에서 지구로의 열전달의 계산에 기반을 둔 것이었다. 그러나 그가 발전시킨 이 수학적 모형은 한참 후에야 과학자들이 발견해낸 태양의 열을 생산해내는 핵융합, 혹은 판 구조론을 포함하지 않았었다. 그렇기는 하지만, 그의 추정치가 틀렸음에도 불구하고 지구의 나이를 측정하는 데에 과학적인 방법을 적용한 첫 번째 시도 중 하나로 인정된다.

Q05 In 1899, Irish physicist John Joly proposed using the salinity of the world's oceans to calculate the age of the ocean, and by extension, the age of the Earth. Theorizing that the salt in the ocean must have come from the erosion of the land into the sea, **Q02** he proposed that the ocean's age could be calculated by knowing the amount of salt that is added each year. Using this approach, Joly calculated the age of the world's oceans to be between 80 to 100 million years. **Q03** Though accepted as the most compelling idea at first, his approach was soon criticized for being inaccurate. However, his idea of measuring elements of matter on the Earth drove him and other scientists to consider new possibilities.

With the discovery of radiation in 1896, scientists began to devise ever more accurate means of measurement. In 1913, British geologist Arthur Holmes developed a method to measure the age of minerals using radiometric dating. His initial estimates put the Earth's age at around 1.6 billion years. Yet as he refined his method, his estimate of the Earth's age continued to grow.

Since Holmes' discovery, scientists have developed and refined the technique of radiometric dating to a great degree. **Q04** Today, radiometric dating has put the age of the Earth to be 4.56 billion years. But this is still much younger than the universe, which is estimated to have come into being 13.7 billion years ago.

01 지문의 Nevertheless 와 의미상 가장 가까운 것은?
(A) 그렇지 않았다면
(B) 그러나
(C) 마침내
(D) 따라서

02 지문의 proposed 와 의미상 가장 가까운 것은?
(A) 제안했다
(B) ~에 반대했다
(C) ~을 고집했다
(D) 끝냈다

03 지문의 most compelling 과 의미상 가장 가까운 것은?
(A) 가장 위험한
(B) 가장 쉬운
(C) 가장 확실한
(D) 가장 예상치 못한

04 지문에서 this 가 가리키는 것은?
(A) Holmes의 발견
(B) 방사성 연대 측정법
(C) 지구의 나이
(D) 우주

05 지문에 따르면, John Joly에 관한 내용 중 옳은 것은?

(A) 방사성 연대 측정법 이론을 발전시켰다.
(B) 지구의 나이를 계산하는 데에 최초로 과학적인 방법을 사용했다.
(C) 자신의 이론에 핵융합을 포함하지 않았다.
(D) 지구의 나이를 알아내기 위해 바다의 나이를 계산했다.

해설 | Factual Information 단락 3에서 아일랜드 물리학자 John Joly는 지구의 나이를 계산하기 위해 해양의 염분을 이용하여 바다의 나이를 계산하는 이론을 제안했다고 설명한다.

어휘 | **calculate** 계산하다 **philosopher** 철학자 **historian** 역사학자 **tackle** (힘든 문제와) 씨름하다 **radiometric dating** 방사성 연대 측정법 **interpretation** 해석, 설명 **employ** 사용하다, 쓰다 **approach** 접근법, 접근 **mathematical** 수학의 **nuclear fusion** 핵융합 **plate tectonics** 판 구조론 **physicist** 물리학자 **salinity** 염분 **erosion** 침식, 부식 **inaccurate** 부정확한 **measure** 측정하다 **matter** 물질, 문제 **possibility** 가능성 **geologist** 지질학자 **mineral** 광물, 미네랄

Chapter 02 Reference

Sample Question   p.37

When people collect in an area to settle down, the area of their settlement can be distinguished based on various criteria. One of the main factors that distinguish the area of their settlement is their population. It creates a settlement hierarchy which sorts human settlements by the size of them. For instance, a hamlet describes a tiny population of less than 100 people. Several hamlets could form a community, having essential service facilities such as hospitals or schools. This community is called a village. A town contains several villages, with a population ranging from at least 1,000 to 20,000 at most.	사람들이 정착하기 위해 한 지역에 모일 때, 그들의 정착지는 다양한 기준에 의해 구분될 수 있다. 정착지를 구분 짓는 주요 요인 중 하나는 인구이다. 그것은 정착지 계급을 만드는데, 이는 인간의 정착지를 그들의 규모로 분류하는 것이다. 예를 들어, 작은 마을(hamlet)은 100명 이하의 적은 인구를 나타낸다. 여러 작은 마을(hamlet)은 공동체를 형성할 수 있고, 이는 병원이나 학교 같은 필수적인 부대복리시설을 갖는다. 이 공동체는 마을(village)이라고 불린다. 소도시(town)는 여러 마을을 포함하며 최소 1,000명부터 최대 20,000명에 이르는 인구를 포함한다.

지문에서 them 이 가리키는 것은?
(A) 부대복리시설
(B) 사람
(C) 요인
(D) 정착지

어휘 | **settle down** 정착하다, 편안히 앉다   **settlement** 정착(지), 합의   **distinguish** 구분하다, 구별하다   **hierarchy** 계급, 계층
service facility 부대복리시설

Basic Drill   p.38

01 (D)	02 (C)	03 (A)	04 (A)	05 (B)	06 (C)	
Vocab Quiz	01 basic	02 attribute	03 native	04 allows	05 influence	06 turned to

01

The first law of thermodynamics is one of the most fundamental laws of the physical world. The first part of the first law of thermodynamics states that energy must be conserved at all times, which is known as the law of conservation of energy. Simply put, energy cannot be created or destroyed. Energy may change forms, or it may be transferred from one object to another, but there is always the same amount of total energy. An important concept in understanding this is the concept of a closed system. A closed system is a set of objects that are not influenced by anything outside of that system. Within a closed system, energy cannot be created or destroyed, but energy may be added to or taken out of a closed system.	열역학 제1법칙은 물리계의 가장 기본적인 법칙 중 하나이다. 열역학 제1법칙의 첫 번째는 에너지는 반드시 보존된다는 것인데, 이는 에너지 보존의 법칙이라고 알려져 있다. 간단히 말해서 에너지는 생성되거나 파괴될 수 없다는 것이다. 에너지는 형태를 바꾸거나 한 물체에서 다른 물체로 옮겨갈 수 있지만, 전체 에너지의 양은 언제나 같다. 이것 을 이해하는 데 있어서 중요한 개념은 폐쇄계라는 개념이다. 폐쇄계란 외부의 영향을 전혀 받지 않는 물체의 집합을 가리킨다. 폐쇄계 안에서 에너지는 생성되거나 파괴될 수 없지만, 폐쇄계 안으로 에너지가 추가되거나 폐쇄계 밖으로 빠져나올 수는 있다.

지문에서 this 가 가리키는 것은?
(A) 폐쇄계
(B) 전체 에너지의 양
(C) 열역학의 법칙
(D) 에너지 보존의 법칙

해설 | this 의 앞에 나온 내용은 전부 에너지 보존의 법칙(law of conservation of energy)을 설명하는 내용이다.

어휘 | **thermodynamics** 열역학   **fundamental** 기본적인   **conserve** 보존하다   **simply put** 간단히 말해서   **transfer** 옮기다

02

The most important scientific tools for astronomers are telescopes. This is demonstrated by the fact that the first major discoveries about the solar system, those of Galileo, accompanied the invention of the telescope. As telescopes have increased in power over the centuries, they have allowed astronomers to make more and more discoveries about the nature of the universe. The first telescopes used glass lenses to focus their light, but most modern telescopes now use mirrors as their major light amplifiers. In a lens telescope, the light must pass through the lens, so the lens must be entirely perfect. But in a mirror telescope, the light simply bounces off the mirror. This means that only the surface of the mirror must be perfect, making it much easier to manufacture large mirrors.

천문학자들에게 가장 중요한 과학 도구는 망원경이다. 이는 Galileo가 발견한 태양계의 가장 첫 번째 주요 발견이 망원경의 발명을 동반했다는 사실에서 입증된다. 수세기에 걸쳐 망원경의 능력이 증가함에 따라, 그것들은 천문학자들이 우주의 본질에 대해 점점 더 많은 것을 발견할 수 있도록 해주었다. 초기 망원경은 빛을 집중시키기 위해 유리 렌즈를 사용했지만, 대부분의 현대 망원경은 광증폭기로 반사경을 사용한다. 렌즈 망원경에서는 빛이 렌즈를 통과해야 하기 때문에 렌즈가 철저히 완벽해야 한다. 하지만 반사망원경에서 빛은 그저 반사경에 반사될 뿐이다. 이는 반사경의 표면만 완벽해야 한다는 것을 의미하는데, 이는 크기가 큰 반사경을 만드는 것을 더 용이하게 만들어준다.

지문에서 they 가 가리키는 것은?

(A) 발견
(B) 과학 도구
(C) 망원경
(D) 수세기

해설 | "As telescopes have increased in power over the centuries …" 를 보면 천문학자들이 우주의 본성에 대해 점점 더 많은 것을 발견할 수 있도록 해준 것은 망원경이라는 것을 알 수 있다.

어휘 | **demonstrate** 입증하다, 실증하다 **solar system** 태양계 **light amplifier** 광증폭기 **entirely** 철저히, 전적으로 **manufacture** 만들다, 제조하다

03

The túngara frog, an indigenous amphibian in Central America, is well known for its distinctive breeding behavior. In order to seduce females, male frogs produce two types of mating calls distinguished by their complexity: a basic one and a complex one. The former one merely consists of a whine, which is sufficient to bring in a female. However, as more complex mating calls can attract more females, males conspicuously add chucks to the whine calls. While making these whine-chuck calls in shallow pools on the forest floor, male túngara frogs leave ripples on the water surface. Although these efforts are much more efficient in grasping the attention of females, male frogs also make themselves vulnerable by leaving physical traces that can draw the unwanted attention of predators.

중앙아메리카의 토착 양서류인 퉁가라 개구리는 독특한 번식 행동으로 잘 알려져 있다. 암컷을 유혹하기 위해 수컷 개구리들은 두 종류의 짝짓기 신호를 보내는데, 이는 복잡성에 따라 구분된다. 기본 신호와 복잡한 신호가 그것이다. 전자는 단지 낑낑거리는 소리로 구성되는데, 이는 암컷을 데려오기에 충분하다. 하지만 더 복잡한 짝짓기 신호가 더 많은 암컷을 유혹할 수 있으므로 수컷들은 구구하는 소리를 낑낑거리는 신호에 뚜렷하게 더한다. 숲 바닥의 얕은 웅덩이에서 이런 낑낑거리고 구구거리는 신호를 보내면서, 수컷 퉁가라 개구리들은 수면에 잔물결을 남긴다. 이런 노력이 암컷의 주의를 끄는 데 훨씬 더 효과적이지만, 수컷 개구리들은 원하지 않던 포식자들의 주의까지 끄는 물리적 흔적을 남기면서 그 자신들 또한 취약하게 만든다.

지문에서 themselves 가 가리키는 것은?

(A) 수컷 개구리
(B) 암컷
(C) 신호
(D) 포식자

해설 | themselves 와 같은 재귀대명사는 동사와 목적어가 같을 때 「주어 + 동사 + 목적어(재귀대명사)」와 같은 형태로 사용된다. 즉, 주어와 목적어 모두 수컷 개구리라고 볼 수 있다.

어휘 | **indigenous** 토착의, 원산의 **amphibian** 양서류 **whine** 낑낑(낄낄)거리는 소리 **conspicuously** 뚜렷하게, 두드러지게 **chuck** 구구거리는 소리 **vulnerable** 취약한, 연약한

04

It is reasonable to suppose that speech was a gradual outgrowth of the system of communication used by our pre-human ancestors — calls, gestures, or a combination of the two. In order for human speech to arise from these systems, however, they first had to undergo significant development. Each ape call is mutually exclusive; one call cannot convey two ideas at the same time. For example, there may be one vocalization that means "food" and another that means "danger." If a chimp notices a ripe banana, but at the same time spots a leopard waiting to pounce, it can send only one of those messages to its fellows, because a call system lacks a way of combining the messages "food" and "danger." Speech, on the other hand, permits such combinations.

언어가 인류 이전의 선조들이 부르거나 몸짓을 하거나 아니면 두 가지 모두를 결합한 의사소통 체계의 점진적 파생물이라고 가정하는 것은 합당하다. 그러나 인간의 언어가 이와 같은 시스템으로부터 생겨나기 위해서는 우선 중대한 발전 과정을 거쳐야 했다. 각 유인원의 소리는 상호배타적이어서 하나의 소리가 두 가지 생각을 동시에 전할 수 없다. 예를 들어, '먹이'를 뜻하는 한 발성과 '위험'을 뜻하는 또 다른 것이 있을 수 있다. 침팬지가 잘 익은 바나나를 발견한 동시에 덮치려고 기다리고 있는 표범을 발견했을 때, 그것은 주위 동료들에게 이 둘 중 한 가지 메시지만을 전달할 수 있다. 왜냐하면 소리 체계에는 '먹이'와 '위험'을 결합할 방법이 없기 때문이다. 반면에 언어는 이런 결합을 가능하게 한다.

지문에서 another 가 가리키는 것은?

(A) 발성
(B) 음식
(C) 침팬지
(D) 위험

해설 | another 앞의 one vocalization(한 발성)을 통해 another 가 가리키는 것도 vocalization(발성)임을 알 수 있다.

어휘 | **outgrowth** 파생물, 부산물 **pre-human** 인류 이전의 **combination** 결합 **mutually** 상호간에, 서로 **exclusive** 배타적인 **convey** 전달하다 **vocalization** 발성 **spot** 발견하다 **pounce** (공격하거나 잡으려고 확) 덮치다 **permit** 가능하게 하다

05

From the very start, the culture of the American colonies was significantly different from its English mother culture. Many of what are seen as "American values" were present from the time of the first colonies. A good example would be the importance that American culture places on independence and individuality. These values played a large role in the shaping of America in a number of aspects.

The first would be the reformation of religion among the early settlers. It is well known that the first settlers were largely motivated by their desire for religious freedom in their choice to come over. Specifically, they felt that church officials in England held too much power over the members of the church by enforcing strict religious obedience. The early settlers practiced a form of Christianity that taught that it was the individual's responsibility to develop his or her own understanding of religion, and rejected the way of the Anglican Church in England, where only priests could interpret the Bible.

The sense of individuality and independence did not just extend to its impact on the religious life in Americans. It also laid the foundation for American democracy as people began to question a person's right to rule another. Instead of following the repressive laws of Britain, America developed its own balance between liberty and equality and eventually adopted the Constitution of the United States of America in 1788, the world's first formal blueprint for a modern democracy.

맨 처음부터 미국 식민지 문화는 그것의 모국 문화인 영국 문화와 상당히 달랐다. '미국의 가치'로 여겨지는 많은 것들이 초기 식민지 시대부터 존재했다. 미국 문화에서 독립성과 개별성을 중요시한다는 것이 그 좋은 예이다. 이 가치들은 많은 측면에서 초기 미국을 형성하는 데 큰 역할을 했다.

첫 번째로는 초기 정착민들의 종교 개혁을 들 수 있다. 처음 정착민들이 그곳으로 건너오는 것을 선택함에 있어서 종교적 자유에 대한 갈망이 큰 동기부여가 된 것은 잘 알려져 있다. 구체적으로 말하면, 그들은 영국 교회의 관리들이 엄격한 종교적 복종을 강요하여 교회 신자들에 대해 너무 많은 권한을 가지고 있다고 느꼈다. 초기 이주민들은 그들 자신의 종교에 대한 이해를 높이는 것이 개인의 책임이라고 가르친 기독교의 예법을 따랐고, 오직 성직자들만 성경을 해석할 수 있었던 영국 국교회의 방식은 거부했다.

개별성과 독립성은 미국인들의 종교적 생활에만 영향을 끼친 것이 아니었다. 이는 또한 사람들이 다른 이를 지배할 수 있는 권리에 의문을 제기하기 시작하면서 미국 민주주의의 토대를 마련했다. 영국의 억압적인 법을 따르는 대신, 미국은 자유와 평등에 대한 균형을 다졌고 결국 1788년에 현대 민주주의의 세계 최초 공적 청사진인 미합중국의 헌법을 채택했다.

지문에서 The first 가 가리키는 것은?

(A) 가치
(B) 측면
(C) 독립성
(D) 역할

해설 | 앞 문장인 "These values played a large role in the shaping of America in a number of aspects"를 보면 많은 측면에서 초기 미국을 형성하는 데 큰 역할을 했다고 하고 바로 The first 로 새로운 문단을 시작했다. 즉, 많은 측면 중 첫 번째 측면을 얘기하고자 했음을 알 수 있다.

어휘 | **colony** 식민지 **independence** 독립성 **individuality** 개별성 **reformation** 개혁 **settler** 정착민 **Anglican Church** 영국 국교회 **priest** 성직자 **interpret** 해석하다 **blueprint** 청사진

06

Eratosthenes, one of the fathers of Greek geometry, was most interested in devising a system of latitude and longitude for navigation. Such a system would allow merchants to find their location accurately at sea. In order to do this, however, Eratosthenes first needed to know the distance around the Earth. At the time, this was impossible to measure through direct observation.

So instead, Eratosthenes resorted to the rules of geometry to solve the problem. As a young man, he had noticed that at noon on the longest day of the summer, the sun did not cast a shadow in his hometown of Cyrene. This meant that the sun was directly overhead. Later, when he studied in Alexandria, he noticed that the sun did in fact cast a shadow at noon on the longest day of the summer. Using a pole and string, he measured the angle of the shadow, which was about 7 degrees. From this, Eratosthenes knew that the distance from Cyrene to Alexandria was also 7 degrees of the Earth's 360-degree circumference, or about 2 percent of the total distance around the Earth. Eratosthenes came up with a figure of 47,000 kilometers as the distance around the Earth. The true distance is 40,008 kilometers. The inaccuracy in his number comes from the fact that he could not accurately measure the distance between the two cities.

그리스 기하학의 아버지 중 한 명인 Eratosthenes는 항해를 위한 위도와 경도의 체계를 고안하는 것에 가장 흥미를 느꼈다. 그러한 시스템은 상인들이 바다에서 그들의 위치를 정확히 알 수 있게 해 줄 것이었다. 이를 위해 Eratosthenes는 먼저 지구의 둘레를 알아야만 했다. 그 당시 이를 직접 관찰하여 측정하는 것은 불가능했다.

대신에 그는 그 문제를 해결하기 위해 기하학의 법칙에 의지했다. 그가 청년이었을 당시, 여름의 가장 긴 날의 정오에 그의 고향 키레네에서는 태양이 그림자를 드리우지 않는다는 사실을 깨달았다. 이것은 태양이 머리 바로 위에 있다는 것을 의미했다. 나중에 그가 알렉산드리아에서 공부할 때 여름의 가장 긴 날의 정오에 사실 태양이 그림자를 드리운다는 사실을 알아차렸다. 그는 막대기와 줄을 사용해서 그림자의 각도를 측정했더니, 약 7도가 나왔다. 이를 통해 Eratosthenes는 키레네에서 알렉산드리아까지의 거리가 지구 360도 둘레 중 7도, 즉 지구 전체 거리의 약 2%에 해당하는 거리에 있다는 사실을 알게 되었다. Eratosthenes는 지구의 거리가 47,000km라는 것을 계산해냈다. 실제 거리는 40,008km이다. 그가 계산한 값이 부정확했던 것은 그가 두 도시 사이의 거리를 정확히 측정할 수 없었기 때문이다.

지문에서 the problem 이 가리키는 것은?

(A) 믿을 만한 항해 체계를 개발할 수 없는 것
(B) 기하학의 실용법을 찾을 수 없는 것
(C) 지구 둘레의 거리를 직접 측정할 수 없는 것
(D) 바다에서 정확한 위치를 기록할 수 없는 것

해설 | 앞 문장에서 지구의 위도와 경도를 측정하려면 지구 둘레의 길이를 알아야 하지만, 직접적인 둘레 측정은 불가능했다고 한다. 지문에서 사용된 the problem 은 지구 둘레의 길이를 직접 측정할 수 없다는 점이다.

어휘 | **geometry** 기하학 **devise** 고안하다 **latitude** 위도 **longitude** 경도 **navigation** 항해 **resort to** ~에 의지하다 **cast** (그림자를) 드리우다 **inaccuracy** 부정확

Reading Practice

01 (A)   02 (C)   03 (B)   04 (B)   05 (D)

ECONOMIES OF THE TANG AND SONG DYNASTIES

The economies of the Chinese Tang and Song Dynasties flourished for more than 600 years from the seventh century to the late thirteenth century. Q01 The population of China began to explode during this time, fueling advancements in technology, as well as an economic revolution. During the Tang Dynasty (618-907 C.E.) the government paid much attention to the development of agriculture and irrigation, which in turn led to greater efficiency in agricultural production for trading with neighboring countries. This dynasty also saw significant growth in the handicraft industry, most notably with silk, as well as pottery, paper-making, and ship-building.

The Song Dynasty (960-1276 C.E.) further expanded these industrial developments and realized that huge sums of money were to be made by increasing the trade of these products. ①As a result, they established numerous markets along the borders of their Northern neighbors and pushed forward with massive sea trade routes, ②primarily with their Korean and Japanese neighbors, but also with regions located as far away as Eastern Africa. In exchange for items such as copper coins, silk, porcelain, spices, tea, and printed books, the Song Dynasty received silver and animals such as horses, camels, and sheep.

However, as trade in the Tang and Song Dynasties increased exponentially, Q03-1 merchants were faced with the problem of cumbersome modes of currency. For hundreds of years, bronze or copper coins had been used as the basic unit of currency in China, each coin having a hole in the middle to allow large amounts of coins to be strung together for larger transactions. Q03-2 Q05 Unfortunately, as these were extremely heavy to carry, Chinese merchants from the Tang Dynasty eventually developed the idea of producing the world's first paper currency to mitigate the burden of carrying around large bunches of coins. As this new currency form began to take precedence, deposit shops were set up in the kingdom, Q04 where merchants were able to acquire receipts of deposit certificates for money or goods they left in these shops. Authorities in the early Song period permitted a select few shops a monopoly on the issuing of deposit certificates, but by the twelfth century, the government took charge of the deposit system and produced the world's first government-issued paper money.

당나라와 송나라의 경제

중국의 당나라와 송나라의 경제는 7세기부터 13세기 후반까지 600년 이상 번영하였다. 이 시기에 중국의 인구가 폭발적으로 증가했고, 이는 경제 혁명뿐만 아니라 기술에서의 발전에도 활기를 불어넣었다. 당나라 시기 (서기 618-907년)에는 정부가 농업과 관개의 발전에 주의를 기울였는데, 이는 결국 주변 국가들과의 교역을 위한 농업 생산에 더 큰 효율성을 가져다주었다. 이 시대는 수공업에서도 상당한 발전을 하였는데, 도자기, 제지, 조선뿐만 아니라 비단에서 특히 발전하였다.

송나라 (서기 960-1276년)는 이런 산업 발전을 더욱 확장했고, 이 상품들의 교역량을 증가시킴으로써 막대한 금액을 벌어들일 수 있음을 깨달았다. 그 결과, 그들은 북쪽 국가들의 경계를 따라 많은 시장을 설립했고, 거대 규모의 해양 교역로를 확장했는데, 상대국은 주로 한국과 일본이었지만 동부 아프리카처럼 먼 거리의 지역들도 포함됐다. 동화, 비단, 자기, 향신료, 차, 활자본과 같은 물품들을 교환하면서 송나라는 은과 말, 낙타, 양과 같은 동물들을 받았다.

하지만 당나라와 송나라의 교역이 기하급수적으로 증가함에 따라, 상인들은 다루기 힘든 통화 형태로 인한 문제에 직면했다. 수백 년 동안 청동화와 동화가 중국에서 통화의 기본 단위로 사용되었고, 이 동전에는 큰 규모의 거래를 할 때 많은 양의 동전을 묶기 위해 가운데에 구멍이 있었다. 불행히도, 이 동전들은 들고 다니기에 너무 무거웠기 때문에 당나라의 중국 상인들은 결국 큰 동전 다발을 갖고 다녀야 하는 부담을 완화하기 위해 세계 최초의 지폐를 만들 생각을 하였다. 이 새로운 통화 형태가 우위를 점하기 시작하면서, 나라에 예치소(deposit shop)들이 세워졌고, 상인들은 이곳에 그들이 맡기는 돈이나 상품에 대한 예치 증서의 인수증을 받을 수 있었다. 초기 송나라 당국은 엄선된 몇몇 예치소들에게 예치증서를 발급할 수 있는 독점권을 주었지만, 12세기에는 정부가 예치 시스템을 담당했고 세계 최초의 정부 발행 지폐를 생산해냈다.

---

01 지문의 flourished 와 의미상 가장 가까운 것은?
- (A) 번창하였다
- (B) 줄어들었다
- (C) 반등하였다
- (D) 대변혁을 하였다

해설 | Vocabulary   flourished 의 의미는 뒤의 문장들에서 힌트를 얻을 수 있다. 인구가 폭발적으로 증가했고, 경제 혁명뿐만 아니라 기술 발전도 이뤘다는 내용을 통해 경제가 번창하였음(thrived)을 알 수 있다.

02 다음 중 지문에서 표시된 문장의 주요 정보를 가장 잘 나타낸 문장은?
정답 외의 보기들은 중요한 의미가 바뀌거나 주요 정보가 빠져 있다.

(A) 그들은 북부 국가들에 시장을 이미 가지고 있었음에도 불구하고, 그들 수입의 대부분이 일본 및 한국과 형성한 거대한 해양 교역로로부터 발생하였다.
(B) 결국, 그들은 그들의 북부 국가들과의 교역을 증가시키기로 했는데, 이는 일본, 한국, 그리고 여러 동부 아프리카 국가들과의 해양 교역로를 확장하는 데 어려움을 겪었기 때문이다.
(C) 그 결과, 가깝고 먼 주변국들과의 해양 교역로를 개척시켰을 뿐만 아니라, 그들의 북부 주변국들과의 교역을 위한 시장도 설치되었다.
(D) 일본, 한국, 아프리카로의 해양 교역로 확장은 북쪽 국경을 따라가는 상품 교역의 감소로 인한 결과였다.

해설 | Sentence Simplification 표시된 문장은 크게 두 의미로 나뉠 수 있다. ① 그들은 북쪽의 국경을 따라 많은 시장을 설립했다. ② 한국, 일본, 동부 아프리카와의 해양 교역로를 확장했다.

03 지문의 cumbersome 과 의미상 가장 가까운 것은?

(A) 혁신적인
(B) 힘든
(C) 만연한
(D) 열등한

해설 | Vocabulary cumbersome 의 의미는 주변 문장을 통해 힌트를 얻을 수 있다. 무거운 동전을 들고 다니는 것이 힘들었다는 것을 알 수 있으므로, cumbersome 은 burdensome(힘든)과 동의어임을 알 수 있다.

04 지문에서 they 가 가리키는 것은?

(A) 영수증
(B) 상인
(C) 당국
(D) 예치증서

해설 | Reference 그들(they)이 맡기는 돈이나 물건들에 대해 상인들이 예치증서를 받을 수 있다는 내용으로 보아 they 가 가리키는 것은 상인들임을 알 수 있다.

05 단락 3에 따르면, 중국 상인들이 많은 양의 돈을 갖고 다녀야 하는 문제를 해결한 방법은?

(A) 정부에게 새로운 통화를 만들라고 강요함으로써
(B) 주변국들과 더 적은 양을 거래함으로써
(C) 새로운 통화 가치를 만듦으로써
(D) 더 가벼운 새 통화 형태를 만듦으로써

해설 | Factual Information 지문의 "… Chinese merchants from the Tang Dynasty eventually developed the idea of producing the world's first paper currency to mitigate the burden of carrying around large bunches of coins"를 통해 중국 상인들은 더 가벼운 새 통화 형태를 만듦으로써 많은 양의 돈을 갖고 다녀야 하는 문제를 해결했음을 알 수 있다.

어휘 | **Tang Dynasty** 당나라 **Song Dynasty** 송나라 **flourish** 번영하다, 번창하다 **irrigation** 관개 **handicraft** 수공업, 수공예(품) **exponentially** 기하급수적으로, 전형적으로 **cumbersome** 다루기 힘든, 크고 무거운 **mitigate** 완화시키다, 경감시키다 **take precedence** 우위를 점하다 **monopoly** 독점권

Chapter 03 Sentence Simplification

Sample Question   p.45

Hummingbirds are a unique family of bird species. Found only in the Western Hemisphere, hummingbirds are the smallest birds in the world, with some species being as small as 6 centimeters and weighing as little as 5 grams. Like most small animals, hummingbirds lead extremely active lives. ① They visit hundreds of flowers daily to eat nectar, a sweet liquid inside certain flowers, at a rate of nearly twice their bodyweight, ② but they also catch insects and spiders now and then to satisfy their nutritional needs, ③ as nectar is a poor source of nutrients.	벌새는 조류 중 독특한 과이다. 서반구에서만 발견되는 벌새는 세계에서 가장 작은 새로, 어떤 것은 6cm의 크기에 무게는 5g 밖에 나가지 않는다. 대부분의 작은 동물처럼, 벌새는 굉장히 활발한 삶을 영위한다. 이들은 특정 꽃 안에 있는 달콤한 액체인 꿀을 자신들 몸무게의 거의 2배에 달하는 비율로 먹기 위해 수백 송이의 꽃을 매일 찾아가지만, 꿀은 부족한 영양 공급원이므로 필요 영양소를 충족시키기 위해 때때로 곤충과 거미를 잡아먹기도 한다.

다음 중 지문에서 표시된 문장의 주요 정보를 가장 잘 나타낸 문장은? *정답 외의* 보기들은 중요한 의미가 바뀌거나 주요 정보가 빠져 있다.

(A) 벌새는 그들의 필요 영양소를 충족시키기 위해 그들 몸무게의 2배에 달하는 달콤한 액체를 먹어야 하므로, 매일 꽃을 찾아간다.
(B) 벌새는 매일 꽃의 꿀을 먹는 것과 더불어, 영양을 위해 때때로 곤충과 거미를 잡아먹는다.
(C) 벌새는 그들 몸무게의 2배에 달하는 양을 매일 먹어야 하므로, 꾸준하게 꿀과 곤충을 찾는다.
(D) 벌새가 필요한 필수 영양소는 꿀을 먹거나 곤충 및 거미를 잡아먹음으로써 충족될 수 있다.

어휘 | **hummingbird** 벌새   **hemisphere** (지구의) 반구   **weigh** (무게가) ~만큼 나가다   **nectar** 꿀   **liquid** 액체   **bodyweight** 몸무게
now and then 때때로, 가끔   **nutrient** 영양소, 영양분

Basic Drill   p.46

01 (B)   **02** (C)   **03** (C)   **04** (B)   **05** (B)   **06** (D)

Vocab Quiz   **01** important   **02** massive   **03** isolated   **04** countless   **05** mostly   **06** earlier

01

Setting tax policy is a [crucial] responsibility of the government, as such policies not only ensure the funding of government programs, but also have a significant impact on the economy in general. A good example of this comes from the early 1980s, when America was faced with a serious recession. The government made significant cuts in the tax rates for companies, but not for regular citizens, even though regular citizens had little money at the time. The logic behind this was that ① cutting individual taxes would not help, ② because it would only increase the amount of money consumers can spend ③ without fixing the problems in supply. By cutting taxes for companies, the government allowed those companies to use the tax money they saved to increase their supply.	세금 정책을 정하는 것은 그러한 정책이 정부 프로그램의 자금을 확보할 뿐만 아니라 전반적인 경제에 상당한 영향을 끼치기 때문에 정부의 [중요한] 의무이다. 이것을 보여주는 좋은 예가 1980년대 초에 있는데, 그때 미국은 심각한 불경기에 직면하게 되었다. 정부는 이 당시 시민들이 돈이 얼마 없음에도 불구하고 일반 시민의 세금은 그대로 두고, 기업이 내는 세율은 상당히 인하했다. 이를 뒷받침하는 논리는 개인의 세금을 줄이는 것이 공급의 문제를 해결하지 않고 소비자가 쓸 수 있는 금액만 늘려주는 것이기 때문에 도움이 되지 않으리라는 것이었다. 정부는 기업에 대한 세금을 줄여줌으로써, 이 기업들이 절약한 세금으로 공급을 늘릴 수 있게 해 준 것이었다.

다음 중 지문에서 표시된 문장의 주요 정보를 가장 잘 나타낸 문장은?
정답 외의 보기들은 중요한 의미가 바뀌거나 주요 정보가 빠져 있다.

(A) 세금을 낮추는 것은 소비자가 가진 돈만 증가시키기 때문에 별 소용이 없을 것이다.
(B) 개인 세금을 낮추는 것은 공급이 아니라 소비자의 돈만 증가시키기 때문에 의미가 없을 것이다.
(C) 개인 세금을 낮추는 것은 공급 문제를 해결할 수 없으며 소비자들의 돈만 절약해 줄 것이다.
(D) 개인 세금을 낮추는 것은 소비자의 지출을 늘리거나 공급 문제를 해결할 수 없을 것이다.

해설 | 표시된 문장은 크게 세 의미로 나뉠 수 있다. ① 개인 세금을 줄이는 것은 도움이 안 된다. ② 소비자의 돈만 늘린다. ③ 공급 문제를 해결하지는 못한다. ②와 ③은 ①에 대한 이유이다.

어휘 | **crucial** 중요한　**ensure** 확보하다　**funding** 자금　**significant** 상당한, 현저한　**impact** 영향　**recession** 불경기, 경기 침체　**supply** 공급

02

It has long been known that communities often choose courses of action that are either very damaging or even fatal to the community. For example, the society that lived on Easter Island practiced extensive logging, even though eventual deforestation of their island led to the destruction of their society. ① Today, many countries around the world continue to pollute the environment, ② despite well-documented evidence that such pollution may make human life much more difficult or even impossible in the future. Such self-destructive behavior is explained by game theory, which states that every decision maker acts in his or her own self-interest, maximizing their own benefit, and the welfare of others is secondary. In such situations, individual interests often conflict with the interests of the group as a whole.

공동체가 종종 그 공동체에 커다란 피해를 주거나 심지어 치명적인 방침을 선택한다는 것은 오래전부터 알려진 사실이다. 예를 들어, 이스터 섬에 살던 사람들은 결과적으로 섬의 삼림 파괴가 그들 사회의 파괴를 가져왔음에도 불구하고, 대규모의 벌채를 했다. 오늘날 전 세계의 많은 국가들은 그러한 오염이 미래에 우리의 삶을 훨씬 더 힘들게 만들거나 혹은 심지어 불가능하게 만들 수 있다는 충분히 입증된 증거들이 있는데도, 계속해서 환경을 오염시키고 있다. 이러한 자기 파괴적 행동은 게임 이론에 의해 설명되는데, 이 이론은 모든 의사 결정자들이 자신의 이익을 극대화하며 자기 이익에 따라 행동하고, 다른 사람들의 복지는 별로 중요하지 않은 것으로 설명한다. 이런 상황에서 개인의 이익은 종종 집단 전체의 이익과 충돌한다.

다음 중 지문에서 표시된 문장의 주요 정보를 가장 잘 나타낸 문장은?
정답 외의 보기들은 중요한 의미가 바뀌거나 주요 정보가 빠져 있다.

(A) 오늘날 많은 국가들은 그 영향에 관해 충분히 입증된 증거들이 부족해서 계속해서 환경을 오염시킨다.
(B) 환경을 오염시키는 많은 국가들은 자신들의 행동에 대해 잘 인지하지 못하고 있으므로 계속해서 그렇게 한다.
(C) 비록 많은 국가들이 자신들의 행동에 대한 미래의 결과를 알고 있지만, 계속해서 환경을 오염시킨다.
(D) 환경 오염이 미래의 삶을 불가능하게 할 것이라는 사실에도 불구하고 많은 국가들이 환경을 오염시킨다는 사실은 기록에 의해 충분히 입증되어 있다.

해설 | 표시된 문장은 크게 두 의미로 나뉠 수 있다. ① 많은 국가는 환경을 오염시키고 있다. ② 환경 오염으로 생겨날 부정적인 결과에 대해 충분히 입증된 증거들이 있다. ①과 ②의 내용은 상반된 내용으로 despite the fact that으로 연결되어 있으며, 정답 문장은 Even though로 연결하였다.

어휘 | **community** 공동체　**fatal** 치명적인　**extensive** 대규모의, 아주 넓은　**logging** 벌채　**eventual** 결과적인　**deforestation** 삼림 파괴　**well-documented** 기록에 의해 충분히 입증된　**self-destructive** 자기 파괴적인　**self-interest** 자기 이익　**conflict** 충돌하다

03

Cave paintings of the early Magdalenian period differed from those of the previous Aurignacian period. Whereas ① Aurignacian painters made use of the natural shape of the rock for modeling, and used sophisticated color pallets to make polychrome images, ② artists of the early Magdalenian period created flat drawings that consisted merely of black outlines with no detail or color. Another difference was that early Magdalenians abandoned the larger compositions favored by Aurignacian artists in favor of solitary figures. However, their style gradually developed over time until the late Magdalenian artists surpassed their Aurignacian predecessors in the creation of more sophisticated designs with beautifully rendered details.

초기 마들렌기의 동굴 벽화는 이전 오리냐크기의 벽화와는 달랐다. 오리냐크 화가들은 모형화에 돌의 자연적인 형태를 사용하고 여러 가지 색채 이미지를 만들기 위해 세련된 색채 팔레트를 사용했던 반면, 초기 마들렌기 예술가들은 어떠한 섬세함 혹은 색채가 없이 검은 윤곽으로만 이루어진 단조로운 그림들을 만들어냈다. 또 다른 점은 초기 마들렌기의 사람들은 독립된 인물들을 선호하며, 오리냐크 예술가들이 좋아했던 큰 구성들을 버렸다. 그러나 이들의 스타일은 마들렌기 후기의 예술가들이 아름답게 표현된 섬세함과 함께 더 정교해진 디자인을 창조함으로써 오리냐크 조상들을 능가할 때까지 서서히 발전했다.

다음 중 지문에서 표시된 문장의 주요 정보를 가장 잘 나타낸 문장은?
정답 외의 보기들은 중요한 의미가 바뀌거나 주요 정보가 빠져 있다.

(A) 오리냐크 예술가들은 단순하게 검정색으로 그리는 것을 선호했던 반면, 마들렌기 예술가들은 돌에 그리는 그들의 대상을 다채로운 모델로 만들었다.
(B) 마들렌기 예술가들은 오리냐크 화가들이 그렸던 깊이와 용적을 가진 세밀한 여러가지 색채의 이미지들을 만들어내는 수단을 가지고 있지 않았다.
(C) 초기 마들렌기의 예술가들은 오리냐크 화가들의 기법에 비해, 비교적 단순한 기법들로 단조로운 그림들을 그렸다.
(D) 초기 마들렌기의 동굴 벽화는 정교한 모형화와 색채 기법들이 사용되었음에도 불구하고 매우 따분했다.

해설 | 표시된 문장은 크게 두 의미로 나뉠 수 있다. ① 오리냐크 화가들은 돌의 자연적인 형태와 세련된 색채를 이용했다. ② 초기 마들렌기 예술가들은 단조로운 그림들을 그렸다. ①과 ②의 내용은 상반된 내용으로 Whereas로 연결되어 있으며, 정답 문장은 이를 compared to를 사용하여 표현했다.

어휘 | **cave** 동굴　**period** 시기　**previous** 이전의　**sophisticated** 세련된　**polychrome** 여러 가지 색채의　**merely** 오로지, 단지
abandon 버리다, 포기하다　**gradually** 서서히　**render** 표현하다, 만들다

04

Psychopharmacology, the study of how mood-altering drugs affect mood, sensation, thinking, and behavior, is a rapidly growing field of medicine. ①While the use of psychiatric drugs has been in existence for over 50 years, ②improvements in the understanding of brain chemistry and the consequent discovery of new drug types have greatly expanded their use over time, and ③there are now drugs available for the treatment of nearly every major form of psychiatric disorder. This has undeniably led to the improvement of innumerable lives, but many are now voicing concerns over the expanded use of drugs in treating the mentally ill and any unforeseen adverse medical and social consequences.

기분을 바꿔주는 약물이 기분, 느낌, 사고, 그리고 행동에 영향을 끼치는 방식에 대해 연구하는 정신약리학은 빠르게 성장하고 있는 의학 분야이다. 정신병 치료 약물의 사용은 50년이 넘게 존재해 왔으며, 뇌의 화학작용에 대한 이해의 발전과 그에 따른 새로운 약 종류의 개발은 시간이 지남에 따라 사용을 크게 확대시켰고, 이제는 거의 모든 주요 형태의 정신 질환 치료에 이용 가능한 약이 있다. 이로 인해 수많은 사람들의 삶이 명백히 향상되었지만, 현재 많은 사람들이 정신 질환을 치료하는 데 있어서의 늘어난 약물 사용과 예상치 못한 약물 부작용, 그리고 사회적 결과에 대해 우려를 표하고 있다.

다음 중 지문에서 표시된 문장의 주요 정보를 가장 잘 나타낸 문장은?
정답 외의 보기들은 중요한 의미가 바뀌거나 주요 정보가 빠져 있다.

(A) 정신 치료 약물은 새로운 것이 아니고 50년 넘게 존재해 왔지만, 뇌 화학작용에 대한 발전으로 최근에서야 이 약물들이 대부분의 정신 질환의 치료에 사용될 수 있었다.
(B) 뇌 화학작용과 관련된 발견들과 이로 인한 새로운 약물의 개발은 정신 치료 약물의 사용을 대부분의 정신 질환의 치료로까지 크게 확대시켰다.
(C) 뇌 화학작용과 신약들의 이해에 관한 많은 발견은 지난 50년간 이루어졌지만, 모든 주요 유형의 정신 질환을 치료하기 위해서는 아직도 더 많은 발견들이 이루어져야 한다.
(D) 정신 치료 약물이 거의 50년 동안 존재했지만, 현재 새로운 약물의 개발로 의사들이 거의 모든 유형의 정신 질환을 치료할 수 있게 되었다.

해설 | 표시된 문장은 크게 세 의미로 나뉠 수 있다. ① 정신 치료 약물은 50년 이상 존재했다. ② 뇌 화학작용에 대한 이해가 깊어져서 새로운 약물이 발견되고, 약물 사용이 늘어났다. ③ 그 결과 현재 거의 모든 정신 질환을 치료할 수 있는 약물이 있다. 이 중에 ①의 내용은 중요하지 않은 내용이므로 정답 문장에서 제거되었다.

어휘 | **psychopharmacology** 정신약리학　**psychiatric** 정신병 치료[법]의, 정신 의학의　**existence** 존재　**improvement** 발전, 개선
available 이용 가능한, 활용할 수 있는　**disorder** 질환, 장애　**unforeseen** 예상치 못한

05

The Earth has layers that were formed during a process known as planetary differentiation, which took place when the Earth was approximately 500 million years old. The young planet was heated up by impacts during its accretion, as well as by the decay of radioactive isotopes, and existed in a primarily liquid state, which allowed heavier material to sink to the center of the planet and lighter material to rise, resulting in the formation of a core, mantle, crust, and gaseous atmosphere.

Since then, the outer crust has cooled enough to support life, but the inner layers of the planet still remain hot. Approximately 90 percent of the heat in the interior of the planet is generated by the decay of radioactive elements in the mantle. The remaining 10 percent is heat left over from planetary formation or a result from the pressure generated deep within the planet. ① The temperature of the Earth's inner core is approximately 7,000 degrees Celsius, more than three times the melting temperature of the iron it is made of; ②yet the inner core is solid because of the great pressure exerted on it. Above the inner core is the outer core, also made of iron, which exists in a liquid state at a cooler temperature of approximately 3,000 degrees Celsius. The mantle, which rests

지구는 여러 층을 가지고 있으며, 이는 지구의 나이가 약 5억 년이었을 때 일어난 행성 분화라고 알려진 과정 동안 형성되었다. 생긴 지 얼마 되지 않은 행성은 방사성 동위원소의 붕괴뿐만 아니라, 부착 성장기의 영향으로 뜨겁게 달구어져서 주로 액체 상태로 존재했고, 이는 더 무거운 물질들이 이 행성의 중앙으로 가라앉게 하고 더 가벼운 물질들은 위로 떠올라 핵, 맨틀, 지각, 그리고 기체의 대기 형성으로 이어졌다.

그 이후, 외부 지각은 생명체가 존재할 수 있을 정도로 충분히 차가워졌지만, 이 행성의 내층은 여전히 뜨겁다. 이 행성(지구)의 내부 열의 90% 가량은 맨틀에서의 방사성 물질 붕괴로 생성되었다. 나머지 10%의 열은 행성의 형성으로부터 남은 것이거나 행성 깊은 곳에서의 압력으로 생성된 것이다. 지구 내핵의 온도는 약 섭씨 7천도이며, 이는 내핵을 구성하는 철이 녹는 온도의 3배가 넘는다. 그러나 내핵은 그것에 가해지는 큰 압력 때문에 고체 상태이다. 내핵 위에는 역시 철로 이루어진 외핵이 있으며, 이보다 낮은 약 섭씨 3천도의 액체 상태로 존재한다. 외핵 위에 존재하며 판 구조론의 작용을 가능하게 하는 맨틀은 대부분이 끈적거리긴 하지만 액체는 아닌, 용해 상태의 감람석으로 이루어져 있다.

above the outer core and drives the process of plate tectonics, largely consists of molten olivine, which is viscous but not liquid.

다음 중 지문에서 표시된 문장의 주요 정보를 가장 잘 나타낸 문장은?
정답 외의 보기들은 중요한 의미가 바뀌거나 주요 정보가 빠져 있다.

(A) 지구의 내핵은 고온과 큰 압력 때문에 용해된 철로 이루어져 있다.
(B) 지구의 내핵에 가해지는 압력은 그 내핵의 고온에서도 고체 상태를 유지하게 한다.
(C) 고온과 큰 압력의 조화로 인해 지구의 내핵은 고체 상태로 존재할 수 있다.
(D) 지구 내핵의 상태는 그것의 온도와 가해지는 압력에 따라 달라진다.

해설 | 표시된 문장은 크게 두 의미로 나뉠 수 있다. ① 지구 내핵의 온도는 고온이다. ② 큰 압력으로 인해 내핵은 고체로 존재한다. ①, ②의 내용은 고온에도 불구하고 내핵이 고체인 이유가 그에 가해지는 큰 압력 때문이라고 설명하고 있다.

어휘 | **planetary** 행성의 **impact** 영향 **accretion** 부착, 응축 **decay** 붕괴, 부식 **isotope** 동위원소 **liquid** 액체 **formation** 형성 **gaseous** 기체의, 가스의 **pressure** 압력, 압박 **temperature** 온도, 기온 **Celsius** 섭씨 **iron** 철 **solid** 고체의, 단단한 **exert** 가하다 **plate tectonics** 판 구조론 **olivine** 감람석 **viscous** 끈적끈적한, 점성이 있는

06

The idea that language determines our thoughts, or at least influences them, is known as linguistic determinism. The theory was first presented in the West by Wilhelm von Humbolt, a famous German linguist of the nineteenth century. His ideas were later expanded upon by Franz Boas, who, through his study of various languages around the world, came to realize how complete and total the differences between those various languages could be. This gave rise to the belief that if languages were so radically different, then the thoughts allowed by those languages must be quite different as well. The assumption was that in order to think something, a person had to be able to say it.

The concepts of linguistic determinism were most clearly focused in the work of Edward Sapir and his protégé Benjamin Whorf. Although Sapir and Whorf never developed an explicit theory of linguistic determinism, the ideas expressed in their numerous writings have come to be known as the Sapir-Whorf hypothesis. The Sapir-Whorf hypothesis is a less rigid theory of linguistic determinism than the previous theories of the German linguists. ① Whereas earlier linguists had claimed that thoughts are impossible without language and are therefore controlled by language, ② Sapir and Whorf claimed that thoughts were merely influenced by language, ③ which gave rise to competing theories of strong and weak linguistic determinism.

언어가 우리의 생각을 결정하거나, 적어도 영향을 끼친다는 개념은 언어 결정론으로 알려져 있다. 이 이론은 19세기 독일의 유명한 언어학자인 Wilhelm von Humbolt에 의해 서양에서 처음으로 제시되었다. 그의 생각은 후에 Franz Boas에 의해 확장되었는데, 그는 세계의 다양한 언어 연구를 통해 그 다양한 언어들이 얼마나 완벽히 다를 수 있는지 발견하였다. 이것은 언어가 그렇게 근본적으로 다르다면, 언어를 사용함으로써 갖게되는 생각 또한 꽤 다를 것이라는 믿음을 낳았다. 이것의 가정은 사람이 무언가를 생각하기 위해선 그것을 말로 할 수 있어야 한다는 것이었다.

언어 결정론의 개념들은 Edward Sapir와 그의 제자인 Benjamin Whorf의 연구에 가장 명확하게 집중되어 있다. 비록 Sapir와 Whorf가 언어 결정론에 관해 뚜렷한 이론을 세우지는 않았지만, 그들의 수많은 글에 남겨진 생각들은 Sapir-Whorf 가설이라고 알려지게 되었다. Sapir-Whorf 가설은 이전 독일 언어학자들의 언어 결정론만큼 강경하진 않았다. 초기 언어학자들은 언어 없는 사고가 불가능하므로 언어에 의해 사고가 지배된다고 주장했지만, Sapir와 Whorf는 사고는 단지 언어에 의해 영향을 받는 것이라고 주장하였고, 이는 강경한 언어 결정론과 완화된 언어 결정론이라는 대립되는 이론들이 생기게 했다.

다음 중 지문에서 표시된 문장의 주요 정보를 가장 잘 나타낸 문장은?
정답 외의 보기들은 중요한 의미가 바뀌거나 주요 정보가 빠져 있다.

(A) 초기 언어학자들은 언어 없이는 사고를 제어할 수 없다고 생각했지만, Sapir와 Whorf는 이러한 생각에 영향을 받지 않았다.
(B) Sapir와 Whorf는 강경한 언어 결정론을 지지했으며, 이는 사고와 언어가 강하게 연결되어 있다는 것을 의미한다.
(C) 초기 언어학자들은 사고와 언어는 늘 연결되어 있다고 주장했지만, Sapir와 Whorf는 이 연결 관계가 그렇게 중요하지 않다고 주장했다.
(D) 초기 언어학자들은 사고가 오로지 언어를 통해서만 존재한다고 주장했지만, Sapir와 Whorf는 언어가 단지 생각을 형성하는 데 도움을 줄 뿐이라고 주장했다.

해설 | 표시된 문장은 크게 세 의미로 나뉠 수 있다. ① 초기 언어학자들은 언어가 없이는 사고가 불가능하다고 주장했다. ② Sapir와 Whorf는 사고는 그저 언어의 영향을 받을 뿐이라고 주장했다. ③ 강경한 언어 결정론과 완화된 언어 결정론으로 나뉘었다. ①, ②의 내용은 언어와 사고의 관계에 대한 서로 다른 주장을 나타낸 것이다.

어휘 | **linguistic** 언어의 **determinism** 결정론 **linguist** 언어학자 **expand** 확장하다 **complete** 완벽한, 완전한 **various** 다양한 **give rise to** ~을 낳다, 일으키다

Reading Practice

p.52

01 (A)   02 (D)   03 (A)   04 (B)   05 (C)

SOLAR ACTIVITY

Like Earth, the Sun has several different forms of visible activity, or weather. But unlike Earth, the Sun's weather is created by forces deep within the Sun rather than in its atmosphere. The Sun is made of electrically charged particles, which create a strong magnetic field around the Sun. Because the Sun rotates slightly faster at its equator than it does at its poles, its magnetic field slowly gets pulled out of balance. A helpful analogy is to think of the Sun's magnetic field as a giant rubber band. As the Sun rotates, the rubber band slowly twists, becoming tighter and tighter.

①As the magnetic field of the Sun gets twisted, resulting in an imbalance of the magnetic field in one part of the Sun, it becomes stronger in one area and ②gives the Sun its first form of weather by preventing heat from rising up from the center of the Sun to this particular area of the surface. The result is a sunspot which is cooler than the rest of the surface. Because they are cooler than the rest of the sun, these sunspots appear to be darker. These dark spots can be several times the size of Earth, and astronomers have been observing them for hundreds of years. Sunspots appear to follow an 11-year cycle of activity. Although no one has been able to adequately explain the causes for this cycle as of yet, it seems that the height of the cycle represents the time of greatest imbalance in the Sun's magnetic field, resulting in more sunspots.

Q04 Eventually, the magnetic field around a sunspot will become so twisted that it will snap. Q05(A) All the energy that has been stored in the twists of the magnetic field will be released in this one moment. The result is a huge jump in temperature called a solar flare. Q05(B) In as little as ten seconds, the temperature will rise to as much as 20 million degrees, up from about 1 million. Q05(D) Solar flares also release huge amounts of radiation, primarily in the form of X-rays, into space. Q05(C) When this radiation reaches the Earth, it can damage satellites and affect weather patterns.

태양 활동

지구와 마찬가지로 태양에도 여러 가지의 가시적인 활동의 형태, 즉 날씨가 있다. 그러나 지구와는 달리 태양 날씨는 대기에 의해서라기보다는 태양의 내부 깊은 곳에 있는 힘 때문에 생긴다. 태양은 전기를 띤 입자들로 구성되어 있는데, 그 입자들은 태양 주위에 강한 자기장을 만들어 낸다. 태양은 극지방보다 적도에서 자전 속도가 약간 더 빠르므로, 이 자기장은 조금씩 균형을 잃게 된다. 태양의 자기장을 거대한 고무밴드로 생각하면 좋은 비유가 될 것이다. 태양이 자전하면 고무밴드는 조금씩 뒤틀리면서 점점 더 팽팽해진다.

태양의 자기장이 뒤틀림에 따라, 태양의 한 부분에서 자기장의 불균형이 생기게 되고, 이것은 한 지역에서 점점 더 강해져 태양의 중심으로부터 특정 표면 지역으로 열이 이동되는 것을 막음으로써 최초의 날씨 형태가 등장하게 한다. 그 결과는 나머지 표면보다 온도가 낮은 흑점이다. 이 흑점들은 태양의 나머지 부분보다 온도가 더 낮으므로 더 어둡게 보인다. 이 어두운 부위는 지구 크기의 몇 배에 이를 수 있으며 천문학자들은 수백 년 동안 이를 관찰해오고 있다. 태양의 흑점은 11년의 활동 주기를 따르는 듯 보인다. 아직은 아무도 이 주기의 원인에 대해 충분히 설명하지 못하지만, 주기의 최고점은 태양의 자기장의 불균형이 가장 커서 더 많은 흑점을 만들어내는 시기를 나타내는 것으로 보인다.

결국 태양의 흑점을 둘러싼 자기장은 너무 많이 뒤틀리게 되고, 그것은 끊어질 것이다. 자기장의 뒤틀린 부분에 저장되어 있던 모든 에너지는 한순간에 방출된다. 그 결과 태양 표면의 폭발이라고 불리는 엄청난 온도의 상승이 일어난다. 10초에 불과한 짧은 시간 동안, 기온은 약 1백만도로부터 2천만도까지 상승할 수 있다. 또 태양 표면의 폭발은 엄청난 양의 복사 에너지를 주로 X선의 형태로 우주로 방출한다. 이러한 복사 에너지가 지구에 도달하면 인공위성에 손상을 입히고 날씨의 패턴에 영향을 미칠 수 있다.

01 다음 중 지문에서 표시된 문장의 주요 정보를 가장 잘 나타낸 문장은? 정답 외의 보기들은 중요한 의미가 바뀌거나 주요 정보가 빠져 있다.

(A) 태양이 뒤틀려짐에 따라 태양의 자기장은 한 구역에서 점점 강해지며, 이 자기장은 태양의 첫 번째 날씨 형태를 일으킨다.
(B) 태양 표면의 특정 지역에서의 더욱 강한 자기장은 뒤틀린 자기장과 태양의 큰 온도 차를 일으킨다.
(C) 태양의 자기장이 뒤틀려지고 표면의 한 부분에 집중될 때, 이것은 열의 이동을 방해한다.
(D) 태양의 특정 표면 지역에서의 자기장 불균형은 자기장이 뒤틀리게 될 것인지 아닌지를 결정한다.

해설 | Sentence Simplification   표시된 문장은 크게 두 의미로 나눌 수 있다. ① 태양의 자기장 뒤틀림은 특정 부분에서의 자기장 불균형을 일으키고, 이것은 한 지역에서 점점 더 강해진다. ② 태양에 최초의 날씨 형태가 등장한다.

02 지문의 result 와 의미상 가장 가까운 것은?
(A) 이유
(B) 조건
(C) 근원
(D) 결과

해설 | Vocabulary   result 는 consequence의 의미가 있다.

03 지문의 adequately 와 의미상 가장 가까운 것은?
(A) 충분히
(B) 과학적으로
(C) 논리적으로
(D) 완전히

해설 | Vocabulary   adequately 는 sufficiently의 의미가 있다.

04 지문에서 it 이 가리키는 것은?
(A) 흑점
(B) 자기장
(C) 에너지
(D) (열, 에너지 등의) 복사

해설 | Reference   단락 3의 첫 문장에서 '자기장(magnetic field)이 너무 많이 뒤틀리게 되면, 마침내 그것(it)은 끊어질 것이다'라고 한다. 여기서 심하게 꼬여서 끊어지는 것은 자기장임을 알 수 있다.

05 태양 표면의 폭발에 관한 내용으로 옳지 않은 것은?
(A) 태양 자기장 불균형의 최종 결과로 생겨난 것이다.
(B) 태양 표면 온도를 급격히 상승시킨다.
(C) 거리 때문에 지구에 영향을 거의 미치지 않는다.
(D) 많은 양의 복사 에너지를 우주로 방출한다.

해설 | Negative Fact   단락 3에서 태양 표면의 폭발이 발생하면 지구의 인공위성에 손상을 입히고 날씨 패턴에 영향을 준다고 말하고 있다. 따라서 (C)는 옳지 않은 내용이다.

어휘 | **visible** 가시적인, 보이는   **atmosphere** 대기   **electrically** 전기로   **particle** 입자   **magnetic field** 자기장   **rotate** 자전하다, 회전하다   **equator** 적도   **pole** 극지방   **analogy** 비유, 유추   **twist** 뒤틀리다   **imbalance** 불균형   **sunspot** 태양의 흑점   **adequately** 충분히   **height** 최고점, 절정   **snap** 끊어지다   **solar flare** 태양 표면의 폭발   **release** 방출하다   **radiation** 복사, 방사선   **primarily** 주로

Chapter 04 Factual Information & Negative Fact

Sample Question   p.55

As psychologists have long argued over whether personality or situation is more influential to a person's behavior, the theory of interactionism was proposed to resolve the debate. Interactionists argue that 02(C) personality traits and situations interact to influence one's behavior, and each variable has an influence on how powerful the other variable is in predicting behavior. For example, 01 some situations, like army boot camp, are where people are not allowed to express their individual personalities. These situations are called "strong situations," in which the situations have a very strong likelihood of accurately predicting behavior. On the contrary, 02(A) "weak situations," such as relaxing alone, allow more freedom for personal expression, so one's personality will be a strong predictor of behavior. Likewise, 02(B) each personality trait can be gauged for how well its presence can predict behavior. For instance, for those who are highly independent, their personality is a strong predictor of behavior, 02(D) while for those who are more self-conscious, the situation may be a stronger predictor of behavior.

성격과 상황 중에 어떤 것이 개인의 행동에 더 영향을 끼치는지를 두고 심리학자들이 오랫동안 논쟁을 해왔는데, 이 논쟁을 해결하기 위해 상호 작용설이 제기되었다. 상호 작용주의자들은 성격 특성과 상황이 개인의 행동에 상호적으로 영향을 미치며, 각각의 변수는 행동을 예측하는 데 있어 나머지 하나의 변수가 행사하는 영향력에 영향을 끼친다고 주장한다. 예를 들어, 신병 훈련소에서와 같이 개인의 성격을 표출하는 것이 허용되지 않는 상황들이 있다. 이러한 상황들은 "강경 상황"이라 불리며, 여기서는 상황이 행동을 정확하게 예측할 가능성이 매우 크다. 반면, 홀로 쉬는 것과 같은 "약한 상황"에서는 개인을 표출할 자유가 더 많이 허락되기 때문에 개인의 성향이 행동의 커다란 예측 변수가 된다. 마찬가지로 각각의 성격 특성은 이것의 존재가 얼마나 행동을 잘 예측할 수 있는지에 따라 측정될 수 있다. 예를 들어, 매우 독립적인 사람들에게는 성격이 행동의 강한 예측 변수가 되지만, 좀 더 남의 시선을 의식하는 사람들에게는 상황이 행동에 대해 더 강한 예측 변수가 될 것이다.

01 지문에 따르면, 다음 중 강경 상황에 관한 내용 중 옳은 것은?
(A) 성격과 상황 모두 행동의 강한 예측 변수이다.
(B) 독특한 성격들의 표현을 허용하지 않을 것이다.
(C) 개인의 성격이 행동을 결정짓는 주요 요소이다.
(D) 매우 독립적인 사람들은 이러한 상황들을 쉽게 이겨낼 수 있다.

02 지문에서 언급되지 않은 것은?
(A) 성격 특성은 약한 상황에서 행동을 예측하는 데 큰 영향을 미칠 것이다.
(B) 각각의 성격 특성은 행동을 예측하는 데 있어 각기 다른 영향력을 가진다.
(C) 상황과 성격 특성 모두 개인의 행동에 영향을 미칠 것이다.
(D) 남의 시선을 매우 의식하는 사람들은 강경 상황에 영향을 받지 않을 것이다.

어휘 | **psychologist** 심리학자   **personality** 성격   **interactionism** 상호 작용설   **variable** 변수   **predict** 예측하다
army boot camp 신병 훈련소   **likelihood** 가능성   **predictor** 예측 변수   **gauge** 측정하다, 판단하다   **self-conscious** 남의 시선을 의식하는

Basic Drill   p.56

| 01 (C) | 02 (B) | 03 (A) | 04 (A) | 05 (D) | 06 (A) |

Vocab Quiz   01 strenuous   02 emitted   03 abandoned   04 delicate   05 prevalent   06 method

01

One may find it intriguing that even prehistoric cave paintings could last intact for over 40,000 years and still show off their vivid colors. The Native Americans used inorganic pigments to color their drawings with materials such as grinded clays and minerals. The color of inorganic pigments varied from red to dark brown, but the extracted pigments were qualitatively undifferentiated. During the Renaissance, master painters threw their souls into finding

사람들은 선사 시대 동굴 벽화가 4만 년 넘게 온전하게 유지되었을 뿐만 아니라, 여전히 선명한 색깔을 뽐낼 수 있다는 점을 흥미롭게 여길 수 있을 것이다. 아메리카 원주민들은 그림에 색을 칠하는 데 빨은 점토 및 광물과 같은 무기 안료를 사용했다. 무기 안료가 가진 색깔은 빨강에서 짙은 갈색까지 다양했지만, 추출된 색소들은 질적으로는 획일적이었다. 르네상스 시대에 거장 화가들은 자신들의 걸작을 위해 풍부하고 광채가 나는 색깔을 찾는 데 온 힘을 쏟았다. 안료를 준비하는 데 있어 가장 힘든 방법 중 하나는 식물 재료를 사용하는 것이었다.

rich and lustrous colors for their masterpieces. One of their arduous methods of preparing pigments was using plant material. Squashed blackberries could create dazzling purple, and the extract of blueberries with a slight hint of vinegar could create a lovely elusive blue. The artists were keen to produce fresh pigments from plants, as they could be easily discolored or denatured.

으깬 블랙베리는 눈부신 자주색을 만들어낼 수 있었으며, 약간의 식초를 첨가한 블루베리 추출물은 아름답고도 찾기 힘든 파란색을 만들어낼 수 있었다. 식물로부터의 안료는 색깔이 쉽게 변색하거나 바뀔 수 있었기 때문에, 예술가들은 신선한 안료를 만들어 내는 것에 상당히 예민하였다.

지문에 따르면, 필자가 언급한 르네상스 시대의 화가들이 식물로부터 만든 색소를 사용한 이유는?

(A) 점토와 진흙에서 얻은 색소는 질이 낮았기 때문에
(B) 지구 광물보다는 식물에서 색소를 추출하기가 더 쉬웠기 때문에
(C) 자신들의 그림을 위해 더욱 다양하고 풍부한 색깔을 원했기 때문에
(D) 식물 외 다른 재료들로부터의 색깔들은 쉽게 못쓰게 되었기 때문에

해설 | 르네상스 시대에는 자신들의 그림에 풍부하고 광채가 나는 색깔을 사용하고 싶어 하는 화가들이 식물로부터 색깔을 추출하여 사용했다고 한다.

어휘 | **intriguing** 흥미로운 **prehistoric** 선사 시대의 **intact** 온전한, 훼손되지 않은 **show off** 뽐내다, 으스대다 **vivid** 선명한 **pigment** 안료, 색소 **clay** 점토 **mineral** 광물 **extract** 추출하다 **qualitatively** 질적으로 **undifferentiated** 획일적인, 구분되지 않는 **lustrous** 광채가 나는, 윤기가 흐르는 **dazzling** 눈부신, 현혹적인 **vinegar** 식초 **elusive** 찾기 힘든, 달성하기 힘든 **keen** 예민한, 날카로운

02

Acid rain is rain that has unusually high levels of acid in it, and is a result of air pollution. When fossil fuels are burned, they release chemicals containing sulfur and nitrogen into the air. Once in the air, these chemicals combine with water vapor to form sulfuric and nitric acids, which then return to Earth when it rains. Since it is the result of burning fossil fuels, acid rain presents the greatest problem to industrial nations that rely heavily on coal as a source of energy. However, more advanced nations, such as the United States and many parts of Western Europe, have developed technology that reduces the amount of sulfur and nitrogen released from their power plants. They are therefore at least partially able to control their acid rain problems.

산성비는 현저하게 높은 산성을 띠고 있는 비를 말하며, 대기 오염의 결과이다. 화석 연료가 타면서 황과 질소를 포함한 화학물질을 대기 중으로 내보낸다. 일단 대기 중에 퍼지게 되면, 이러한 화학물질들은 수증기와 결합하여 황산이나 질산을 형성하고, 그것들은 비가 내릴 때 지상으로 돌아오게 된다. 산성비는 화석 연료 연소의 결과물이기 때문에, 석탄을 주 에너지원으로 쓰고 있는 공업 국가들에서 가장 큰 문제가 된다. 그러나 미국 및 서유럽의 많은 나라와 같이 더 선진화된 국가들은 자국의 발전소에서 배출되는 황과 질소의 양을 줄이는 기술을 개발해냈다. 그러므로 그 나라들은 적어도 부분적으로는 그들의 산성비 문제를 조절할 수 있다.

지문에 따르면, 선진국이 산성비의 피해가 덜한 이유는?

(A) 개발 도상국에 비해 에너지를 덜 소비하기 때문에
(B) 더 깨끗한 에너지 생산 기술이 있기 때문에
(C) 비에서 산을 분리해 낼 수 있는 기술이 있기 때문에
(D) 화석 연료를 태우는 것에 관한 더욱 엄격한 환경 법률이 있기 때문에

해설 | 미국과 서부 유럽과 같은 선진국은 황과 질소를 줄일 수 있는 기술이 있어서 산성비 문제를 일부 조절할 수 있다고 한다.

어휘 | **unusually** 현저하게 **fossil fuel** 화석 연료 **sulfur** 황 **nitrogen** 질소 **vapor** 수증기 **sulfuric** 황을 함유한 **nitric** 질소를 함유한 **industrial** 공업 국가의 **power plant** 발전소 **partially** 부분적으로, 일부분

03

Modernism was probably the most influential intellectual and artistic movement of the twentieth century. Modernism is difficult to define because it has many aspects, but it is essentially the complete rejection of the artistic values of the previous centuries. Artists like Pablo Picasso discarded traditional attitudes toward perspective and realism, and created highly fragmented and abstract works. Similarly, many writers left traditional structures of writing. T. S. Eliot dispensed with structure and organization in his poetry to create free verse, which followed none of the established poetic rules. In the sphere of music, composers began to experiment with new sounds, focusing on the destruction of harmony rather than the creation of it.

모더니즘은 20세기에 가장 영향력이 컸던 지적·예술적 운동이었을 것이다. 모더니즘에는 많은 양상이 있었기 때문에 이를 정의하기가 어렵지만, 본질적으로는 이전 세기들의 예술적 가치를 완전히 거부하는 것이다. Pablo Picasso와 같은 예술가들은 원근법과 사실주의에 대한 전통적 태도를 버리고, 극도로 파편화되고 추상적인 작품을 창조해 냈다. 마찬가지로 많은 작가들은 전통적인 글의 구성을 포기했다. T. S. Eliot은 그의 시에서 구조와 구성을 없애고 자유시를 만들어냈는데, 이것은 기존 시의 규칙 중 어느 것도 따르지 않았다. 음악 분야에서 작곡가들은 새로운 소리로 실험하기 시작했고 하모니를 만들어내기보다 그것을 파괴하는 것에 초점을 맞추었다.

지문에 따르면, 모든 모더니즘 유형의 공통적인 특징은?

(A) 예술의 전통적인 가치 부정
(B) 각기 다른 견해의 통합
(C) 사실주의의 추구
(D) 기존 구성의 분열

해설 | 두 번째 문장에서 모더니즘은 본질적으로 이전 세기의 예술적 가치를 완전히 거부하는 것이라 말한다.

어휘 | **modernism** 모더니즘, 현대주의   **influential** 영향력 있는   **intellectual** 지적인   **define** 정의하다   **aspect** 양상, 견해   **complete** 완전한, 온전한   **rejection** 거부   **discard** 버리다, 폐기하다   **perspective** 원근법   **fragmented** 파편화된   **abstract** 추상적인   **similarly** 마찬가지로   **dispense with** ~을 없애다   **free verse** 자유시   **poetic** 시의   **sphere** 분야, 영역

04

To the naked eye, planets and stars may appear to be similar. However, unlike stars, which are very hot and shine with their own light, planets are much cooler and (A) do not shine on their own. (D) The light one can see from a planet is actually reflected sunlight, as some of the light is reflected back into space when the Sun's light hits a planet. (B) Planets maintain the same orbit, century after century, through a fragile balance of speed and gravity. As the planets orbit around the Sun, their circular motion tends to push them outwards. However, (C) that outward push is exactly balanced by the Sun's gravity, which pulls the planets towards the Sun. This balance keeps the planets in their assigned orbits.

육안으로 보면, 행성과 항성은 비슷하게 보일지도 모른다. 그러나 아주 뜨겁고 스스로 빛나는 항성과는 다르게, 행성은 훨씬 더 차갑고 스스로 빛을 내지 않는다. 행성으로부터 볼 수 있는 빛은 실제로는 반사된 햇빛으로, 태양의 빛이 행성에 다다랐을 때 그 빛 중 일부가 우주로 반사되는 것이다. 행성은 속도와 중력의 섬세한 균형을 통해 같은 궤도를 수세기 동안 유지한다. 행성들이 태양 주위를 돌 때, 이러한 순환 운동은 행성들을 밖으로 밀어내는 경향이 있다. 그러나 그렇게 밖으로 밀어내는 힘은 행성들을 태양 방향으로 잡아당기는 태양의 중력과 정확하게 균형이 맞는다. 이러한 균형은 행성의 지정된 궤도를 유지한다.

행성에 관한 내용 중 옳지 않은 것은?

(A) 스스로 빛을 발한다.
(B) 고정된 궤도를 돈다.
(C) 태양 중력의 영향을 받는다.
(D) 그들의 빛은 단지 햇빛이 반사된 것이다.

해설 | 행성은 스스로 빛을 발하는 것이 아니라, 빛이 반사된 것뿐이라고 한다.

어휘 | **naked eye** 육안   **star** 항성, 별   **reflect** 반사하다   **orbit** 궤도   **fragile** 섬세한, 연약한   **gravity** 중력   **outwards** 밖으로   **assign** 지정하다

05

During the advent of the Industrial Revolution, widespread social acceptance of child labor meant that children made up a large percentage of those who moved from the farm to the factory. In 1833, nearly two-thirds of the factory workers in Leeds, a major industrial center in England, were under the age of 15. England was hardly the only nation where children formed a majority of the factory workforce. As the Industrial Revolution spread throughout Europe and the United States, so did this new form of child labor. Child labor in Industrial Revolution factories, however, quickly proved to be far less benign than child labor on the homestead. With no legal safeguards, children working in the factories of this time were little more than the property of indifferent factory owners. (A) (B) It was typical for a child to work more than ten hours a day under miserable conditions for 30 to 40 percent of the wages for an adult. (C) Furthermore, children were subjected to harsh punishments when they failed to keep pace with older workers. Children were routinely whipped, dunked in cold water, and subjected to other inhumane punishments when they failed to meet their work quotas. Children who tried to run away to escape such treatment were occasionally chained to their work stations.

산업 혁명이 도래하면서, 미성년 노동에 대한 널리 퍼진 사회적 수용은 농장에서 공장으로 옮겨간 사람들의 많은 비율을 어린이들이 차지했다는 것을 의미했다. 1833년에는 영국의 주요 공업 중심지 중 하나인 리즈의 공장 노동자들 중 거의 3분의 2가 15세 이하였다. 어린이들이 공장 노동력의 대부분을 차지한 국가가 영국이 유일하다고는 할 수 없었다. 산업 혁명이 유럽과 미국으로 퍼져나가면서, 이런 새로운 형태의 미성년 노동도 퍼져나갔다. 그러나 곧 산업 혁명 공장들에서의 미성년 노동은 농장에서의 미성년 노동보다 훨씬 더 양호하지 않다는 것이 드러났다. 법적 안전망 없이, 이 당시에 공장에서 일했던 어린이들은 무관심한 공장 주인들의 소유물에 지나지 않았다. 어린이 노동자가 성인 임금의 30~40%만을 받으며 비참한 환경에서 하루 10시간 이상 일하는 것은 일반적이었다. 게다가 어린이들은 성인 노동자들의 작업 속도를 따라가지 못했을 때 가혹한 처벌을 당했다. 어린이들은 작업 할당량을 맞추지 못하면 일상적으로 채찍질 당하고, 차가운 물에 빠뜨려졌고, 다른 여러 형태의 비인간적인 처벌에 처해졌다. 그런 대우에서 벗어나기 위해 도망치려 했던 어린이들은 때때로 그들의 작업장에 사슬로 묶여 있기도 했다.

산업 혁명 당시 어린이 노동자들이 처한 어려움에 관한 내용으로 지문에서 언급되지 않은 것은?

(A) 긴 노동 시간
(B) 성인 노동자에 비해 낮은 임금
(C) 극도로 가혹한 처벌
(D) 무작위적이고도 정당하지 않은 해고

해설 | 지문에서 어린이는 하루에 10시간 이상 노동하고, 성인 임금의 30-40% 밖에 받지 못했다고 말했으므로 (A)와 (B)는 옳은 내용이다. 또한 하루에 정해진 업무 할당량을 채우지 못한 경우 가혹한 처벌을 받았다고 했으므로 (C)도 옳은 내용이다. (D)에 관한 내용은 언급되지 않았다.

어휘 | **advent** 도래, 출현　**widespread** 널리 퍼진　**acceptance** 수용　**workforce** 노동력　**benign** 양호한, 인자한　**homestead** 농장　**property** 소유물, 재산　**indifferent** 무관심한　**wage** 임금, 봉급　**be subjected to** ~을 당하다　**punishment** 처벌　**routinely** 일상적으로　**whip** 채찍질하다　**dunk** (무엇을 물 속에) 빠뜨리다　**inhumane** 비인간적인　**quota** 할당량　**treatment** 대우

06

Map making, or cartography, is an activity of vital importance for human civilization. (B) Maps improve the speed and safety of travel, allow civilizations to set the boundaries of their territories, and occasionally by their absence inspire further exploration of the world. The first known maps date back to around 7,000 B.C. (C) The earliest maps are maps of cities and may have been used by city planners. World maps at this time were next to useless. Early civilizations knew very little about the wider world around them. Long-distance travel was extremely difficult, and so the world maps of early civilizations were based largely on the map makers' religious beliefs.

The first civilization to take a scientific approach to map making was the ancient Greeks. The ancient Greeks, incidentally, were also the first to have an accurate view of the shape of the world. This knowledge was a crucial element in the Greek system of map making. It was the Greeks who first developed the system of latitude and longitude that we still use on maps today. Understanding that the world is a sphere allowed (D) the Greeks to divide their maps according to a 360-degree system. This turned the world into a grid, on which they could precisely describe any location. While the Greek system of map making was a good one, (A) Greek maps were still quite faulty because they had no accurate means of measuring distance at the time.

지도 제작은 인간 문명에 있어 굉장히 중요한 활동이다. 지도는 여행의 속도와 안전을 개선하고, 문명사회가 영토의 경계를 설정하게 해주며, 지도의 부재는 종종 미지의 세계로의 탐험을 고무하기도 한다. 최초로 알려진 지도들은 약 기원전 7천 년으로 거슬러 올라간다. 최초의 지도들은 도시들의 지도였고, 도시 계획가들에 의해 사용되었을 것이다. 이 당시의 세계지도는 거의 쓸모가 없었다. 초기 문명은 그들 주위의 더 넓은 세상에 대해 거의 아는 것이 없었다. 장거리 여행은 굉장히 어려웠으므로, 초기 문명의 세계지도는 주로 지도 제작자의 종교적 믿음에 기반을 두었다.

지도 만드는 것에 과학적인 접근법을 취한 첫 번째 문명은 고대 그리스인들이다. 덧붙여 말하자면, 고대 그리스인들은 또한 세계의 정확한 모양을 알게 된 최초의 사람들이기도 했다. 이러한 지식은 그리스인들의 지도를 만드는 방식에 있어 중요한 요소였다. 우리가 오늘날의 지도에서 아직도 사용하고 있는 경도와 위도 체계를 처음으로 발전시킨 사람들도 그리스인들이었다. 세계가 구형(球形)이라는 점을 이해하는 것은 그리스인들이 360도 체계에 맞추어 지도를 나눌 수 있게 했다. 이것은 세계를 격자의 틀에 맞추었고, 이것을 통해 어떤 위치도 정확하게 설명할 수 있었다. 그리스의 지도 제작 체계가 훌륭하긴 했지만, 그리스 지도는 그 당시에 거리를 재는 정확한 방법이 없었기 때문에 여전히 꽤 큰 결함이 있었다.

지문에 따르면 지도 제작에 관한 내용으로 옳지 않은 것은?

(A) 경도와 위도의 사용으로, 그리스 지도는 여전히 매우 정확하다.
(B) 지도 제작이 발전한 결과, 더 빠르고 더 안전한 여행이 가능했다.
(C) 지도는 본래 도시 계획가들에 의해 도시 지도로 사용되었다.
(D) 그리스 지도는 360도 체계에 기반을 두고 개발되었다.

해설 | 지문의 단락 1에서 지도 덕분에 여행 속도와 안전이 개선되고, 최초의 지도들은 도시 계획가들에 의해 사용되었던 도시 지도였다고 말하고 있다. 또한 단락 2에서는 세계가 구형임을 이해한 그리스인들이 360도 체계에 기반을 두어 지도를 제작했다고 하였다. 그러나 거리를 재는 정확한 방법이 없었기 때문에 여전히 그리스 지도는 부정확하다고 하였으므로 (A)는 옳지 않은 내용이다.

어휘 | **map** 지도　**cartography** 지도 제작(법)　**territory** 영토　**absence** 부재　**inspire** 고무시키다　**exploration** 탐험　**next to** 거의 ~하는　**be based on** ~에 기반을 두다　**largely** 주로, 대부분　**approach** 접근법　**incidentally** 덧붙여 말하자면, 우연히　**latitude** 위도　**longitude** 경도　**sphere** 구형(球形)　**grid** 격자　**precisely** 정확히　**accurate** 정확한

Reading Practice

01 (A), (B) 02 (B) 03 (D) 04 (C) 05 (A)

THE ROBBER BARONS

As an economic system, capitalism assumes that open markets and free competition are always of benefit to the customer. **Q01(B)** the idea is that in order to compete in an open market, a company must offer higher-quality products at a lower cost than its competitors. The result of this competition is that the consumer gets the best possible product at the lowest possible cost. **Q02** Another assumption of capitalism is that governments must refrain from regulating or interfering in the business practices of companies because this prevents free competition. **Q01(A)** The problem, however, is that this system relies on companies operating in an honest and ethical manner, which is not always the case.

In the nineteenth century, America was still a developing nation in many ways. **Q03** Although the Industrial Revolution was rapidly transforming much of the nation, the United States was still a rustic, backward nation when compared with the great nations of Europe. Much of the country's territory was undeveloped and lacked even basic infrastructures, such as usable roads and electricity. Therefore, the focus of the United States during this period was on development, and the men driving this development were the robber barons.

Q04 The robber barons were not actual nobility, but rather were the leading businessmen of the time. They owned the factories, shipyards, and railway companies that built the infrastructure America lacked, and these entrepreneurial activities helped them accumulate great wealth. The robber barons got their name from the fact that many of the business practices they engaged in were unethical and sometimes even criminal. Willing to do whatever was necessary to ensure their dominance in business, the robber barons used ruthless practices and unscrupulous approaches to their business, such as bribing officials, threatening competitors, taking advantage of their employees, and caring little for the environmental impacts of their industries. ①In creating their vast business empires, the robber barons routinely engaged in anti-competitive business practices to destroy their competitors, ②which resulted in a powerful monopoly that gave them the power to regulate the supply and price of commodities, in contrast to the original intention of capitalism. Without the threat of real competition, helpless consumers had no choice but to pay the unreasonable prices set by the robber barons.

---

01 자본주의에 관해 옳은 문장 2개를 선택하시오. 점수를 받기 위해서 반드시 2개의 답을 선택하시오.

(A) 자본주의의 본래 의도한 기능을 수행하기 위해서 기업은 윤리적인 방식으로 운영해야 한다.
(B) 자본주의가 만들어내는 경쟁은 더 낮은 가격과 높은 품질의 상품을 보장한다.
(C) 자본주의는 정부가 사업에 개입하는 것을 막는다.
(D) 자본주의는 높은 품질의 제품을 구매하려는 소비자들 사이의 경쟁을 높인다.

해설 | **Factual Information** 단락 1에 의하면 자본주의에서 경쟁의 결과로 낮은 가격에 품질 좋은 상품을 살 수 있다고 하였고, 이 체제는 윤리적으로 경영되는 기업에 달려 있다고 한다.

02 지문에서 this system 이 가리키는 것은?

(A) 자유 시장
(B) 자본주의
(C) 자유 경쟁
(D) 문제

해설 | Reference 단락 1에서 this system 은 정직하고 윤리적으로 경영되는 기업에 달려 있다고 말하고 있다. 정직하고 윤리적인 사업 운영은 앞에서 설명한 사업체 간의 자유 경쟁으로 싼 값에 질 좋은 상품을 사도록 함으로써, 소비자의 이익을 증진할 수 있는 자본주의의 전제 조건임을 알 수 있다.

03 단락 2에 따르면, 19세기에 미국이 직면했던 문제점은?

(A) 효율적인 사업 운영 방식이 부족했다.
(B) 선진국이 되기 위한 노동력이 부족했다.
(C) 산업 혁명의 빠른 변화에 대응할 수 없었다.
(D) 미국의 많은 지역이 유럽 국가보다 훨씬 더 낙후되어 있었다.

해설 | Factual Information 단락 2에서 당시 미국은 유럽의 강대국보다 낙후되어 있었다고 말하고 있다.

04 지문의 accumulate 와 의미상 가장 가까운 것은?

(A) 소비하다
(B) 투자하다
(C) 축적하다
(D) 공유하다

해설 | Vocabulary 당시 강도 귀족은 미국에서 부족했던 기반 시설들을 만드는 회사를 소유하고 있었다는 내용으로부터 accumulate 의 의미를 추론하면 '축적하다'라는 의미임을 알 수 있다.

05 다음 중 지문에서 표시된 문장의 주요 정보를 가장 잘 나타낸 문장은? 정답 외의 보기들은 중요한 의미가 바뀌거나 주요 정보가 빠져 있다.

(A) 강도 귀족은 산업을 독점하기 위해 수많은 부정직한 방법들을 자주 사용했다.
(B) 강도 귀족은 그 분야에서 우세했기 때문에 종종 비윤리적인 사업 관행을 사용했다.
(C) 강도 귀족은 시장을 통제하기 위해 자본주의의 본래 목적을 변화시키고 싶어 했다.
(D) 강도 귀족은 자신만의 사업 왕국을 만들기 위해 무엇이든 하려고 하였다.

해설 | Sentence Simplification 표시된 문장은 크게 두 의미로 나뉠 수 있다. ① 강도 귀족은 경쟁자를 무너뜨리려고 반경쟁적인 관행을 일삼았다. ② 강력한 독점주의를 만들어 냈다.

어휘 | robber baron 강도 귀족 **capitalism** 자본주의 **assume** 가정하다, 추정하다 **competition** 경쟁 **be of benefit to** ~에게 이익이 되다 **refrain from** ~을 삼가다, 자제하다 **regulate** 규제하다 **interfere** 간섭하다, 끼어들다 **ethical** 윤리적인 **transform** 변형시키다 **rustic** 낙후된, 시골의 **infrastructure** 사회 기반 시설 **nobility** 귀족, 귀족 계급 **shipyard** 조선소 **accumulate** 축적하다, 모으다 **unethical** 비윤리적인 **dominance** 우위, 장악 **ruthless** 무자비한, 가차 없는 **unscrupulous** 부도덕한 **bribe** 뇌물을 주다 **threaten** 협박하다, 위협하다 **vast** 광대한 **anti-competitive** 반경쟁적인 **monopoly** 독점, 전매 **commodity** 상품, 물품 **have no choice but to** ~할 수 밖에 없다

Chapter 05 Inference

Sample Question
p.63

Midden analysis is the analysis of the discarded artifacts of ancient civilizations. What people throw away can tell archaeologists a great deal about a culture. Animal bones and vegetable remains can provide important clues about the diet of ancient peoples. Discarded tools tell us of their occupations. Broken pottery, scraps of clothing, and other personal objects can tell us of their lifestyles. Furthermore, midden analysis can often tell us a great deal about the habitat in which a people lived. Chemical analysis of plant matter, for example, provides information regarding temperatures, average rainfall, and other climatic information about the time period.

패총 분석은 고대 문명에서 버려진 인공 유물들을 분석하는 것이다. 사람들이 버렸던 것들은 고고학자들에게 한 문화에 대해 엄청나게 많은 것들을 이야기해준다. 동물의 뼈와 채소의 잔해는 고대 사람들의 식습관에 대해 중요한 실마리를 제공할 수 있다. 버려진 도구는 그들의 직업을 말해준다. 깨진 도자기, 옷 조각, 기타 여러 개인적 물건을 통해서 우리는 그들의 생활양식을 알 수 있다. 게다가 패총 분석은 종종 우리에게 한 종족이 살았던 거주지에 대한 많은 정보를 주기도 한다. 예를 들어, 식물 물질을 화학적으로 분석하면 당시의 기온, 평균 강수량, 그리고 기타 기후 정보에 대한 정보를 얻을 수 있다.

지문에서 추론할 수 있는 것은?
(A) 패총 분석은 특정 기후에서만 가능한다.
(B) 기후는 식물의 화학적 구성 요소에 영향을 준다.
(C) 버려진 도구들은 고대 식습관에 대한 좋은 단서이다.
(D) 잔해들은 보통 기온 변화에 따라 층으로 쌓인다.

어휘 | **midden** (고고학) 패총, 조개무지   **artifact** 인공 유물, 공예품   **ancient** 고대의   **civilization** 문명   **archaeologist** 고고학자   **bone** 뼈   **diet** 식습관   **discard** 버리다   **occupation** 직업   **scrap** 조각, 파편   **habitat** 거주지   **chemical** 화학의   **temperature** 기온, 온도   **rainfall** 강수(량)   **climatic** 기후의

Basic Drill
p.64

| 01 (B) | 02 (C) | 03 (B) | 04 (B) | 05 (A) | 06 (B) |

Vocab Quiz   01 reflects   02 property   03 substitute   04 reasonably   05 proper   06 prospective

01

Core sampling is an essential tool for scientists wishing to investigate the fundamental data of the Earth in biological, chemical, and geological aspects. In core sampling, a hollow drill is used to drill into the substance of the Earth, for example, sediment or rock. The material contained in the hollow section of the drill can then be brought up and studied. Core sampling can be conducted in any areas with any material where the Earth is stable enough to form layers. A good example would be the ocean floor. On the ocean floor, there is almost no activity to disturb the layering process, such as waves or human activity. Therefore, sediment builds up in progressive layers, with each layer being older than the one on top of it. The sedimentation on the seafloor helps scientists to understand the climate pattern over time, since the seafloor mirrors changes in the Earth's climate.

코어 채취는 생물학적, 화학적, 그리고 지질학적 면에서 지구에 대한 기초 자료를 조사하고자 하는 과학자들에게 필수적인 수단이다. 코어 채취에서는 퇴적물 혹은 암석과 같은 지구의 물질에 구멍을 내기 위해 속이 빈 천공기가 사용된다. 그 빈 구멍 부분에 담아진 물질을 끌어올려 연구할 수 있다. 코어 채취는 지구가 지층이 형성될 만큼 충분히 안정된 곳이라면 어느 장소에서나 어떤 물질로든 행해질 수 있다. 좋은 예로는 대양저를 들 수 있다. 대양저에는 파도나 인간 활동 등의 지층 형성 작용을 방해할 만한 활동이 거의 일어나지 않는다. 그 때문에 침전물은 연속하는 층으로 쌓이며 각 층은 그 위층보다 오래된 것이다. 해저는 지구의 기후 변화를 반영하기 때문에, 해저의 퇴적 작용은 과학자들이 시간에 걸쳐 이루어진 기후 패턴을 이해할 수 있게 돕는다.

지문의 정보를 바탕으로, 코어 채취에 대해 추론할 수 있는 것은?
(A) 지질학 분야에서 상대적으로 새로운 기술이다.
(B) 인구가 집중된 지역의 인근에서는 그렇게 유용하지 않다.
(C) 심해 탐사를 위해 처음 개발되었다.
(D) 퇴적물이 섞인 경우에도 적용할 수 있다.

해설 | 지문에서 코어 채취는 지층이 안정적으로 쌓인 곳에서 이루어질 수 있으며, 그 예로 지층에 영향을 줄 수 있는 파도나 인간의 활동이 없는 해저층을 언급했다. 이를 바탕으로 코어 채취는 인구가 집중된 지역 인근에서는 그렇게 유용하지 않음을 알 수 있다.

어휘 | **investigate** 조사하다 **geologic** 지질학적인 **sediment** 침전물 **hollow** 속이 빈, 구멍 **drill** 천공기 **conduct** 행하다 **layer** 층
disturb 방해하다 **progressive** 연속하는

02

Redox reactions involve the transfer of electrons between two chemical species as a result of the differences in the electronegativities of two chemicals. Electronegativity is a chemical attribute which describes the ability to draw electrons from other chemicals. Chemicals that have the ability to take electrons from other chemicals are said to be highly electronegative, while those that tend to lose electrons easily are said to be electropositive. A common example of a redox reaction would be the formation of rust. Rust forms when iron, a highly electropositive metal, comes into contact with water. When this happens, iron loses electrons to the oxygen atoms in water. The oxygen atoms and the iron are then bound together to form a new chemical compound called iron oxide, or rust. The formation of rust happens more quickly in salt water because salt water is more electrically conductive than regular water and thus allows the electrons to move from the iron atoms to the oxygen atoms more easily.

산화 환원 반응이란 두 화학 물질의 전기음성도 차이의 결과로 생겨나는 것으로, 두 개의 화학종 사이에서 전자들이 이동하는 것을 포함한다. 전기음성도는 다른 화학 물질로부터 전자를 끌어당길 수 있는 화학적 특성을 가리킨다. 다른 화학 물질로부터 전자를 끌어당기는 능력을 갖춘 화학 물질은 음전성이 크다고 표현되며, 쉽게 전자를 잃어버리는 경향이 있는 화학 물질들은 양전성이라고 표현된다. 산화 환원 반응의 흔한 예는 녹이 스는 것이다. 녹은 양전성이 큰 금속인 철이 물과 접촉할 때 생긴다. 이때 철은 물속의 산소 원자에게 전자를 빼앗긴다. 그러면 산소 원자와 철은 서로 결합하여 산화철이라고 불리는 새로운 화합물, 즉 녹을 생성한다. 녹의 형성은 소금물에서 더 빠르게 일어나는데, 이는 소금물이 보통 물보다 전기 전도성이 높아서 전자가 철 원자에서 산소 원자로 보다 쉽게 이동하도록 하기 때문이다.

지문에 따르면 필자가 산소에 대해 암시하는 것은?
(A) 모든 산화 환원 반응에 필요하다.
(B) 소금물의 밀도가 더욱 높은 곳에서 존재한다.
(C) 음전성 화학 물질이다.
(D) 오직 철하고만 결합할 수 있다.

해설 | 지문에서 다른 화학 물질에서 전자를 뺏는 성질을 음전성(electronegativity)이라고 했다. 철을 물에 담갔을 때 녹이 스는 것은 물속에 있는 산소가 철 속에 있는 전자를 빼앗아가기 때문이라고 설명하고 있다. 이를 바탕으로 산소는 음전성 화학 물질임을 알 수 있다.

어휘 | **redox reaction** 산화 환원 반응 **electron** 전자 **chemical** 화학의, 화학 물질 **electronegativity** 전기음성도 **attribute** 특성, 자질
electronegative 음전성의 **tend to** ~하는 경향이 있다 **electropositive** 양전성의 **rust** (금속의) 녹 **iron** 철
come into contact with ~와 접촉하다 **oxygen** 산소 **atom** 원자 **iron oxide** 산화철 **conductive** 전도성의, 도체의

03

Opera is an extended art form where singers and musicians perform a dramatic work combining text and musical score in a theatrical setting, called an opera house. The first composition considered opera, *Dafne*, was developed in the Italian city of Florence during the 1590s. At the time, a group of humanists, musicians, poets, and intellectuals known as the Camerata were interested in injecting storytelling into music, as they were inspired by the belief that the great tragic plays of ancient Greece had been sung rather than simply acted. Another motivation may have been the desire of the composers to find an alternative to the production of music for the Church, which they found rigid, conventional, and oppressive. This is supported by the selection of material for the opera. Early composers took their material from the mythologies of ancient Rome and Greece, which were full of plots, betrayals, and love affairs. From the very beginning, the sobriety of the Church had little place in opera.

오페라는 가수와 음악가가 오페라 하우스라고 부르는 공연 장소에서 글과 음악을 결합한 극적인 공연을 하는 확장된 예술 형태이다. 최초의 오페라 작품으로 여겨지는 『다프네』는 1590년대에 이탈리아의 도시 피렌체에서 처음으로 만들어졌다. 당시 카메라타로 알려진 인문주의자, 음악가, 시인, 그리고 지식인들은 고대 그리스의 위대한 비극적인 연극들이 단순히 연기되기보다는 노래로 불렸을 것이란 믿음에 영감을 받아, 음악 안에 이야기하는 것을 주입하는 것에 관심을 가졌다. 또 다른 동기는 작곡가들이 엄숙하고, 진부하고, 또한 억압적이라고 생각했던 교회 음악에 대한 대안을 찾고자 했던 욕구였을 것이다. 이것은 오페라를 위해 선택되었던 소재로 뒷받침될 수 있다. 초기의 작곡가들은 고대 로마와 그리스의 신화에서 소재를 취했는데, 그 안에는 음모와 배신, 연애 사건이 가득했다. 첫 시작부터 교회의 근엄함은 오페라에서 찾아볼 수 없었다.

지문에서 초기 오페라에 대해 추론할 수 있는 것은?
(A) 항상 그리스에서 공연되었다.
(B) 종교적인 주제가 다뤄지는 경우는 드물었다.
(C) 질적인 면보다는 창의성에 중점을 두었다.
(D) 작곡가들에 의해서만 만들어졌다.

해설 | 지문에서 오페라가 탄생한 이유 중의 하나로 엄숙하고 진부한 교회 음악의 대안을 찾는 작곡가들의 욕망이 언급되었고, 오페라에서는 교회에 관한 내용은 거의 찾아볼 수 없었다고 설명한다. 이를 바탕으로 초기 오페라는 종교적 주제를 드물게 다루었음을 알 수 있다.

어휘 | **combine** 결합하다　　**composition** 작품　　**humanist** 인문주의자, 인도주의자　　**poet** 시인　　**intellectual** 지식인　　**inject** 주입하다, 도입하다　　**inspire** 영감을 주다　　**tragic** 비극적인　　**motivation** 동기　　**alternative** 대안　　**rigid** 엄숙한　　**conventional** 진부한, 판에 박힌　　**oppressive** 억압적인　　**mythology** 신화　　**plot** 음모　　**betrayal** 배신　　**love affair** 연애 사건　　**sobriety** 근엄함, 진지함

04

Both temperature and salinity affect the density of water. In turn, density affects the ability of a substance to float. Less-dense substances will rise above denser substances, which can be seen with oil and water. Sea water is not perfectly clear, as sunlight only penetrates through the first few hundred feet of sea water and, as a result, all of the sun's heat is absorbed by the upper surface layer of sea water. Wave action mixes this upper-level water together fairly evenly, and so the temperature remains relatively uniform. Beyond the reach of sunlight and wave action, however, the temperature of the ocean drops rapidly by more than 20 degrees Celsius after a few hundred feet, and then continues to drop at a far slower rate. The rapid temperature change results in two layers of water with very different densities, surface water and deep water, separated by the thin layer called thermocline. Nearly 90 percent of the world's water is below the thermocline, but the vast majority of sea life lives above it.

온도와 염분은 물의 밀도에 영향을 미친다. 마찬가지로, 밀도는 물질이 뜰 수 있는 능력에 영향을 준다. 밀도가 낮은 물질은 밀도가 높은 물질 위로 떠오르는데, 이는 기름과 물의 예에서 볼 수 있다. 해수는 완전히 투명하지 않으며, 햇빛은 해수의 처음 몇백 피트만을 통과함에 따라 모든 태양열은 해수의 위 표면층에만 흡수된다. 파도의 작용으로 위에 있는 층의 물은 모두 꽤 균등하게 섞이게 되며, 그래서 온도는 비교적 균일한 상태로 유지된다. 그러나 햇빛과 파도의 작용이 미치는 범위를 벗어나면 수백 피트 아래 바다의 수온은 섭씨 20도 이상 급격하게 떨어지며, 그러고 나서는 더 완만한 속도로 온도가 계속 떨어진다. 급격한 온도 변화는 매우 다른 밀도를 가진 두 개의 물의 층, 즉 수온약층이라고 불리는 얇은 층에 의해 나누어진 지표수와 심층수를 야기한다. 지구의 물 중 약 90%가 수온약층 아래에 존재하지만, 바다 생물의 대다수는 수온약층 위에서 살아간다.

지문에서 심층수에 대해 추론할 수 있는 것은?
(A) 도달하는 햇빛의 양에 쉽게 영향을 받는다.
(B) 다른 층들에 비해 밀도가 높다.
(C) 바다 생물에게 적절한 환경을 제공한다.
(D) 지구상의 물 중 작은 부분만 차지한다.

해설 | 지문에서 온도는 물의 밀도에 영향을 미치며 밀도가 높은 것이 아래로 내려간다고 했다. 또한, 수백 피트 아래의 바다의 수온은 급격한 온도 차를 갖고 있으며 수온약층에 의해 매우 다른 밀도를 가진 지표수와 심층수로 나뉜다고 한다. 이를 바탕으로 심층수는 바다의 다른 층들에 비해 밀도가 높음을 알 수 있다.

어휘 | **temperature** 온도　　**salinity** 염분　　**density** 밀도　　**penetrate** 통과하다, 꿰뚫다　　**absorb** 흡수하다, 빨아들이다　　**layer** 층, 막　　**fairly** 꽤　　**evenly** 균등하게　　**relatively** 비교적, 상대적　　**rapidly** 급격하게　　**Celsius** 섭씨　　**thermocline** 수온약층(바다나 호수의 수온이 급격히 변하는 부분)

05

The custom of paying a bride price before marriage is still a well-established part of many African cultures. In paying a bride price, the family of the groom must provide payment to the family of the bride before the marriage is allowed. The bride price can vary greatly from culture to culture in Africa. In the Zulu and Swazi tribes of southern Africa, the bride price often takes the form of cattle. The actual payment of money sometimes takes place, but payment in goods is more frequent. The amount paid in a bride price can also vary. In modern times, the bride price is usually quite small, and its value is mainly symbolic. However, the bride price can still be quite high, especially among prominent or highly traditional families.

There are a number of justifications used to explain the payment of a bride price. The first is that the bride price represents an acknowledgement of the expense the bride's family has gone to in order to raise her and bring her up as a suitable bride for the groom. It also represents payment for the loss of a family member, since the bride will officially become a member of her husband's family and will leave her own. On a deeper level, the bride price represents payment for the fact that the bride will bring children into the family of the groom, thereby increasing the wealth of the

결혼 전에 신부값을 지급하는 풍습은 많은 아프리카 문화에서 여전히 흔들리지 않고 있다. 신부값을 지급할 때 신랑의 가족은 결혼이 허락되기 전에 신부의 가족에게 대가를 지급해야 한다. 아프리카에서 신부값은 문화에 따라 크게 다르다. 남아프리카의 줄루와 스와지 부족 사회에서 신부값은 종종 가축으로 지급된다. 실제로 돈을 지급하는 일도 가끔은 있지만, 물건으로 지급하는 것이 더 흔하다. 신부값에 지불되는 양 또한 다르다. 현대에는 신부값이 때때로 아주 적고 대개 상징적인 가치를 지닌다. 그러나 특히 저명하거나 전통 있는 가문 사이에서는 신부값이 여전히 꽤 높다.

신부값을 지급하는 것을 설명하는 데에 사용되는 여러 정당화하는 이유가 있다. 첫째로 신부값은 신부를 키우고 신랑에게 적합한 신부로 성장시키기 위해 신부의 가족이 치른 비용을 인정하는 의미를 나타낸다. 또한 신부가 공식적으로 신랑 집안의 구성원이 되고 자신의 가족을 떠날 것이기 때문에, 신부값은 가족 구성원의 손실에 대한 대가를 의미하기도 한다. 더 깊은 의미에서 신부값은 신부가 신랑의 집안에 자식을 낳아줌으로써 그 집안의 부를 증가시킬 것이라는 사실에 대한 지급을 의미한다. 이러한 개념은 신부가 아이를 낳지 못하면 신부값을 종종 돌려주어야 한다는 사실로 뒷받침된다.

family. This concept is reinforced by the fact that the bride price must often be returned if the bride fails to bear children.

단락 2에서 필자가 아프리카의 가정에 대해서 암시하는 것은?
(A) 자녀 출산을 매우 중요시한다.
(B) 결혼한 딸을 다시는 볼 수 없다.
(C) 결혼식 날 신부값을 지불한다.
(D) 높은 신부값을 받기 위해 딸을 키우는 데 큰 노력을 들인다.

해설 | 지문 마지막 부분에서 신부값은 가족의 부를 늘려줄 수 있는 자녀 출산에 대한 대가이고, 아이를 낳지 못한 경우에 신부값은 다시 되돌려 받는다고 한다. 이를 바탕으로 아프리카 가정에서는 자녀 출산이 무척 중요시되고 있음을 알 수 있다.

어휘 | **custom** 풍습, 관습 **bride price** 신부값 **cattle** 가축 **symbolic** 상징적인 **prominent** 저명한 **justification** 정당화하는 이유 **represent** 나타내다 **acknowledgement** 인정 **officially** 공식적으로 **reinforce** 뒷받침하다 **bear** (아이를) 낳다, 출산하다

06

From the thirteenth to the fifteenth century, the wool trade was the foundation of the British economy. The British held a monopoly on the finest grade of wool that was being produced in Europe at the time. However, relatively little of the wool the island produced was actually spun into yarn to produce cloth. Rather, the bulk of the raw wool was shipped across the channel to Flanders, where the best weavers produced very high-quality cloth. It is true that wool was produced elsewhere, but it was often of such poor quality and roughness that it could not compete with the quality that came from England.

Because the export of raw wool was extremely lucrative, the trade became the target of the British Crown, who sought to control it and, by extension, profit from it. Customs and taxes were levied on wool exports to mainland Europe. Because the King was so closely tied to the Church of England at this time in history, many of these profits made their way back to the Church. Consequently, the Church also took a vested interest in the wool trade and the potential profits that could be reaped from it.

Despite the high demand for British wool and the involvement of the Crown and the Church, England remained solely focused on the production and export of raw wool. Refinement of the wool into higher-value cloth was done almost exclusively in Flanders, which imported the raw wool and shipped the cloth back to England at a profit. English manufacturers only began to focus on producing high-grade cloth in the eighteenth century with the arrival of the Industrial Revolution and the large-scale mechanization of weaving and production.

13~15세기에 양모 무역은 영국 경제의 토대였다. 그 당시 영국은 유럽에서 생산되고 있던 고품질의 양모에 대한 독점권을 가지고 있었다. 그러나 실제로는 그 섬에서 생산되던 양모 중 상대적으로 적은 양이 실로 만들어져 옷으로 만들어졌다. 대신 많은 원모는 해협을 통해 플랑드르로 보내졌는데, 이곳에서는 최고의 방직공들이 매우 높은 품질의 옷을 만들었다. 다른 곳에서도 양모가 생산되었지만, 질이 좋지 않고 거칠어서 영국 양모의 질과는 경쟁이 안 됐다.

원모의 수출이 매우 수익성이 좋았기 때문에, 이 무역은 이것을 통제하고 더 나아가 이로부터 이익을 얻으려 하는 영국 왕실의 표적이 되었다. 유럽 대륙으로 수출되는 양모에 관세와 세금이 부과되었다. 역사상 이 시기의 왕실은 영국 국교회와 밀접히 묶여있었기 때문에, 대부분 수익은 교회로 되돌아갔다. 결과적으로 교회는 양모 무역에서 기득권을 가지고 있었을 뿐만 아니라 이로부터 거둘 수 있는 잠재적 이익까지 가졌다.

영국산 양모에 대한 높은 수요와 영국 왕실과 교회의 관여에도 불구하고, 영국은 오로지 원모의 생산과 수출에만 집중했다. 양모를 사용해 가치가 높은 옷을 만드는 것은 거의 플랑드르에서만 행해졌으며, 이곳에서는 원모를 수입하여 영국으로 옷을 다시 팔아 이익을 남겼다. 영국 제조사들은 산업 혁명과 대규모로 기계화된 제직 및 생산의 도래로 인해 18세기에 고품질 옷을 생산하는 데에 초점을 맞추기 시작했다.

단락 3에서 필자가 산업 혁명 동안의 옷 생산에 대해 암시하는 것은?
(A) 원모의 수출은 여전히 왕실의 주요 관심사였다.
(B) 기술 진보는 영국에서 방모 직물의 생산을 가능하게 했다.
(C) 플랑드르는 곧바로 최고의 방모 직물 생산국이라는 위치를 잃었다.
(D) 원모와 가공한 양모의 수출에 세금을 부과함으로써 교회는 새로운 이익을 챙겼다.

해설 | 지문에서는 산업 혁명 전에 영국은 양모의 무역에만 집중했지만, 산업 혁명 후 옷 생산에 초점을 맞추었다고 했다. 이를 바탕으로 산업 혁명의 기술 진보가 영국의 방모 직물을 가능하게 하였음을 알 수 있다.

어휘 | **wool trade** 양모 무역 **hold a monopoly** 독점권을 갖다 **relatively** 상대적으로 **channel** 해협 **the bulk of** 많은, 대부분의 **compete** 경쟁하다 **lucrative** 수익성이 좋은 **Church of England** 영국 국교회 **vested interest** 기득권 **reap** 거두다, 수확하다 **Industrial Revolution** 산업 혁명

Reading Practice

p.68

01 (C)   02 (D)   03 (D)   04 (A)   05 (B)

THE EVOLUTION OF HUMAN SOCIETY

Anthropologists consider the evolution of human society to involve four social revolutions: hunter-gatherer, agrarian, industrial, and post-industrial. The first two of these are considered to have had a profound influence on each other, despite being quite different in nature.

A hunter-gatherer society is perhaps the earliest form of human groups. They lived by hunting, fishing, and gathering wild sources of food. Q01(B) Because they had to follow the animals and the seasons, they led a nomadic life. This lifestyle dictated many aspects of their society and culture. Q01(C) Hunter-gatherer societies were typically small groups of people, numbering between 20 to 30 for small groups, and up to 150 for larger ones. Q01(D) Consequently, many of their possessions were small, portable, and sourced directly from the animals they hunted or their surrounding natural environment. The clothing they wore was made from animal skins and hides, and their tools were from scavenged wood or stone. Q02 In most cases, their shelters were portable or semi-permanent, allowing them to readily follow their food sources with the seasons and migration patterns. Labor was typically divided along gender lines, with men usually responsible for hunting while women most of the gathering. This distinction was not exclusive, though, as many aspects of daily life were shared between men and women. Q01(A) Childcare, for instance, was typically a cooperative affair, where a child would be cared for by the community to a large degree, rather than exclusively by its mother.

①Because of the permanent nature of its food source and higher level of productivity, ②agrarian societies were able to support a much denser population base, ③with the result that many aspects of culture, economy, and society evolved in ways markedly different from the nomadic hunter-gatherers. Q04 As a result of the excess food which could be stored and sold later at a profit, complex economies evolved to manage and grow the surpluses. Q05 Consequently, agrarian societies heralded the development of permanent dwellings, community spaces, and utilities such as roads and running water, as well as the evolution of more complex governing structures.

In short, the emergence of agrarian societies established the foundation for many aspects of our modern culture today. Our systems of governance, transportation, and communication all had their early start in an agrarian society. Agrarian societies were also the foundation for the move toward industrial technology and our modern society.

인류 사회의 진화

인류학자들은 인류 사회의 진화가 '수렵·채집인 사회, 농경 사회, 산업 사회, 그리고 탈공업화 사회'라는 네 가지 사회 혁명을 포함한다고 생각한다. 이 중 수렵·채집인 사회와 농경 사회는 사실상 굉장히 다른 것임에도 불구하고 서로에게 상당한 영향을 끼쳤다고 여겨진다.

수렵·채집인 사회는 아마도 인간 집단의 가장 초기 형태일 것이다. 이들은 사냥, 낚시, 그리고 야생에서의 음식 재료 채집을 통해 살았다. 그들은 동물과 계절을 따라 움직여야 했기 때문에, 유목 생활을 했다. 이러한 생활 양식은 그들의 사회와 문화에 영향을 주었다. 수렵·채집인 사회는 적게는 20~30명, 많게는 150명까지로 이루어진 사람들의 소규모 집단이었다. 그 결과, 소유물 중 상당수는 크기가 작고, 휴대가 쉬운 것들이었으며 그들이 사냥한 동물 혹은 자연 환경에서 직접 얻은 것들이었다. 그들이 입던 옷은 동물의 가죽으로 만들어졌으며, 도구는 버려진 나무나 돌들로 만들어졌다. 대부분의 경우에 그들의 주거지는 이동할 수 있거나 반영구적이어서 계절과 이동 방식에 맞춰 식재료들을 따라 쉽게 옮겨 다닐 수 있었다. 노동은 일반적으로 성별에 따라 분배되었으며, 여자는 채집 대부분을 책임졌던 반면 남자는 사냥을 책임졌다. 그러나 많은 일상생활의 양상이 남성과 여성에 공유되었기에 이러한 구분은 배타적인 것은 아니었다. 예를 들어, 양육은 아이의 엄마에 의해서만 배타적으로 이루어진 것이 아니라 상당 부분 공동체로부터 보살핌을 받는 협동적인 일이었다.

지속해서 구할 수 있는 식재료와 높은 수준의 생산성 덕분에, 농경 사회에서는 더 많은 인구가 살아갈 수 있었고, 문화·경제·사회적으로 많은 면에서 발달함에 따라 유목의 수렵·채집인 사회와는 두드러지게 달라졌다. 저장이 가능하여 후에 이익을 남기고 팔 수 있는 초과 식량의 결과로 이 과잉을 처리하고 증가시키기 위해 복잡한 경제가 발달했다. 따라서 농경 사회는 복잡한 지배 구조의 진화뿐만 아니라 영구적인 주거, 공동체 공간, 그리고 도로와 유수 같은 시설들의 발전을 예고했다.

요컨대, 농경 사회의 출현은 오늘날 현대 문화의 많은 양상의 기반을 구축했다. 우리의 통치, 교통, 의사소통의 시스템 모두 농경 사회에서 처음 시작했다. 또한 농경 사회는 산업 기술 및 현대 사회로 향해가는 토대였다.

---

01 단락 2에 따르면, 수렵·채집인 사회에 관한 내용으로 옳지 <u>않은</u> 것은?

(A) 아이들은 공동체에 의해 협력하여 길러졌다.
(B) 유목하고 계절과 동물을 따라가는 경향이 있었다.
(C) 주거지는 많은 사람을 수용할 정도로 컸다.
(D) 도구는 가까이에 있는 재료들로부터 발전했다.

해설 | Negative Fact   단락 2에서 수렵·채집인 사회의 주거지는 이동할 수 있거나 반영구적이라고 했으며, 크기에 대해서는 뚜렷하게 언급되지 않았다.

02 단락 2의 정보에 따르면, 수렵·채집인 사회에 대해 추론할 수 있는 것은?

(A) 영구적인 주거지의 발달은 식량 안보의 비결이었다.
(B) 동물의 가죽은 그 사회에서 종종 기준 통화로 사용되었다.
(C) 단체에서 개인의 사회적 위치는 물질적인 부에 의해 결정되었다.
(D) 초기 도구와 주거지는 유목 생활에서 비롯된 직접적인 결과였다.

해설 | Inference   계절과 이동 방식에 맞춰 이주하는 생활을 했기 때문에 초기 도구는 작고, 주거지는 이동할 수 있거나 반영구적이었다고 하였다. 이를 바탕으로 수렵·채집인 사회의 초기 도구와 주거지는 그들의 생활 양식의 직접적 결과임을 알 수 있다.

03 다음 중 지문에서 표시된 문장의 주요 정보를 가장 잘 나타낸 문장은? **정답 외의 보기들은 중요한 의미가 바뀌거나 주요 정보가 빠져 있다.**

(A) 그들의 특성에 따라, 많은 인구는 농경 사회 및 수렵·채집인 사회와의 많은 차이점의 예가 된다.
(B) 농경 사회와 유목 사회의 다른 문화·경제·사회적 특징들은 인구 밀도 및 음식의 생산성의 차이를 야기했다.
(C) 수렵·채집인 사회와는 달리, 농경 사회의 문화 및 경제가 음식의 과잉으로 인해 각기 독립적으로 발전했다.
(D) 농경 사회의 식량 과잉과 높은 생산성은 더 많은 인구로 이어졌으며, 수렵·채집인 사회와 여러 측면에서 다르게 되었다.

해설 | Sentence Simplification   표시된 문장은 크게 세 의미로 나뉠 수 있다. ① 농경 사회에서는 지속해서 구할 수 있는 식재료(즉, 식량 과잉)와 높은 수준의 생산성이 가능했다. ② 이로 인해 농경 사회는 더 높은 인구가 살아갈 수 있었다. ③ 많은 문화·경제·사회적 발달로 수렵·채집인 사회와는 두드러지게 달라졌다.

04 단락 3에서 농경 사회에 관해 추론할 수 있는 것은?

(A) 농경 사회는 복잡한 사회가 되기 위한 전제 조건을 충족했다.
(B) 더 밀집된 인구는 농경 사회에 의해서만 유지될 수 있었다.
(C) 농경 사회에서 넘쳐나는 음식은 다른 집단과의 무역을 북돋았다.
(D) 농경 사회 사람들은 수렵·채집인 사회의 사람들보다 더 나은 교육을 받았었다.

해설 | Inference   단락 3에서 농경 사회에서 초과 식량의 결과로 이 과잉을 처리하고 증가시키기 위해 복잡한 경제 구조와 그에 따른 많은 시설이 발달했다고 하였다. 이를 바탕으로 농경 사회는 복잡한 사회가 되기 위한 전제 조건을 갖췄음을 알 수 있다.

05 지문의 emergence 와 의미상 가장 가까운 것은?

(A) 능력
(B) 출현
(C) 구조
(D) 발전

해설 | Vocabulary   emergence 의 바로 앞 문장에서 농경 사회가 여러 발전을 예고했다고 했으므로, 농경 사회의 '출현(emergence)'이 현대 문화의 많은 양상의 기반을 구축했음을 알 수 있다. 따라서 emergence 는 advent와 같은 의미를 지녔음을 알 수 있다.

어휘 | **anthropologist** 인류학자   **evolution** 진화   **agrarian** 농경의, 농업의   **post-industrial** 탈공업화의   **in nature** 사실상, 현실적으로
nomadic life 유목 생활   **lifestyle** 생활 양식   **dictate** 영향을 주다, 좌우하다   **up to** ~까지   **possession** 소유물, 소지품
portable 휴대가 쉬운, 이동이 쉬운   **hide** 동물의 가죽   **shelter** 주거지, 거주지   **semi-permanent** 반영구적인   **readily** 쉽게, 순조롭게
migration 이동, 이주   **labor** 노동   **be responsible for** ~에 책임이 있다   **exclusive** 배타적인, 독점적인   **aspect** 양상, 측면
permanent 지속적인, 영구적인   **productivity** 생산성   **population** 인구   **markedly** 두드러지게, 현저하게   **surplus** 과잉
herald 예고하다, 알리다   **emergence** 출현, 발생

Chapter 06 Rhetorical Purpose

Sample Question p.71

Changes in environment and evolution are completely intertwined and cannot be considered separate matters, since environmental changes present new challenges that a species must adapt to or it may face extinction. Instances illustrating this fact are numerous. Dramatic climatic changes 64 million years ago led to the extinction of the dinosaurs and the flourish of mammals. Also, rapid changes in the African climate led early hominids to develop bigger and more complex brains to deal with unpredictable weather, which would become the base of modern human beings. The introduction of antibiotics in medicine has led the evolution of antibiotic-resistant strains of bacteria. These are just a few of the ways in which environmental changes help drive evolution.

환경의 변화는 하나의 종이 적응하지 못하면 멸종에 직면할 수도 있다는 새로운 위기를 제시하기 때문에, 환경의 변화와 진화는 전적으로 서로 얽혀 있으며 각기 다른 문제로 여겨질 수 없다. 이러한 사실을 설명하는 예는 수없이 많다. 6천 4백만 년 전의 급격한 기후 변화는 공룡의 멸종과 포유류의 번영을 가져왔다. 또한 아프리카의 급격한 기후 변화는 원시 인류로 하여금 종잡을 수 없는 날씨에 대처하기 위해 더욱 크고 더욱 복잡한 뇌를 발달시키게 했으며, 이는 현대인의 기반을 마련했다. 의학에서의 항생제의 도입은 항생제에 내성을 가진 박테리아 종의 진화를 이끌었다. 이런 것들은 환경의 변화로 진화가 발생한 단 몇 개의 예일 뿐이다.

필자가 항생제를 언급하는 이유는?
(A) 항생제의 다양한 쓰임을 언급하기 위해
(B) 유기체가 적응한 환경적 변화의 예를 들기 위해
(C) 약의 개발로 인간의 건강이 어떻게 위험해지는지 논의하기 위해
(D) 진화의 결과가 늘 긍정적이지만은 않다는 것을 보여주기 위해

어휘 | **evolution** 진화　**intertwine** 서로 얽히게 하다　**extinction** 멸종　**climatic** 기후의　**hominid** 원시 인류　**antibiotic** 항생제

Basic Drill p.72

01 (B)　**02** (D)　**03** (A)　**04** (B)　**05** (B)　**06** (B)

Vocab Quiz　**01** approximately　**02** fundamental　**03** combination　**04** whole　**05** hostile　**06** chief

01

The Earth's magnetic field is roughly in line with its axis of rotation, and in some places extends for tens of thousands of miles beyond the Earth. The magnetic field of the Earth, however, is not entirely stable, since it is generated by a geodynamo, the kinetic energy derived from the Earth's liquid core. The Earth's magnetic field has undergone a large number of major shifts and reversals throughout the history of the Earth. Any number of factors can lead to local or temporary disturbances in the magnetic field. Firstly, according to the Earth's geologic record, its magnetic field flips on average about once every 200,000 years. Also, its pattern of declination has shown westward drifting features for more than 400 years. In addition, the overall strength of the Earth's magnetic field weakens and causes greater instability when a newly generated field lines up in the opposite direction of an existing magnetic field, or when a new field continues to grow.

지구 자기장은 자전축과 거의 일치하며, 일부 지역에서는 지구 밖으로 수만 마일을 뻗어 나가기도 한다. 그러나 지구 자기장은 지구 액체 핵으로부터 나온 운동 에너지인 지오다이너모로부터 발생하기 때문에, 완전히 안정된 것은 아니다. 지구 자기장은 지구 역사상 수많은 주요 변화와 전환을 겪었다. 꽤 많은 수의 요인들이 자기장에서의 지역적 혹은 일시적 변동을 가져올 수 있다. 첫째로, 지구의 지질 기록에 따르면 지구 자기장은 평균 약 20만 년 마다 뒤집힌다. 또한 서쪽으로 이동하는 특징적인 양상이 400년 이상 동안 보인다. 게다가 새로운 자기장이 기존의 자기장과 반대 방향에서 생기거나 새로운 자기장이 계속해서 커지게 되면, 지구 자기장의 전반적인 세기가 약해지고 굉장히 불안정해진다.

지문에서 필자가 지구 자기장을 설명하는 방법은?
(A) 다른 행성의 자기장과 대조함으로써
(B) 지구 자기장의 불안정성의 원인이 되는 요인들의 예를 제시함으로써
(C) 지구 자기장을 불안정하게 만드는 데에 있어 지구 액체 핵의 역할을 설명함으로써
(D) 지구 자기장의 불안정성을 일으키는 원인에 대한 다양한 이론을 언급함으로써

해설 | 지문의 주제는 지구의 자기장이 불안정하다는 내용이다. 필자는 지구 자기장은 지오다이너모로부터 발생하기 때문에 완전히 안정된 것은 아니고, 많은 요인으로 인해 불안정하게 될 수 있다고 하며 그 요인의 예시들을 제시하고 있다.

어휘 | **magnetic field** 자기장 **kinetic** 운동의 **any number of** 꽤 많은 수의 **temporary** 일시적인 **disturbance** 변동, 방해
instability 불안정(성) **opposite** 반대의, 다른 편의

02

The Nile is the longest river in the world, flowing from Lake Victoria of Uganda to the Mediterranean Sea. It is considered a primary water source to a number of countries in Africa. Even in ancient times, the Nile had such a crucial role in the lives of Egyptians that many believed the great civilization of Ancient Egypt was indebted to the Nile. Although the inundation of the Nile was a great threat to the Egyptians, as the overflowing water often ravaged communities near its banks, the Egyptians relied on the regular occurrence of inundation in their agricultural practices by using a calendar. The water level of the river would rise from June to September, depositing a layer of mineral-rich soil on the river's banks. As the inundation receded in October, farmers plowed and planted crops to well-watered and fertile soil called silt. Egyptians' unique farming practices using the Nile allowed them to devote more time and resources to cultural, technological, and artistic pursuits.

나일 강은 세계에서 가장 긴 강으로, 우간다의 빅토리아 호수에서부터 지중해까지 흐른다. 나일 강은 아프리카 여러 국가에 주요한 수원으로 여겨진다. 고대 시대에도 나일 강은 이집트인들의 삶에서 굉장히 중요한 역할을 했기에 많은 사람들은 고대 이집트의 위대한 문명이 나일 강의 덕분이었다고 생각한다. 넘쳐난 물은 종종 둑 근처의 지역 사회를 황폐하게 하였기 때문에 나일 강의 범람은 이집트인들에게 굉장한 위협이기도 했지만, 이집트인들은 그들의 달력을 사용하여 이러한 범람의 주기적인 발생을 농업 활동에 잘 이용했다. 강의 수위는 6~9월에 높아져 강의 둑에 무기물이 풍부한 흙 층을 만들었다. 10월에는 강의 범람이 약해져, 농부들은 세사(silt)라고 불리는 관개가 잘되고 비옥한 흙을 갈고 작물들을 심었다. 나일 강을 이용한 이집트인들의 독특한 농사법은 이들이 많은 시간과 자원들을 문화적·기술적·예술적 소일거리에 사용할 수 있게 하였다.

지문에서 필자가 달력을 언급하는 이유는?
(A) 고대 이집트 문명의 발전을 증명하기 위해
(B) 이집트의 달력 체계를 다른 문화의 달력 체계와 비교하기 위해
(C) 이집트인들이 자신들만의 달력을 만든 본질적 이유를 알려주기 위해
(D) 이집트인들이 강의 범람 주기를 예측했던 방법을 설명하기 위해

해설 | "… the Egyptians relied on the regular occurrence of inundation in their agricultural practices by using a calender"에서 이집트인들은 달력을 사용하여 강의 범람 주기를 예측했고 이를 농업 활동에 사용했다고 말해주고 있다.

어휘 | **flow** 흐르다 **Mediterranean Sea** 지중해 **primary** 주요한, 주된 **crucial** 중요한, 결정적인 **civilization** 문명
be indebted to ~의 덕분이다, 신세를 지다 **inundation** 범람, 침수 **ravage** 황폐하다 **bank** 둑, 제방 **plow** 갈다, 경작하다
crop (농)작물 **fertile** 비옥한, 기름진

03

In his experiment conducted in 1928, Griffith used two types of bacteria: type III-S (smooth) and type II-R (rough). The former type of bacteria had a capsule that protected itself from the host's immune system, resulting in the death of the host, while the latter lacked the capsule and was killed by the host's immune system. During the experiment, Griffith discovered that once bacteria from III-S were killed by heat, they were no longer lethal. In the following stage of the observation, Griffith injected a combination of heat-killed III-S and live II-R into mice. Surprisingly, this mixture of nonlethal bacteria became virulent and killed the mice. Griffith concluded that some part of dead III-S somehow transferred to the II-R and allowed the II-R to create a protective coat, eventually killing the host. Today, we know the transformed information that survived the heating process is called DNA and that it can be transferred through a process known as transformation.

Griffith는 1928년 자신의 실험에서 III-S형 (smooth)과 II-R형 (rough)의 두 가지 박테리아를 사용했다. III-S형 박테리아는 숙주의 면역 체계로부터 자신을 보호하는 캡슐을 가지고 있어 숙주를 죽게 하는 반면, II-R형 박테리아는 캡슐이 없어 숙주의 면역 체계 때문에 사라졌다. 이 실험 동안 Griffith는 III-S형 박테리아를 가열해 없애면 이 박테리아는 더이상 치명적이지 않게 된다는 것을 발견했다. 다음 단계의 관찰에서, 그는 열을 가해 독성을 죽인 III-S형 박테리아와 살아 있는 II-R형 박테리아의 조합을 쥐에게 주입했다. 놀랍게도 이 치명적이지 않던 박테리아의 혼합물은 독성을 갖게 되어 쥐를 죽였다. Griffith는 독성을 죽인 III-S형 박테리아의 일부가 어떤 이유에서 II-R형 박테리아로 들어가 II-R형 박테리아에게 보호막을 형성하게 했고, 이것이 숙주를 죽였다고 결론을 내렸다. 오늘날 우리는 열 과정에서 생존한 변형된 정보가 DNA이며, 이것이 형질 변환이라고 알려진 과정을 통해 옮겨질 수 있다는 것을 알게 되었다.

지문에서 필자가 형질 변환을 설명하는 방법은?
(A) Griffith 실험에서 뜻밖이었던 결과를 설명함으로써
(B) 쥐에서 발견된 몇몇 박테리아 종류들을 대조함으로써
(C) Griffith 실험에서 사용된 과정을 분석함으로써
(D) 면역 체계에서 보호 캡슐의 중요성을 강조함으로써

해설 | 열 과정에서 생존한 변형된 정보가 DNA이고, 이것은 형질 변환이라는 과정을 통해 옮겨질 수 있다고 하는 발견들은 Griffith의 실험에서 예상치 못한 실험의 결과로 우연히 발견된 것들임을 설명하고 있다.

어휘 | **immune system** 면역 체계　**host** (기생 생물의) 숙주　**lethal** 치명적인　**virulent** 독성을 가진, 악성의　**protective coat** 보호막

04

Cultivation theory, first developed by sociologist George Gebner in the 1960s, attempts to explain the effects that mass media have on the attitudes of the public. In its simplest form, cultivation theory says that mass media, such as television and radio, help to form our view of the world. Our understanding of how the world works and our feelings about the world are heavily influenced by mass media. This is important because what is shown as reality in mass media is often quite different from what actually happens in the real world. For example, if a person watches a great number of police dramas on TV, that person might believe that police are frequently involved in gun battles with criminals. However, in real life, most police go through their entire careers without ever firing their weapons. This is just one example of how mass media can give the public an inaccurate view of reality.

1960년대에 사회학자 George Gebner가 처음 진전시킨 문화계발효과이론은 대중매체가 대중의 태도에 미치는 영향을 설명하고자 하는 것이었다. 간단하게 말해서 문화계발효과이론은 텔레비전과 라디오와 같은 대중매체가 세계관을 형성하는 데 도움을 준다는 것이다. 우리는 세상이 어떻게 돌아가는지 이해하는 것과 세상에 대해 어떻게 느끼는지에서 대중매체의 영향을 많이 받는다. 대중매체에서 실제인 것처럼 보여지는 것이 종종 현실 세계에서 일어나는 일과는 다르므로 이것은 중요하다. 예를 들어, 어떤 사람이 TV에서 경찰 드라마를 많이 시청한다면 그 사람은 경찰이 범죄자와 총격전을 자주 벌인다고 생각하게 될 것이다. 하지만 실제 대부분의 경찰은 전체 경력 기간 내내 무기를 써보지도 못하고 퇴직한다. 이것은 대중매체가 대중에게 부정확한 현실을 보여주는 하나의 예일 뿐이다.

지문에서 필자가 경찰 드라마 를 언급하는 이유는?
(A) 사회의 폭력의 원인을 암시하기 위해
(B) 대중매체가 어떻게 잘못된 현실 인식을 하게 만드는지 보여주기 위해
(C) 폭력적인 TV 프로그램의 부정적 영향을 설명하기 위해
(D) 사람들이 그러한 TV 프로그램을 보지 말아야 한다는 점을 주장하기 위해

해설 | 지문에서 필자는 실제 대부분의 경찰은 경찰 드라마 속의 총격전과는 다르게 경력 기간 내내 무기를 써보지 못하고 퇴직한다고 한다. 필자가 경찰 드라마를 언급한 이유는 그 다음 문장인 "This is just one example of how mass media can give the public an inaccurate view of reality"에서 직접 드러나 있다.

어휘 | **cultivation theory** 문화계발효과이론　**sociologist** 사회학자　**attitude** 태도　**be influenced by** ~에 영향을 받다　**frequently** 자주　**criminal** 범죄자　**weapon** 무기

05

The end of the American Civil War was supposed to bring freedom to African-American slaves, and for a while it did. After the war, the Southern states were controlled by the Northern army via a military government. During this time, African-Americans enjoyed relatively equal treatment in the South. As the Southern states were slowly readmitted into the Union and the Northern army withdrew, however, many of the freedoms that African-Americans had gained were again taken from them.

The first attack on African-American freedoms came in the election of 1876. White Southerners used violence and intimidation to keep African-Americans from voting in this election. The result was a Southern government that was entirely white and inimical to African-Americans. Southern states quickly passed a number of laws intended to keep African-Americans from enjoying the freedoms they had won. Informally known as the Jim Crow laws, these laws basically separated whites and African-Americans in the South. African-Americans were prohibited from eating in the same restaurants, going to the same schools, and even using the same water fountains as whites.

The most damaging laws to African-Americans, however, were the voting laws. The Southern states passed laws requiring literacy tests and a special voting tax for all voters. While some African-Americans could pass the literacy test, few could afford to pay the voting tax. These two laws were very effective in limiting

남북 전쟁의 종식은 흑인 노예들에게 자유를 가져다주기로 되어 있었고, 실제로 한동안은 그랬다. 전쟁 이후 남부의 주들은 군사 정부 아래에서 북부 군대에 의해 통치되었다. 이 기간에 흑인들은 남부에서 비교적 평등한 대우를 받을 수 있었다. 하지만 남부 주들이 천천히 연방으로 다시 받아들여지고 북부 군대가 철수하면서 흑인들은 그들이 얻은 자유 대부분을 다시 빼앗겼다.

흑인의 자유에 대한 첫 번째 공격은 1876년 선거와 함께 시작되었다. 남부 백인들은 이 선거에서 흑인들이 투표를 못하도록 하기 위해서 폭력과 협박을 사용하였다. 그 결과 백인으로만 이루어지고 흑인을 적대하는 남부 정부가 수립되었다. 남부 주들은 흑인들이 쟁취한 자유를 빼앗기 위해 많은 법을 재빨리 통과시켰다. 비공식적으로 Jim Crow 법이라고 알려진 이 법들은 남부에서 백인들과 흑인들을 근본적으로 갈라놓았다. 흑인들은 백인들과 같은 식당에서 식사하거나 같은 학교에 다닐 수 없었으며, 심지어 같은 식수대를 사용하는 것조차 금지되었다.

그러나 흑인들에게 가장 불리한 법은 선거법이었다. 남부 주들은 모든 유권자가 읽기·쓰기 능력 검사를 받고 특별 투표세를 내야 한다는 법들을 통과시켰다. 읽기·쓰기 능력 검사를 통과할 수 있었는지는 몰라도, 투표세를 낼 수 있는 흑인은 거의 없었다. 이 두 법은 흑인들의 정치적 힘을 제약하는 데 매우 효과적이었다. 1900년에 앨라배마주에는 투표할 수 있을 정도로 나이가 든 흑인 유권자가

the political power of African-Americans. In 1900, Alabama had 181,000 African-Americans who were old enough to vote, yet only 3,000 were actually registered to do so. The voting laws ensured that African-Americans had no voice in government and no effective way to fight against their unfair treatment.

181,000명이 있었는데 이들 중 단지 3,000명만이 실제로 투표 등록을 할 수 있었다. 이 선거법은 흑인들이 정부에 발언권을 가지거나 그들의 불공정한 대우에 맞설 효과적 방법을 가지는 것을 확실하게 막았다.

단락 3에서 필자가 앨라배마주의 흑인 유권자에 대해 자세히 언급하는 이유는?
(A) Jim Crow 법이 앨라배마주에서 가장 심했음을 암시하기 위해
(B) 흑인 유권자들을 배제하는 데 있어 선거법의 효과를 보여주기 위해
(C) 흑인들의 수는 많았지만 정치적 조직이 부족했음을 보여주기 위해
(D) 미국 흑인 중 읽고 쓸 수 있는 인구 비율이 낮았음을 보다 자세히 보여주기 위해

해설 | 지문은 흑인들에게 적대적인 정부가 흑인들에게 불리하도록 제정한 법률들을 나열하고 있다. 단락 3에서 필자는 선거법의 언어 능력 검사와 투표세가 흑인의 정치적 발언권을 배제하는 효과를 앨라배마주 실제 투표 등록을 한 흑인 유권자의 수를 언급하며 설명하고 있다.

어휘 | **American Civil War** 남북 전쟁 **be supposed to** ~하기로 되어 있다 **freedom** 자유 **relatively** 비교적, 상대적으로 **readmit** 다시 받아들이다 **withdraw** 철수하다 **intimidation** 협박 **water fountain** 식수대(분수식의 물 마시는 곳) **register** 등록하다 **ensure** 확실히 하다 **unfair** 불공정한, 부당한

06

Establishing the dates for found artifacts is one of the principal jobs of archaeologists. Modern archaeologists have a number of highly accurate scientific methods to determine the date of an artifact, but in the early days of archaeology, this was mainly done through guesswork. The first attempt to develop an organized system for dating artifacts came in 1820, when Christian Thomsen, a Danish archaeologist, suggested his three-age system. The basis of Thomsen's dating system was the examination of tools found at an archaeological site. According to Thomsen, all early cultures had progressed from first using stone tools to bronze tools and finally to iron tools. Thus, if bronze tools were found at a site, an archaeologist could say with certainty that the site came after the Stone Age but before the Iron Age. Analyzing the sophistication with which tools were made could help further determine a more detailed time period for a site.

Thomsen's dating system, however, had a number of problems. First, while his system was helpful for dating sites within the same culture, it was not very effective in dating sites from multiple cultures. Different civilizations adopted bronze and iron technology at different times, and one culture may have still been in the Bronze Age while another culture had already progressed to the Iron Age. Furthermore, some civilizations never adopted these technologies, or they skipped steps. The peoples of the Sahara, for example, went directly from using stone tools to iron tools, skipping the Bronze Age entirely. Another example would be the Maya civilization in Central America, which never progressed beyond stone tools.

발굴된 유물의 연대를 규명하는 것은 고고학자들에게 가장 중요한 일 중 하나이다. 현대 고고학자들은 유물의 연대를 추정하는 여러 가지 매우 정확한 과학적 방법들을 가지고 있지만, 고고학의 초기에는 연대 추정이 주로 추측으로 이루어졌다. 유물의 연대를 추정하는 조직적인 체계를 만들려는 첫 번째 시도는 1820년에 이루어졌는데, 이때 덴마크의 고고학자 Christian Thomsen이 3시기법을 제안했다. Thomsen의 연대 추정법의 기본은 유적지에서 발굴된 도구들을 자세히 조사하는 것이었다. Thomsen에 의하면 모든 초기 문화는 석기에서 청동기로, 그리고 결국 철기로 진행했다고 한다. 따라서 어떤 유적지에서 청동 도구가 발견되면 고고학자는 그 유적지가 석기 시대보다는 나중이고 철기 시대보다는 먼저라고 분명히 말할 수 있다는 것이다. 도구의 정교함을 분석하는 것은 그 유적지의 더 자세한 연대를 밝히는 데에 도움이 될 수 있었다.

그러나 Thomsen의 연대 추정법에는 여러 문제가 있었다. 우선, 그의 방법은 같은 문화권 내의 유적지 연대를 추정하는 데에는 도움이 되었지만, 다른 문화권에 속한 유적지의 연대 추정에는 그다지 효과적이지 않았다. 각 문명은 저마다 다른 시기에 청동기와 철기 기술을 받아들였고, 한 문화가 여전히 청동기 시대에 머물러 있는 시기에 다른 문화는 이미 철기 시대로 진입했을 수 있다. 게다가 어떤 문명은 이러한 기술을 아예 받아들이지 않거나 단계를 건너뛰기도 했다. 예를 들어, 사하라 부족민들은 청동기 시대를 아예 거치지 않고 석기 도구에서 철기 도구를 바로 사용했다. 또 다른 예는 중앙아메리카의 마야 문명인데, 이 문명은 석기 도구 이후로 발전하지 않았다.

단락 2에서 전반적으로 말하고 있는 논의의 목적은?
(A) 3시기법과 새롭게 개발된 연대 추정법을 비교한다.
(B) 3시기법에 결함이 있음을 알려주기 위한 예들을 제시한다.
(C) 3시기법을 사용하는 절차를 자세히 설명한다.
(D) 유물의 시기를 결정하는 데 있어 대안을 제시한다.

해설 | 단락 2의 첫 문장 "Thomsen's dating system, however, had a number of problems"에서 Thomsen의 연대 추정법인 3시기법의 결함에 관해 설명할 것이라는 것을 알 수 있다.

어휘 | **establish** (사실을) 규명하다 **artifact** 유물 **principal** 중요한, 주요한 **archaeologist** 고고학자 **accurate** 정확한 **guesswork** 추측 **bronze** 청동 **iron** 철 **sophistication** 정교함 **date** (유물에) 연대를 매기다 **adopt** 받아들이다, 입양하다 **directly** 바로, 곧장

Reading Practice

01 (A) 02 (B) 03 (C) 04 (C) 05 (D)

METAMORPHOSIS IN THE ANIMAL KINGDOM

Q02 Metamorphosis refers to a biological process where an animal goes through a sudden, drastic change in its physiology. Generally, animals that undergo metamorphosis begin in a larvae state and then transform into a physiologically different adult state, each state exhibiting dramatically different characteristics. This change in form is largely due in part to either a change in the functions carried out by a particular species or a change in the species' lifestyle and environment.

Q04 Environment plays a crucial role in the metamorphosis of animals that are born in water but later need to prepare themselves physiologically for a terrestrial life. In other words, their bodies need to change to adapt to a life on land. **Q01 Q04** Salamanders demonstrate an example of this need to adapt to a life on land, as a large majority of salamanders will lose their tail fin and external gills, originally used for swimming, which are replaced with a new layer of skin more suitable for land. **A** In the case of tadpoles and frogs, tadpoles lose their tails, which are replaced by limbs, allowing adult frogs to easily move around on more solid surfaces. **B** An interesting feature of the tadpole's metamorphosis results from its diet. **C** **Q05** As it loses its strong teeth, necessary for the consumption of pond plants, the adult frog ends up developing strong tongue muscles to accommodate a change to a more carnivorous diet. **D** In a similar vein, the transition of its eyes from the side to the front of its head also allows it to locate and catch prey more easily.

The majority of insects also go through some form of metamorphosis, although their changes can be classified into ametabolous, hemimetabolous, and holometabolous stages. Ametabolous insects, like the mayfly, have no larvae stage and undergo an immediate transformation to adult stage. Hemimetabolous insects, such as the grasshopper, go through a gradual transformation into adult state. Lastly, holometabolous insects, such as the caterpillar and butterfly, **Q03** undergo a complete physiological transformation from larvae to adult state.

When amphibians evolved for life on land, they still kept a connection to their original aquatic environments. **Q04** On the other hand, reptiles, which were the first vertebrates, or animals with a backbone, were some of the first species to settle on land and therefore did not develop a radical physiological need to adapt to a terrestrial environment. Some reptiles do undergo small changes, such as a snake shedding its skin, but these changes are extremely gradual. In addition, while some reptiles do spend time in aquatic environments, they are generally born on land and do not go through severe physiological changes that occur in species that undergo metamorphosis.

동물계에서의 변태

변태는 동물이 생리학적으로 갑작스럽고 극단적인 변화를 겪는 생물학적 과정을 일컫는다. 보통 변태를 겪는 동물들은 유충 상태에서 시작하여 성충기에는 생리학적으로 다르게 되며, 각각의 단계는 굉장히 다른 특징들을 가진다. 이러한 형태의 변화는 주로 특정 종에 의한 기능의 변화 혹은 그 종의 생활양식 및 환경의 변화에서 기인한다.

환경은 물에서 태어났지만, 나중에는 생리학적으로 땅에서 사는 것을 준비해야 하는 동물들의 변태에서 중요한 역할을 한다. 다시 말해 그들의 몸은 육지 생활에 적합하도록 바뀌어야 한다. 도롱뇽은 육지 생활에 적응해야 하는 예를 보여주는데 다수의 도롱뇽은 수영에 사용되던 꼬리지느러미와 겉 아가미를 잃게 되고, 대신 육지에 더 적합한 새로운 피부층을 얻게 된다. **A** 올챙이와 개구리의 경우, 올챙이의 꼬리는 팔다리로 대체되고 이는 성인 개구리가 더 단단한 지면에서 쉽게 돌아다닐 수 있게 한다. **B** 올챙이의 변태 중 흥미로운 특성 하나는 그것들의 식습관에서 비롯된다. **C** 연못에 있는 식물들을 섭취하기 위해 필요했던 강한 이빨은 사라지고, 성인 개구리는 육식으로의 변화에 순응하기 위해 단단한 혀 근육을 발달시키게 된다. **D** 비슷한 맥락에서, 머리 양옆으로부터 앞면으로의 눈의 위치 변화는 먹이를 좀 더 쉽게 찾고 잡을 수 있도록 해준다.

대다수의 곤충 역시 변태를 경험하는데, 이들의 변화는 불변태, 불완전 변태, 완전 변태의 단계로 분류될 수 있다. 하루살이와 같은 불변태 곤충들은 유충 단계가 없으며 성충기로 즉각적으로 변화한다. 메뚜기와 같은 불완전 변태 곤충들은 성충기까지 서서히 진행되는 변태를 겪는다. 마지막으로 애벌레와 나비 와 같은 완전 변태 곤충들은 유충에서 성충기에 다다를 때 완전한 생리적 변화를 겪는다.

양서류는 육지 생활을 위해 진화하긴 하지만, 여전히 기존 물속 환경과의 관련성을 가지고 있다. 반면, 최초의 척추동물이나 파충류나 척추를 가진 동물들은 육지에 살기 시작한 첫 번째 종들이었으므로 육지 환경에 적응하기 위한 급격한 생리적 필요가 발생하지 않았다. 몇몇 파충류들은 뱀이 허물을 벗는 것과 같은 작은 변화를 겪긴 하지만, 이러한 변화는 매우 점진적인 것이다. 게다가 몇몇 파충류들은 물속 환경에서 시간을 보내기도 하는데 이들은 본래 육지에서 태어나며 변태하는 종들에게 일어나는 극심한 생리학적 변화를 겪진 않는다.

01 단락 2에서 필자가 언급하는 것은?
(A) 도롱뇽은 그들이 태어난 곳과는 다른 환경에 적응하기 위해 변태한다.
(B) 개구리는 올챙이였던 때와 같은 식습관을 유지한다.
(C) 올챙이의 육식 식습관은 그들의 변태를 촉진한다.
(D) 도롱뇽은 환경에 따라 그들의 생리학적 기능을 바꿀 수 있다.

해설 | Factual Information 단락 2에서 필자는 환경에 적응하기 위해 변태하는 동물의 예로 도롱뇽을 들고 있다.

02 단락 1과 단락 2의 관련성은?
(A) 단락 2는 단락 1에서 설명된 이론의 추가적인 증거들을 제공한다.
(B) 단락 1은 단락 2에서 논의되는 주제의 개요를 제시한다.
(C) 단락 2는 단락 1에 제시된 결과들을 요약한다.
(D) 단락 1은 단락 2에서 주장된 논란의 주제를 소개한다.

해설 | Rhetorical Purpose 단락 1은 주제의 개요(동물의 변태)를 제시하고, 단락 2에서는 환경에 따른 동물들의 변태 예시들을 설명하고 있다.

03 필자는 무엇의 예로써 애벌레와 나비 를 언급했는가?
(A) 성충기로의 즉각적인 변태
(B) 성충기로까지 신체적 불변
(C) 성충기로까지 완전한 생리학적 변태
(D) 성충기로의 점진적인 변화

해설 | Rhetorical Purpose 애벌레와 나비 같은 완전 변태 곤충들은 완전한 생리적 변화를 겪는다고 설명하고 있다.

04 지문에서 추론할 수 있는 것은?
(A) 완전 변태 곤충들은 불변태 곤충들보다 더욱 진화되었다고 여겨진다.
(B) 파충류는 살아남기 위해 극단적인 상황에서 변태를 겪을 것이다.
(C) 새로운 환경에 적응해야 할 필요가 없는 종들은 변태할 필요가 적다.
(D) 더욱 다양한 변태를 겪는 종일수록 생존 확률이 높다.

해설 | Inference 환경은 동물들의 변태에 중요한 역할을 하며, 그에 대한 예시로 도롱뇽을 언급했다. 살아가는 환경이 물에서 육지로 달라지는 도롱뇽의 경우에는 많은 변화를 겪으며 그렇지 않은 파충류들은 적은 변태를 한다고 하였다. 이를 바탕으로 새로운 환경에 적응할 필요를 느끼는 종들만 변태를 한다는 것을 알 수 있다.

05 다음 문장이 지문에 들어갈 곳을 나타내는 네 개의 사각형[■]을 보시오.

> 비슷한 맥락에서, 머리 양옆으로부터 앞면으로의 눈의 위치 변화는 먹이를 좀 더 쉽게 찾고 잡을 수 있도록 해준다.

이 문장이 들어갈 가장 적절한 위치는?
(A) A (B) B (C) C (D) D

해설 | Sentence Insertion 삽입 문장의 In a similar vein을 통해 삽입 문장 앞에는 먹이와 관련하여 바뀐 신체 변화의 예가 나와야 한다는 것을 알 수 있다.

어휘 | **metamorphosis** 변태, 변화 **biological** 생물학의 **physiology** 생리, 생리학 **larvae** 유충, 애벌레 **terrestrial** 땅의, 육생의 **salamander** 도롱뇽 **tail fin** 꼬리지느러미 **external gill** 겉 아가미 **suitable** 적합한 **tadpole** 올챙이 **limb** 팔다리 **surface** 지면, 수면 **consumption** 섭취, 소비 **tongue** 혀, 혓바닥 **carnivorous** 육식성의 **immediate** 즉각적인 **grasshopper** 메뚜기 **go through** ~을 겪다 **caterpillar** 애벌레 **amphibian** 양서류 **reptile** 파충류 **vertebrate** 척추동물 **backbone** 척추 **radical** 급격한 **shed** 벗다, 갈다

Chapter 07 Sentence Insertion

Sample Question
p.79

Coral reefs, often called "rainforests of the sea," are some of the most diverse ecosystems on Earth. Although coral reefs add up to less than half a percent of the ocean floor, more than a quarter of all marine species spend part of their lives in the reefs. **A** Relying on them for food and shelter, these species live in symbiosis with the reefs. **B** **Therefore, keeping this mutualism under control is crucial in maintaining a healthy marine ecosystem.** Unfortunately, due to overfishing and coastal waste water, the ecosystem has been interrupted and this has resulted in endangerment to the coral reefs. **C** The disrupted balance has induced a higher level of algae, which threatens the reefs by decreasing the coral growth rate. **D**

종종 '바다의 우림'이라고도 불리는 산호초는 지구에서 가장 다양한 생태계 중 일부이다. 산호초가 해저의 0.5% 미만을 차지하지만, 모든 해양 생물 종의 4분의 1 이상이 산호초에서 생의 일부를 보낸다. **A** 이 종들은 먹이와 은신처를 위해 산호초에 의지하면서 산호초와 공생 관계를 맺고 산다. **B** 따라서 이 상리공생 관계를 잘 관리하는 것은 건강한 해양 생태계를 유지하는 데 중요하다. 불행하게도, 남획과 해안의 폐수 때문에 생태계는 혼란에 빠졌고, 이는 산호초가 멸종 위기의 상황에 처하도록 만들었다. **C** 파괴된 균형은 높은 수준의 조류를 발생시켰는데, 이는 산호의 성장 속도를 감소시키면서 산호초를 위협한다. **D**

다음 문장이 지문에 들어갈 곳을 나타내는 네 개의 사각형[■]을 보시오.

따라서 이 상리공생 관계를 잘 관리하는 것은 건강한 해양 생태계를 유지하는 데 중요하다.

이 문장이 들어갈 가장 적절한 위치는?
(A) **A**   (B) **B**   (C) **C**   (D) **D**

어휘 | **coral reef** 산호초   **rainforest** (열대) 우림   **ecosystem** 생태계   **symbiosis** 공생   **mutualism** 상리공생, 상호부조론
overfishing 남획   **endangerment** 멸종 위기의 상황   **alga**(pl. algae) 조류, 바닷말

Basic Drill
p.80

| 01 (B) | 02 (C) | 03 (B) | 04 (D) | 05 (D) | 06 (A) |

Vocab Quiz 01 unveil 02 model 03 exact 04 extend 05 principle 06 purpose

01

Stoicism is the study of the unified account of the world through three main approaches: logic, monistic physics, and naturalistic ethics, with the most emphasis on the latter, which focused on the divine principle of pervading nature. The stoic philosophers believed that generative, divine principles of the universe can ultimately reveal the essential reasons for and virtues of human life. They believed that human beings are part of nature and also possess ultimate knowledge within themselves. Ultimate knowledge relates to qualities that form human personalities and comprise human life. **A** It emphasizes the core, or so-called cardinal virtues: wisdom, courage, self-control, and justice. **B** **But among all virtues, why these four?** The stoic philosophers viewed these virtues as ways of mapping the main areas of human experience and expertise. **C** They believed, when taken together, these virtues are essential to leading a full human life because the correct exercise of any one virtue depends on possessing and exercising the others as well. **D**

스토아 철학은 세 가지 주요 접근법을 통해 세상을 통합적으로 해석한 학문이다. 논리학, 일원론적 물리학, 자연주의 윤리학이 그것이며, 후자에 가장 큰 주안점을 두었는데, 이는 고루 퍼져나가는 자연이라는 신성한 원칙에 초점을 둔다. 스토아 철학자들은 우주의 생성력이 있고 신성한 원칙들은 궁극적으로 인간의 삶의 본질적 이유와 덕목을 밝혀낼 수 있다고 믿었다. 그들은 인간이 자연의 일부이며 또한 인간 자신들 내부에 궁극적인 지식을 갖고 있다고 믿었다. 궁극적인 지식은 인간의 성격을 형성하고 인간의 삶을 구성하는 자질과 관련이 있다. **A** 이는 핵심, 또는 소위 기본적 덕목이라고 불리는 것을 강조한다. 지혜, 용기, 자제력, 그리고 정의가 그것이다. **B** 그런데 많은 덕목 중에서 왜 이 네 가지인가? 스토아 철학자들은 이 덕목들을 인간의 경험과 전문성의 주요 분야를 상세하게 그려내는 방법이라고 생각했다. **C** 그들은 이 덕목들이 합쳐졌을 때 완전한 인간의 삶을 이끄는 데 필수적이라고 생각했는데, 왜냐하면 어느 하나의 덕목을 올바르게 실천하는 것이 다른 덕목들을 소유하고 실천하는 것에 달려 있기 때문이다. **D**

주어진 문장이 들어갈 알맞은 사각형[■]을 선택하시오.

> 그런데 많은 덕목 중에서 왜 이 네 가지인가?

(A) A (B) B (C) C (D) D

해설 | 삽입 문장에서 말하는 these four는 지문에서 언급된 wisdom, courage, self-control, justice임을 알 수 있다. 따라서 삽입 문장은 이 네 가지 덕목이 나열된 문장의 뒤에 위치하고, 이 네 가지 덕목이 구체적으로 언급된 문장 앞에 위치해야 한다.

어휘 | **Stoicism** 스토아 철학(주의)   **logic** 논리(학)   **monistic** 일원론적인   **naturalistic** 자연주의적인   **ethics** 윤리학   **virtue** 덕목, 미덕
cardinal 기본적인, 가장 중요한

02

Although the works of James Fenimore Cooper are considered to be of low literary quality by modern standards and quite unlike what people think of as classics, Cooper's novels have an important place in the history of American literature for a number of reasons. First, the hero of his novels, Natty Bumppo, served as a prototype for later heroes in American fiction. More than 150 years later, one can still see Bumppo's qualities of rugged individualism mirrored in the modern action heroes of books and films. Secondly, Cooper's novels awakened a hunger for truly American novels. Before Cooper's time, American readers had generally looked to European authors as the source of much of their literature. These novels naturally dealt with European issues rather than American ones. A After the success of Cooper's novels, however, Americans were no longer content with this situation. B They began to demand novels that took place in American settings and dealt with American issues. C **In short, they wanted novels for Americans, written by Americans.** Therefore, Cooper's novels were influential in promoting the growth of American literature in general. D

James Fenimore Cooper의 작품들이 현재 기준에 의하면 문학적으로 수준이 낮으며, 사람들이 고전이라고 생각하는 것과는 많이 다르다고 여겨지지만, Cooper의 소설은 많은 이유에서 미국 문학사의 중요한 위치를 차지한다. 우선, 소설의 주인공인 Natty Bumppo는 이후 미국 소설 주인공의 전형 역할을 했다. 150년이 지난 후에도 Bumppo의 강인한 개인주의적 면모가 현대 소설과 영화에 등장하는 액션 영웅에 반영되어 있음을 볼 수 있다. 둘째로, Cooper의 소설은 진정한 의미에서의 미국 소설에 대한 갈망을 불러일으켰다. Cooper 이전 시기의 미국 독자들은 일반적으로 유럽 작가들에게서 읽을거리를 찾으려 했다. 이런 소설들은 자연히 미국의 문제보다는 유럽의 문제들을 다루었다. A 그러나 Cooper의 소설이 성공을 거둔 후, 미국인들은 이런 상황에 더는 만족하지 않았다. B 그들은 미국을 배경으로 미국의 문제를 다룬 소설을 요구하기 시작했다. C **요약하면, 그들은 미국인을 위한 미국인이 쓴 소설을 원했다.** 그리하여 Cooper의 소설은 미국 문학의 전반적인 성장을 활성화하는 데 있어서 큰 영향력을 미쳤다. D

주어진 문장이 들어갈 알맞은 사각형[■]을 선택하시오.

> 요약하면, 그들은 미국인을 위한 미국인이 쓴 소설을 원했다.

(A) A (B) D (C) C (D) D

해설 | 삽입 문장 중 In short로부터 이 문장이 바로 앞에 언급된 내용을 요약해주는 역할을 한다는 것을 알 수 있다. 따라서 미국인들이 미국을 배경으로 한 미국의 문제를 다룬 소설을 요구하기 시작했다는 내용 뒤에 자연스럽게 연결될 수 있다.

어휘 | **rugged** 강인한, 튼튼한   **individualism** 개인주의   **mirror** 반영하다   **awaken** (감정을) 불러일으키다, (잠에서) 깨우다   **hunger** 갈망, 열망
content 만족하는   **setting** (문학의) 배경   **promote** 활성화하다

03

The ideas of Charles Darwin had significant effects well beyond the areas of biology and ecology. The basic premise of Darwin's ideas — the concept that organisms must adapt or face extinction — made its way into the social theories of the nineteenth century as well. Social Darwinism, the adaptation of Darwin's ideas to human societies, was the dominant social philosophy of the nineteenth century. In its basic form, Social Darwinism claimed that the same forces which cause the evolution of organisms caused the evolution of societies as well. A According to this view, it was natural that societies which were better adapted to the pressures of the era would advance and oppress those which were not so well adapted. B **In other words, the rise and fall of the societies were determined by the law of survival of the fittest.** Social Darwinist groups had different perspectives about the precise mechanism that enables the theory. C However, the most common opinion was that the competition between

Charles Darwin의 사상은 생물학과 생태학을 넘어선 영역에도 상당한 영향을 끼쳤다. 생물이 적응하지 않으면 멸종한다는 Darwin 사상의 기본적인 전제는 19세기의 사회 이론에도 들어갔다. 인간 사회에 Darwin의 사상을 응용시킨 사회다원주의는 19세기의 지배적인 사회철학이 되었다. 기본적으로 말해서 사회다원주의는 생명체를 진화하게 하는 힘은 사회 역시 진화하게 한다고 주장하였다. A 이 관점에 따르면, 시대의 압박에 더 잘 적응한 사회만이 발전하며 그만큼 잘 적응하지 못한 사회를 억압하는 것은 자연스러운 것이었다. B **다시 말해, 사회의 흥망성쇠는 적자생존의 법칙에 의해 결정된다는 것이었다.** 사회다원주의 집단들은 그 이론을 가능케 하는 정확한 메커니즘에 대해 서로 다른 관점을 갖고 있었다. C 하지만 가장 일반적인 의견은 자유방임적 자본주의에서 개개인의 경쟁이 이 메커니즘의 역할을 수행했고, 여기서 강자의 이익을 위해 약자를 착취하는 것은 자연적이고 타당한 것이라고 여겨졌다는 것이다. D

individuals in laissez-faire capitalism served as this mechanism, where it was considered natural and proper to exploit the weak to benefit the strong. ■D

주어진 문장이 들어갈 알맞은 사각형[■]을 선택하시오.

> 다시 말해, 사회의 흥망성쇠는 적자생존의 법칙에 의해 결정된다는 것이었다.

(A) ■A (B) ■B (C) ■C (D) ■D

해설 | 삽입 문장에 사용된 In other words는 이전에 언급된 내용을 바꿔 말하거나 보충 설명해주는 역할을 한다. 삽입 문장의 survival of the fittest는 지문의 내용 중 "… societies which were better adapted … oppress those which were not so well adapted"를 바꿔 쓴 내용이다.

어휘 | **premise** 전제 **make one's way into** ~로 들어가다(나아가다) **adaptation** 응용, 적응 **dominant** 지배적인 **oppress** 억압하다 **rise and fall** 흥망성쇠 **survival of the fittest** 적자생존 **laissez-faire capitalism** 자유방임적 자본주의

04

The forest canopy is defined as the upper reaches of the forest. It is composed of large, slow-growth trees, which rise high above the forest floor and then spread their branches over a wide area. ■A Examples of canopy trees include pines, oaks, and redwoods. ■B The uppermost layer of the canopy is sometimes 120 feet off the forest floor, which can soar 20 to 100 feet above the next-tallest trees. ■C They rise as a straight column of wood for many feet and then, at their tops, branch out and spread in a heavy layer of leaves. ■D **Due to this formation, canopy trees are able to absorb the greatest amount of sunlight.** The billions of leaves of the canopy act as solar panels and convert sunlight to energy through photosynthesis. In fact, canopy trees have such a monopoly on sunlight in the forest that they are responsible for nearly 90 percent of all photosynthesis that occurs, so they support the majority of the production of fruits, seeds, and flowers.

임관은 숲의 상층부를 가리킨다. 이는 크고 천천히 자라는 나무들로 구성되고, 숲의 지면 위로 아주 높이 올라 넓은 지역을 덮는 나뭇가지를 뻗는다. ■A 임관수의 예로는 소나무, 오크, 삼나무가 있다. ■B 숲 윗부분의 맨 위층은 가끔 임상으로부터 120피트 위에 있는데, 이는 그 다음으로 큰 나무들보다 20~100피트나 솟아 있을 수 있다. ■C 이들은 수직으로 뻗은 기둥으로 수 피트를 뻗어 올라가 꼭대기에 이르러서 가지를 뻗고 수많은 나뭇잎을 펼친다. ■D **이 형성 과정으로 인해 임관수는 가장 많은 양의 햇빛을 흡수할 수 있다.** 셀 수 없이 많은 임관수 나뭇잎들은 태양판 역할을 하고 광합성을 통해 햇빛을 에너지로 전환한다. 사실 임관수는 숲의 햇빛을 독점하며 그 결과 숲에서 일어나는 총 광합성의 거의 90%를 차지한다. 따라서 대부분의 과일, 씨앗, 꽃 생산을 지원한다.

주어진 문장이 들어갈 알맞은 사각형[■]을 선택하시오.

> 이 형성 과정으로 인해 임관수는 가장 많은 양의 햇빛을 흡수할 수 있다.

(A) ■A (B) ■B (C) ■C (D) ■D

해설 | 삽입 문장의 Due to this formation을 통해 이 문장이 어떠한 형성 과정을 설명하는 문장 뒤에 위치해야 하며, 그 문장에는 햇빛을 많이 흡수할 수 있도록 도움을 준다는 내용도 포함되어 있어야 함을 알 수 있다. 즉, 수 피트를 뻗어 올라가 꼭대기에서 가지를 뻗고 수많은 나뭇잎을 펼친다는 내용의 문장 뒤에 삽입 문장이 위치해야 자연스럽다.

어휘 | **forest canopy** 임관 **be composed of** ~로 구성되다 **pine** 소나무 **oak** 오크(떡갈나무·참나무의 총칭) **redwood** 삼나무 **column** 기둥 **branch out** 가지를 뻗다, 가지를 치다 **monopoly** 독점, 독차지

05

Direct democracy, sometimes called pure democracy, is a form of democracy where the power of decision making lies directly with the public. It is usually contrasted with a representative democracy, where the general public votes for representatives, who then make laws on the public's behalf. In a direct democracy, the public chooses its leaders, votes on its laws, and is actively involved in the major decisions of society. The power of a direct democracy is based on three tenets: the power of initiative, the power of referendum, and the power of recall. ■A The power of initiative is the power to raise issues that should be voted on. ■B In a direct democracy, any citizen can, in theory, suggest a new law or policy. ■C In practice, issues are usually raised through petitions. ■D **If a**

가끔 순수 민주주의라고도 불리는 직접민주주의는 의사 결정의 권한이 직접적으로 대중에게 있는 민주주의의 한 형태이다. 이는 보통 대의민주주의와 대비되는데, 대의민주주의에서는 일반 대중이 투표를 통해 대표자들을 뽑고 그들은 대중을 대신하여 법을 제정한다. 직접민주주의에서 대중은 그들의 지도자를 선출하고, 법안을 투표로 정하고, 사회의 중요 사안을 결정하는 데 직접 관여한다. 직접민주주의는 세 개의 원칙에 그 기반을 두는데, 국민 발의권, 투표권, 그리고 해임권이 그것이다. ■A 국민 발의권은 투표할 안건을 제기할 수 있는 권리이다. ■B 직접민주주의에서는 이론적으로 국민 누구나 새로운 법안이나 정책을 제안할 수 있다. ■C 실제로는 이런 사안들이 청원에 의해 제기된다. ■D **만일 한 국민이 자신의 아이디어에 대해 일정 수의 서명을 얻으면, 그 사람은 자신의 아이디어에 대해 투표를 하도록 만들 수 있게 된다.** 투표권은 간단히 말해 발의된 사항을 직접 투표를 통해 승인 및 거부할 수 있는 권리이다. 이 방법으로 직접

citizen can get a certain number of signatures for his or her idea, that person can force the society to vote on the idea. The power of referendum is simply the power to approve or reject initiatives through a direct vote. In this way, citizens in a direct democracy are actively involved in creating their own laws. Initiatives and referendums together dramatically reduce the direct costs, time, and effort spent on government decisions. The final tenet of a direct democracy is the power of recall. Under the power of recall, the public has the right to remove government officials it is unhappy with. This means that the leaders of the nation are directly accountable to the public, since they can basically be removed from office at any time. Proponents of direct democracy believe these aspects have positive net social benefits and limit the influence of numerically small but politically powerful pressure groups.

민주주의를 시행하는 시민들은 스스로 법을 만드는 데 적극 참여하는 것이다. 국민 발의권과 국민 투표는 정부 결정에 소요되는 직접적인 비용, 시간, 노력을 상당히 감소시킨다. 직접민주주의의 마지막 원칙은 해임권이다. 대중은 해임권에 의해 만족스럽지 않은 정부 관료를 해임할 수 있는 권리를 가진다. 이는 한 국가의 지도자들은 언제든지 공직에서 해임될 수 있으므로, 대중에게 직접적인 책임이 있다는 것을 뜻한다. 직접민주주의 옹호자들은 이런 측면들이 긍정적인 사회적 순편익을 갖고, 수적으로는 적지만 정치적으로 권력이 있는 압력 집단의 영향력을 제한시킨다고 생각한다.

주어진 문장이 들어갈 알맞은 사각형[■]을 선택하시오.

만일 한 국민이 자신의 아이디어에 대해 일정 수의 서명을 얻으면, 그 사람은 자신의 아이디어에 대해 투표를 하도록 만들 수 있게 된다.

(A) A (B) B (C) C (D) D

해설 | 삽입 문장은 지문의 내용 중 '청원(petition)'의 정의를 자세히 설명한 것이다. 따라서 삽입 문장은 국민 발의권의 절차 중 하나인 청원이 언급된 문장 뒤에 자연스럽게 연결될 수 있다.

어휘 | direct democracy 직접민주주의 **initiative** (국민) 발의권 **referendum** 국민 투표 **recall** 해임권, 소환 **raise** (문제를) 제기하다 **issue** 안건, 사안 **in practice** 실제로 **approve** 승인하다, 찬성하다

06

White's law, named after the famous anthropologist Leslie White, is a theory which attempts to explain how the availability of energy affects the speed of advancement in a civilization. **A** **White's law basically states that civilization evolves as the amount of energy harnessed per person is increased, or as the efficiency of energy usage is increased.** The basic assumption of White's law is that out of the three major aspects of civilization — technological, sociological, and ideological — the technological aspect plays the greatest role in driving the evolution of a civilization. **B** White thought that the intent of all technology is to help people overcome the challenges of survival. **C** Farming technology provides us with greater amounts of food, and housing technology provides us with shelter. **D** Since all technology requires some form of energy to operate, greater amounts of energy should allow us to use greater amounts of technology, which in turn should allow society to advance. The same would be true of more efficient energy usage. If technology is created to use less energy, that should have the same basic effect as increasing the total amount of energy available.

White distinguished five different stages in the evolution of civilization, according to the different forms of energy used to power technology. In the first stage, energy is provided by our own muscles and humans must do all of their own work. In the second stage of development, humans begin to use animals to power their technology, as a farmer does when he uses a horse to pull his plow. The third stage occurs when humans begin to use plants as a source of power. This stage can be identified by a huge increase in the efficiency of farming. In the fourth stage, humans begin to rely on natural resources such as coal and oil as their primary sources of energy. In the final stage, nuclear power is utilized to provide energy.

유명한 인류학자인 Leslie White의 이름을 딴 White의 법칙은 이용 가능한 에너지가 문명의 발달 속도에 미치는 영향을 설명하고자 하는 이론이다. **A** **White의 법칙은 기본적으로 한 사람 당 사용하는 에너지의 양이 증가하거나 에너지 사용의 효율성이 높아짐에 따라 문명이 진화한다는 것이다.** White의 법칙에 깔린 기본 전제는 문명의 세 가지 주요 측면(기술적 측면, 사회학적 측면, 사상적 측면) 중에서 기술적인 측면이 문명의 진화를 추진하는 데 있어서 가장 큰 역할을 한다는 것이다. **B** White는 모든 기술의 의도는 사람들이 생존에 대한 문제를 극복하는 데 도움을 주는 것에 있다고 생각했다. **C** 농업 기술은 우리에게 더 많은 양의 식량을 주며, 주택 기술은 우리에게 거처를 마련해 준다. **D** 모든 기술은 어떤 형태든 작동하는 데에 에너지를 필요로 하므로, 더 많은 양의 에너지가 있다면 우리는 더 많은 기술을 이용할 수 있으며, 그에 따라 사회는 더 발달하게 된다. 더욱 효율적인 에너지의 사용도 마찬가지이다. 더 적은 양의 에너지를 사용하는 기술을 만든다면, 그것은 이용 가능한 에너지의 총량이 증가하는 것과 기본적으로 같은 효과를 갖게 될 것이다.

White는 기술을 작동시키는 데 사용되는 에너지의 여러 형태에 따라 문명의 진화를 다섯 단계로 구분했다. 첫 단계는 우리의 근육에 의해 에너지가 제공되는 단계인데, 이 단계에서 인간은 모든 일을 자신의 힘으로 해야 한다. 두 번째 발전 단계에서 인간은 동물을 이용하여 기술을 작동시키기 시작한다. 농부가 말을 이용해서 쟁기를 끄는 것처럼 말이다. 세 번째 단계는 인간이 동력의 원천으로 식물들을 이용하기 시작할 때 일어난다. 이 단계는 농업 효율성이 획기적으로 향상되는 단계로 식별될 수 있다. 네 번째 단계에서 인간은 석탄이나 석유와 같은 천연자원을 주된 에너지원으로 의존하기 시작한다. 마지막 단계에서는 원자력이 에너지원으로 사용된다.

주어진 문장이 들어갈 알맞은 사각형[■]을 선택하시오.

> White의 법칙은 기본적으로 한 사람 당 사용하는 에너지의 양이 증가하거나 에너지 사용의 효율성이 높아짐에 따라 문명이 진화한다는 것이다.

(A) A (B) B (C) C (D) D

해설 | 삽입 문장은 White의 법칙이 주장하는 것이 무엇인지에 대한 보충 설명을 하고 있으므로 White의 법칙이 소개된 문장과 White의 법칙 속 문명의 진화에 대해 자세히 언급한 문장 사이에 자연스럽게 위치할 수 있다.

어휘 | anthropologist 인류학자 availability 이용 가능성 harness 이용하다 efficiency 효율성 sociological 사회학적인 ideological 사상적인 distinguish 구분하다 power 작동시키다, 동력을 공급하다 plow 쟁기

Reading Practice

p.84

01 (C) 02 (B) 03 (A) 04 (B) 05 (B)

ATMOSPHERIC CIRCULATION

Much of the world's weather is determined by two atmospheric cells: the Hadley cell and the Polar cell. Cells are atmospheric cycles that are driven by thermal energy. Q04 As the sun heats the air near the surface of the earth, the air begins to rise. At a certain point, however, this air encounters a barrier and cannot rise any further. As new air is heated and begins to rise, the warm air near this barrier is pushed sideways, since it cannot move vertically anymore. As it moves, it begins to lose its heat, until it once again begins to sink towards the earth, pushing the cooler air below it sideways and forming a circular movement of air, which is called a cell.

The Hadley cell begins about 5 degrees north or south of the equator, where the sun's heating effect is the strongest. Q03-1 The high temperatures near the equator allow the air to pick up tremendous amounts of moisture from the oceans before it begins to rise. The energy contained in the warm, moist air causes violent thunderstorms, which transport that energy high into the atmosphere. As the warm, moist air begins its horizontal movement, it begins to lose energy in the form of heat. By the time it reaches a latitude of about 30 degrees north or south, it has lost enough heat energy to once again sink towards the earth. In the last part of the cycle, the air flows back towards the equator to begin the cycle again. Q01 An important effect of this is that the Hadley cell creates the strong trade winds that early sailors used to cross the seas.

A Q05-1 The Polar cell begins at much higher latitudes, where the air is considerably cooler and drier. B Although these atmospheric conditions are somewhat different, the mechanics that drive the Polar cell are the same as those for the Hadley cell. Q05-2 At about 60 degrees north or south, the air still has enough heat to drive a cell cycle. C Q02 Q03-2 As the air rises, it encounters a similar barrier and begins to move laterally instead of vertically. D By the time it reaches the North or South Pole, it has lost nearly all of its heat and sinks back down to the earth. The major difference is that the air was never warm enough to pick up much moisture, so this part of the cycle involves much less water loss than it does in the Hadley cell. The major effect of the Polar cell on weather is that it creates a jet stream, the strong eastern wind pattern that controls much of the weather at northern and southern latitudes.

대기의 순환

세계의 날씨 중 많은 경우가 두 종류의 대기 세포에 의해 결정된다. 해들리 세포와 극세포가 그것이다. 세포는 열에너지에 의해 이루어지는 대기 순환을 가리킨다. 태양이 지표 근처의 공기를 데우면 그 공기는 상승하기 시작한다. 그러나 어떤 지점에 이르면 이 공기는 어떤 장벽에 부딪혀서 더는 위로 올라갈 수 없다. 새로운 공기가 가열되고 상승하기 시작하면, 이 장벽 부근의 따뜻한 공기는 더이상 수직으로 움직일 수 없으므로 옆으로 밀려난다. 이 공기는 움직이면서 열을 잃고, 결국 다시 지표 쪽으로 가라앉게 되는데 그 과정에서 아래쪽의 차가운 공기를 옆으로 밀어내어 공기의 순환을 형성하며, 이를 세포라고 부른다.

해들리 세포는 적도의 남북위 5도 지점에서 발생하는데, 이 지점은 태양열의 영향이 가장 큰 곳이다. 적도 부근의 고온 때문에 공기는 바다에서 엄청난 양의 습기를 얻게 되고, 상승하기 시작한다. 고온 다습한 공기에 포함된 에너지는 격렬한 뇌우를 일으키는데, 이 뇌우는 그 에너지를 대기 상층부로 이동시킨다. 고온 다습한 공기가 수평 이동을 하면 에너지가 열의 형태로 상실되기 시작한다. 이 공기가 남북위 30도 지점에 도달할 무렵, 그것은 충분히 많은 열에너지를 상실해서 다시 지표로 내려온다. 순환의 마지막 단계에서 공기는 적도 쪽으로 돌아 다시 순환을 시작한다. 이로부터 발생하는 중요한 영향은 초기 항해자들이 바다를 건너는 데 이용했던 강력한 무역풍을 만들어낸다는 것이다.

A 극세포는 훨씬 높은 위도에서 시작되는데, 그곳의 공기는 훨씬 더 차고 더 건조하다. B 비록 이 대기 상태들이 다소 다르긴 하지만, 극세포를 움직이게 하는 원리는 해들리 세포를 움직이게 하는 원리와 똑같다. 남북위 60도에서의 공기는 여전히 세포의 순환을 만들 수 있을 만큼의 에너지가 있다. C 공기가 상승하면서 비슷한 장벽에 부딪히고 수직으로 가는 것 대신 측면으로 이동한다. D 그것이 북극이나 남극에 다다르면, 대부분의 열을 잃고 다시 지표로 내려온다. 중요한 차이점은 이 공기는 많은 습기를 취할 만큼 따뜻한 적이 없었다는 점이다. 그래서 이 순환 과정에서는 해들리 세포보다 훨씬 적은 양의 수분을 잃는다. 극세포가 날씨에 미치는 주된 영향은 제트 기류를 만들어낸다는 점이다. 제트 기류는 동쪽으로 흐르는 강한 기류로, 북위와 남위에서 일어나는 기상 현상을 많이 통제한다.

01 필자가 무역풍을 언급하는 이유는?

(A) 해들리 세포의 발견을 논하기 위해
(B) 해들리 세포의 뇌우의 위험성을 설명하기 위해
(C) 해들리 세포가 날씨에 미치는 영향을 설명하기 위해
(D) 무역 역사에서 해들리 세포의 중요성을 강조하기 위해

해설 | Rhetorical Purpose 필자는 단락 2에서 해들리 세포의 형성 과정을 설명하며, 그것의 대기 순환으로부터 발생하는 중요한 영향으로 초기 항해자들이 바다를 건너는 데 이용했던 무역풍을 언급했다.

02 지문에서 it 이 가리키는 것은?

(A) 열
(B) 공기
(C) 장벽
(D) 순환 과정

해설 | Reference 공기(air)가 상승하면서 비슷한 장벽에 부딪히고 측면으로 이동한다는 문장 뒤에 그것이(it) 북극이나 남극에 다다르면 열을 잃고 다시 지표로 내려온다는 내용을 통해 it 이 공기(air)를 지시하는 대명사임을 알 수 있다.

03 필자는 해들리 세포와 극세포에서의 공기 이동을 어떻게 설명하는가?

(A) 공기의 이동에서 열의 역할을 논의함으로써
(B) 각 세포가 다른 세포에게 어떻게 영향을 미치는지 명확히 설명함으로써
(C) 각 세포 내에서 이동의 방향을 대비함으로써
(D) 날씨가 각 세포의 일반적인 이동을 어떻게 방해할 수 있는지 설명함으로써

해설 | Rhetorical Purpose 해들리 세포에서의 공기는 열에너지를 상실했을 때 지표로 내려오며, 극세포에서의 공기는 북극이나 남극에 다다르면 대부분 열을 잃고 다시 지표로 내려온다고 설명한다. 두 세포 모두 공기의 이동에 관해 설명할 때 열의 역할에 따른 이동의 변화를 토대로 한다.

04 지문에서 공기의 이동에 대해 추론할 수 있는 것은?

(A) 적도 부근의 공기는 극지방의 공기보다 더 빠르게 움직인다.
(B) 차가운 공기는 따뜻한 공기 아래로 내려앉는 경향이 있다.
(C) 수분이 사라지면 공기의 이동이 느려지는 경향이 있다.
(D) 공기의 이동은 날씨 패턴 변화의 영향을 받는다.

해설 | Inference 가열된 공기로 인해 순환되는 대기를 설명하는 단락 1을 바탕으로 따뜻한 공기는 위로 이동하고, 차가운 공기는 아래로 내려앉는 성질이 있음을 알 수 있다.

05 다음 문장이 지문에 들어갈 곳을 나타내는 네 개의 사각형[■]을 보시오.

> 비록 이 대기 상태들이 다소 다르긴 하지만, 극세포를 움직이게 하는 원리는 해들리 세포를 움직이게 하는 원리와 똑같다.

이 문장이 들어갈 가장 적절한 위치는?

(A) A (B) B (C) C (D) D

해설 | Sentence Insertion 삽입 문장의 these atmospheric conditions 는 단락 3의 첫 문장 "… the air is considerably cooler and drier"를 가리키는 지시어이다. 그리고 극세포의 대기 순환 원리는 해들리 세포를 움직이게 하는 원리와 똑같다는 삽입 문장의 내용은 극세포의 대기 순환 원리를 본격적으로 설명하기 시작하는 문장 "At about 60 degrees north or south, the air still has enough heat to drive a cell cycle"과 자연스럽게 연결된다.

어휘 | **atmospheric** 대기의　**circulation** 순환　**thermal** 열의　**encounter** 부딪히다, 마주치다　**vertically** 수직으로　**tremendous** 엄청난　**moisture** 습기, 수분　**transport** 이동시키다　**horizontal** 수평의　**trade wind** 무역풍　**laterally** 측면으로, 옆쪽으로　**stream** 기류

Chapter 08 Prose Summary

Sample Question

Numerous studies were undertaken to determine the exact nature of the risk windfarms pose to avian populations, particularly birds and bats. As a whole, bird and bat fatalities differ greatly among facilities and regions, but were in the range of 4 to 14 per wind turbine per year.

Most birds killed by wind turbines were song birds. Since most of these birds migrate at night at altitudes far above wind turbines, it is believed that the majority of these deaths take place during take-off and landing, at resting areas near wind turbine sites. Regarding bats, one of the primary causes of death is direct collision with the turbine blades or poles. Another main cause of death is barotrauma, an injury normally caused by changes in atmospheric pressure, which in the case of bats results from spinning turbine blades.

In response to this growing problem, extensive monitoring has been added at numerous wind turbine sites, and researchers and operators have come up with several options for minimizing or mitigating mortality of birds and bats. Some of these examples are using lighting or noise generators to repel them, ceasing operation during periods that could increase mortality rates, and adopting newer turbine designs in areas with lower avian populations. Fortunately, it was reported that these endeavors to reduce the mortality rates in avian populations are bringing about encouraging results in some regions.

새의 개체군, 특히 새와 박쥐에게 풍력 발전 지역이 가하는 정확한 위험성을 알아보고자 많은 연구가 시행되었다. 전체적으로 새와 박쥐의 폐사는 시설과 지역에 따라 매우 달랐지만, 연간 평균 한 대의 풍력 발전용 터빈에서 네 마리에서 열네 마리가 죽었다.

풍력 발전용 터빈으로 인해 죽은 대부분의 새는 명금이었다. 이 새들은 풍력 발전용 터빈보다 훨씬 더 높은 고도에서 밤에 이동을 하므로, 이 죽음의 상당수는 이륙 및 착륙 동안 풍력 발전용 터빈 근처의 휴식처에서 일어난 것으로 보인다. 박쥐의 경우, 주요 죽음의 원인 중 하나는 터빈의 날개 혹은 기둥과의 직접적인 충돌이다. 죽음의 또 다른 주요 원인은 주로 기압의 변화로 야기되는 피해인 기압 장애인데, 박쥐의 경우 돌아가는 터빈 날로부터 발생한다.

점점 커지고 있는 문제에 대응하여, 많은 풍력 발전용 터빈 장소를 광범위하게 관찰하고 있으며, 연구진과 기계 조작자들은 새와 박쥐의 폐사를 최소화하고 줄이기 위한 여러 선택사항들을 고안해냈다. 이러한 예의 몇몇은 그것들을 쫓아내기 위해 빛과 소음 발생기를 사용하는 것, 폐사율이 높은 시간에 작동을 멈추는 것, 새의 개체군이 적은 곳에 새로운 터빈 디자인을 쓰는 것이다. 다행히 새의 폐사율을 줄이기 위한 이러한 노력은 일부 지역에서 고무적인 결과를 나타내고 있다고 보고되었다.

지문을 간략히 요약하기 위한 도입 문장이 아래 제시되어 있다. 지문에서 가장 중요한 내용을 표현한 세 개의 문장을 골라 요약문을 완성하시오. 일부 문장은 지문에 나오지 않았거나 중요하지 않은 내용이기 때문에 요약문에 포함되지 않는다. *이 문제는 2점이다.*

> 풍력 발전 지역은 새와 박쥐에게 위험하다.

(A) 이동하는 명금은 풍력 발전용 터빈에 의한 새의 개체군 죽음 중 가장 많다.
(B) 밤에 높은 고도로 나는 새들은 풍력 발전용 터빈에 의한 죽음의 위험이 더 크다.
(C) 시설과 지역은 풍력 발전용 터빈에 의한 새와 박쥐 폐사를 가장 많이 변하게 하는 변수이다.
(D) 풍력 발전용 터빈이 새와 박쥐에게 가하는 위험에 대한 많은 연구는 아직 해결책을 찾지 못했다.
(E) 새와 박쥐의 폐사율을 줄이기 위한 다양한 노력이 긍정적인 결과들을 보여주고 있다.
(F) 풍력 발전용 터빈과의 직접적인 충돌과 기압 장애는 박쥐가 죽게되는 두 가지 주요 원인이다.

어휘 | windfarm 풍력 발전 지역 **avian** 새의, 조류의 **population** 개체군, 인구 **differ** 다르다 **song bird** 명금(고운 소리로 우는 새) **take-off** 이륙 **primary** 주요한 **collision** 충돌 **barotrauma** 기압(압력) 장애 **generator** 발생기 **mortality rate** 폐사율

Basic Drill

| 01 (B), (D), (F) | 02 (A), (B), (D) | 03 (B), (C), (E) | 04 (A), (D), (E) |

| **Vocab Quiz** | 01-1 exact | 01-2 time | 02-1 ultimately | 02-2 notably | 03-1 precise | 03-2 increases |
| | 04-1 survive | 04-2 excess | | | | |

01

THE DARK AGE OF GREECE

Many civilizations undergo a series of high points and low points during their history. Among early civilizations, we call the low points "dark ages" because civilizations often fell apart to such a point that it is hard to get an accurate picture of their history during these periods. During a dark age, a civilization may not have produced monuments, statues, or other objects which we use to learn about early civilizations.

One of the most significant dark ages was the dark age of Greece, which lasted from about 1100 BC to 900 BC. Prior to that time, Greece had a highly advanced society called the Mycenaean civilization. The Mycenaeans were a trading civilization, and they did much to spread their culture across the eastern Mediterranean. In fact, the Mycenaean civilization was so important that when it collapsed in the twelfth century BC, most other civilizations in the region collapsed as well. The next 200 years are like a blank page to historians, and thus we know very little about this period. One major reason for this is that writing basically stopped. The collapse of the Mycenaeans brought an end to writing in the area, and thus an end to the written records historians rely on.

The little that we know about this period has been learned from archaeology. It seems that civilization became much less advanced. The pottery from this period is much simpler and less artistic. This suggests that there was a lack of wealthy people to buy higher-quality products. Another interesting point is that most of the large cities of earlier time periods appear to have been abandoned in favor of much smaller settlements. This would suggest a large decrease in population, possibly due to a widespread lack of food and consequent starvation.

Sometime around 800 BC, the Greeks began to emerge from this dark age, most likely due to the influence of other civilizations. They had lost their early writing system, but began to use the writing system of the Phoenicians. They began constructing larger cities and trading with their neighbors again. Over the next 300 years, their civilization continued to rise, and their dark age was left behind.

지문을 간략히 요약하기 위한 도입 문장이 아래 제시되어 있다. 지문에서 가장 중요한 내용을 표현한 세 개의 문장을 골라 요약문을 완성하시오. 일부 문장은 지문에 나오지 않았거나 중요하지 않은 내용이기 때문에 요약문에 포함되지 않는다. *이 문제는 2점이다.*

> 그리스의 암흑시대는 기원전 1100년부터 900년까지 이어진 문명의 멸망 시기였다.

(A) 고도로 발달한 그리스 사회인 미케네 문명은 동부 지중해 지역에 지대한 영향을 끼쳤다.
(B) 미케네 문명의 멸망과 함께 시작된 그리스의 암흑시대는 동부 지중해의 대부분 문명을 포함했다.
(C) 기록의 분실과 대규모 건축의 종말에도 불구하고 역사학자들은 그리스의 암흑시대에 대해 알아낼 수 있었다.
(D) 그리스 암흑시대는 덜 발달한 문명과 인구의 급감으로 특징지어진다.
(E) 많은 증거들은 그리스 암흑시대 동안 인구가 대폭으로 늘어났다는 것을 암시한다.
(F) 그리스는 페니키아인들과 같은 다른 문명들의 도움으로 암흑시대에서 벗어날 수 있었다.

그리스의 암흑시대

많은 문명은 역사 속에서 절정과 침체의 연속을 겪는다. 우리는 초기 문명에서 이런 침체의 순간을 '암흑시대'라고 부르는데, 이는 문명들이 종종 너무 무너져 버려서 이 기간의 그들 역사에 대해 정확한 상황을 알 수 없기 때문이다. 암흑시대 동안의 문명은 초기 문명에 대한 연구에 사용되는 기념물이나 조각상 혹은 다른 물건을 제작하지 않았을 수 있다.

가장 중요한 암흑시대 중 하나는 기원전 1100년부터 900년에 있었던 그리스의 암흑시대였다. 이 시대 이전에 그리스는 미케네 문명이라고 불리던 고도로 발전된 사회였다. 미케네인들은 무역 문명이었고 지중해 동부 전역에 걸쳐 그들의 문화를 전파하기 위해 많은 것을 했다. 사실, 미케네 문명은 매우 중요했기 때문에, 기원전 12세기에 미케네 문명이 멸망하자 이 지역의 다른 문명들도 대부분 멸망해 버렸다. 이후 200년은 역사가들에게 빈 페이지로 남아 있어서 우리는 이 시기에 대해 거의 알 수 없다. 이에 대한 주요 이유 중 하나는 기본적으로 기록이 중단된 것에 있다. 미케네 문명의 멸망은 그 지역에 대한 기록을 중단시켰고, 그렇게 역사가들이 의존하는 문서 기록도 끝나 버렸다.

우리가 그나마 이 시대에 대해 아는 것은 고고학을 통해 깨달은 것이다. 문명은 훨씬 덜 발전했던 것으로 보인다. 이 시대의 도자기는 훨씬 더 단순하고 예술성이 떨어진다. 이것은 양질의 물건들을 살 만한 부유층이 없었다는 것을 암시한다. 다른 한 가지 흥미로운 점은 대부분의 초기 시대 큰 도시들이 훨씬 더 작은 정착지의 선호에 따라 버려진 것으로 보이는 것이다. 이것은 만연한 식량 부족과 그에 따른 굶주림으로 인해 인구가 대폭으로 감소했다는 것을 암시한다.

기원전 800년 전후로 그리스인들은 아마도 다른 문명들의 영향으로 암흑시대에서 벗어나기 시작했다. 그들은 초기의 문자 체계를 잃었지만, 페니키아인들의 문자 체계를 사용하기 시작했다. 큰 도시를 짓기 시작하고 이웃 문명과도 다시 교역하기 시작했다. 이후 300년에 걸쳐 그들의 문명은 계속해서 발전했고 암흑시대를 뒤로 했다.

해설 | (B)는 그리스 암흑시대의 배경을 설명한 단락 2의 내용을 요약해 놓은 것이다. (D)는 고고학 연구를 통해 발견된 그리스 암흑시대의 특징을 서술한 단락 3의 내용을 요약해 놓은 것이다. (F)는 그리스 암흑시대의 종지부를 언급한 단락 4의 내용을 요약해 놓은 것이다.

어휘 | **dark age** 암흑시대　**civilization** 문명　**monument** 기념물　**statue** 조각상　**prior to** ~의 전에, ~에 앞서서　**Mycenaean** 미케네(문명)의
Mediterranean 지중해의　**collapse** 멸망하다　**bring an end to** ~을 중단하다, 끝내다　**archaeology** 고고학　**pottery** 도자기
abandon 버리다　**settlement** 정착지　**widespread** 만연한, 널리 퍼진　**consequent** 결과적인　**starvation** 굶주림
emerge from 벗어나다　**Phoenician** 페니키아인

02

EARTH'S ENERGY BUDGET

The Earth has three major naturally occurring energy sources: solar radiation, tidal energy caused by the moon's gravitational pull on the oceans, and internal heating caused mostly by the radioactive decay of metals deep inside the Earth. Of these three sources, solar radiation accounts for 99.97 percent of all the energy available on Earth. In fact, the amount of energy contributed by tidal action and internal heating is less than the annual fluctuation in solar radiation. The total amount of incoming energy and the amount of energy either used or emitted into space are roughly equal. This balance is called the energy budget.

Of all the solar energy that reaches the Earth, 6 percent is reflected back into space by the upper atmosphere. Another 20 percent is reflected by the tops of clouds, and 4 percent is reflected from the surface. This means that 30 percent of all the solar energy reaching the Earth immediately escapes back into space. Of the remaining 70 percent, 19 percent is absorbed into the atmosphere — 3 percent by clouds and 16 percent by atmospheric gases and dust. That means that 51 percent of all solar energy is absorbed by ground sources.

The 70 percent of the solar energy that is absorbed by the Earth must also eventually be released into space, or the temperature of the Earth would continuously rise. This energy is released through indirect radiation. All ground heat is eventually radiated back into the atmosphere, where it eventually escapes into space. Indirect ground radiation occurs through three processes. The surface radiates 21 percent of the solar energy it absorbs directly as heat. Another 23 percent is transferred back into the atmosphere through the evaporation of surface water. The remaining 7 percent is lost as the ground heats the air near its surface.

This complex balance of incoming and outgoing energy is controlled by a number of factors. One such factor is the reflectivity of different surface materials. For example, ice reflects about 35 percent of solar energy, while forests only reflect 5 percent. Therefore, environmental changes, such as the melting of glaciers and deforestation, can affect the Earth's energy budget. In addition, gases in the atmosphere, especially carbon dioxide, play an important role in the absorption of solar energy, so changes in their levels affect the energy budget as well.

지구의 에너지 수지

지구는 천연으로 얻어지는 세 가지의 주요 에너지원을 갖고 있다. 태양 복사열, 해수에 대한 달의 중력에 의해 발생하는 조수 에너지, 그리고 대부분 지구 내부 깊은 곳에서 일어나는 금속의 방사성 붕괴로 발생하는 내부열이 그것이다. 이 세 가지 에너지원 중에서 태양 복사열이 지구에서 이용 가능한 모든 에너지의 99.97%를 차지한다. 사실 조수 에너지와 내부열에 의한 에너지는 태양 복사열의 연간 변동에도 미치지 못한다. 흡수되는 에너지의 총량과 사용되거나 우주로 방출되는 에너지의 총량은 대략 같다. 이 균형을 에너지 수지라고 한다.

지구에 도달하는 모든 태양 에너지 중 6%는 상층 대기에 의해 우주로 반사되어 돌아간다. 그리고 20%는 구름 상층부에 의해 반사되며 4%는 지표면으로부터 반사된다. 이는 곧 지구에 도달하는 태양 에너지의 30%가 즉시 우주로 빠져 나가는 것을 의미한다. 나머지 70% 중에서 19%는 대기에 의해 흡수되는데, 3%는 구름에 의해, 16%는 대기의 가스와 먼지에 의해 흡수된다. 이는 전체 태양 에너지 중 51%가 지상의 여러 곳으로 흡수됨을 의미한다.

지구에 흡수되는 태양 에너지의 70%도 궁극적으로 우주로 방출되어야만 하며, 그렇지 않으면 지구의 기온은 계속 상승할 것이다. 이 에너지는 간접 복사를 통해 방출된다. 지상의 모든 열은 궁극적으로 대기로 다시 방출되며, 거기서 다시 우주로 빠져 나간다. 지상의 간접 복사는 세 가지 과정을 통해 일어난다. 지표는 흡수했던 태양 에너지의 21%를 열의 형태로 직접 방출한다. 23%는 지표수의 증발을 통해 대기로 이동된다. 나머지 7%도 지면이 지표면 부근의 공기를 가열시키면서 사라진다.

이처럼 흡수되고 방출되는 복잡한 에너지의 균형은 여러 가지 요인에 의해 통제된다. 그러한 요인 중 하나는 여러 지표면 물질의 반사율이다. 가령 얼음은 35%의 태양 에너지를 반사하는 반면 숲은 5%만을 반사한다. 그러므로 빙하의 해빙이나 삼림 벌채와 같은 환경의 변화는 지구의 에너지 수지에 영향을 미칠 수 있다. 또한 대기에 있는 가스들, 특히 이산화탄소는 태양 에너지의 흡수에 중요한 역할을 하며, 이러한 가스의 수치 변화 또한 에너지 수지에 영향을 준다.

지문을 간략히 요약하기 위한 도입 문장이 아래 제시되어 있다. 지문에서 가장 중요한 내용을 표현한 세 개의 문장을 골라 요약문을 완성하시오. 일부 문장은 지문에 나오지 않았거나 중요하지 않은 내용이기 때문에 요약문에 포함되지 않는다. *이 문제는 2점이다.*

> 에너지 수지는 지구로 들어오고 나가는 에너지의 균형을 가리킨다.

(A) 모든 태양 에너지는 에너지 수지를 유지하기 위해 직접 반사 혹은 간접 복사의 형태로 우주 밖으로 이동되어야만 한다.

해설 | (A)는 에너지 수지의 과정을 설명하는 단락 2와 3의 내용을 요약해 놓은 것이다. (B)는 지구의 에너지원들을 설명한 단락 1의 내용을 요약해 놓은 것이다. (D)는 에너지의 균형에 영향을 주는 요인들을 설명한 단락 4의 내용을 요약해 놓은 것이다.

(B) 지구의 전체 에너지 투입 총량의 대부분은 태양으로부터 오고, 다른 에너지 원이 제공하는 양은 조금밖에 되지 않는다.
(C) 모든 태양 에너지의 70%만이 지구의 대기와 표면에 흡수된다.
(D) 지표면의 반사력과 대기의 흡수 능력에 영향을 미치는 환경적 변화는 에너지 수지에 많은 영향을 미칠 수 있다.
(E) 구름은 태양 에너지를 반사하고 흡수하는 데 중요한 역할을 하고 에너지 수지에 필수적이다.
(F) 지표면에 흡수된 태양 에너지는 세 가지 대기 과정을 통해 우주 밖으로 복사되어 나갈 수 있다.

어휘 | **radiation** 복사　**tidal** 조수의　**gravitational pull** 중력　**radioactive** 방사성[능]의　**decay** 붕괴　**account for** ~를 차지하다　**fluctuation** 변동　**reflect** 반사하다　**immediately** 즉시　**atmospheric** 대기의　**continuously** 계속　**evaporation** 증발　**reflectivity** 반사율　**deforestation** 삼림 벌채　**absorption** 흡수

03

WORKING MEMORY

The development of the first computers in the 1960s had an important influence on psychology. As computers became more advanced and began to "think" in more complex ways, psychologists began to make comparisons between the workings of computers and the human brain. Many of these comparisons have turned out to be wrong or inaccurate; the human brain is quite different from a computer. But the comparison between human memory and computer memory has stood up to rigorous testing.

A computer has two forms of memory. While its hard drive stores all the information in the computer over long periods of time, its RAM, or Random Access Memory, stores the files that the computer needs to use at the present time. Once the computer stops using a file, it is "forgotten" by its RAM and returned to the hard drive. The human brain works in a similar way. Psychologists call our "hard drive" long-term memory, and our "RAM" working memory.

Working memory serves a number of functions. This is where new information is stored before it is processed into long-term memory. Working memory also allows us to call up information from our long-term memory when we need to use it. For example, a person's address is stored in his or her long-term memory, but it is called up to working memory when that person fills out an envelope at the post office. Working memory also allows us to integrate old information with new information. If a person studied sociology several years ago, all that information would be in their long-term memory. If that same person takes a new sociology class, some of that old information will be called up to working memory, so connections can be made between the new and the old information.

With so many important jobs to do, working memory plays a vital role in our intelligence. Just as a computer's performance is partially limited by its RAM capacity (computers with too little RAM cannot run larger, more complex programs), so is our ability to process and handle information partially determined by our working memory. A person who can store more pieces of information in working memory can work with more information at one time. That person can also make a greater number of connections between new and old information. Therefore, a higher capacity for working memory boosts human mental performance just as more RAM does for a computer.

작동 기억

1960년대 첫 컴퓨터의 개발은 심리학에 중요한 영향을 끼쳤다. 컴퓨터가 더 발달하고 더 복잡한 방식으로 '생각'하게 되면서, 심리학자들은 컴퓨터와 인간 뇌의 작동을 비교하기 시작했다. 이런 비교 사항의 많은 부분이 틀리거나 부정확한 것으로 밝혀졌는데 이는 인간의 뇌가 컴퓨터와는 꽤 다르기 때문이다. 그러나 인간의 기억과 컴퓨터 기억장치의 비교는 엄격한 테스트를 잘 견뎌냈다.

컴퓨터에는 두 가지 기억장치가 있다. 하드 드라이브는 컴퓨터의 모든 정보를 오랜 시간에 걸쳐 저장하는 반면, 램, 즉 랜덤 액세스 메모리는 컴퓨터가 그 당시 사용해야 하는 파일을 저장한다. 일단 컴퓨터가 파일 사용을 중지하면 램에서 '잊혀지고' 하드 드라이브로 돌아간다. 인간의 뇌도 비슷한 방식으로 작용한다. 심리학자들은 우리의 '하드 드라이브'를 장기 기억으로, 우리의 '램'을 작동 기억으로 부른다.

작동 기억은 많은 기능을 수행한다. 이곳은 새로운 정보가 장기 기억으로 처리되기 전에 저장되는 곳이다. 또 작동 기억은 우리가 사용해야 할 정보를 장기 기억으로부터 가져오는 역할을 하기도 한다. 예를 들어, 장기 기억에 저장되어 있던 어떤 사람의 주소는 우체국에서 봉투를 작성할 때 작동 기억으로 불려 오게 된다. 작동 기억은 또한 오래된 정보와 새로운 정보를 통합할 수 있게 해 주기도 한다. 몇 년 전에 사회학을 공부했다면, 그에 대한 모든 정보는 장기 기억에 있을 것이다. 만약 똑같은 사람이 새로운 사회학 수업을 듣는다면, 과거의 기억 중 일부가 작동 기억으로 불려와서 새로운 정보와 예전 정보가 연결될 수 있다.

많은 중요한 역할을 가진 작동 기억은 우리의 지능에 중대한 역할을 한다. 컴퓨터의 성능이 램의 용량에 의해 부분적으로 제한되는 것과 마찬가지로 (너무 적은 용량의 램을 가진 컴퓨터는 더 크고 더 복잡한 프로그램을 실행할 수 없다) 우리가 정보를 공정하고 처리하는 능력도 우리의 작동 기억에 의해 일부 결정된다. 작동 기억에 더 많은 정보 조각들을 저장할 수 있는 사람은 동시에 더 많은 정보를 가지고 작업할 수 있다. 또한 이런 사람은 새로운 정보와 오래된 정보를 더 많이 연결할 수 있다. 따라서 더 큰 용량의 작동 기억은 램이 컴퓨터에 그러듯 인간의 정신 활동을 증진시킨다.

지문을 간략히 요약하기 위한 도입 문장이 아래 제시되어 있다. 지문에서 가장 중요한 내용을 표현한 세 개의 문장을 골라 요약문을 완성하시오. 일부 문장은 지문에 나오지 않았거나 중요하지 않은 내용이기 때문에 요약문에 포함되지 않는다. *이 문제는 2점이다.*

> 심리학자들은 컴퓨터 기억장치의 구조와 인간의 기억 사이에서 강한 유사점을 찾아냈다.

(A) 컴퓨터의 램 용량은 컴퓨터가 정보를 효과적으로 처리할 수 있는 능력을 결정한다.
(B) 컴퓨터의 하드 드라이브는 인간의 장기 기억과 유사하고, 컴퓨터의 램은 인간의 작동 기억과 유사하다.
(C) 작동 기억은 새로운 정보를 저장하고 기존 정보를 처리하는 데 사용되는 것을 말한다.
(D) 작동 기억은 인간이 새로운 주제를 공부하거나 예전에 배웠던 주제를 복습할 때 필수적이다.
(E) 작동 기억은 정보를 처리하는 역할을 맡기 때문에 지능과 깊은 연관성이 있다.
(F) 각기 다른 정보 조각들을 연결하는 것은 작동 기억의 가장 중요한 기능이다.

해설 | (B)는 인간의 뇌와 컴퓨터를 비교한 단락 2의 내용을 요약해 놓은 것이다. (C)는 인간의 작동 기억의 기능에 관해 기술한 단락 3의 내용을 요약해 놓은 것이다. (E)는 작동 기억의 정보 처리 능력에 관해 서술한 단락 4의 내용을 요약해 놓은 것이다.

어휘 | **working memory** 작동 기억　**psychologist** 심리학자　**turn out** ~임이 밝혀지다　**stand up to** ~를 잘 견디내다, ~와 맞서다　**hard drive** (컴퓨터의) 하드 드라이브　**Random Access Memory** 랜덤 액세스 메모리, 임의 추출 기억 장치　**long-term** 장기의　**process** (정보 등을) 처리하다　**call up** 불러내다　**fill out** (서류 등을) 작성하다　**integrate** 통합하다　**sociology** 사회학　**connection** 연결　**vital** 중대한, 필수적인　**intelligence** 지능, 지성　**performance** 성능, 수행　**partially** 부분적으로　**capacity** 용량, 능력　**boost** 증진시키다, 돋우다

04

OSMOREGULATION

Different from terrestrial mammals, marine mammals must constantly maintain and regulate the concentration and volume of their internal body fluid, as water and electrolytes constantly cross back and forth through their body walls. This active maintenance and regulation of internal water and electrolyte concentration is referred to as osmoregulation. To maintain a constant internal fluid balance with little deviation, the amount of water and electrolytes entering the animal must be equal to that going out. For instance, if a dolphin takes in a great amount of water and electrolytes, it must be able to excrete an equal amount through breathing, feces and urine, or milk during lactation. On the other hand, when a seal is fasting, it needs to have the capability to endure the absence of food and water by having a unique mechanism to reduce water loss and produce water from its metabolism.

Marine mammals take in water and electrolytes through the ingestion of food and water. Compared to land mammals, the diet of marine mammals consists of a far greater amount of water, up to 80 percent of what they ingest. Due to this, most marine mammals do not ingest seawater, although they have the capacity to do so. The ratio of water to electrolytes can differ according to the type of an organism consumed; the electrolyte content of a vertebrate food source is usually one third that of the seawater, while an invertebrate is essentially the same as the surrounding seawater. As such, an organism's diet has a significant impact on the degree to which it must actively manage its electrolyte intake. In addition, animals can also produce water as a by-product of metabolism, which is called metabolic water production. Likewise, the amount of metabolic water varies according to their diets.

삼투압 조절

육지 포유동물과는 달리, 해양 포유동물은 물과 전해질이 피부 벽을 통해 끊임없이 오가므로 내부 체액의 농도와 양을 끊임없이 유지하고 조절해야 한다. 물과 전해질 농도의 활발한 유지 및 조절 활동은 삼투압 조절 작용이라 불린다. 최소의 편차로 체액을 일정하게 보존하기 위해 체내로 들어가는 물과 전해질의 양은 나가는 양과 같아야 한다. 예를 들어, 돌고래 한 마리가 엄청난 양의 물과 전해질을 흡수했다면 같은 양을 호흡, 분뇨 및 소변, 또는 수유 동안의 젖으로 배출해야 한다. 반면, 바다표범은 금식할 때 음식과 물 없이도 견딜 수 있는 능력이 있는데, 이는 물 손실을 줄이면서도 물을 생산해 내는 특별한 신진대사를 가지고 있으므로 가능하다.

해양 포유동물은 음식과 물의 섭취를 통해 물과 전해질을 흡수한다. 육지 포유동물과 비교했을 때, 해양 포유동물의 먹이에서 물은 그들이 섭취하는 것의 80%까지 차지하며 많은 양을 포함한다. 그래서 대부분의 해양 포유동물들은 바닷물을 마실 수 있는 능력이 있음에도 불구하고 마시지 않는다. 전해질과 물의 비율은 유기체가 먹는 종류에 따라 다르다. 척추동물 식량원의 전해질 양은 바닷물의 3분의 1가량이지만, 무척추동물의 경우 주변 바닷물과 같다. 그와 같이 한 유기체가 먹는 것은 그것이 어느 정도로 전해질 흡수를 유지해야 하는지에 대해 중요한 영향을 미친다. 또한, 동물들은 신진대사의 부산물로서 물을 생산해 낼 수 있는데, 이것은 대사성 수분 생산이라고 불린다. 마찬가지로 대사수의 양도 동물들이 먹는 것에 따라 다르다.

There are several methods marine mammals use to control their output of water and electrolytes. The methods to get rid of the surplus water in their internal fluid are excretion and evaporation. Water is evaporated through the skin and lungs. No electrolytes are lost in the process of evaporation because marine mammals lack sweat glands, which would allow salt to pass through to the surface of the skin. However, by excreting water through urine or feces, both water and electrolytes can be removed from the body. Because salt, comprising a large portion of electrolytes, must be excreted by the kidney, marine mammals have developed a specialized kidney that can accommodate the high volume of water and electrolytes that must be processed. This specialized kidney regulates the internal fluid balance by controlling the concentration of the urine.

해양 포유동물이 물과 전해질의 생산을 조절하기 위해 사용하는 방법에는 여러 가지가 있다. 체내에 있는 과잉의 물을 없애는 방법은 배설과 증발이다. 물은 피부와 허파를 통해 증발한다. 해양 포유동물은 피부층을 통해 염분을 배출해내는 땀샘이 없으므로, 이러한 증발 과정에서 전해질의 손실은 없다. 그러나 소변이나 배설을 통한 배출은 물과 전해질 모두를 체내로부터 제거할 수 있다. 전해질의 많은 부분을 차지하는 염분은 반드시 신장을 통해 배출되어야 하므로, 해양 포유동물은 처리되어야 하는 물과 전해질을 많이 수용할 수 있는 특별한 신장을 발달시켰다. 이 특별한 신장은 소변의 농도를 조절함으로써 체액의 균형을 조절한다.

지문을 간략히 요약하기 위한 도입 문장이 아래 제시되어 있다. 지문에서 가장 중요한 내용을 표현한 세 개의 문장을 골라 요약문을 완성하시오. 일부 문장은 지문에 나오지 않았거나 중요하지 않은 내용이기 때문에 요약문에 포함되지 않는다. 이 문제는 2점이다.

> 해양 포유동물은 체액 균형을 조절하기 위해 특별한 방법들을 사용한다.

(A) 해양 포유동물은 음식과 물의 섭취를 통해 물과 전해질을 흡수하며, 신진대사를 통해 물을 생산한다.
(B) 돌고래와 바다표범은 염분이 있는 환경에 적응한 해양 포유동물의 전형적인 예이다.
(C) 해양 포유동물은 전해질 생산량을 통제하기 위해 특별한 땀샘과 신장을 발달시켰다.
(D) 해양 포유동물은 삼투압 조절이라고 불리는 체액 균형을 유지하고 조절하는 능력을 갖고 있다.
(E) 배설과 증발은 해양 포유동물이 물과 전해질 생산을 조절하기 위해 사용하는 전형적인 방법들이다.
(F) 전해질 함유 비율은 먹이에 따라 다르며, 무척추동물은 척추동물보다 3배 더 많은 전해질을 갖고 있다.

해설 | (A)는 해양동물의 음식과 물의 섭취를 통한 삼투압 조절을 설명한 단락 2의 내용을 요약해 놓은 것이다. (D)는 해양동물과 삼투압 조절에 관해 기술한 단락 1의 내용을 요약해 놓은 것이다. (E)는 해양동물의 배설과 증발을 통한 삼투압 조절을 설명한 단락 3의 내용을 요약해 놓은 것이다.

어휘 | osmoregulation 삼투압 조절 **terrestrial** 육지의, 지생의 **body fluid** 체액 **electrolyte** 전해질, 전해액 **deviation** 편차, 차이 **excrete** 배출하다, 배설하다 **lactation** 수유, 젖의 분비 **fasting** 금식, 단식 **metabolism** 신진대사 **ingestion** 섭취 **compared to** ~와 비교하여 **capacity** 능력 **ratio** 비율, 비 **vertebrate** 척추동물의 **invertebrate** 무척추동물의 **by-product** 부산물 **metabolic water production** 대사성 수분 생산 **evaporation** 증발 **lung** 허파, 폐 **sweat gland** 땀샘 **kidney** 신장, 콩팥

Reading Practice

p.96

01 (D) **02** (C) **03** (D) **04** (B) **05** (A), (D), (F)

THE IMPACT OF GLOBAL WARMING ON OCEAN TEMPERATURES

Most researchers agree that the recent global warming trend is due to greenhouse gases humans have put into the atmosphere. Over the past few decades, there has been an intense scientific debate over whether global warming would affect the oscillations between El Niño and La Niña. El Niño is characterized by unusually warm ocean temperatures in the Equatorial Pacific, as opposed to La Niña, which is characterized by unusually cold ocean temperatures in the Equatorial Pacific. For the past several millennia, the Pacific Ocean has alternated between these two states in an irregular, though basically balanced oscillation. Some theorize that if the oscillation stops, the Earth will go through a continuous El Niño-like state which could warm the Earth very quickly.

지구 온난화가 해수 온도에 미치는 영향

대부분의 연구진은 최근의 지구 온난화 추세가 인간이 대기 중에 방출해온 온실가스 때문이라는 것에 동의한다. 지난 수십 년간, 엘니뇨와 라니냐 현상의 규칙적인 움직임에 지구 온난화가 영향을 미치는지의 여부를 두고 격렬한 과학적 논쟁이 이어져 왔다. 적도 부근 태평양에서 해수 온도가 대단히 차가운 현상의 라니냐와 반대로, 엘니뇨는 적도 부근 태평양의 해수 온도가 몹시 뜨거운 현상으로 특징지어진다. 지난 수천 년 동안, 태평양은 기본적으로 균형 잡힌 움직임이긴 했지만, 이 두 가지의 상태가 불규칙적으로 번갈아 일어났다. 몇몇 이들은 이러한 움직임이 멈추게 되면 지구는 지속적인 엘니뇨 상태를 겪게 될 것이고 이것이 결국에는 지구를 빠른 속도로 뜨겁게 달굴 것이라는 이론을 제시한다.

Q01 Ordinarily the cool surface layer of the eastern Pacific Ocean acts as a water-cooled radiator and removes heat from the tropical atmosphere by carrying it hundreds of meters below the surface. The ocean currents act as the coolant that absorbs atmospheric heat, but in an El Niño year, both the shallow and deep waters are too hot to diffuse the atmospheric heat, causing a warming and strange weather patterns. Although El Niño events are too short to have lasting effects nowadays, some climate scientists question the tropical Pacific's ability to cool the atmosphere under growing global warming effects. However, recent studies into the ancient climate of the Eocene Epoch indicate that the tropical Pacific may actually be more resilient to global warming than the current climate theory claims.

A **Q02** **Q04** Some of the researchers hypothesized that the Eocene Epoch would be the best period to compare with if a continuous El Niño-like state had ever existed. **B** Based on this hypothesis, they stimulated the computer model of a "hothouses" climate in the Eocene Epoch to see the tropical Pacific's role under a continuous El Niño-like state. Contrary to most beliefs that the Pacific Ocean consists of two layers with shallows absorbing heat and depths carrying it away, it has been proven that the tropical eastern Pacific also has a third layer wedged between the two. **C** Because this third layer historically remained cool and acted as a barrier between the warmer shallow and depth water, Eocene tropics were not much different than they are today. **D** This finding was further supported by other studies which used sediment records of ancient lakebeds in present-day Wyoming and Germany. **Q03** These sediment records demonstrated that El Niño events occurred with identical regularity in the Eocene Epoch's climate computer model, indicating that there was no continuous El Niño state, even though the climate was significantly warmer.

보통 때는 동태평양의 차가운 표면층이 수랭식 냉각기 역할을 하며, 열대 지방의 대기에 있는 열을 수백 미터 표면 아래로 옮겨서 이것을 없앤다. 냉각수 역할을 하는 해류는 대기 중의 열을 흡수하지만, 엘니뇨 현상이 있는 해에는 얕고 깊은 물 모두가 너무 뜨거워, 대기의 열을 분산시킬 수 없고 덥고 이상한 기후 패턴을 만들어낸다. 엘니뇨 현상은 매우 짧아서 오늘날 지속적인 영향을 끼치진 않지만, 일부 기상 과학자들은 심화되는 지구 온난화 현상에서 대기를 차갑게 해주는 열대 태평양의 기능에 대해 의문을 던진다. 그러나 에오 세의 고대 기후에 대한 최근 연구는 열대의 태평양이 현재 기후 이론이 주장하는 것보다 지구 온난화에 대해 더 탄력적일 수 있다는 것을 보여준다.

A 일부 연구진들은 계속되는 엘니뇨와 같은 상태가 있었더라면 에오 세가 가장 비교할 만한 최적의 시기라고 가정한다. **B** 이 가정에 기반을 두어, 그들은 지속적인 엘니뇨 현상과 같은 상황에서 열대 태평양의 역할을 알아보기 위해 에오 세의 '온실' 기후의 컴퓨터 모델을 활성화했다. 태평양이 열을 흡수하는 얕은 층과 이것을 옮기는 깊은 층의 두 개의 층으로 이루어져 있다는 일반적인 믿음과 달리, 열대의 동태평양은 이 두 개의 층에 끼인 세 번째 층을 가지고 있다는 것이 증명되었다. **C** 역사상 이 세 번째 층은 차가운 채로 남아 더 따뜻하고 얕은 층과 깊은 물 사이에서 장벽 역할을 해왔기 때문에, 에오 세의 열대 역시 지금과 별다르지 않았다. **D** 이러한 사실은 현재의 와이오밍 주와 독일에 있는 고대 호수 바닥의 퇴적물 기록을 사용한 다른 연구들에 의해서도 뒷받침되었다. 이 퇴적물 기록에 의하면 엘니뇨 현상은 에오 세의 기후 컴퓨터 모델과 동일한 규칙적 패턴으로 일어나며, 기후가 아무리 현저하게 따뜻해도 지속적인 엘니뇨 현상이 일어나진 않았음을 보여준다.

01 지문에서 it 이 가리키는 것은?
(A) 대기
(B) 냉각기
(C) 표면
(D) 열

해설 | Reference 동태평양의 차가운 표면층은 이것(it)을 수백 미터 표면 아래로 옮김으로써 대기의 열을 없앤다고 했으므로, 열(heat)을 이동시키는 것임을 알 수 있다.

02 지문의 ancient 와 의미상 가장 가까운 것은?
(A) 습한
(B) 모순되는
(C) 아주 옛날의
(D) 불변의

해설 | Vocabulary ancient 의 의미는 뒤 문장의 '에오 세가 가장 비교할 만한 시기'라고 한 것에서 먼 옛날의 시기를 언급하고 있음을 추론할 수 있다.

03 단락 3에서 필자가 퇴적물 기록 에 대해 자세히 언급하는 이유는?
(A) 와이오밍 주와 독일 사이의 지질학적 유사성을 증명하기 위해
(B) 에오 세 동안 열대 태평양의 세 번째 층에 대한 역할을 설명하기 위해
(C) 에오 세 열대가 어떻게 따뜻한 기후를 유지할 수 있었는지를 설명하기 위해
(D) 지속적인 엘니뇨와 같은 현상은 일어날 가능성이 작다는 이론을 지지하기 위해

해설 | Rhetorical Purpose 단락 3의 중심 내용은 지속적인 엘니뇨 현상이 일어나는 것이 가능한지에 대한 것이며, 필자는 퇴적물 기록에 의하면 엘니뇨 현상이 지속해서 일어나진 않을 것이라고 설명하고 있다.

04 다음 문장이 지문에 들어갈 곳을 나타내는 네 개의 사각형[■]을 보시오.

> 이 가정에 기반을 두어, 그들은 지속적인 엘니뇨 현상과 같은 상황에서 열대 태평양의 역할을 알아보기 위해 에오 세의 '온실' 기후의 컴퓨터 모델을 활성화했다.

이 문장이 들어갈 가장 적절한 위치는?
(A) A　　(B) B　　(C) C　　(D) D

해설 | Sentence Insertion　삽입 문장의 this hypothesis는 앞 문장에서 언급된 '일부 연구진들이 가정한 계속되는 엘니뇨와 같은 상태가 있었더라면 에오 세가 가장 비교할 만한 최적의 시대'라는 내용을 가리킨다.

05 지문을 간략히 요약하기 위한 도입 문장이 아래 제시되어 있다. 지문에서 가장 중요한 내용을 표현한 세 개의 문장을 골라 요약문을 완성하시오. 일부 문장은 지문에 나오지 않았거나 중요하지 않은 내용이기 때문에 요약문에 포함되지 않는다. *이 문제는 2점이다.*

> 지구 온난화가 지구 기온에 지대한 영향을 끼치는지에 대해 논쟁적 토론이 있어왔다.

(A) 지속적인 엘니뇨와 같은 상태에서의 열대 태평양의 역할을 알아보기 위해 에오 세 기후가 연구됐다.
(B) 고대 호수 바닥의 퇴적물 기록은 에오 세 기후 모델에서 일관성 없는 엘니뇨 주기를 보여주었다.
(C) 인간에 의해 야기되는 온실가스가 지구 온난화의 주범이라는 사실을 뒷받침하는 증거들은 많다.
(D) 일부 연구진들은 지구 온난화가 열대의 대기를 식혀주는 열대 태평양의 역할을 무력화시킬 것이며, 이는 지속적인 엘니뇨 현상을 야기할 것이라고 믿는다.
(E) 라니냐 현상이 일어나는 해에, 무더운 기후를 식혀주기 때문에 열대 태평양의 역할은 중요하다.
(F) 몇몇 증거들은 태평양이 열대 대기의 열을 없앨 것이므로, 미래에 엘니뇨와 같은 현상은 없을 것이라고 말한다.

해설 | Summary　(A)와 (D)는 전반적으로 커지는 지구 온난화 현상으로 인해 계속되는 엘니뇨의 가능성에 대한 우려를 설명한 단락 2의 내용을 요약해 놓은 것이다. (F)는 연구 결과를 통해 앞선 우려가 기우였음을 나타내는 단락 3의 내용을 요약해 놓은 것이다.

어휘 | **global warming** 지구 온난화　**temperature** 온도, 기온　**greenhouse gas** 온실 가스　**oscillation** 움직임, (규칙적인)진동　**radiator** 냉각기, 방열기　**tropical** 열대의　**ocean current** 해류　**absorb** 흡수하다　**diffuse** 분산시키다　**ancient** 고대의　**resilient** 탄력성 있는, 회복력 있는　**hypothesize** 가정하다, 가설을 세우다　**shallow** 얕은　**barrier** 장벽, 벽　**lakebed** 호수 바닥　**regularity** 규칙적인 패턴, 정기적임

Chapter 09 Fill in a Table

Sample Question
p.99

One of the central ideas behind the United States government is the separation of powers. All powers of the central government are divided among three co-equal departments — the executive, the legislative, and the judiciary. The idea of dividing the powers of the government in this way was to ensure that no one body could take control and override the will of the people. For the founding fathers of the United States, protecting America from tyranny was one of the most important goals.

[B] The executive branch is headed by the President of the United States. [E] Today, the President's power has grown substantially from what it was when America was first founded. For example, America's first President had only four Cabinet departments — State, Treasury, War, and Justice. Today, there are 15 departments.

[D] The legislative branch of government is the Congress. This is the part of government responsible for making the laws of the land. [G] The American Congress is divided into two parts — the House of Representatives and the Senate. The House of Representatives has 435 members who are elected on the basis of state population. The Senate has 100 members, two per state regardless of state size. Together, these two bodies balance the will of the majority with the needs of individual states.

The judicial branch of the United States government is the Supreme Court. There are nine members of the Supreme Court, including the Chief Justice. The Supreme Court is the only one of the three branches whose members are not directly elected. [C] Instead, the President nominates a person to the court and the Senate confirms the nomination. Once appointed, Supreme Court justices can serve for life.

미국 정부의 이면에 놓인 중요한 개념 중 하나는 권력의 분립이다. 중앙 정부의 모든 권력은 세 개의 동등한 부처인 행정부, 입법부, 사법부로 분리된다. 정부의 권력을 이처럼 분리한 것은 어떤 조직이 국민의 뜻을 마음대로 조종하고 그보다 우선할 수 없도록 하기 위해서였다. 미국 건국의 아버지들에게 있어서 독재로부터 미국을 보호하는 것은 가장 중요한 목표 중 하나였다.

행정부는 미국 대통령이 이끈다. 오늘날 대통령의 권력은 미국이 건국된 시대보다 상당히 확대되었다. 예를 들면 미국의 초대 대통령은 휘하에 네 개의 내각 부서, 즉 국무부, 재무부, 국방부, 법무부만을 거느렸다. 오늘날에는 15개 부서가 있다.

정부의 입법부는 국회이다. 이는 나라의 법을 만드는 임무를 갖는 정부 부처이다. 미국 국회는 하원과 상원의 두 부분으로 나누어진다. 하원은 435명의 의원으로 구성되며, 이들은 주의 인구를 기준으로 하여 선출된다. 상원은 100명의 의원으로 구성되며, 주의 크기에 관계없이 각 주당 2명이 선출된다. 하원과 상원은 공동으로 다수의 의지를 각 주의 필요와 조율한다.

미국 정부의 사법부는 대법원이다. 대법원에는 대법원장을 비롯하여 9명이 있다. 대법원은 세 개의 부처 중 유일하게 구성원들이 직접 선출되지 않는 부처이다. 그 대신 대통령이 법관 후보를 지명하고 상원이 지명을 승인한다. 대법관은 일단 임명되면 평생 근무할 수 있다.

보기에서 적절한 문구를 골라 관련된 부처의 종류와 연결하시오.
보기 중 2개는 사용되지 않는다. *이 문제는 3점이다.*

보기	부처
(A) 12명으로 구성되어 있다. (B) 미국 대통령이 이끈다. (C) 대통령과 상원에 의해 권한을 부여받은 법관들에 의해 운영된다. (D) 법을 제정한다. (E) 권력이 강해졌다. (F) 주의 규모에 따라 구성원 수를 결정한다. (G) 하원과 상원으로 이루어진다.	**행정부** • (B) • (E) **입법부** • (D) • (G) **사법부** • (C)

어휘 | **co-equal** 동등한　**the executive** 행정부　**the legislative** 입법부　**the judiciary** 사법부　**override** 우선하다, 우위에 서다　**founding father** [미국사] 미국 건국의 아버지, 미국 헌법 제정자　**tyranny** 독재, 전제 정치　**Cabinet** 내각　**State (Department)** 국무부　**Treasury (Department)** 재무부　**War (Department)** 국방부　**Justice (Department)** 법무부　**elect** 선출하다　**regardless of** ~과는 관계없이　**majority** 다수　**Supreme Court** 대법원　**Chief Justice** 대법원장　**nominate** (후보로) 지명하다　**confirm** 승인하다　**nomination** 지명　**appoint** 임명하다　**serve** 근무하다

Basic Drill

p.100

01 [*Australopithecus* – (C), (D)], [*Homo Erectus* – (A), (B), (F)]
02 [Western Church – (C), (F)], [Eastern Church – (A), (D), (E)]
03 [Advanced Termites – (D), (E), (G)], [Primitive Termites – (A), (C)]
04 [Associative Learning – (B), (D)], [Imitative Learning – (C), (E)], [Both – (A)]

Vocab Quiz	01-1 locations	01-2 supplanted	02-1 countless	02-2 aspects
	03-1 series	03-2 transform	04-1 specific	04-2 simply

01

THE BONE RECORD OF HUMAN ANCESTORS

Archaeologists and anthropologists interested in tracing the evolution of the human species must rely largely on what is commonly called the bone record. The bone record is the collection of fossilized bones gathered from different sites. By dating these bones and placing them in chronological order, scientists can trace both the evolution and movement of the human species.

The oldest bones in the bone record belong to a species named *Australopithecus*. *Australopithecus* first emerged about 4.4 million years ago, and is the first human ancestor to definitively diverge from ape species. The primary distinction between apes and *Australopithecus* is that *Australopithecus* was a fully bipedal creature; it walked in an upright manner on two feet. While some apes are able to stand upright, they can only do so for short periods of time. Nevertheless, the brain of *Australopithecus* was only about 35 percent of the size of a modern human's, and **(C) its intelligence was probably not much higher than a chimpanzee's.** *Australopithecus* was also much smaller than modern humans. Typical heights for the species were about 1.2 to 1.4 meters, with males being significantly larger than females. *Australopithecus* did not make tools, but it did use rocks and sticks to reach for food, to crush nuts, and for other purposes. **(D) Because of its small size and lack of weapons for defense, *Australopithecus* was a common prey for lions and other predators of western and southern Africa where it lived.**

The bones of *Australopithecus* began to disappear from the bone record around 1.8 million years ago, when the species was quickly replaced by the more advanced *Homo erectus*. **(F) *Homo erectus* was a much more "human" species.** **(A) It stood at around 1.75 meters, about the same height as the average modern human.** Its brain was about 75 percent of the size of a modern human's, and **(B) this larger brain size allowed it to fashion a number of stone tools and weapons.** With its larger size and new weapons, *Homo erectus* quickly went from being hunted to being the hunter. *Homo erectus* was a far more successful species than *Australopithecus*, and spread from Africa into southern Europe and Asia. *Homo erectus* still was not fully human, however. The structure of its vocal cords suggests that it was incapable of forming speech and was limited to grunts and growls for communication.

인류 조상의 뼈 기록

인류의 진화를 추적하는 데 관심이 있는 고고학자들과 인류학자들은 주로 뼈 기록이라고 불리는 것에 상당히 의지해야 한다. 뼈 기록은 여러 장소에서 모은 화석화된 뼈를 수집하는 것이다. 이러한 뼈들의 연도를 추정하고 시간 순서대로 배열함으로써 과학자들은 인류 종의 진화와 이동 모두를 추적할 수 있다.

뼈 기록에서 가장 오래된 뼈는 오스트랄로피테쿠스라는 종에 속한다. 오스트랄로피테쿠스는 440만 년 전에 최초로 나타났으며, 유인원으로부터 분명히 갈라져 나온 최초의 인류 조상이다. 유인원과 오스트랄로피테쿠스의 주요 차이점은 오스트랄로피테쿠스는 완전한 양족 동물이었다는 것이다. 즉, 그것은 똑바로 두 발로 서서 걸었다. 일부 유인원들은 똑바로 서 있을 수 있지만, 잠깐 동안만 그럴 수 있다. 그럼에도 불구하고, 오스트랄로피테쿠스의 뇌는 현대 인류의 뇌의 35% 크기에 불과했으며, 지능은 아마도 침팬지보다 아주 높지는 않았을 것이다. 오스트랄로피테쿠스는 또한 현대 인류보다 훨씬 더 작았다. 오스트랄로피테쿠스의 평균 신장은 1.2~1.4 미터 정도였고, 남성이 여성보다 훨씬 더 컸다. 오스트랄로피테쿠스는 도구를 만들지는 않았지만, 식량에 도달하거나 견과류를 깨고 또 다른 목적을 위해 돌과 막대기를 사용했다. 오스트랄로피테쿠스는 몸집이 작고 자신을 방어할 무기가 없었기 때문에, 그들이 살았던 서부 아프리카와 남부 아프리카에서 사자를 비롯한 다른 포식자의 일반적인 먹잇감이었다.

오스트랄로피테쿠스의 뼈는 약 180만 년 전 무렵부터 뼈 기록에서 사라지기 시작했는데, 이때 오스트랄로피테쿠스는 더욱 진화된 호모 에렉투스로 빠르게 대체되었다. 호모 에렉투스는 훨씬 더 '인간을 닮은' 종이었다. 서 있을 때 키가 약 1.75 미터로, 이는 보통의 현대 인류와 거의 같은 크기였다. 호모 에렉투스의 뇌는 현대 인류의 뇌의 약 75% 크기였으며, 이렇게 더 큰 뇌로 많은 수의 석기와 무기를 만들 수 있었다. 호모 에렉투스는 몸집이 더 크고 새로운 무기가 있었기 때문에, 사냥당하는 쪽에서 사냥하는 쪽으로 빠르게 처지가 바뀌었다. 호모 에렉투스는 오스트랄로피테쿠스보다 훨씬 더 성공적인 종이었고, 아프리카에서 남부 유럽과 아시아로 퍼져나갔다. 그러나 호모 에렉투스도 아직은 완전한 인간은 아니었다. 호모 에렉투스의 성대 구조는 그들이 언어를 구사할 수 없었으며, 의사소통이 앓는 소리와 으르렁거리는 소리로 제한되어 있었음을 암시한다.

보기에서 적절한 문구를 골라 관련된 인류 조상의 종과 연결하시오.
보기 중 2개는 사용되지 않는다. *이 문제는 3점이다.*

(A) 현대 인류와 크기가 거의 비슷하다.	오스트랄로피테쿠스
(B) 자신의 도구를 만들 수 있다.	• (C)
(C) 침팬지와 지능이 비슷하다.	• (D)
(D) 포식자로부터 무방비 상태이다.	호모 에렉투스
(E) 고기만을 먹는다.	• (A)
(F) 인간에 더 가깝다.	• (B)
(G) 잠시 동안만 똑바로 서 있을 수 있다.	• (F)

해설 | 지문에 따르면, 오스트랄로피테쿠스는 침팬지와 지능이 비슷했고, 몸집이 현대 인류보다 훨씬 더 작으며 무기를 스스로 만들 수 없어 포식자에게 쉽게 공격당했다. 호모 에렉투스는 현대 인류와 신장이 거의 비슷하고, 스스로 도구를 만들었으며, 오스트랄로피테쿠스보다는 인간에 더 가까운 종이었다.

어휘 | trace 추적하다   fossilize 화석화되다[하다]   chronological 시간 순서대로 된, 연대순의   definitively 분명히, 명확하게   diverge 갈라지다   ape 유인원   distinction 차이점, 구별   bipedal 양족 동물의   upright 똑바로   significantly 훨씬, 상당히   prey 먹잇감   predator 포식자   disappear 사라지다   fashion 만들다   vocal cord 성대   incapable ~를 할 수 없는   grunt 앓는 소리, 꿀꿀거리는 소리   growl 으르렁거리는 소리

02

THE SPLIT OF THE CHRISTIAN CHURCH

The division of the Christian Church has its roots in the division of the Roman Empire. (C) The Christians in the Latin-speaking Western Empire slowly began to drift apart from the Greek-speaking Christians of the Eastern Empire. While the gaps between these two groups steadily grew over the next 700 years, they were still technically members of the same Christian faith. In 1054, however, the Christian Church was irrevocably split into the Western Catholic Church and the Eastern Orthodox Church.

The causes for this split were innumerable. Certainly, the language barrier between the two churches played a major role, but there were other, more decisive factors in the breakup of the Christian Church. The power of the Pope was one such issue. The early Christian Church was ruled by five prelates, or church fathers. These prelates were stationed in the five most-prominent cities of the Roman world, with the Roman prelate receiving the most honor. In the early church, while the Roman prelate had been entitled to a greater amount of the respect, all five prelates wielded the same amount of power within the church. (A) (E) As the divisions between eastern and western Christians grew, the Roman prelate began to claim authority over his four eastern colleagues. The eastern prelates rejected the supremacy of the Roman Pope, and this was the first major source of tension within the church.

The other factor leading to the Great Schism of 1054 was the more complex issue of religious belief. Since the earliest days of the church, people had debated the exact nature of Christ. Was Christ a man, or was he a god? If he was a god, was he the equal of his father, or was he a lesser god? (F) To solve such difficult questions, the Christians had developed a complex concept called the Trinity. The idea of the Trinity maintained that the three divine beings mentioned in the Bible — the Father, the Son(Christ), and the Holy Spirit — were in fact different facets of the same god. They were at once divided and the same. The Western Church, under the guidance of the Pope, had explicitly stated this to be true. (D) The Eastern prelates, however, were not as vocal on the matter. They preferred to leave their beliefs unstated. These differences ultimately led to the split of the Christian Church in 1054.

기독교 교회의 분열

기독교 교회의 분열은 로마 제국의 분열에 그 기원을 두고 있다. 라틴어를 사용하는 서로마 제국의 기독교인들은 그리스어를 사용하는 동로마 제국의 기독교인들과 서서히 사이가 멀어지기 시작했다. 이후 700년에 걸쳐 이 두 집단 사이의 괴리는 꾸준히 커졌지만, 그들은 엄밀히 말해서 여전히 같은 기독교 신앙의 구성원들이었다. 그러나 1054년에 기독교 교회는 서방 가톨릭 교회와 동방 정교회로 돌이킬 수 없이 분열되었다.

분열의 원인은 셀 수 없이 많았다. 기독교의 분열에서 두 교회 사이의 언어 장벽이 분명 커다란 역할을 했지만, 더욱 결정적인 다른 요인들이 있었다. 교황의 권력 문제가 그중 하나였다. 초기의 기독교 교회는 다섯 명의 고위 성직자가 다스렸다. 이 고위 성직자들은 로마 영토의 주요 5개 도시에 배치되었으며, 로마의 고위 성직자가 가장 큰 영예를 누렸다. 초기 교회에서는 비록 로마의 고위 성직자가 더 많이 추앙받기는 했지만, 다섯 명의 고위 성직자 모두가 교회 내에서 같은 권력을 행사했다. 동서 기독교인들 사이의 분열이 커짐에 따라 로마의 고위 성직자는 네 명의 동로마 동료들에 대해 권위를 내세우기 시작했다. 동로마의 고위 성직자들은 로마 교황의 지배권을 거부했고, 이것이 교회 내의 갈등을 가져온 첫 번째 주된 원인이었다.

1054년의 교회의 대분열을 일으킨 또 다른 요인은 더욱 복잡한 신앙 문제였다. 사람들은 초기 교회 시대부터 그리스도의 정확한 본질에 대해 논쟁을 벌였다. 그리스도는 인간이었는가, 아니면 신이었는가? 신이었다면 그의 아버지와 동등한가, 아니면 지위가 더 낮은 신인가? 이러한 어려운 문제를 해결하기 위해 기독교인들은 삼위일체라는 복잡한 개념을 발전시켰다. 삼위일체의 개념은 성경에 언급된 세 가지 성스러운 존재, 즉 성부, 성자(그리스도), 그리고 성령이 사실은 같은 하느님의 여러 다른 측면이라는 것이었다. 그들은 하나인 동시에 여럿이었다. 서방 교회는 교황의 인도 하에 삼위일체설이 사실이라고 명백히 선언했다. 그러나 동로마의 고위 성직자들은 그 문제에 대해 그렇게 적극적으로 의견을 표명하지 않았다. 그들은 그들의 믿음을 말하지 않은 채로 남겨두길 선호했다. 이러한 차이점들이 궁극적으로 1054년의 기독교 교회의 분열로 이어졌다.

보기에서 적절한 문구를 골라 관련된 기독교 집단과 연결하시오. 보기 중 2개는 사용되지 않는다. *이 문제는 3점이다.*

(A) 고위 성직자 간의 동등한 지위를 원했다.	서방 교회
(B) 성경을 단 하나의 권위로 인정했다.	• (C)
(C) 라틴어를 사용했다.	• (F)
(D) 삼위일체의 개념을 공식적으로 옹호하지 않았다.	동방 교회
(E) 교황의 권력을 인정하지 않았다.	• (A)
(F) 삼위일체의 개념을 지지했다.	• (D)
(G) 교회의 분열을 적극적으로 추진했다.	• (E)

해설 | 지문에 따르면, 서방 교회는 라틴어를 사용하며, 삼위일체의 개념을 지지하였다. 동방 교회는 다른 성직자보다 높은 지위를 원하는 교황의 요구를 받아들이지 않고 동등한 지위를 원했다. 그리고 삼위일체에 대한 개념을 공식적으로 옹호하지 않고 말하지 않은 채로 남겨두었다.

어휘 | **division** 분열, 분리 **drift apart** 사이가 멀어지다 **technically** 엄밀히 말해서 **faith** 신앙 **irrevocably** 돌이킬 수 없이 **split** 분열되다 **Orthodox Church** 동방 정교회 **decisive** 결정적인 **breakup** 분열, 붕괴 **prelate** 고위 성직자 **station** 배치하다 **prominent** 주요한 **wield** (권력을) 행사하다 **authority** 권위 **reject** 거부[거절]하다 **supremacy** 지배권 **Great Schism** 교회의 대분열 **debate** 논쟁하다 **Trinity** [신학] 삼위일체 **divine** 성스러운 **the Father** 성부 **the Son** 성자 **the Holy Spirit** 성령 **explicitly** 명백하게 **vocal** 적극적으로 의견을 표명하는 **ultimately** 궁극적으로, 마침내

03

CELLULOSE DIGESTION IN TERMITES

Cellulose, the world's most abundant carbohydrate, is an endless string of 3,000 or more sugar molecules. Although it is a very common substance on the Earth, most organisms lack the ability to digest cellulose and have difficulty ingesting it as an energy source. Grazing mammals, such as cows and goats, are able to digest cellulose directly, but in a time-consuming way. Termites, one of the smallest orders of insects, receive their nutrition from cellulose with help of certain microorganisms. Termites use two distinct feeding strategies to assimilate cellulose indirectly depending on their degree of evolution.

[A] Primitive termites digest cellulose by means of tiny one-celled animals in their digestive tract. These one-celled microorganisms, called protozoa, do the actual work of breaking down the cellulose. Termites swallow grass, leaves, and branches that are delivered to the fermentation chamber, where protozoa reside and do the work. These tiny workers then break the cellulose down into sugar and enable their host to take in the sugar as an energy source. Since termites and protozoa are two different organisms, the culture of cellulose digesters is passed along through a special process from one generation to the next. Initially, newly hatched termites lack these microorganisms for their cellulose digestion. [C] Therefore, adults secrete a special liquid, rich in digesters, for young termites to feed on, thereby allowing young termites to obtain protozoa. When treated with antibiotics or an anti-protozoan solution, the protozoa in their digestive system will die and the termites will slowly starve to death, unable to digest cellulose into absorbable sugar molecules.

More-advanced termite species practice a different type of feeding strategy. Unlike their primitive brethren, advanced termites break down cellulose outside their body. Without going through a time-consuming fermentation chamber process, [E] these species are more nimble and efficient in comparison. In order to digest cellulose in the air, advanced termites live in symbiosis with fungi, the only organism able to break down cellulose in the

흰개미의 셀룰로스 소화

세상에서 가장 풍부한 탄수화물인 셀룰로스는 3,000개 이상의 무한한 일련의 당 분자이다. 지구에서 매우 흔한 물질이지만, 대부분 유기체들은 이 셀룰로스를 소화하지 못하고 에너지 자원으로 섭취하는 데 어려움을 겪는다. 소나 염소 같은 방목 포유류들은 셀룰로스를 직접 소화할 수 있지만, 시간이 걸린다. 곤충의 가장 작은 종 중 하나인 흰개미는 특정한 미생물의 도움으로 셀룰로스로부터 영양분을 얻는다. 흰개미는 그들의 진화 정도에 따라, 셀룰로스를 간접적으로 소화하는 데 두 가지 다른 전략을 사용한다.

초기의 흰개미는 소화관내에 있는 작은 단세포 동물이라는 수단을 통해 셀룰로스를 소화한다. 원생동물이라고도 불리는 이 단세포 미생물은 셀룰로스를 분해하는 실질적인 역할을 한다. 흰개미는 발효실로 전달되는 풀, 나뭇잎, 나뭇가지를 삼키는데, 원생동물이 여기 발효실에서 살면서 그들의 임무를 수행한다. 그리고 나서 이 작은 일꾼들은 셀룰로스를 당으로 분해하고 그들의 숙주가 당을 에너지 자원으로 흡수할 수 있도록 해준다. 흰개미와 원생동물은 서로 다른 두 종류의 생물이기 때문에, 셀룰로스를 소화하는 배양 조직은 특수한 절차를 통해 다음 세대로 옮겨진다. 처음에 새로 부화된 흰개미들은 셀룰로스 소화를 위한 이 미생물을 가지고 있지 않다. 그러므로 성체 흰개미들은 새끼 흰개미들에게 먹일 소화 물질이 풍부한 특수한 액체를 분비하는데, 그렇게 함으로써 새끼 흰개미들이 원생동물을 갖게 한다. 항생물질이나 항원생동물 물질로 처리되면, 소화계의 원생동물이 죽어 흰개미는 셀룰로스를 흡수 가능한 당 분자로 소화할 수 없으므로 천천히 굶어 죽게 된다.

좀 더 진화한 흰개미 종은 다른 영양 섭취 전략을 사용한다. 초기 흰개미들과는 달리, 고등 흰개미는 체외에서 셀룰로스를 분해한다. 시간이 오래 걸리는 발효실 과정을 거치지 않아, 이 종들은 비교적 좀 더 빠르고 효과적이다. 공기 중에서 셀룰로스를 소화하기 위해, 고등 흰개미는 균류와 공생 관계를 맺고 사는데, 이는 산소가 있는 곳에서 셀룰로스를 분해할 수 있는 유일한 생물이다. 흰개미는 풀, 잔가지, 그리고 다른 목재의 물질을 모으는데, 이것들을 씹어서 개미집으로 가져온다. 씹어진 나무는 개미집에서 comb이라고 불리는 작은 환기실에 쌓인다.

presence of oxygen. (G) Termites gather grass, twigs and other woody materials by chewing up and delivering them to their nest. In the nest, the chewed-up wood is piled up in a small ventilated chamber called a comb. (D) The termites then place spores of a special fungus called *Termitomyces* on the comb, and as the spores grow on the comb, they convert the cellulose from woody pulp into sugars and nitrogen for termites to intake. Needless to say, termites and their micro-digesters rely on each other for survival.

그리고 나서 흰개미는 흰개미버섯이라고 불리는 특정한 균류의 포자를 comb에 살포한다. 그리고 comb에서 포자가 자라면서 목재의 펄프를 흡수 가능한 당과 질소로 전환시킨다. 말할 필요도 없이, 흰개미와 아주 작은 이 소화 물질은 생존을 위해 서로 의존한다.

보기에서 적절한 문구를 골라 관련된 흰개미 종과 연결하시오. 보기 중 2개는 사용되지 않는다. *이 문제는 3점이다.*

(A) 소화관에서 셀룰로스를 분해한다. (B) 소화 물질을 가진 채로 태어난다. (C) 분비를 통해 미생물을 전달한다. (D) 균류가 소화한 것을 섭취한다. (E) 시간을 좀 더 절약하는 방법으로 셀룰로스를 소화한다. (F) 직접 셀룰로스를 소화할 수 있다. (G) 개미집에 초목을 쌓는다.	고등 흰개미 • (D) • (E) • (G) 초기 흰개미 • (A) • (C)

해설 | 지문에 따르면, 좀 더 진화한 고등 흰개미는 초기 흰개미보다 좀 더 시간을 절약하는 방법으로 셀룰로스를 소화하는데, 초목으로 지은 구조물에 균류의 포자를 살포하고, 그 균류가 분해한 셀룰로스를 흡수한다. 초기 흰개미는 소화관에서 원생동물을 이용해 셀룰로스를 흡수하고, 이 원생동물을 다음 세대로 전달할 때는 특수한 분비 작용을 통해 전달한다.

어휘 | **cellulose** 셀룰로스, 섬유소 **termite** 흰개미 **carbohydrate** 탄수화물 **sugar molecule** 당 분자, 설탕 분자 **ingest** 섭취하다, 삼키다 **time-consuming** 시간이 걸리는 **assimilate** 소화하다, 동화시키다 **primitive** 초기의, 원시의 **digestive tract** 소화관 **protozoan**(pl. protozoa) 원생동물 **break down** 분해하다 **fermentation** 발효 (작용), 소동 **host** 숙주 **secrete** 분비하다 **antibiotic** 항생물질, 항생제 **absorbable** 흡수 가능한, 흡수되는 **nimble** 빠른, 민첩한 **symbiosis** 공생 **fungus**(pl. fungi) 균류, 곰팡이 **ventilate** 환기하다, 표명하다 **spore** 포자 ***Termitomyces*** 흰개미버섯

04

ASSOCIATIVE AND IMITATIVE LEARNING

Most animal species are capable of at least some level of learning. Animal learning mechanisms appear in large part to be quite similar to the learning mechanisms of human infants. (A) While explicit instruction is nearly impossible, most animals are capable of learning through association and imitation.

Associative learning is the most widely known form of animal learning. (D) In associative learning, the animal begins to associate a particular action with a particular outcome. The most famous example of this is that of Pavlov's dogs. In Pavlov's famous experiment, his dogs began to associate the ringing of a bell with the result of being fed. In time, they began to get excited merely by the ringing of the bell, even if they were not fed. This kind of learning is common in the wild. For example, a bear that breaks into a beehive to get the honey may receive many painful stings. If this happens several times, the bear may begin to associate beehives with pain and begin to avoid them. Another example comes from the island of Koshima, where Japanese scientists were studying macaques, a species of monkey. The scientists left potatoes on the beach for the monkeys each morning. Eventually the monkeys began to associate the action of going to the beach, which they did not do before, with the finding of food. Now the macaques on Koshima walk down to the beach each morning.

연상 학습과 모방 학습

대부분의 동물 종은 최소한 일정 수준의 학습이 가능하다. 동물의 학습 방법은 인간 유아들의 학습 방법과 많은 부분에서 꽤 흡사하게 보인다. 명시적인 지도는 거의 불가능하지만, 대부분의 동물은 연상과 모방을 통해 학습할 수 있다.

연상 학습은 가장 널리 알려진 동물의 학습 형태이다. 연상 학습에서 동물은 특정 행동과 특정 결과를 연관짓기 시작한다. 가장 유명한 예는 Pavlov의 개이다. Pavlov의 유명한 실험에서 그의 개들은 종소리를 먹이를 먹는 것과 연관시키기 시작했다. 얼마 지나지 않아 개들은 먹이를 주지 않고 단지 종소리만 들려줘도 흥분하게 되었다. 이런 종류의 학습은 야생에서 흔하게 나타난다. 예를 들어, 어떤 곰이 꿀을 먹기 위해 벌통을 뒤지다가 고통스러운 벌침에 많이 쏘일 수 있다. 만약 이것이 여러 번 반복되면, 그 곰은 벌통과 고통을 함께 연상하게 되어 벌통을 피하기 시작할 것이다. 또 다른 예는 일본 과학자들이 원숭이의 한 종류인 짧은꼬리원숭이를 연구하던 코시마 섬에서 찾아볼 수 있다. 과학자들은 매일 아침 해변에 감자를 놓았는데, 결국 원숭이들은 이전에는 하지 않았던 해변에 가는 행동과 먹이 찾는 것을 연관 지어 생각하게 되었다. 이제 코시마의 짧은꼬리원숭이는 매일 아침 해변으로 걸어 나온다.

Another type of learning common in animals is imitative learning. (B) (E) Unlike associative learning, imitative learning does not rely on the animal's past experiences. Imitative learning may occur simply by watching others. After the macaques on Koshima learned to walk to the beach for food, they saw one macaque washing her potatoes in the ocean before eating them. Slowly the other macaques began to imitate her behavior, and now all the macaques on the island wash their potatoes before eating them. The macaques have also developed a taste for salt and even dip their potatoes into the water between bites. The macaques also picked up a number of new behaviors from imitating individuals in their species. The macaques now go down to the beach to splash and swim in the ocean on especially hot days. They were not rewarded for this behavior by the scientists, so they could not have possibly learned this through associative learning. The only explanation is that they saw one of their members splashing in the water and learned from her example that splashing in the water helps cool their bodies down. (C) Thus, imitative learning is thought to be an important mechanism in the development of new behaviors in a species.

보기에서 적절한 문구를 골라 관련된 학습 종류와 연결하시오.
보기 중 2개는 사용되지 않는다. *이 문제는 3점이다.*

	연상 학습
(A) 대부분 동물에게 나타난다.	• (B)
(B) 반복된 경험으로 인해 형성된다.	• (D)
(C) 새로운 행동을 개발하도록 도와준다.	모방 학습
(D) 뚜렷한 행동과 결과물 사이의 관계에 기초한다.	• (C)
(E) 행동을 보이기 위해 다른 이들에게 의존한다.	• (E)
(F) 동물의 학습으로서 가장 드문 종류이다.	둘 다
(G) 사람을 통해 배운다.	• (A)

어휘 | **mechanism** 방법 **infant** 유아 **explicit** 명시적인 **association** 연상, 연합 **imitation** 모방 **associate** 연관짓다, 연상하다 **outcome** 결과 **experiment** 실험 **beehive** 벌집 **painful** 고통스러운 **sting** (곤충 따위의) 침[가시] **macaque** 짧은꼬리원숭이 **dip** 담그다 **splash** 첨벙거리다, (물을) 튀기다 **cool something down** ~을 식히다

Reading Practice

p.108

| 01 (C) | 02 (B) | 03 (B) | 04 (D) | 05 [Tikopia – (C), (D)], [Easter Island – (B), (G)], [Both – (A)] |

TIKOPIA AND EASTER ISLAND SOCIETIES

The challenges faced by the Easter Island and Tikopia societies were some of the most extreme that have confronted any society in the history of human civilization. Q05(A) Located on small, isolated islands, as both societies were, nearly every social pressure, from resource allocation to population control, was exacerbated by their isolation. Yet despite facing similar environmental pressures, the Tikopia have survived for nearly 3,000 years, while the Easter Island society completely failed in the late 1500s. The answer to the different fates of these two societies lies primarily in their management of resources.

While Tikopia society has a very high population density, its total population is small enough that all members of the society know each other personally. **Q05(D) The Tikopia have a powerful sense of the common good of their society, and all decisions are considered with respect to how they will affect the society as a whole.** In addition, the Tikopia have long understood that their island simply cannot support a larger population, and important cultural taboos were designed to ensure population stability. The Tikopia feel it is immoral to have large families, and thus practice extensive family planning, even resorting to infanticide in earlier times.

A Q05(C) The Tikopia also have strict rules designed to prevent the overexploitation of their limited resources. **B** If a person wishes to catch or eat fish, he or she must first seek the permission of the chief so as to prevent the depletion of fish stocks. **C** Q04 In addition, the trees on the island all produce edible fruit and have been cultured in such a way to replicate the natural tree cover of the rainforest, creating an extremely efficient and environmentally friendly agricultural system. **D In fact, this system is so advanced and environmentally sound that modern day ecologists are trying to replicate it in other parts of the world.**

Easter Island society, in contrast, is a lesson in overexploitation, poor resource planning, and negligent environmental practices that eventually doomed the society. **Q02 Q05(B) Easter Island society was a typical Polynesian culture in that it had an elite, royal class of chiefs who lived far above the conditions of the rest of society.** Q03 Q05(G) Enormous amounts of manpower went into meeting the needs of the chiefs, and first among those needs was the construction of moai, the giant stone heads for which Easter Island is now famous. Moai were built essentially as a form of competition between rival chiefs, with larger moai signifying greater power. Monument construction required cutting down large numbers of trees to transport and lift the huge stone blocks. Trees were also heavily harvested for the construction of canoes and for use as firewood. The result was massive deforestation. By 1500, the large palms used in canoe and monument construction were gone, and so these activities stopped. Within another 100 years, the island had been completely deforested, and the islanders were reduced to using grasses and leaves for their cooking fires. Deforestation also led to massive soil erosion, which reduced crop yields as well as migrating bird species, eliminating an important source of protein. Without the food resources to feed the population, Easter Island society collapsed.

티코피아 사회는 인구 밀도가 매우 높지만, 총인구는 사회의 모든 구성원이 서로를 개인적으로 알 수 있을 정도로 적다. 티코피아 사람들은 사회의 공익에 대한 강한 인식을 갖고 있고, 모든 결정은 그것이 사회 전체에 미칠 영향과 관련하여 고려된다. 덧붙여, 티코피아 사람들은 오래전부터 그들의 섬이 더 많은 인구를 지탱할 수 없다는 것을 알았고, 인구의 안정성을 위해 중요한 문화적 금기들이 고안되었다. 티코피아 사람들은 대가족을 거느리는 것이 비도덕적인 일이라 생각하며 광범위한 가족 계획을 실천하는데, 심지어 옛날에는 영아 살해까지 행해졌다.

A 또한 티코피아 사람들에게는 제한된 자원을 과잉 개발하는 것을 방지하기 위해 고안된 엄격한 규칙이 있다. **B** 어떤 사람이 물고기를 잡거나 먹고 싶으면, 물고기 수의 고갈을 막기 위해 우선 부족장의 허가를 받아야 한다. **C** 게다가 섬의 나무들은 모두 먹을 수 있는 과일을 생산하며 열대 우림의 삼림 밀도와 똑같이 길러져, 매우 효율적이고 환경친화적인 농경 체계를 만들어 낸다. **D** 사실 이 시스템은 매우 진보되고 환경친화적이기 때문에 현대 생태학자들이 다른 곳에서 이 방법을 그대로 사용하려고 노력 중이다.

반대로 이스터 섬 사회는 사회를 결국에는 불행한 결말로 이끈 자원의 과잉 개발, 엉성한 자원 활용 계획, 그리고 태만한 환경 관리를 보여주는 교훈적 사례이다. 이스터 섬 사회는 사회 대부분의 사람보다 훨씬 높은 생활 수준을 영위했던 부족장들로 이루어진 엘리트 계급이 있었다는 점에서 전형적인 폴리네시아 사회였다. 부족장들의 요구를 충족하기 위해 엄청난 인력이 동원되었으며, 이러한 요구 중 첫 번째는 모아이를 만드는 것이었다. 모아이는 돌로 만들어진 거대한 두상으로, 오늘날 이스터 섬은 이것으로 유명하다. 모아이는 원래 경쟁 관계에 있는 부족들 사이의 경쟁의 한 형태로 만들어졌는데, 더 큰 모아이는 더 큰 권력을 의미했다. 석상을 제작할 때 거대한 돌덩이를 운반하고 끌어올리기 위해 많은 수의 나무를 베었다. 또한 카누 제작과 땔감용으로 나무를 심하게 벌목하였다. 그 결과 대규모 삼림 벌채가 일어났다. 카누와 건축에 쓰인 커다란 야자수는 1500년경에 사라졌고, 이러한 활동은 중단되었다. 100년 후에는 섬 전체가 완전히 벌채되어 주민들은 요리용 불을 때기 위해 풀과 나뭇잎만을 이용해야 하는 처지가 되었다. 또 삼림 벌채는 엄청난 토양 침식으로 이어졌고 이는 철새 종뿐만 아니라 곡류의 생산량을 감소시켜 주요 단백질 공급원이 사라지고 말았다. 인구를 지탱할 식량 자원이 없어짐으로 인해 이스터 섬 사회는 붕괴되었다.

01 지문의 exacerbated 와 의미상 가장 가까운 것은?

(A) 재현되었다
(B) 야기되었다
(C) 악화되었다
(D) 처리되었다

해설 | Vocabulary exacerbated 는 '악화되었다'라는 의미가 있다.

02 단락 4의 정보를 토대로 이스터 섬 사회에 대해 추론할 수 있는 것은?

(A) 이스터 섬의 인구 증가는 섬 사회에서 전례가 없던 일이었다.
(B) 일반 대중과 부족장 사이에는 상당한 경제적, 정치적 격차가 있었다.
(C) 삶의 대부분 양상이 철저히 통제되었다.
(D) 모아이 건설이 그 사회의 유일한 문화적 업적이었다.

해설 | Inference 단락 4에 따르면, 이스터 섬 사회에서는 사회 대부분의 사람보다 부족장이 훨씬 높은 생활 수준을 영위했다고 한다. 이를 바탕으로 일반 대중과 부족장 사이에는 큰 경제적, 정치적 격차가 있었음을 알 수 있다.

03 필자가 지문에서 모아이 를 언급하는 이유는?

(A) 이스터 섬 사회의 가장 위대한 업적에 대해 논의하기 위해
(B) 이스터 섬 사회의 형편없는 자원 관리에 대한 예를 제시하기 위해
(C) 티코피아와 이스터 섬 사회 사이의 팽팽한 경쟁관계에 대해 설명하기 위해
(D) 이스터 섬 주민들의 건축 방법에 관해 논의하기 위해

해설 | **Rhetorical Purpose** 모아이가 언급된 단락의 주제는 이스터 섬 사회가 생존과는 관계없는 곳에 인력과 자원을 낭비하고 있었다는 내용이다. 필자가 제시한 모아이 제작은 이 내용을 뒷받침하기 위해 사용된 예시이다.

04 다음 문장이 지문에 들어갈 곳을 나타내는 네 개의 사각형[■]을 보시오.

> 사실 이 시스템은 매우 진보되고 환경친화적이기 때문에 현대 생태학자들이 다른 곳에서 이 방법을 그대로 사용하려고 노력 중이다.

이 문장이 들어갈 가장 적절한 위치는?

(A) A (B) B (C) C (D) D

해설 | **Sentence Insertion** 삽입 문장 중 In fact는 앞에 언급된 내용을 다시 언급하며 강조하는 역할을 함을 알 수 있다. 따라서 삽입 문장의 this system이 가리키는 것은 앞 문장의 "… an extremely efficient and environmentally friendly agricultural system"임을 알 수 있다.

05 보기에서 적절한 문구를 골라 관련된 사회와 연결하시오. 보기 중 2개는 사용되지 않는다. *이 문제는 3점이다.*

(A) 지리적으로 고립되었다.	티코피아
(B) 매우 계급화된 사회이다.	• (C)
(C) 가능한 모든 자원의 사용은 엄격하게 통제된다.	• (D)
(D) 공익에 대해 강조했다.	이스터 섬
(E) 자원이 더 많았다.	• (B)
(F) 존재하는 자원을 거의 활용하지 않았다.	• (G)
(G) 인력과 자원을 생존에 필수적이지 않은 곳에 투입했다.	둘 다
	• (A)

해설 | **Fill in a Table** 지문에 따르면, 티코피아 사회와 이스터 섬은 둘 다 외부로부터 고립된 사회였다. 티코피아 사회는 삶에 대한 모든 결정을 공동체의 안위와 연결지어 결정하고 한정된 자원의 사용을 엄격하게 통제했다. 이스터 섬 사회는 계급화된 사회이고, 자원과 인력을 지도층의 권력 과시에 낭비하여 생존에 필수적이지 않은 곳에 이를 투입했다.

어휘 | **isolated** 고립된 **allocation** 배분 **population control** 인구 조절 **exacerbate** 악화시키다 **fate** 운명 **primarily** 주로 **density** 밀도 **common good** 공익 **taboo** 금기 **stability** 안정성 **immoral** 비도덕적인 **extensive** 광범위한 **infanticide** 영아 살해 **overexploitation** (천연자원의) 과잉 개발 **permission** 허가, 허락 **depletion** 고갈, 소모 **edible** 먹을 수 있는, 식용의 **tree cover** 삼림 밀도, 수목피도 **in contrast** 반대로, 대조적으로 **negligent** 태만한 **doom** 불행한 결말[운명]을 맞게 하다 **manpower** 인력, 인원수 **signify** 의미하다 **harvest** 거두어들이다 **massive** 대규모의 **deforestation** 삼림 벌채 **soil erosion** 토양 침식 **crop yield** 곡류의 생산량 **protein** 단백질 **collapse** 붕괴되다

PART B | Approaching Themes

Chapter 10 Humanities I

Intensive Drill 1 p.114

01 (B) **02** (D) **03** (A) **04** (C) **05** (A), (C), (D)

THE TRANSCONTINENTAL RAILROAD

Before the middle of the nineteenth century, major trading centers only existed along America's coastlines, in large port towns where much of the population was concentrated. However, as more settlers moved westward, cities sprang up along the frontier, and new centers of trade began to open in the interior of the United States. Unfortunately, the development of effective overland transportation lagged behind this rapid westward expansion. The construction of canals helped, but they were limited in the amount of goods they could transport and did not extend past the Mississippi River. **Q01** In order to solve this problem, it was determined that a major railroad system into the West would be indispensable. By 1828, some short rail lines had already been constructed, though they were designed only to connect major cities within the same region, like New York and Boston. Several companies had provided railroads as far as Indiana and Missouri by the middle of the century, but pressure was mounting to construct a railway that would lead all the way from the East Coast to California.

Such a feat required cooperation between the federal government and private companies. Several projects took shape in the 1840s, when surveyors began to plot different competing routes from Mid-American railroad stations to territories in the West, such as Oregon and California. To resolve these differences and devise a plan for an official railroad, the government conducted its own study, the Pacific Railroad Survey, which compared all of the potential routes. **Q02** The government decided to provide funding for a railroad that ran from Nebraska to Utah, where it would meet up with a second railway that would be built from Utah to California. Two companies were commissioned by the government to build the railroads: the Union Pacific Company would build the eastern half, while the Central Pacific Company would build the western section.

Q03 Construction began in 1862, but the outbreak of the Civil War slowed progress considerably on the Union Pacific line when workers were called away to serve in the army. However, workers further west on the Central Pacific were able to continue construction in Utah and California. For this reason, the Central Pacific Railroad advanced far more quickly than the Union Pacific. A compromise was made to extend the Central Pacific further to the east, to make up for the time lost building the Union Pacific line. The lines finally met one another in 1869, at the newly determined junction in Promontory, Utah.

대륙횡단 철도

19세기 중반 이전에 주요 무역 중심지는 미국의 해안선을 따라 많은 인구가 집중적으로 사는 거대 항구 도시에만 존재했다. 그러나 더 많은 정착민이 서쪽으로 이동하면서, 국경 지역에 도시들이 생겨났고, 새로운 무역 중심지가 미국 내륙에 생기기 시작했다. 불행히도 효과적인 육상 운송 수단의 발전은 이러한 서부로의 빠른 발전보다 뒤쳐졌다. 운하의 건설이 도움되기는 했지만, 운송할 수 있는 물품의 양이 한정되어 있었고 미시시피 강 너머로 확장될 수 없었다. 이 문제를 해결하기 위해 서부 지방으로 향하는 주요 철도 건설은 필수적이라는 것이 결정되었다. 1828년에 일부 단거리 노선들이 이미 완공되어 있기는 했으나, 이것들은 뉴욕에서 보스턴을 연결하는 것처럼 같은 지역 안의 주요 도시들만을 연결하도록 설계되었다. 몇몇 회사들이 19세기 중반까지 멀리는 인디애나와 미주리까지 가는 철도를 제공하기는 했지만, 동부 해안지역에서 캘리포니아를 잇는 철도 건설의 압력은 계속해서 증가했다.

이런 위업은 연방 정부와 민간 회사 간의 협력을 필요로 했다. 1840년대에 조사관들이 미국 중부에 있는 철도역에서 오리건과 캘리포니아 같은 서부 지역을 잇는 다른 경쟁 노선을 계획하면서 몇몇 사업이 구체화되었다. 이런 차이점을 해결하고 공식 철도 건설을 고안하기 위해 정부는 모든 가능한 노선들을 비교하는 '태평양 철도 조사'라는 연구를 진행했다. 정부는 유타와 캘리포니아를 잇게 될 두 번째 철도와 만나는 네브래스카–유타 구간 철도에 자금을 대주기로 했다. 정부는 두 회사에 철도 건설을 위탁했는데 유니언 퍼시픽 회사가 동부를, 센트럴 퍼시픽 회사가 서부 구역의 철도 건설을 담당했다.

1862년에 공사가 시작되었으나, 유니언 퍼시픽 철도는 남북 전쟁이 발발하면서 노동자들이 군대에서 복무하도록 소집되는 바람에 공사가 상당히 지연됐다. 그러나 멀리 서부에서 일하던 센트럴 퍼시픽 노동자들은 유타–캘리포니아 구간 공사를 계속할 수 있었다. 이런 이유로 센트럴 퍼시픽 철도가 유니언 퍼시픽보다 훨씬 빠르게 진행될 수 있었다. 유니언 퍼시픽 철도 공사의 지연을 만회하기 위해서 센트럴 퍼시픽이 동쪽으로 공사를 확장하는 절충안이 제안되었다. 1869년에 마침내 두 철도가 새롭게 지정된 합류점인 유타 프로몬토리에서 만났다.

A The transcontinental railroad was completed before there was substantial need for its services. B Q04 In the early years, one train a week was all it took to deliver all the supplies needed by settlers in the West. C **Thus, expansion of the rail system could hardly be justified.** However, as settlements in the West expanded, so did the railroad. By the 1880s, new rail lines ran the entire length of the West Coast, from Washington state in the north to Los Angeles in the south. D

A 이 대륙횡단 철도는 이것에 대한 거대한 수요가 있기도 전에 완공되었다. B 초창기에는 일주일에 열차 한 대가 전부여서, 서부 정착민들에게 필요한 모든 물품을 운반했다. C 따라서 철도 확장에 정당성을 부여하기 힘들었다. 그러나 서부 식민지가 확장되면서 철도도 확장되었다. 1880년대까지 새로운 철도가 북쪽의 워싱턴 주에서 남쪽의 로스앤젤레스까지 서해안 전역에 깔렸다. D

---

01 지문의 indispensable 과 의미상 가장 가까운 것은?

(A) 치우친
(B) 필수적인
(C) 중단된
(D) 불가능한

해설 | Vocabulary indispensable 의 의미는 "In order to solve this problem, it was determined that a major railroad system into the West would be indispensable"에서 힌트를 얻을 수 있다. this problem은 새로 생긴 무역 중심지에 운송 수단이 없는 상황을 가리킨다. 이런 상황에서 철도를 건설하는 것은 '필수적인' 조치였을 것이다.

02 첫 대륙횡단 철도를 잇는 주요 거점으로 단락 2에서 언급되지 않은 곳은?

(A) 네브래스카
(B) 유타
(C) 캘리포니아
(D) 워싱턴

해설 | Negative Fact 단락 2에서 첫 대륙횡단 철도를 잇는 거점으로 네브래스카, 유타, 캘리포니아가 언급되고 있다.

03 단락 3에서 필자가 남북 전쟁 기간 당시 서부에 대해 암시하는 것은?

(A) 전쟁에서 큰 역할을 하지 않았다.
(B) 대부분의 전투가 서부에서 일어났다.
(C) 가장 강력한 군사력을 가지고 있었다.
(D) 전쟁에서 일찍 항복했다.

해설 | Inference 단락 3에서 서부에서 일하던 센트럴 퍼시픽 노동자들은 전쟁과 관계없이 철도를 계속 건설할 수 있었다고 설명하고 있다. 이를 바탕으로 서부 쪽은 전쟁의 영향이 크지 않았음을 알 수 있다.

04 다음 문장이 지문에 들어갈 곳을 나타내는 네 개의 사각형[■]을 보시오.

> 따라서 철도 확장에 정당성을 부여하기 힘들었다.

이 문장이 들어갈 가장 적절한 위치는?

(A) A   (B) B   (C) C   (D) D

해설 | Sentence Insertion 삽입 문장의 Thus를 통해 이 문장이 바로 앞에 언급된 내용에 대해 결론을 내리는 역할을 한다는 것을 알 수 있다. 따라서 삽입 문장은 이 철도 확장에 정당성을 부여하기 힘든 상황을 나타낸 문장 바로 뒤에 위치해야 한다.

05 지문을 간략히 요약하기 위한 도입 문장이 아래 제시되어 있다. 지문에서 가장 중요한 내용을 표현한 세 개의 문장을 골라 요약문을 완성하시오. 일부 문장은 지문에 나오지 않았거나 중요하지 않은 내용이기 때문에 요약문에 포함되지 않는다. 이 문제는 2점이다.

> 미국에서 건설된 첫 대륙횡단 철도는 정부와 민간 기업 간의 대규모 협력이 필요했다.

(A) 정부는 모든 가능한 철도 노선을 비교하고 미국을 횡단하는 가장 좋은 노선을 계획하기 위해 '태평양 철도 조사'라는 연구를 실시하였다.
(B) 남북 전쟁 때문에 센트럴 퍼시픽은 원래 유니언 퍼시픽 것이었던 공사를 해야 했다.
(C) 정부는 유니언 퍼시픽과 센트럴 퍼시픽 두 회사에 철도의 두 주요 구간 건설을 위탁했다.
(D) 대륙횡단 철도는 1869년에 완공되었지만, 많은 서부 지역의 인구가 천천히 증가함에 따라, 그 철도의 가치가 입증된 것은 훨씬 이후였다.
(E) 초기 철도는 너무 짧아서 주로 보스턴이나 뉴욕 같은 동해안의 주요 도시들을 연결하는 역할만 했다.
(F) 대륙횡단 철도가 건설되기 전에 물자는 주로 미시시피 강을 지나도록 확장된 운하를 통해 운송되었다.

해설 | Summary (A)와 (C)는 '태평양 철도 조사'의 상황적 배경을 설명한 지문의 내용을 요약해 놓은 것이다. (D)는 대륙횡단 철도의 완공과 영향에 대한 내용을 요약해 놓은 것이다.

어휘 | **population** 인구　**westward** 서쪽으로　**spring up** 생겨나다　**overland** 육상[육로]의　**lag behind** ~보다 뒤처지다　**expansion** 발전, 확장　**construction** 건설　**canal** 운하　**indispensable** 필수적인　**mount** 증가하다　**cooperation** 협력　**federal government** 연방 정부　**private** 민간의　**resolve** 해결하다　**devise** 고안하다　**potential** 가능한　**funding** 자금　**meet up with** ~와 만나다　**commission** 위탁하다　**outbreak** (전쟁의) 발발　**considerably** 상당히　**serve** (군대에) 복무하다　**compromise** 절충안, 타협　**substantial** 거대한, 상당한　**deliver** 운반하다, 수송하다

Intensive Drill 2   p.116

01 (C)　**02** (D)　**03** (A)　**04** (C)　**05** (C), (D), (F)

MEXICAN MURALISM

The Mexican mural movement came out of the aftermath of the Mexican Revolution, which took place from 1910 to 1920. Q04(A) The Mexican government at that time began to fund large-scale wall paintings in civic buildings and structures, with the objective of creating a historical narrative and identity for the general public, of which most were poor and illiterate. Q04(B) The government felt that through the creation of massive, public murals, a new kind of Mexican sentiment embodying the cultural values of Mexico would instill a greater sense of pride and sentiment in the general population. One of the main concerns of the government was to unify the population under one ideology, thereby encouraging artists to produce works that would educate and benefit the masses.

Q01-1 Many artists at the time seized the opportunity to produce these artworks, claiming that muralism would be an art of social and political discourse. In other words, they saw it as a creative opportunity to blend art and politics together, which was a quite radical idea at the time. Q01-2 Q04(D) Although many of the artists commissioned to produce murals had different ideologies, styles, and personalities, their desire to use art as a means for social revolution is evident in their works.

Three artists grew in prominence out of the movement and are widely recognized for their innovative and influential art pieces today. The first of these artists, David Siqueiros, is considered to have been the most innovative. His artworks are characterized by bold lines and brushstrokes that stood out prominently, as well as their tendency to use overly exaggerated perspectives. Q02 His goal in mural painting was to create a new type of mural that incorporated modern technology. In order to carry out his vision and break from traditional forms of painting, he would spray, pour, drip, or splatter paint onto his murals.

Diego Rivera was also a significant artist of the Mexican mural movement, but unlike Siqueiros, he favored a more traditional style of painting. His artworks incorporated bright, vibrant colors, with a heavy emphasis placed on oranges, reds, and earthy browns. The most prevalent scenes he created were market scenes that were reminiscent of Mexico's historically indigenous cultures. He firmly believed that Mexicans needed to be imbued with a new vision of life, and he tried to instill Mexicans with a strong sense of pride in their cultural heritage.

멕시코 벽화 운동

멕시코 벽화 운동은 1910년부터 1920년에 일어난 멕시코 혁명의 여파로 생겨났다. 이 시기 멕시코 정부는 대다수가 가난하고 문맹이었던 일반 대중들을 위한 역사적 서사 및 정체성을 만들어 주기 위한 목적으로, 시의 건물과 구조물들에 큰 벽화를 그리는 데 자금을 지원해주기 시작했다. 정부는 이러한 거대한 대중 벽화를 만듦으로써 멕시코의 문화적 가치를 포함하고 있는 새로운 멕시코적 감성이 일반 시민들에게 큰 자부심과 정서를 불어넣을 수 있다고 생각했다. 정부의 주요 관심사는 하나의 이념 아래 국민을 통합시키는 것이었기 때문에, 화가들이 대중을 교육하고 유익하게 하는 작품들을 만들도록 장려했다.

당시 많은 화가들은 이러한 예술 작품을 만들 기회를 잡았으며, 벽화주의가 사회적·정치적 담화의 예술이 될 수 있을 것이라 주장했다. 다시 말해, 그들은 벽화가 예술을 정치와 함께 결합할 수 있는 독창적인 기회라고 생각했으며 이러한 생각은 그때 당시에는 굉장히 급진적인 생각이었다. 벽화 제작을 의뢰받은 많은 화가들은 각기 다른 이념과 스타일, 개성을 가지고 있었지만, 예술이 사회 혁명의 수단으로 사용되길 원하는 바람은 그들의 작품 속에서 분명하게 나타난다.

3명의 화가가 이 운동에서 두각을 나타냈으며, 오늘날 그들의 혁신적이고 영향력 있는 미술 작품으로 널리 인정받고 있다. 이들 중 첫 번째 화가인 David Siqueiros는 가장 혁신적이었다고 여겨진다. 그의 미술 작품들은 현저하게 눈에 띄는 굵은 선과 붓놀림, 그리고 지나치게 과장된 원근법을 사용하는 경향으로 특징지어진다. 벽화를 그리는 데 있어 그의 목표는 현대 기술을 포함하는 새로운 종류의 벽화를 탄생시키는 것이었다. 그의 비전을 이뤄내고 전통적인 그림 양식에서 탈피하기 위해, 그는 벽화에 물감을 뿌리고, 붓고, 방울로 떨어뜨리거나 튀기기도 했다.

Diego Rivera 역시 멕시코 벽화 운동에서 중요한 화가였지만, Siqueiros와는 달리 좀 더 전통적인 그림 스타일을 선호했다. 그의 작품은 주황색, 빨간색, 갈색에 큰 중점을 두며 밝고, 선명한 색깔을 사용했다. 그가 만든 것 중 가장 일반적인 장면은 시장으로, 이것은 멕시코의 역사적인 토착 문화를 연상하게 했다. 그는 멕시코인들이 새로운 삶의 비전으로 가득 채워져야 한다고 강하게 믿었으며, 멕시코인들에게 멕시코의 문화 유산에 대한 강한 자부심을 주입하려 노력했다.

The last artist, Jose Clemente Orozco, took an entirely different approach from Siqueiros and Rivera in creating murals. Q03 He focused more on depictions of human suffering and the atrocities that had become common during the Mexican Revolution. His objective in portraying the horrors of war was to provide what he felt was an honest portrayal of Mexico's heritage. Despite producing some artistically astounding murals, his work was heavily criticized by both the government and art critics for failure to capture the essence of providing the Mexican people with a new sense of cultural pride and identity.

마지막 화가인 Jose Clemente Orozco는 벽화 작업에 있어 Siqueiros와 Rivera와는 완전히 다른 접근법을 택했다. 그는 멕시코 혁명 동안 흔한 일이 되었던 인간의 고통과 잔혹 행위를 묘사하는 데에 초점을 두었다. 이러한 전쟁의 공포 를 묘사하는 그의 목적은 그가 멕시코 유산의 진솔한 묘사라고 생각하는 것을 제공하는 것이었다. 예술적으로 놀라운 벽화를 몇 점 만들어냈음에도 불구하고, Orozco의 작품은 멕시코 국민에게 문화적 자긍심과 정체성을 부여해야 한다는 본질을 포착하는 데 실패했다는 점에서 정부와 미술 비평가들 양쪽에서 거센 비판을 받았다.

---

01 단락 2에 따르면, 멕시코 벽화에 관한 내용 중 옳은 것은?
 (A) 멕시코의 화가들은 그림을 그릴 때 다른 화가들과 비슷한 예술 양식을 이용했다.
 (B) 예술과 정치의 융합은 그 당시 널리 받아들여졌다.
 (C) 벽화에 대한 화가들의 동기는 정치적·사회적인 것이었다.
 (D) 화가들은 동일한 이념을 가지고 벽화를 그리도록 의뢰받았다.

해설 | Factual Information 단락 2에서 화가들은 벽화주의가 사회적·정치적 담화가 될 수 있을 것이라 하였으며, 각기 다른 이념을 가진 화가들도 예술이 사회적·정치적으로 사용되길 원하는 같은 바람을 가지고 있었다고 하였다.

02 지문에서 his vision 이 가리키는 것은?
 (A) 가난하고 문맹인 사람들을 벽화로 깨우치는 것
 (B) 전통적인 양식과 현대 양식을 통합하는 것
 (C) 그림에 굵은 선과 붓놀림을 사용하는 것
 (D) 현대 기술을 사용하여 벽화를 그리는 것

해설 | Reference 그의 목표는 현대 기술을 포함하여 새로운 종류의 벽화를 탄생시키는 것이라고 한 바로 앞 문장을 통해 his vision 이 가리키는 내용을 알 수 있다.

03 필자는 지문에서 무엇의 예로 전쟁의 공포 를 언급하는가?
 (A) 멕시코 혁명에 대한 묘사
 (B) 멕시코 문화 유산에 대해 적대심을 표현하는 벽화
 (C) 굉장히 과장된 원근법을 강조한 예술 작품
 (D) 멕시코의 문화적 가치를 육성하려는 정부의 바람을 나타내는 벽화

해설 | Rhetorical Purpose 바로 앞 문장에서 멕시코 혁명 동안 인간의 고통과 잔혹 행위가 흔한 일이 되었다고 설명한다. 필자는 the horrors of war 를 멕시코 혁명에 관해 묘사하기 위해 언급했음을 알 수 있다.

04 지문에 따르면, 멕시코 벽화에 관한 내용으로 옳지 않은 것은?
 (A) 멕시코인들을 위한 역사적 서술 및 정체성을 제공하는 데 사용되었다.
 (B) 멕시코인들에게 자긍심과 정서를 불어넣기 위한 의도였다.
 (C) 예술가들은 추상적인 개념을 표현하기 위한 수단으로 생각했다.
 (D) 예술가들에 의해 사회적 혁명을 위한 도구로 여겨졌다.

해설 | Negative Fact 멕시코 벽화는 일반 대중들에게 역사적 서술 및 정체성을 제공하는 데 사용되었으며, 자부심을 불어넣는 용도로 사용되었다고 하였으므로 (A)와 (B)는 옳은 내용이다. 이러한 벽화를 그리는 예술가들은 벽화를 사회적 혁명의 수단으로 여겼다고 했으므로 (D) 또한 옳은 내용이다. (C)에 관한 내용은 언급되지 않았다.

05 지문을 간략히 요약하기 위한 도입 문장이 아래 제시되어 있다. 지문에서 가장 중요한 내용을 표현한 세 개의 문장을 골라 요약문을 완성하시오. 일부 문장은 지문에 나오지 않았거나 중요하지 않은 내용이기 때문에 요약문에 포함되지 않는다. 이 문제는 2점이다.

> 1920년대에 멕시코 정부는 멕시코 국민을 통합하려는 수단으로써 벽화를 그리도록 의뢰했다.

 (A) 예술 비평가들은 전쟁의 공포를 묘사한 Orozco의 작품을 크게 비난했다.
 (B) Siqueiros의 작품은 여성과의 관계로부터 지대한 영향을 받았다.
 (C) Siqueiros는 현대 기술에 영감을 받은 독창적인 벽화를 그렸다.
 (D) Orozco의 작품은 멕시코 혁명의 잔혹 행위에 초점을 맞췄다.
 (E) Rivera는 그의 벽화에 흙색조를 즐겨 사용했다.
 (F) Rivera의 작품은 일반적으로 토착 멕시코인들의 풍경을 묘사했다.

해설 | Summary 멕시코 정부는 1920년대에 멕시코 국민을 통합시키기 위해 벽화 운동을 시작했으며, 대표적인 화가로 Siqueiros, Rivera, Orozco를 언급하고 있다. (C), (D), (F)는 각 작가의 작품에 대해 요약한 문장이다.

어휘 | **mural** 벽화　**aftermath** 여파　**take place** 일어나다, 발생하다　**objective** 목적, 목표　**illiterate** 문맹의, 글을 읽고 쓸 줄 모르는　**opportunity** 기회　**muralism** 벽화주의　**political** 정치적　**blend** 결합하다, 섞다　**radical** 급진적인　**commission** 의뢰하다　**personality** 개성, 성격　**innovative** 혁신적인, 독창적인　**influential** 영향력 있는　**brushstroke** 붓놀림　**exaggerated** 과장된　**perspective** 원근법, 균형감　**prevalent** 일반적인, 널리 행해지는　**reminiscent** 연상시키는　**indigenous** 토착, 원산의　**imbue** 가득 채우다　**heritage** 유산　**entirely** 완전히　**depiction** 묘사, 서술　**portray** 묘사하다　**astounding** 놀라운, 놀랄 만한　**criticize** 비판하다

Intensive Drill 3　　　　　　　　　　　　　　　　　　　　　　　p.118

01 (B)　**02** (C)　**03** (A)　**04** (B)　**05** [Baroque Music – (A), (D), (E)], [Medieval Music – (B), (G)]

FIGURED BASS IN BAROQUE MUSIC

Q02-1 As the Baroque Period of music came into prominence during the time from 1600 to 1750 A.D., composers wanted to move away from the somber, simplistic musical styles of the preceding Medieval Period and instead produce music that was richer in melody and rhythm. Q01 The music of the Medieval Period was almost exclusively composed for religious purposes, primarily church masses. Q05(B) Due to the solemn, venerable mood of the mass in churches, composers had little room for any kind of musical variation or experimentation. Q05(G) In addition, music during the Medieval Period predominantly consisted of chants and madrigals that used the human voice as its principal musical instrument. Although harpsichords and organs were sometimes used for musical accompaniment, their overall musical presence was generally subdued.

A Q04 However, by the 1600s, Baroque composers began to write music not only for religious services, but also wrote secular compositions for royalty and the general public, who started to favor more lively and intricate styles of music. **B** Especially chamber music, one of the more complicated forms of music developed at that time, was among their most beloved. Q02-2 As Baroque music began to break with strictly religious music and experiment increasingly with musical creativity, elaborate musical compositions became the dominant style. **C** Q05(D) These compositions were rich in new rhythmic structures, introducing more complex melodies and other forms of musical ornamentation that created a heightened sense of dynamism and energy. **D**

One of the most popular compositional techniques to emerge in this new brand of musical composition was figured bass, sometimes referred to as thoroughbass, which was essentially a form of musical shorthand written into the bass line of the music score. Composers used figured bass to provide musical accompaniment to their compositions by incorporating instruments such as the harpsichord and a predecessor to the modern guitar. The orchestra would play the composed music as it was, note-by-note, while the figured bass would be roughly sketched out. The figured bass provided a framework for these instruments to play the bass line of the musical composition by giving them basic chords to follow. Q05(A) However, unlike the uniform musical arrangements characteristic of the Medieval Period, these accompanying instruments were given greater creative freedom to improvise on these chords. This is of particular importance, since improvisation was a common feature in Baroque music and reflected the musical ideals of the composers at that time.

바로크 음악의 통주 저음

바로크 시대 음악이 서기 1600~1750년에 두드러지게 되면서, 작곡가들은 이전 중세 시대 음악의 어둡고 단순한 음악 양식에서 벗어나길 원했으며, 대신 더 풍부한 멜로디와 리듬의 음악을 만들고 싶어 했다. 중세 시대 음악은 거의 대부분 주로 교회 미사를 위한 종교적인 목적으로만 만들어졌다. 교회 미사는 엄숙하고 숭엄한 분위기였기 때문에, 작곡가들이 음악적 변형이나 실험을 해볼 만할 여지가 거의 없었다. 게다가 중세 시대의 음악은 주된 악기로 사람의 목소리를 사용하는 성가 또는 마드리갈로 대개 이루어져 있었다. 음악 반주를 위해 하프시코드와 오르간이 가끔 사용되긴 했지만, 전체적인 음악적 분위기는 보통 가라앉아 있었다.

A 그러나 1600년대에 바로크 작곡가들은 종교적인 목적으로 음악을 작곡했을 뿐만 아니라, 더 생생하고 복잡한 음악 양식을 좋아하기 시작한 왕족과 일반 대중들을 위한 세속적인 작품도 만들었다. **B** 특히 그 당시에 발전되었던 더욱 복잡한 음악 형식인 실내악은 그들이 가장 사랑하는 것 중 하나였다. 바로크 음악은 엄격한 종교 음악과 단절하고, 음악적 창의성으로 더 많은 실험을 하기 시작함에 따라, 정교한 음악 작품들이 지배적인 양식이 되었다. **C** 이러한 작품들은 리듬 구조가 풍성했으며, 고조된 활력과 에너지를 만드는 더욱 복잡한 멜로디와 여러 음악적 장식을 도입했다. **D**

이 새로운 작곡 유형에서 떠오른 가장 인기 있는 작곡 기술 중 하나는 통주 저음이었는데, 때때로 도로우베이스(thoroughbass)라 불리고 근본적으로 악보의 저음부에 표기된 음악적 속기 형태였다. 작곡가들은 하프시코드나 현대 기타의 초기 형태와 같은 악기들을 사용하여 그들 작품에 반주를 만들기 위해 통주 저음을 사용했다. 통주 저음은 개략적으로 제시된 데 반해, 오케스트라는 악보에 적혀진 대로 곡을 연주하곤 했다. 통주 저음은 악기들이 음악 작품의 저음 선율을 연주할 수 있도록 이들이 따라야 할 기본적인 화음들을 제공함으로써 뼈대를 제공했다. 그러나 중세 시대의 특징인 획일적인 음악 편곡과는 달리, 이들 반주하는 악기들은 화음에 맞춰 즉흥적으로 연주할 수 있는 더 큰 자유가 주어졌다. 즉흥 연주가 바로크 음악의 공통적인 특징이었고, 그 당시 작곡가들의 음악적 이상을 반영하는 것이었기 때문에 이것은 특히 중요하다.

Although these accompanists were required to follow and observe the underlying rhythmic and harmonic structure of the compositions, the development of figured bass musical shorthand provided just enough information for the accompanist to improvise these melodies and rhythms. Baroque composers generally conceded that writing out every note for these accompanists would restrict the freedom of well-trained accompanists, as well as prevent them from fully demonstrating the extent of their ability. Q03 Q05(E) Therefore, in order to better showcase these accompanists' skills, composers used figured bass to write compositions with more complex harmonies, contrasting musical themes, and innovative melodies and sequences of chords, which gave rise to a new form of musical variance unfathomed in the Medieval Period.

반주자는 곡의 기본 리듬과 화성 구조를 따르고 지키도록 요구되긴 했지만, 통주 저음 음악의 약기(略記)의 발전은 반주자가 멜로디와 리듬을 즉흥적으로 연주할 수 있을 정도의 충분한 정보를 제공했다. 바로크 시대 작곡가들은 모든 음을 적는 것이 잘 훈련된 반주자의 자유를 제한할 뿐만 아니라, 이들의 실력을 완전히 발휘하지 못하게 한다는 것을 인정했다. 따라서 반주자의 실력을 더 잘 보여줄 수 있게 하려고, 작곡가들은 통주 저음을 사용하여 좀 더 복잡한 하모니, 대조되는 음악적 테마, 획기적인 멜로디와 화음의 배열을 가진 곡을 만들었으며, 이는 중세 시대에는 없던 새로운 음악적 변형을 가져다주었다.

01 단락 1에서 필자가 중세 음악에 대해 암시하는 것은?
(A) 중세 음악은 유럽의 귀족들 사이에서 인기 있었다.
(B) 중세 음악은 일반적으로 대중들을 위해 작곡되지 않았다.
(C) 중세 음악은 교회 미사에서 사용된 다양하고 정교한 양식들을 진화시켰다.
(D) 중세 음악은 새로운 종류의 리듬을 서서히 도입했다.

해설 | Inference 단락 1에서 중세 시대 음악은 주로 교회를 위한 종교적인 목적으로만 만들어졌다고 하였다. 이를 바탕으로 중세 음악은 일반적으로 대중들을 위해 작곡되지는 않았다는 것을 알 수 있다.

02 지문의 break with 와 의미상 가장 가까운 것은?
(A) ~을 다루다
(B) 선호하다
(C) ~에서 분리하다
(D) 닮다

해설 | Vocabulary 단락 1에서 바로크 시기 음악은 주로 종교적인 목적으로만 만들어진 중세 시대의 음악에서 벗어나길 원했다고 설명하고 있다. 여기에서 break with 는 '~에서 분리하다'의 의미가 있음을 알 수 있다.

03 단락 4에서 필자가 언급하는 것은?
(A) 통주 저음 표기법은 반주자들이 그들의 능력을 발휘하게 하였다.
(B) 바로크 시대의 작곡가들은 각각의 음악가를 위해 모든 음을 적었다.
(C) 복잡하고 혁신적인 음악 구조는 중세 시대 양식으로부터 발전되었다.
(D) 통주 저음은 오케스트라 모든 음악가들을 위한 음악적 속기 형식이었다.

해설 | Factual Information 통주 저음 음악의 발전은 반주자가 멜로디와 리듬을 즉흥 연주할 수 있도록 하여 능력을 발휘할 수 있도록 해주었다고 하였다.

04 다음 문장이 지문에 들어갈 곳을 나타내는 네 개의 사각형[■]을 보시오.

특히 그 당시에 발전되었던 더욱 복잡한 음악 형식인 실내악은 그들이 가장 사랑하는 것 중 하나였다.

이 문장이 들어갈 가장 적절한 위치는?
(A) A (B) B (C) C (D) D

해설 | Sentence Insertion 삽입 문장에서 the more complicated forms 라고 했으므로, 지칭 대상인 intricate styles of music이 언급된 문장 뒤에 위치해야 자연스럽다.

05 보기에서 적절한 문구를 골라 관련된 음악 시대와 연결하시오. 보기 중 2개는 사용되지 않는다. *이 문제는 3점이다.*

(A) 즉흥성이 더 많다.	바로크 음악
(B) 변화가 거의 없는 엄격한 음악 양식이다.	• (A)
(C) 많은 음악가를 필요로 한다.	• (D)
(D) 복잡한 음악 스타일과 구조를 갖는다.	• (E)
(E) 음악가들이 그들의 능력과 실력을 보여줄 수 있다.	중세 음악
(F) 귀족들을 위한 음악이며, 매우 종교적이다.	• (B)
(G) 주요 악기로 인간의 목소리가 사용되었다.	• (G)

해설 | Fill in a Table 바로크 시대 음악은 통주 저음으로 즉흥성이 많고, 음악가들이 능력을 발휘할 수 있었으며, 복잡한 음악 구조를 가졌다고 하였다. 이전의 중세 시대 음악은 주로 종교적인 목적으로 만들어진 엄격한 음악 형식이었고, 주요 악기로는 인간의 목소리가 사용됐다고 하였다.

어휘 | **composer** 작곡가 **somber** 어두운, 검은 **Medieval Period** 중세 시대 **religious** 종교적인 **solemn** 엄숙한, 근엄한
variation 변형, 변화 **madrigal** 마드리갈(반주 없이 여러 명이 부르는 노래) **harpsichord** 하프시코드(현을 뜯어 소리를 낸던 피아노 비슷한 중세 악기)
secular 세속적인, 일반 대중들 속에 사는 **intricate** 복잡한 **elaborate** 정교한 **ornamentation** 장식 **framework** 뼈대 **chord** 화음

Mini Test 1   p.120

01 (C)   **02** (B)   **03** (B)   **04** (D)   **05** (B), (D), (F)

CHARLEMAGNE AND THE HOLY ROMAN EMPIRE

Q02 By the fifth century A.D., the Roman Empire, once the largest and most powerful on Earth, had finally collapsed after years of fighting with Germanic tribes from the north of Europe. The remnants of the once mighty Roman Empire lay to the east, in Constantinople, the royal seat of the Byzantine Empire. Meanwhile, in central and western Europe, a new superpower was rising to prominence: the Frankish kingdom, which included several of the independent Germanic tribes that had aided in the overthrow of the Western Roman Empire. Within 100 years of the Romans' defeat, the Frankish kingdom expanded to include much of eastern and central Europe. Under their legendary king Charlemagne, the Franks rose to such prominence in the region that a weakened Rome, now little more than a religious center, would appeal to them in an effort to reestablish the former glory of the Roman Empire.

Several factors led to the Franks, under Charlemagne, becoming the protectors of the Roman Empire. This honor was traditionally left to the Byzantines, but infighting among the ruling elites there led to instability, and the Romans lost confidence in their ability to defend the Pope and the Catholic Church. At the same time, around 799 A.D., Pope Leo III was having trouble with his own country as well. The Roman nobles were intent upon taking his title, for the simple reason that Leo was of peasant birth. Q03 They laid accusations of an array of crimes against the Pope in the hopes that at least one of them would lead to a conviction and force him from power. The tension led to a vicious physical attack on the Pope, in which rebels attempted to gouge out his eyes and cut off his tongue. Leo fled to Paderborn, a city within the Frankish kingdom, where he met Charlemagne for the first time.

Having accepted Christianity as the state religion some time back, the Franks gladly took the Pope in. Charlemagne resolved to help him, and called a meeting with his enemies to try to quell the violent opposition. When the talks fell apart, Charlemagne traveled to Rome in person, along with the Pope, to see that the uprising was stopped. ①He met again with supporters and opponents of the Pope to discuss the situation, but ②this time, he was able to sway the committee of friends and enemies to cease attacks on the Pope and ③allow him to officially declare his innocence of all the charges falsely brought against him by the nobles. His enemies were thus exiled, and Leo was pardoned.

While still in Rome, Charlemagne attended Christmas Mass at the Vatican, at the Pope's request. As he knelt down to pray, the Pope placed a crown on his head, officially making him Emperor of the Romans. For the Pope, the act served to thank Charlemagne for his defense and to increase the influence of the Catholic Church across the vast Frankish territory. Charlemagne, meanwhile, seized upon the opportunity to renew the Roman Empire under the rule of the Franks. This did not become official until two centuries later, when a portion of the Frankish lands was renamed the Holy Roman Empire, an institution that would persist for nearly a thousand years.

래에 로마 제국을 부활시킬 기회를 잡을 수 있었다. 이런 일은 2세기가 지나 프랑크 왕국 일부가 신성 로마 제국으로 개명되어서야 공식화 되었는데, 이 제국은 이후 1000년 가까이 지속하였다.

01 지문의 remnants 와 의미상 가장 가까운 것은?
(A) 적
(B) 통치자
(C) 나머지
(D) 구성원

해설 | Vocabulary   remnants 는 '나머지, 잔류'의 의미이다.

02 단락 1에 따르면, 로마 제국을 멸망시킨 것은?
(A) 비잔틴 제국
(B) 게르만 부족
(C) 가톨릭 교회
(D) 프랑크 왕국

해설 | Factual Information   단락 1의 첫 문장에서 로마 제국은 게르만 족과의 전쟁 끝에 멸망했다고 설명한다.

03 지문에서 them 이 가리키는 것은?
(A) 귀족들
(B) 죄목들
(C) 희망들
(D) 반역자들

해설 | Reference   그것들 중 하나라도(at least one of them) 유죄 선고로 이어지기를 바랐다는 내용으로부터 them 은 문장 앞부분에 나온 an array of crimes임을 알 수 있다.

04 다음 중 지문에서 표시된 문장의 주요 정보를 가장 잘 나타낸 문장은? 정답 외의 보기들은 중요한 의미가 바뀌거나 주요 정보가 빠져 있다.
(A) 로마 귀족들과의 두 번째 회합에서 Charlemagne 대제는 교황을 공격한 반역자들의 결백을 확신하게 되었다.
(B) Charlemagne 대제는 교황의 반대 세력과 지지 세력을 만나 교황의 무죄를 주장하기 위해 로마로 건너갔다.
(C) 교황을 공격한 것으로 인해 로마 귀족들은 Charlemagne 대제에게 동의하고 Leo 3세가 모든 혐의로부터 무죄임을 선언하게 되었다.
(D) Charlemagne 대제가 로마 귀족들과 두 번째 만났을 때, 귀족들은 교황의 무죄를 인정하고 공격을 중단할 것에 동의했다.

해설 | Sentence Simplification   표시된 문장은 크게 세 의미로 나뉠 수 있다. ① Charlemagne 대제가 지지자와 반대자를 두 번째로 만났다. ② Charlemagne 대제는 교황에 대한 공격을 멈추도록 지지 세력과 반대 세력의 마음을 움직였다. ③ 교황이 모든 혐의로부터 무죄하다는 것을 선언할 수 있었다.

05 지문을 간략히 요약하기 위한 도입 문장이 아래 제시되어 있다. 지문에서 가장 중요한 내용을 표현한 세 개의 문장을 골라 요약문을 완성하시오. 일부 문장은 지문에 나오지 않았거나 중요하지 않은 내용이기 때문에 요약문에 포함되지 않는다. *이 문제는 2점이다.*

> 프랑크 왕국의 Charlemagne 대제는 로마의 영향력을 서방으로 확장하게 한 가톨릭 교회와의 동맹 관계를 구축했다.

(A) 로마 제국의 왕좌는 서로마 제국이 침략자에 의해 멸망하면서 동쪽의 콘스탄티노플로 이동했다.
(B) 교황 Leo 3세는 그의 명성을 무너뜨리고 지위에서 그를 밀어내려는 로마 귀족들과의 맹렬한 대립에 부딪혔다.
(C) 프랑크 왕국은 몇몇 게르만 부족이 연합해 형성됐고 유럽에서 강대국으로 성장했다.
(D) Charlemagne 대제는 귀족들을 설득해서 교황에 반대하는 적대행위를 멈추게 할 수 있었고, 로마에 다시 평화를 가져왔다.
(E) 비잔틴 제국은 정부 관료들 사이의 싸움으로 불안정한 상태가 되었다.
(F) 교황은 Charlemagne 대제에게 감사를 표하고 가톨릭 교회의 영향력을 프랑크 왕국으로 확대하기 위해 그를 로마 제국의 황제로 만들었다.

해설 | Summary   지문은 프랑크 왕국이 로마 제국의 수호자가 된 경위를 설명하고 있다. (B)는 교황이 소작농 출신이라는 이유로 모함을 당하는 단락 2의 내용을 요약해 놓은 것이다. (D)는 프랑크의 왕 Charlemagne 대제가 교황을 돕는 단락 3의 내용을 요약해 놓은 것이며, (F)는 교황이 Charlemagne 대제를 로마 황제로 등극시키는 단락 4의 내용을 요약해 놓은 것이다.

어휘 | **collapse** 멸망하다　**tribe** 부족　**mighty** 강력한　**superpower** 초강대국　**prominence** 명성, 우위　**overthrow** 멸망
legendary 전설적인　**appeal** 애원하다, 호소하다　**protector** 수호자　**traditionally** 전통적으로　**infighting** 내분　**instability** 불안정
confidence 신뢰, 자신감　**peasant** 소작농, 농민　**accusation** 고발　**conviction** 유죄 판결　**tension** 긴장　**vicious** 잔악한, 악의적인
rebel 모반자, 반역자　**gouge something out** ~을 파내다　**state religion** 국교　**fall apart** 실패하다　**quell** 누그러뜨리다, 진압하다
uprising 반란　**declare** 선언하다　**innocence** 무죄　**charge** 혐의, 죄　**exile** 추방하다　**pardon** 사면하다　**Mass** 미사
kneel down 무릎을 꿇다　**seize upon** (기회 등을) 잡다　**persist** 지속하다

Mini Test 2　　　　　　　　　　　　　　　　　　　　　　　　　　　　　　　　p.122

01 (A)　　**02** (D)　　**03** (B)　　**04** (C)　　**05** (A), (C), (D)

THE ANCIENT CITY OF PETRA

One of the most amazing relics of the ancient world is Petra, an archaeological site in the country of Jordan. Petra is an ancient city that was literally carved out of the walls of a mountain in a style known as rock-cut architecture. The city was founded in 100 BC by a group of Arab peoples called the Nabataeans, who made it the capital city of their kingdom. In ancient times, Petra was a major center of trade in the Middle East, as it lay at the intersection of several different trade routes. [A] Petra also rose to prominence because of its water supply, which made the desert city habitable. [B] [Q04] The city sits in a low-lying valley among several large mountains, along the route of several mountain streams. [C] Unfortunately, this also makes it a frequent victim of floods. [Q01] The Nabataeans, however, constructed dams and special channels that could divert the water either away from the city or into special holding tanks, where it was stored to be used in times of drought. [D] The fact that Petra had a constant store of water made the city even more popular with passing traders, as they could buy some of the city's water when it had become scarce elsewhere during the dry seasons.

The city had the advantage of being a natural fortress, as it was surrounded on all sides by high mountains. The main entrance to the city, called the *siq*, was its main point of defense. The *siq* was a long chasm that cut through the giant sandstone cliffs. It was created by a fault in the mountain which had been slowly worn away by water over the years. It was only a few meters wide but stretched for nearly a mile, with towering cliff walls on each side. Visitors had to navigate this long corridor in order to reach the city. The end of the narrow *siq* opened into the city's most spectacular ruin, called the treasury. The facade of the treasury was heavily influenced by Greek architecture, with stately columns and sculptures decorating the outward facing wall. [Q02] The city was also home to several ancient tombs, which have since allowed archaeologists to trace the history of this site according to the style in which these tombs were built — most reflected the early Nabataean style, while others were influenced by later inhabitants such as the Romans and Muslims.

Despite the defenses and riches of the city, the Nabataeans were unable to defend Petra against Roman attacks, and it fell to the Empire in 106 AD, having been under Nabataean rule for just over 200 years. Under Roman rule, the city continued to prosper for a time, as evidenced by the Roman additions to the city's original architecture. [Q03] But when major trade routes began to shift in the fifth century, the city saw a decline in commerce, and it slowly fell into ruin. Islamic forces invaded Petra and took control of

고대 도시 페트라

고대의 가장 놀라운 유적 중 하나는 요르단에 있는 고고학적 유적지 페트라다. 페트라는 돌을 깎아서 짓는 건축 양식으로 문자 그대로 산의 절벽을 깎아서 만든 고대 도시다. 도시는 기원전 100년에 나바테아인이라고 불리는 아랍계 민족에 의해 건설되었고, 그들은 이곳을 왕국의 수도로 삼았다. 고대에 페트라는 여러 무역로의 교차점에 위치하여 중동의 주요 무역 중심지였다. [A] 페트라는 또한 사막 도시에서 사람이 살 수 있도록 물을 공급할 수 있었기 때문에 중요한 도시가 되었다. [B] 페트라는 여러 산속의 개울을 따라 큰 산들의 저지대의 골짜기에 있다. [C] 불행하게도 이로 인해 종종 홍수의 피해를 보았다. 그러나 나바테아인은 도시에서 먼 곳으로 또는 가뭄이 닥쳤을 경우에 사용할 수 있는 특별 저장 물탱크 안으로 물의 방향을 바꿀 수 있게 하는 댐과 특별한 수로를 건설했다. [D] 페트라가 물을 항상 저장할 수 있다는 사실은 지나가는 상인들 사이에서 이 도시를 더욱 인기 있게 만들었는데, 다른 곳에서 물을 구하기 힘든 건기에도 페트라에서는 물을 살 수 있었기 때문이다.

도시는 사방이 높은 산들로 둘러싸여 있었기 때문에 자연적으로 생성된 요새라는 이점을 가지고 있었다. 도시로 들어가는 정문은 시크(siq)라고 불렸는데 방어의 핵심이었다. 시크는 거대한 사암 절벽을 통과하는 긴 협곡이었다. 시크는 수년 동안 물에 의해 깎여나가며 형성된 산의 균열 때문에 만들어졌다. 폭은 불과 몇 미터밖에 되지 않지만, 높게 솟은 절벽 사이로 1마일가량 뻗어 있었다. 방문객들은 도시에 도달하려면 이 긴 통로를 지나가야 했다. 좁은 시크가 끝나는 지점에는 보물창고라고 불리는 도시에서 가장 장관인 유적지가 있었다. 보물창고의 정면은 그리스 건축 양식의 영향을 크게 받아 벽의 외관이 장엄한 기둥과 조각들로 장식되어 있었다. 도시에는 또한 고고학자들이 무덤이 지어진 양식에 따라 이곳의 역사를 추적할 수 있도록 해주는 고대 무덤들이 있는데, 대부분은 초기 나바테아 양식이 반영됐고 다른 무덤들은 로마인이나 이슬람교도 같은 이후 거주자들의 영향을 받았다.

도시의 방어력과 부에도 불구하고 나바테아인들은 로마의 공격으로부터 페트라를 지킬 수 없었고, 도시는 200년 조금 넘게 나바테아인이 지배하고 있다가 서기 106년 로마 제국의 손에 넘어갔다. 로마 통치 하에서도 도시는 한동안 번영을 이어갔는데, 도시의 원래 건축물에 로마 양식이 더해진 것이 그 증거다. 그러나 5세기에 주요 무역로가 바뀌기 시작하면서 도시의 상업은 쇠퇴했고 서서히 폐허가 되어갔다. 100년 뒤 이슬람 군대가 페트라를 침공해 도시의 통제권을 장악하면서, 남아 있던 나바테아 문화는 빠르게 사라졌다. 1812년 탐험 당시 현지

the city a hundred years later, and what remained of Nabataean culture quickly disappeared. The city remained largely unknown to the modern Western world until Swiss explorer Johann Burckhardt was shown the ruins by local Bedouins on an 1812 expedition, and reported back to his colleagues in Europe. In 1985, the United Nations named it a World Heritage Site, and it was later also named one of the New Seven Wonders of the World.

베두인족이 스위스 탐험가 Johann Burckhardt를 유적지로 안내하고 그가 유럽 동료들에게 보고하기 전까지, 도시는 현대 서구 사회에 거의 알려지지 않았었다. 이 유적지는 1985년 유엔에 의해 세계문화유산에 등재되었고, 이후 세계 신 7대 불가사의에 이름을 올렸다.

01 지문의 divert 와 의미상 가장 가까운 것은?
(A) 방향을 바꾸다
(B) 획득하다
(C) 순환시키다
(D) 방출하다

해설 | Vocabulary 문장에서 물을 도시에서 먼 곳이나 특별 저장 물탱크 안으로 보낼 수 있다는 내용에서 divert 는 '방향을 바꾸다'의 의미임을 알 수 있다.

02 지문에서 this site 가 가리키는 것은?
(A) 보물창고
(B) 유적지
(C) 시크
(D) 도시

해설 | Reference 도시에는 또한 고고학자들이 무덤이 지어진 양식에 따라 이곳(this site)의 역사를 추적할 수 있도록 해주는 고대 무덤들이 있다고 했다. 즉, 지문에서 this site 는 도시(city)를 가리킨다.

03 단락 3에 따르면, 페트라의 상업이 쇠퇴하게 된 첫 번째 주요 원인은?
(A) 나바테아인들의 패전
(B) 주요 무역로의 변경
(C) 서구인들에 의한 발견
(D) 자연 재해로부터의 피해

해설 | Factual Information 단락 3에서 5세기에 무역로가 바뀌면서 페트라의 상업이 쇠퇴하게 되었다고 설명한다.

04 다음 문장이 지문에 들어갈 곳을 나타내는 네 개의 사각형[■]을 보시오.

불행하게도 이로 인해 종종 홍수의 피해를 보았다.

이 문장이 들어갈 가장 적절한 위치는?
(A) A (B) B (C) C (D) D

해설 | Sentence Insertion 삽입 문장은 페트라가 불행히도 이로 인해 종종 홍수의 피해를 보았다고 한다. 따라서 삽입 문장은 페트라의 홍수에 취약한 지형적 조건을 설명한 문장 뒤에 위치해야 적절하다.

05 지문을 간략히 요약하기 위한 도입 문장이 아래 제시되어 있다. 지문에서 가장 중요한 내용을 표현한 세 개의 문장을 골라 요약문을 완성하시오. 일부 문장은 지문에 나오지 않았거나 중요하지 않은 내용이기 때문에 요약문에 포함되지 않는다. *이 문제는 2점이다.*

고대에 활발한 무역의 중심지였던 고대 도시 페트라는 현재 귀중한 고고학적 유적지이다.

(A) 페트라는 상인들이 사용하던 여러 무역로의 교차점에 위치하고 수자원이 풍부해 성장할 수 있었다.
(B) 몇몇 다른 양식들로 지어진 무덤들은 고고학자들이 누가 도시에 살았는지를 통해 유적지 일부의 연대를 측정할 수 있도록 도와주었다.
(C) 페트라는 시크라고 불리는 정문의 도움으로 자연적 요새로 만들어진 것과 보물창고 및 고대 무덤들과 같은 유적지를 가진 것으로 특징지어진다.
(D) 다양한 민족이 지배해 왔던 페트라는 19세기에 재발견되어 세계문화유산으로 지정되었다.
(E) 페트라의 수자원은 나바테아인에게 필요한 물을 공급해 줬지만, 많은 홍수의 원인이 되기도 하였다.
(F) 현지 베두인족의 안내로 스위스 탐험가 Johann Burckhardt가 페트라를 발견했으며, 그는 후에 이 장소를 세계문화유산으로 지정되게 만들기 위해 노력했다.

해설 | Summary (A)는 페트라의 지형을 설명한 단락 1의 내용을 요약해 놓은 것이다. (C)는 페트라의 지형적 특징으로 인한 유적지를 설명한 단락 2의 내용을 요약해 놓은 것이다. (D)는 페트라의 몰락과 재발견을 설명한 단락 3의 내용을 요약해 놓은 것이다.

어휘 | **relic** 유적, 유물　**archaeological** 고고학적인　**literally** 문자 그대로　**carve out of** ~을 깎아서 만들다　**intersection** 교차점　**prominence** 중요함, 유명　**habitable** 거주할 수 있는, 살 만한　**low-lying** 저지대의　**divert** 방향을 바꾸다　**drought** 가뭄　**fortress** 요새　**chasm** 협곡, 균열　**sandstone** 사암　**fault** 균열　**spectacular** 장관의　**ruin** 유적　**treasury** 보물창고, 금고　**facade** 건물 정면　**stately** 장엄한, 위풍당당한　**inhabitant** 거주자, 주민　**Muslim** 이슬람교도

iBT Practice   p.124

01 (D)　**02** (C)　**03** (A)　**04** (C)　**05** (C)　**06** (C)　**07** (B)　**08** (D)　**09** (B)　**10** (B)　**11** (C)　**12** (C)
13 [Eastern Pueblos – (C), (F)], [Western Pueblos – (A), (B), (D), (H)], [Both – (G)]

CULTURE OF THE PUEBLO PEOPLES

Q02 In the southwestern region of the United States reside several tribes of Native Americans known as the Pueblo peoples, who derive their name from the fact that their ancestors lived in pueblos that traditionally consisted mostly of houses made from mud-bricks and straw. **Q01** While they originally descended from a single ancestral group thousands of years ago, the Pueblo peoples gradually fragmented into different tribes, each with a distinct culture. The cultures of these tribes were further altered by the Spanish, who took over the Pueblos' territory in the seventeenth century and transformed Pueblo life in ways which can still be seen today. Despite the numerous developments throughout their long history, the Pueblo peoples have maintained many core features of their cultures, in particular their social structure and ceremonial practices. Recurring distinctions in both social structure and ceremonial practices allow researchers to divide modern Pueblo peoples into two basic categories: the Western Pueblo and the Eastern Pueblo.

The Western Pueblo tribes reside in the deserts of northern Arizona and western New Mexico. **Q05** The Western Pueblo tribes all feature a similar social organization based around the clan, the central social unit in these societies. These clans are large families that trace their ancestry through the mother's side of the family. **Q03** Upon marriage, a man will live with his wife's mother, and the couple's children belong to their mother's clan. **Q04** **Q13(B)** There are rigid rules about whom people can and cannot marry, as tribe members must marry outside of their particular clans. **Q13(D)** In this social structure, women own the farming property and have a good deal of social power. All other organizations such as business in a tribe are owned and operated by individual clans.

Besides the organization of communities by clan membership, the other distinctive feature of the Western Pueblos is their set of ceremonial practices. While influenced by the introduction of Christianity, **Q13(G)-1** the Western Pueblo have retained most of their traditional religious practices, at the center of which lies the *kachina* cult. **A** Originally, the *kachina* cult attempted to communicate with spirits that could bestow good fortune upon the tribe, particularly in the form of greater rainfall. **B** **Q13(A)-1** This was important because farming in such arid regions is difficult, **Q12** **Q13(A)-2** since adequate rainfall is rare and unpredictable. **C** **The activities of the cult are an attempt to mitigate this and bring some level of stability.** An important part of these ceremonies involves the men dressing up as the spirits they pray to and playing the role of these characters. **D** **Q13(H)** This practice is fundamental to the Western Pueblo peoples, as evidenced by the fact that many communities have myriad places of worship.

푸에블로족의 문화

미국 남서부 지역에는 푸에블로족으로 알려진 아메리칸 원주민 부족 여럿이 주거하고 있는데, 그들의 명칭은 그들의 조상이 전통적으로 진흙 벽돌과 짚으로 만든 집들로 구성된 푸에블로에서 살던 것에서 유래되었다. 푸에블로족은 본래 수천 년 전에 살았던 단일 조상 집단의 자손이지만, 각자의 독특한 문화를 가진 다른 부족들로 점차 나뉘게 되었다. 이 부족들의 문화는 스페인 사람들로 인해 더욱 변화했는데, 이들은 17세기에 푸에블로족의 영토를 차지하고 푸에블로족의 생활을 오늘날까지 이어지는 방식으로 변화시켰다. 오랜 역사를 통해 많은 변화를 겪었지만, 푸에블로족들은 많은 부분에서 자신들 문화의 주요 특성을 유지해 왔으며, 특히 사회 구조나 의식적 관행에 있어서 그러하다. 연구자들은 사회 구조와 의식적 관행에서 반복되는 차이점들을 바탕으로 푸에블로족들을 두 가지 범주, 즉 서부 푸에블로와 동부 푸에블로로 나눈다.

서부 푸에블로 부족들은 애리조나 북부와 뉴멕시코 서부에 주거한다. 서부 푸에블로 부족 모두는 주요 사회 단위인 씨족을 중심으로 한 비슷한 사회 조직으로 이루어져 있다. 이런 씨족들은 가족 중 모계 쪽으로 조상을 거슬러 올라가는 대가족이다. 남자는 결혼을 하면 부인의 모친과 함께 살며 부부의 아이들은 그들의 어머니 씨족에 속한다. 부족 구성원이 결혼할 때는 반드시 자신의 씨족 밖에서 배우자를 찾아야 해서, 결혼할 수 있는 상대에 대한 엄격한 규칙이 있다. 이러한 사회적 구조에서 여자들은 농장의 소유지를 가지며 사회적 권력을 상당 부분 차지한다. 부족 내 사업과 같은 다른 모든 조직은 개별 씨족이 소유하고 운영한다.

씨족 구성원에 의해 부족이 구성된다는 점 외에 서부 푸에블로족의 다른 고유한 특성으로 들 수 있는 것은 일련의 의식적 관행이다. 기독교가 도입되면서 영향을 받기는 했지만, 서부 푸에블로족은 대부분 전통적 종교 관행을 유지해왔으며, 그 중심에는 카치나(*kachina*) 의식이 있다. **A** 본래 카치나 의식은 특히 큰 강우의 경우처럼 부족에게 행운을 줄 수 있다는 정령들과 소통하려는 시도에서 비롯되었다. **B** 충분한 비가 올 때가 드물며 예측도 할 수 없는 그런 메마른 지역에서는 농업 활동이 힘들기 때문에 이는 매우 중요했다. **C** 이런 의식 활동은 이를 경감시키고 어느 정도의 안정을 불러오기 위한 시도이다. 남자들이 자신의 기도 대상인 정령들처럼 차려입고서 그 정령 역할을 연기하는 부분이 이 의식의 중요한 부분이다. **D** 많은 부족에 수많은 숭배 장소가 있다는 사실에서 증명되듯이, 이 관습은 서부 푸에블로족에게 핵심적이다.

The Eastern Pueblo, who are primarily located in the valley along the Rio Grande River in New Mexico, have different social structures and ceremonial practices from their western counterparts. Q07 First, the Eastern Pueblo do not strictly adhere to a clan system, so clans do not play as critical a social role as they do in the Western Pueblo society. Q13(F) Lineage is usually traced along both the mother's and father's families, with members from both groups living among an extended family. Second, most Eastern Pueblos are divided into two moieties, or central social groups: the Summer People and the Winter People. These terms come from a traditional method of sharing power in the Eastern Pueblo societies: Q13(C) the Summer People would rule for the six months of summer and the Winter People would rule for the six months of winter. Q08-1 To offset the political discrepancy such an arrangement could potentially cause, Q09 the community also has numerous smaller groups that are in charge of hunting, medicine, ceremonial rituals, and other such activities. These secondary groups operate throughout the year and consist of members from both moieties. This unites members of both moieties and limits the power of the ruling moiety, Q08-2 maintaining peace between the two.

Q13(G)-2 Ceremonial practices are also an important part of the Eastern Pueblo culture, though there are significant differences from those of the Western Pueblo. Individual Eastern Pueblo communities have far fewer places of worship than the Western Pueblo have. Q10 Furthermore, the *kachina* cults have little influence among the Eastern Pueblo, and in some communities they are not present at all. The ceremonies also differ in their focus. Due to their location, these tribes do not feel the need to focus primarily on weather-centric ceremonies for assistance with growing crops. Instead, their ceremonies traditionally place more emphasis on activities that are considered more masculine, particularly hunting, at least for part of the year. ①The various tribes emphasize different concerns, like hunting and farming, to different degrees and at different times, ②a noticeable distinction from the singular focus of the Western Pueblo ceremonial practices.

동부 푸에블로족은 주로 뉴멕시코의 리오그란데 강변 계곡에 위치하며, 서부 푸에블로족과는 다른 사회적 구조와 의식적 관행을 가지고 있다. 첫째, 동부 푸에블로족은 씨족 제도를 엄격히 고수하지 않으며, 그러므로 씨족이 서부 푸에블로 사회에서처럼 중요한 역할을 하지 않는다. 혈통은 보통 모계와 부계 두 쪽을 모두 따르고, 두 쪽 모두의 구성원들이 함께 대가족을 이루고 산다. 둘째, 대부분 동부 푸에블로족은 사회의 중심 집단인 두 개의 반족으로 나뉘는데, 여름족과 겨울족이 그것이다. 이 이름은 동부 푸에블로 사회의 전통적 권력 분배 방식에서 유래했는데, 여름족이 여름이 속한 6개월을 통치하면, 겨울족이 겨울이 속한 6개월을 번갈아 가며 통치한다. 이러한 제도가 잠재적으로 초래할 수 있는 정치적 차이를 상쇄하기 위해, 부족 안에는 또한 수많은 소집단이 있어 사냥, 의술, 의식 제도 및 다른 활동들을 관장한다. 이런 부수 집단은 연중 내내 운영되며, 양쪽 반족 출신의 구성원들로 조직된다. 이를 통해 두 반족의 구성원들이 결속할 수 있고 지배 반족의 권력이 제한되어, 두 반족 사이의 평화가 유지된다.

동부 푸에블로 문화에서도 의식적 관행은 중요한 부분을 차지하지만, 서부 푸에블로족의 의식적 관행과는 현저한 차이를 보인다. 동부 푸에블로 부족에는 서부 푸에블로족보다 숭배 장소가 훨씬 적다. 그리고 동부 푸에블로족에서는 카치나 의식이 별 영향을 미치지 못하며, 어떤 부족에서는 그것이 아예 존재하지 않기도 한다. 의식은 그 목적에서도 차이를 보인다. 동부 푸에블로 부족들은 그들의 위치 덕분에 작물 재배를 위해 날씨에 초점을 맞춘 의식들에 중점을 둬야 한다고 생각하지 않았다. 대신 그들의 의식에서는 적어도 연간 몇 달 동안은 좀 더 남성적인 활동이라고 여겨지는 활동, 특히 수렵을 강조한다. 여러 부족은 정도와 시기에 따라 다르게 수렵과 농업 등 각기 다른 관심 분야를 강조하는데, 이는 하나에 목적을 두는 서부 푸에블로족의 의식적 관행과 현저한 차이를 보인다.

---

01 필자가 지문에서 스페인 사람들을 언급하는 이유는?
(A) 푸에블로족이 폭넓게 끼친 영향에 관해 설명하기 위해
(B) 푸에블로족이 어떻게 많은 부족으로 나뉘었는지 설명하기 위해
(C) 푸에블로족 문화의 놀라운 회복력을 보여주기 위해
(D) 푸에블로족 문화의 변화에 관해 설명하기 위해

해설 | Rhetorical Purpose 지문은 푸에블로족이 단일 부족에서 내려왔지만, 각자 독특한 문화를 지닌 다른 부족들로 나뉘어 갔다고 말함으로써, 푸에블로족 문화에 변화가 일어났음을 드러내고 있다. 이 뒤에 스페인 사람들의 영향을 덧붙여 언급하고 푸에블로족 문화에 일어난 변화에 대해 추가로 설명하고 있다.

02 단락 1에 따르면, 푸에블로족 이름의 기원은?
(A) 가족 구조
(B) 지리적 위치
(C) 주거 형태
(D) 종교적 믿음

해설 | Factual Information 단락 1의 첫 번째 문장에서 푸에블로족의 이름은 진흙 벽돌과 짚으로 만든 푸에블로라고 불리는 주택에서 유래되었다고 설명한다.

03 지문에서 their가 가리키는 것은?
(A) 아이들
(B) 가족들
(C) 씨족들
(D) 구성원들

해설 | Reference 그들의 어머니(their mother)는 필연적으로 어머니가 낳은 자녀들을 가리킨다. 이 지시어가 가리키는 것은 동일 문장의 아이들(the couple's children)이다.

04 지문의 rigid 와 의미상 가장 가까운 것은?

(A) 관대한
(B) 수많은
(C) 엄격한
(D) 소소한

해설 | Vocabulary rigid 의 의미는 "… whom people can and cannot marry, as tribe members must marry outside of their particular clans" 에서 힌트를 얻을 수 있다. 즉, 결혼 상대는 다른 씨족 사람이어야 한다는 내용으로부터 rigid 가 '엄격한'이라는 의미임을 추론할 수 있다.

05 단락 2에 따르면, 서부 푸에블로족의 기본적 사회 단위는?

(A) 마을
(B) 가족
(C) 씨족
(D) 부족

해설 | Factual Information 단락 2에서 서부 푸에블로족은 씨족(clan)을 중심으로 이루어졌음을 알 수 있다.

06 지문의 myriad 와 의미상 가장 가까운 것은?

(A) 외딴
(B) 거대한
(C) 수많은
(D) 훌륭한

해설 | Vocabulary myriad 는 numerous의 뜻이 있다.

07 지문의 critical 과 의미상 가장 가까운 것은?

(A) 고정된
(B) 중요한
(C) 활동적인
(D) 사소한

해설 | Vocabulary critical 이 포함된 문장에서 동부 푸에블로족은 서부 푸에블로 사회와는 다르게 씨족 제도를 엄격히 따르진 않았다고 하였으므로, 씨족은 그들에게 '중요하지' 않은 사회적 역할을 했음을 유추할 수 있다.

08 지문의 discrepancy 와 의미상 가장 가까운 것은?

(A) 독재
(B) 협력
(C) 영향
(D) 차이

해설 | Vocabulary 반의어 단서를 찾을 수 있는 문제이다. "To offset the political …"과 단락 4의 마지막 부분에서 "… maintaining peace between the two"는 결국 같은 의미임을 알아야 한다. 평화를 유지하는 것은 곧, 차이를 방지한다는 뜻으로 discrepancy 는 '차이'의 의미임을 알 수 있다.

09 단락 4에 따르면, 동부 푸에블로 사회에서 특별히 선택된 구성원들이 행해야 했던 의무가 아닌 것은?

(A) 의식
(B) 농업
(C) 의술
(D) 사냥

해설 | Negative Fact 단락 4에서 특별히 뽑힌 구성원들의 의무로써 사냥, 의술, 의식이 언급되고 있다.

10 지문에서 they 가 가리키는 것은?

(A) 의식
(B) 카치나 의식
(C) 공동체
(D) 숭배 장소

해설 | Reference 동부 푸에블로족에서는 카치나 의식들의 영향이 작으며 어떤 부족에서는 그것들이 아예 존재하지 않기도 한다고 한다. 따라서 they 는 kachina cults를 가리킨다.

11 다음 중 지문에서 표시된 문장의 주요 정보를 가장 잘 나타낸 문장은? 정답 외의 보기들은 중요한 의미가 바뀌거나 주요 정보가 빠져 있다.

(A) 동부 푸에블로족은 각기 다른 시간에 다른 범위로 정령의 도움을 구하기 위해 종교 의식을 행했다.
(B) 동부 푸에블로족의 종교 의식은 하나의 목적을 가지고 있는데, 그 점으로 인해 서부 푸에블로족과 구별된다.

해설 | Sentence Simplification 표시된 문장은 크게 두 의미로 나뉠 수 있다. ① 동부 푸에블로족에는 다양한 관심사에 따라 중요성과 시기를 달리한 여러 가지 의식이 있다. ② 서부 푸에블로족은 하나의 관심사에 집중해서 의식을 행한다.

(C) 서부 푸에블로족과는 달리 동부 푸에블로족은 특정 필요와 시기에 따라 다양한 경우에 종교 의식을 사용한다.
(D) 서부 푸에블로족의 종교 의식은 큰 필요가 있을 때만 행해지는데, 이것은 동부 푸에블로족과 매우 반대된다.

12 다음 문장이 지문에 들어갈 곳을 나타내는 네 개의 사각형[■]을 보시오.

> 이런 의식 활동은 이를 경감시키고 어느 정도의 안정을 불러오기 위한 시도이다.

이 문장이 들어갈 가장 적절한 위치는?
(A) A   (B) B   (C) C   (D) D

해설 | Sentence Insertion   삽입 문장 중 "an attempt to mitigate this and bring some level of stability"를 통해 푸에블로족이 겪고 있는 어떠한 어려움에 관련된 내용의 문장 뒤에 삽입 문장이 위치해야 함을 알 수 있다.

13 보기에서 적절한 문구를 골라 관련된 푸에블로족과 연결하시오.
보기 중 2개는 사용되지 않는다. *이 문제는 4점이다.*

보기	푸에블로족
(A) 강수량이 적을 때가 많고 예측하기 힘든 지역에 산다. (B) 다른 씨족 사람과 결혼해야 한다. (C) 부족을 번갈아 지배했던 두 집단으로 나뉜다. (D) 여자들이 농장을 소유하며 상당한 사회적 영향력을 갖는다. (E) 결혼은 동일 씨족 안에서만 허락된다. (F) 조상은 모계와 부계를 모두 거슬러 올라간다. (G) 종교 의식을 통해 정령에게 행운을 구한다. (H) 많은 숭배 장소를 갖고 있는 공동체를 포함한다. (I) 부족 구성원들이 정치적 영향력을 차지하기 위해 서로 경쟁한다.	**동부 푸에블로족** • (C) • (F) **서부 푸에블로족** • (A) • (B) • (D) • (H) **둘 다** • (G)

해설 | Fill in a Table   서부 푸에블로족과 동부 푸에블로족은 모두 종교 의식이 있다. 동부 푸에블로족은 겨울족과 여름족이 반년씩 번갈아 통치하며, 조상은 모계와 부계 모두를 따른다. 서부 푸에블로족은 강수량이 적고 예측하기 힘들어 카치나 의식이 중요하게 취급되었고, 부족마다 수많은 숭배 장소가 있다고 한다. 또한, 결혼은 다른 씨족 구성원과 해야 하며, 모계 사회로 여성들이 사회적으로 영향력이 강하다.

어휘 | **tribe** 부족   **straw** 짚   **descend from** ~의 자손이다   **fragment** 나뉘다, 분리되다   **territory** 영토   **transform** 변화시키다   **practice** 관행, 관습   **recur** 반복되다   **distinction** 차이점   **clan** 씨족   **rigid** 엄격한   **property** 소유지, 재산   **distinctive** 고유한   **retain** 유지하다   **bestow** 주다, 수여하다   **fortune** 행운   **arid** 메마른   **adequate** 충분한   **unpredictable** 예측할 수 없는   **fundamental** 중요한   **counterpart** 상대방   **strictly** 엄격하게   **adhere to** ~을 고수하다   **lineage** 혈통   **moiety** 반족(半族)   **offset** 상쇄하다   **discrepancy** 차이   **arrangement** 제도   **potentially** 잠재적으로

Chapter 11 Humanities II

Intensive Drill 1

p.130

01 (C)   02 (C)   03 (A)   04 (B)   05 [*Salon de Paris* – (A), (D), (E)], [*Salon des Independants* – (C), (F)]

THE SALON OF PARIS

Q02 Today, Paris is well known for its contributions to new and daring art movements. However, early attempts at experimental art in the city actually faced strong opposition from the government, which favored art that was of a more classical, academic nature. Until the late nineteenth century, the art world of Paris revolved around the *Salon de Paris*, a regular exhibition of painting and sculpture by the French government. Q01 Q05(E) If an artist had any hopes of becoming a great success, it was mandatory that he or she be accepted to the Paris Salon, as this was the only great form of exposure available at the time. In addition, its influence on French painting, artistic style in particular, painterly conventions, and the reputation of artist was enormous.

The Salon of Paris was first opened as a way of exhibiting work from the city's premier art academy in 1667, Q05(D) and was not initially available to the public. This changed over the years as the exhibition grew to greater prominence, but even after it opened to the public and art from outside the school became more frequently accepted, the Salon maintained a reputation for art that reflected only the conventional styles taught in art schools. Beginning in 1725, the Salon was held in the prestigious Louvre Palace, Q05(A) and in 1748 the Salon adopted a system in which prominent teachers from the art academy judged the works and awarded medals to the best. The judges were extremely selective in what art was to be included in the exhibition, and their tastes were very conservative in nature. Q03 Many rising artists who found themselves being rejected year after year complained to the authorities, who moved to establish the *Salon des Refuses*, or the "Salon of Rejects," in which they allowed some of the art rejected by the Salon to be shown.

However, by the late nineteenth century, this measure was not enough to satisfy artists of new and emerging styles. **A** In response to the conservative Salon, a small group of artists was allowed to organize its own yearly exhibition in 1884, featuring works from all styles, called the *Salon des Indépendants*. **B** **The people who established this new exhibition were members of the Impressionist movement, whose work was especially disliked by the Salon.** Q04 The values of the new exhibition were very different from those of the official Salon. **C** Q05(C) First of all, the system of judges was abandoned, and the public was allowed to judge works of art based on their own values rather than the opinions of academics. **D** Q05(F) In addition, no work of art was rejected, and all submissions found a place on the exhibition grounds. This free-thinking approach gave much-needed exposure to France's rising artists, many of whom represented the very future of modern art. For instance, the works of now-legendary painters such as Henri Matisse, Georges Braque, and Vincent Van Gogh made some of their first appearances here.

파리 살롱전

오늘날 파리는 새롭고 도전적인 예술 운동에 대한 기여로 잘 알려져 있다. 그러나 사실은 이 도시에서 실험적 예술에 대한 초기의 시도는 고전적이고 학구적 성격의 예술을 선호했던 정부로부터의 강한 반대에 직면했다. 19세기 후반까지 파리의 예술계는 파리 살롱전을 중심으로 돌아갔는데, 이 파리 살롱전은 프랑스 정부가 주관하는 그림과 조각의 정기 전시회였다. 이 살롱전은 그 당시에 작품 발표를 위해 열린 하나밖에 없는 좋은 수단이었기 때문에, 성공하고 싶은 예술가라면 누구나 파리 살롱전에 출품하는 것이 필수적이었다. 게다가 이것이 프랑스 미술, 특히 예술적 형식, 화가 특유의 관습, 그리고 예술가의 명망에 끼친 영향은 엄청났다.

원래 파리 살롱전은 1667년에 파리 최고의 미술학교에서 배출된 작품을 전시하려는 방편으로 개최됐었고, 처음엔 대중에게 공개되지 않았다. 이는 여러 해가 지나면서 전시회가 커지고 명성을 얻으면서 변하였는데, 전시회가 대중에 공개되고 학교 외부 작품들이 더 빈번하게 출품되기는 했지만 살롱전은 여전히 미술학교에서 가르치는 전통 양식을 반영한 예술만을 고집한다는 평판을 유지했다. 1725년부터는 살롱전이 명망 높은 루브르 박물관에서 열렸으며, 1748년에는 예술학교 출신의 저명한 교수들이 작품을 심사하고 최고 작품에 메달을 수여하는 방식을 도입하였다. 심사위원들은 전시회에 무슨 작품이 출품될지를 매우 까다롭게 골랐으며, 그들의 취향은 사실상 매우 보수적이었다. 해마다 출품을 거절당했던 많은 유망한 예술가들이 당국에 불만을 표시했고, 당국은 살롱전 출품이 거부된 작품 일부를 전시하도록 살롱데레퓨제, 즉 "낙선전"을 도입하게 된다.

그러나 19세기 후반까지 이 조치는 새롭게 떠오르는 양식을 추구했던 예술가들을 충분히 만족시킬 수 없었다. **A** 보수적 살롱전에 대한 대응으로, 1884년에 한 작은 예술가 집단은 모든 양식의 예술품을 다루는 연례 전시회 조직을 허가받았으며, 그 전시회는 독립전이라는 이름으로 불렸다. **B** 이 새로운 전시회를 조직한 사람들은 인상주의 운동 회원들이었고 그들의 작품은 살롱전에서 특히 환영받지 못했다. 이 새로운 전시회의 성격은 공식 살롱전과는 매우 달랐다. **C** 우선, 심사위원 체제를 채택하지 않았으며, 학회의 의견보다는 대중이 자신의 판단에 근거해 작품을 심사했다. **D** 그리고 어떤 작품도 거절당하지 않았으며, 모든 출품작이 전시회장에서 자리를 얻었다. 이런 자유로운 접근법은 프랑스의 유망한 예술가들에게 절실하던 출품 기회를 부여했으며, 이들 중 많은 이들은 현대 예술의 미래를 대표했다. 예를 들어, 지금은 전설적인 화가로 추앙 받는 Henri Matisse나 Georges Braque, Vincent Van Gogh와 같은 화가들의 작품 일부가 이곳에서 처음으로 발표되었다.

01
지문의 mandatory와 의미상 가장 가까운 것은?

(A) 중요한
(B) 흔히 있는
(C) 필수의
(D) 타당한

해설 | Vocabulary 살롱전은 작품 발표를 할 수 있는 유일한 수단이었다고 했으므로, 성공하고 싶은 예술가에게 이 살롱전에 출품하는 것이 '필수적'이었음을 유추할 수 있다.

02
단락 1에서 필자가 실험적 예술에 대한 현대 파리의 명성에 대해 자세히 언급하는 이유는?

(A) 파리에서 활동했던 위대한 몇몇 예술가에 대해 감탄을 표현하기 위해
(B) 파리가 왜 모든 양식의 예술가들에게 중요한 도시인지 설명하기 위해
(C) 그 도시의 평판과 놀랍게 모순되는 상황을 소개하기 위해
(D) 프랑스의 실험 예술 상황에 대해 질문을 던지기 위해

해설 | Rhetorical Purpose 도입 문단의 첫 문장은 파리가 실험적 예술로 유명하다는 사실을 언급한 뒤, 예전의 파리 예술계의 보수적인 분위기와 대조시키고 있다.

03
단락 2에 따르면, 당국이 낙선전을 조직하게 된 계기는?

(A) 예술가들이 자신들의 작품이 너무 자주 거절된다며 불만을 표시했다.
(B) 정부가 거절된 예술가들을 이용하고자 했다.
(C) 심사위원들이 한 가지 양식의 예술만 받아들였다.
(D) 대중이 그 예술가들의 작품을 전시하라고 요구했다.

해설 | Factual Information 예술가들은 자신들의 작품이 낙선하자 당국에 항의하였고 당국은 낙선된 작품만을 전시하는 낙선전을 열게 되었다.

04
다음 문장이 지문에 들어갈 곳을 나타내는 네 개의 사각형[■]을 보시오.

> 이 새로운 전시회를 조직한 사람들은 인상주의 운동 회원들이었고, 그들의 작품은 살롱전에서 특히 환영받지 못했다.

이 문장이 들어갈 가장 적절한 위치는?

(A) A (B) B (C) C (D) D

해설 | Sentence Insertion 삽입 문장의 this new exhibition이 이전 문장에서 언급된 "the Salon des Indépendants"를 가리킨다는 것을 알 수 있다. 그리고 삽입 문장의 살롱전 심사위원들이 독립전을 개설한 인상주의 화가들의 작품을 싫어했다는 사실은 다음 문장에 제시된 이 새로운 전시회의 성격이 공식 살롱전과는 매우 달랐다는 내용과 자연스럽게 연결된다.

05
보기에서 적절한 문구를 골라 관련된 살롱전과 연결하시오. 보기 중 2개는 사용되지 않는다. *이 문제는 3점이다.*

보기	살롱전
(A) 유명 예술 교수들이 작품을 심사함	**파리살롱전**
(B) 이전에 거절당한 작품만 출품됨	• (A)
(C) 평가는 학회가 아닌 대중에게 맡겨짐	• (D)
(D) 한때 대중에 공개되지 않았음	• (E)
(E) 예술가로서의 명성을 얻기 위한 단 하나의 수단으로 여겨졌음	**독립전**
(F) 제대로 된 출품작은 절대 거절하지 않음	• (C)
(G) 실험적인 예술만 받아들임	• (F)

해설 | Fill in a Table 파리 살롱전은 유명 예술 교수들이 작품을 심사하였고, 한때 대중에게는 공개되지 않았으며, 예술가로서 명성을 얻기 위한 하나의 통로였다. 반면, 독립전은 대중이 작품을 심사했으며, 출품되는 모든 작품은 다 받아들였다.

어휘 | **contribution** 기여, 헌신 **experimental** 실험적인 **revolve around** (관심·주제가) ~을 중심으로 돌아가다 **mandatory** 필수의, 의무적인 **influence** 영향(력) **initially** 처음에 **reputation** 명성 **conventional** 전통적인 **prestigious** 명망 높은, 유명한 **selective** 까다로운, 선택적인 **authority** 당국 **judge** 심사위원, 심사하다 **submission** 출품작, 제출

Intensive Drill 2

p.132

01 (C)　**02** (A)　**03** (D)　**04** (D)　**05** (A), (B), (F)

ART RESTORATION AND CONSERVATION

Great masterpieces of art are destined to live forever as a beloved part of our cultural heritage. However, works of art are inherently fragile. Paint may chip or flake off over the years; canvases may bend or warp. For this reason, experts are continually making efforts to restore and conserve great works of art so that they may survive in perpetuity.

Conservation and restoration have a long history in the art world, but until the nineteenth century, most of the work had been done by isolated individuals, and involved simply cleaning or touching up pieces of art for themselves or other collectors. The methods used were often only temporarily effective, and sometimes caused long-term damage to the "restored" pieces. For example, Q01(B) it was not uncommon to apply varnish to a painting to serve as a protective coating. However, these conservators unknowingly used inferior materials that, in just a few years' time, would yellow and peel. Q01(A) In addition, early conservators used paints that had no more permanent value than the originals, and sometimes even less. Q01(D) Thus, paintings had to be restored quite frequently. Q02 With each restoration, the paintings lost more and more of their original integrity and sustained more long-term damage.

①During the nineteenth century, however, renowned scientists like Louis Pasteur and Michael Faraday began to study the effects of the environment on works of art, and ②their findings served to inform museum curators about the best ways to maintain their precious art collections. In 1888, Friedrich Rathgen became the first chemist to be employed directly by a museum, the Royal Museum of Berlin, thus officially transforming the practice of art conservation into a profession. Shortly after World War I, the British Museum hired chemist Harold Plenderleith to restore paintings that had suffered damage while hidden from enemies in the London Underground. These chemists and others identified and created pigments that would keep their color longer. They also discovered that ultraviolet radiation, such as that from the sun, had a profound effect on the brilliance of the paint. In response to this, museum curators placed their most sensitive paintings in display areas with a minimum of sunlight to keep them from fading.

Today, art conservators are careful not to alter a work of art in any way that is not absolutely necessary to its survival. They normally practice one of two methods: interventive conservation and preventive conservation. Q04 Interventive conservation is similar to the restoration techniques of old, in that the conservator actually interacts with a work of art directly in order to clean it or to remedy some flaw. Even the most advanced interventive techniques can cause damage to artwork, so ample justification is required before a conservator can undertake such a process. More common is preventive conservation, in which measures are taken to prevent any future damage to a work of art. This involves simply protecting the art from environmental factors that can contribute to decay, so that little or no interventive work will be needed in the future.

미술 복원과 보존

위대한 걸작품들은 우리의 문화유산의 사랑 받는 일부분으로 영원히 남도록 운명 지어졌다. 그러나 미술 작품은 본래 훼손되기 쉽다. 페인트는 시간이 지남에 따라 부스러지거나 파편이 떨어지며, 캔버스는 굽거나 뒤틀어지기도 한다. 이런 이유로 전문가들은 위대한 미술 작품들이 영구히 살아남을 수 있도록 끊임없이 복원 및 보존하려고 노력한다.

보존과 복원은 미술계에서 긴 역사를 가지고 있지만, 19세기까지 대부분의 작품 복원은 개별적으로 진행되었고, 자기 자신이나 다른 수집가를 위해서 단순히 작품을 청소하거나 다듬는 정도에 그쳤다. 이때 사용된 방법은 보통 일시적으로만 효과가 있었고, 오히려 '복원된' 작품에 장기적인 해가 되는 경우도 있었다. 예를 들어, 보호막을 입힌다는 명분으로 그림에 광택제를 입히는 일은 흔했다. 그러나 이 보존가들은 무지하게도 저급 재료를 사용하여 불과 몇 년 만에 누레지거나 벗겨지곤 했다. 게다가 초기 보존가들은 원본에 쓰였던 것과 지속성이 비슷한 페인트나, 때로는 오히려 더 저급한 페인트를 사용했다. 그래서 그림은 꽤 자주 복원되어야 했다. 복원 작업을 할 때마다, 그림은 더욱더 본래의 온전함을 잃었고 더 많은 장기적 손상을 입었다.

그러나 19세기에 Louis Pasteur와 Michael Faraday 같은 저명한 과학자들이 미술 작품에 미치는 환경의 영향에 대해 연구하기 시작하였고, 그들의 발견은 미술관 관장들이 소중한 미술작품 유지를 위해 제일 나은 방법을 알리는 데 유용하게 쓰였다. 1888년에 Friedrich Rathgen은 베를린 왕립 미술관에 고용됨으로써 박물관에 직접 고용된 최초의 화학자가 되었는데, 이는 공식적으로 미술 보전 작업을 하나의 전문 직업으로 바꾸어 놓았다. 제1차 세계 대전 직후, 대영박물관은 화학자 Harold Plenderleith를 고용하여 런던 지하철에 적으로부터 숨겨났던 손상된 미술품을 복원하게 하였다. 이런 화학자들을 비롯한 사람들은 색깔이 더 오래 유지되는 물감을 찾아내고 만들어내었다. 그들은 또한 햇빛 등으로부터 발생하는 자외선이 페인트의 광택에 큰 영향을 미친다는 사실을 알아냈다. 이점에 대처하기 위해 미술관 관장들은 가장 민감한 작품들을 퇴색되지 않도록 태양 빛이 가장 적게 드는 전시 구역에 배정하였다.

오늘날 미술 보존가들은 미술품의 존속에 절대적으로 필요하지 않으면 어떤 방식으로도 작품을 변화시키지 않도록 주의를 기울인다. 이들은 보통 개입적 보존과 예방적 보존 방법 중 한 가지 방법을 사용한다. 개입적 보존은 작품의 결점을 청소하거나 보완하기 위하여 보존가가 미술 작품에 직접 작업한다는 점에서 과거의 보존 기술과 비슷하다. 개입적 보존은 최고도의 기술일지라도 작품에 손상을 입힐 수 있으므로, 보존가가 그런 작업을 맡기 전에 충분한 정당성이 요구된다. 더욱 흔하게 쓰이는 방법은 예방적 보존 방법인데, 여기에서는 미술 작품에 추후 손상을 예방하기 위한 조치를 취한다. 이때는 훗날 개입적 조치를 최소화하거나 개입적 조치가 필요치 않도록 부패를 일으키는 환경 요소로부터 작품을 보호하는 조치만을 취한다.

01 단락 2에 따르면, 초기 복원 노력과 관련된 문제점으로 옳지 않은 것은?
(A) 저급한 페인트 사용하기
(B) 해로운 광택제를 칠하기
(C) 햇볕으로부터 작품 이전하기
(D) 미술품 자주 복원하기

해설 | Negative Fact 지문에서 초기 그림 복원자들은 미술작품 복원에 대한 충분한 이해 없이 저급한 광택제와 페인트를 사용하여 그림을 꽤 자주 복원했고, 복원 작업마다 그림은 더욱 손상되었다고 한다. (C)에 관한 내용은 언급되지 않았다.

02 단락 2에 따르면, 초기 미술 보존가들에 대해 추론할 수 있는 것은?
(A) 그들은 미술 작품을 보존하는 데 필요한 지식이 충분하지 않았다.
(B) 그들은 예술 영역을 잘 모르는 비전문가였다.
(C) 그들은 미술품을 단순히 복원하는 대신에 개선하려 하였다.
(D) 그들은 품질이 좋은 물감을 사용하였다.

해설 | Inference 초기 예술 복원은 해로운 광택제를 사용하거나 원래 쓰인 물감보다도 질이 좋지 않은 물감을 사용하는 등 오히려 작품에 피해가 가는 경우가 많았다. 이를 바탕으로 초기 그림 복원자들은 예술 작품의 보존력을 높이는 데 필요한 지식이 충분하지 않았음을 알 수 있다.

03 다음 중 지문에서 표시된 문장의 주요 정보를 가장 잘 나타낸 문장은? 정답 외의 보기들은 중요한 의미가 바뀌거나 주요 정보가 빠져 있다.
(A) 환경이 미술 작품에 미치는 영향은 19세기 미술관 관장들이 연구하면서 완전히 이해되게 되었다.
(B) 연구를 위해 화학자들을 고용한 후로 미술관은 환경적 손상으로부터 미술 작품을 보호하는 방법을 바꾸기 시작하였다.
(C) 19세기의 과학자들은 나쁜 환경이 미술 작품에 손상을 입힐 수 있다는 사실을 알고 미술관 관장들에게 자신들의 연구 결과를 고려하라고 촉구했다.
(D) 19세기 유명 과학자들의 연구는 미술관 관장들이 미술 작품을 환경적 손상으로부터 보호하는 방법에 영향을 주었다.

해설 | Sentence Simplification 표시된 문장은 크게 두 의미로 나뉠 수 있다. ① 과학자들이 미술 작품에 미치는 환경적 영향에 대해 연구했다. ② 이러한 연구로부터 나온 지식은 미술관에서 미술 작품을 보존하는 데 사용되었다.

04 지문에서 such a process 가 가리키는 것은?
(A) 환경적 요인으로부터 작품 보호하기
(B) 충분한 정당성
(C) 예방적 보존 방법
(D) 개입적 보존 방법

해설 | Reference '개입적 보존은 최고도의 기술일지라도 작품에 손상을 입힐 수 있으므로, 그런 과정(such a process)을 맡기 전에 충분한 정당성이 요구된다'에서 such a process 가 개입적 보존 방법을 가리킨다는 것을 알 수 있다.

05 지문을 간략히 요약하기 위한 도입 문장이 아래 제시되어 있다. 지문에서 가장 중요한 내용을 표현한 세 개의 문장을 골라 요약문을 완성하시오. 일부 문장은 지문에 나오지 않았거나 중요하지 않은 내용이기 때문에 요약문에 포함되지 않는다. *이 문제는 2점이다.*

> 위대한 예술작품을 복원하고 보존하려는 지속적인 노력은 전문가들에 의해 계속되고 있다.

(A) 수백 년 동안 미술 보존가들은 미술 작품 보존을 하는 데 오히려 해가 되는 기술과 저급 재료를 사용하였다.
(B) 소중한 미술 작품을 보존하기 위한 노력으로, 미술관은 보존 과정에서의 화학자들의 기술을 인정하기 시작했다.
(C) 미술 보존은 미술사에서 화학에 이르기까지 여러 다양한 학문을 포함한 복잡한 작업이다.
(D) 미술관 관장들은 작품의 질을 크게 저하할 수 있는 자외선에 미술품이 노출되지 않도록 보호한다.
(E) 과학적 연구는 안료의 지속성과 관련하여 어느 물감이 최고인지 결정하는 데 필수적이다.
(F) 현재 미술 보존가들은 개입적 보존 방법과 예방적 보존 방법 둘 다를 사용하지만, 미술 작품에 불필요한 수정을 가하지 않으려 한다.

해설 | Summary (A)는 19세기의 미술 작품의 보존과 복원의 실태를 설명한 단락 2의 내용을 요약해 놓은 것이다. (B)는 19세기의 미술 작품의 보존과 복원을 이해하기 위한 노력을 설명한 단락 3의 내용을 요약해 놓은 것이다. (F)는 오늘날의 미술 작품의 보존과 복원을 위한 노력을 설명한 단락 4의 내용을 요약해 놓은 것이다.

어휘 | **restoration** 복원 **conservation** 보존 **destine** 운명 지어지다 **heritage** 유산 **inherently** 본래 **chip** 부스러지다 **flake off** 파편이 떨어지다 **restore** 복원하다 **in perpetuity** 영구히 **varnish** 광택제 **unknowingly** 모르고 **integrity** 온전함 **renowned** 저명한 **curator** (미술관) 관장 **chemist** 화학자 **suffer damage** 손상을 입다 **ultraviolet** 자외선 **profound** 큰, 깊은 **fading** 퇴색, 색이 바램 **alter** 변하다, 바꾸다 **absolutely** 절대적으로 **interventive** 개입적 **preventive** 예방적인 **undertake** 맡다, 착수하다 **decay** 부패하다

Intensive Drill 3

01 (A) 02 (D) 03 (D) 04 (C) 05 (B), (C), (E)

THEATER ACTING AND FILM ACTING

Q01(B) Though live performance on a stage and performing on screen are both considered part of the dramatic arts, there are several fundamental differences between them. The first difference comes from scripts. In stage acting, the audience is often very familiar with the performance materials even before they see the acting. Q01(A) Because theater by its nature is repetitive and familiar to the audience, the audience is expected to know the plot of the story. Q01(C) The script, which is written by the playwright, is sacrosanct in stage acting. Neither errors nor deviations from it are tolerated by actors or audiences alike. In this way, the performance aims to be as truthful a representation of the playwright's words as possible. In filmmaking, on the other hand, the audience has not seen the script before watching the film. Therefore they have no expectation that the actors or directors are following a script with great fidelity. It is not uncommon, in fact, for the script for a film to be written or rewritten on the fly. Q01(D) The audience is unaware of this and only ever sees one version, which they consider to be the faithful version.

Similar expectations hold true for how characters are portrayed in theater as compared to film. In theater, the characters, their roles, mannerisms, tone of voice, intents, and even costume are more or less well defined. The audience arrives at the theater with a preconceived notion of what a given character looks and sounds like. Likewise, one actor's performance of a character will be compared and critiqued with another's. Q02 In film, the characters are defined by the actors and directors. When casting a part, directors look for a person who fits the world they are trying to create. The job of the film actor is to imbue the role with personality and presence that convinces the audience the character is a real person.

Another difference between stage and film acting comes from the physical location where they are performed. On a stage, actors must convey their acting even to audience members in the back row. A This means that the performances should be "larger than life"; louder voices and more dramatic and defined movements are required. B Q04 All this is necessary for the audience to engage with the actors and the material while seated in the theater, particularly if they are seated at some distance from the performers. **C This is why actors often remark that they feed off the energy of the audience, something that film actors cannot experience directly.** In film, on the other hand, actors behave more naturally, speaking in a normal volume and moving and gesturing in a natural way. D Technical elements such as lighting, sound, camera angles, and musical score add additional impact to the acting.

Stage acting happens in real time without any editing. The actors work intensely to capture and maintain the audience's attention. The live performance creates a strong, intimate connection between the actors and the audience, something that a film cannot do to the same degree. This is the reason some people say that live performances leave a stronger lasting impression on their audience.

연극에서의 연기와 영화에서의 연기

무대에서의 라이브 공연과 화면 속의 공연 모두 극예술의 일부로 간주되지만, 이들 사이에는 몇 가지 본질적인 차이점들이 있다. 그 중 첫 번째 차이는 대본에서 온다. 무대 연기에서 청중들은 간혹 연기를 보기도 전에 공연 내용들에 대해 매우 잘 알고 있다. 연극은 본래 반복적이고 대중에게 친숙하므로, 관객들은 이야기의 줄거리를 알고 있으리라 예상된다. 극작가가 쓴 대본은 무대 연기에서 침범할 수 없는 부분이다. 그래서 대본을 틀리거나 벗어나는 것은 배우와 관객들에게 용인되지 않는다. 이러한 방식에서, 공연의 목적은 극작가의 언어를 최대한 진실되게 재현하는 것이다. 반면, 영화 제작에서 관객들은 영화를 보기 전까지는 대본을 보지 못했기 때문에, 배우와 감독이 대본을 충실히 따랐으리라 예상하지 않는다. 사실 영화의 대본은 현장에서 쓰이거나 다시 쓰이는 경우가 흔하다. 관객은 이러한 것들을 인지하지 못하며 그들은 오직 한 가지 버전만을 보게 되는데, 이것이 가장 충실한 버전이라 여기게 된다.

이러한 예상은 영화와 비교하여 연극에서 인물이 묘사되는 방법에서도 마찬가지이다. 연극에서는 등장인물과 그들의 역할, 매너리즘, 목소리 톤, 의도, 심지어 의상까지 대개 분명하게 정해진다. 관객들은 특정 등장인물의 생김새와 목소리 등을 이미 예상한 채 극장에 온다. 이처럼 한 배우가 인물을 연기하는 것이 다른 것과 비교되고 비평된다. 영화에서의 등장인물은 배우와 감독에 의해 정의된다. 감독은 배역을 맡길 때, 그들이 구현하고자 하는 세계와 맞아떨어지는 배우를 찾는다. 영화배우의 역할은 관객들이 등장인물이 실재 인물이라고 믿을 수 있도록 배역의 성격과 존재로 가득 채우는 것이다.

연극에서의 연기와 영화에서의 연기의 또 한 가지 차이점은 그들이 연기하는 물리적 장소에서부터 온다. 무대에서 배우는 뒤쪽 열에 앉은 관객에게까지 연기를 전달해야 한다. A 이것은 연기가 "평소보다 더 과장되어야" 한다는 것을 의미한다. 즉, 더 큰 목소리와 더욱 과장되고 분명한 동작이 요구된다. B 이 모든 것들은 관객이 극장에 앉아있을 때, 특히 공연되는 장소로부터 멀리 떨어져 있더라도 이들이 배우와 내용에 집중하는 데 필요하다. **C 이것이 바로 배우가 관객들의 에너지를 먹고 산다고 말하는 이유이며, 이는 영화배우가 직접 경험할 수 없다.** 반면에, 영화에서 배우는 정상 크기의 목소리와 자연스러운 움직임과 몸짓으로 좀더 자연스럽게 연기한다. D 조명과 음향, 카메라 앵글, 음악 등 기술적인 요소들이 연기에 보태어진다.

무대 연기는 편집 없이 실시간으로 일어난다. 배우는 관객이 집중하고 이를 유지하도록 만들기 위해 열심히 연기한다. 라이브 공연은 배우와 관객 사이에 영화에서는 이루어질 수 없는 정도의 강하고 끈끈한 관계를 형성한다. 이것이 바로 몇몇 사람들이 라이브 공연이 관객에게 지속적인 더욱 강한 인상을 남긴다고 말하는 이유이다.

01
단락 1에서 언급되지 않은 것은?

(A) 관객들은 무대 연기에 대한 선입견이 거의 없다.
(B) 무대 연기와 영화 제작 모두 극예술로 간주된다.
(C) 무대 연기에서의 대본은 침범할 수 없는 부분이며 변경되어서는 안 되는 것으로 간주된다.
(D) 관객들은 영화의 최종 버전만을 볼 수 있다.

해설 | Negative Fact   단락 1에서 무대에서의 공연과 화면 속의 공연 모두 극예술로 간주되고 무대 연기는 본래 반복적이고 친숙한 내용으로 대본 수정이 불가하지만 영화는 수정 가능하며 관객은 최종 버전만을 보게 된다고 한다. (A)는 단락 1의 내용과 일치하지 않는다.

02
단락 2에 따르면, 영화에서의 연기에 관한 내용 중 옳은 것은?

(A) 배우는 캐릭터가 이전에 묘사된 방법을 따라야만 한다.
(B) 감독은 역할에 대한 관객의 기대를 충족시킬 만한 배우를 선택한다.
(C) 캐릭터는 이전에 연기된 역할과의 비교 되기 쉽다.
(D) 배우와 감독은 그 줄거리에 맞는 캐릭터를 함께 그려나간다.

해설 | Factual Information   단락 2에서 영화의 등장인물은 배우와 감독에 의해 만들어진다고 하였다.

03
단락 2는 각기 다른 공연 환경에 갖는 관객의 기대에 대한 앞서서의 언급과 어떻게 관련되어 있는가?

(A) 관객이 왜 각기 다른 공연 환경에 다른 기대를 갖는지 설명한다.
(B) 다른 환경들의 장점이 합쳐진 새로운 종류의 공연을 설명한다.
(C) 각기 다른 공연 유형에 따라 본래의 내용을 변경하는 것에 대한 허용 정도를 대조한다.
(D) 관객들이 각기 다른 공연 환경으로부터 예상하는 것들의 다른 예를 설명한다.

해설 | Rhetorical Purpose   단락 1에서는 연극은 대본에 충실한 데 반해, 영화는 그렇지 않기 때문에 관객들이 예상할 수 없다고 하였다. 이어 단락 2에서는 관객들이 연극과 영화에서 예상하는 또 다른 예시인 인물이 묘사되는 방법을 설명하고 있다.

04
다음 문장이 지문에 들어갈 곳을 나타내는 네 개의 사각형[■]을 보시오.

> 이것이 바로 배우가 관객들의 에너지를 먹고 산다고 말하는 이유이며, 이는 영화배우가 직접 경험할 수 없다.

이 문장이 들어갈 가장 적절한 위치는?

(A) A   (B) B   (C) C   (D) D

해설 | Sentence Insertion   삽입 문장의 "… something that film actors cannot experience directly"로부터 삽입 문장 뒤에는 영화가 언급될 것이고 문장의 이전에는 그와 대조되는 내용의 연극에 관한 묘사가 언급되었을 것임을 알 수 있다.

05
지문을 간략히 요약하기 위한 도입 문장이 아래 제시되어 있다. 지문에서 가장 중요한 내용을 표현한 세 개의 문장을 골라 요약문을 완성하시오. 일부 문장은 지문에 나오지 않았거나 중요하지 않은 내용이기 때문에 요약문에 포함되지 않는다. *이 문제는 2점이다.*

> 영화와 라이브 연극의 차이점은 관객에게 각기 다른 경험을 선사한다.

(A) 영화에서의 잘 짜인 줄거리는 무대 연기보다 더욱 실감 나는 경험을 제공한다.
(B) 대본은 영화에서는 그때그때 변경될 수 있지만, 무대 연기에서는 바뀌어서는 안 된다.
(C) 영화에서는 캐릭터가 수정될 수 있지만, 연극에서는 변경 가능한 대상이 아니다.
(D) 영화는 무대 연기보다 관객들에게 더욱 강한 인상을 남기고자 기술적인 효과를 사용한다.
(E) 무대 위에서는 배우가 과장하여 연기하는 데 반해 영화에서 배우는 자연스러운 연기를 한다.
(F) 연극 대본이 수정될 수 있는데 반해 영화 대본은 변경될 수 없다.

해설 | Summary   (B)는 연극과 영화에서 대본의 수정을 언급한 단락 1에 대한 내용을, (C)는 연극과 영화의 캐릭터 묘사를 비교하는 단락 2에 대한 내용을, (E)는 물리적인 장소에서 비롯된 연극에서의 연기와 영화에서의 연기 차이에 관해 설명한 단락 3의 내용이다.

어휘 | **fundamental** 본질적인, 근본적인   **repetitive** 반복적인   **plot** 줄거리, 음모   **playwright** 극작가   **sacrosanct** 침범하지 않는, 신성불가침의   **portray** 묘사하다, 그리다   **compared to** ~와 비교하여   **costume** 의상, 복장   **given** 특정의, 주어진   **imbue** 가득 채우다   **personality** 성격, 인격   **physical** 물리적인, 신체적인   **location** 장소   **row** 열, 좌석   **editing** 편집   **intimate** 끈끈한, 친밀한   **lasting** 지속적인, 영속적인

Mini Test 1

01 (D)　　02 (A)　　03 (C)　　04 (A), (D)　　05 [The *Iliad* – (F), (G)], [The *Odyssey* – (A), (B), (E)]

THE *ILIAD* AND THE *ODYSSEY*

The Greek poet Homer is widely held to be the earliest and most important Greek writer. His works were written at a turning pointing in Greek history when verse was turning from an oral tradition to written words. At the same time, Greek society was developing and changing, and ideas of social organization, economics, philosophy, and politics were emerging and evolving. Many of these ideas went on to form important and defining elements upon which Western civilization developed. Consequently, Homer's works not only mirrored the ideas of his contemporaries, but also went on to greatly influence Western literature.

Q01 Nothing definitive is known of Homer the man; indeed, there is much conjecture as to whether he really existed. Numerous scholars have shown that except for the works the *Iliad* and the *Odyssey*, other works attributed to him may have been written by anonymous writers. It was not uncommon for writers to attribute epic poems to being "of Homer," further obscuring the issue. Furthermore, the stories bear many similarities to popular oral poems and stories, so that some scholars argue that his poems were merely amalgamations of numerous oral stories. What is roundly accepted, though, is that the *Iliad* and the *Odyssey* share many stylistic similarities, enough that they appear to be written by the same author.

Q02 Q04(D) For the Greeks, Homer's works the *Iliad* and the *Odyssey* highlighted and celebrated how they had become the dominant power in the Mediterranean region. The former is essentially a story of military dominance. Q05(G) It tells of the Mycenaean victory at Troy, which was a battle for control of a valuable sea passage. Q05(F) Many of the characters in the *Iliad* choose military glory over family life, willingly sacrificing the chance to live a long life with those they love. Q05(E) The *Odyssey*, on the other hand, focuses more on characteristics and attributes that Greeks should aspire to. Q05(B) One of the most important values in the *Odyssey* is loyalty, as Odysseus's devotion to his family, his country, and his god is unwavering. This value stands out continuously during the course of the book by describing the faithful wife waiting patiently for years for her husband to return, and the hero who acts courageously and honorably for his country. Q05(A) It also described in great detail the gods and how they behaved, in effect setting the template for how we understand Greek mythology today.

Q04(A) In this way, Homer's epic poems became a template for the further stories of Greece's rise to power in the region. Homer's work was written as Greek civilization was emerging, and thus his writings capture many of the ideas and beliefs that would come to be defining elements of Western civilization. We see in his writings examples of the common good outweighing the power of the individual, the obligations that men have to their leaders, and obligations that women and men have to each other. Q03 The stories are, in a sense, morality tales that show how one should behave in the new civilization the Greeks were forging. Homer's writings have also gone on to influence countless forms of western literature, from *Don Quiote* to recent films such as *O Brother Where Art Thou?*

01 지문의 definitive 와 의미상 가장 가까운 것은?

(A) 엄청난
(B) 인상적인
(C) 상세한
(D) 명백한

해설 | Vocabulary 다음 문장에서 Homer에 대해 여러 추측이 있다고 했고, 주어진 단어가 수식하는 것이 부정어 Nothing이므로, definitive 의 의미는 '확실한, 명백한'임을 유추할 수 있다.

02 지문에서 The former 가 가리키는 것은?

(A) 일리아드
(B) 지중해 지역
(C) 오디세이
(D) Homer

해설 | Reference 이전 문장에서 『일리아드』와 『오디세이』를 언급했으므로 앞의 것(The former)은 『일리아드』임을 알 수 있다.

03 단락 4에서 추론할 수 있는 것은?

(A) 그리스인들이 Homer의 작품은 사회의 일반적인 견해와 다르다고 생각하는 것은 흔한 일이었다.
(B) Homer의 이야기는 도덕적 가치관에 대해 제한된 초점을 맞추기 때문에 구식이라고 여겨진다.
(C) Homer의 이야기 속의 도덕적 신념은 당대의 도덕적 기준과 부합했다.
(D) Homer 작품의 의의를 지금도 알아보는 비평가들은 거의 없다.

해설 | Inference Homer의 이야기가 그리스인들이 행동해야 할 바를 보여주는 도덕적 이야기였다는 단락 4의 내용을 바탕으로 그의 이야기 속의 도덕적 신념은 당대의 도덕적 기준과 부합했음을 알 수 있다.

04 『일리아드』와 『오디세이』에 관해 옳은 문장 2개를 선택하시오. 점수를 받기 위해서 반드시 2개의 문장을 선택하시오.

(A) 『일리아드』와 『오디세이』는 그리스 지배에 관한 더 많은 이야기의 지침이 되었다.
(B) 학자들은 Homer가 『일리아드』와 『오디세이』를 동시에 집필했는지를 두고 논쟁을 벌인다.
(C) 『일리아드』와 『오디세이』가 여러 작가에 의해 쓰였음을 보여주는 충분한 증거들이 있다.
(D) 그리스인들은 『일리아드』와 『오디세이』를 지중해 지역에서의 그리스 지배의 상징으로 간주한다.

해설 | Factual Information 단락 1과 3에서 『일리아드』와 『오디세이』는 지중해 지역에서의 그리스의 지배적인 권력을 강조하고 기념했다고 하며, 단락 4에서는 이 작품들이 그리스가 이 지역에서 권력을 장악하게 되는 것을 다루는 더 많은 이야기들의 본보기가 되었다고 한다.

05 보기에서 적절한 문구를 골라 관련된 Homer의 시와 연결하시오. 보기 중 2개는 사용되지 않는다. *이 문제는 3점이다.*

(A) 신들을 자세히 묘사한다.
(B) 충성심의 가치를 강조한다.
(C) 힘보다 지혜의 가치를 중시한다.
(D) 그리스 문명을 묘사한다.
(E) 그리스의 이상적인 가치들을 강조한다.
(F) 가족보다 군사적 영예를 강조한다.
(G) 군사적 승리의 이야기를 설명한다.

『일리아드』
• (F)
• (G)

『오디세이』
• (A)
• (B)
• (E)

해설 | Fill in a Table 『일리아드』는 트로이 전쟁에서의 승리를 이야기하며, 가족보다 군사적 영예를 강조한 이야기라고 설명하고 있고, 『오디세이』는 신들을 자세히 묘사하며, 충성심의 가치를 강조함으로써 그리스의 이상적인 가치들을 강조하고 있다고 한다.

어휘 | **poet** 시인 **verse** 시, 운문 **oral tradition** 구전 **philosophy** 철학 **politics** 정치 **contemporary** 동시대인, 동시대의 **literature** 문학 **definitive** 확실한, 확정적인 **conjecture** 추측 **anonymous** 익명의 **scholar** 학자 **merely** 단지 **amalgamation** 병합 **dominant** 지배적인 **region** 지역 **dominance** 지배 **sacrifice** 희생하다 **unwavering** 변함없는, 확고한 **stand out** 두드러지다 **mythology** 신화

Mini Test 2

01 (B) 02 (A) 03 (A) 04 (B) 05 (A), (C), (F)

POTTERY OF THE HOPI INDIANS

The pottery of the Hopi Indian tribe of southwestern America is among the most vibrant Native American traditions. The Hopi and their neighboring tribes began making pottery over 2,000 years ago, and the traditional process of pottery making has changed very little since then. The potter, almost always a woman in Hopi culture, first must obtain the clay that is needed to make the pot. Clay is traditionally gathered near the home, simply by digging small pits in the ground. Q01 Larger mines do exist, and many of them are kept secret from outsiders by members of the tribe, as clay is often seen as an almost sacred material. Traditional prayers are offered up to the spirits when the clay is taken from the earth. The clay must be conditioned for several days before it is ready to be used, and the women do this by Q02 grinding the hard substance into a fine powder and soaking it in water until it is soft and flexible.

After this step is completed, the clay can be molded into the shape of the pot. Most often, the pot is carefully molded by hand, using small amounts of water to keep the clay soft and smooth throughout the process. Another popular method, most often used for much larger objects, is to use long coils of clay that can be stacked. A base is made from a flat piece of clay, and the pot is literally built from the ground up by stacking the coils on top of one another. Once molded, the pot is left to dry for a short time before the potter returns to polish it. Polishing involves the use of a small, wet pebble, which is scraped up and down the sides of the pot at a rapid pace. This ensures that there are no imperfections such as air bubbles in the clay, which can ruin the pot when it goes into the firing stage.

Designs for the pot are often in the form of pictures or shapes that are scratched into the clay surface with a special tool. ①This process is known as scraffito, and it must be done very carefully, ②because marks that are too shallow may not show up after firing, ③while marks that are too deep risk breaking the inner surface, which can cause the pot to shatter when heated. Traditional designs often feature the Avanyul, a feathered serpent from Hopi folklore, and several other symbols that have a personal, spiritual significance to the potter, such as wolves or waterfowl. Painting is not uncommon either, and is traditionally done with a piece of a yucca plant that has been chewed at one end to form a brush.

Finally, the pot is placed in a shallow pit to be fired. **A** Q04 Placed on a bed of large broken pottery shards, the pot is then covered further with more shards. **B** **The space between the pieces allows air to pass into the furnace and feed the flames.** The whole arrangement is then covered with a mound of dried cow or sheep feces, and wood is used to set the feces ablaze. **C** The potter recites a traditional prayer for good luck in completing her work of art, as any number of things can go wrong during the firing. **D** A gust of wind, for instance, can blow ashes or feces onto the pot which may stick to the clay, ruining the design of the pot and the many days of work that went into shaping it. After several hours of cooking, the pot is hardened and ready for use.

호피 인디언의 도기

남서아메리카 호피 인디언 족의 도기는 가장 찬란한 아메리카 원주민 전통 중 하나이다. 호피족과 그 인근 부족들은 2,000년 전부터 도기를 만들기 시작했으며, 그 전통 도기 제조 방식은 그 이래로 거의 변하지 않았다. 호피족 문화에서 도공은 대개 여자가 담당하는데, 우선 도자기 만들기에 필요한 점토를 확보해야 한다. 점토는 전통적으로 땅에 작은 구덩이를 파는 단순한 방법으로 집 근처에서 채취한다. 큰 규모의 채취장도 존재하긴 하지만, 점토가 주로 신성한 물질로 여겨지기 때문에, 부족 일원들은 그중 많은 곳을 외부인에게 비밀로 유지한다. 땅에서 점토를 채취할 때는 신령에게 전통 기도를 올린다. 며칠에 걸쳐 점토는 사용할 수 있는 상태가 되도록 준비되어야 하는데, 이 작업은 여자들이 딱딱한 입자를 갈아서 고운 가루로 만들고 부드럽고 유연해질 때까지 물에 담가 놓는 방식으로 행해진다.

이 단계가 끝나면, 점토는 도자기 형태로 만들어질 수 있다. 대부분의 경우 전 과정 내내 점토를 부드럽고 매끄럽게 유지하기 위해 도자기는 소량의 물을 사용해서 손으로 조심스럽게 만들어진다. 또 하나 많이 쓰이는 방법은, 대개 훨씬 더 큰 도기를 만들 때 쓰이는 방법인데 점토를 긴 코일 형태로 켜켜이 쌓는 것이다. 바닥은 점토를 납작하게 편 조각으로 만들며, 도자기는 바닥에서부터 위로 말 그대로 코일을 하나하나 쌓아서 만든다. 일단 도자기 모양이 만들어지면, 도공이 다시 다듬기 전까지 잠시 두어 말린다. 다듬는 과정에는 작고 축축한 조약돌을 사용하는데, 조약돌로 도자기 표면을 위아래로 빠른 속도로 문지른다. 이것은 점토에 공기 방울과 같은 불순물을 확실하게 제거하는데, 불순물은 굽는 단계에서 도자기를 망칠 수도 있다.

도자기의 문양은 그림이나 형상의 형태인 경우가 많으며, 특별한 도구로 점토 표면을 긁어서 만든다. 이 과정은 스크라피토라고 알려져 있으며 매우 주의해서 행해져야 하는데, 그 이유는 긁힌 정도가 너무 얕으면 구운 다음 문양이 안 보일 수도 있고, 반면 긁힌 정도가 너무 깊으면 도자기 내부 표면에 균열이 생겨 구울 때 도자기가 산산조각이 날 수도 있기 때문이다. 전통적 문양으로는 호피 민속신앙에 등장하는 깃털 달린 뱀인 아바뉼이 쓰일 때가 많으며, 늑대나 물새 등 도공에게 개인적·영적으로 의미가 있는 다른 상징물도 여럿 쓰인다. 그림을 그려 넣는 방법도 드물지 않게 쓰이며, 전통적으로 유카 식물 한쪽 끝을 씹어 붓 형태로 만든 도구를 써서 행해졌다.

마지막으로 도자기를 굽기 위해 얕은 구덩이 안에 놓는다. **A** 깨진 큰 도자기 파편 조각들 위에 놓인 이 도자기는 더 많은 도자기 파편들로 덮인다. **B** **조각들 사이의 공간은 공기가 화로 속으로 들어가 불길을 계속 유지하게 한다.** 이렇게 모두 준비되고 나면, 소나 양의 말린 배설물로 다시 덮으며, 나무를 사용해 그 배설물을 타오르게 한다. **C** 작품이 완성되기까지 도공은 행운을 빌기 위해 전통 기도문을 읊는데, 많은 것들이 굽는 동안 잘못되는 경우가 빈번하기 때문이다. **D** 예를 들어, 돌풍은 재나 배설물이 도자기로 날아가 점토에 붙어, 도자기의 문양과 그 형태를 빚느라 들인 여러 날의 시간을 허사로 만들 수 있다. 몇 시간 동안 굽고 나면, 도자기는 단단해지고 사용될 수 있다.

01 지문에서 them 이 가리키는 것은?
(A) 작은 구덩이
(B) 채취장
(C) 일원
(D) 외부인

해설 | Reference 큰 규모의 채취장(mines)도 존재하지만, 그중(them) 많은 곳을 외부인에게 비밀로 유지했다는 문장에서 them 은 mines를 가리킴을 알 수 있다.

02 지문의 flexible 과 의미상 가장 가까운 것은?
(A) 유연한
(B) 깨지기 쉬운
(C) 촘촘한
(D) 무거운

해설 | Vocabulary 딱딱한 물질을 갈아서 고운 가루로 만든 다음 물에 적시면 그 결과 딱딱한 것이 부드럽고(soft) 말랑말랑해질 것이다. 이를 통해 flexible 은 '유연한'의 의미임을 유추할 수 있다.

03 다음 중 지문에서 표시된 문장의 주요 정보를 가장 잘 나타낸 문장은? *정답 외의 보기들은 중요한 의미가 바뀌거나 주요 정보가 빠져 있다.*

(A) 문양을 너무 깊게 새기면 도자기를 손상시킬 수 있고, 문양을 너무 얕게 새기면 구운 후에 나타나지 않을 수도 있으므로, 스크라피토는 매우 주의해서 행해져야 한다.
(B) 도자기가 오븐에 들어갈 때 깨지지 않게 하려면 스크라피토로 도자기를 장식하는 일을 조심해서 해야 한다.
(C) 점토에 충분히 깊이 새겨지지 않은 문양은 도자기를 구울 때 사라지는 일이 많으므로, 스크라피토는 표면에서 깊게 새겨져야 한다.
(D) 스크라피토는 잘못하다 도자기를 망칠 수 있는 위험스런 작업이기 때문에, 대부분은 이를 과정에서 가장 필요 없는 단계로 여긴다.

해설 | Sentence Simplification 표시된 문장은 크게 세 의미로 나눌 수 있다. ① 스크라피토는 주의가 필요한 작업이다. ② 문양을 너무 얕게 새기면 나중에 문양이 제대로 드러나지 않는다. ③ 문양을 너무 깊게 새기면 도자기를 구울 때 깨질 수 있다.

04 다음 문장이 지문에 들어갈 곳을 나타내는 네 개의 사각형[■]을 보시오.

조각들 사이의 공간은 공기가 화로 속으로 들어가 불길을 계속 유지하게 한다.

이 문장이 들어갈 가장 적절한 위치는?
(A) A (B) B (C) C (D) D

해설 | Sentence Insertion 삽입 문장에서 조각 사이의 공간(The space between the pieces)이 의미하는 것은 단락 4의 두 번째 문장의 깨진 도자기 조각(broken pottery shards) 더미의 틈새를 가리킨다.

05 지문을 간략히 요약하기 위한 도입 문장이 아래 제시되어 있다. 지문에서 가장 중요한 내용을 표현한 세 개의 문장을 골라 요약문을 완성하시오. 일부 문장은 지문에 나오지 않았거나 중요하지 않은 내용이기 때문에 요약문에 포함되지 않는다. *이 문제는 2점이다.*

호피족 인디언들의 전통 도기를 만드는 길고 집중적인 과정은 수백 년 동안 거의 변하지 않고 유지되었다.

(A) 점토가 적절한 상태가 되면, 손으로 만들어지거나 긴 띠로 만들어 쌓아 올려진다.
(B) 전통적으로 호피족 사회에서 도기를 만들 기회는 남자나 여자에게 모두 비슷하게 주어지지만, 대개는 여자가 도기 만드는 일을 한다.
(C) 도공은 직접 문양을 새겨 넣거나 색칠을 하여 도자기 표면에 문양을 넣는다.
(D) 도기에 그림을 그리는 경우에는, 일반적으로 도공에게 영적인 의미가 있는 동물의 이미지가 쓰인다.
(E) 점토 표면의 아주 작은 결함은, 도자기가 오븐에서 구워질 때 깨지도록 할 수 있다.
(F) 마지막 단계에서 도자기는 도기 조각과 동물 배설물로 덮이며, 사용될 수 있는 상태로 단단해지기까지 불에 구워진다.

해설 | Summary (A)는 점토를 도자기로 빚어내는 과정을 설명한 단락 2에 대한 내용을, (C)는 도자기의 문양에 관한 단락 3에 대한 내용을, (F)는 도자기를 구워내는 단락 4에 대한 내용을 요약한 것이다.

어휘 | **pottery** 도기, 도자기 **vibrant** 찬란한, 힘찬 **clay** 점토, 찰흙 **pot** 도자기, 냄비 **sacred** 신성한, 성스러운 **prayer** 기도, 기도하는 사람 **condition** ~에 맞게 준비하다 **grind** 갈다 **substance** 입자, 물질 **soak** 물에 담그다, 흠뻑 적시다 **mold** (틀에 넣어) …을 만들다 **stack** 쌓다, 쌓아 올리다 **polish** 다듬다 **pebble** 조약돌, 자갈 **imperfection** 불순물, 결함 **bubble** 공기 방울 **shallow** 얕은 **folklore** 민속신앙, 민속학 **shard** 도자기의 파편 **feces** 배설물 **recite** 읊다, 낭송하다 **gust of wind** 돌풍

iBT Practice   p.140

01 (C) 02 (A) 03 (B) 04 (C) 05 (D) 06 (B) 07 (A) 08 (D) 09 (C) 10 (D) 11 (B) 12 (D)
13 (B), (C), (D)

DADA

The course of Western art forever changed after World War I. **Q03** The brutality and violence of the war affected an entire generation of young poets, writers, painters, and other artists. They were disappointed that Western ideals like peace and democracy had not prevented such violence. The outrage felt by these artists gave rise to the most subversive art movement the world had ever seen. Its practitioners called it Dada, and it stood for everything that art was not; it was, in a sense, "anti-art." **Q10(C)** Instead of pleasing the tastes of viewers, Dada artists sought to shock and offend them. **Q01 Q10(B)** Dadaists sought to challenge people's traditional beliefs by challenging the ways in which they viewed art. Dada artists wanted not only to change the art world, but to change the beliefs and attitudes of the people as well. **Q02** Throughout its short history, Dada spread to several cities around the world, taking on a new and unique form wherever it appeared.

Dada was begun by a small group of artists in Zurich, Switzerland. **Q04** Switzerland was neutral in the war, and it was a refuge for people from nearby warring countries such as Germany and Austria. Artists moved to Switzerland both to escape the war and to protest it. The movement centered on a local nightclub called the Cabaret Voltaire, where performance art was the main attraction. **Q05 Q11(D)** In one early performance, poet Hugo Ball read three pieces of experimental poetry while bouncing around the stage in a costume made of cardboard cylinders and a pair of cardboard wings. In short, the performance was completely absurd, and **Q06** audiences left the club both shocked and confused at such disregard for their own pleasure. This, of course, was Ball's intention. Similar performances at the Cabaret included many important artists who would later go on to achieve great fame. One of them was Max Ernst, who, with the help of fellow artists, established a Dada group in Cologne, Germany shortly after the war.

A From Zurich, some members of the original Dada group moved to New York City to join an already thriving community of Dada artists there. **B** The atmosphere in New York was much different from that of Zurich and Cologne. **C Q07-1 Q12** New York artists practiced what was perhaps the most playful form of Dada to date. **D** These artists were less burdened by the violence in Europe, and the result was this relatively carefree attitude. **Q07-2** Whereas cynicism played a major role in European Dada, irony and humor were important to the New York scene. The basic goals, however, remained the same: the creation of anti-art that challenged the beliefs of mainstream society. **Q11(A)** French artist Marcel Duchamp created one of the best-known artworks here, a sculpture called *Fountain*, which featured an overturned bathroom urinal. Audiences reacted with disgust to the piece, and the work was almost universally reviled by the mainstream art community. However, it did spark a great deal of lively debate, as the artist had hoped it would.

다다

제1차 세계 대전 후 서양 예술의 행로는 완전한 변화를 겪었다. 전쟁의 잔인성과 폭력성은 젊은 시인, 작가, 화가 및 다른 예술가들의 세대 전체에 영향을 미쳤다. 그들은 평화와 민주주의와 같은 서구의 이상향이 이러한 폭력을 막지 못한 데에 실망하였다. 이런 예술가들이 느낀 분노는 전 세계가 한 번도 보지 못했던 가장 전복적인 예술 운동을 일으켰다. 이를 실천하는 이들은 이런 예술을 다다라고 불렀는데, 다다는 예술이 아닌 모든 것을 나타내는 개념으로, 즉 '반(反) 예술'을 의미했다. 다다 예술가들은 관람객들의 취향을 만족시켜 주는 대신, 관객에게 충격을 주고 불쾌감을 줄 방법을 찾았다. 다다 예술가들은 그들이 예술을 바라보는 방법에 도전하는 것으로 사람들의 전통적 믿음에 도전하고자 했다. 다다 예술가들은 예술 세계만이 아니라 사람들의 믿음과 태도도 바꾸고자 했다. 이것의 짧은 역사 동안, 다다는 나타나는 곳마다 새롭고 독특한 형태를 취하며 세계 전역의 도시로 퍼져나갔다.

다다는 스위스의 취리히에 있던 작은 예술가 집단에서 시작되었다. 스위스가 전쟁에서 중립이었기 때문에, 독일과 오스트리아와 같은 전쟁 중이던 인근 나라 사람들에게 피난처가 되었다. 예술가들은 전쟁을 피하는 동시에 전쟁에 반대하기 위해 스위스로 이주했다. 다다 예술 운동은 카바레 볼테르라는 지역 나이트클럽이 중심이 되었는데, 이곳에선 행위예술이 주 관심사였다. 초기에 행해졌던 한 공연 중에 시인 Hugo Ball은 판지로 만든 원통 복장을 하고 판지 날개를 달고서 무대를 뛰어다니면서 실험적 시 세 편을 낭독했다. 한 마디로 그 공연은 완전히 터무니없었고, 관객들은 자신들의 즐거움을 경시한 그런 공연을 보고 충격과 혼란에 휩싸여 클럽을 나섰다. 물론 이것은 바로 Ball이 의도한 바였다. 그 카바레에서의 비슷한 공연들에는 훗날 대단한 명성을 얻은 많은 중요한 예술가들이 포함되어 있었다. 그중 하나는 Max Ernst로, 그는 전쟁이 끝난 직후에 다른 동료 예술가들의 도움을 받아 독일의 쾰른에 다다 예술 집단을 창설했다.

A 초기 다다 예술 집단의 멤버 일부는 취리히를 떠나 뉴욕으로 이주했는데, 이는 이곳에서 이미 번성한 다다 예술가 집단에 참여하기 위함이었다. **B** 뉴욕의 분위기는 취리히나 쾰른의 분위기와는 사뭇 달랐다. **C** 뉴욕의 예술가들은 아마도 역사상 가장 익살스러운 형태라고 할 수 있는 다다 예술을 구현했다. **D** 이 예술가들은 유럽의 폭력성으로 인한 부담을 덜 받았고, 그 결과로 비교적 심각하지 않은 태도를 지닐 수 있었다. 유럽의 다다 예술에서 냉소주의가 주요 역할을 했다면, 뉴욕에서는 아이러니와 유머가 중요한 역할을 했다. 그렇지만 기본 목표는 모두 같았는데, 바로 주류 사회의 믿음에 도전하는 반예술의 확립이 그것이었다. 프랑스 예술가 Marcel Duchamp은 가장 유명한 예술품 중 하나로 알려진 조각상 〈샘〉을 창작했는데, 이것은 뒤집힌 화장실 소변기를 나타낸 것이었다. 관객들은 이 작품에 혐오감을 드러냈고, 거의 모든 주류 예술 집단으로부터 경멸을 받았다. 그러나 어쨌든 이 작품은 원작자가 바랐던 대로 매우 큰 논란의 발단이 되었다.

Q10(D) Artists in Paris had been closely following the work of various Dada groups around the world, but a real movement of Dada did not begin in Paris until 1920, when several of the movement's original members moved there. For many years prior to this, the city had held a stronger reputation for its literature than for its art. However, once an array of artists began pouring into the city, Dada succeeded in Paris more than in any other city. Q10(A)-1 Writers such as Andre Breton took up the cause of the Dadaists and published essays on the Dada philosophy. Q10(A)-2 Q11(C) French painter Jean Crotti held the first exhibition of Dada paintings at the Society of Independent Artists. Q10(A)-3 Composer Erik Satie collaborated with Pablo Picasso and others to create one of the most bizarre and scandalous ballets of the time. ①Whereas most ballets include graceful dancing and beautiful music, ②Satie and Picasso's ballet featured Cubist-style sets, an orchestra of noisemaking instruments, and costumes so large and awkward that few of the dancers could move with ease. Despite the wide array of art produced in Paris, the Dada movement began to go out of style in 1922, and by 1924 it had all but disappeared. Though Dada may be gone, the lasting influence of Dada can still be found in modern styles of music such as punk rock, and it is also alive and well in many modern art films.

파리의 예술가들은 그때까지 세계 전역의 다양한 다다 예술가 집단의 동향을 관심 있게 주시해왔지만, 파리에서의 진정한 다다 운동은 다다 초기 멤버들 몇몇이 파리로 이주해온 1920년이 되어서야 시작되었다. 이전에 파리는 수년 동안 예술보다 문학에 대한 명성이 더 강했다. 그러나 다수의 예술가가 파리로 몰려오기 시작하자, 파리의 다다는 다른 어떤 도시에서보다 더 크게 번창하였다. Andre Breton 같은 작가들은 다다이스트들의 이념을 받아들여 다다 철학에 대한 수필을 출판하였다. 프랑스 화가인 Jean Crotti는 독립예술가 사회에서 최초로 다다 미술품 전시회를 열었다. 작곡가인 Erik Satie는 Pablo Picasso 등 다른 예술가들과 협력하여 그 시대의 가장 기이하고 물의를 빚은 발레 공연을 창작했다. 대부분 발레 공연이 우아한 춤동작과 아름다운 음악을 동반하는 데 반해, Satie와 Picasso의 발레 공연은 입체파 스타일의 세트와 소음을 내는 악기로 구성된 오케스트라, 그리고 너무 크고 어색해서 무용수들이 편하게 움직일 수 없었던 의상으로 이루어졌다. 파리에서 이렇게 넓은 방면으로 많은 예술이 만들어졌음에도 불구하고, 1992년에 이르러 다다 예술운동은 인기를 잃기 시작하고, 1924년에 이르러서는 거의 소멸하게 되었다. 비록 다다는 사라졌을지 모르지만, 다다의 지속적인 영향은 펑크록 같은 현대 음악에서 아직 찾을 수 있으며, 다수의 현대 예술 영화에서도 여전히 살아 있다.

01 지문에서 they 가 가리키는 것은?
(A) 예술가들
(B) 믿음들
(C) 사람들
(D) 다다 예술가들

해설 | Reference "Dadaists sought to challenge people's traditional beliefs by challenging the ways in which they viewed art"에서 밑줄 친 부분을 비교해 볼 때, 둘 다 동사가 challenge이고, traditional belief와 the ways in which they viewed art는 서로 일맥상통하는 내용이다. 이를 바탕으로 they 가 people을 가리킨다는 것을 알 수 있다.

02 지문에서 its 가 가리키는 것은?
(A) 다다
(B) 예술계
(C) 형식
(D) 역사

해설 | Reference 이것의(its) 짧은 역사 동안, 다다는 나타나는 곳마다 새롭고 독특한 형태를 취하며 세계전역의 도시로 퍼져나갔다는 내용을 보아 its 가 가리키는 것은 다다임을 알 수 있다.

03 단락 1에 따르면, 제1차 세계 대전이 예술가들에게 미친 영향에 대해 추론할 수 있는 것은?
(A) 많은 유명한 예술가들의 죽음을 초래했다.
(B) 예술가들이 사회에 대한 믿음을 상실하게끔 했다.
(C) 예술가들의 표현의 자유를 제한했다.
(D) 예술로 생계를 유지하기가 더욱 어려워졌다.

해설 | Inference 예술가들은 제1차 세계 대전의 잔인함을 목격하고 평화와 민주주의 사상이 폭력을 막지 못한 것에 대해 분노했다. 이를 바탕으로 그들이 전쟁으로 인해 자신들의 사회에 대한 믿음을 상실했음을 알 수 있다.

04 지문의 refuge 와 의미상 가장 가까운 것은?
(A) 경로
(B) 예배실
(C) 피난처
(D) 여행

해설 | Vocabulary 스위스는 전쟁에서 중립적인 태도를 보인 국가였고, 예술가들이 전쟁을 피해 스위스로 왔다는 사실에서 refuge 는 '피난처'의 의미임을 알 수 있다.

05 지문의 absurd 와 의미상 가장 가까운 것은?
(A) 청소년의
(B) 잔인한
(C) 천박한
(D) 터무니없는

해설 | Vocabulary 그 공연이 absurd 했는데, 그 공연이 판지로 만든 복장으로 하는 공연이었다고 했으므로 absurd 는 '터무니없는'이라는 의미임을 유추할 수 있다.

06 지문에서 This 가 가리키는 것은?

(A) Ball 공연의 모순
(B) Ball 공연에 대한 관객들의 반응
(C) 공연가가 큰 명성을 얻음
(D) 새로운 예술 운동의 시초

해설 | Reference This 앞에 있는 "… audiences left the club both shocked and confused at such disregard for their own pleasure"를 가장 잘 요약한 어구는 Ball 공연에 대한 관객들의 반응이다.

07 단락 3에 따르면, 뉴욕의 다다 예술 운동이 다른 도시들과 달랐던 점은?

(A) 다른 곳보다 좀 더 명랑했다.
(B) 세계의 관심을 더 많이 끌었다.
(C) 그곳의 예술가들은 다른 대부분의 예술가들보다 더 유명했다.
(D) 다다 예술 운동의 마지막을 장식했다.

해설 | Factual Information 뉴욕의 다다는 유럽의 다다에 비해 덜 심각하고 웃음을 유발하려는 측면이 많았다.

08 지문의 collaborated 와 의미상 가장 가까운 것은?

(A) 경쟁했다
(B) 의사소통했다
(C) 동의하지 않았다
(D) 협동했다

해설 | Vocabulary collaborated 는 '협동했다'는 의미로 쓰였다.

09 다음 중 지문에서 표시된 문장의 주요 정보를 가장 잘 나타낸 문장은? 정답 외의 보기들은 중요한 의미가 바뀌거나 주요 정보가 빠져 있다.

(A) Satie와 Picasso는 본래의 우아한 발레 춤과 음악에 입체파 스타일의 기호를 더했다.
(B) Satie와 Picasso는 정통 발레에 실험적 변경을 시도하긴 했지만, 관중들은 입체파 스타일의 발레에 무관심했다.
(C) 섬세한 전통 발레와는 반대로, Satie와 Picasso의 입체파 스타일 발레는 비정형의 배경으로 구성되었다.
(D) 전통 발레에 입체파를 더하려는 Satie와 Picasso의 노력은 가장 혁신적인 접근법 중 하나로 여겨진다.

해설 | Sentence Simplification 표시된 문장은 크게 두 의미로 나뉠 수 있다. ① 대부분 발레 공연이 우아한 춤동작과 아름다운 음악을 동반한다. ② Satie와 Picasso의 발레 공연은 입체파 스타일의 무대 장치와 너무 크고 어색해서 무용수들이 편하게 움직일 수 없었던 의상으로 이루어졌다.

10 지문에 따르면, 다다에 관한 내용으로 옳지 않은 것은?

(A) 문학, 순수미술, 발레 등 다양한 예술 장르를 포함했다.
(B) 주류 사회의 믿음과 전통적인 예술에 대한 반발로 나타났다.
(C) 다다 예술가들은 관객의 취향을 충족시키지 않았다.
(D) 다다는 프랑스에서 처음 생겨나 다른 도시들로 퍼졌다.

해설 | Negative Fact 프랑스는 다른 곳보다 상대적으로 늦게 다다 운동이 시작되었다.

11 지문에서 다다 예술 작품으로 언급되지 않은 것은?

(A) 조각상
(B) 패션
(C) 그림
(D) 시

해설 | Negative Fact (A)는 단락 3에 나온 Duchamp의 〈샘〉에서 언급되었고, (C)는 단락 4의 프랑스 화가 Jean Crotti에 대한 내용에서, (D)는 단락 2에서 Hugo Ball의 실험적인 시에 대한 내용에서 언급되었다. 패션에 관한 내용은 언급되지 않았다.

12 다음 문장이 지문에 들어갈 곳을 나타내는 네 개의 사각형[■]을 보시오.

> 이 예술가들은 유럽의 폭력성으로 인한 부담을 덜 받았고, 그 결과로 비교적 심각하지 않은 태도를 지닐 수 있었다.

이 문장이 들어갈 가장 적절한 위치는?

(A) A (B) B (C) C (D) D

해설 | Sentence Insertion 삽입 문장의 These artists는 이전 문장의 New York artists를 가리키며, 삽입 문장은 뉴욕 예술가들의 다다가 유럽의 다다에 비해 익살스러울 수 있었던 이유가 될 수 있다.

13 지문을 간략히 요약하기 위한 도입 문장이 아래 제시되어 있다. 지문에서 가장 중요한 내용을 표현한 세 개의 문장을 골라 요약문을 완성하시오. 일부 문장은 지문에 나오지 않았거나 중요하지 않은 내용이기 때문에 요약문에 포함되지 않는다. *이 문제는 2점이다.*

> 다다는 전통적인 예술과 사회에 대한 개념을 흔들려고 시도한 세계적인 예술 운동이었다.

(A) 제1차 세계 대전은 파리, 취리히, 심지어는 뉴욕에 있는 예술가들에게까지 본국에 대한 긍지를 나타낼 수 있는 좀 더 애국적인 예술을 창조하도록 영감을 불어넣었다.
(B) 예술가 단체는 취리히에서 전복적인 예술인 다다 운동을 만들어냈고, 그들은 터무니없는 공연으로 관객들에게 충격을 주었다.
(C) 유럽의 다다 운동은 심각하고 냉소적인 것이 특징인 것에 반해, 미국의 다다는 아이러니와 유머와 같은 독특한 특성을 지녔다.
(D) 다다는 파리에서 그 절정에 이르렀는데, 이곳에서는 예술가들이 협력하여 기이한 형태의 다다 발레를 상연했다.
(E) 스위스가 전쟁 당시 중립적 태도를 보임으로써, 취리히는 예술 운동이 시작될 수 있는 이상적 도시가 되었다.
(F) 프랑스 화가 Jean Crotti가 최초로 다다 그림 전시회를 개최함에 따라, 다다는 다른 도시들보다 파리에서 가장 성공했다.

해설 | Summary (B)는 취리히에서 열렸던 행위예술에 관한 내용을 설명한 단락 2의 내용을, (C)는 뉴욕의 다다에 대해 설명한 단락 3의 내용을, (D)는 프랑스의 다다에 대해 설명한 단락 4의 내용을 요약한 것이다.

어휘 | **brutality** 잔인성 **outrage** 분노 **subversive** 전복적인 **taste** 취향 **offend** 불쾌감을 주다 **challenge** 도전하다 **unique** 독특한 **performance art** 행위예술 **absurd** 터무니없는 **disregard** 경시 **intention** 의도 **establish** 창설하다 **thrive** 번성하다, 잘 자라다 **cynicism** 냉소주의 **irony** 아이러니 **overturned** 뒤집힌 **urinal** 소변기 **disgust** 혐오감, 반감 **revile** 경멸하다 **spark** 발단이 되다 **reputation** 명성, 평판 **array** 다수 **pour** 몰려들다 **collaborate** 협력하다 **bizarre** 기괴한 **scandalous** 물의를 빚는 **graceful** 우아한 **awkward** 어색한

Chapter 12 Life Science I

Intensive Drill 1   p.146

01 (B)   02 (C)   03 (A)   04 (B)   05 (B), (C), (E)

SLEEP DEPRIVATION

Sleep is an essential part of our mental and physical health, so a lack of adequate sleep can be physically and mentally detrimental to our health. Physically speaking, our body needs sleep to recover and rejuvenate. Q01-1 Because our body releases human growth hormone, HGH, when it is sleeping, this enables our body to maintain healthy muscle mass, thicker skin, and stronger bones. Q01-2 Q02(D) However, poor sleep habits reduce the amount of HGH that is released, which has an effect on the physical health and strength of muscles, skin, and bones. Q02(A) In addition, with little sleep, our body is typically under greater amounts of stress and Q02(B) releases the stress hormone cortisol, which in excess amounts can start to break down collagen, the critical protein in our skin that keeps it elastic.

In addition, lack of sleep has been correlated with an increase in appetite and cravings for certain high-fat and high-carbohydrate foods. There is a link between sleep and the peptides that regulate appetite, and when the amount of sleep is reduced, the levels and effectiveness of the peptides are altered detrimentally. Research shows that people who get less than six hours of sleep a night are 30 percent more likely to be overweight. The increased chance to become overweight also raises the risk of problems with our cardiovascular system. Because sleep has a vital role in our body's ability to repair our blood vessels and heart, its deprivation can lead to higher risk of chronic health problems such as high blood pressure, heart disease, and strokes.

Above all, the most obvious effect poor sleep has is on our cognitive abilities. Q03-1 Poor sleep affects our everyday life with impaired alertness, concentration, reasoning, and problem solving. It gets in the way of our decision-making process and stifles creativity too. Q03-2 Obviously, this has the greatest impact on students. It has been shown that students with minor sleep deprivation tend to receive lower grades compared to students who get sufficient sleep. Also, studies have shown that a lack of sleep and Q03-3 poor-quality sleep actually lead to an increase in accidents on the job. Factory workers reported a greater frequency of accidents, and drivers operating cars and heavy machinery under the effects of little sleep have been shown to have the same reaction times as drunk drivers.

A Likewise, lack of sleep makes it harder to recall and assimilate past knowledge with new knowledge and experiences, while sufficient sleep helps to consolidate memories. B **Sleep deprivation can also affect how we interpret events and the world around us.** In particular, sleep-deprived people are particularly poor at recognizing and assessing how their lack of sleep is affecting them physically and emotionally. C This is particularly concerning for people who work in professions such as judges, airline pilots, or doctors, where they must constantly assess their ability to perform their tasks safely and accurately. D

수면 부족

수면은 우리의 정신적·신체적 건강에서 중요한 부분을 차지하며, 적절한 수면의 부족은 신체적·정신적 건강에 해로울 수 있다. 신체적으로 말하자면, 우리의 몸은 회복과 원기 회복을 위해 수면이 필요하다. 우리의 몸은 잠을 잘 때 인간 성장 호르몬인 HGH를 분비하는데, 이것은 건강한 근육량, 두꺼운 피부, 튼튼한 뼈를 유지할 수 있게 해준다. 그러나 좋지 않은 수면 습관은 분비되는 HGH 양을 줄어들게 하여 근육, 피부, 그리고 뼈의 신체적인 건강에 영향을 미치게 된다. 또한 수면 부족으로 인해 우리 몸은 굉장한 스트레스를 받게 되어 스트레스 호르몬인 코르티솔을 분비하게 되는데, 과도한 양의 코르티솔은 피부를 탄력 있게 해주는 중요한 단백질인 콜라겐을 파괴하기 시작한다.

게다가 수면 부족은 식욕을 북돋워 고지방·고탄수화물 음식을 갈망하게 하는 것과 연관이 있다. 식욕을 통제하는 펩티드와 수면은 연관되어 있어, 수면양이 줄어들게 되면 펩티드의 수치와 효율성이 해롭게 바뀌게 된다. 한 연구결과에 따르면 6시간 미만의 수면을 취하는 사람은 과체중이 될 확률이 30%나 더 높은 경향이 있다고 한다. 과체중이 될 확률이 높아질수록 심혈관 체계에 문제를 일으킬 확률도 높아진다. 수면은 우리의 혈관과 심장 기능을 회복하는 중요한 역할을 하고 있으므로, 수면 부족은 고혈압, 심장병, 그리고 뇌졸중과 같은 만성적인 건강 질환 발생 위험을 높일 수 있다.

무엇보다 수면 부족의 가장 명백한 영향은 인지 능력에 대한 것이다. 수면 부족은 일상생활의 민첩성, 집중력, 추론력, 그리고 문제 해결 능력을 손상시킨다. 이것은 우리의 의사 결정 과정을 방해하고 창의력 또한 줄어들게 한다. 명백하게도, 수면 부족은 학생들에게 가장 큰 영향을 끼친다. 수면이 부족한 학생들은 충분히 잠을 자는 학생들에 비해 낮은 학점을 받는 경향을 보였다. 또한, 연구들은 수면 부족 혹은 질 낮은 수면이 일터에서도 잦은 사건 사고로 이어짐을 보여주었다. 공장 근로자들은 더 빈번한 사고를 냈으며, 수면이 부족한 상태로 자동차 혹은 중장비를 운전하는 기사들은 음주 운전자와 동일한 반응 시간을 보였다.

A 마찬가지로 수면 부족은 과거의 지식을 상기해내고 새로운 지식과 경험에 동화시키는 것을 어렵게 만든다. 반면에 충분한 수면은 기억을 강화시키는 것을 돕는다. B **수면 부족은 우리 주변의 사건과 세계를 이해하는 데에도 영향을 미친다.** 특히 수면이 부족한 사람들은 수면 부족이 그들에게 신체적, 감정적으로 어떠한 영향을 미치고 있는지를 인식하고 가늠하는 것에 취약하다. C 이것은 특히 일을 안전하고 정확하게 수행하기 위해 자신들의 능력을 끊임없이 검토해야 하는 판사, 비행기 조종사, 의사와 같은 전문직 종사자들에 있어 더욱 그러하다. D

01
지문의 reduces와 의미상 가장 가까운 것은?

(A) 신장시키다
(B) 줄이다
(C) 바꾸다
(D) 막다

해설 | Vocabulary 앞에서 HGH는 잠을 잘 때 분비된다고 했으므로, 수면 부족 습관은 HGH를 '줄어들게(reduces)' 한다는 것을 알 수 있다. 이 의미와 가장 가까운 단어는 (B)이다.

02
단락 1에서 언급되지 않은 것은?

(A) 우리의 몸은 충분한 수면이 부족할 때 굉장한 스트레스를 받는다.
(B) 코르티솔이 과다하게 되면 콜라겐을 파괴한다.
(C) 콜라겐은 근육과 피부, 뼈의 힘을 증대시킨다.
(D) 수면 부족은 분비되는 HGH 양을 감소시킨다.

해설 | Negative Fact 단락 1에서 수면 부족은 스트레스 호르몬인 코르티솔을 분비하게 하고, 코르티솔은 콜라겐을 파괴한다고 했다. 또한 수면 부족은 인간의 성장 호르몬인 HGH의 양을 줄인다고 설명하고 있다.

03
단락 3에서 추론할 수 있는 것은?

(A) 충분한 수면은 일과 학교에서 성공하기 위해 필수이다.
(B) 더 높은 학점을 받는 학생들은 시간을 잘 관리한다.
(C) 수면 부족은 기대 수명을 줄어들게 한다.
(D) 수면 부족의 정도는 직업군에 의해 결정된다.

해설 | Inference 단락 3에서 수면 부족은 인지 능력에 큰 영향을 미치며 학생들의 학점과 일에서의 실수 발생 정도와 관련이 있다고 하였다.

04
다음 문장이 지문에 들어갈 곳을 나타내는 네 개의 사각형[■]을 보시오.

> 수면 부족은 우리 주변의 사건과 세계를 이해하는 데에도 영향을 미친다.

이 문장이 들어갈 가장 적절한 위치는?
(A) A   (B) B   (C) C   (D) D

해설 | Sentence Insertion 삽입 문장의 also로부터 삽입 문장 앞에는 수면 부족이 미치는 영향이 나오고 이후에는 수면 부족이 주위 사건과 세계를 이해하는 데 영향을 미치는 예가 나와야 한다는 것을 알 수 있다.

05
지문을 간략히 요약하기 위한 도입 문장이 아래 제시되어 있다. 지문에서 가장 중요한 내용을 표현한 세 개의 문장을 골라 요약문을 완성하시오. 일부 문장은 지문에 나오지 않았거나 중요하지 않은 내용이기 때문에 요약문에 포함되지 않는다. *이 문제는 2점이다.*

> 수면 부족은 우리 신체와 정신에 지대한 신체적 · 정신적 해를 끼칠 수 있다.

(A) 수면 부족은 집중력, 추리력, 문제 해결 능력에 필요한 콜라겐을 손상시킨다.
(B) 수면 부족은 HGH 양을 줄어들게 하고 스트레스 호르몬인 코르티솔을 분비한다.
(C) 수면 부족은 손상된 펩티드 조절로 식욕을 부추기고 체중의 증가를 일으킨다.
(D) 수면 부족의 악영향은 낮은 점수를 유발할 수 있기에 학생들에게 특히 중대하다.
(E) 잠이 부족할 때 중요 인지 능력과 기억 강화가 손상된다.
(F) 수면이 부족한 사람들은 그것의 악영향을 간과한다.

해설 | Summary (B)는 단락 1을, (C)는 단락 2를, (E)는 단락 3과 4를 요약한 것이다.

어휘 | **physical** 신체의, 육체의   **adequate** 적절한, 적당한   **detrimental** 해로운, 손해를 입히는   **rejuvenate** 원기를 회복하다
muscle 근육   **bone** 뼈   **protein** 단백질   **elastic** 탄력 있는   **correlate** 서로 관련시키다   **appetite** 식욕   **crave for** ~을 갈망하다
carbohydrate 탄수화물   **peptide** 펩티드(두 개 이상의 아미노산 분자로 이뤄지는 화학 물질)   **effectiveness** 효율성, 효과성
be likely to ~할 확률[가능성]이 크다   **overweight** 과체중의, 비만의   **cardiovascular** 심혈관의   **vital** 중요한, 생사가 걸린
blood vessel 혈관   **stroke** 뇌졸중   **obvious** 명백한, 분명한   **cognitive** 인지의, 인식의   **impair** 손상시키다, 해치다
alertness 민첩성, 빈틈없음   **reasoning** 추론력, 추리   **stifle** 줄어들게 하다, 억압하다   **creativity** 창의력   **sufficient** 충분한
heavy machinery 중장비   **recall** 상기하다, 생각해내다   **assimilate** 동화하다   **consolidate** 강화하다   **assess** 검토하다, 평가하다

Intensive Drill 2

01 (B)   02 (A)   03 (C)   04 (A)   05 [Viruses – (A), (E)], [Bacteria – (B), (D)], [Both – (C)]

VIRUSES AND BACTERIA

Bacteria and viruses are often spoken of in similar terms, especially in regard to their ability to cause disease. However, beyond this common trait, the two differ in a number of important ways. For instance, Q05(D)-1 bacteria are living organisms, and as such can survive independently of other living things. Q05(A) Viruses, on the other hand, are inactive unless they find their way into a living host, at which time they are able to grow and reproduce.

One major difference between bacteria and viruses is their composition. Bacteria are the simplest forms of life on Earth, but are rather complex in their makeup when compared to viruses. Like any cell, Q01 a bacterium is surrounded by a protective wall, or membrane, that holds its contents together. 05(C) Inside the membrane is a bundle of DNA that carries the bacterium's genetic information. Viruses are similar in that they also contain genes in the form of either DNA or RNA, though in far smaller quantities. In viruses, however, these materials are contained not in a cell membrane, but in a thinner outer coating of proteins.

Bacteria and viruses also differ greatly in their methods of reproduction. Again, it is Q05(D)-2 the bacterium's status as a single-celled living organism that sets it apart from the virus. Bacteria reproduce asexually through cell division. ① Once they grow to a certain size, the DNA inside splits into two identical structures called progeny cells, ② and slowly the cell breaks apart, with one group of DNA in each new cell. Reproduction of bacteria is limited, however, by the nutrients available in the environment. Viruses, on the other hand, cannot reproduce until they have latched onto a host. After a virus attaches itself to a host cell, the virus works its way into the cell through the membrane. Q05(E) As the virus's protein shell dissolves, the genetic information in the virus is released into the cell where it can reproduce and spread. Q03 Viruses will continue to reproduce rapidly until the host's resources have been completely used up, at which time they will simply look for a new host.

A Most types of bacteria are beneficial to humans, and not all viruses carry disease, but both can be harmful when they disrupt the normal functions of the human body. Q04 Diseases caused by viruses range from the common cold to HIV, and can be either temporary and relatively harmless or life-long and potentially deadly. B While there is no real cure for viral diseases, vaccines and antiviral drugs can help. C Vaccines introduce a very small portion of the virus into the body, so that if a person does come in contact with the virus, he or she is already immune to its effects. D Antiviral drugs have only come into being in the last 20 years or so, and they work by halting the reproduction of the virus rather than killing it. Q05(B) Bacterial infections are far easier to treat; antibiotic drugs work with the immune system to quickly kill most infections.

01
지문에서 its가 가리키는 것은?

(A) 세포
(B) 박테리아
(C) 세포막
(D) 구성

해설 | Reference "… a bacterium is surrounded by a protective wall, or membrane, that holds its contents together"에서 세포막(membrane)은 이것(bacterium)의 내용물을 수용하는 역할을 한다. 따라서 its는 bacterium을 가리킨다.

02
다음 중 지문에서 표시된 문장의 주요 정보를 가장 잘 나타낸 문장은?
정답 외의 보기들은 중요한 의미가 바뀌거나 주요 정보가 빠져 있다.

(A) 세포가 커지면서 동일한 두 개의 세포로 각기 분열되고, 각 세포는 원래 세포와 동일한 유전 물질을 포함한다.
(B) 세포가 두 개로 분리되면, 그 DNA가 복제되어 새로운 세포를 만들 수 있을 만큼 커진다.
(C) DNA는 세포 안에서 복제되며, 그 시점에서 세포가 더욱 커져서 결국 두 개의 다른 세포로 분열한다.
(D) 세포는 다른 유전 물질을 포함한 두 개의 개별 세포로 스스로 분열하면서 생식한다.

해설 | Sentence Simplification 표시된 문장은 크게 두 의미로 나뉠 수 있다. ① 일정 크기로 자란 박테리아의 DNA는 두 개의 같은 구조로 분열한다. ② 분열하는 이 구조들은 같은 DNA를 한 세트씩 포함한다.

03
단락 3에 따르면, 바이러스의 번식에 대해 추론할 수 있는 것은?

(A) 늘 일정한 개체 수를 생산한다.
(B) 단세포의 분열을 통해 일어난다.
(C) 살아 있는 숙주가 있으면 끊임없이 번식한다.
(D) 숙주 세포 밖에서 일어날 수 있다.

해설 | Inference 단락 3의 마지막 부분에서 바이러스는 숙주의 영양분이 다 없어질 때까지 번식하고, 영양분이 고갈되면 새로운 숙주를 찾을 거라고 했으므로, 숙주가 충분하면 계속해서 번식할 것임을 추론할 수 있다.

04
다음 문장이 지문에 들어갈 곳을 나타내는 네 개의 사각형[■]을 보시오.

> 대부분 박테리아 종류는 인간에게 이로우며 모든 바이러스가 질병을 옮기지는 않지만, 둘 다 인체의 정상적 기능을 방해하게 되면 해로울 수 있다.

이 문장이 들어갈 가장 적절한 위치는?

(A) A (B) B (C) C (D) D

해설 | Sentence Insertion 삽입 문장은 "… both can be harmful when they disrupt the normal functioning of the human body"에 근거하여 바이러스가 인간에게 일으키는 질병에 대해 처음 언급하고 있는 단락 4의 첫 문장 앞에 위치하는 것이 가장 적절하다.

05
보기에서 적절한 문구를 골라 관련된 미생물의 종과 연결하시오. 보기 중 2개는 사용되지 않는다. *이 문제는 3점이다.*

보기	
(A) 숙주 밖에서는 번식할 수 없다.	바이러스: (A), (E)
(B) 항생제에 의해 치료될 수 있다.	박테리아: (B), (D)
(C) 중심에 DNA 다발이 있다.	둘 다: (C)
(D) 독립적으로 살 수 있는 단세포 생물체이다.	
(E) 세포에 유전 정보를 주입함으로써 번식한다.	
(F) 유전 물질을 보호할 외피가 없다.	
(G) 인체의 기능을 방해하지 않는다.	

해설 | Fill in a Table 바이러스는 숙주 없이는 비활성화되고 세포에 유전 정보를 넣음으로써 번식하는 반면, 박테리아는 항생제로 치료될 수 있고 독립적으로 살 수 있는 단세포 생물이다. 바이러스는 DNA 다발을, 박테리아는 DNA나 RNA의 형태로 유전자 정보를 갖고 있다.

어휘 | term 용어, 말 trait 특징 inactive 비활성의 host 숙주 reproduce 번식하다 composition 구성 make-up 구조 compared to ~에 비해서 protective 보호하는 membrane 세포막 bundle 묶음, 다발 gene 유전자 coating 외피 reproduction 번식 set apart 구별하다 asexually 무성생식으로, 성(性)과 관계없이 cell division 세포 분열 split 분열하다 identical 동일한 nutrient 영양소 latch onto ~에 붙어다니다 attach oneself to ~에 붙어다니다 dissolve 녹다 release 풀다 beneficial 이로운 disrupt 방해하다 harmless 해가 없는 potentially 잠재적으로 deadly 치명적인 viral 바이러스성의 antiviral 항바이러스성의 immune 면역된 halt 멈추다 antibiotic 항생물질의 immune system 면역 체계

Intensive Drill 3

p.150

01 (C)　02 (C)　03 (A)　04 (A)　05 (A), (C), (E)

FEEDING MECHANISMS OF MARINE ORGANISMS

The oceans are vast and cover two-thirds of the Earth's surface. Q02 They are organized into various layers based on depth and the amount of light received from the Sun. Q01 Each layer consists of a different mixture of marine species that are adapted to its light levels, pressures, and temperatures. One such adaptation can be found in the feeding behavior of ocean creatures. Marine organisms adopt various types of distinctive features and feeding mechanisms that acclimate to the environment in different zones of the ocean.

Filter-feeding is one of the most common feeding strategies in aquatic habitats where sunlight penetrates the water. This layer of ocean, also known as the sunlight zone, contains plentiful but tiny organisms that are suspended in water such as plankton and krill, providing the foundation of the marine food chain. Filter-feeding is a method in which animals take in mouthfuls of water, filter out undesirable parts through structures that act as sieves, and swallow the food left in their mouths. Filter feeders range from small creatures like sponges to enormous mammals like blue whales. Each has its own specialized equipment for filter-feeding. For example, immobile organisms like sponges have a water current system made of chambers and canals for water to flow through them. The system pumps in water, filters the food from the water, then expels the water out. Baleen whales, instead of teeth, have fringe-like hair called baleen that traps prey and forces out water. Basking sharks and whale sharks have bristle-like gill rakers that strain food as they swim through the water with their mouths open.

Unlike the sunlight zone, the deep sea or midnight zone lacks sunlight and is as dark as night. Q04-1 Deep-sea organisms living in this layer of ocean have evolved different types of feeding mechanisms for survival. Q03 Due to the absence of photosynthesis, food is scarce and hard to find in deep-sea regions. Q04-2 As a result, deep-sea creatures have developed physical features to ensure that captured prey has little chance of escape. Some have extremely long fang-like teeth that point inward to trap prey up in their mouths. Furthermore, many have large mouths, huge hinged jaws, and bulky and expandable stomachs to capture and process large quantities food at once. Deep-sea creatures do not expend much energy for swimming in search of food. Instead, they either sit and wait for prey or attract prey using clever adaptations such as lures. Anglerfish have a long fin sprouting from middle of their heads, like a fishing rod. By wiggling their fins, anglerfish draw prey close enough for them to ingest as whole. Some anglerfish even emit light at the edge of their fins to seduce more quarries.

바다 생물의 섭식 메커니즘

바다는 광활하며 지구 표면의 3분의 2를 덮는다. 바다는 깊이와 태양으로부터 받는 빛의 양에 따라 다양한 층으로 나뉜다. 각각의 층에는 이것의 햇빛 양, 압력, 그리고 온도에 맞게 적응한 다양한 해양 생물 종들이 혼합되어 있다. 이러한 적응의 한 가지 예로 해양 생물들의 섭식 행동을 들 수 있다. 해양 생명체들은 바다의 각기 다른 층에 적응하기 위해 여러 종류의 독특한 특징과 섭식 메커니즘을 채택했다.

햇빛이 물을 통과하는 바닷속 서식지에서 여과 섭식은 가장 흔한 섭식 전략 중 하나이다. 햇빛 지역이라고도 알려진 이 바다 층은 바다의 먹이 사슬의 기초가 되는 플랑크톤 및 크릴 새우 등의, 개체 수가 풍부하긴 하지만 작은 생물체들이 있는 곳이다. 여과 섭식이란 동물이 입안 가득 물을 마셔 원하지 않은 부분을 체로 거르는 역할을 하는 구조를 통해 내보낸 후, 입에 남은 음식을 삼키는 방법이다. 여과 섭식은 해면과 같이 작은 생명체부터 큰 포유동물인 흰긴수염고래까지 사용하는 방법이다. 각각은 여과 섭식에 자신들만의 특정 방법을 가지고 있다. 예를 들어, 해면과 같이 움직이지 않는 유기체는 물이 왔다 갔다 할 수 있는 공간 및 관으로 만들어진 해류 시스템을 가지고 있다. 이 시스템에서 물이 들어오면 물속의 음식만 걸러 물은 다시 내보내게 한다. 수염고래는 이빨 대신 실처럼 생긴 수염으로 먹이를 가두고 물을 내보낸다. 돌묵상어와 고래상어는 헤엄칠 때 입을 벌려 털처럼 생긴 아가미 갈퀴로 먹이를 가둔다.

햇빛 지역과는 다르게, 심해 혹은 자정 지역은 햇빛이 부족하여 밤처럼 어두운 곳이다. 심해층에 사는 유기체들은 생존을 위해 다른 섭식 유형을 발전시켜왔다. 심해 지역에는 광합성이 없기 때문에 먹이가 드물고 찾기가 어렵다. 그 결과 심해에 사는 생명체들은 포획한 먹잇감이 거의 빠져나갈 수 없도록 하는 신체적 특징들을 발달시켰다. 일부는 입으로 먹이를 가둘 수 있게끔 안쪽으로 송곳니같이 생긴 매우 긴 이빨들이 있다. 또한, 대다수는 큰 입과 턱, 그리고 커다랗고 늘어날 수 있는 위를 가지고 있어 한 번에 많은 양의 먹이를 잡고 소화할 수 있다. 심해에 사는 생물들은 먹이를 찾기 위한 수영에 큰 에너지를 쏟지 않는다. 대신 먹이를 꾀어낼 수 있도록 영리하게 적응하여, 앉아서 먹이를 기다리거나 유인한다. 아귀는 머리의 중간부터 뻗어 나온 긴 지느러미가 있으며, 이는 낚싯대처럼 생겼다. 아귀는 지느러미를 흔들며 먹잇감이 통째로 삼켜질 수 있을 만큼 충분히 가까이 오도록 유인한다. 몇몇 아귀는 더 많은 사냥감을 꾀어내기 위해 지느러미 끝에서 빛을 발산하기도 한다.

01 지문에서 its 가 가리키는 것은?

(A) 혼합
(B) 태양
(C) 층
(D) 깊이

해설 | Reference 이것의(its) 햇빛 양, 압력, 온도에 따라 적응한 다양한 해양 생물 종들이 혼합되어 각각의 층에 산다는 내용을 통해 its 가 가리키는 것이 층임을 알 수 있다.

02 단락 1에 따르면, 해양층이 구분되는 방법은?

(A) 해양 동물의 섭식 행동에 의해
(B) 바다 색에 의해
(C) 통과하는 햇빛의 양에 의해
(D) 수온에 의해

해설 | Factual Information 단락 1에서 바다는 깊이와 태양으로부터 받는 빛의 양에 따라 다양한 층으로 나뉜다고 설명하고 있다.

03 지문의 scarce 와 의미상 가장 가까운 것은?

(A) 드문
(B) 보이지 않는
(C) 특별한
(D) 사소한

해설 | Vocabulary 동의어 단서를 찾을 수 있는 문제이다. "… food is scarce and hard to find in deep-sea regions"의 밑줄 친 부분에서 scarce 는 '드문'의 의미임을 알 수 있다.

04 단락 3에서 필자가 신체적 특징들 에 대해 자세히 언급하는 이유는?

(A) 해양 생물들이 어떻게 심해에 적응했는지 설명하기 위해서
(B) 각기 다른 해양층이 해양 동물들의 생김새에 영향을 준다는 개념을 반박하기 위해서
(C) 심해 생물들이 어떻게 포식자들을 피하는지 설명하기 위해서
(D) 심해 동물들이 어떻게 음식을 먹는지에 대한 흥미로운 사실을 알려주기 위해서

해설 | Rhetorical Purpose 햇빛 지역과는 다르게 빛이 부족한 심해층의 생명체들은 생존을 위해 독특한 신체적 특징들을 발달시켰다.

05 지문을 간략히 요약하기 위한 도입 문장이 아래 제시되어 있다. 지문에서 가장 중요한 내용을 표현한 세 개의 문장을 골라 요약문을 완성하시오. 일부 문장은 지문에 나오지 않았거나 중요하지 않은 내용이기 때문에 요약문에 포함되지 않는다. 이 문제는 2점이다.

| 해양 동물은 섭식 메커니즘을 위해 특수화된 특징들을 가지고 있다. |

(A) 바다는 깊이와 햇빛의 양에 따라 여러 개의 층으로 나뉘며, 이것은 해양 동물들의 특성에 영향을 끼친다.
(B) 햇빛 지역에는 통과하는 햇빛으로 인해 다량의 플랑크톤이 존재한다.
(C) 자정 지역에서 해양 동물들은 많은 에너지를 쓰지 않고도 효율적으로 사냥할 수 있게 진화했다.
(D) 심해의 해양 동물들이 가진 가장 흔한 두 가지 섭식 습관은 여과 섭식과 꾀어내기이다.
(E) 햇빛 지역의 많은 해양 생물들은 음식을 섭취할 때 물 거르개 역할을 하는 특정 신체 부위를 사용한다.
(F) 상어는 매우 짧은 시간 내에 먹잇감을 잡을 수 있게 해주는 독특한 신체적 특징들을 갖도록 진화되었다.

해설 | Summary (A)는 바다는 여러 층으로 나뉘며 이는 해양 동물들의 특성에 영향을 끼친다는 단락 1의 내용을, (C)는 자정 지역 해양 동물들의 섭식 메커니즘을 설명하는 단락 3의 내용을, (E)는 햇빛 지역의 해양 동물들의 경우를 설명하는 단락 2의 내용을 요약한 것이다.

어휘 | **adapt** 적응시키다, 맞추다 **distinctive** 독특한, 변별적인 **acclimate** 적응하다, 순응하다 **strategy** 전략 **habitat** 서식지 **penetrate** 관통하다, 뚫고 들어가다 **plentiful** 풍부한 **krill** 크릴 새우 **food chain** 먹이 사슬 **filter-feeding** 여과 섭식 **undesirable** 원하지 않은, 달갑지 않은 **sieve** 체(가루, 물 등을 거르는데 쓰는 부엌 도구) **sponge** 해면, 스펀지 **blue whale** 흰긴수염고래 **immobile** 움직이지 않는 **water current** 해류 **baleen whale** 수염고래 **fringe** 실, 솔 **prey** 먹이, 먹잇감 **basking shark** 돌묵상어 **gill raker** 아가미 갈퀴 **photosynthesis** 광합성 **scarce** 드문, 진귀한 **physical** 신체적, 육체의 **trap** 가두다 **jaw** 턱 **quantity** 양 **anglerfish** 아귀 **fin** 지느러미 **sprout** 뻗어 나오다, 자라기 시작하다 **fishing rod** 낚싯대 **wiggle** 흔들다 **emit** 발산하다, 내뿜다 **seduce** 꾀다, 유혹하다 **quarry** 사냥감

Mini Test 1

01 (A) **02** (C) **03** (D) **04** (B) **05** (C), (D), (F)

COLONIZATION OF PLANT LIFE ON EARTH

Millions of plant species are present across the globe, but like all life on earth, they originated in the ocean and gradually made their way to land. The first organisms to settle on land more than a billion years ago are called cyanobacteria. Since these organisms are able to photosynthesize sunlight, they released huge amounts of oxygen into the atmosphere, easing the migration of other plant forms from the ocean to land. There were several reasons that settling on land was beneficial to plants.

First, plants were able to photosynthesize sunlight easier, as the passage of sunlight to plants on land is more direct than to plants in water. In addition, the greater presence of carbon dioxide in the atmosphere than in the ocean facilitated the process of transforming carbon dioxide into oxygen. Lastly, the earth's soil was deeply rich in mineral nutrients, which were not as plentiful in the ocean. However, the plants also encountered several obstacles to survival as they made the switch from life in the ocean to life on land. Because plants were used to living in a constantly moist, aquatic environment, they needed to make sure that they did not dry out as they settled on land. Moreover, they had little gravitational support on land and needed to adapt to this environmental change.

One of the most significant organisms to help plant life make the transition from water to land was soil fungi, Q01 and plants and soil fungi ended up forming a mutual relationship with each other. ①The soil fungi provided the plants with essential nutrients that helped the plants to grow and spread, and ②in return, the fungi received the carbon dioxide processed from the plants, which they stored in the soil.

Plants also underwent dramatic physiological changes as they accustomed themselves to an environment with less water. While the original algae ancestors of plants had fairly simple bodies, plants needed to develop new structures to live on land, such as roots, leaves, and vascular tissue. Q03 The development of these physiological structures was crucial, as plants needed a way to transport water and nutrients through their bodies. Consequently, the first plants to grow on land were quite small and needed to grow in environments close to water. However, over time plants grew larger and deeper roots, which provided them with a more stable foundation to stand upright, thereby solving the gravitational problem. More importantly, roots allowed the plants to access nutrients and water in the soil, which traveled through newly developed vascular tissue, resulting in plants growing faster and taller. Leaves also evolved to capture larger amounts of sunlight, which aided in plants' developmental process.

Q04 As plants grew stronger and ubiquitously spread across the globe, they had a very significant ecological impact on the planet. Whereas carbon dioxide levels in the atmosphere were originally very high, the amount of oxygen released into the air greatly increased and allowed for other life forms to thrive. The larger amount of oxygen in the atmosphere also contributed to an increase in wildfires that are essential for plant species to produce seeds, grow, and reproduce.

지구상 식물의 이주

전 세계에 수많은 식물 종들이 있는데, 지구의 모든 생명이 그러했듯이, 이들은 원래 바다에 있었다가 차츰 육지로 올라오게 되었다. 10억 년도 더 이전에 육지에 처음 자리를 잡게 된 유기체는 시아노박테리아라고 불린다. 이 유기체는 햇빛으로부터 광합성을 해서 많은 양의 산소를 대기에 방출했고, 바다에 있는 다른 식물들이 육지로 오는 것을 용이하게 하였다. 식물이 육지에 정착하는 것이 더 좋은 데에는 몇 가지 이유가 있다.

첫 번째로, 식물에 도달하는 햇빛의 경로가 수중에서보다는 육지에서 더 직접적이므로 식물은 광합성을 더 쉽게 할 수 있었다. 게다가 바다에서보다 훨씬 많은 대기 중의 이산화탄소는 이산화탄소를 산소로 바꾸는 과정을 촉진시켰다. 마지막으로, 땅의 토양은 미네랄 영양분이 매우 풍부했는데, 해양에서는 그렇게 많지 않았다. 그러나 바다 속 생명체이던 식물이 육지 생명체로 변하면서 생존을 위해 여러 장애물에 부딪히기도 했다. 지금껏 촉촉한 물속 환경에서 살아온 것에 익숙한 식물들은 땅 위에 자리 잡으며 마르지 않도록 해야 했다. 더욱이 식물들은 육지에서 중력의 도움을 거의 받지 못했으므로 이러한 환경적인 변화에 적응해야만 했다.

식물이 물에서 육지로 이주하는 데 도움을 준 가장 중요한 유기체 중 하나는 토양균류였고, 식물균과 토양균류는 서로 상호 관계를 형성했다. 토양균류는 식물이 자라고 뻗어 나가는 데 도움을 주는 필수 영양분을 제공했고, 대신 식물에서 생산되는 이산화탄소를 받아 땅속에 저장했다.

식물은 물이 적은 환경에 적응하면서 극적인 생리적 변화도 겪었다. 식물의 본래 조류 선조는 꽤 간단한 신체 구조로 되어 있던 반면, 식물은 육지에 적응하기 위해 뿌리, 잎, 그리고 관다발 조직과 같은 새로운 구조를 발달시켜야 했다. 이러한 생리적 구조의 발달은 식물이 그들 몸을 통해 물과 영양분을 옮기려는 방법을 필요로 했으므로 매우 중요했다. 따라서 육지 상의 첫 번째 식물은 매우 작고 물이 근처에 있는 환경에서 자라야 했다. 그러나 시간이 지날수록 더 크고 더 깊은 뿌리를 가지게 되었고 더 안정되게 똑바로 설 수 있는 기반을 제공하게 되어 중력 문제를 해결하였다. 더욱 중요한 것은 뿌리가 식물이 흙 속의 영양분과 물에 접근할 수 있게 만들었으며, 이것들은 새롭게 발달된 관다발 조직을 통해 식물들이 더 빠르고 더 크게 성장할 수 있게 만들었다. 잎 또한 더 많은 양의 태양을 받을 수 있게 발달하여 식물의 발육 과정을 도왔다.

식물이 강성해지고 전 세계 곳곳으로 퍼지면서, 지구 생태계에 매우 큰 영향을 끼쳤다. 대기 중의 이산화탄소의 양은 본래 높았지만, 공기 중으로 방출되는 산소의 양이 많이 증가했고 이는 다른 생명체들이 잘 자랄 수 있게 해주었다. 대기 중 더 많아진 산소의 양은 들불이 자주 나게 하기도 하였는데, 이는 식물 종들이 씨앗을 만들어내고, 자라고, 번식하는 데에 필수이다.

01 단락 3에 따르면, 토양균류에 관한 내용 중 옳은 것은?

(A) 토양균류와 식물은 생존을 위해 서로 없어서는 안 되는 관계를 형성했다.
(B) 토양균류는 식물로부터 필수 영양분을 흡수한다.
(C) 토양균류는 대기 중의 이산화탄소 증가의 원인이 되었다.
(D) 식물이 땅으로 이주할 때 토양균류는 처음에 살아남기 위해 고군분투했다.

해설 | Factual Information   토양균류는 식물에 필수 영양분을 주고, 이산화탄소를 받음으로써 서로 상호 호혜 관계를 형성했다.

02 다음 중 지문에서 표시된 문장의 주요 정보를 가장 잘 나타낸 문장은? *정답 외의 보기들은 중요한 의미가 바뀌거나 주요 정보가 빠져 있다.*

(A) 식물은 육지로 이주하면서 토양균류로부터 성장하기 위한 필요 영양분을 받으며 이와 상호 관계를 형성했다.
(B) 오직 식물만 균류로부터 이득을 취했기 때문에 식물과 토양균류는 단일 방향의 관계였다.
(C) 식물은 토양균류로부터 필수 영양분을 받고, 그 대신 이산화탄소를 제공한다.
(D) 식물은 균류가 살아남는 데 필요한 필수 영양분을 주었고, 균류는 이산화탄소를 내뿜으로써 식물에 도움을 주었다.

해설 | Sentence Simplification   표시된 문장은 크게 두 의미로 나뉠 수 있다. ① 토양균류는 식물에 필수 영양분을 제공한다. ② 대신에 식물에서 생산되는 이산화탄소를 받는다.

03 지문의 Consequently 와 의미상 가장 가까운 것은?

(A) 비슷하게
(B) 한편
(C) 더욱이
(D) 따라서

해설 | Vocabulary   식물이 육지 환경에 적응하기 위해 새로 발달시킨 구조를 설명하고 있다. 이어지는 내용은 앞 내용의 결과적인 내용이므로 Consequently 는 '따라서'의 의미임을 알 수 있다.

04 단락 5에서 필자가 식물에 대해 암시하는 것은?

(A) 식물은 대기 중의 높은 이산화탄소를 빠르게 감소시킬 수 있었다.
(B) 식물의 이주가 없었더라면, 다른 생물들이 진화는 좀 더 어려웠을지도 모른다.
(C) 들불은 식물들의 이주를 막는 데에 큰 역할을 할 수 있었다.
(D) 대기 중의 높은 이산화탄소 수치는 식물 이주에 해로운 영향을 끼쳤다.

해설 | Inference   식물이 땅 위로 이주하게 되면서 대기 중의 산소량이 증가했고 이는 다른 생명체들이 잘 자랄 수 있게 했다.

05 지문을 간략히 요약하기 위한 도입 문장이 아래 제시되어 있다. 지문에서 가장 중요한 내용을 표현한 세 개의 문장을 골라 요약문을 완성하시오. 일부 문장은 지문에 나오지 않았거나 중요하지 않은 내용이기 때문에 요약문에 포함되지 않는다. *이 문제는 2점이다.*

> 시아노박테리아의 육지로의 정착은 다른 식물 종들이 땅으로 이주하기 더 편한 환경을 만들어주었다.

(A) 육지에서의 중력 증가는 식물들이 더 크게 자라고 더 깊은 뿌리를 내려 똑바로 서게 하였다.
(B) 식물은 대기 중의 이산화탄소를 관의 구조에 저장함으로써 육지로 이주했다.
(C) 몇몇 난관에도 불구하고, 많은 식물 종은 더 좋은 삶을 살기 위해 바다에서 육지로 이주했다.
(D) 육지에서의 환경적인 변화에 적응하기 위해, 식물은 다른 종들과 상호 관계를 맺고, 새로운 구조를 발달시켰으며, 신체 구조를 향상시켰다.
(E) 식물의 뿌리는 안정적인 중력 지지를 제공할 뿐만 아니라 흙으로부터 영양분과 물을 공급했다.
(F) 전 세계의 성공적인 식물 번영은 다른 생물 종들이 지구에서 번영하기 더 쉽게 만들었다.

해설 | Summary   (C)는 식물의 육지로의 이주에 따른 장단점을 설명한 단락 2의 내용을 요약해 놓은 것이다. (D)는 식물이 육지에 적응하기 위해 선택한 생존 전략을 설명한 단락 3과 4의 내용을 요약해 놓은 것이다. (F)는 식물의 육지로의 이주가 지구 생태계에 끼친 영향을 설명하는 단락 5의 내용을 요약해 놓은 것이다.

어휘 | **species** 종　**cyanobacteria** 시아노박테리아　**photosynthesize** 광합성하다　**release** 방출하다, 뿜다　**oxygen** 산소　**atmosphere** 대기　**carbon dioxide** 이산화탄소　**facilitate** 촉진하다, 가능하게 하다　**plentiful** 풍부한　**gravitational** 중력의　**soil fungi** 토양균류　**mutual** 상호 간의, 서로의　**relationship** 관계　**physiological** 생리학상의, 생리적인　**algae** 조류　**ancestor** 선조, 조상　**fairly** 꽤, 상당히　**root** 뿌리　**vascular tissue** 관다발 조직　**stable** 안정된

Mini Test 2　　　　　　　　　　　　　　　　　　　　　　　　p.154

01 (B)　02 (C)　03 (B)　04 (B)　05 (A), (C), (E)

CELL STRUCTURE

Cells are often called the building blocks of life, as they are the smallest functional unit of all life on Earth. Some life forms, like bacteria, consist of only one cell, while the human body is estimated to contain over 100 trillion cells. Q01 While every cell is a mostly autonomous unit, cells can also join with one another or work in cooperation to make up extremely complex forms of life. Cells vary in size and shape across different living organisms, depending upon their function or the organism in which they are found, but all are composed of the same basic parts.

Every cell has a protective covering that holds together its many parts and prevents interference from outside forces. This is called the cell membrane, and may be thought of as the skin of the cell. A The cell membrane is selectively permeable — Q04 this means that it can choose to let some materials pass through it and to block others. B In this way, the cell is able to absorb the nutrients it needs without letting in unnecessary or harmful elements. Q02(A) (B) Attached to the cell membrane is the cytoskeleton, a rigid structure that helps the cell maintain its shape. C Like a human skeleton, the cytoskeleton forms a defensive grid-like pattern around the cell that holds the membrane in place and Q02(D) protects the internal components of the cell. D The cytoskeleton may serve other purposes as well: it may contain what are called flagella, small hairs that help the cell move through external liquid.

Inside the cell membrane is a fluid called cytoplasm, which surrounds and cushions all of the internal cell parts. Located within the cytoplasm are organelles, small parts of the cell that serve specific functions to promote the cell's well-being. What organs are to the human body, organelles are to the cell. Of the several existing organelles, one of the most significant is the mitochondrion. Q03 Mitochondria are often called the power plants of the cell, as they produce the energy needed by the cell. They do this by taking various nutrients from the cytoplasm, which they use as their "fuel," and mix them with oxygen in a process called cellular respiration. The result is the creation of another substance, called ATP, which provides the cell with ample energy to survive by regulating its internal metabolism.

The most important part of the cell as a whole is the nucleus, or the control center of the cell. Safe within the nucleus is the genetic information that determines every characteristic and trait of that cell. The nucleus is constructed much like a smaller cell within a larger cell. It is protected by a double-layered membrane that separates the material inside from the cytoplasm floating around it. It also has its own type of skeleton, called a nuclear lamina, which gives support to the structure of the nucleus. The nucleus

세포의 구조

세포는 지구의 모든 생명체의 가장 작은 기능적 단위이므로 흔히 생명의 기본 단위라고 불린다. 박테리아 같은 일부 생명체는 단일 세포로 구성되지만, 인체는 100조 개가 넘는 세포로 구성되어 있다고 추정된다. 모든 세포는 거의 **독립적** 단위이지만, 또한 서로 결합하거나 협력하여 극도로 복잡한 생명체를 구성할 수도 있다. 세포는 각기 다른 생물마다 크기와 모양이 다르고, 이러한 차이는 세포의 기능과 그들이 발견되는 유기체에 달려있지만, 모두 동일한 기본 요소로 되어 있다.

모든 세포는 많은 요소를 한데 모으고 외부 힘이 간섭하는 것을 막는 보호막을 갖추고 있다. 이는 세포막으로 불리며, 세포의 피부라고 할 수 있다. A 세포막에는 선별적 투과성이 있어서, 세포가 통과할 물질과 그렇지 않은 물질을 선별적으로 고를 수 있게 해준다. B **이런 방법으로 세포는 불필요하거나 해로운 요소를 걸러내고 필요한 영양소를 흡수할 수 있다.** 세포막에는 세포 골격이 붙어 있는데, 이는 세포가 형태를 유지할 수 있게 도와주는 딱딱한 구조체이다. C 인간의 골격처럼 세포 골격도 세포 주위에서 방어적 격자 문양으로 형성되어 있으며, 세포막을 제자리에 유지하고 세포의 내부 요소를 보호한다. D 세포 골격은 다른 역할을 하기도 하는데, 편모라고 불리는 작은 털이 외부 액체를 통해 세포가 움직이도록 도와주기도 한다.

세포막 안에는 세포질이라고 불리는 액체가 있는데, 세포질은 세포 내 모든 요소를 둘러싸고 보호한다. 세포질 안에는 세포 기관이 있는데, 이는 세포가 잘 살 수 있게 촉진하게 하는 특별한 기능을 수행하는 세포의 작은 부분이다. 인체에 장기가 있다면, 세포에는 세포 기관이 있다. 존재하는 여러 세포 기관 중 가장 중요한 기관 중 하나는 미토콘드리아이다. 미토콘드리아는 흔히 세포의 발전소라고 불리는데, 세포가 필요로 하는 에너지를 생성하기 때문이다. 미토콘드리아는 세포질에 있는 다양한 영양소를 가져다가 연료로 사용하고 세포 호흡이라고 불리는 과정을 통해 산소와 혼합한다. 이 결과로 ATP라고 불리는 또 다른 물질이 생성되는데, ATP는 내부 신진대사를 조절함으로써 세포가 살 수 있는 충분한 에너지를 공급한다.

세포 전체에서 가장 중요한 부분은 세포의 통제 센터인 세포핵이다. 이 세포핵 안에 안전하게 있는 유전자 정보는 해당 세포의 모든 성격과 특성을 결정한다. 세포핵은 큰 세포 안에 있는 작은 세포와 같이 구성되어 있다. 세포핵은 두 겹의 세포막으로 보호되는데, 이 점막은 안에 있는 물질을 그 주위로 흐르는 세포질로부터 분리해준다. 또한 세포핵은 핵막하층이라고 불리는 일종의 골격도 갖추고 있어서, 핵의 조직을 지탱해 준다. 세포핵은 점막 안에 있는 구멍을 통해 유전자 정보를 세포의 다른 부분으로 전달, 세포 전체의 대체적인 형태 및 유지, 생식에 대한 정보를 알려준다. 세포가 증식할 때, 모든 미래 세포의 생김새와 기능을

transmits genetic information through pores in the membrane to other parts of the cell about the formation, maintenance, and reproduction of the cell as a whole. When the cell reproduces, it is this important DNA that determines how all future cells will look and function.

결정하는 것이 바로 이 중요한 DNA이다.

---

01 지문의 autonomous 와 의미상 가장 가까운 것은?
(A) 응집력이 있는
(B) 독립적인
(C) 중요한
(D) 종속된

해설 | Vocabulary 해당 문장은 While이 쓰여 두 절의 내용이 서로 대조되고 있다. 종속절의 autonomous 의 의미는 주절 join with one another or work in cooperation의 반대의 뜻을 떠올리면 된다.

02 단락 2에 따르면, 세포 골격에 관한 내용으로 옳지 않은 것은?
(A) 세포가 형태를 유지하도록 해 준다.
(B) 세포막에 붙어 있다.
(C) 구멍이 있어 영양소가 들어오도록 해 준다.
(D) 세포 내부가 손상되지 않게 보호해 준다.

해설 | Negative Fact 세포 골격은 세포막과 붙어 있고, 세포의 형태를 유지시키고, 세포 안의 내용물을 보호한다.

03 필자가 지문에서 발전소 를 언급하는 이유는?
(A) 세포 기관의 중요성을 설명하기 위해
(B) 미토콘드리아의 기능을 설명하기 위해
(C) 세포가 얼마나 많은 에너지를 필요로 하는지 보여주기 위해
(D) 세포가 자가충족할 수 있다는 것을 증명하기 위해

해설 | Rhetorical Purpose 해당 문장의 후반부에서 필자가 발전소를 언급한 이유를 알 수 있다. 미토콘드리아는 세포가 필요로 하는 에너지를 만들어내는 기능이 있다는 점을 설명하려고 발전소 를 언급했다.

04 다음 문장이 지문에 들어갈 곳을 나타내는 네 개의 사각형[■]을 보시오.

> 이런 방법으로 세포는 불필요하거나 해로운 요소를 걸러내고 필요한 영양소를 흡수할 수 있다.

이 문장이 들어갈 가장 적절한 위치는?
(A) A (B) B (C) C (D) D

해설 | Sentence Insertion 삽입 문장의 내용은 세포가 불필요한 물질을 걸러내고 영양소를 흡수할 수 있다는 내용인데, In this way로부터 삽입 문장의 바로 앞에는 세포가 물질을 선택적으로 받아들일 수 있다는 내용이 나와야 자연스럽게 연결됨을 알 수 있다.

05 지문을 간략히 요약하기 위한 도입 문장이 아래 제시되어 있다. 지문에서 가장 중요한 내용을 표현한 세 개의 문장을 골라 요약문을 완성하시오. 일부 문장은 지문에 나오지 않았거나 중요하지 않은 내용이기 때문에 요약문에 포함되지 않는다. *이 문제는 2점이다.*

> 세포들은 크기와 모양에 있어 다양하지만, 세포의 건강과 안녕을 보장하는 동일한 기본 구성으로 이루어져 있다.

(A) 세포막 안에는 여러 세포 기관들이 있는데, 이 중 미토콘드리아는 산소와 다른 영양분들을 에너지로 바꾼다.
(B) 세포는 세포 골격으로부터 형태를 얻는데, 세포 골격은 세포벽 아래서 지탱하는 단단한 격자 문양을 하고 있다.
(C) 세포의 제일 바깥쪽 부분은 세포막과 세포 골격인데, 이 둘은 각각 선택적으로 필요한 물질을 통과시키고, 세포의 모양을 유지시켜준다.
(D) 세포막에 튀어나와 있는 편모라 불리는 작은 털은 세포가 주변 액체 사이로 움직일 수 있게 하는 역할을 한다.
(E) 세포핵은 여러 세포 기관을 통제하고, 많은 기관과의 소통을 담당하는 DNA 다발과 다른 물질로 구성되어 있다.
(F) 핵막하층은 핵막의 안쪽 벽을 형성하며, 안에 있는 물질을 보호한다.

해설 | Summary (C)는 세포의 바깥쪽에 있는 세포막과 세포 골격에 대해 설명한 단락 2에 대한 내용을, (A)는 세포막 안쪽의 세포의 구조와 기능에 대해 설명한 단락 3의 내용을, (E)는 세포의 정중앙에 위치한 세포핵에 대해 설명한 단락 4의 내용이다.

어휘 | **building block of life** 생명체의 기본 단위　**functional** 기능적인　**estimate** 추정하다　**autonomous** 독립적인　**cooperation** 협력　**hold together** 한데 모으다　**interference** 방해　**membrane** 세포막　**selectively** 선별적으로　**permeable** 투과성의　**cytoskeleton** 세포 골격　**rigid** 딱딱한　**defensive** 방어하는　**grid-like** 격자 모양의　**flagellum** (pl. flagella) 편모　**cushion** 보호하다　**organelle** 세포 기관　**promote** 촉진하다　**mitochondrion** (pl. mitochondria) 미토콘드리아　**power plant** 발전소　**respiration** 호흡　**regulate** 조절하다　**metabolism** 신진대사　**nucleus** 세포핵　**construct** 구성하다　**double-layered** 두 겹의　**separate** 분리하다　**nuclear lamina** 핵막하층　**pore** 구멍　**maintenance** 유지

iBT Practice   p.156

| 01 (C) | 02 (B) | 03 (D) | 04 (C) | 05 (C) | 06 (C) | 07 (A) | 08 (A) | 09 (C) | 10 (D) | 11 (D) | 12 (B), (D), (E) |

CIRCADIAN RHYTHM

The health and well-being of humans, animals, and even plants are largely dependent on natural biological rhythms that help regulate bodily functions and optimize an organism's ability to carry out vital tasks. Most organisms are subject to what is called a circadian rhythm, a roughly 24-hour cycle that is divided into periods of sleep and wakefulness. The circadian rhythm has a far-reaching influence on the daily lives of organisms, regulating physical activity, chemical processes, and behavior. Although circadian rhythms are generated internally, they are heavily influenced by environmental cues, most notably the difference between day and night. However, circumstances do arise in which organisms lack the ability to pick up on such cues, or the cues are altogether absent. In such cases, circadian rhythms are regulated almost entirely by an "internal clock" that informs an organism's biological processes. For the most part, though, circadian rhythms are uniform and predictable across a vast range of species.

The circadian rhythm is controlled by a part of the brain called the hypothalamus, which acts as a clearing house for internal and external cues, collecting and interpreting them to ultimately determine one's sleep patterns. Sleep is induced naturally by a chemical called melatonin, and melatonin production is directly associated with activity in the hypothalamus. The retina of the eye contains special cells that, when activated by light, send signals to the hypothalamus that tell it that surroundings are lit. Q02 Q03 The hypothalamus sends this information on to the pineal gland, also in the brain, which either produces or inhibits the production of melatonin, depending on the information it receives. Q04 If the retina detects light, then the pineal gland halts production of melatonin, and as the hormone cycles out of the brain, wakefulness follows. The wavelength of the light detected determines how much melatonin should be produced. Q05 The opposite is true when night falls; the lack of light stimulates the pineal gland to produce more melatonin in preparation for the organism's coming sleep. Some other preparations include lowering body temperature and blood pressure.

Humans and other animals follow this basic model most of the time, but under unusual circumstances, this is not always possible. ①In the extreme northern and southern parts of the world, Q07 where the sun does not set for months at a time, ②the environmental cues that would generally control the circadian rhythm are not always present. Q08 Studies have produced mixed results in regard to how Arctic animals respond to sustained sunlight. Reindeer will display no consistent circadian rhythm for several months out of the year. This is called a free-running rhythm

24시간 주기 리듬

인간과 동물, 그리고 심지어 식물의 건강과 안녕은 신체 기능을 조절하고 생명유지 활동을 수행하는 생물의 능력을 최적화해주는 것을 돕는 자연 생체 리듬에 크게 의존한다. 대부분 생물이 24시간 주기 리듬이라고 불리는 이것의 영향을 받는데, 이는 자는 기간과 깨어 있는 기간으로 나뉘는 약 24시간 주기를 말한다. 이 24시간 주기 리듬은 신체 활동과 화학 작용, 행동을 조절하며, 생명체의 일상생활에 매우 광범위한 영향을 미친다. 24시간 주기 리듬은 본래 내부적으로 생성되지만, 환경적 신호, 특히 낮과 밤의 변화에 가장 큰 영향을 받는다. 그러나 생명체가 이러한 신호를 감지할 능력이 부족하거나 신호 자체가 완전히 없는 상황도 있게 마련이다. 이런 상황에서 24시간 주기 리듬은 거의 전적으로 생명체의 생물학적 과정을 알려주는 '체내 시계'에 의해 조절된다. 그러나 대부분의 경우, 이 24시간 주기 리듬은 넓은 범위 의 종에 걸쳐 일정하며 예측이 가능하다.

24시간 주기 리듬은 시상하부라고 불리는 뇌의 한 부분에서 통제되는데, 시상하부는 체내·체외의 신호 교환소 기능을 하며, 신호를 모으고 해석하여 궁극적으로 생물의 수면 패턴을 결정한다. 수면은 멜라토닌이라고 불리는 화학 물질에 의해 자연적으로 유도되며, 멜라토닌 생성은 시상하부의 활동과 직접 관계가 있다. 눈의 망막에는 특수한 세포가 있는데, 이 세포가 빛에 의해 활성화되면 주위 환경이 밝은지를 알려주는 신호를 시상하부에 보낸다. 시상하부는 역시 뇌에 있는 송과선에 이 정보를 보내며, 송과선은 그것 이 받는 정보에 따라 멜라토닌을 생성하거나 억제한다 . 만약 망막이 빛을 감지하면, 송과선은 멜라토닌의 생성을 멈추고, 그러면 호르몬이 뇌를 벗어나는 주기가 오면서 잠이 깨게 된다. 감지된 빛의 파장은 멜라토닌이 얼마나 많이 생성되어야 하는지를 결정한다. 밤이 되면 반대 현상이 일어나는데, 빛의 부재가 송과선을 자극하면 생명체가 잠 오는 것에 대비하도록 멜라토닌을 더욱 많이 생성한다. 다른 대비 과정으로 체온과 혈압을 낮추기도 한다.

인간과 그 외 동물들은 거의 대부분 이런 기본 유형을 따르는데, 특이한 상황에서는 그렇지 않은 때도 있다. 지구의 극북지방이나 극남지방에서는 해가 한 번에 몇 달 동안 지지 않는데, 이런 곳에서는 24시간 주기 리듬을 일반적으로 조절하는 환경적 신호가 늘 존재하는 것이 아니다. 북극 동물들이 지속되는 햇빛에 어떻게 반응하는지에 관해 조사한 연구 결과들은 각양각색이었다. 순록 은 일 년의 몇 달 동안 일정한 24시간 주기 리듬을 보이지 않는다. 이것은 자율주기라고 불리며, 자율주기는 동물이 먹거나 잠자려는 등의 욕구를 자각하는 경우에만 조절된다. 밤낮의 주기가 다시 시작되면, 순록은 다시 규칙적인 24시간 주기 리듬으로 복귀한다. 다른 연구를 통해서는 알래스카에 사는 다람쥐들이 낮이나 밤이

and is regulated only by the animal's awareness of its needs, like those for food and sleep. When the day-night cycle does resume, the reindeer return to a regular circadian rhythm. In another study, squirrels in Alaska were found to follow a strict circadian rhythm year round, despite constant sunlight or darkness. Q09 The reason for this is unknown, except that perhaps the sun's position relative to the horizon is enough of a cue to maintain a cycle.

While some organisms can successfully maintain a free-running rhythm, it can be harmful for humans to do so. Not getting sufficient sleep at regular intervals can cause hormones in the brain to become unbalanced. Q10 If a deficiency of sleep continues for long enough, it may even result in mental illness. By ignoring the circadian rhythm, one's waking and sleeping schedule becomes out of sync with the biological processes that occur during regular sleep, in which muscles regenerate, memories are stored, and a number of other important processes are carried out. Missing out on any one of these processes can have serious negative physical effects like muscle loss and even heart failure. Sometimes a person's circadian rhythm can become inconsistent when he or she travels a long distance across many time zones. A This is commonly called "jet lag," since it mostly applies to air travel. B While the body is still accustomed to the rhythms it established at the place of departure, it is suddenly faced with new environmental cues. C This can result in irregular sleep patterns, fatigue, and mental exhaustion. D Over time, however, the human body can adapt to the new cues if effort is taken to follow them.

계속되는지의 여부에 상관없이 일년 내내 24시간 주기 리듬을 엄격히 따라 생활하는 것이 밝혀졌다. 이 이유는 밝혀지지 않았고, 다만 지평선 대비 태양의 위치가 주기 유지를 위한 충분한 신호가 될 것이라는 추측만 할 수 있을 뿐이다.

자율주기를 성공적으로 유지하는 생명체가 있지만, 인간이 자율주기를 갖는 것은 해로울 수 있다. 규칙적 간격을 두고 충분한 수면을 하지 않으면 뇌에 있는 호르몬의 불균형이 일어난다. 수면 부족이 장기간 계속되면, 심지어 정신 질환에 이를 수도 있다. 규칙적 수면을 취하면 근육이 재생되고 기억이 저장되며 그 밖의 수많은 다른 중요한 작용이 발생하는데, 24시간 주기 리듬을 무시하면 사람의 기상 및 취침 시간이 규칙적인 수면을 취할 때 일어나는 생물학적 작용과 서로 맞지 않게 된다. 이런 작용 중 하나라도 제대로 일어나지 않으면 근육의 손실이나 심지어는 심장 마비처럼 심각하고 부정적인 신체적 영향을 미칠 수 있다. 때로 24시간 주기 리듬은 여러 다른 시간대를 지나는 장거리 여행을 하면서 불일치할 수도 있다. A 이 현상은 대부분 비행기 여행을 할 때 나타나기에 흔히 '시차증'이라고 불린다. B 몸은 아직 출발지의 주기에 적응되어 있는데, 갑자기 새로운 환경적 신호에 맞닥뜨리는 것이다. C 이는 불규칙한 수면 패턴이나 피로, 정신적 피로를 초래할 수 있다. D 그러나 시간이 지남에 따라 새로운 신호를 따르려고 노력하면, 인간의 몸은 그 새로운 신호에 적응할 수 있게 된다.

01 지문의 range 와 의미상 가장 가까운 것은?

(A) 다수
(B) 사회
(C) 범위
(D) 숫자

해설 | Vocabulary　range 는 '범위'라는 의미이다.

02 지문의 inhibits 와 의미상 가장 가까운 것은?

(A) 균형을 맞추다
(B) 억제하다
(C) 자극하다
(D) 지연시키다

해설 | Vocabulary　반의어 단서를 찾을 수 있는 문제이다. "… either produces or inhibits …"에서 inhibits 는 produces와 반대 의미를 가졌음을 알 수 있다.

03 지문에서 it 이 가리키는 것은?

(A) 시상하부
(B) 멜라토닌
(C) 뇌
(D) 송과선

해설 | Reference　해당 문장의 "the information it receives"와 문장 전반부의 "The hypothalamus sends this information on to the pineal gland"를 비교해 보면 it 이 곧 pineal gland임을 알 수 있다.

04 단락 2에 따르면, 멜라토닌의 생성량을 결정하는 것은?

(A) 시상하부에서 내보내는 신호
(B) 몸이 잠들어 있는 시간
(C) 눈이 감지하는 빛의 파장
(D) 뇌에 있는 호르몬의 양

해설 | Factual Information　망막이 빛을 감지하면 송과선은 멜라토닌의 생성을 억제하며, 감지된 빛의 파장에 따라 멜라토닌이 생성되는 양이 달라진다.

05 단락 2에 따르면, 수면을 대비하는 것으로 언급되지 않은 것은?

(A) 체온의 하강
(B) 멜라토닌의 증가
(C) 정신적 각성도의 감소
(D) 혈압의 변화

해설 | Negative Fact 마지막 두 문장에서 수면 준비 단계로 멜라토닌의 증가, 체온과 혈압이 내려가는 것을 언급하고 있다.

06 다음 중 지문에서 표시된 문장의 주요 정보를 가장 잘 나타낸 문장은? 정답 외의 보기들은 중요한 의미가 바뀌거나 주요 정보가 빠져 있다.

(A) 극지방에서는 심지어 한 달이 될 수도 있는 긴 기간 동안 햇빛이 드물게 나타나는데 이는 환경적 신호에 영향을 미친다.
(B) 환경적 신호는 극남지방에 비해 햇빛이 더 많은 극북지방에서 더 미세하다.
(C) 극지방에서는 대개 24시간 주기 리듬을 조절하는 환경적 신호가 제한된다.
(D) 몇 달 동안 지속되는 햇빛으로 인해 저위도 지역에서는 기존의 환경적 신호를 감지하기가 힘들 수 있다.

해설 | Sentence Simplification 표시된 문장은 크게 두 의미로 나뉠 수 있다. ① 북극과 남극 지방에서는 ② 24시간 주기 리듬을 조절하는 환경적 신호는 항상 존재하지는 않는다.

07 지문의 sustained 와 의미상 가장 가까운 것은?

(A) 지속되는
(B) 강렬한
(C) 갑작스러운
(D) 약해진

해설 | Vocabulary sustained 의 의미는 앞 문장의 "… where the sun does not set for months at a time …"으로부터 알 수 있다. 해가 몇 달간 지지 않으므로 일광 시간이 지속됐을(sustained) 것이다.

08 필자가 지문에서 순록 을 언급하는 이유는?

(A) 일부 동물이 어떻게 불규칙 주기를 지내는지 보여주려고
(B) 일부 동물에서는 왜 24시간 주기 리듬이 나타나지 못하는지 설명하려고
(C) 엄격한 24시간 주기 리듬을 가지고 있는 동물의 예를 들어 주려고
(D) 여러 동물의 24시간 주기 리듬에 대한 결론을 내리려고

해설 | Rhetorical Purpose 길어진 일광 시간에 대해서 여러 동물이 어떻게 반응하는지 보여주고 있다. 순록은 길어진 일광 시간에 따라 생체 주기도 변화하는 동물의 예로 제시되었다.

09 단락 3에 따르면, 과학자들이 제시한 이론에서 알래스카 다람쥐의 24시간 주기 리듬을 조절하는 것은?

(A) 해의 일출과 일몰
(B) 배고픔과 피곤함과 같은 기본적 욕구
(C) 지평선 대비 태양의 위치
(D) 몇 달 동안 계속되는 낮 혹은 밤

해설 | Factual Information 단락 3의 맨 마지막 문장에서 다람쥐가 일광 시간에 관계없이 일정한 생체 주기를 보이는 이유에 대해 과학자들이 추정한 바를 소개하고 있다.

10 지문의 sufficient 와 의미상 가장 가까운 것은?

(A) 편안한
(B) 가벼운
(C) 깊은
(D) 충분한

해설 | Vocabulary sufficient 의 의미는 뒷 문장 "If a deficiency of sleep continues …"에서 힌트를 얻을 수 있다. 수면 부족의 현상을 설명하는 것으로 보아 sufficient 는 '충분한'의 의미임을 알 수 있다.

11 다음 문장이 지문에 들어갈 곳을 나타내는 네 개의 사각형[■]을 보시오.

> 그러나 시간이 지남에 따라 새로운 신호를 따르려고 노력하면, 인간의 몸은 그 새로운 신호에 적응할 수 있게 된다.

이 문장이 들어갈 가장 적절한 위치는?

(A) A (B) B (C) C (D) D

해설 | Sentence Insertion 삽입 문장의 "Over time, however …"는 앞서의 설명을 뒤집으며, 시간이 지나고 노력하면 문제가 해결될 것이라고 말한다. 삽입 문장 앞에 구체적인 문제들이 언급되고 이 문장 뒤에는 그 문제들이 재언급되기 어색하므로 가장 마지막인 D에 위치하는 것이 자연스럽다.

12 지문을 간략히 요약하기 위한 도입 문장이 아래 제시되어 있다. 지문에서 가장 중요한 내용을 표현한 세 개의 문장을 골라 요약문을 완성하시오. 일부 문장은 지문에 나오지 않았거나 중요하지 않은 내용이기 때문에 요약문에 포함되지 않는다. *이 문제는 2점이다.*

> 24시간 주기 리듬이라고 알려진 수면과 각성의 회복 주기는 생물적 작용을 조절할 수 있게 돕는다.

(A) 밤과 낮 같은 명백한 환경적 신호가 없으면 어떤 동물들은 비정상적인 행동을 보인다.
(B) 24시간 주기 리듬은 세포와 분비선, 그리고 뇌에 있는 호르몬들의 복잡한 연결고리를 통해 조절된다.
(C) 생체 주기를 이루도록 돕는 신호는 주로 유기체의 체내 시계로부터 온다.
(D) 24시간 주기 리듬은 건강을 유지하는 데 매우 중요하기 때문에, 무시하면 인간의 건강에 심각한 영향을 미칠 수 있다.
(E) 어떤 동물들은 몇 달간 낮만 지속되는 한정된 상황에서도 24시간 주기 리듬을 성공적으로 조절한다.
(F) 인간의 24시간 주기 리듬은 여러 시간대를 지나는 여행을 하며 침해될 수 있고, 그로 인해 피로함과 정신적 혼란 등이 초래될 수 있다.

해설 | Summary   (B)는 24시간 주기 리듬을 조절하는 생리학적 과정을 설명한 단락 2의 내용을 요약해 놓은 것이다. (D)는 24시간 주기 리듬과 인간 건강의 관계를 설명한 단락 4의 내용을 요약해 놓은 것이다. (E)는 24시간 주기가 아닌 특정 상황에서의 24시간 주기 리듬 조절을 설명하는 단락 3의 내용을 요약해 놓은 것이다.

어휘 | **regulate** 조절하다   **optimize** 최적화하다   **carry out** 수행하다   **circadian** 24시간 주기의   **wakefulness** 깨어있음, 각성상태   **far-reaching** 광범위한   **internally** 내부적으로   **cue** 신호   **notably** 특히   **circumstance** 상황, 환경   **altogether** 완전히, 전혀   **absent** 없는, 부재의   **uniform** 일정한   **predictable** 예측 가능한   **hypothalamus** 시상하부   **clearing house** 정보 교환소   **interpret** 해석하다   **induce** 유도하다   **melatonin** 멜라토닌   **be associated with** ~와 관계가 있다   **retina** 망막   **activate** 활성화하다   **pineal gland** 송과선   **inhibit** 억제하다   **detect** 감지하다   **wavelength** (빛 등의) 파장   **opposite** 정반대의 상황   **stimulate** 자극하다   **blood pressure** 혈압   **present** 존재하는   **in regard to** ~에 관해   **respond to** ~에 반응하다   **reindeer** 순록   **consistent** 일정한   **free-running** 자율적으로 운영되는   **awareness** 자각, 인식   **resume** 다시 시작하다   **unbalanced** 불균형적인   **deficiency** 부족   **out of sync** 서로 맞지 않은, 조화되지 않은   **regenerate** 재생시키다   **heart failure** 심장 마비   **inconsistent** 일치하지 않는   **jet lag** 시차증   **be accustomed to** ~에 적응하다, 익숙하다   **exhaustion** 피로

Chapter 13 Life Science II

Intensive Drill 1

p.162

| 01 (D) | 02 (B) | 03 (B) | 04 (D) | 05 [Crocodiles – (A), (D)], [Birds – (B), (F), (G)] |

PARENTAL CARE OF BIRDS AND CROCODILES

Q01-1 Both birds and crocodiles, modern descendants of the archosaur, still share several physiological and behavioral traits. Anatomically speaking, they have evolved similar four-chambered hearts, as well as a one-way passage of air through their lungs. However, their behavioral similarities, especially in relation to fostering their offspring in nests, deserve particular attention, as both adult crocodiles and birds spend time nurturing their young to various degrees. One of the biggest questions still debated among researchers is whether or not these similarities in parental care between birds and crocodiles evolved independently or as the result of a common ancestor. Recent fossil evidence dated about 200 million years ago suggests that common ancestors, such as non-avian dinosaurs and pterosaurs, also provided extended care for their young in nests.

In the case of modern-day crocodiles, Q02(A) females still watch over their eggs in their nest, using their own urine as a means to moisten their nest and keep the eggs warm. Q05(D) Because the temperature of the eggs during their incubation period is a determining factor in the sex of the baby, the female crocodile meticulously regulates the temperature of her nest. As soon as the babies hatch from their eggs, Q02(C) Q05(A) the mother carries her newborn babies to shallow water, where they gradually accustom themselves to moving in the water and hunting for prey. At first, the young spend a lot of time around their mother, Q02(D) feeding off of bits of food that fall down from the mother's mouth. Q01-2 This process of newborn acquisition of food from the mother's mouth is moderately akin to Q05(F) the process of regurgitation that adult birds use to feed their young. However, after several weeks of intense care provided by their mother, sometimes up to two months, the young crocodiles are finally able to function independently and leave the nesting site.

In the case of adult birds taking care of their young, although parental care patterns vary greatly from species to species, they all still retain some inherently common traits. Q03 Q05(G) One of the most notable nurturing traits shared among bird species is that both the male and female parents contribute to varying degrees in raising their young. In many cases, the father will leave the nest to gather food, whereby he will regurgitate his food findings to the mother, who will then in turn pass some of the food from her mouth to the children's mouths. ① During the period when the young birds grow from helpless beings to adults, the mother continuously Q05(B) broods her young, guarding them and keeping them warm, and also ② protects them from predators and any environmental factors that could lead to their death. Despite some bird species being able to leave their nests a few weeks after birth, most young birds need their parents' care for a longer period of time before they are able to leave the nest.

새와 악어의 어버이 양육

새와 악어는 모두 조룡의 현대 후손이며, 여전히 몇몇 생리적·행동적 특성들을 공통적으로 지닌다. 해부학적으로 말하자면, 이들은 비슷하게 4개의 심실을 가진 심장을 발달시켰으며, 폐를 통해 공기가 한 방향으로 움직이는 하나의 통로가 있다. 하지만 그들의 행동적인 유사성, 특히 둥지에서 새끼들을 양육하는 것과 관련하여서는 특히 주목할 만하다. 어른 새와 악어 모두 다양한 정도로 어린 새끼를 양육하기 때문이다. 연구자들 사이에서 여전히 논란이 되는 질문 중 하나는 새와 악어가 양육에서 보이는 유사성이 각자 독립적으로 발달한 것인지 아니면 공통의 조상을 가진 것의 결과로 나타난 것인지에 대한 것이다. 2억 년 전까지 거슬러 올라가는 화석의 최근 증거들은 날지 못하는 공룡 및 익룡과 같은 공통 조상 역시 둥지에서 새끼들을 돌보았다는 사실을 보여준다.

현생 악어의 경우, 암컷은 자신의 소변을 사용하여 둥지를 촉촉하게 하고 알을 따뜻한 상태로 유지하며 둥지에서 알을 보살핀다. 부화 기간 동안 알 온도가 새끼의 암수를 결정하는 인자가 되기 때문에, 암컷 악어는 둥지 온도를 세심하게 조절한다. 새끼가 알에서 부화하면, 어미는 태어난 새끼들을 얕은 물로 데려가 이들이 물에서 움직이고 먹이를 사냥하는 것에 서서히 익숙해지도록 한다. 처음에 이 어린 새끼들은 어미 곁에서 많은 시간을 보내며, 어미의 입으로부터 떨어진 먹이를 먹는다. 갓 태어난 새끼가 어미의 입으로부터 음식을 습득하는 이 과정은 어른 새가 새끼들에게 먹이를 줄 때 사용하는 토해내는 과정과 유사하다. 그러나 몇 주, 경우에 따라서는 최대 2달간의 집중적인 양육 시기가 지나고 나면 어린 악어는 마침내 독립적으로 기능하고 둥지를 떠날 수 있게 된다.

새끼를 돌보는 어른 새의 경우, 양육 방식은 종마다 굉장히 다를 수 있지만, 어느 정도 본질적으로 공통된 특성을 갖는다. 조류에서 보이는 가장 두드러진 양육 특성은 암컷과 수컷 부모 모두 새끼를 기르는 데 다양한 정도로 기여를 한다는 점이다. 많은 경우에 아빠 새는 먹이를 구하기 위해 둥지를 떠난 후, 찾은 음식을 토해내어 어미 새에게 주고 어미 새는 다시 이 음식을 입에서 꺼내 새끼에게 먹인다. 무력한 새끼가 성인이 되는 기간 동안, 어미 새는 계속해서 새끼를 보호하고 따뜻하게 하며 품고, 또한 새끼를 포식자와 이들을 죽게 만들 수 있는 모든 환경 요인들로부터 보호한다. 일부 조류는 태어난 지 몇 주 후에 둥지를 떠날 수 있지만, 대부분의 새끼는 둥지를 떠나기까지 더 많은 기간 동안 부모의 보살핌을 필요로 한다.

01
지문의 akin to 와 의미상 가장 가까운 것은?

(A) ~와 관련된
(B) ~에 상반되는
(C) ~와 비교하여
(D) ~와 비슷한

해설 | Vocabulary akin to 의 의미는 단락 1의 "Both birds and crocodiles, modern descendants of the archosaur, still share …"에서 힌트를 얻을 수 있다. 즉, 악어와 새는 비슷한 특성을 공유한다고 하였다. 여기에서 어미 악어가 새끼에게 먹이를 주는 행동은 새와 비슷하다는 것을 유추할 수 있다.

02
단락 2에 따르면, 암컷 악어에 관한 내용으로 옳지 않은 것은?

(A) 알 온도를 조절한다.
(B) 수컷 악어가 새끼에게 먹이를 제공하길 기대한다.
(C) 새끼가 물속에서 움직이는 것에 적응하도록 도와준다.
(D) 새끼가 자신의 입에서 음식을 먹을 수 있게 한다.

해설 | Negative Fact (A), (C), (D)는 단락 2에서 언급된 내용이다. 그러나 단락 2에서 수컷 악어에 대한 언급은 없다.

03
단락 3에서 필자가 새의 어버이 양육 방식을 설명하는 방식은?

(A) 다양한 종들의 양육 방식을 비교함으로써
(B) 자녀를 키우는 데 있어 각각의 부모 역할을 상세히 설명함으로써
(C) 음식을 모아오는 아빠 새의 중요성을 설명함으로써
(D) 포식자로부터 새끼를 보호하는 데 있어 각각의 부모 역할을 설명함으로써

해설 | Rhetorical Purpose 단락 3에서 조류에서 가장 두드러진 양육 특성을 설명하기 위해 암컷과 수컷이 각각 양육에 어떠한 역할을 하는지 설명하고 있다.

04
다음 중 지문에서 표시된 문장의 주요 정보를 가장 잘 나타낸 문장은? 정답 외의 보기들은 중요한 의미가 바뀌거나 주요 정보가 빠져 있다.

(A) 새끼 새는 부모로부터 지속적인 보호를 받으며 자라기 때문에, 그들이 다 자랐을 때도 할 수 있는 것이 없게 될 가능성이 크다.
(B) 조류는 어미 새가 지속해서 새끼를 보호하고 따뜻하게 하는 등 과도한 어버이 양육을 하는 것으로 알려져 있다.
(C) 어미 새는 환경적 요인 혹은 포식자들과 같이 있음직한 위험으로부터 그들 자신을 보호하려 한다.
(D) 새끼 새가 성인으로 자라는 동안, 어미들은 끊임없이 이들을 돌보고, 있음직한 위협으로부터 지킨다.

해설 | Sentence Simplification ① 아기 새는 성인이 될 때까지 어미 새의 보살핌을 받는다. ② 환경적 요인 혹은 포식자로부터 아기 새를 보호한다. 표시된 문장을 가장 잘 나타낸 것은 (D)이다. 보기에서 ①은 "look after their young", ②는 "defend them from possible threats"로 바뀌어 표현되었다.

05
보기에서 적절한 문구를 골라 관련된 동물의 종과 연결하시오. 보기 중 2개는 사용되지 않는다. *이 문제는 3점이다.*

보기	
(A) 얕은 물에서 새끼가 먹이를 사냥하도록 자극한다.	악어
(B) 포식자로부터 새끼를 지킨다.	• (A)
(C) 새끼에게 음식을 모으는 것을 가르친다.	• (D)
(D) 성별 결정을 위해 알 온도를 조절한다.	새
(E) 태어난 후 새끼들이 둥지를 떠나도록 자극한다.	• (B)
(F) 음식물을 토해냄으로써 새끼에게 먹이를 준다.	• (F)
(G) 암수 모두의 어버이 양육을 통해 새끼를 기른다.	• (G)

해설 | Fill in a Table 단락 2와 3에서 새와 악어의 양육에 대해 설명하고 있다. 악어는 새끼에게 물에서 먹이를 사냥하도록 하고 암컷이 부화 기간에 성별 결정을 위해 알의 온도를 조절한다고 하였다. 이후 새의 경우를 설명한다. 새는 포식자와 위험한 환경적 요인으로부터 새끼를 지키고, 토해냄을 통해 수컷이 암컷에게, 그리고 암컷은 새끼에게 먹이를 주며 암수 모두가 양육에 참여한다고 하였다.

어휘 | **descendant** 후손, 후예 **archosaur** (고생물) 조룡 **physiological** 생리적 **behavioral** 행동적인 **anatomically** 해부학적으로 **chamber** 심실, 심방 **foster** 양육하다, 기르다 **offspring** 새끼, 자식 **nest** 둥지, 집 **fossil** 화석 **pterosaur** (고생물) 익룡 **incubation** 부화 **meticulously** 세심하게, 꼼꼼하게 **hatch** 부화되다 **shallow** 얕은 **accustom** 익숙하게 하다 **prey** 먹이, 사냥감 **regurgitation** 토해냄, 되새김 **inherently** 본질적으로, 선천적으로 **notable** 두드러진, 눈에 띄는 **contribute to** ~에 기여하다 **helpless** 무력한, 속수무책인 **brood** 품다 **predator** 포식자

Intensive Drill 2 p.164

01 (C)   02 (C)   03 (A)   04 (C)   05 [Altricial – (A), (G)], [Precocial – (B), (D), (F)]

PRECOCIAL AND ALTRICIAL SPECIES

Most animals, when they are born, require a great deal of care from one or more of their parents before they are fit enough to survive on their own. Others, however, are ready from a very early point in their development to leave the nest and fend for themselves. These two broad groups of animals can be characterized as either precocial or altricial. Precocial refers to animals that require little care after birth, while altricial refers to those that rely on their parents for a longer period. **Q03** The characteristics of each group can vary widely depending on the type of animal in question, and it can sometimes be difficult to distinguish one from the other.

Precocial animals have a much longer gestation period than altricial animals. For this reason, they are more fully developed when they are finally born. **Q05(F)** Animals can present precocial habits across a broad spectrum, and nowhere in nature is this better exemplified than in birds. **A** **Q05(D)** The young of most precocial bird species are born with well-developed skeletons, feathers, and an excellent sense of sight. **B** **Q01 Q04 Q05(B)** Some species of birds have young that are ready to leave the nest within 24 hours of hatching, and may be called superprecocial because of this amazing ability. **C** Another such species can actually dig its way out of the nest after hatching and leave immediately. Less precocial chicks still require some care; for instance, some are born without the ability to regulate their body temperature, and must rely on the mother to their warmth for a short period of time until they are able to regulate it themselves. **D** There are also some mammals, such as deer and goats, which are precocial to a certain degree, though they number far fewer than birds.

Q02 The other group of animals, those said to be altricial, require a great deal more care before they become independent. **Q05(A)** This group comprises most mammal species. Altricial young are often born without a number of basic survival traits, such as a coat of fur or fully open eyes. For this reason, they must be allowed some time to develop before they can be expected to survive without direct care from the mother. Humans are included among altricial species, and require one of the longest periods of care of any species. Other mammals, such as giraffes, display much shorter periods. It is believed by many scientists that this is due to their large size as adults. The young can gestate for a longer period within a larger adult, one result of which is that the young mammal is larger and more developed when it leaves the womb. In comparison to humans, giraffes have a gestation period of 15 months, whereas the gestation period for humans is only 9.

조성 동물과 만성 동물

대부분 동물들은 태어나면, 혼자서 살아남을 수 있을 때까지 부모 중 한쪽 혹은 양쪽 모두의 많은 보살핌을 받아야 한다. 그러나 어떤 다른 동물들은 발육 초기 단계에서부터 둥지를 떠나 스스로를 돌볼 준비가 되어 있기도 하다. 이 두 종류의 동물은 크게 조성 동물 혹은 만성 동물로 나눌 수 있다. 조성 동물은 태어난 후 보살핌이 거의 필요하지 않은 동물을 가리키고, 만성 동물은 부모에게 좀 더 긴 기간 동안 의존하는 동물을 가리킨다. 각 집단의 특징은 동물의 종류에 따라 매우 다양하며 때론 구별하기가 어려울 수도 있다.

조성 동물은 만성 동물보다 잉태 기간이 훨씬 더 길다. 이런 이유로 훨씬 성숙한 상태에서 태어난다. 동물들은 넓은 범위로 조성 습성을 나타내지만, 새만큼 이런 특징을 잘 보여주는 동물은 없다. **A** 대부분의 조성 조류의 새끼는 잘 발달된 골격과 깃털, 뛰어난 시력을 갖추고 탄생한다. **B** 일부 종류는 부화 후 24시간 이내에 둥지를 떠날 준비가 되며, 이런 뛰어난 능력 덕분에 초조성이라고 불린다. **C** 사실상 부화 직후 둥지를 떠날 수 있는 종도 있다. 이보다 조성이 적은 새끼들은 약간의 보살핌을 필요로 하는데, 예를 들어 일부는 체온을 조절할 능력이 없이 태어나서 스스로 조절할 수 있을 때까지 단기간 어미에게 의존해야 한다. **D** 포유 동물 중에서도 사슴과 염소같이 어느 정도는 조성 습성을 가지고 태어나는 동물도 있지만, 새만큼 그 수가 많지는 않다.

나머지 다른 집단의 동물, 즉 만성 동물은 독립하기까지 많은 보살핌을 필요로 한다. 포유동물의 대부분이 이 집단 에 속한다. 만성 동물의 새끼는 생존에 필요한 기본 특징 상당수를 갖추지 못하고 태어나는데, 그 예로 몸의 털이 없거나 눈을 다 뜨지 못한 상태를 들 수 있다. 이런 이유로 그들은 어미의 직접적인 보살핌 없이 살아남을 수 있을 때까지 시간이 필요하기도 하다. 인간은 만성 종류에 속하는데, 다른 어떤 종보다 더욱 장시간의 보살핌 기간이 필요하다. 기린과 같은 다른 포유동물은 훨씬 더 짧은 기간이 걸린다. 많은 과학자는 이것이 그들이 성숙했을 때의 커다란 몸 크기 때문이라고 생각한다. 크기가 큰 동물의 새끼는 오랫동안 태내에서 성장할 수 있기 때문에 태어날 때 더 크고 더 성숙한 상태에서 태어난다. 인간과 비교했을 때 기린의 임신 기간은 15개월인데 반해, 인간의 임신 기간은 9개월밖에 되지 않는다.

01 단락 2에 따르면, 초조성 동물이 될 수 있는 조건은?
   (A) 태어날 때 잘 발달된 골격을 갖추고 있다.
   (B) 태어나면서 생존에 필요한 특성을 다 갖추고 있다.
   (C) 거의 즉시 어미를 떠날 수 있다.
   (D) 완전히 발달한 시력을 필요로 한다.

해설 | Factual Information   지문에서는 알에서 부화한 지 24시간 이내에 둥지를 떠날 수 있는 일부 새를 초조성 동물로 분류하고 있는데, 조류에 국한시키지 않고 동물 전체에 적용한다면 초조성 동물이란 태어난 지 얼마 되지 않아 독립할 수 있는 동물을 가리킬 수 있다.

02 지문에서 This group 이 가리키는 것은?
(A) 포유동물
(B) 인간
(C) 만성 동물
(D) 조성 동물

해설 | Reference 바로 앞 문장에서 언급되고 있는 동물의 종류는 만성 동물이다.

03 지문에서 만성 동물과 조성 동물의 습성을 구별하는 것에 대해 추론할 수 있는 것은?
(A) 습성의 종류가 매우 다양하기 때문에 항상 확실히 구별되지는 않는다.
(B) 같은 종의 동물 사이에서는 뚜렷하게 구별된다.
(C) 조성 동물은 크기가 상대적으로 크고, 만성 동물은 대개 크기가 작다.
(D) 만성 동물은 조성 동물보다 더 진화했다고 여겨진다.

해설 | Inference 지문에서는 같은 만성, 조성 동물이라도 종류에 따라 매우 다양하며, 때론 종류를 구별하기가 어려울 수도 있다고 설명하고 있다.

04 다음 문장이 지문에 들어갈 곳을 나타내는 네 개의 사각형[■]을 보시오.

| 사실상 부화 직후 둥지를 떠날 수 있는 종도 있다. |

이 문장이 들어갈 가장 적절한 위치는?
(A) A   (B) B   (C) C   (D) D

해설 | Sentence Insertion 삽입 문장의 Another such species는 "Some species of birds have young that are ready to leave the nest within 24 hours of hatching, and may be called superprecocial because of this amazing ability"에서 언급한 태어난 지 얼마 안 되어 둥지를 떠나는 조류의 종류를 가리킨다. 따라서 삽입 문장의 적절한 위치는 **C**이다.

05 보기에서 적절한 문구를 골라 관련된 동물의 종류와 연결하시오.
보기 중 2개는 사용되지 않는다. *이 문제는 3점이다.*

(A) 대부분 포유동물을 포함한다.	만성 동물
(B) 태어난 후 몇 시간 안에 둥지를 떠날 수 있다.	• (A)
(C) 하나의 종 안에서도 다르다.	• (G)
(D) 태어날 때 잘 발달한 골격을 갖추고 있다.	조성 동물
(E) 알을 낳는 종만 해당한다.	• (B)
(F) 대부분 예로 새를 들 수 있다.	• (D)
(G) 상대적으로 긴 보살핌 기간이 필요하다.	• (F)

해설 | Fill in a Table 지문은 만성 동물과 조성 동물을 비교해 놓았다. 만성 동물은 태어날 때 자립 능력이 떨어져 어미의 보살핌이 필요한 기간이 상대적으로 긴 동물을 가리키고, 조성 동물은 태어나서 상대적으로 이른 시일 내에 자립할 수 있는 동물을 가리킨다. 조성 동물로는 조류가 대표적인데, 이들은 잘 발달한 골격, 깃털, 시력을 갖고 태어난다. 심지어는 태어난 후 몇 시간 안에 둥지를 떠날 수 있는 종류도 있다. 반면, 만성 동물은 포유류가 많으며, 조성 동물보다 어미의 보살핌이 오랜 시간 필요하다.

어휘 | **precocial** 조성의   **altricial** 만성의   **fend** 돌보다   **distinguish** 구별하다   **gestation** 잉태 기간   **spectrum** 범위   **exemplify** 예증하다   **skeleton** 골격, 뼈대   **feather** 깃털   **nest** 둥지, 보금자리   **superprecocial** 초조성의   **mammal** 포유동물   **gestate** 잉태하다, 서서히 성장하다

Intensive Drill 3   p.166

01 (A)   **02** (B)   **03** (B)   **04** (D)   **05** (B), (D), (E)

KUDZU

The American Southeast is famous for its beautiful rural areas that are home to a wide array of flora, including several species of trees and flowering plants. One particular plant that became dominant in this region within the past century is kudzu. Kudzu is a distinctive plant, immediately recognizable by its hairy vines, big leaves, and purple flowers blooming from long stems. ①Kudzu is not native to the United States, though; its origins can actually be traced to East Asia, particularly China and Japan, ②where its starchy roots were often eaten and its stems were used to produce fiber for ropes. However, since its introduction into the American Southeast, it has spread out over most of the area and become a threat that must be constantly and closely watched.

칡

미국의 남동부는 아름다운 시골 지역으로 유명한데, 이 지역에는 여러 종류의 나무와 꽃을 포함한 다양한 식물이 자라고 있다. 지난 백 년간 이 지역을 장악하게 된 특정 식물이 있는데, 바로 칡이다. 칡은 독특한 식물종이며 털이 많은 줄기와 큰 잎사귀, 그리고 긴 줄기에서 피어나는 보라색 꽃으로 한눈에 알아볼 수 있다. 칡은 본래 미국의 토종 식물은 아니고 사실 동아시아 지역, 특히 중국과 일본에서 그 근원을 찾을 수 있는데, 이곳에서는 탄수화물이 많은 뿌리를 종종 식용으로 사용했고 줄기는 밧줄용 섬유를 만드는 데 사용했다. 하지만 미국 남동지역에 칡이 도입된 이후, 이것은 전역으로 퍼져나가 계속해서 면밀히 주시해야 하는 위협적인 식물이 되었다.

Kudzu first became popular among people in the United States during the 1880s. Q02(B) Q02(C) The pleasant appearance of the plant, as well as its rapid growth, made it an attractive provider of shade in the warm, sunny climate of the Southeast. Fifty years later, beginning in the 1930s, farmers found other uses for kudzu. Due to its high protein content, Q02(D) it served as a convenient food source for livestock, and Q02(A) its deep roots helped anchor soil in order to prevent erosion. Q03 It became so popular that people would grow millions of seeds at a time and planted kudzu almost anywhere that they could, particularly in Alabama, Georgia, North Carolina, Virginia, and other such southeastern states.

However, such avid promotion of kudzu proved to have harmful consequences. Kudzu's quick rate of growth — up to a foot a day — soon became a major problem. It grew over open fields, up the trunks of trees, along sides of highways, and anywhere else, quickly overtaking land, vegetation, and infrastructure. Q04 By the 1950s, kudzu was hated by most farmers as an invasive plant species that could not be contained, and the U.S. government subsequently removed its status as an acceptable cover crop. Studies have shown that kudzu has cost agricultural and lumber industries several millions of dollars each year. The primary threat it poses is by blocking out sunlight other plants need, thus interfering with crop and timber production.

Fortunately, there are a few ways to counteract kudzu's spread. The most effective way of removing, or at least controlling, an infestation is the removal of the plant's root crown. These are knobs of plant tissue at the top of the root. By closely cutting this knob away from the root system, people can slow down the plant's growth. The leftover root system, which runs very deep, is then normally treated with herbicide. While this helps control the spread, it cannot stop it. Another proposed method would include using natural agents like bacteria or animals to destroy the plant, but currently this is not feasible, and kudzu remains a prevalent pest.

---

01 다음 중 지문에서 표시된 문장의 주요 정보를 가장 잘 나타낸 문장은? 정답 외의 보기들은 중요한 의미가 바뀌거나 주요 정보가 빠져 있다.

(A) 칡은 근원지가 동아시아이고 여기에서는 음식과 도구의 재료로 사용되었다.
(B) 칡은 근원지는 중국과 일본이고 미국에서는 여러 섬유를 만들기 위해 자주 쓰인다.
(C) 미국에서 칡은 동아시아 국가에서와는 다르게 녹말 식품과 도구에 쓰이는 섬유를 만드는 데 사용되었다.
(D) 미국에서 칡은 관상용 식물로 간주하였지만, 동아시아 국가들에서는 쓰임이 매우 많았다.

02 단락 2에 따르면, 미국에서 칡이 인기를 끌었던 이유로 옳지 않은 것은?

(A) 토양을 보존하는 데 도움이 되었다.
(B) 빨리 성장하지 않았다.
(C) 아름다운 장식용 식물이었다.
(D) 소의 먹이로 유용했다.

03 지문의 avid 와 의미상 가장 가까운 것은?

(A) 위험한
(B) 열렬한
(C) 간결한
(D) 희귀한

04 단락 3에서 필자가 칡에 대한 미국 정부의 결정과 연구 결과를 언급하는 이유는?
(A) 칡이 성장하는 데 필요한 최적의 환경을 지적하기 위해
(B) 미국과 다른 나라에서의 칡의 인기를 비교하기 위해
(C) 미국 전역으로 어떻게 칡이 퍼져나갔는지를 설명하기 위해
(D) 칡이 야기하는 피해가 매우 심각하다는 것의 증거를 제시하기 위해

해설 | Rhetorical Purpose 단락 3의 중심 내용은 칡이 미치는 피해에 대한 내용이다. 칡은 성장 속도가 너무 빨라서 주변 환경에 오히려 피해를 끼치고 결과적으로 정부가 나서서 칡을 허용 가능한 피복 식물에서 제외하기에 이르렀고, 농업과 목재 산업에 미치는 어마어마한 손해액이 언급되었다. 미국 정부의 움직임과 칡 연구 결과는 칡이 미치는 피해가 얼마나 심각한지를 짐작할 수 있게 하는 대목이다.

05 지문을 간략히 요약하기 위한 도입 문장이 아래 제시되어 있다. 지문에서 가장 중요한 내용을 표현한 세 개의 문장을 골라 요약문을 완성하시오. 일부 문장은 지문에 나오지 않았거나 중요하지 않은 내용이기 때문에 요약문에 포함되지 않는다. *이 문제는 2점이다.*

> 칡은 1880년대에 미국에서 인기 있는 식물이었지만, 현재는 침입종으로 간주되며 지속적인 관리 노력을 필요로 한다.

(A) 주로 큰 잎과 자주색 꽃, 긴 줄기로 인한 아름다운 외관 때문에 많은 양의 칡이 심어졌다.
(B) 처음에 미국인들은 칡을 농사와 장식을 위한 다양한 목적으로 사용했다.
(C) 칡의 뿌리는 얕아서 쉽게 뽑히고 없앨 수 있으며, 침략을 예방한다.
(D) 칡을 제거하는 가장 효과적인 방법은 뿌리의 윗부분을 없애고 뿌리에 독을 치는 것이다.
(E) 칡이 생겨난 후, 이것은 넓은 지역에서 급격히 성장하여 땅과 식물, 그리고 기반 시설에 피해를 주었다.
(F) 칡은 19세기에 처음 아시아에서 미국으로 건너왔으며, 여전히 사랑받는 식물이다.

해설 | Summary (B)는 칡의 다양한 사용에 대해 설명한 단락 2의 내용, (D)는 칡의 피해를 최소화하는 방법에 대해 설명한 단락 4, (E)는 칡의 피해를 설명한 단락 3을 요약했다.

어휘 | **rural** 시골의, 전원의 **dominant** 장악한 **recognizable** 알아볼 수 있는 **hairy** 털이 많은 **livestock** 가축 **avid** 열렬한 **promotion** 장려 **consequence** 결과 **overtake** 덮치다 **infrastructure** 사회 기반 시설 **invasive** 침입성의, 침략적인 **contain** 억제하다 **subsequently** 그에 따라 **lumber** 목재 **infestation** 횡행, 퍼짐 **leftover** 남은 **herbicide** 제초제 **feasible** 실현 가능한 **prevalent** 만연한, 일반적인 **pest** 골칫거리

Mini Test 1

01 (A) 02 (B) 03 (C) 04 (D) 05 (B), (D), (F)

HONEYBEE COMMUNICATION

Honeybees are very social creatures, as they live together in large hives that are divided into a highly structured hierarchy. Honeybees function as a collective unit: they depend on each other to build, defend, and sustain their hives. Thus, they have various methods of communicating with each other, including releasing various scents and dancing. Extensive research has shown that the purpose of their dance is twofold: to inform other members of the colonies of the location of nectar that bees use to make honey, their primary staple, and to recruit other bees to retrieve this nectar. In spite of numerous theories about the particular significance of the modes of communication used, researchers generally agree that there are essentially three: dance, sounds emitted during dance, and the distribution of odors from the food source.

꿀벌의 의사소통

꿀벌은 매우 사회적인 생물이며 상당히 조직적인 계급제로 나누어진 큰 벌집에서 모여 산다. 꿀벌은 공동체 단위를 이루어 역할하는데, 서로 의지하여 벌집을 만들고, 방어하고, 지켜낸다. 그래서 꿀벌은 다양한 방법으로 의사소통하는데, 여기에는 몇 가지 냄새를 분비하는 것과 춤이 포함된다. 광범위한 연구를 통해 이 춤에는 두 가지 목적이 있다는 것을 알아냈다. 꿀벌의 주요 산물인 꿀을 만드는 데 쓰는 화밀의 장소를 공동체의 다른 벌들에게 알려주는 것과 화밀을 가져올 다른 동료 벌들을 모집하는 것이 그것이다. 벌들의 의사소통 방식이 전하는 의미에 대해서는 여러 이론들이 있지만, 과학자들은 기본적으로 세 가지가 있다는 데 대부분 의견을 같이한다. 그것은 바로 춤과 춤을 출 때 나는 소리, 그리고 먹이의 근원지에서 나는 냄새의 배포이다.

The most immediate mode of communication that honeybees use is dance. These movements have been noticed by observers since the ancient days of Aristotle, but their exact purpose was not discovered until after the mid-twentieth century. Q01 An audience of honeybees from a hive must watch the dance closely and catch every detail in order to understand the message correctly. The dancer provides crucial information through various movements. Some of these movements include the rotation of the bee's tail a certain number of times and positioning its body at specific angles, and they are incorporated into two possible dances. The round dance is used to indicate food sources that are nearby, and Q02 the more complicated waggle dance indicates the location of food sources that are further away. This particular dance indicates the exact direction in which a food source is located and how far away it is.

In addition to the dance itself, different sounds are made by the dancer and detected through the antennae of honeybees. Ultimately, both visual movement and sound are necessary to relay the information properly. Moreover, the specific sounds must be made correctly to create a successful dance. A Q03 Experiments with bees that had artificially clipped wings or mutated, shorter wings showed that they produced a higher vibration when dancing, and as a result they could not recruit members from the colony to seek out the food source. B By comparing the dances of various other species of bees and the conditions in which these dances are performed, researchers now believe sounds are an adaptation to dancing in locations with little light. C Q04 The sounds supposedly help the audience bees follow the dancer's movements in these environments, but this is still speculative. D **Another theory is that certain sounds inform the audience that the food source is of a particularly desirable quality.**

The use of odor is another important mode of communication, though its usefulness in finding food is highly debated among researchers. Some have suggested that picking up these odors, instead of dancing, is the primary method bees use to find available food sources, but most believe that it plays a secondary role. The scent of certain flowers, nectar, and other properties of the food source rubs off on the scout as it searches for food. As the scout dances, the audience will pick up on this scent. This action is supposed to help them detect the exact location of the food source, as they can trace the smell to the spot.

꿀벌이 취하는 가장 즉각적인 의사소통 방법은 춤이다. 이 움직임은 Aristotle이 살던 고대 시대부터 관찰자들에 의해 인지되어 왔지만, 이 춤의 정확한 목적은 20세기 중반이 되어서야 밝혀졌다. 벌집에 있는 꿀벌은 춤의 뜻을 정확히 이해하기 위해서 춤을 자세히 관찰하고 모든 세부적인 움직임을 포착해야 한다. 춤을 추는 벌은 여러 움직임을 통해 중요한 정보를 제공한다. 이런 움직임의 예로 특정 숫자만큼 꼬리를 회전하고 몸을 특정 각도로 트는 방법 등이 있으며, 이 움직임들은 두 가지 가능한 춤으로 분류된다. 원무는 근처에 있는 먹이의 근원지를 알리기 위해서 쓰이는 춤이며, 좀 더 복잡한 8자로 움직이는 춤은 좀 더 멀리 있는 먹이의 장소를 알려주는 춤이다. 이 특별한 춤은 먹이가 있는 곳의 정확한 방향과 거리를 나타낸다.

춤 외에도 춤추는 벌이 내는 여러 소리는 꿀벌의 더듬이를 통해 감지된다. 결국, 정보를 정확히 전달하기 위해선 시각적인 움직임과 소리 모두가 필요하다. 또한 성공적으로 춤을 추기 위해서는 특정 소리를 정확하게 내야 한다. A 인위적으로 날개를 자르거나 변화시켜 날개가 짧은 벌을 실험한 결과, 이들은 춤을 출 때 높은 진동을 일으키는데, 이 때문에 먹이를 수집하러 갈 다른 동료들을 부르지 못하게 되었다. B 여러 다른 종의 벌춤과 이런 춤을 추는 다른 조건들을 비교한 결과, 연구자들은 소리가 빛이 적은 장소에서 춤을 인지하기 좋게 적응시킨 것으로 생각하게 되었다. C 소리는 아마 이런 환경에서 다른 벌들이 춤추는 벌의 움직임을 이해하도록 도와주는 것이라 추측되지만, 아직 추측에 불과하다. D **또 다른 이론에서 특정 소리는 동료들에게 먹이가 특히 좋은 질이라는 정보를 준다고 한다.**

냄새를 사용하는 것 역시 중요한 의사소통의 한 가지 방법이지만, 먹이를 찾는 데 이 방법이 유용한지는 연구자들 사이에서 의견이 분분하다. 일부는 먹이를 찾는 데 사용하는 주요 수단이 춤이 아니라 냄새를 알아차리는 것이라고 주장하지만, 대부분은 냄새가 부차적인 역할을 한다고 생각한다. 일부 꽃과 화밀, 그리고 먹이 근원지의 다른 특성에서 나오는 냄새가 벌이 먹이를 찾아다닐 때 이 벌에 옮는다. 정찰하는 벌이 춤을 추면 이를 보는 꿀벌들이 이 냄새를 알아차린다. 이 행동은 먹이가 있는 장소에서 나는 냄새를 맡아 먹이의 정확한 위치를 추적할 수 있도록 도움을 주는 것으로 추정된다.

01 지문의 provides 와 의미상 가장 가까운 것은?

(A) 제공하다
(B) 비틀다
(C) 억제하다
(D) 받다

해설 | Vocabulary   provides의 의미는 앞 문장에서 힌트를 얻을 수 있다. "An audience of honeybees from a hive must watch the dance closely and catch every detail in order to understand the message correctly"에서 벌이 춤을 추면 다른 벌들은 그 춤이 전달하는 메시지를 정확히 이해해야 한다는 사실로부터, 춤추는 벌(the dancer)은 다양한 춤을 통해서 중요한 정보를 제공한다(provides)는 것을 알 수 있다.

02 단락 2에 따르면, 8자 모양 춤이 이를 보는 꿀벌들에게 전달하는 메시지는?

(A) 오직 가까운 거리에 먹이가 있다는 것
(B) 먹이의 거리와 방향
(C) 먹이의 질
(D) 먹이가 있는 정확한 장소

해설 | Factual Information   단락 2의 마지막 문장에서 8자 모양 춤은 먹이가 있는 곳의 방향과 거리를 알려준다고 설명한다.

03 단락 3에 따르면, 짧은 날개의 벌들이 메세지를 효과적으로 전달하지 못하는 이유는?

(A) 날개로 먹이의 냄새를 충분히 전달하지 못해서
(B) 춤을 출 때 더 낮은 진동음을 만들어서
(C) 춤을 출 때 잘못된 소리가 나서
(D) 춤을 출 때 빨리 몸을 움직일 수 없어서

해설 | Factual Information 단락 3에서 소리도 메세지를 정확하게 전달하는 역할을 한다고 설명한다. 이것을 뒷받침하는 실험으로 벌의 날개를 자르면, 날개를 자르지 않은 벌보다 높은 진동수를 일으키는데, 그 결과 먹이를 수집할 벌을 모으지 못했다고 설명한다. 결국 벌의 날개를 자르면 잘못된 소리가 나기 때문에 정확한 메시지가 전달되지 않았음을 알 수 있다.

04 다음 문장이 지문에 들어갈 곳을 나타내는 네 개의 사각형[■]을 보시오.

> 또 다른 이론에서 특정 소리는 동료들에게 먹이가 특히 좋은 질이라는 정보를 준다고 한다.

이 문장이 들어갈 가장 적절한 위치는?

(A) A   (B) B   (C) C   (D) D

해설 | Sentence Insertion 삽입 문장은 벌의 소리가 전달하는 메시지에 대한 이론을 이야기하고 있다. 삽입 문장의 Another theory를 통해 벌의 소리에 대한 한 가지 이론이 소개된 다음에 삽입 문장이 와야 함을 알 수 있다.

05 지문을 간략히 요약하기 위한 도입 문장이 아래 제시되어 있다. 지문에서 가장 중요한 내용을 표현한 세 개의 문장을 골라 요약문을 완성하시오. 일부 문장은 지문에 나오지 않았거나 중요하지 않은 내용이기 때문에 요약문에 포함되지 않는다. *이 문제는 2점이다.*

> 먹이에 대한 정보를 제공하는 과정에서, 꿀벌은 여러 가지 방법으로 의사소통해야 한다.

(A) Aristotle은 꿀벌의 춤이 벌집을 위해 화밀을 수집하기 위한 행동이라는 것을 처음으로 발견한 사람이었다.
(B) 꿀벌은 다른 동료 벌들이 먹이의 장소를 정확히 찾을 수 있도록 화밀의 냄새를 제공한다.
(C) 더듬이가 평균 길이보다 짧은 꿀벌은 8자 춤을 이해하는 데 필요한 소리를 감지할 수 없다.
(D) 꿀벌의 날개에서 나는 소리는 다른 꿀벌들이 춤의 의미를 이해하도록 도와주는 중요한 역할을 한다.
(E) 변이된 꿀벌은 여러 종류의 춤에서 꿀벌이 만들어내는 정확한 움직임을 찾아내는 데 아주 중요하게 사용된다.
(F) 꿀벌은 벌집에 있는 다른 동료들에게 먹이의 장소를 알려주기 위한 주요 방법으로 두 종류의 춤을 춘다.

해설 | Summary 지문은 꿀벌이 먹이의 위치를 다른 꿀벌에게 전달할 때 사용하는 의사소통 수단에 대해 언급하고 있다. 단락 2에서는 춤, 단락 3에서는 소리, 단락 4에서는 냄새에 대해 설명하고 있다. (B)는 단락 4의 내용을, (D)는 단락 3의 내용을, (F)는 단락 2의 내용을 요약한 것이다.

어휘 | **hierarchy** 계급제 **extensive** 광범위한 **staple** 주요 산물 **recruit** 모집하다 **retrieve** 가져오다 **emit** (소리를) 내다 **distribution** 배포 **odor** 냄새 **rotation** 회전 **crucial** 중요한 **waggle** (8자로 움직이는) 춤 **detect** 탐지하다 **antennae** 더듬이 **clipped** 짧게 잘린 **mutate** 변화시키다 **vibration** 진동 **adaptation** 적응 형태 **supposedly** 아마 **speculative** 추측에 근거한 **scent** 냄새

Mini Test 2
p.170

| 01 (D) | 02 (A) | 03 (B) | 04 (C) | 05 [Seed Plants – (B), (E)], [Spore Plants – (C), (F), (G)] |

SEEDS AND SPORES

There are several ways to categorize the many types of plants on Earth, but when it comes to reproduction, plants can generally be divided into two basic categories: those which reproduce by means of seeds, and those which reproduce through the use of spores. Though they serve the same basic functions, the differences between these two reproductive units and the methods of reproduction they represent are many.

종자와 포자

지구의 많은 종류의 식물을 분류하는 데는 여러 방법이 있지만, 번식 방법으로 분류할 때 식물은 보통 기본적인 두 가지 종류로 구분된다. 종자(씨앗)로 번식하는 종류와 포자를 사용해 번식하는 종류이다. 이 두 종류는 동일한 기본 역할을 하지만, 이 두 가지 번식 종류의 차이점과 그들이 나타내는 번식 방법은 다양하다.

The more familiar of the two categories is the seed-bearing plant. Seeds are basically small, enclosed units that contain an embryo of the parent plant. The embryo, an undeveloped version of the parent plant, is the most important component, as it can eventually grow into a new plant. Q05(B) All seeds feature certain protective structures to ensure the health of the embryo. For instance, ①it is usually protected by an outer covering known as a seed coat, ②a layer of material that helps both to retain moisture in the seed and to keep it from becoming damaged by environmental factors. Q02 Seeds also contain a source of food for the embryo to feed on as it develops. This food is usually a combination of oils, starches, and proteins, which occupies the space between the embryo and the seed coat.

Seeds are considered the end stage in the process of reproduction in seed plants, having been preceded by other familiar processes such as pollination and flowering. All that remains is for the seeds to be spread, which may be accomplished with the help of wind, water, or even animals. Q03 Q05(E) Seed plants are the most advanced form of plant in evolutionary terms. For this reason, they often dominate their respective ecological niches, like forests and grasslands. Those few plants that still reproduce entirely asexually — without a partner — represent the most basic form. Between them lies an intermediate stage in the evolution of plants: the spore plant.

Spores are much simpler in their makeup than seeds, and are a common reproductive unit of bacteria and fungi in addition to plants. Q04 One of the key differences between seeds and spores is that spores do not have the same support mechanisms, such as stored food resources or defensive coverings. Q05(F) So spores from plants are less able to survive in unfavorable conditions for long periods of time before growing into a full plant. Q05(C) As a rule, spores are released in large numbers as a way of giving them a better chance of growing to maturity.

Despite their many shortcomings, spores do have some advantages over seeds. Q05(G) Spores are extremely light compared to seeds, and can thus be dispersed more easily and over greater distances, even by light breezes. The most common type of spore plant is the fern, which releases spores from the underside of its leaves. Some species of fern may be said to bridge the evolutionary gap between spore-producing plants and seed-producing plants. The presence of ferns dates back over 300 million years, and over the course of their long evolution, some have evolved into seed-bearing plants.

두 가지 종류 중 조금 더 우리에게 친숙한 것은 종자를 맺는 식물이다. 씨앗은 기본적으로 어미 식물의 배(胚)를 품고 있는 작고 껍질로 싸여 있는 기관이다. 식물로 발달하기 전 단계인 배는 자라서 최종에는 새 식물이 될 수 있으므로 가장 중요한 요소이다. 모든 종자는 배를 지키기 위해 특정한 보호막을 구축한다. 예를 들어, 보통 배는 종피라는 껍질로 보호되는데, 이는 종자의 수분을 유지하며 환경적 요소로 인해 배가 손상되는 것을 막도록 하는 물질로 이루어진 피막이다. 종자는 또한 배가 자라는 데 필요한 영양물을 포함하고 있다. 이 영양물은 지방, 탄수화물, 단백질의 배합으로 이루어진 것으로 배와 종피 사이의 공간을 차지한다.

종자는 종자식물 번식에서 마지막 단계로 생각되는데, 수분(受粉)과 개화 같은 비슷한 단계의 다음에 온다. 이제는 종자가 퍼지는 일만 남았는데, 이는 바람과 물 혹은 동물의 힘을 빌려서 완성된다. 종자식물은 진화적으로 가장 발달한 형태의 식물이다. 이런 이유로 각각의 적합한 생태적 장소, 즉 산림이나 초원에서 우월한 위치를 차지한다. 완전 무성(암수의 구분 없이)으로 번식하는 몇 안 되는 식물들은 가장 기본적인 형태이다. 식물 진화의 중간 단계가 이들 사이에 있는데, 이것이 바로 포자식물이다.

포자는 종자보다 구성이 훨씬 더 간단한데, 식물뿐만 아니라 박테리아와 진균의 흔한 번식 구조이다. 종자와 포자의 주요 차이점 중 하나는 바로 포자에는 저장된 영양분이나 보호막 같은 보호 메커니즘이 없다는 사실이다. 그러므로 식물의 포자는 완전한 식물로 자라기 전에 장기간 불리한 상황에 놓이면 잘 살아남지 못한다. 일반적으로 포자식물은 성체로 자랄 수 있는 더 많은 기회를 얻기 위한 한 가지 방법으로 많은 수의 포자를 퍼뜨린다.

많은 단점이 있기는 하지만 포자는 종자보다 나은 이점이 몇 가지 있다. 포자는 종자와 비교했을 때 상당히 가벼우므로 심지어 약한 미풍에도 더욱 쉽고 더욱더 멀리 퍼져나갈 수 있다. 포자식물의 가장 흔한 종류로 고사리가 있는데, 잎의 밑부분에서 포자를 퍼트린다. 고사리의 일부 종류가 포자식물과 종자식물의 진화론적 공백 부분을 잇는 다리일 것이라는 설이 있다. 고사리의 존재는 3억 년 전으로 거슬러 올라가는데, 기나긴 진화 과정에서 일부가 종자를 맺는 식물로 진화했다는 것이다.

01 다음 중 지문에서 표시된 문장의 주요 정보를 가장 잘 나타낸 문장은? 정답 외의 보기들은 중요한 의미가 바뀌거나 주요 정보가 빠져 있다.

(A) 수분은 배의 종자에 저장되는데, 배는 종피라는 보호막 안에 있다.
(B) 종피라고 불리는 바깥 껍질은 배에 수분을 공급해주어 그것을 잠재적 위험으로부터 스스로 보호할 수 있도록 한다.
(C) 배는 종자 안에서 손상되지 않도록 수분에 의해 보호받는데, 종피는 씨앗이 마르지 않도록 한다.
(D) 종피는 배가 마르지 않고 외부 손상을 받지 않도록 보호한다.

해설 | Sentence Simplification   ①은 배는 종피가 보호해준다는 내용, ②는 종피는 수분을 유지하고 외부 요인으로부터 보호해준다는 내용이다. ②는 ①보다 좀 더 구체화한 내용이라고 할 수 있다. 원문의 내용을 가장 잘 옮긴 것은 (D)이다.

02 단락 2에서 종자식물에 관한 내용 중 옳은 것은?
(A) 종자는 배를 위한 영양분을 제공한다.
(B) 종피는 새로운 식물에 필요한 유전적 정보를 담고 있다.
(C) 모든 종자식물이 배에 대한 보호막을 가지고 있는 것은 아니다.
(D) 배의 먹이는 종피의 표면에 있다.

해설 | Factual Information 단락 2에서 종자식물의 종자는 안에 배의 생명을 유지해주는 영양분이 있다고 설명한다.

03 지문에서 this reason 이 가리키는 것은?
(A) 종자가 바람과 물, 동물들의 도움을 받아 퍼져나가는 것
(B) 종자식물이 가장 발달한 형태의 식물이라는 것
(C) 종자 안에 배의 영양분이 있다는 것
(D) 종자가 번식 과정의 마지막 단계라는 주장

해설 | Reference this reason 은 앞 문장 "Seed plants are the most advanced form of plant …"를 가리킨다.

04 단락 4에 따르면, 포자가 취약한 이유는?
(A) 아주 넓은 지역으로 분포될 수 없다.
(B) 지상에서 포식자를 끌어들인다.
(C) 영양분과 보호 수단이 없다.
(D) 땅에 뿌리를 내리지 못한다.

해설 | Factual Information 포자식물이 종자식물보다 취약한 이유로 영양분을 비축해둔 것이나 보호막이 없다는 점을 들고 있다.

05 보기에서 적절한 문구를 골라 관련된 식물의 종과 연결하시오. 보기 중 2개는 사용되지 않는다. 이 문제는 3점이다.

(A) 포식자에게 취약하다.	종자식물
(B) 보호 외피가 있다.	• (B)
(C) 많은 양으로 퍼진다.	• (E)
(D) 녹색 식물에만 한정된다.	포자식물
(E) 가장 진보된 식물 형태로 여겨진다.	• (C)
(F) 불리한 환경에서 살아남을 가능성이 적다.	• (F)
(G) 무게로 인해 먼 거리까지 퍼질 수 있다.	• (G)

해설 | Fill in a Table 종자식물은 식물 중에서도 가장 진화된 형태로 씨앗은 배를 지키기 위한 보호막과 영양분을 담고 있어 좋지 않은 환경에도 잘 견딜 수 있고 우월한 생태적 지위를 갖고 있다. 이에 반해 포자식물은 불리한 환경에 취약하므로 포자를 대량으로 뿌리는 형태로 생존확률을 높인다. 그리고 포자는 가벼우므로 멀리까지 날아갈 수 있다.

어휘 | **reproduction** 번식 **reproduce** 번식하다 **spore** 포자 **reproductive** 번식하는 **seed-bearing** 종자를 맺는 **embryo** 배(胚) **starch** 탄수화물, 녹말 **precede** 먼저 일어나다 **pollination** 수분(작용) **flowering** 개화, 꽃이 핌 **respective** 각각의 **asexually** 무성(無性)으로 **fungus** (pl. fungi) 진균, 균류 **unfavorable** 불리한 **maturity** 성체, 성숙기 **shortcoming** 단점 **disperse** 퍼지다, 흩어지다 **breeze** 미풍 **fern** 고사리 **presence** 존재

iBT Practice
p.172

| 01 (B) | 02 (B) | 03 (B) | 04 (C) | 05 (A) | 06 (D) | 07 (D) | 08 (B) | 09 (B) | 10 (B) | 11 (C) | 12 (C) |
| 13 (B) | 14 (B), (C), (E) | | | | | | | | | | |

CARNIVOROUS PLANTS

All plants rely on nutrients taken from the soil in order to survive. Q02 However, in areas where the soil does not contain enough vital nutrients, some plants have adapted to supplement their diets from another source: living organisms. Though they are few in number, carnivorous plants are nonetheless fascinating beings whose "diets" range from one-celled organisms to insects in order to survive. They are commonly found in marshlands. Q01 Carnivorous plants feature one of several types of "traps" to capture prey, which they consume to make up for nutrients that may be missing from the soil.

식충 식물

모든 식물은 생존하기 위해 흙에서 나오는 영양분에 의지한다. 하지만 토양에 필수 영양분이 충분히 없는 지역의 식물은 다른 공급원, 즉 다른 생명체를 통해 필요한 양분을 보충해야 한다. 식충 식물은 수적으로는 얼마 안 되지만, 생존을 위해 미생물에서부터 벌레까지 '잡아먹는' 굉장히 흥미로운 식물이다. 이 식물은 흔히 습지대에 발견된다. 식충 식물에는 그 주요한 특징으로 먹이를 잡기 위한 여러 종류의 '덫' 중 한 가지를 가지고 있다는 것인데, 이들은 먹이를 섭취하여 토양에서 빠져있는 영양분들을 보충한다.

The most well-known of these plants are the snap traps, which includes the Venus flytrap. Q03 Snap traps are easily identified by their leaves, which are separated into two lobes that have the ability to fold together. These carnivorous plants capture prey through mechanisms that are not unlike the common household mousetrap. Q04(D) Inside the lobes, the surface is covered with tiny hairs that are sensitive to movement. Q04(A) When the plant's prey brushes against the hairs, it triggers a closing mechanism that rapidly brings the two lobes together, trapping the prey securely inside. Q05 The speed at which the traps respond is unheard of for most plant life: the time between triggering the hairs and snapping shut is less than a second. As the prey struggles inside the trap, it only triggers more hairs, causing the leaves to tighten their grip. Q04(B) The plant then secretes liquid chemicals from special glands into the trap to dissolve the prey and absorb all of its nutrients. Besides the Venus flytrap, only one other type of snap trap exists today, referred to as the waterwheel plant. The two share a common ancestor and differ only in a few ways. Q04(C) For instance, the waterwheel is an aquatic plant, while the flytrap is exclusively terrestrial. In addition, the flytrap feeds primarily on arthropods like spiders, while the waterwheel lives off of simple invertebrates, like certain types of plankton.

Pitfall traps are among the most strangely beautiful types of carnivorous plants, though they may also be the most primitive. They function much more simply than snap traps, though the wide variety of pitfall traps, also known as pitcher plants, means that some are more complex than others. The simplest type of this carnivorous plant is best exemplified by the sun pitcher plant. It consists of tall leaves that roll into a tubular shape. The mouth of the leaf, and the opening of the trap are wider than the rest of the body. Q06 Q09-1 The sun pitcher plant simply waits for unsuspecting prey to slip down the sides of the tube, where digestive enzymes wait in a small pool to drown and ingest it. Q07 Q09-2 More complex forms of pitfall traps use basically the same mechanism for killing and eating their prey, but the actual trap can be far more elaborate. The cobra plant features a large, vacant bulb at its tip with small transparent dots that let sunshine in. ① When insects, mostly ants, crawl into the bulb, they struggle to escape through these "false exits," but ② eventually they tire themselves out and Q09-3 fall down the tube into the digestive chamber, ③ where they are dissolved by the plant's digestive enzymes.

A third type of carnivorous plant uses flypaper traps to capture its prey. A Q13 This plant is extremely numerous and varies greatly in appearance from species to species. B **However, all of them share the same basic trapping mechanism.** Q10 Their leaves contain glands that release a sticky type of mucus which can be used to trap insects that unknowingly land on them. C One type of flypaper trap is the butterwort plant. D The butterwort has broad, bright green leaves that are grouped closely together. Q11 Flying insects are attracted to the butterwort because the thin layer of mucus on its leaves has the semblance of dew, making the plant look like it is covered in water droplets. When the insect lands, the leaves release more of this sticky substance, which further traps the insect. Another type of flypaper trap is the cape sundew, which has an appearance quite unlike its distant cousin the butterwort. The leaves of the cape sundew are long and thin, like tentacles. Tiny hairs run up and down the length of the tentacles, each containing a large drop of mucus. Q12 As with the butterwort, insects are attracted to the cape sundew, expecting to find water, but instead become trapped in the mucus. The tendrils then curl up, enclosing the insect in a tight coil that aids in digestion.

그중에서도 가장 잘 알려진 종은 파리지옥을 포함하는 포획형이다. 포획형은 잎으로 쉽게 구별할 수 있는데, 둘로 나누어진 두 열편은 접힐 수 있다. 이 종류의 식충 식물은 흔히 볼 수 있는 가정용 쥐덫과 비슷한 방법으로 먹이를 잡는다. 열편 안은 움직임을 감지할 수 있는 예민한 감각모로 덮여 있다. 이 식물의 먹이가 감각모를 건드릴 때, 이것은 문을 닫게 하는 메커니즘을 촉발하여 두 열편은 빠르게 닫히고 먹이를 완전히 안에 가두어 버린다. 덫이 반응하는 속도는 대부분 식물에서는 찾아볼 수 없을 정도이다. 감각모를 자극하고 잎이 닫히는 순간까지 걸리는 시간은 1초도 되지 않는다. 먹이가 덫 안에서 발버둥칠수록 감각모를 더 많이 건드리게 되어 열편은 더 단단히 닫힌다. 그 후에 식물은 특수한 분비샘에서 덫 안으로 액체 화학물을 분비하여 먹이를 분해하고, 모든 영양분을 섭취한다. 파리지옥 외에 현존하는 유일한 포획형 종류는 벌레잡이말이다. 두 식물은 공통된 조상에서 시작되어 크게 다르지 않다. 예를 들어, 파리지옥은 오로지 육지에서만 사는 반면, 벌레잡이말은 수중에서 산다. 그리고 파리지옥은 거미와 같은 절지동물을 주로 섭취하는 반면에, 벌레잡이말은 특정 플랑크톤류와 같은 단순 무척추동물을 먹으며 살아간다.

포충낭형은 식충 식물 중에서 가장 원시적이지만 묘하게도 가장 화려한 종이기도 하다. 포획형보다 훨씬 더 간단한 기능을 하지만, 함정형이라고도 알려진 포충낭형의 종류가 워낙 다양해 어떤 종은 다른 종보다 더 복잡하기도 하다. 그중에서 제일 간단한 식충 식물의 종류로는 해받이병풀을 예로 들 수 있다. 이것은 관 모양으로 말아지는 큰 잎들로 이루어져 있는데, 잎의 입구와 덫이 열리는 부분은 다른 부위보다 더 넓다. 해받이병풀은 의심하지 않는 먹이가 소화 효소로 이루어진 작은 연못의 관 밑으로 들어올 때까지 기다려 물에 빠뜨려 이것을 먹는다. 더욱 복잡한 형태의 포충낭형도 기본적으로 같은 방법으로 먹이를 잡아먹는데, 함정 자체는 훨씬 더 복잡하다. 달링토니아는 크고 속이 빈 구근의 끝 쪽에 있는 투명한 작은 구멍을 통해 햇빛을 받아들이는 것이 특징이다. 대부분 개미인 벌레들이 구근 안으로 들어오면 이 '가짜 출구'를 통해 밖으로 도망치려 애쓰다가 결국에는 지쳐 포충낭 아래의 소화기관에 떨어져 소화 효소에 의해 분해되고 만다.

세 번째 식충 식물 종류는 먹이를 포획하기 위해 끈끈이 덫을 사용한다. A 이 식물은 무수히 많고 종류에 따라 생김새도 매우 다양하다. B **하지만 모든 종류는 기본적으로 같은 방식의 덫을 사용한다.** 잎에는 끈끈한 점액을 분출하는 샘이 있는데 그것을 모르고 그것들 위에 내려앉은 벌레를 포획하는 데 이 점액이 사용된다. C 끈끈이형의 하나로 벌레잡이제비꽃이 있다. D 벌레잡이제비꽃은 서로 가까이 붙어있는 넓고 밝은 녹색 잎을 갖고 있다. 잎에 있는 얇은 점액막이 이슬의 모습을 해서 마치 물방울이 잎에 붙어 있는 것처럼 보이는데, 이를 통해 날개 달린 곤충을 유인한다. 벌레가 잎 위에 앉으면 잎에서 끈끈한 점액을 더욱 많이 분출하여 벌레를 더욱 확실히 잡는다. 끈끈이형의 또 한 종류로는 끈끈이귀개가 있다. 생김새는 많이 다르지만 벌레잡이제비꽃의 먼 친척쯤 된다. 끈끈이귀개의 잎은 길고 얇아 마치 촉수처럼 생겼다. 이파리 위쪽부터 아래까지 짧은 털로 덮여 있으며 각각의 털에는 큰 점액 방울들이 있다. 벌레잡이제비꽃에서처럼 벌레가 물을 찾기 위해 끈끈이귀개로 다가가는데 물 대신 점액에 빠지게 된다. 그 후 덩굴은 둥글게 말려, 소화를 돕는 단단한 고리 안에 벌레를 가둔다.

01 지문의 capture 와 의미상 가장 가까운 것은?

(A) 감시하다
(B) 잡다
(C) 소화하다
(D) 유혹하다

해설 | Vocabulary   capture 앞에 있는 traps라는 단어를 통해 단어 의미의 힌트를 얻을 수 있다.

02 단락 1에 따르면, 식충 식물이 살아 있는 생명체로부터 영양분을 얻는 이유는?

(A) 해충에 대항하는 면역력을 발달시켜야 하기 때문에
(B) 그들이 사는 토양으로부터 필요한 영양분을 얻을 수 없기 때문에
(C) 토양에 있는 해로운 화학물질로부터 자신을 보호해야 하기 때문에
(D) 습지대에는 고단백질의 생명체가 풍부하기 때문에

해설 | Factual Information   지문에서 어떤 지역에는 식물이 필요로 하는 영양분이 토양에 없기 때문에 그곳에 사는 식물은 다른 먹이 원천, 즉 살아 있는 생명체에서 영양분을 취하도록 진화되었다고 설명한다.

03 필자가 지문에서 쥐덫 을 언급하는 이유는?

(A) 포획형의 약점을 설명하기 위해
(B) 포획형이 어떻게 기능하는지 더욱 잘 설명하기 위해
(C) 포획형의 잎의 강점을 강조하기 위해
(D) 파리지옥을 다른 포획형과 비교하기 위해

해설 | Rhetorical Purpose   단락 2에서 파리지옥이 먹이를 잡는 과정에 대해 설명하고 있다. 파리지옥은 둘로 나누어진 열편을 접어 먹이를 잡는다. 이어서 덫이 언급되었는데, 파리지옥이 먹이를 잡는 것은 덫의 원리와 비슷하다고 설명하고 있다. 여기에는 파리지옥을 독자가 잘 알고 있는 도구인 쥐덫에 비유해서 설명함으로써 독자의 이해력을 높이려는 목적이 있다.

04 단락 2에 따르면, 포획형 식물에 관한 내용으로 옳지 않은 것은?

(A) 열편을 닫아 먹이를 잡는다.
(B) 화학물질로 먹이를 녹여 섭취한다.
(C) 대부분 육지 식물이다.
(D) 작은 털로 먹이의 존재를 감지한다.

해설 | Negative Fact   포획형 식물은 육지 식물과 수중 식물로 나누어진다.

05 단락 2에 따르면, 포획형 식물에 대해 추론할 수 있는 것은?

(A) 일단 먹이를 잡으면, 그 먹이가 빠져나갈 가능성은 희박하다.
(B) 주로 크기가 크고 영양분이 많은 곤충을 섭취한다.
(C) 사냥 방법 면에서 다른 다양한 종류가 있다.
(D) 서식지가 파괴되면서 멸종 위기에 처해 있다.

해설 | Inference   먹이가 포획형 식물의 열편의 미세한 털을 건드리는 순간 매우 빠른 속도로 열편을 닫아 먹이를 잡으며, 먹이가 빠져나가려고 발버둥칠수록 열편은 더욱 꽉 닫힌다. 이 사실로 미루어 보아, 먹이는 일단 잡히면 빠져나가기 힘들다는 것을 알 수 있다.

06 지문의 ingest 와 의미상 가장 가까운 것은?

(A) 잡다
(B) 이용하다
(C) 독살하다
(D) 먹다

해설 | Vocabulary   "The sun pitcher plant simply waits for unsuspecting prey to slip down the sides of the tube, where digestive enzymes wait in a small pool to drown and ingest it"의 밑줄 친 부분에서 힌트를 얻을 수 있다. 먹이가 소화액 속으로 미끄러져 떨어진다는 것으로부터 ingest 는 '먹다'의 의미임을 유추할 수 있다.

07 지문의 elaborate 와 의미상 가장 가까운 것은?

(A) 원시적인
(B) 깊은
(C) 산성의
(D) 복잡한

해설 | Vocabulary   동의어 단서를 찾을 수 있는 문제이다. 해당 문장의 complex와 뜻이 같다.

08 다음 중 지문에서 표시된 문장의 주요 정보를 가장 잘 나타낸 문장은? 정답 외의 보기들은 중요한 의미가 바뀌거나 주요 정보가 빠져 있다.

(A) 달링토니아는 소화액을 생산하는 구근으로 먹이를 유인하여 잡는다.
(B) 달링토니아의 구근은 곤충을 잘못된 출구로 속여서 지치게 한 다음 소화기관으로 떨어지도록 유인한다.
(C) 곤충들은 달링토니아의 밝은색에 의해 이 식물의 '위'로 유인되어 구근 안에 갇히게 된다.
(D) 개미가 달링토니아의 구근으로 들어오면 달링토니아는 출구를 막아 소화기관에 가둔다.

해설 | Sentence Simplification   표시된 문장은 복잡해 보여도 시간적인 순서로 이어져 있다. ①, ②, ③은 각각 먹이를 잡는 단계를 나타내는데, ①은 곤충이 구근 안으로 들어오면, 가짜 출구로 빠져나오려고 계속해서 시도한다는 내용, ②는 먹잇감이 지쳐서 소화액이 있는 방으로 떨어지게 된다는 내용, ③은 식물의 소화액에 녹아 분해된다는 내용이다. 원문의 내용을 가장 잘 옮긴 것은 (B)인데, 정답에는 ③의 과정이 생략되어 있다. ③과 같은 정보는 이미 ②에 내포된 정보이므로 없어도 무관하다.

09 단락 3에 따르면, 포충낭형 식물에 관한 내용 중 옳은 것은?
(A) 먹이를 죽이는 메커니즘은 포획형과 비슷하다.
(B) 소화 물질로 가득 차 있다.
(C) 다른 식충 식물과 같이 화려하지 않다.
(D) 식충 식물 중 가장 진화된 형태이다.

해설 | Factual Information 포충낭형 식물의 공통적인 특징은 주머니처럼 생긴 조직에 소화액이 들어있다는 점이다.

10 지문에서 them 이 가리키는 것은?
(A) 곤충
(B) 잎
(C) 분비샘
(D) 종

해설 | Reference 잎에서 끈끈한 액체를 분비하는 것은 곤충이 그것들(them)에 내려앉을 때, 곤충들이 꼼짝없이 잡히기 때문이라고 설명했다. 여기서 그것들은 끈끈한 액체를 분비하는 잎을 가리킨다.

11 지문의 semblance 와 의미상 가장 가까운 것은?
(A) 가치
(B) 구성
(C) 모습
(D) 본질

해설 | Vocabulary "Flying insects are attracted to the butterwort because the thin layer of mucus on its leaves has the semblance of dew, making the plant look like it is covered in water droplets"에서 밑줄 친 부분의 의미가 똑같다는 것을 알면 semblance의 의미는 쉽게 찾을 수 있다.

12 단락 4에 따르면 끈끈이형 식물에 유인당하는 벌레가 찾는 것은?
(A) 먹이
(B) 은신처
(C) 물
(D) 짝

해설 | Factual Information 끈끈이형 식물은 식물에서 분비되는 점액이 마치 물처럼 보이도록 만들어 곤충들을 유인한 뒤 곤충이 끈끈한 점액에 붙으면 이것을 먹는다.

13 다음 문장이 지문에 들어갈 곳을 나타내는 네 개의 사각형[■]을 보시오.

> 하지만 모든 종류는 기본적으로 같은 방식의 덫을 사용한다.

이 문장이 들어갈 가장 적절한 위치는?
(A) ■A (B) ■B (C) ■C (D) ■D

해설 | Sentence Simplification However는 삽입 문장이 앞에 언급된 내용과 대조적인 내용이 나와야 함을 암시한다. 삽입 문장의 내용은 먹이를 잡는 기본적인 원리는 모두 똑같다는 내용인데, 이 내용은 지문 중에서 끈끈이 덫은 종류별로 생김새가 천차만별이라고 언급한 "This plant is extremely numerous and varies greatly in appearance from species to species"와 내용상 대조를 이루고 있다. 따라서 삽입 문장은 이 문장 뒤에 오는 것이 적절하다.

14 지문을 간략히 요약하기 위한 도입 문장이 아래 제시되어 있다. 지문에서 가장 중요한 내용을 표현한 세 개의 문장을 골라 요약문을 완성하시오. 일부 문장은 지문에 나오지 않았거나 중요하지 않은 내용이기 때문에 요약문에 포함되지 않는다. 이 문제는 2점이다.

> 많은 종류의 식충 식물이 있는데, 그들은 먹이를 잡는데 각각 고유한 방법이 있다.

(A) 벌레잡이말과 파리지옥은 포획형 식물의 유일한 두 종류이다.
(B) 가장 원시적인 식충 식물은 곤충이 스스로 덫에 걸리도록 한다.
(C) 몇몇 식충 식물은 벌레를 유혹하기 위해 끈끈한 점액을 사용하고 이것이 잎에 닿으면 못 움직이게 한다.
(D) 식충 식물은 식물에 필요한 모든 필수 영양분을 제공하지 못하는 지역에서 가장 일반적으로 발견된다.
(E) 몇몇 식충 식물은 예민한 감각모를 건드리면 반사적으로 반응하는 방법으로 먹이를 공격적으로 잡는다.
(F) 식충 식물 중 몇 종류는 토양 환경에서 자라지 못하기 때문에 물에서만 발견된다.

해설 | Summary 지문은 식충 식물의 대표적인 3가지 종류를 설명하고 있다. 쥐덫의 원리로 먹이를 붙잡는 포획형, 소화액이 든 주머니에 벌레가 빠지면 그것을 섭취하는 포충낭형, 식물에서 점액을 분비시키고 이것을 물이라고 착각하고 찾아오는 곤충을 잡는 끈끈이형에 대해 설명하고 있다. (B)는 포충낭형에 대한 내용, (C)는 끈끈이형에 대한 내용, (E)는 포획형에 대한 내용을 요약한 것이다.

어휘 | carnivorous 식충성의 **supplement** 보충하다 **organism** 생명체, 유기체 **fascinating** 흥미로운 **marshland** 습지대 **make up for** ~을 보충하다 **lobe** 열편(裂片) **mechanism** 방법, 원리 **trigger** 촉발하다 **secrete** 분비하다 **gland** 분비샘, 선 **dissolve** 분해하다 **exclusively** 오로지 **terrestrial** 육지에 사는, 육생의 **arthropod** 절지동물 **invertebrate** 무척추동물 **primitive** 원시적인 **exemplify** 예가 되다 **tubular** 관의 **digestive** 소화의 **enzyme** 효소 **bulb** 구근 **transparent** 투명한 **chamber** 방 **mucus** 점액 **butterwort** 벌레잡이제비꽃 **sundew** 끈끈이주걱 **tentacle** 촉수 **tendril** 덩굴손

Chapter 14 Physical Science

Intensive Drill 1 p.178

01 (B) 02 (B) 03 (D) 04 (B) 05 (B), (D), (E)

ISAAC NEWTON

Q01 One of the most influential figures in modern history was Isaac Newton, a British scholar whose work led to breakthroughs in many different sciences, including mathematics, astronomy, biology, and chemistry. Surprisingly, for a man with such a brilliant mind, Newton performed below average in his school years. He was admitted to the prestigious Trinity College, but neglected classes to work on his own private studies. When the school closed because of an outbreak of the plague, Newton finally had the time he needed to develop his many theories in math and science. It is often said that Newton made some of his most important discoveries within the year that followed, which is why it is called his *annus mirabilis*, or "year of miracles." His discoveries were later recorded in his famous book *Philosophiae Naturalis Principia Mathematica*, often referred to as simply the *Principia*, widely considered the most important work of science in history.

The highlight of Newton's book was his three laws of motion. Q02 The first law explained the force of inertia, stating that an object will remain either still or moving at a constant speed and direction until acted upon by another force. For example, a satellite moving through space will continue to move at a constant speed and direction unless it encounters an obstacle that alters its speed and direction.

According to the second law, acceleration is produced when a force acts on a mass; hence, the greater the mass, the greater the amount of force is needed to move it. It proposes a direct relationship between force, mass, and acceleration, and a way to calculate the force acting on an object by multiplying the object's mass by the rate at which its speed changes. In the third law, Newton states that every time a force acts on an object, that object also exerts an equal force in return. Take, for example, a man pushing a large rock up a hill: the man exerts force on the rock to move it, while the rock exerts an equal amount of force on the man's muscles.

These three simple rules laid the groundwork for another of Newton's most famous theories, that of gravitation, which also appears in the *Principia*. Newton theorized that Q03(A),(C) each body with mass attracts other bodies with mass, the attraction being stronger for greater masses and at shorter distances. This attraction is of course the force of gravity, Q03(D) and it is an illustration of his third law of motion, that every force creates an opposite and equal force. A Q03(B) Newton applied this theory to an important problem of his day: why the planets move in circular orbits. B **Newton combined gravitation with his laws of motion to find the solution.** Q04 The moon orbits the Earth, he theorized, because it is held there by Earth's gravity. C However, the force exerted back onto the Earth by the moon keeps it at a distance. D

ISAAC NEWTON

현대사에 가장 큰 영향을 끼친 인물 중 한 명인 Isaac Newton은 영국의 학자로 수학, 천문학, 생물학, 화학을 포함한 많은 과학 분야에서 여러 큰 발전을 이끌었다. 놀랍게도 그런 뛰어난 능력의 소유자인 Newton은 학창 시절에는 평균 이하의 성적을 보였다. 그는 명문 트리니티 대학에 입학했지만, 자신의 별도 연구를 위해 학교 공부를 소홀히 하였다. 전염병 발발로 학교가 문을 닫았을 때, Newton은 비로소 수학과 과학의 많은 이론을 발전시키는 데 필요한 시간을 가질 수 있게 되었다. 바로 이다음 해에 Newton의 가장 중요한 발견들이 이루어졌다고 알려져 있는데, 그렇기 때문에 이 해를 그의 *annus mirabilis*, 즉 '경이적인 해'라고 부른다. 그의 발견은 이후 역사상 가장 중요한 과학 업적으로 여겨지며, 종종 『프린키피아』라고도 불리는 그의 유명한 저서인 『자연 철학의 수학적 원리』에 기록되었다.

Newton 저서의 하이라이트는 세 개의 운동 법칙이었다. 제1법칙은 관성의 힘을 설명한 것인데 물체는 다른 힘으로 저지될 때까지 계속해서 일관된 속도와 방향으로 움직이고 있거나 혹은 정지해 있을 거라는 법칙이다. 예를 들어, 우주에서 움직이고 있는 위성은 속도나 방향을 바꾸게 하는 장애물을 만나지 않는 한 한결같은 속도와 방향으로 계속해서 움직이고 있을 것이다.

제2법칙에 따르면, 가속은 질량에 힘이 가해질 때 발생한다. 따라서 질량이 크면 클수록 이를 움직이기 위한 힘의 양은 더 많이 필요하다. 이는 힘, 질량, 그리고 가속도 사이의 직접적인 관계와 물체의 가속도와 물체의 질량을 곱해서 물체에 작용하고 있는 힘을 계산하는 방법을 제공한다. 제3법칙에서 Newton은 물체에 힘이 작용할 때마다 물체가 반작용으로 같은 힘을 낸다고 진술했다. 예를 들어, 언덕 위로 큰 바위를 밀어 올리는 남자가 있다고 할 때, 그 남자가 바위를 움직이기 위해 바위에 힘을 가하면, 바위도 같은 양의 힘을 남자의 근력에 가한다는 뜻이다.

이 세 가지 간단한 법칙은 Newton의 또 다른 가장 유명한 이론이자 『프린키피아』에도 등장하는 만유인력 이론을 위한 토대를 제공한다. Newton은 모든 질량이 있는 물체는 다른 질량이 있는 물체를 끌어당기며, 인력은 질량이 크고 거리가 짧을수록 커진다는 이론을 폈다. 이 인력은 물론 중력의 힘이며, 모든 힘은 동일한 반작용적 힘을 만들어낸다고 하는 그의 제3운동법칙의 실례가 된다. A Newton은 이 이론을 그가 살던 당시의 중요한 문제, 즉 행성이 왜 원형 궤도로 돌까 하는 문제에 적용했다. B **Newton은 그 해답을 찾기 위해 그의 운동 법칙과 중력을 결합했다.** 그가 이론화한 바에 따르면 달은 지구의 중력에 이끌려서 지구를 돈다. C 그러나 반대로 달이 지구에 역으로 가하는 힘으로 인해 그 거리가 유지된다. D

01
지문의 breakthroughs 와 의미상 가장 가까운 것은?
(A) 혼란
(B) 발전
(C) 개혁
(D) 토대

해설 | **Vocabulary** 현대사에 가장 큰 영향을 끼친 인물 중 한 명이라고 하였으므로, breakthroughs 는 '발전'의 의미임을 알 수 있다.

02
필자가 지문에서 위성을 언급하는 이유는?
(A) 그의 운동 법칙에 의해 영향을 받는 물체의 종류를 보여주기 위해
(B) 관성이 어떻게 움직이고 있는 물체의 움직임을 결정하는지 설명하기 위해
(C) 관성의 힘이 물체마다 어떻게 다른지 설명하기 위해
(D) 그의 운동 법칙이 전체 자연계에서 보편적이라는 사실을 강조하기 위해

해설 | **Rhetorical Purpose** "For example, a satellite moving through space …"에서 앞에 언급된 관성의 법칙에 대한 예로 satellite 를 언급한 것이다. 앞 문장 중 "… an object will remain either still or moving at a constant speed and direction until acted upon by another force"는 관성의 법칙에 따라 물체가 어떻게 움직이는지 설명하고 있다. 가장 타당한 보기는 (B)이다.

03
단락 4에 따르면, 중력에 관한 내용으로 옳지 않은 것은?
(A) 질량이 큰 물체에서 더욱 강하다.
(B) 행성이 원형 궤도로 공전하는 이유를 설명해준다.
(C) 질량이 있는 모든 물체에서 나오는 힘이다.
(D) Newton의 제2법칙에 따라 작용한다.

해설 | **Negative Fact** 단락 4에 따르면, 중력은 제2법칙이 아닌 제3운동법칙의 실례가 된다.

04
다음 문장이 지문에 들어갈 곳을 나타내는 네 개의 사각형[■]을 보시오.

> Newton은 그 해답을 찾기 위해 그의 운동 법칙과 중력을 결합했다.

이 문장이 들어갈 가장 적절한 위치는?
(A) A (B) B (C) C (D) D

해설 | **Sentence Insertion** 삽입 문장의 to find the solution은 행성이 원형 궤도로 공전하는 이유에 대한 해답을 말한다. 지문의 마지막 두 문장은 바로 행성이 공전하는 이유에 대해 설명해 놓은 것이다. 따라서 가장 적절한 위치는 B이다.

05
지문을 간략히 요약하기 위한 도입 문장이 아래 제시되어 있다. 지문에서 가장 중요한 내용을 표현한 세 개의 문장을 골라 요약문을 완성하시오. 일부 문장은 지문에 나오지 않았거나 중요하지 않은 내용이기 때문에 요약문에 포함되지 않는다. 이 문제는 2점이다.

> Isaac Newton은 역사상 가장 큰 영향력을 미친 과학자이며, 그의 업적은 물리학의 기본 원리 연구의 토대를 마련했다.

(A) Newton은 물리학 외의 모든 방면의 과학, 특히 수학을 연구했고, 또한 미적분학의 창설로 유명하다.
(B) Newton은 대학이 학사를 중단했던 시기에 충분한 시간이 있었고, 곧 『프린키피아』로 그의 이론을 출간하였다.
(C) 훗날 과학자와 교사로서 성공하긴 하였지만, 대학 다닐 때 Newton은 평균 이하의 학생이었다.
(D) Newton 이론 중 가장 유명한 것은 3개의 운동 법칙인데, 그것은 물체가 어떻게 그것에 가해지는 힘에 대응해 움직이는지를 설명해준다.
(E) Newton은 운동 법칙을 사용해 중력 이론에 다다랐으며, 이로 인해 행성의 움직임을 설명할 수 있었다.
(F) Newton의 운동 법칙은 원자나 다른 미시적 현상의 움직임을 설명할 만큼 자세하지는 못하다.

해설 | **Summary** (B)는 단락 1을, (D)는 Newton의 운동법칙에 대해 설명한 단락 2와 3을 (E)는 Newton의 중력 이론을 설명한 단락 4를 요약한 것이다.

어휘 | **breakthrough** 큰 발전, 약진 **admit** 입학시키다 **prestigious** 명문의, 명성 있는 **neglect** 소홀히 하다 **outbreak** (전쟁, 질병의) 발발 **plague** 전염병 **inertia** 관성 **constant** 일관된 **encounter** 만나다 **obstacle** 장애물 **alter** 바꾸다 **mass** 질량 **calculate** 계산하다 **object** 물체 **multiply** 곱하다 **exert** 힘을 가하다 **groundwork** 토대 **theorize** 이론화하다 **attraction** 인력, 끄는 힘 **gravity** 중력 **illustration** 실례, 설명 **circular** 원형의

Intensive Drill 2

01 (A)　02 (C)　03 (D)　04 (D)　05 [Organic Chemistry – (B), (E), (F)], [Inorganic Chemistry – (C), (G)]

ORGANIC AND INORGANIC CHEMISTRY

The field of chemistry is a complex one involving many sub-disciplines and applications. However, at its simplest, the study of chemistry can be divided into two main groups according to the structure of the chemicals being studied: organic chemistry and inorganic chemistry. Q05(B) Organic compounds contain a carbon compound in its structure and other elements such as hydrogen, oxygen, and nitrogen are attached to this carbon backbone. Carbon is an extremely versatile atom Q01 with the potential to form many kinds of bonds with a myriad of atoms. In addition, carbon is one of the few elements that can bond with itself to form straight chains, branched chains, rings, and other shapes. Organic compounds are also formed from a relatively small number of elements, but due to the nature of carbon, Q05(E) these elements are able to be combined in an almost unlimited number of combinations. Q05(F) ①Consequently, living things have taken advantage of the flexibility of carbon and ②possess it in the chemical structures of their DNA, lipids, and fatty acids, as well as proteins and enzymes, ③which are the foundations for cellular processes within organisms.

Opposite organic chemistry, inorganic chemistry is concerned with molecules that do not contain the carbon compound. There are countless compounds and numerous amounts of applications that fall under the realm of inorganic. Q05(C) Contrary to organic compounds' biological nature, inorganic compounds have a geologically-based nature and are associated with the nonliving portion of the world. Not all, but most inorganic compounds contain metal, and Q04 because of this characteristic, inorganic compounds tend to conduct electricity, which organic compounds are not capable of. In terms of complexity, they are less complex in their structure, hence less stable than organic compounds.

The applications for both types of chemistry are wide-ranging and often overlap. Organic chemistry is a highly creative science field in which chemists create new molecules and explore the properties of existing compound, and is a foundation of biochemistry, biotechnology, and medicine, since they play such a critical role in life processes. It has a vital role in economic growth and is essential to a diverse range of industries including rubber, plastics, fuel, pharmaceutical, and agrichemical industries. Meanwhile, inorganic chemistry is a highly practical science and useful for specific purposes due to the thermal-stability of high melting points and electrical conductivity properties. Usually inorganic chemistry focuses on how inorganic elements can be modified, separated, or used in products. Q05(G) As such, inorganic chemistry is a key element of environmental science, particularly the recovery and prevention of pollution. Microchip industries, fibers, and mining are also areas where inorganic chemistry plays an important role.

유기 화학과 무기 화학

화학 분야는 많은 하위 분야와 응용 분야를 포함하는 복잡한 분야이다. 하지만 가장 간단하게 말하자면, 화학 연구는 연구되는 화학 물질의 구조에 따라 두 가지의 주요 그룹으로 나뉠 수 있다. 즉, 유기 화학과 무기 화학으로 나뉜다. 유기 화합물은 그 구조에 탄소 화합물을 포함하고, 수소, 산소, 질소와 같은 다른 원소들이 이 탄소 골격에 붙는다. 탄소는 무한한 원자와 수많은 종류의 결합을 형성할 수 있는 잠재력을 지닌 매우 다용도의 원자이다. 게다가 탄소는 자신과 결합하여 직쇄, 분기 사슬, 고리 및 다른 형태를 형성할 수 있는 몇 안 되는 원소 중 하나이다. 유기 화합물은 또한 비교적 적은 수의 원소들로 형성되지만, 탄소의 본질로 인해 이 원소들은 거의 무한한 숫자의 결합물로 결합될 수 있다. 그 결과, 생물은 탄소의 유연성을 이용해왔고, 생물 내 세포 과정의 기초가 되는 단백질과 효소뿐만 아니라 DNA, 지질, 지방산의 화학 구조에도 탄소를 지닌다.

유기 화학의 반대인 무기 화학은 탄소 화합물을 포함하지 않는 분자들과 관련이 있다. 무기 화학의 영역에는 무한한 혼합물과 수많은 응용이 있다. 유기 화합물의 생물학적인 성질과는 반대로, 무기 화합물은 지질학에 기반을 둔 성질을 가졌고, 세상의 무생물 부분과 관련이 있다. 모두 그렇지는 않지만, 대부분의 무기 화합물은 금속을 포함하고, 이런 특징으로 인해 무기 화합물은 전기를 전도하는 경향이 있는데, 이는 유기 화합물에게는 불가능한 일이다. 복잡성이라는 측면에서 그들은 구조상 덜 복잡하고, 따라서 유기 화합물보다 덜 안정적이다.

두 화학 분야의 응용은 범위가 넓고 종종 겹치기도 한다. 유기 화학은 화학자들이 새로운 분자를 만들어내고, 기존에 존재하던 화합물의 성질을 분석한다는 점에서 매우 창의적인 과학 분야이며, 생명 과정에서 중요한 역할을 하므로 생화학, 생명공학, 의학의 기초가 된다. 경제적 성장에서 필수적인 역할을 하며 고무, 플라스틱, 연료, 약학, 그리고 농화학 산업을 포함한 다양한 범위의 산업에서 필수적이다. 반면 무기 화학은 매우 실용적인 과학이며, 매우 높은 용해점과 전기 전도도 성질로 인해 특수한 목적을 수행하는 데 유용하다. 보통 무기 화학은 무기 원소가 수정되고, 분리되거나 제품에서 사용될 수 있는 방법에 초점을 둔다. 이러한 점에서 무기 화학은 특히 오염의 회복이나 방지와 같은 환경 과학의 핵심 요소이다. 마이크로칩 산업, 섬유 산업, 그리고 광산업 또한 무기 화학이 중요한 역할을 하는 분야이다.

01
지문의 versatile 과 의미상 가장 가까운 것은?
(A) 유연성이 있는
(B) 생산적인
(C) 이로운
(D) 포괄적인

해설 | Vocabulary 무한한 원자와 수많은 종류의 결합을 형성할 수 있는 잠재력을 지녔다고 설명하고 있으므로 versatile 의 의미는 '융통성이 있는'이라는 의미의 adaptable과 유의어로 볼 수 있다.

02
다음 중 지문에서 표시된 문장의 주요 정보를 가장 잘 나타낸 문장은? 정답 외의 보기들은 중요한 의미가 바뀌거나 주요 정보가 빠져 있다.
(A) 그러므로 탄소의 화학적 구성을 사용하는 것은 모든 생물의 세포 과정에서 필수적이다.
(B) 따라서 융통성 있는 탄소의 유전적 구성은 생물이 가질 수 있는 가장 좋은 이점으로 여겨진다.
(C) 그 결과, 생물은 다양한 생물학적 구성의 화학적 구성에 탄소의 유연성을 이용한다.
(D) 따라서 모든 생물의 DNA, 지질, 지방산, 단백질, 효소는 화학적 구성에 탄소를 지닌다.

해설 | Sentence Simplification 표시된 문장을 가장 잘 옮긴 것은 (C)이다. 표시된 문장에서 ①은 "living beings utilize carbon's adaptability"로, ②와 ③은 "in their chemical makeup of various biological compositions"로 바뀌었다.

03
지문의 realm 과 의미상 가장 가까운 것은?
(A) 경계
(B) 결과
(C) 측면
(D) 영역

해설 | Vocabulary realm 은 영역이라는 의미의 sphere와 유의어이다.

04
필자가 지문에서 금속 을 언급하는 이유는?
(A) 유기 화합물과 무기 화합물의 공유된 성질을 강조하기 위해
(B) 무기 화합물 사용에 대한 예를 설명하기 위해
(C) 무기 화합물의 본질을 묘사하기 위해
(D) 무기 화합물의 전기 전도도를 언급하기 위해

해설 | Rhetorical Purpose 지문에서 무기 화합물이 금속 을 포함하는 본질로 인해 전기를 생산하는 경향이 있다고 설명하고 있으므로, 금속 을 언급한 이유는 무기 화합물의 전기 전도도를 언급하기 위해서이다.

05
보기에서 적절한 문구를 골라 해당하는 화학의 분야와 연결하시오. 보기 중 2개는 사용되지 않는다. 이 문제는 3점이다.

(A) 다른 분야보다 더 발전했다.	유기 화학
(B) 화합물에 탄소를 지닌다.	• (B)
(C) 무기물의 특성을 갖는다.	• (E)
(D) 수소 골격에 원소를 결합한다.	• (F)
(E) 거의 무한한 원소 혼합물을 가질 수 있다.	무기 화학
(F) 주로 생물과 관련된다.	• (C)
(G) 환경 과학에서 필수적인 역할을 한다.	• (G)

해설 | Fill in a Table 지문에 의하면, 유기 화합물에는 탄소 화합물이 포함되며, 거의 무한한 원소 혼합물을 가질 수 있고, 주로 생물과 관련이 있다. 반면 무기 화학은 유기 화학과 달리 무기물의 특성을 가지며, 오염 회복이나 방지와 같은 환경 과학에서 필수적인 역할을 한다.

어휘 | **sub-discipline** 하위 분야 **organic chemistry** 유기 화학 **inorganic chemistry** 무기 화학 **straight chain** 직쇄 **branched chain** 분기 사슬 **flexibility** 유연성, 변통성 **lipid** 지질 **fatty acid** 지방산 **protein** 단백질 **enzyme** 효소 **overlap** 겹치다 **biochemistry** 생화학 **biotechnology** 생명공학 **pharmaceutical** 약학의, 제약의 **agrichemical** 농화학의, 농약(의) **thermal-stability** 열 안정성 **melting point** 용해점, 녹는점 **electrical conductivity** 전기 전도도[전도성]

Intensive Drill 3

p.182

01 (D) 02 (C) 03 (A) 04 (B) 05 [Mountain Glacier – (A), (B), (C)], [Continental Glacier – (E), (G)]

MOUNTAIN AND CONTINENTAL GLACIERS

Glaciers can be roughly divided into two very different types: mountain glaciers and continental glaciers. The most well-known type of glacier is the mountain variety, also called an alpine glacier. Q05(B) Mountain glaciers form when valleys become filled with ice after years of continuous freezing snow, which condenses into ice and slowly begins its descent down the valley slope. ①The shape taken by mountain glaciers is largely determined by the topography of the area in which they form, and ②in general they are longer than they are wide, ③due to their gradual momentum in one fairly specific direction. Q05(A) The shape generally conforms to the rocky passes that they fill as they flow toward lower elevations. One exception to this is a type of mountain glacier called a piedmont glacier, which forms at the bottom of a mountain or valley. Because it flows outward rather than in a single direction, it can have more of a circular shape than other mountain glaciers. Q02 Q05(C) Because mountain glaciers exist in subarctic climates, they are affected by the elements in ways that continental glaciers are not, sometimes even putting them in danger of collapse. For example, rainfall can melt small portions of mountain glaciers, forming icy streams of water that can, over long periods of time, carve elaborate ice caves ever deeper into the glacier.

Continental glaciers are quite different. As their name suggests, they are massive in size and far more expansive. Today, the only continental glaciers in existence are the ice sheets of the Arctic and Antarctic regions. These continental glaciers formed over millions of years, as layer after layer of snow fell to the Earth and became compacted into one thick sheet of ice weighing millions of tons. The bedrock of the continent of Antarctica is almost completely covered in glacier ice, with only a few isolated mountain ranges penetrating the thick ice sheet. Q04 In some areas, the ice is so plentiful that it extends beyond the edge of the continent and into the ocean, forming what are known as ice shelves. On the Antarctic mainland, the ice can reach depths of over a mile. Q03 Q05(E) The effect of such a thick, heavy layer of ice is that it depresses the actual land mass so that most of it is below sea level. The pressure exerted on the deepest layers of the ice sheet by the denser and heavier upper layers causes some of this deeper ice to melt, creating a slippery layer of ice and water below the ice sheet. Q05(G) Unlike mountain glaciers, continental glaciers do not flow in any consistent manner, but gravity may cause portions of the continental glacier to slide along the fine bottom layer of ice down any slopes.

산악 빙하와 대륙 빙하

빙하는 크게 두 종류, 산악 빙하와 대륙 빙하로 나눌 수 있다. 가장 잘 알려진 빙하 종류는 고산 빙하라고 불리는 산 위에 있는 빙하이다. 산악 빙하는 골짜기에 몇 년간 지속해서 눈이 쌓여 얼게 되면서 형성되고, 얼음으로 압축되어 점차 계곡의 경사면으로 하강하기 시작한다. 산악 빙하의 형태는 이것이 형성되는 지역의 지형에 의해 결정되는데, 한 특정 방향을 향한 점진적 운동력 때문에 보통 넓이보다 길이가 더 길다. 빙하가 고도가 낮은 곳으로 움직이기 때문에 빙하의 형태는 그것이 채우는 산길과 일치한다. 이것의 예외로 산록 빙하가 있는데, 산이나 골짜기의 밑부분에서 형성된다. 산록 빙하는 한 방향보다는 바깥 방향으로 움직이기 때문에 다른 산악 빙하보다 둥그런 형태를 띠운다. 산악 빙하는 북극에 가까운 기후에서 발달하기 때문에 대륙 빙하와는 다르게 주위 요소들에 영향을 받는데, 때로는 이 때문에 붕괴할 위험에 놓이기도 한다. 예를 들어, 강우 때문에 산악 빙하 일부가 녹아 얼음 물줄기가 생기면 장기간에 걸쳐 빙하의 아주 깊숙한 곳에 얼음 동굴이 생길 수도 있다.

대륙 빙하는 많이 다르다. 이름에서 알 수 있듯이, 크기도 거대하고 더 광대하다. 오늘날까지 유일하게 존재하는 대륙 빙하는 북극과 남극지역의 빙상이다. 이 대륙 빙하는 수백만 년에 걸쳐 생겨났는데, 눈이 땅에 내려와 계속 쌓이면서 수백만 톤에 달하는 무게를 지닌 두꺼운 빙상으로 압축된 것이다. 남극 대륙의 기반암은 거의 빙하로 덮여 있고, 몇 개 안 되는 산맥만이 두꺼운 빙상을 뚫고 솟아 있다. 일부 지역에서는 얼음이 너무 커져 대륙의 끝을 넘어서 바다에까지 뻗쳐 있는데, 이것이 바로 빙붕이다. 남극 대륙에서 얼음의 두께는 1마일이 넘기도 한다. 이렇게 두껍고 무거운 얼음층의 영향 중 하나는 이것이 대륙을 내리 눌러서 땅 대부분을 해수면 밑으로 밀어버리는 현상이다. 무겁고 밀도가 높은 얼음층이 가장 두꺼운 층의 빙상에 압력을 가하면서 이 압력이 밑부분의 얼음을 녹여, 빙상 밑에 얼음과 물로 된 미끄러운 층을 만들게 된다. 산악 빙하와 다르게 대륙 빙하는 일관된 방식으로 움직이지 않지만, 중력에 의해서 빙하 일부가 섬세한 바닥 층을 따라 경사 밑으로 미끄러져 내려가기도 한다.

| 01 | 다음 중 지문에서 표시된 문장의 주요 정보를 가장 잘 나타낸 문장은? 정답 외의 보기들은 중요한 의미가 바뀌거나 주요 정보가 빠져 있다.

(A) 산악빙하는 골짜기와 산에서 형성되는데, 이 골짜기와 산은 빙하를 길고 넓은 형태로 만들어 아래로 이동하게 한다.
(B) 산악빙하가 일정한 속도로 움직일 때 지형이 이동 방향을 결정한다.
(C) 한쪽으로만 향하는 산악빙하의 움직임은 폭이 길이보다 넓어지도록 만든다.
(D) 산악빙하는 이동하는 주변 지역의 모양에 따라 주로 길고 폭이 좁은 형태가 된다.

해설 | Sentence Simplification 표시된 문장을 가장 잘 옮긴 것은 (D) 이다. 표시된 문장에서 ①은 "Mountain glaciers take the shape of the surrounding area through which they travel"로, ②는 "and mostly in a long and narrow form"으로 바뀌었다.

| 02 | 단락 1에 따르면, 얼음동굴에 대해 추론할 수 있는 것은?

(A) 동굴 속의 물이 얼면 얼음으로 가득 찬다.
(B) 긴 기간에 걸쳐 정교하게 만들어진 것이다.
(C) 빙하를 약하게 만들어 일부분을 움푹 들어가게 할 수 있다.
(D) 수마일을 뻗어갈 수 있는 빙하수의 강을 형성한다.

해설 | Inference 산악 빙하는 여러 가지 자연적인 요소로 인해 붕괴할 수도 있다고 설명하고 있다. 강우로 인해 산악빙하가 일부 녹아 형성되는 얼음 동굴을 예로 제시하고 있다.

| 03 | 지문에서 it 이 가리키는 것은?

(A) 얼음층
(B) 효과
(C) 덩어리
(D) 수준

해설 | Reference 해당 문장에서 땅덩어리를 누르는 것은 얼음층이다.

| 04 | 단락 2에 따르면, 빙붕이 형성되는 시기는?

(A) 장기 침식으로 인해 빙하가 붕괴할 때
(B) 빙상이 대륙 바깥으로 뻗어 나갈 때
(C) 빙하 일부가 바다로 떨어져 나갈 때
(D) 빙상이 너무 무거워 지탱할 수 없을 때

해설 | Factual Information 지문에서 빙붕이란 얼음의 양이 너무 많아 대륙 바깥까지 뻗어 나간 것을 가리킨다고 설명한다.

| 05 | 보기에서 적절한 문구를 골라 해당하는 빙하의 종류와 연결하시오. 보기 중 2개는 사용되지 않는다. 이 문제는 3점이다.

(A) 이동하는 길에 따라 형성된다.	산악 빙하
(B) 높은 지형의 골짜기에 계속해서 눈이 쌓이면서 형성된다.	• (A)
(C) 자연적 요소에 더욱 많이 노출된다.	• (B)
(D) 기후 변화에 따라 급속한 속도로 가라앉고 있다.	• (C)
(E) 대륙을 해수면 아래로 밀어낼 수 있을 정도로 무겁다.	대륙 빙하
(F) 다양한 야생동물의 서식처이다.	• (E)
(G) 불규칙적으로 움직인다.	• (G)

해설 | Fill in a Table 지문에서 단락 1은 산악 빙하에 대해, 단락 2는 대륙 빙하에 대해 설명하고 있다. 산악 빙하의 형태는 지형에 따라 영향을 많이 받고, 높은 지형의 골짜기에 계속 눈이 쌓이면서 발생하며, 대륙 빙하보다 자연적인 요소에 노출되어 붕괴 가능성도 있다. 대륙 빙하는 지면을 해수면 아래로 밀 정도로 무게가 상당하다. 대륙 빙하는 지면과 맞닿아 있는 부분이 녹아 지면의 고도에 따라 불규칙적으로 이동하기도 한다. (D)와 (F)에 관한 내용은 언급되어 있지 않다.

어휘 | **continental** 대륙의   **alpine** 고산의, 산악의   **continuous** 지속적인   **condense** 압축되다, 밀집되다   **descent** 하강   **topography** 지형, 지세   **conform to** ~와 일치하다   **elevation** 높이, 고도   **exception** 예외   **piedmont** 산록 지대   **subarctic** 북극에 가까운   **collapse** 붕괴   **rainfall** 강우   **massive** 거대한, 큰   **expansive** 광대한   **existence** 존재   **compacted** 압축된   **bedrock** 기반암   **penetrate** 뚫다   **depress** 내리누르다   **dense** 밀도가 높은   **slippery** 미끄러운   **consistent** 일관된

Mini Test 1 p.184

01 (C)   02 (B)   03 (D)   04 (D)   05 (A), (B), (D)

NUCLEAR POWER

Nuclear power is the subject of much controversy around the world. Despite the fact that it is a clean and efficient source of electricity, it comes with some very serious risks. Today, there are over 400 nuclear power plants in operation worldwide, and countries like France get as much as 77 percent of their energy from this source. Few people fully understand the mechanism that drives this energy source. In many ways, it is similar to more traditional sources such as coal-fired power plants. Both nuclear and coal-fired plants rely on pressurized steam to drive electric generators. The controversy surrounding nuclear power stems from how this steam is produced — the process of nuclear fission.

The term nuclear fission refers simply to the splitting of an atom. It occurs regularly in nature, albeit much more slowly than in power plants, and is the reason we call certain elements "radioactive." In the case of power plants, the substance that is used is uranium-235, which is unique among the different types of uranium in that it can undergo induced fission — nuclear fission that is created by human intervention under artificial conditions. Q01 An atom of uranium-235 releases a great deal of energy when it absorbs a neutron from outside itself. In less than a second, the neutron creates unstable conditions within the atom that cause a very sudden reaction. When the atom bursts apart, energy is released and heat is created. In the presence of other uranium-235 atoms, the particles released by the first instance of fission cause fission in the surrounding atoms, creating a chain reaction that results in the release of massive amounts of energy.

However, this is not the same energy that is used to power homes and businesses. Q03(C) The purpose of fission reactions is simply to create heat. This is used to heat a store of water to its boiling point so that it rapidly evaporates, letting off steam. The steam is the real source of the power, since, like the water in a hydroelectric dam, the force of its movement sets in motion a series of electric generators that ultimately produce the plant's energy. Q03(A) After the electricity is produced, the steam goes through a cooling phase and is released into the atmosphere by way of giant concrete towers. The steam released from these cooling towers does not contain harmful radiation, as the water never comes into contact with the radioactive materials in the plant.

A Q03(B) Admittedly, nuclear power faces a big problem when it comes to the disposal of the spent uranium. B Once the element is no longer useful for production, it must be thrown away or stored somewhere, and though its radioactivity is diminished through use in the plant, it is still a dangerous and deadly substance. C Improperly stored uranium can contaminate the ground and the water supply around it, posing a serious threat to public health. D **Only after tens of thousands of years of natural decay will the uranium reach levels that are safe again.** Q03(D) Q04 For this reason, radioactive waste is stored in secure facilities under the strict supervision of experts, where it is allowed to cool and decay without threatening the environment. As the number of nuclear power plants grows, and the waste they produce increases, storing nuclear waste becomes a serious problem with nuclear power.

원자력

원자력은 세계적으로 많은 논란이 되는 주제이다. 원자력은 깨끗하고 효율적인 전기 공급원이지만, 동시에 매우 심각한 위험을 수반한다. 오늘날 세계적으로 400개가 넘는 원자력 발전소가 가동 중이고, 프랑스 같은 나라는 원자력으로부터 77%에 달하는 에너지를 얻는다. 이 에너지를 생성하는 원리를 완전히 이해하고 있는 사람은 별로 없다. 원자력은 많은 점에서 화력 발전소 같은 전통적 공급원과 유사하다. 원자력 발전소나 화력 발전소 모두 전기 발전기를 돌리기 위하여 압축 증기에 의존한다. 원자력에 대한 논란은 바로 이 증기를 생성하는 방법인 핵분열 과정에서 비롯된다.

핵분열이라는 용어는 단순히 원자의 분열을 가리킨다. 비록 발전소에서보다 훨씬 천천히 발생하기는 하지만, 핵분열은 자연에서도 흔히 발생하며, 그 이유로 특정 원소에 '방사능이 있다'고 하는 것이다. 발전소에서 사용되는 물질은 우라늄235이며, 유도 분열, 즉 인공적 조건으로 사람이 개입하여 조작하는 핵분열이 가능하다는 점에서 이 우라늄은 다른 우라늄과 비교할 때 독특하다. 우라늄235의 원자는 그것이 주위의 중성자를 흡수할 때 대량의 에너지를 방출한다. 1초도 안 되는 순간에 중성자는 원자 안에서 순식간에 반응을 일으키는 불안정한 상태를 만들어낸다. 원자가 산산조각이 나며 폭발하면서, 에너지가 방출되고 열이 생성된다. 다른 우라늄235 원자가 주위에 있으면, 최초 핵분열로 방출된 입자는 주위 원자에서도 분열을 일으키며 대량의 에너지를 방출하는 연쇄반응을 일으킨다.

그러나 가정과 산업 현장에서 쓰이는 에너지는 이 에너지가 아니다. 핵분열 반응의 목적은 단순히 열을 생성하는 데 있다. 이 열은 저장고에 있는 물을 끓는점까지 데워서 빠르게 증발시키고 증기를 내보내기 위해 쓰인다. 이 증기가 바로 에너지의 진정한 공급원인데, 수력 발전 댐의 물이 하는 것처럼, 최종적으로 발전소에서 에너지를 내는 일련의 전기 발전기를 이 증기의 움직임이 가동시키기 때문이다. 전기가 생성된 후에 증기는 냉각 단계를 거치게 되고, 거대한 콘크리트 탑을 통해 대기로 방출된다. 여기서 물은 발전소 안의 방사능 물질과 절대 접촉하지 않기 때문에, 이런 냉각탑에서 방출된 증기에는 해로운 방사능이 들어있지 않다.

A 인정하건대, 원자력은 다 쓴 우라늄의 처리에서 큰 문제에 직면한다. B 우라늄이 원자력 생성에 더이상 필요 없게 되면, 이 우라늄은 반드시 폐기되거나 어딘가에 저장되어야 한다. 그리고 발전소에서 사용되면서 방사능이 줄어들기는 하지만, 우라늄은 여전히 위험하고 치명적인 물질이다. C 우라늄이 제대로 저장되지 않으면 땅과 그 주위의 물을 오염시켜, 공중 보건에 심각한 위협을 가한다. D **수만 년 동안의 자연 부식이 있고 난 뒤에야, 우라늄은 다시 안전한 수준이 될 것이다.** 이런 이유로 방사능 폐기물은 전문가들의 철저한 관리 아래 안전한 시설에 저장되어, 환경에 대한 위협 없이 냉각되고 분해된다. 원자력 발전소가 늘어나고 여기에서 발생하는 폐기물도 증가하면서, 핵폐기물을 저장하는 문제는 원자력의 심각한 문제가 되고 있다.

01 지문에서 it 이 가리키는 것은?

(A) 핵분열
(B) 에너지
(C) 원자
(D) 반응

해설 | Reference "An atom of uranium-235 releases a great deal of energy when it absorbs a neutron from outside itself"에서 it 은 주절의 주어 "An atom of uranium-235"를 가리킨다.

02 지문의 diminished 와 의미상 가장 가까운 것은?

(A) 방출되었다
(B) 줄어들었다
(C) 강해졌다
(D) 변화되었다

해설 | Vocabulary diminished 는 '줄어들었다'의 의미이다.

03 지문에 따르면, 원자력 발전에 관한 내용으로 옳지 않은 것은?

(A) 증기는 냉각탑을 거쳐 대기로 방출된다.
(B) 원자력 발전은 핵폐기물을 만들어낸다.
(C) 핵분열은 증기를 생성하기 위해 사용된다.
(D) 발전 과정에서 나온 폐기물은 식을 때까지 땅속에 저장된다.

해설 | Negative Fact (D)는 옳지 않은 설명이다. 단락 4에서 핵폐기물은 안전한 시설에 보관되어 냉각되고 분해된다고 설명한다.

04 다음 문장이 지문에 들어갈 곳을 나타내는 네 개의 사각형[■]을 보시오.

> 수만 년 동안의 자연 부식이 있고 난 뒤에야, 우라늄은 다시 안전한 수준이 될 것이다.

이 문장이 들어갈 가장 적절한 위치는?

(A) A (B) B (C) C (D) D

해설 | Sentence Insertion 지문에서 For this reason이라는 연결어가 나오고 방사능 폐기물은 전문가들의 철저한 관리 아래 안전한 시설에 저장된다는 내용이 나온다. 따라서 수만 년 동안의 자연 부식이 필요하다는 내용의 삽입 문장은 이 앞부분에 위치하는 것이 자연스럽다.

05 지문을 간략히 요약하기 위한 도입 문장이 아래 제시되어 있다. 지문에서 가장 중요한 내용을 표현한 세 개의 문장을 골라 요약문을 완성하시오. 일부 문장은 지문에 나오지 않았거나 중요하지 않은 내용이기 때문에 요약문에 포함되지 않는다. 이 문제는 2점이다.

> 전기는 원자력으로 생성할 수 있는데, 그 과정은 어느 정도의 위험을 수반한다.

(A) 원자력 발전소는 중성자를 주입하여 우라늄 원자가 분열될 때까지 불안정하게 만들고 우라늄이 분열되도록 유도한다.
(B) 원자력 발전소의 전기 발전기는 핵분열로 물을 급속히 가열하여 생긴 증기로 가동된다.
(C) 원자력은 유럽 전역에 걸쳐 널리 쓰이긴 하지만, 아직도 미국 등지의 다른 곳에서는 논란거리로 여겨진다.
(D) 발전소에서 나온 핵폐기물은 수백 년 동안 대중에 위험스런 요소가 될 수 있으므로 반드시 특별 시설에 보존되어야 한다.
(E) 특별 종류의 우라늄인 우라늄235는 특히 불안정한 동위원소이기 때문에 원자력 발전소에서 요구된다.
(F) 발전소에서 생긴 증기는 대기로 방출되기 전에 냉각을 위한 어떤 과정을 거친다.

해설 | Summary 지문은 핵분열이 일어나는 과정, 핵분열이 전기 발전에 이용되는 과정, 쓰고 남은 핵폐기물을 처리하는 방법에 대해 차례로 설명하고 있다. (A)는 단락 2의 내용을, (B)는 단락 3의 내용을, (D)는 단락 4의 내용을 요약한 것이다.

어휘 | **controversy** 논란 **in operation** 가동 중인 **mechanism** 원리 **coal-fired** 화력에 의한 **pressurized** (액체, 기체가) 압축된 **generator** 발전기 **nuclear fission** 핵분열 **splitting** 분열, 분리 **occur** 발생하다 **albeit** 비록 ~이기는 하지만 **radioactive** 방사능의 **neutron** 중성자 **unstable** 불안정한 **reaction** 반응 **burst apart** 산산조각나다 **chain reaction** 연쇄반응 **release** 방출하다 **boiling point** 끓는점 **evaporate** 증발하다 **let off** 내보내다 **hydroelectric** 수력 발전의 **ultimately** 최종적으로 **radiation** 방사선 **admittedly** 인정하건대 **disposal** 처리, 폐기 **diminish** 줄어들게 하다 **improperly** 제대로, 부적절하게 **contaminate** 오염시키다 **pose a threat** 위협을 가하다 **secure** 안전한 **supervision** 관리, 감독

Mini Test 2

01 (A) 02 (B) 03 (C) 04 (A) 05 (C)

VOLCANO MONITORING

One of the most reliable and frequently employed methods of monitoring volcanoes and predicting eruptions is through the measurement of local seismic disruptions. This is because impending volcanic eruptions frequently lead off with minor earthquakes. As magma rises in the volcano, it must squeeze through a constricted chamber or series of chambers while under great pressure. The force will crack some of the rock or force rocks with pre-existing cracks to convulse, setting off tremors of varying frequencies. This seismic activity is relatively weak and occurs roughly ten kilometers beneath the volcano. Q01 In order to detect such weak quakes, scientists must set up a network of seismometers around the volcano in order to catch the slightest fluctuations in seismic activity that are usually a prelude to a volcanic eruption. About four to eight seismometers are placed about twenty kilometers from one of the vents, and several more are placed on the volcano itself. All of these have to be close in order to catch the quakes, as a seismometer being placed too far away could not detect subtle shifts in seismic activity. Fortunately, this method has been used so extensively that it is quite advanced, and scientists are experienced in detecting crucial seismic activity quickly, accurately, and in real time.

While seismic monitoring is the most widely used and trusted method of monitoring volcanoes, there are other technologies that allow scientists to observe landscape deformation, which usually accompanies volcanic activity. A ①In addition to causing quakes, ②the increased magma flow will also make the volcano swell and alter the surrounding landscape, particularly its evenness and elevation, ③though these changes are too slight to be noticed with the naked eye. B Q05 Scientists use a variety of tools to observe such changes. C One major tool is the satellite. In particular, scientists use Global Positioning System (GPS) satellites to study a very detailed map of the earth's surface, though GPS is not primarily used to study volcanoes. D Additionally, scientists have Interferometric Synthetic Aperture Radar (InSAR) satellites. These satellites use radar to map out changes in the landscape and the development of deformations very accurately, detecting possible volcanic activity.

In addition to the deformations in the ground caused by volcanic activity, Q03 scientists can measure chemical gaseous emissions. Gauging the emission of certain gases like sulfur dioxide and carbon dioxide is helpful. As magma rises to the surface, it will give off greater amounts of these two gases, so increased amounts around a volcanic area would be a good indication of increased activity. While it is possible to monitor such activity at a safe distance via satellite, Q04 weather can interfere with accurate readings. Therefore, the direct sampling of these emissions by people is a more accurate method, though this means having to get near an active vent to retrieve the samples. This is difficult because acidic gases like sulfur dioxide easily dissolve in bodies of water, skewing precise measurements. Carbon dioxide is less likely to vanish in such a manner, though, so it could be more helpful in predicting volcanic activity.

화산 감시

화산을 감시하고 폭발을 예상하는 활동에서 가장 믿을 수 있고 자주 사용되는 방법 중 하나는 지역의 지진 활동을 측정하는 것이다. 그 이유는 화산 폭발이 임박했을 때 가벼운 지진이 자주 일어나기 때문이다. 마그마는 화산 안으로 차오를 때 엄청난 압력 하에서 비좁은 한 공간 혹은 일련의 공간들을 비집고 들어가게 된다. 이 힘은 일부 바위에 균열을 일으키거나 기존의 균열이 진동하게 하면서, 다양한 주파수의 진동을 유발한다. 이런 지진 활동은 비교적 미약하며, 대략 화산 10km 밑에서 일어난다. 이런 미약한 지진을 감지하기 위해 과학자들은 화산 주변에 화산 폭발의 전조인 지진 활동의 미세한 변동을 감지하기 위한 지진계 네트워크를 설치한다. 네 개에서 여덟 개 정도가 분화구 중 하나에서 대략 20km 지점에 설치되고 추가로 몇 개가 화산에 설치된다. 지진계 하나가 너무 멀리 있으면 지진 활동의 미묘한 변동을 감지하지 못하기 때문에, 이것들은 지진을 감지하기 위해 가깝게 있어야 한다. 다행히도 이런 방법은 매우 광범위하게 사용되어 왔고 상당히 발전했으며, 과학자들은 중요한 지진 활동을 빠르고 정확하며 실시간으로 탐지할 수 있는 경험을 쌓았다.

지진 활동 감시가 화산을 감시하는 방법으로 가장 널리 사용되고 신뢰를 받고 있지만, 과학자들이 화산 활동과 동반되는 풍경 변화를 관찰할 수 있게 해주는 다른 기술들도 있다. A 마그마 흐름의 증가는 지진을 일으키는 것 외에 화산을 위로 부풀어 오르게 하고 주변 풍경 특히 평편함과 고도를 변화시키지만, 이런 변화는 육안으로 인식하기에는 너무 미세하다. B 과학자들은 이런 변화를 관찰하기 위해 다양한 도구를 사용한다. C 주요 도구 중 하나는 인공위성이다. 특히, GPS가 화산 연구에 주로 쓰이지는 않지만, 과학자들은 지구 표면의 매우 상세한 지도를 연구하기 위해 GPS 위성을 이용한다. D 이에 더해 과학자들은 레이더 영상 간섭 기법(InSAR) 위성을 가지고 있다. 이 위성들은 지형의 변화와 변화의 추이를 매우 정밀하게 표시하기 위해 레이더를 이용하며 화산 활동 가능성을 탐지한다.

화산 활동으로 인해 지면이 변화하는 것에 더해 과학자들은 화학 가스 배출물들을 측정할 수도 있다. 이산화황이나 이산화탄소 같은 특정 가스의 배출을 측정하는 것이 도움이 된다. 마그마가 지표면으로 상승하면 이 두 가스를 대량으로 뿜어내기 때문에 화산 주변 가스의 양이 증가하면 활동이 증가하고 있다는 사실을 알려준다. 위성을 통해 안전한 거리에서 이런 활동을 감시하는 것이 가능하긴 하지만 날씨가 정확한 해석을 방해할 수 있다. 따라서 인간이 직접 배출물의 표본을 추출하는 것이 더 정확한 방법이기는 하지만, 이것은 표본을 추출하기 위해 화산 분화구 가까이 가야 한다는 것을 뜻한다. 이산화황 같은 산성 가스는 물에 쉽게 용해되면서 정확한 측정을 왜곡하기 때문에 이러한 방법은 어렵다. 이런 면에서 이산화탄소는 사라질 가능성이 적기 때문에 화산 활동을 예측하는 데 더 유용할 수 있다.

01
단락 1에 따르면, 과학자들이 화산 주변에 지진계 네트워크를 이용해야만 하는 이유는?

(A) 발생하는 지진이 그렇게 강하지 않기 때문에
(B) 손상된 장비를 교체하기 위해 준비해야 하기 때문에
(C) 다음 화산 폭발의 정확한 강도를 예측하기 때문에
(D) 진동이 어디서 발생할지 확신하지 못하기 때문에

해설 | Factual Information 지진 활동은 미약하고 화산 10km 밑에서 일어나기 때문에 지진계 네트워크를 사용한다.

02
다음 중 지문에서 표시된 문장의 주요 정보를 가장 잘 나타낸 문장은?
정답 외의 보기들은 중요한 의미가 바뀌거나 주요 정보가 빠져 있다.

(A) 화산이 폭발하기 전에 지역 주변 지면의 고도와 평편함이 깨지긴 하지만, 이는 관찰하기 어렵다.
(B) 증가한 마그마 흐름은 지진을 일으키는 것 이외에도, 감지하기 어려운 방식으로 주변 지역을 변화시킨다.
(C) 지진은 주변 지역의 고도와 평편함을 변화시키고 화산 마그마가 부풀어 오르도록 한다.
(D) 폭발하기 직전에 화산이 부풀어 오르는 것은 지면 고도를 바꾸는 지진 때문이다.

해설 | Sentence Simplification 표시된 문장에서 ②는 마그마가 증가하면 주변의 지형을 바꾸어 놓는다는 내용, ③은 지형의 변화가 육안으로는 포착하기 힘들다는 내용, ①은 마그마의 증가로 지진이 발생한다는 내용이다. 표시된 문장을 가장 잘 나타낸 것은 (B)이다. 보기에서 ②는 "The increased magma flow transforms neighboring areas"로 ③은 "in ways that are hard to detect"로 ①은 "as well as causing quakes"로 바뀌어 표현되었다.

03
지문의 Gauging 과 의미상 가장 가까운 것은?

(A) 예방하다
(B) 흡수하다
(C) 측정하다
(D) 발견하다

해설 | Vocabulary 동의어 단서를 찾을 수 있는 문제이다. 앞 문장의 "... scientists can measure chemical gaseous emissions"에서 이 단어가 measure와 의미와 같다는 것을 알 수 있다.

04
단락 3에 따르면, 마그마에서 배출되는 가스를 직접 추출하는 이유는?

(A) 좋지 않은 날씨로 인해 정확한 화산 가스 배출 측정이 방해될 수도 있기 때문에
(B) 위성으로 화산 가스 배출을 측정하는 것이 불가능하기 때문에
(C) 마그마에서 가스를 추출하는 방법이 가장 간단하기 때문에
(D) 물에 녹은 가스를 추출하는 작업이 필요하기 때문에

해설 | Factual Information 지문에서 위성으로 화산 가스를 측정할 수 있지만, 날씨 때문에 정확한 판독이 불가능해질 수도 있으므로 직접 표본을 추출한다고 설명한다.

05
다음 문장이 지문에 들어갈 곳을 나타내는 네 개의 사각형[■]을 보시오.

> 주요 도구 중 하나는 인공위성이다.

이 문장이 들어갈 가장 적절한 위치는?

(A) **A** (B) **B** (C) **C** (D) **D**

해설 | Sentence Insertion "과학자들은 이런 변화를 관찰하기 위해 다양한 도구를 사용한다"는 내용 뒤에 삽입 문장이 위치해야 자연스럽다.

어휘 | **impending** 임박한 **squeeze** 비집고 들어가다 **constricted** 비좁은 **pre-existing** 기존의 **convulse** 진동하다 **set off** 유발하다 **tremor** 진동 **frequency** 진동수, 주파수 **detect** 감지하다 **seismometer** 지진계 **prelude** 전조, 징후 **subtle** 미묘한 **extensively** 광범위하게 **real-time** 실시간 **accompany** 동반하다 **evenness** 평편함 **elevation** 고도 **satellite** 인공위성 **in particular** 특히 **primarily** 주로 **gaseous** 가스의 **sulfur dioxide** 이산화황 **interfere** 방해하다 **sampling** 표본 추출 **skew** 왜곡하다 **vanish** 사라지다

iBT Practice

p.188

01 (C) 02 (B) 03 (A) 04 (B) 05 (C) 06 (A) 07 (C) 08 (C) 09 (B) 10 (B) 11 (C) 12 (C)
13 (A), (E), (F)

COMETS

In ancient cultures, the abrupt appearance of a comet was taken as a mysterious omen of bad fortune, inspiring predictions of famine, disease, and flood. This was not the only fallacious belief attached to comets. The Greek philosopher Aristotle reasoned that, since the heavens were essentially perfect, such a temporary and unpredictable occurrence as a comet must instead come from the Earth. Q02 Thus, he believed comets were pieces of the Earth that had somehow been ignited and blown into space. Surprisingly, this view remained unchallenged for nearly 2,000 years after Aristotle's death. Today, astronomers are able to study comets in close detail through the use of advanced telescopes and satellite images, and as a result have a far more informed understanding of what makes a comet.

The best way to illustrate the basic makeup of a comet is to liken it to a "dirty snowball." The mass of the comet consists of ice intermixed with rock and dust. Q03 Many of these small celestial bodies are believed to originate in the Oort Cloud, which is Q04 a giant spherical mass of floating ice, debris, and gases that surrounds our solar system, extending to distances thousands of times farther than the orbit of Pluto. Scientists believe that these elements may collide and conjoin within the Oort Cloud. When large objects pass through the cloud, they knock some of these pieces out of their regular orbits and into the inner solar system, where their new orbits make them visible from the Earth. Comets appear to observers as bright white streaks, with a rounded head and a long, shimmering tail. However, this common image represents only a brief phase in the comet's life cycle. Further examination of the comet's various components helps to explain why comets appear as they do.

The nucleus is the most basic, and the only consistent, component of a comet. The nucleus of a comet comprises the core of what appears to be the comet's head, and consists of a densely packed mixture of mostly ice and rock. The nucleus of a comet can measure anywhere from 100 meters to 30 miles in diameter, but most average about 10 miles across. Q05 The nuclei of comets are some of the darkest bodies in the heavens; they only reflect about 4 percent of the sunlight that shines on them. Q08 The intense darkness of the nucleus is generally attributed to an accretion of rock and dust on the surface that covers the ice trapped within. ①Offsetting this darkness only slightly is the thick shroud of dust and debris that surrounds the nucleus bound by its gravitational pull, but ②even though this covering reflects more light than the surface of the nucleus, ③it still does not account for the bright appearance of comets in the sky.

혜성

고대 문화에서는 혜성의 갑작스러운 출현을 불운의 이상한 징조로 보았고, 이를 통해 기근과 질병, 홍수를 예측하였다. 혜성에 관한 잘못된 생각은 이뿐만이 아니었다. 그리스의 철학자 Aristotle은 하늘이 본질적으로 완벽하기 때문에 혜성의 일시적이고 예견할 수 없는 현상은 지구에서 비롯된 것이 틀림없다고 주장하였다. 그리하여 그는 혜성이 지구의 조각이 어떤 방법으로 발화되어 우주로 날아간 것이라 믿었다. 놀랍게도 이 주장은 Aristotle가 죽은 후에도 약 2천 년 동안 의문 제기 없이 계속되어 왔다. 오늘날 천문학자들은 첨단 망원경과 위성 사진으로 더욱더 자세하게 혜성 연구를 할 수 있게 되었고, 결과적으로 혜성이 어떻게 만들어지는지에 대해 훨씬 더 많은 정보를 알게 되었다.

혜성의 기본 구성을 가장 잘 설명하는 방법은 이를 '먼지 눈덩어리'로 비유하는 것이다. 혜성은 얼음과 돌과 먼지의 혼합으로 구성된다. 이 작은 천체들은 오르트 구름이라는 곳에서 비롯되었다고 여겨지는데, 오르트 구름은 떠다니는 얼음, 잔해, 가스 등이 결합된 거대한 둥근 띠 모양의 집합체로 태양계를 감싸고 있으며, 명왕성 궤도의 몇천 배 정도가 되는 곳까지 뻗어 있다. 과학자들은 이러한 요소들이 오르트 구름 안에서 충돌하거나 결합한다고 믿고 있다. 큰 물체가 구름을 지나치면 이런 조각들을 쳐서 정상 궤도에서 벗어나게 해 태양계 안쪽으로 보내는데, 곧 지구에서 보이는 새 궤도로 진입하게 하는 것이다. 혜성은 밝은 하얀 광선으로 보이는데 둥그런 머리 부분과 길면서 희미하게 빛나는 꼬리를 갖고 있다. 하지만 이런 일반적 모습은 혜성 주기의 짧은 한 단계를 설명할 뿐이다. 혜성의 여러 구성에 관한 깊은 연구는 혜성이 왜 나타나는지 설명할 수 있도록 도와준다.

혜성의 핵은 가장 기본적이면서 유일하게 변하지 않는 요소이다. 핵은 혜성의 머리 부분으로 보이는 중심 부분을 구성하는데, 대체로 얼음과 돌로 단단하게 결합해 있다. 혜성의 핵의 크기는 직경 100m에서 30마일까지 다양한데, 대부분은 평균적으로 10마일 정도의 크기를 보인다. 놀랍게도 혜성의 핵은 하늘에서 보이는 가장 어두운 부분으로 그것들은 혜성에 비치는 태양 빛의 약 4%만을 반사한다. 핵이 이렇게 매우 어둡게 보이는 것은 그 안에 갇힌 얼음을 감싸고 있는 표면의 먼지와 돌이 축적된 결과이다. 이 어두운 부분을 조금이라도 밝히는 것은 중력으로 인해 핵을 감싸고 있는 먼지와 잔해 층이지만, 이 층은 핵의 표면보다도 더 많이 빛을 반사하는데도 불구하고 하늘에서 혜성을 밝게 보이게 하는 데는 아무런 설명도 주지 못한다.

What produces the bright image that is visible to humans, sometimes even with the naked eye, is the other two major components of comets, the coma and tail. It should be noted that these two phenomena are relatively rare during the entire lifespan of a comet, and only occur under special conditions. The coma is a nebulous cloud of gases and dust particles that forms a giant gaseous ball around the nucleus. **Q11** This formation is much larger than the nucleus, however, measuring tens of thousands of times its size. A coma cannot form around the comet until it passes into the inner solar system, where it is exposed to the heat of the sun. When this happens, **Q10** the ice inside the comet turns to vapor through a process called sublimation, and is then ejected from the comet through holes in the surface of the nucleus. This highly reflective water vapor forms a temporary atmosphere around the comet that shines brightly when exposed to the sun's rays. In addition to the sun's heat, the comet is also subject to solar winds and radiation pressure. **A** For this reason, portions of the coma are forced away from the comet, leaving a trail in the sky that is known as the comet's tail. **B** **Q12** Contrary to popular belief, the direction in which the tail points is not related to the comet's forward momentum. **C** **Instead, the tail always points away from the sun.** **Q09** As the comet revolves around the sun, the tail is continually changing directions in relation to its position to the solar winds and other forces. **D**

---

01 지문의 abrupt 와 의미상 가장 가까운 것은?

(A) 빛나는
(B) 주기적인
(C) 갑작스러운
(D) 계속되는

해설 | Vocabulary abrupt 는 '갑작스러운'이라는 의미로 sudden과 의미가 비슷하다.

02 단락 1에 따르면, 혜성에 관한 Aristotle의 이론은?

(A) 자연재해가 온다는 불길한 조짐
(B) 폭발로 인해 지구에서 우주로 떨어져 나간 조각들
(C) 지구에서 멀리 떨어진 곳에 있는 하늘의 물체
(D) 지구와 하늘이 혼합된 조각

해설 | Factual Information Aristotle은 하늘은 완벽하기 때문에 혜성은 하늘로부터 생겨난 것이 아니라 지구의 조각이 떨어져 나간 것이라고 보았다.

03 필자가 지문에서 오르트 구름 을 언급하는 이유는?

(A) 혜성의 생성지를 설명하기 위해
(B) 혜성의 풍부함을 설명하기 위해
(C) 혜성의 꼬리가 어떻게 생기는지 설명하기 위해
(D) 혜성의 생김새를 설명하기 위해

해설 | Rhetorical Purpose 필자는 혜성이 오르트 구름 에서 나온 것이라고 설명함으로써 혜성의 생성 장소를 밝히고 있다.

04 지문에서 these elements 가 가리키는 것은?

(A) 돌과 먼지
(B) 얼음, 잔해, 그리고 가스
(C) 천체
(D) 물체

해설 | Reference these elements 는 앞 문장에 설명된 오르트 구름을 이루는 구성 성분을 가리킨다. 즉, 얼음, 잔해, 가스 등의 물질을 가리킨다.

05 지문에서 they 가 가리키는 것은?

(A) 몸통
(B) 혜성
(C) 핵
(D) 하늘

해설 | Reference 지문에서 they 는 햇빛의 4%만을 반사한다고 설명한다. 그런데 they 앞뒤 문맥을 살펴보면 핵은 매우 어두운 색을 가졌다는 설명이 나오고 있다. 따라서 they 는 핵을 가리킨다는 것을 알 수 있다.

06 지문의 accretion 과 의미상 가장 가까운 것은?
(A) 축적
(B) 혼합
(C) 형성
(D) 부식

해설 | Vocabulary accretion은 '축적, 첨가, 증대'라는 의미이다.

07 다음 중 지문에서 표시된 문장의 주요 정보를 가장 잘 나타낸 문장은? 정답 외의 보기들은 중요한 의미가 바뀌거나 주요 정보가 빠져 있다.
(A) 핵은 태양 빛을 흡수하고 늘상 밝은 혜성을 어둡게 하는 먼지와 파편으로 이루어진 구름층으로 둘러싸여 있다.
(B) 먼지와 잔해 층이 혜성의 밝기에 부분적으로 영향을 주지만 이들은 자신이 둘러싸고 있는 핵보다는 여전히 더 어둡다.
(C) 혜성을 둘러싸고 있는 먼지와 파편의 두꺼운 구름층은 핵보다는 더 많은 빛을 반사하지만 혜성의 밝기를 설명해 줄 정도로 충분히 밝은 것은 아니다.
(D) 핵에서 반사되는 빛은 먼지와 잔해 층에 흡수되는데 이러한 현상이 혜성의 밝기를 설명해 줄 수 있을 것이다.

해설 | Sentence Simplification ①과 ②는 서로 비슷한 내용으로, 핵을 감싸고 있는 먼지와 잔해가 햇빛을 반사하기 때문에 핵의 어두운 색이 조금이라도 밝게 만들어진다는 뜻이다. ③은 ①과 ②에서 제시된 설명으로는 혜성의 밝은 빛을 설명하기에는 역부족이라는 내용이다. 원문을 가장 잘 옮긴 것은 (C)이다.

08 단락 3에 따르면, 혜성의 핵이 아주 어두운 이유는?
(A) 핵은 얼음과 돌의 결합체이기 때문이다.
(B) 보기보다 훨씬 더 멀리 떨어져 있기 때문이다.
(C) 먼지와 돌의 층으로 둘러싸여 있기 때문이다.
(D) 빛을 반사하지 않는 가스로 덮여 있기 때문이다.

해설 | Factual Information 단락 3에서 핵의 색깔이 어두운 것은 핵 안에 있는 얼음 주위를 돌과 먼지가 감싸고 있기 때문이라고 설명한다.

09 지문의 revolves 와 의미상 가장 가까운 것은?
(A) 일어나다
(B) 회전하다
(C) 폭발하다
(D) 머무르다

해설 | Vocabulary "As the comet revolves around the sun …"은 혜성이 태양 주위를 '공전한다'는 의미이므로 '회전하다'라는 뜻의 rotates가 정답이다.

10 단락 4에 따르면, 승화의 의미로 추론할 수 있는 것은?
(A) 액체가 고체로 변하는 과정
(B) 고체가 기체로 변하는 과정
(C) 기체가 액체로 변하는 과정
(D) 액체가 기체로 변하는 과정

해설 | Inference 승화는 혜성 안의 얼음(고체)이 수증기(기체)로 변하는 과정이라고 설명하고 있다.

11 단락 4에 따르면, 혜성에 관한 내용 중 옳은 것은?
(A) 대부분은 태양계 안쪽에서 형성된다.
(B) 꼬리는 혜성이 움직이는 방향을 가리킨다.
(C) 코마의 크기는 핵보다 몇 배 크다.
(D) 반사되는 표면이 태양에 노출되면 빛난다.

해설 | Factual Information 단락 4에서 코마는 혜성보다 몇만 배 정도 크다고 설명한다. 따라서 (C)가 정답이다. (B)는 틀린 설명이다. 혜성의 꼬리는 혜성이 움직이는 방향을 일러주는 것이 아니라, 태양 위치의 반대 방향을 가리키는 것이다.

12 다음 문장이 지문에 들어갈 곳을 나타내는 네 개의 사각형[■]을 보시오.

> 대신, 꼬리는 항상 태양 위치의 반대 방향을 가리킨다.

이 문장이 들어갈 가장 적절한 위치는?
(A) A (B) B (C) C (D) D

해설 | Sentence Insertion 혜성의 꼬리는 태양이 있는 곳에서 반대 방향으로 뻗는다는 삽입 문장의 내용은 "Contrary to popular belief, the direction in which the tail points is not related to the comet's forward momentum"의 밑줄 친 부분의 내용을 추가로 덧붙이는 역할을 할 수 있다.

13 지문을 간략히 요약하기 위한 도입 문장이 아래 제시되어 있다. 지문에서 가장 중요한 내용을 표현한 세 개의 문장을 골라 요약문을 완성하시오. 일부 문장은 지문에 나오지 않았거나 중요하지 않은 내용이기 때문에 요약문에 포함되지 않는다. *이 문제는 2점이다.*

> 혜성의 모양은 기본 세 요소인 핵과 코마, 꼬리를 이해하면 잘 알 수 있다.

(A) 코마는 혜성 안의 얼음이 태양열로 인해 빛에 반사가 잘 되는 가스로 유출되면서 생성된다.
(B) 보통 혜성에 뒤에 있는 먼지와 가스로 이루어진 꼬리의 길이는 1 천문단위 또는 1억5천만 킬로미터다.
(C) 핵은 주위의 코마보다 몇천 배나 작기 때문에 육안으로는 볼 수 없다.
(D) 혜성은 큰 물체가 태양계 바깥쪽 궤도에 있는 혜성을 칠 때 태양계 바깥으로 떠밀려 나간다.
(E) 태양풍에서 오는 압력은 혜성의 먼지와 가스를 거꾸로 향하게 하여 꼬리처럼 보이는 것을 형성하게 된다.
(F) 혜성의 수명 동안 계속해서 남아 있는 부분은 얼음을 감싸고 있는 돌과 먼지의 어둡고 빽빽한 집합체인 핵밖에 없다.

해설 | Summary 지문은 혜성의 구조인 핵, 코마, 꼬리에 대해 설명하고 있다. (A)는 혜성의 코마에 대한 내용, (E)는 혜성의 꼬리에 대한 내용, (F)는 핵에 대한 내용이다.

어휘 | **prediction** 예측 **famine** 기근, 굶주림 **fallacious** 잘못된 **ignite** 불을 붙이다 **satellite image** 위성 사진 **makeup** 구성 **intermixed** 혼합된 **celestial body** 천체 **spherical** 둥근, 구의 **debris** 잔해 **collide** 충돌하다 **conjoin** 결합하다 **shimmering** 희미하게 반짝이는 **component** 구성 **nucleus** 핵(核) **consistent** 변하지 않는, 일관된 **comprise** 구성하다 **diameter** 직경, 지름 **accumulation** 축적 **gravitational** 중력의 **account for** ~를 설명하다 **coma** 코마 (혜성 주위의 성운 모양의 물질) **lifespan** 수명 **nebulous** 희미한, 흐린 **gaseous** 기체의 **sublimation** [물리] 승화 **eject** 방출하다 **solar wind** 태양풍 **radiation pressure** 방사압 **revolve** 공전하다

Chapter 15 Social Science

Intensive Drill 1   p.194

| 01 (D) | 02 (C) | 03 (D) | 04 (A) | 05 (B), (D), (E) |

THOMAS MALTHUS AND POPULATION CONTROL

Thomas Malthus was a nineteenth-century British scholar who did influential work in the field of demography, the mathematical study of populations. His most famous work, *An Essay on the Principles of Population*, has influenced countless scientists since its first publication. In this essay, Malthus argued that population growth would always exceed man's ability to produce enough food and other goods to support the population. He believed that population would always grow to the farthest limits of subsistence, but ruinous forces such as war or famine would keep it from growing any farther. Malthus argued that this phenomenon was responsible for the high rate of poverty during his time, since a limited food supply had to continually provide for a growing population. If population were in line with production, however, then society as a whole would experience greater well-being.

To this end, Malthus argued for population control as a means of righting the balance between population growth and food supply. In *An Essay on the Principles of Population*, he stated that natural forms of population control often worked, to a degree. Human vice, or moral weakness, whether in the form of violent crime or life-threatening habits such as alcoholism, would often be enough to do the unpleasant job of keeping the population from growing beyond the point of subsistence. However, if this failed, then the consequences would become far worse. Widespread famine, deadly diseases, and even plagues would then step in to decrease the population. Q02 The conditions of overpopulation and the spread of poverty and poor living conditions would be such that these forces would occur quite naturally. Q03 Malthus went so far as to argue that the Black Death of the Middle Ages was a plague brought on by an unsafe surge in the European population.

To an extent, Malthus believed that these tragedies could be avoided if humans were to conduct their own sort of population control. He had a number of suggestions for how societies could control their populations to avoid famine or plague. One of them was the teaching of moral restraint in regard to sexual activity. In his day, it was believed that producing many children made a nation strong, and that it should be allowed to go on unchecked. ①Malthus argued that having many children had quite the opposite effect, and ②believed that the people, especially poor people, should be conditioned to avoid most relationships that might lead to having children. In addition, Malthus did not rule out the possibility of controlled breeding among people. He proposed the idea that the most healthy and intelligent people be allowed to breed with few limits, while strict limits should be placed on the poor and less fit. In this way, the population could be managed and a stronger breed of people could be created that were less likely to drain society of its resources.

Thomas Malthus와 인구 조절

Thomas Malthus는 인구를 수학적으로 연구하는 학문인 인구학 분야에 중요한 업적을 남긴 19세기 영국 학자였다. 그의 가장 유명한 책 『인구론』은 출판 당시부터 수많은 과학자에게 영향을 주었다. 이 책에서 Malthus는 인구 증가는 이를 뒷받침해 줄 충분한 음식 및 물자를 생산하는 인간의 능력을 언제나 능가할 것이라고 주장했다. 그는 인구가 최대 생존 한계점에 다다를 때까지 증가하겠지만, 전쟁이나 기아 같은 파괴적인 힘이 그 이상의 증가를 억제할 것이라고 믿었다. Malthus는 이 현상이 바로 그 당시 높았던 빈곤율의 이유라고 주장했는데, 왜냐하면 제한된 식량 공급이 증가하는 인구를 계속해서 뒷받침해야 했기 때문이다. 그러나 인구가 생산량에 맞추어 증가한다면, 사회 전체가 더 큰 번영을 누릴 것이라고 믿었다.

이 때문에 Malthus는 인구 증가와 식량 공급 간의 균형을 바로 세우기 위해서는 인구를 조절해야 한다고 주장했다. 『인구론』에서 그는 자연적 인구 조절 방식이 어느 정도까지는 효과가 있곤 했다고 진술했다. 폭력 범죄 또는 알코올 중독처럼 생명을 위협하는 습관의 형태로 나타나는 인간의 악행, 혹은 도덕적 해이가 생존 한계점을 넘을 만큼 인구가 증가하지 못하게 하는 즐겁지 않은 작업을 충분히 수행할 수 있을 것이었다. 그러나 만약 이것이 실패한다면, 그 결과는 훨씬 더 심각하게 나타날 것이다. 그때는 광역적으로 퍼지는 기아와 치명적 질병, 심지어는 전염병까지 인구를 감소시키기 위해 끼어들 것이다. 인구 과잉 현상, 빈곤의 확산, 열약한 생활 환경이 매우 심해지면, 이러한 힘이 자연적으로 발생할 것이다. Malthus는 더 나아가 중세 시대의 흑사병이 유럽의 인구가 위험할 정도로 급증하면서 생긴 전염병이었다고까지 주장했다.

Malthus는 인간이 자체적으로 인구 조절을 하면, 이런 비극적 상황을 어느 정도까지는 피할 수 있다고 믿었다. 그는 기아나 전염병을 피하기 위해 사회가 어떤 방법으로 인구 조절을 할 수 있는지에 대해 여러 가지 제안을 하였다. 그중 하나는 성행위에 관한 도덕적 제재를 교육하는 것이었다. 그 당시에는 아이를 많이 낳을수록 나라가 부강해지므로 아이를 제한 없이 낳을 수 있게 해야 한다고 여겼다. Malthus는 아이를 많이 낳는 것은 그 반대의 결과를 불러올 수 있다고 주장하며, 사람들, 특히 가난한 사람들은 웬만하면 아이가 생길 수 있는 관계를 피하도록 조절되어야 한다고 믿었다. 게다가 Malthus는 사람들의 출산을 조절해야 할 가능성도 제외하지 않았다. 그는 최상의 건강하고 지적인 사람들은 거의 제한 없이 출산할 수 있게 하지만, 가난하고 허약한 사람들은 출산이 엄격하게 제한되어야 한다고 제안했다. 이렇게 되면 인구 조절이 가능하고, 더 강한 혈통의 사람들이 만들어져서 사회 자원을 고갈시키지 않을 수 있을 것이다.

01
지문의 ruinous 와 의미상 가장 가까운 것은?

(A) 위험한
(B) 강한
(C) 내부의
(D) 파괴적인

해설 | Vocabulary ruinous 는 '파괴적인'의 의미이다.

02
단락 2에 따르면, 인구가 생존 한계점을 넘어서지 않는 이유는?

(A) 그때가 되면 사용 가능한 자원이 제한될 것이다.
(B) 정점에 다다른 후에 감소하기 시작할 것이다.
(C) 자연적 힘으로 결국은 억제될 것이다.
(D) 가난한 사람들의 인구 규모가 커질 것이다.

해설 | Factual Information Malthus는 음주와 같은 올바르지 못한 생활 습관이 인구 조절을 하지 못한다면 기아나 전염병과 같은 자연적 힘으로 결국 인구는 생존 한계점을 넘지 않는다고 보았다.

03
필자가 지문에서 흑사병 을 언급하는 이유는?

(A) 열악한 생활 환경의 치명적인 결과 중 하나를 시사하기 위해
(B) Malthus의 『인구론』의 기본 전제를 설명하기 위해
(C) 억제되지 않은 인구 증가는 항상 자연재해로 이어진다는 점을 보여주기 위해
(D) 자연이 어떻게 인구 과잉을 억제할 수 있는지에 대한 Malthus 견해의 예를 들기 위해

해설 | Rhetorical Purpose 단락 2는 인구 증가는 자연적인 힘으로 생존 한계점을 넘지 않는다는 Malthus의 주장에 대한 내용이다. 지문에서 흑사병의 예는 인구 과잉이 자연적으로 어떻게 억제되는지 보여주는 예로 사용되었다.

04
다음 중 지문에서 표시된 문장의 주요 정보를 가장 잘 나타낸 문장은? 정답 외의 보기들은 중요한 의미가 바뀌거나 주요 정보가 빠져 있다.

(A) Malthus는 특히 가난한 사람들 사이의 제한 없는 출산은 나라에 부정적인 영향을 줄 수 있기 때문에 억제되어야 한다고 주장했다.
(B) Malthus는 가난한 사람들의 출산을 억제하면 나라를 부강하게 할 수 있다고 믿었다.
(C) Malthus는 경제적 조건에 상관없이 모든 계급 사람들의 출산이 제한되어야 한다는 의견을 지지했다.
(D) Malthus는 출산을 장려함으로 나라를 부강하게 만드는 그 당시 사회 정책에 동조했다.

해설 | Sentence Simplification 표시된 문장은 크게 두 의미로 나뉠 수 있다. ① Malthus는 아이를 많이 갖는 것은 반대 결과를 갖는다고 주장했다. ② 특히 가난한 사람들은 그런 대부분의 관계를 피하도록 조절되어야 한다.

05
지문을 간략히 요약하기 위한 도입 문장이 아래 제시되어 있다. 지문에서 가장 중요한 내용을 표현한 세 개의 문장을 골라 요약문을 완성하시오. 일부 문장은 지문에 나오지 않았거나 중요하지 않은 내용이기 때문에 요약문에 포함되지 않는다. *이 문제는 2점이다.*

> Thomas Malthus는 인구 증가가 억제되지 않으면 재난으로 이어질 수 있으며, 어느 정도 조절이 필요하다고 믿었다.

(A) 가난한 사람들이 처해 있는 불결한 생활 환경은 질병을 낳는 산실이었다.
(B) Malthus 이론의 기본은 인간의 인구가 늘 식량 공급 한계점까지 증가해 사회를 위험하게 한다는 것이었다.
(C) Malthus의 연구는 지도자로 하여금 인간의 번식에 대한 태도를 바꾸도록 했다.
(D) Malthus는 자연에 자체적으로 인구 조절을 하는 수단이 있지만, 항상 효과가 있지는 않다고 생각했다.
(E) Malthus는 사회 번영을 위해서는 출산 조절 같은 인위적 수단으로 인구 증가를 억제해야 한다고 주장했다.
(F) 기아와 전염병은 자연적인 형태의 인구 조절의 가장 일반적인 예시이다.

해설 | Summary (B)는 Malthus의 이론을 설명한 단락 1의 내용을 요약해 놓은 것이다. (D)는 자연적 인구 조절 방식을 설명한 단락 2의 내용을 요약해 놓은 것이다. (E)는 사회적 인구 조절 수단을 설명한 단락 3의 내용을 요약해 놓은 것이다.

어휘 | **demography** 인구학 **publication** 출판, 발표 **subsistence** 생존 **famine** 기아, 굶주림 **phenomenon** 현상 **right** (정상적인 위치가 되도록) 바로 세우다 **vice** 악행 **alcoholism** 알코올 중독 **consequence** 결과 **plague** 전염병 **Black Death** 흑사병 **restraint** 제한, 제재 **rule out** 제외하다 **breeding** 출산 **drain** (힘·돈 등을) 고갈시키다

Intensive Drill 2

p.196

01 (C)   **02** (D)   **03** (B)   **04** (C)   **05** (A), (C), (F)

SOCIAL ACCULTURATION

Social acculturation is the process through which immigrants or minority groups adapt and eventually integrate into the larger or dominant culture of their society. The standard model for social acculturation was first proposed by Kalvero Oberg in 1954. Oberg described social acculturation as a four-step process: euphoria, frustration, negotiation, and assimilation. The euphoric stage typically only lasts for several weeks. In this stage, nearly everything about the new culture is seen in a positive light. The euphoria that people often feel in this stage is strongly related to a sense of novelty. **Q01** New experiences are often greeted with enthusiasm, and the first few weeks in a new culture are typically nothing but a string of novel experiences.

Once the initial period of novelty has worn off, immigrants often experience a period of frustration. Immigrants must relearn most of the skills that are needed in everyday life. Language is obviously the greatest part of this process, but even in situations where the immigrant is fluent in the new language, a learning curve still exists. Immigrants are typically unaware of, or at least not totally familiar with, the cultural practices of their new society. They may lack knowledge that is considered common sense in the new culture, and this can make even simple tasks, such as going to the doctor, more difficult. **Q02** Individuals in this stage often express their frustration by finding fault with the society around them and treating their mother culture with feelings of nostalgia. They may be reluctant or unwilling to take part in the new culture and may seek to close themselves off from it as much as possible.

Q03 The phase of frustration can vary greatly for different people because they all have very different personalities. Indeed, some never progress beyond this stage. Eventually, however, most people enter the stage of negotiation, in which they learn to adapt and deal with the problems that they experience in the new society. Slowly, they become more familiar with the culture and more proficient at social tasks. There may be some temporary slippage back into the frustration stage when they are confronted with a particularly challenging social situation, but for the most part, immigrants tend to continue to make forward progress once they have entered this stage.

In the final phase, assimilation, the immigrants become fully integrated into their new culture, to the point where they can be seen as regular members of that society. Assimilation can take an extremely long time, and may not even occur in the lifetime of first-generation immigrants. **Q04** In many cases it is only the children of immigrants, who are born in the new culture, who can be said to have truly assimilated.

사회 문화 변용

사회 문화 변용은 이민자들이나 소수 집단이 그들 사회보다 더 크거나 지배적인 문화로 적응하고 결국에는 융합되는 과정이다. 사회 문화 변용의 표준적인 모델은 1954년 Kalvero Oberg에 의해 처음 제안되었다. Oberg는 사회 문화 변용에는 4단계 과정이 있다고 설명했다: 행복, 좌절, 타협, 그리고 동화이다. 행복 단계는 일반적으로 몇 주 동안만 지속된다. 이 단계에서는 새 문화에 대한 거의 모든 것이 긍정적으로 보여진다. 이 단계에서 사람들이 종종 느끼는 행복은 새로움과 깊게 연관되어 있다. 새로운 경험들은 종종 의욕적으로 받아들여지고, 새로운 문화에서 처음 몇 주는 일반적으로 새로운 경험의 연속일 따름이다.

초기 새로움의 기간이 지나고 나면, 이민자들은 흔히 좌절의 기간을 경험한다. 이민자들은 일상생활에 필요한 대부분 기술을 다시 배워야 한다. 언어는 명백히 이 과정의 가장 큰 부분을 차지하지만, 이민자들이 새 언어를 유창하게 구사하는 상황이라 할지라도 학습의 굴곡은 여전히 있다. 이민자들은 대체로 새 사회의 문화적 관습을 알지 못하거나, 적어도 완전히 친숙하지는 않다. 그들은 새 문화에서 상식으로 간주되는 지식이 부족할 수 있으며, 이 때문에 심지어 의사를 찾아가는 것과 같은 간단한 일도 어려울 수 있다. 이 기간을 거치는 사람들은 그들 주위 사회 탓을 하거나 모국의 문화를 향수 어린 마음으로 대하면서 종종 좌절감을 표현한다. 그들은 새로운 문화에 참여하는 것을 망설이거나 내켜 하지 않으며, 새 문화로부터 자신들은 최대한 고립시키려 할 수 있다.

좌절 단계는 사람마다 모두 성격이 많이 다르기 때문에 크게 달라질 수 있다. 물론, 일부는 절대 이 단계를 넘어서지 못한다. 하지만 결국, 대부분의 사람은 타협의 단계로 들어서는데, 이 단계에서 그들은 그들이 새 사회에서 경험하는 문제들에 적응하고 대처하는 법을 배운다. 서서히 그들은 문화에 더 친숙해지고, 사회 업무에 더 능숙하게 된다. 특별히 어려운 사회적 상황에 직면했을 때 좌절 단계로의 일시적인 회귀가 있을 수 있지만, 대부분의 경우 이민자들은 그들이 이 단계에 들어선 이상 보통 앞으로 나아가는 경향이 있다.

마지막 단계, 즉 동화 단계에서 이민자들은 그 사회의 전형적인 구성원으로 여겨질 정도로 그들의 새로운 문화에 완전히 통합된다. 동화는 아주 긴 시간이 걸릴 수 있으며, 이민 첫 세대의 일생 동안에는 일어나지 않을 수도 있다. 그 새로운 사회에서 태어난 이민자들의 아이들만 완전히 동화되었다고 할 수 있는 경우가 많다.

01 지문의 novel 과 의미상 가장 가까운 것은?
(A) 익숙한
(B) 호의적인
(C) 색다른
(D) 흥미로운

해설 | Vocabulary 첫 문장의 New experience에서 novel은 '색다른'이라는 의미임을 알 수 있다.

02 단락 2에서 좌절 단계의 영향으로 언급되지 않은 것은?
(A) 사회로부터 회피
(B) 새로운 사회에 대해 비판
(C) 예전 문화에 대한 향수
(D) 간단한 업무조차도 거절

해설 | Negative Fact 단락 2의 마지막에서 좌절 단계에 있는 사람은 주변 사회 탓을 하고, 모국 문화에 향수를 느끼고, 자신을 사회로부터 격리시킬 수 있다고 설명하고 있다. 좌절 단계에 있는 사람은 간단한 업무도 어렵게 느낄 수 있다는 내용이 언급되었지만, 간단한 업무를 거절한다는 말은 없다.

03 지문에서 some 이 가리키는 것은?
(A) 문제
(B) 사람
(C) 인격
(D) 일

해설 | Reference 바로 앞 문장 "The phase of frustration can vary greatly for different people because they can have very different personalities"의 밑줄 친 부분을 통해 some은 some people을 가리킨다는 것을 알 수 있다.

04 단락 4에 따르면, 동화 단계가 일어나는 시기는?
(A) 이민자가 새 언어를 완벽하게 숙달했을 때
(B) 나이가 어린 이민자가 새 문화에서 청소년기를 보냈을 때
(C) 새로운 문화에 2세대가 태어났을 때
(D) 이민자가 새로운 문화와 교류하고자 결심할 때

해설 | Factual Information 단락 4의 마지막 부분에 동화 단계를 보이는 상당수가 이민 2세대라고 설명한다.

05 지문을 간략히 요약하기 위한 도입 문장이 아래 제시되어 있다. 지문에서 가장 중요한 내용을 표현한 세 개의 문장을 골라 요약문을 완성하시오. 일부 문장은 지문에 나오지 않았거나 중요하지 않은 내용이기 때문에 요약문에 포함되지 않는다. 이 문제는 2점이다.

> Kalvero Oberg는 사회 문화 변용에 대한 표준 모델을 제시했는데, 이는 이민자들이 새로운 문화에 적응하는 과정을 말한다.

(A) 문화 변용 과정 동안 이민자들은 새로운 문화에 대해 긍정적으로 또는 부정적으로 느끼게 되는 다양한 단계를 거치게 된다.
(B) 문화 변용 과정은 Kalvero Oberg가 이민자들이 새로운 문화에 동화되는 것을 돕기 위해 1954년 처음 개발했다.
(C) 모든 사람이 문화 변용 과정을 똑같은 속도로 거쳐 가는 것은 아니지만, 사람들은 보통 똑같은 전체적인 과정을 밟는다.
(D) 사회 문화 변용의 첫 단계에서 이민자들은 종종 새로운 문화의 색다름에 강한 인상을 받는다.
(E) 많은 이민자들은 사회 문화 변용 과정 중 마지막 단계에 이르지 못하고 좌절하여 모국 문화로 되돌아간다.
(F) 이민자들은 새로운 문화에 완전히 적응하기 전까지는 익숙하지 않은 생활의 어려움을 극복해야만 한다.

해설 | Summary (A)는 Oberg의 사회 문화 변용 모델을 설명한 단락 1의 내용을 요약해 놓은 것이다. (C)는 사회 문화 변용의 각 단계를 설명한 단락 2, 3, 4의 내용을 요약해 놓은 것이다. (F)는 사회 문화 변용 속 이민자들이 겪는 어려움을 설명한 단락 2와 3의 내용을 요약해 놓은 것이다.

어휘 | acculturation 문화 변용 adapt 적응하다 integrate 융합하다, 통합되다 dominant 지배적인 euphoria 행복 frustration 좌절
negotiation 타협 assimilation 동화, 융화 novelty 새로움 initial 초기의, 처음의 obviously 명백히, 뚜렷이 fluent 유창한
curve 굴곡 unaware ~를 알지 못하는 mother culture 모국문화 nostalgia 향수 reluctant 내키지 않는
take part in ~에 참여하다 close off ~을 고립시키다 proficient 능숙한 slippage 하락, 미끄러짐
be confronted with ~에 직면하다 challenging 어려운, 까다로운 phase 단계

Intensive Drill 3

| 01 (B) | 02 (C) | 03 (C) | 04 (B) | 05 (B), (C), (F) |

RENAISSANCE ARCHITECTURE

The period of European history known as the Renaissance was marked by a renewed interest in learning and the arts. Q01 Having just emerged from the Middle Ages, a time during which the Catholic church largely suppressed the pursuit of science and art, artists and thinkers who were disappointed with the failings of their own culture turned to a culture predating their own for inspiration. Ancient Rome became the model for bold new intellectuals who wished to revitalize their weakened culture. One of the earliest and most pronounced examples of Renaissance principles can be found in the architecture of the period. Drawing inspiration from the ruins of ancient Rome, architects reinvented the European skyline, constructing cathedrals and castles that featured a marked departure from the styles of the previous medieval period.

Q02 Q03-1 The two dominant styles of medieval architecture produced massive, hulking buildings that were more threatening than beautiful. The Romanesque style was often fortress-like in design, with its lack of decoration and use of hard lines. The Gothic style, on the other hand, was far more ornamental, with statuettes of various saints and demons adorning the exterior, and steep, pointed spires that reached to heights unprecedented in medieval construction. However, even the Gothic style inspired far more dread than it did artistic appreciation. Q03-2 In contrast to both styles, Renaissance architecture was a lively celebration of the art form, in turns both majestic and lighthearted, that gladly disposed of the dreary conventions of the past.

The birthplace of Renaissance architecture was the city of Florence, Italy, in the early fifteenth century. Here, an architect by the name of Filippo Brunelleschi started a new artistic trend with his work on the city's main cathedral. Though the cathedral itself was built in the Gothic style more common to the Middle Ages, Q04 Brunelleschi designed its giant dome based on that of the Pantheon of ancient Rome. He had studied the structure at great length and admired the style in which it was built for its orderly and symmetrical appearance. These same characteristics showed up in his design for the church of San Lorenzo, a strict geometrical design which featured Roman columns and archways. Throughout his career, Brunelleschi relied on these basic principles in his work as an architect, initiating a new style based on classical guidelines that would quickly become popular throughout Europe.

Perhaps the second most influential architect of the Renaissance was Donato Bramante, whose work is typical of what is called High Renaissance architecture. The High Renaissance period took place during the late fifteenth and early sixteenth centuries, and is characterized by an almost universal mastery of classical forms by architects from all over Italy. Often cited as a near-perfect piece of High Renaissance architecture, Bramante's *Tempietto* was built on the supposed place where St. Peter was killed in ancient times, and is thus the most sacred site in Rome. The small, round monument was built in explicit imitation of ancient Roman temples. Bramante later participated in the design and construction of the giant dome atop St. Peter's Basilica at the Vatican, a monumental achievement in Renaissance design for which he is best known today.

르네상스 건축

유럽 역사에서 르네상스로 알려진 시기는 배움과 예술에 다시금 관심을 가지게 된 시기로 유명하다. 가톨릭 교회가 과학·예술에 대한 추구를 크게 억눌렀던 중세 시대에서 막 벗어나, 자신들의 문화가 실패한 것에 실망했던 예술가와 사상가들은 영감을 얻기 위해 이전 시대의 문화로 눈을 돌렸다. 약화된 문화를 다시 회복시키고 싶어 했던 대담하고 새로운 지식층에게 고대 로마가 모델이 되었다. 초기의 가장 확연한 르네상스 원리의 예를 이 시대의 건축물에서 찾아볼 수 있다. 건축가들은 고대 로마 유적에서 영감을 받아, 이전 중세 시대 양식에서 뚜렷이 벗어난 특징을 한 대성당과 성을 건축하여 유럽의 스카이라인을 다시 새롭게 그려냈다.

중세 건축의 주요한 두 양식은 아름답기보다는 위협적인, 둔탁하게 크고 거대한 건물을 양산해냈다. 로마네스크 양식은 장식의 부재와 굵은 선의 사용으로 디자인적인 면에서 성곽 같은 느낌을 줄 때가 많았다. 반면에 고딕 양식은 훨씬 더 장식적이어서, 중세 건축물에서 전례 없이 높게 뻗은 가파른 첨탑이 사용되고 외곽 장식을 위해 여러 성자상과 악마상이 사용되었다. 그러나 고딕 양식도 예술적 감탄보다는 경외를 일으키는 경우가 훨씬 더 많았다. 이 두 가지 양식과 대조적으로 르네상스 건축은 과거의 음울한 양식을 기꺼이 버리고, 생동감 넘치는 예술 형식의 축전인 것처럼 웅장하면서도 가벼운 느낌을 주었다.

르네상스 건축은 15세기 초 이탈리아의 도시 피렌체에서 탄생했다. 여기에서 Filippo Brunelleschi라는 이름의 건축가가 도시의 대성당을 지을 때 그의 작품에 새로운 예술적 경향을 시작하였다. 성당 자체는 중세 시대에 더욱 일반적이었던 고딕 양식으로 지어졌지만, Brunelleschi는 고대 로마의 판테온에 기반을 두고 그 거대한 돔을 설계했다. 그는 그 구조를 면밀히 연구했고, 그 정돈되고 대칭적인 모습으로 지어진 양식을 높이 샀다. 이러한 특성이 로마식 기둥과 아치 통로를 사용한 엄격한 기하학적 디자인의 산 로렌초 성당의 설계에 잘 드러나 있다. Brunelleschi는 활동하는 동안 건축가로서 자신의 작품에 이런 기본 원리에 충실하였으며, 고전 건축물들에 기반을 둔 새로운 양식을 탄생시켰고 이것은 유럽 전역에서 빠르게 인기를 얻어갔다.

아마도 두 번째로 영향력 있는 르네상스 건축가는 Donato Bramante일 것이며, 그의 작품은 전성기 르네상스 건축물의 전형이라고 할 수 있다. 전성기 르네상스 시기는 15세기 후반에서 16세기 초반에 걸쳐 있었으며, 이탈리아 전역의 건축가들이 고전 형식을 거의 보편적으로 통달했다는 점을 특징으로 한다. 흔히 전성기 르네상스 건축의 거의 완벽한 건축물로 불리는 Bramante의 템피에토는 고대에 성 베드로가 순교한 곳이라고 여겨지는, 로마 안에서도 가장 성스러운 곳에 지어졌다. 이 작고 둥근 기념물은 고대 로마 신전을 그대로 모방하여 지어졌다. Bramante는 훗날 바티칸 성 베드로 성당 위의 거대한 돔 설계 및 건설에 참여하기도 하였는데, 오늘날 그는 이 르네상스 디자인의 기념비적인 업적으로 가장 잘 알려져 있다.

01 단락 1에 따르면, 르네상스 사상가들이 영감을 얻기 위해 고대 로마로 눈을 돌린 원인은?

(A) 로마를 세계에서 가장 위대한 제국으로 여겼다.
(B) 예술과 교육을 자신들의 문화에 다시 들여오고자 했다.
(C) 고대 로마인과 같은 위상에 도달하고자 했다.
(D) 고대 로마의 대담한 지식층을 이상화했다.

해설 | Factual Information 중세 시대에 과학과 예술의 발전이 크게 억압을 당하자, 자신들의 문화가 쇠퇴하는 것에 크게 실망해, 이전 시대의 문화에서 예술과 학문을 다시 배우고자 했다. 이전 시대의 문화 중 고대 로마 시대의 문화가 그 모델이 되어준 것이다.

02 지문의 threatening 과 의미상 가장 가까운 것은?

(A) 고무하는
(B) 매혹적인
(C) 위협적인
(D) 중요한

해설 | Vocabulary 지문의 massive, hulking과 관련이 있으며, beautiful 과는 반대되는 의미여야 하므로, threatening 은 '위협적인'의 의미임을 알 수 있다.

03 단락 2에서 필자가 로마네스크 양식 과 고딕 양식 에 대해 자세히 설명하는 이유는?

(A) 르네상스 양식이 로마네스크 양식과 고딕 양식에 큰 영향을 끼쳤다는 것을 보여주기 위해
(B) 르네상스 건축이 가장 진보된 건축 양식이라는 것을 강조하기 위해
(C) 르네상스 건축이 이전 양식과 어떻게 다른지 좀 더 분명히 보여주기 위해
(D) 로마네스크 양식과 고딕 양식에 대해 좀 더 자세히 설명하기 위해

해설 | Rhetorical Purpose 로마네스크 양식과 고딕 양식은 모두 르네상스 이전 시대의 건축 양식이었다. 이 두 가지 양식 모두 외관적으로 두려움을 심어주는 특징이 있었는데, 이러한 특징은 생동감 있고 가벼운 느낌을 주는 르네상스 양식과 대조를 이루고 있다. 필자는 르네상스 양식과 르네상스 이전의 대표적인 양식 두 가지를 비교해서 르네상스 양식이 그 이전 양식과 어떻게 다른지를 보여주고 있다.

04 지문에서 the structure 가 가리키는 것은?

(A) 대성당
(B) 판테온
(C) 돔
(D) 교회

해설 | Reference "He had studied the structure at great length and admired the style in which it was built for its orderly and symmetrical appearance"에서 the structure 는 밑줄 친 부분에서 말해주듯 Filippo Brunelleschi를 감동하게 한 건축물이다. 이 문장의 앞 문장에 Brunelleschi는 고대 로마의 판테온 신전을 모델로 돔(dome)을 설계했다는 말이 있다.

05 지문을 간략히 요약하기 위한 도입 문장이 아래 제시되어 있다. 지문에서 가장 중요한 내용을 표현한 세 개의 문장을 골라 요약문을 완성하시오. 일부 문장은 지문에 나오지 않았거나 중요하지 않은 내용이기 때문에 요약문에 포함되지 않는다. 이 문제는 2점이다.

> 르네상스 시기에는 고대 로마 건축의 수많은 요소들이 유럽 문화에 유입되어 건축 예술을 완전히 변화시켰다.

(A) 그 시기 지식인들 덕분에 르네상스 시기의 철학과 예술은 다시 새롭게 피어났다.
(B) 여러 르네상스 건물은 피렌체에 기원을 갖고, 오랫동안 로마의 유적을 연구한 Brunelleschi에 의해 지어졌다.
(C) 전성기 르네상스 시기는 전통 양식으로의 명백한 회귀를 특징으로 하며, 이를 가장 잘 보여주는 예는 Bramante에 의해 지어진 템피에토라는 기념물이다.
(D) 르네상스 건축 양식은 이탈리아에서 매우 인기가 많았지만, 영향이 그 너머로 퍼지지는 않았다.
(E) 고딕 양식의 위업은 성당을 역사상 가장 높게 만든 높고 뾰족한 첨탑 사용에 있다.
(F) 중세 시대의 음울한 건축과 대조적으로 르네상스 건축 양식은 활기찬 때가 많았다.

해설 | Summary (B)는 Brunelleschi의 건축에 대해 설명한 단락 3의 내용을, (C)는 르네상스의 전성기 때의 건축을 설명한 단락 4의 내용을, (F)는 르네상스 건축과 르네상스 이전 시대의 건축을 비교한 단락 2의 내용을 요약한 것이다.

어휘 | suppress 억누르다　pursuit 추구　inspiration 영감　revitalize 새로운 힘을 주다　pronounced 확연한　cathedral 대성당　medieval 중세의　dominant 두드러진, 주요한　hulking (부피가) 큰　ornamental 장식적, 장식용의　demon 악마　spire 첨탑　unprecedented 전례 없는　dread 경외, 두려움　majestic 웅장한　dispose of ~를 버리다　dreary 음울한　convention 관례　symmetrical 대칭적인　geometrical 기하학적인　monumental 기념비적인

Mini Test 1

01 (D) 02 (B) 03 (A) 04 (C) 05 (B), (C), (D)

SLUMS OF THE INDUSTRIAL REVOLUTION

During the Industrial Revolution, England's towns and villages were transformed over just a few decades into major industrial centers. Factories were built in towns such as Manchester and Birmingham due to their access to shipping routes, and these factories required a great deal of workers. Q01 These were often people whose former trades had been taken over by machines, leaving them out of work and desperate for income. While the upper-class factory owners lived in large houses outside the city, the workers generally lived together in filthy apartment houses at the city's center, near their places of work. Factory owners would often set up "company towns," sections of the city in which the apartment buildings, grocery stores, and schools were all owned by the factory owners. Whatever money the workers were able to earn was often paid right back to the factory owners in the form of rent and food bills.

Q02 Q04 Because of the massive influx of workers moving from the country into the industrial centers, tenements went up all over the industrial centers to house workers, but the residents there faced squalid living conditions. The houses were very small and were built side by side in very close quarters, making for dirty, crowded neighborhoods known as slums, which were characterized by high crime rates and poor living conditions. The neighborhoods would often have little better than open sewer systems. Several neighbors often had to share the same toilet facilities as well. The growth of such tenements was such that it put a special strain on the cities' water and sewage systems, so that it was not uncommon for sewage to be running into the streets and the yards of the tenement houses. Given these living conditions, it is not surprising that ①disease sprang up quickly in these areas due to sewage problems and contaminated water, and ②spread rapidly from one person to another due to the close proximity in which everyone lived. Large numbers of workers died from cholera and typhoid, which were spread through the bad water.

Conditions did slowly improve throughout the nineteenth century, as the government intervened and introduced several reforms. Parliament member Michael Thomas Sadler was a major supporter of workers' rights, and authored the Sadler Report in 1832 to show the government that factory owners were engaging in terrible abuse of workers, including women and children. In addition to reducing the average workday and limiting child labor, Sadler worked to ensure that factory owners provided their workers with decent living conditions, as well as education for their children. Further reforms limited the number of homes that could be built in a specific area. The Public Health Act of 1875 forced towns to pave and clean the roads, and a combination of gas lighting and new police forces improved the safety conditions on the streets. Closed, underground sewer systems were finally built, and all water was filtered for purity. New regulations also sought to help the poor and unemployed, providing soup kitchens for those who could not afford to feed themselves.

산업 혁명 시기의 빈민가

산업 혁명 당시 단 몇십 년의 기간 동안, 영국의 소도시와 마을들은 주요 산업 중심지로 변모했다. 해상 운송로와의 접근이 용이하기 때문에 맨체스터와 버밍햄 같은 소도시에는 공장들이 들어섰고, 이런 공장들은 많은 노동력이 필요했다. 여기서 일한 사람들은 원래 있던 일자리를 기계에 빼앗기고 일할 곳이 없어 소득원을 절실히 원하던 사람들인 경우가 많았다. 상위 계층에 속한 공장 소유주들이 도시 외곽의 대저택에 살았던 반면, 노동자들은 보통 일터 근처인 도시 중심의 더러운 아파트에 모여 살았다. 공장 소유주들은 보통 '회사 소도시'를 세우곤 했는데, 이 도시 구역에 있는 아파트 건물과 식료품점, 학교는 모두 공장 소유주의 소유였다. 노동자들이 벌었던 돈이란 돈은 그대로 다시 집세나 식료품 값의 형태로 공장 소유주에게 돌아가는 경우가 많았다.

시골 출신 노동자들이 산업 중심지로 대규모 유입 되었기 때문에, 산업 중심지 전역에서 이 노동자들을 수용하기 위한 주택이 늘어났지만, 그곳 거주자들은 불결한 생활 환경에 직면해야 했다. 집들은 매우 비좁거나, 주택이 매우 인접한 거리에 빼곡히 붙어 지어지다 보니, 빈민가라고 알려진 더럽고 북적거리는 동네가 조성되었는데, 이런 곳은 높은 범죄율과 형편없는 생활 환경으로 특징지어졌다. 이런 지역의 하수구 시설은 개방 하수 시설보다 별로 나을 게 없었다. 여러 이웃이 하나의 화장실 시설을 함께 써야 할 때도 흔했다. 이러한 공동주택이 많이 늘어나면서 도시의 상하수도 시설에는 감당하기 힘든 부하가 걸리는 경지에 이르렀고, 그런 나머지 오물이 길가나 공동주택의 마당에 흘러드는 적도 적지 않았다. 이러한 생활 환경을 고려했을 때, 이런 지역에서 오물이나 오수 문제로 질병이 급속히 생겨나고, 모두가 밀접한 거리에 살다 보니 사람들 사이에 질병이 빠르게 퍼졌다는 사실은 놀랍지 않다. 많은 수의 노동자가 오수를 통해 퍼진 콜레라와 장티푸스로 사망했다.

19세기 전반에 걸쳐 정부가 개입해 몇 가지 개혁 조치를 도입하면서, 이런 환경은 점차 개선되었다. 국회의원이던 Michael Thomas Sadler는 노동자 권리를 적극적으로 옹호했고, 공장 소유주들이 여자나 아이들을 포함한 노동자를 혹독히 착취하고 있다는 사실을 정부에 알리기 위해 1832년에 Sadler 보고서를 저술했다. 평균 근무 일수를 줄이고 어린이 노동에 제한을 가하는 데에 그치지 않고, Sadler는 공장 소유주가 노동자의 아이들 교육과 적절한 생활 환경을 제공하게 하려고 노력했다. 추후 개혁 조치를 통해 특정 지역에 지을 수 있는 주택의 수가 제한되었다. 1875년 제정된 공공보건법으로 도시 길거리가 포장되고 청소되었으며, 가스등과 새로운 경찰력의 조합으로 거리의 안전 환경이 개선되었다. 밀폐식의 지하 하수 시설이 마침내 지어졌으며, 모든 수도가 정화되기 위해 여과됐다. 또한 새로운 규제들을 통해 먹을 것을 살 수 없는 사람들을 위한 무료 급식소 운영 등의 가난한 사람 및 일자리가 없는 사람들을 도우려는 방안도 강구되었다.

01
단락 1에 따르면, 많은 사람들이 일을 하기 위해 공장에 온 이유는?
(A) 제대로 된 교육을 받지 않았기 때문에
(B) 산업 혁명으로 인해 그들의 인력이 필요했기 때문에
(C) 더 나은 일자리를 얻을 자격이 안 되었기 때문에
(D) 기계 노동력 때문에 직업을 잃었기 때문에

해설 | Factual Information 공장 직원들은 노동력이 기계로 대체되면서 일자리를 잃어 수입이 절실하게 필요했던 사람들이다.

02
지문의 influx 와 의미상 가장 가까운 것은?
(A) 숫자
(B) 유입
(C) 변화
(D) 집단

해설 | Vocabulary "moving from the country into the industrial centers"와 일맥상통하는 의미이므로 influx 는 '유입'의 의미임을 알 수 있다.

03
다음 중 지문에서 표시된 문장의 주요 정보를 가장 잘 나타낸 문장은?
정답 외의 보기들은 중요한 의미가 바뀌거나 주요 정보가 빠져 있다.
(A) 이 지역의 나쁜 위생 조건과 인구 과잉은 필연적으로 공동주택과 빈민가를 통해 질병이 발생하고 급속히 퍼져나가도록 만들었다.
(B) 비위생적인 생활 조건은 낙후된 하수 시설을 가진 사람들 사이에 질병이 급속도로 퍼지도록 만들었다.
(C) 사람이 서로 너무 밀접하게 몰려 살았기 때문에 하수 문제가 있었던 빈민가는 질병의 주요 번식지였다.
(D) 거주 지역의 열악한 위생 환경이 가난한 사람들 사이에 질병이 널리 퍼지게 만든 것은 우연이 아니었다.

해설 | Sentence Simplification 표시된 문장은 크게 두 의미로 나뉠 수 있다. ① 오물과 오수로 인해 질병이 급속히 생겨났다. ② 빼곡히 붙어서 사는 환경 때문에 질병이 급속히 전파되었다.

04
단락 2에 따르면, 산업 중심지의 생활 조건에 대해 추론할 수 있는 것은?
(A) 생활 환경의 기준이 정부에 의해 규제되었다.
(B) 노동자들을 위한 주거 지역이 세워지기 훨씬 이전부터 범죄율이 높았다.
(C) 소도시가 갑작스러운 인구 증가에 대처할 수 없었기 때문에 생활 조건이 악화되었다.
(D) 산업 혁명 이전부터 이미 살기에 알맞지 않았다.

해설 | Inference 두 번째 단락의 전체적인 내용은 주거 공간과 시설들이 한정된 상황에서 엄청난 인구가 도시로 유입되면서 나타난 생활 환경 관련 문제점들이다.

05
지문을 간략히 요약하기 위한 도입 문장이 아래 제시되어 있다. 지문에서 가장 중요한 내용을 표현한 세 개의 문장을 골라 요약문을 완성하시오. 일부 문장은 지문에 나오지 않았거나 중요하지 않은 내용이기 때문에 요약문에 포함되지 않는다. *이 문제는 2점이다.*

> 산업 혁명으로 노동자들이 대규모로 도시로 이주하였는데, 수년간 도시의 생활 환경은 빈민가와 다름없었다.

(A) 공장 소유주들이 교외의 대저택에서 살 수 있었던 반면, 노동자들은 공장 근처에 살아야 했다.
(B) 노동자들은 북적거리고 불결한 경우가 다반사인 비좁은 아파트 건물에 살았다.
(C) 빈민가의 불결한 생활 환경은 높은 범죄율과 치명적인 질병 확산의 한 원인이 되었다.
(D) 정부 주도의 개혁은 공장 노동자들의 삶이 현저히 개선되는 결과를 낳았다.
(E) 노동자들은 빈민가에 살아야 하는데도 대부분 산업이 도시에 집중되었기 때문에 도시로 몰려들었다.
(F) 이후 정부의 규제를 통해 공장 소유주들은 아이들에게 교육을 제공하게 되었다.

해설 | Summary (B)는 노동자들의 생활 환경을 설명한 단락 2의 전반부를 요약한 것이다. (C)는 열악한 생활 환경의 결과를 설명한 단락 2의 후반부를 요약한 것이다. (D)는 19세기 정부의 개혁 조치를 설명한 단락 3의 내용을 요약한 것이다.

어휘 | transform 변모하다, 변화시키다 filthy 더러운 massive 대규모의 influx 유입 tenement 공동주택 squalid 불결한 sewer 하수 sewage 오물 spring up 생겨나다 contaminatd 오염된 proximity 밀접, 근접 typhoid 장티푸스 intervene 개입하다 reform 개혁 author 저술하다 abuse 혹사 decent (사회 기준에) 적절한 pave (도로를) 포장하다 combination 조합 filter 여과하다 purity 청결 soup kitchen 무료 급식소

Mini Test 2 p.202

01 (B)   02 (C)   03 (D)   04 (C)   05 [Sensory Memory – (B)], [Short-term Memory – (D), (G)], [Long-term Memory – (C), (E)]

MEMORY

In the past few decades, researchers have learned a great deal about how memory works, most notably that the process of creating memories can be separated into three stages or types: sensory memory, short-term memory, and long-term memory. Q02(B) The first of these three, sensory memory, is by far the most fleeting and insubstantial of the three stages. Sensory memory is different from what is usually thought of as memory, in that it refers to the ability to retain important information while ignoring everything else. Q05(B) In this way, it is closely related to attention and concentration. Q01 Q02(A) When one is focusing most of his or her attention on a specific task, for instance, any stimulus not related to that task is unlikely to be noticed, though it may superficially be perceived. Q02(D) This filter of sorts is very helpful in eliminating sounds or sights that may distract from the task at hand, thereby increasing one's ability to concentrate on what is most important at that moment.

When pertinent information is allowed into one's consciousness, however, it enters the domain of the short-term memory. Q05(G) Short-term memory has been shown to have a duration of just a few seconds to a few minutes, and is most useful in quickly recalling information most relevant to specific tasks, so for information to be successfully retrieved from short-term memory, it must be used within a very brief time period, or else the memory will decay. One example is reading a phone number from a phone book and then looking away to dial the number on a phone. A If a distraction comes in the middle of this process, it takes only seconds for the memory of the phone number to disappear. B Q05(D) One way that the effectiveness of short-term memory can be increased is Q04 by sorting information into small clusters. C This involves breaking down large amounts of information into small parts that are easier to digest. Q03 In the example of the telephone number, a person who tries to remember the number in its entirety will more quickly forget it before dialing. D However, if this same person memorizes the number in groups of digits rather than as a whole, then the memory is likely to endure longer.

Long-term memory is much more complex, as it can retain many decades' worth of information. Q05(C) Long-term memories may be very old, such as the recollection of a childhood birthday party, or they may be recent, such as the top story on the morning news. This represents two distinct types of memories: episodic and semantic. Memories of events such as a party are called episodic memories, because they recall episodes from one's experience. Of course, there are also memories that are not connected to some specific time, place, or event. Q05(E) These are called semantic memories, and can include a wide variety of factual information, such as the rules of grammar or the lyrics to one's favorite song. Memories that are stored for the long term can be one or the other, and are often some mixture of the two as well. Distinctions between these two different types of memories serve as a kind of filing system that allows the brain to more easily recall individual memories.

기억

지난 몇십 년 동안 학자들은 기억의 작용에 대해 많은 것을 알아냈는데, 그중에서도 기억을 만들어내는 과정이 지각 기억, 단기 기억, 장기 기억의 세 단계 혹은 종류로 나뉠 수 있다는 점이 가장 두드러진다. 세 가지 중 첫 번째로 지각 기억은 세 단계 기억 중 무엇보다도 가장 순간적으로 실체가 없는 기억이다. 지각 기억은 다른 모든 것을 무시하면서 중요한 정보만을 간직하는 능력을 가리킨다는 점에서, 일반적으로 기억이라고 여겨지는 것과는 사뭇 다르다. 이런 면에서 지각 기억은 주의·집중과 밀접한 관련이 있다. 예를 들어, 누군가가 특정 작업을 하느라 주의를 쏟고 있을 때, 이 작업과 관련 없는 자극은 그것이 피상적으로 지각될지라도 쉽게 인지되지는 않는다. 이런 종류의 필터 작용은 진행 중인 일에 주의를 흩뜨릴 수 있는 소리나 광경을 없애버리는 데 큰 도움을 주는데, 그렇게 함으로써 바로 그 순간 가장 중요한 일에 집중할 수 있는 능력을 향상시켜준다.

그러나 관련된 정보가 일단 사람의 의식 속으로 들어오면, 그것은 단기 기억의 영역에 속하게 된다. 단기 기억은 몇 초에서 몇 분 동안의 지속 기간을 갖는 것으로 알려져 왔으며, 특정 작업에 제일 많이 관련되는 정보를 빠르게 기억해 내는 데 가장 유용하다. 그래서 정보를 단기 기억으로부터 성공적으로 기억해내려면, 그 기억을 매우 짧은 시간 안에 사용해야 하며, 그렇게 하지 않으면 그 기억은 사라질 것이다. 하나의 예로 전화번호부에서 전화번호를 읽고 전화에 번호를 누르기 위해 돌아보는 때가 있다. A 이 과정 중간에 방해를 받게 되면, 이 전화번호는 불과 몇 초 사이에 기억에서 사라진다. B 단기 기억의 효과를 증진시킬 수 있는 한 가지 방법은 정보를 작은 단위로 나누는 것이다. C 이것은 많은 양의 정보를 소화하기 더 쉽도록 작은 조각으로 나누는 것이다. 전화번호의 경우에서, 전화번호를 통째로 기억하려고 하면 다이얼을 누르기도 전에 잊어버릴 확률이 높다. D 그러나 통째로 기억하기보다 몇 개씩 그룹으로 끊어서 기억하면, 기억이 더 오래 지속될 확률이 높아진다.

장기 기억의 경우는 수십 년 분량의 기억을 저장할 수 있다는 점에서 훨씬 더 복잡하다. 장기 기억은 어린 시절 생일 파티의 회상과 같이 매우 오래된 기억일 수도 있고, 아침 뉴스 시간의 주요 기사처럼 최근의 기억일 수도 있다. 이것은 두 가지 고유 영역의 기억을 나타내는데, 삽화적 기억과 의미적 기억이 그것이다. 파티와 같은 사건의 기억은 개인적 경험에 있었던 일을 회상한다는 점에서 삽화적 기억이라고 불린다. 물론, 특정 시간, 장소, 사건에 연결되지 않은 기억도 있다. 이런 기억들은 의미적 기억이라고 불리며, 문법 법칙이나 가장 좋아하는 노래의 가사 같은 다방면의 사실적 정보가 이에 속한다. 오랫동안 저장되는 기억은 이 둘 중의 하나이거나, 두 가지가 섞인 경우도 흔하다. 이 두 가지 다른 종류의 기억을 구분하는 것은 뇌가 개별 기억을 좀 더 쉽게 기억할 수 있게 해주는 일종의 분류 체계로 작용한다.

01 지문에서 it 이 가리키는 것은?

(A) 작업
(B) 자극
(C) 주의
(D) 필터 작용

해설 | Reference "… any stimulus not related to that task is unlikely to be noticed, though it may superficially be perceived"에서 밑줄 친 부분은 it과 동일한 대상을 설명하고 있다. 따라서 it은 작업과 관련 없는 자극(stimulus)임을 알 수 있다.

02 단락 1에 따르면, 지각 기억에 대한 내용으로 옳지 않은 것은?

(A) 연관되지 않은 정보를 걸러내는 데 유용하다.
(B) 장기 기억이나 단기 기억에 비해 일시적이다.
(C) 너무 많은 자극이 있으면 과부하 되기 쉽다.
(D) 대부분의 방해를 무시함으로써 집중력을 향상시킨다.

해설 | Negative Fact 지각 기억은 세 가지 기억 유형 중 가장 빨리 사라지고, 중요하지 않은 것은 걸러내고 필요한 정보만 처리해서 집중력을 향상시킬 수 있다.

03 필자가 지문에서 전화번호 를 언급하는 이유는?

(A) 단기 기억이 일상생활의 일 처리에 어떻게 도움을 주는지 논의하기 위해
(B) 정보를 반복하는 것이 암기에 어떻게 도움이 되는지 보여주기 위해
(C) 장기 기억이 유용한 상황에 대한 예를 들어주기 위해
(D) 단기 기억의 한계점과 향상 방법에 대해 설명하기 위해

해설 | Rhetorical Purpose 단락 2의 중심 내용은 단기 기억의 한계성과 단기 기억을 향상시킬 수 있는 방법이며, 전화번호는 이 중심 내용을 뒷받침하기 위한 예시로 사용되었다.

04 다음 문장이 지문에 들어갈 곳을 나타내는 네 개의 사각형[■]을 보시오.

> 이것은 많은 양의 정보를 소화하기 더 쉽도록 작은 조각으로 나누는 것이다.

이 문장이 들어갈 가장 적절한 위치는?

(A) A (B) B (C) C (D) D

해설 | Sentence Insertion 삽입 문장 "This involves breaking down large amounts of information into small parts that are easier to digest"에서 This는 단기 기억을 향상시키는 방법으로 소개된 "… sorting information into small clusters …"를 가리키는 지시어이다.

05 보기에서 적절한 문구를 골라 관련된 기억의 종류와 연결하시오. 보기 중 2개는 사용되지 않는다. *이 문제는 3점이다.*

보기	기억의 종류
(A) 지식인들에게서만 발견된다.	지각 기억
(B) 주의와 집중과 관련 있다.	• (B)
(C) 옛날 기억을 포함한다.	단기 기억
(D) 정보가 덩어리로 처리될 때 강화될 수 있다.	• (D)
(E) 사실적인 정보를 저장한다.	• (G)
(F) 가장 진화된 형태의 기억이다.	장기 기억
(G) 짧은 시간 동안만 지속된다.	• (C)
	• (E)

해설 | Fill in a Table 지문에 따르면, 지각 기억은 주의, 집중과 관련이 있고, 단기 기억은 짧은 시간 동안만 지속되긴 하지만 작은 덩어리로 처리될 때 강화될 수 있다고 한다. 장기 기억은 생일 파티와 같은 옛날 경험을 회상하는 삽화적 기억과 사실적인 정보 등의 의미적 기억으로 나뉠 수 있다.

어휘 | short-term 단기간의 long-term 장기간의 fleeting 순간의 insubstantial 실체가 없는 retain 간직하다 concentration 집중 stimulus 자극 superficially 피상적으로 perceive 인지하다 eliminate 없애다 distract 주의를 흩뜨리다 pertinent 관련된 consciousness 의식, 지각 domain 영역 duration 지속 기간 relevant 관계 있는 retrieve 되찾아오다 decay 없어지다 distraction 주의 산만 effectiveness 효과 break down 나누다, 분해하다 digest 소화하다 recollection 회상 represent 나타내다 episodic 삽화적인 semantic 의미적인 recall 기억하다

iBT Practice

01 (C) 02 (D) 03 (B) 04 (B) 05 (C) 06 (A) 07 (A) 08 (D) 09 (C) 10 (A) 11 (B) 12 (C)
13 (B), (D), (F)

ADAM SMITH AND *THE WEALTH OF NATIONS*

In 1776, the same year America gained independence from the British, philosopher Adam Smith wrote a book that would Q01 earn him a permanent place in history, as well as the title "the father of modern economics." The book that made him such an esteemed figure was *The Wealth of Nations*, in which he outlined his theories on Q02 political economy — the ways in which human behavior, market factors, government regulations, and several other factors together drive business and commerce. Smith's work laid the foundation for the modern study of economics, most notably the classical school of economics, from which principles of capitalism and the free market economy originated. More than an economist, however, Smith had a keen interest in human nature, and it was his study of the interaction of human nature with social institutions that led to his groundbreaking work in economics.

At the age of 14, Smith began a long and intensive study of philosophy at the University of Glasgow in his home country of Scotland, later moving to Oxford. Upon graduating, he obtained his first job as a lecturer. It was through his lectures that he gained much positive attention from both his students and his contemporaries, eventually becoming a professor of moral philosophy back at the University of Glasgow. It was in this subject that he published his first book, *The Theory of Moral Sentiments*, which dealt mainly with his ideas about human nature. He believed human nature was an unchanging and universal characteristic of human beings that could be used to predict the behavior of people within societies. Q03 Q06 Smith wrote of how humans seemed to possess two different, seemingly conflicting tendencies: on one hand, they are passionate beings driven by self-preservation; on the other hand, they are Q04 rational beings with the ability to discriminate right from wrong. Q05 These two opposing forces seemed to regulate one another in human behavior, he said, since passionate, self-interested beings were still capable of establishing organized institutions for the betterment of all men.

The ideas put forth in *The Theory of Moral Sentiments* would lay the infrastructure for his study of political economy later on. In fact, it can be said that *The Wealth of Nations* was not its own separate economic treatise, but rather a continuation of the philosophical writings of his earlier work. Smith expanded on his idea of the duality of human nature to examine the workings of the ideal society in terms of its economy. According to his theory, the best society was one in which its participants were dependent upon one another to meet their economic needs. **A** Smith envisioned what he called a "system of perfect liberty," in which the market was left untouched by government institutions, and in which the terms of business were determined instead by "natural" forces. **B** Q12 Economic factors like supply and demand would serve as an "invisible hand" that could guide the markets toward prosperity without any need for government regulations. **C** An example of this economic factor's impact on the market is producers and consumers working together to make sure goods were both bought and sold. Q08 This idea would later become known as laissez-faire capitalism. **D**

Q11 Under this condition, Smith argued, people can improve their own lot while also improving society. This is because the capitalist system exploits the duality of human nature, as discussed in his previous book. According to Smith's model, competition would become the factor that balances man's selfish tendencies with his more rational ones. ① Because individual producers would be forced to compete with one another both for business and for good labor, ② prices would be determined by what consumers were willing and able to pay, and ③ wages would be determined by how much workers are willing to sell their labor for, ④ which would help commerce. The combined effect would create a healthy and robust economy driven both by consumers' freedom of choice and by producers' desire to outcompete other businesses to achieve unlimited wealth. **Q10** In this way, self-interest could actually work for the good of society on the whole. Unfortunately, time proved Smith's theories somewhat idealistic, as fierce competition would lead to such villainy as the labor abuses of the Industrial Revolution just decades later. However, despite the introduction of certain government regulations, the basic tenets of Smith's philosophy still underpin the economic policies of most civilized nations today.

Smith는 이런 상황에서 사람들이 사회를 발전시키는 동시에 그들 스스로를 개선시킬 수 있다고 주장했다. 이것은 이전 저서에서 논의된 바 있는 것처럼 자본주의가 인간 본성의 이중성을 이용하기 때문이다. Smith 이론에 의하면, 경쟁은 인간의 이기성과 이보다 이성적인 성향 간의 균형을 맞춰준다. 각 생산자가 사업과 양질의 노동력을 확보하기 위해 경쟁할 수밖에 없기 때문에, 가격은 소비자들이 흔쾌히 돈을 지급할 수 있는 만큼에 의해 결정되고 임금은 노동자가 자신의 노동 대가로 얼마나 받기를 바라느냐에 따라 결정되는데, 이것이 상업 활동에 도움을 준다. 이런 효과가 결합되면, 소비자의 선택의 자유, 그리고 무한한 부를 손에 넣기 위해 다른 사업 경쟁자들을 뛰어넘으려는 생산자의 욕구로 움직이는 건전하고 활기찬 경제가 창조된다. 이런 식으로 이기심은 전반적으로는 사회에 이로운 일을 한다. 불행하게도 시간이 지나고 바로 수십 년 뒤 산업 혁명의 노동력 착취와 같은 치열한 경쟁으로 인한 악행이 나타나면서 Smith 이론이 다소 이상주의적임이 드러났다. 그러나 특정한 정부 규제가 도입되기는 했지만, Smith 철학의 기본 신조는 오늘날의 가장 선진 문명국가에서 여전히 경제 정책의 근간이 되고 있다.

01 지문의 esteemed 와 의미상 가장 가까운 것은?
(A) 재능 있는
(B) 기이한
(C) 존경받는
(D) 참을성 있는

해설 | Vocabulary   esteemed 의 의미는 앞문장의 "… earn him a permanent place in history, as well as the title of the father of modern economics"로부터 추측할 수 있다.

02 단락 1에 따르면, Smith가 정의한 정치경제는?
(A) 경제 활동에서 사업과 상업의 척도
(B) 인간 본성이 사회 제도를 변화시키는 방법
(C) 고전 경제 개념이 이끄는 시장 활동
(D) 인간, 시장, 그리고 정부의 상호작용

해설 | Factual Information   지문에서 정치경제란 인간 행동, 시장 요소, 정부 규제 등이 사업과 상업을 움직이는 것이라고 설명한다.

03 지문의 conflicting 과 의미상 가장 가까운 것은?
(A) 매혹적인
(B) 상반되는
(C) 의심스러운
(D) 실제적인

해설 | Vocabulary   동의어 단서를 찾을 수 있는 문제이다. "Smith wrote of how humans seemed to possess two different, seemingly conflicting tendencies …"에서 인간은 두 개의 다른 성향을 갖는다고 했으므로 conflicting 은 '상반되는'의 의미임을 알 수 있다.

04 지문의 discriminate 와 의미상 가장 가까운 것은?
(A) 고립시키다
(B) 구별하다
(C) 보호하다
(D) 제외하다

해설 | Vocabulary   "rational beings with the ability to discriminate right from wrong", 즉 잘잘못을 구별할 줄 아는 이성적 존재라는 내용이므로, discriminate 은 '구별하다'의 의미임을 알 수 있다.

05 단락 2에서 필자가 언급하는 것은?
(A) Smith는 『도덕 감정론』이라는 책을 낸 후 유명해졌다.
(B) Smith는 인간의 본성이 대중의 행동을 예측하는 데 사용되어서는 안 된다고 생각했다.
(C) Smith는 인간이 서로 균형을 맞추는 두 가지의 경향을 보인다고 주장했다.
(D) Smith는 그의 연구 분야를 정치경제에서 도덕 철학으로 변경하였다.

해설 | Factual Information   지문에 따르면, Smith는 인간이 두 개의 상반된 경향을 보이고 있지만, 인간 행동에서 이 반대되는 두 힘이 서로를 조절하는 것처럼 보인다고 말했다.

06 단락 2에 따르면, Adam Smith가 인간을 모순적인 존재로 본 이유는?

(A) 인간은 자신의 이익을 추구하는 동시에 도덕적인 분별력이 있기 때문에
(B) 인간은 자유를 추구하는 동시에 사회적 질서를 세우려 하기 때문에
(C) 인간은 개인적으로 행동하면서도 단체적으로 행동하기 때문에
(D) 인간은 사회적 평등을 추구하면서 동시에 사회적 신분 상승을 얻고 싶어 하기 때문에

해설 | Factual Information 단락 2에서 Smith는 인간은 자기 보호를 위해 움직이는 감정적인 존재인 동시에 옳은 것과 옳지 않은 것을 구분하는 능력이 있는 상반된 성격을 지닌 존재라고 보았다.

07 지문의 infrastructure와 의미상 가장 가까운 것은?

(A) 기초
(B) 과정
(C) 규정
(D) 지시

해설 | Vocabulary infrastructure는 '기초'라는 의미이다.

08 지문에서 this condition이 가리키는 것은?

(A) 건전한 경제를 위해 필요한 규제
(B) 개인이 이기적으로 행동하는 경향
(C) 인간이 두 가지 본성을 가지고 있다는 생각
(D) 어떤 개입도 없는 시장

해설 | Reference this condition이 가리키는 것은 앞 단락의 laissez-faire capitalism을 가리킨다. laissez-faire capitalism에 대한 설명은 이 어구의 바로 앞 부분에 있는 설명, 즉 정부의 규제 없이 시장이 번영할 수 있는 체제를 가리킨다.

09 다음 중 지문에서 표시된 문장의 주요 정보를 가장 잘 나타낸 문장은? 정답 외의 보기들은 중요한 의미가 바뀌거나 주요 정보가 빠져 있다.

(A) 노동력과 사업을 확보하기 위해 경쟁하는 생산자들은 그들에게 가장 큰 이익을 가져다주는 선에서 가격을 책정할 것이다.
(B) 만약 사업들이 서로 경쟁을 해야 한다면 가격과 임금은 소비자들의 요구에 따라 결정될 것이다.
(C) 사업 간 경쟁이 소비자와 노동자에게 크게 유리한 가격과 임금을 책정할 것이고, 결과적으로 이것이 상업에 이득이 될 것이다.
(D) 소비자는 생산자가 사업과 노동력을 확보하기 위해 서로 경쟁하는 것에 몰두하기 때문에 스스로 가격과 임금을 책정한다.

해설 | Sentence Simplification 표시된 문장은 크게 네 의미로 나뉠 수 있다. ① 개인 생산자는 사업과 좋은 노동력 확보를 위해 서로 경쟁한다. ② 가격은 소비자가 원하는 가격대로 정해진다. ③ 임금은 노동자가 원하는 노동비에 따라 정해지며, ④ 이는 상업 활동에 도움을 준다.

10 필자가 지문에서 산업 혁명의 노동력 착취를 언급하는 이유는?

(A) Smith의 사상이 부도덕한 인간에 의해 악용될 수 있었음을 시사하기 위해
(B) 현대 경제에서 Smith의 사상은 매우 현실적인 선택이라는 것을 주장하기 위해
(C) 산업 혁명의 비인간적인 면을 보여주려고
(D) 시장의 힘만으로 노동력 착취를 막을 수 있다는 것을 보여주기 위해

해설 | Rhetorical Purpose 산업 혁명의 노동력 착취는 Smith의 경제학의 이론적인 면과 현실적인 면이 어떻게 다른지 보여주는 예이다. Smith는 자기 이익 추구는 궁극적으로 사회 전반에 이익을 준다고 주장했지만, 현실에서는 노동 착취로 이어질 수 있음을 예로 들어, Smith의 사상이 부도덕한 인간에 의해 악용될 수 있었음을 시사하고 있다.

11 단락 4에 따르면, Smith가 구상한 경제에 대해 추론할 수 있는 것은?

(A) 정부에게 지나치게 의존적이어서 제대로 기능할 수 없다.
(B) 사회를 발전시키기 위해 인간 본성에 의지한다.
(C) 매우 가난한 사람들을 감안하지 않는다.
(D) 지금까지 성공적으로 실행된 적이 없다.

해설 | Inference 단락 4에 따르면, Smith가 주장하기를 자본주의가 인간 본성의 이중성을 이용하기 때문에, 사람들이 사회를 발전시키고 그들 스스로도 개선시킬 수 있다고 한다.

12 다음 문장이 지문에 들어갈 곳을 나타내는 네 개의 사각형[■]을 보시오.

> 시장에 대한 이 경제 요소의 영향과 관련된 한 예시는 생산자와 소비자가 함께 역할을 하여 상품이 사고 팔리도록 한다는 것이다.

이 문장이 들어갈 가장 적절한 위치는?
(A) A   (B) B   (C) C   (D) D

해설 | Sentence Insertion 삽입 문장은 어떤 개념의 예를 든 것이다. 삽입 문장은 지문 중에서 "invisible hand"의 예로서, 소비자와 생산자가 물건을 사고 팔기 위해 서로 협의한다는 사실을 들고 있으므로 invisible hand 설명 뒤에 위치해야 자연스럽다.

13 지문을 간략히 요약하기 위한 도입 문장이 아래 제시되어 있다. 지문에서 가장 중요한 내용을 표현한 세 개의 문장을 골라 요약문을 완성하시오. 일부 문장은 지문에 나오지 않거나 중요하지 않은 내용이기 때문에 요약문에 포함되지 않는다. *이 문제는 2점이다.*

> 『국부론』에서 Adam Smith는 이상적인 경제 구조를 설명하기 위해 인간 본성에 대한 그의 철학을 이용했다.

(A) 정치경제에 대한 Smith의 관심은 이후 업적에 중대한 영향을 준 『도덕 감정론』을 쓰도록 이끌었다.
(B) Smith는 인간 본성에 두 가지 경쟁적인 성향이 있는 것으로 설명했는데 하나는 감정과 이기심에 의해, 그리고 다른 하나는 이성과 연민에 의해 작용한다.
(C) Smith는 유럽을 여행하는 동안 일부 대륙의 위대한 정치와 경제 이론들의 영향을 받았다.
(D) Smith 이론은 생산자 사이의 경쟁이 이기심과 이성의 균형을 맞추고 소비자와 생산자 모두에게 이득을 가져다준다는 사상에 기초하고 있다.
(E) Smith의 첫 번째 저서인 『도덕 감정론』은 경제학에서 여전히 영향력 있는 『국부론』이라는 유명한 책의 기초가 되었다.
(F) Smith의 주장에 따르면 가장 번영한 사회는 시장 요소가 전적으로 개인 소비자와 생산자 사이의 상호작용에 의해 결정되는 사회이다.

해설 | Summary (B)는 Smith의 인간 본성에 대한 생각을 설명한 단락 2의 내용을 요약해 놓은 것이다. (D)는 Smith의 자본주의 이론을 설명한 단락 4의 내용을 요약해 놓은 것이다. (F)는 Smith가 지지하는 이상적인 경제 체계를 설명한 단락 3의 내용을 요약해 놓은 것이다.

어휘 | **esteemed** 존경받는 **outline** 기술하다 **regulation** 규제 **lay the foundation for** ~의 기반을 다지다 **groundbreaking** 획기적인
intensive 집중적인 **contemporary** 동시대인 **passionate** 감정적인 **self-preservation** 자기 보호
self-interested 이기적인, 자기 본위의 **capable of** ~를 할 수 있는 **treatise** 논문 **continuation** 연장, 지속
expand 폭을 넓히다, 확장하다 **duality** 이중성 **participant** 구성원 **envision** 구상하다, 상상하다 **institution** 기관
invisible 보이지 않는 **prosperity** 번영 **laissez-faire** 자유방임주의 **capitalism** 자본주의 **exploit** 이용하다 **determine** 결정하다
unlimited 무한한 **idealistic** 이상적인 **villainy** 악행 **tenet** 신조, 교의 **underpin** 근간이 되다

Actual Test 1

Passage 1
01 (A)   02 (D)   03 (B)   04 (C)   05 (A)   06 (B)   07 (D)   08 (D)   09 (B)   10 (C)   11 (B)   12 (A)
13 (D)   14 (B), (D), (F)

Passage 2
15 (C)   16 (A)   17 (A)   18 (C)   19 (C)   20 (B)   21 (D)   22 (B)   23 (B)   24 (B)   25 (D)   26 (A)
27 (A)   28 (A), (C), (F)

Passage 3
29 (C)   30 (C)   31 (D)   32 (D)   33 (A)   34 (B)   35 (B)   36 (D)   37 (C)   38 (B)   39 (D)   40 (B)
41 (D)   42 [New England – (A), (B), (G)], [The Southern Colonies – (C), (E)]

Passage 1   p.210

01 (A)   02 (D)   03 (B)   04 (C)   05 (A)   06 (B)   07 (D)   08 (D)   09 (B)   10 (C)   11 (B)   12 (A)
13 (D)   14 (B), (D), (F)

CAMERA OBSCURA

Camera obscura is a Latin term that means "dark chamber," generally referring to a dark room that only has a tiny amount of light let in through a small pinhole. As sunlight enters the room through the miniscule pinhole, an image is created on the opposite wall of the room. Q02(A) Although the image would be a scene from whatever is outside the room, the image would be reflected upside down on the wall. The original concept of the camera obscura dates back as far as 400 B.C.E. when Q02(D)-1 Chinese philosopher Mozi was the first in history to mention Q01 the basic scientific principles of the camera after he noticed light entering a room through a small pinhole. Q02(D)-2 Subsequent writings by the ancient Greek philosopher Aristotle detail how he perceived this phenomenon by describing the passage of light through a small hole into a room during an eclipse. Q02(B) During the late Renaissance period, special rooms were designed for the public to experience this phenomenon by viewing luminous images of the outside world as they were reflected onto a wall. In the late sixteenth century, Q02(C) Italian artists developed this practice even further by shrinking down the large room used for viewing into a small portable box and replacing the pinhole with a lens.

However, it was not until the sixteenth century that the camera obscura became an invaluable tool for late Renaissance artists who used it to produce drawings and artwork with new perspective and detail. ① As artists during this period began to perfect the use of the camera obscura to produce what would go on to be considered masterpieces, ② its further development would even lead to the basis and foundation of the modern camera and photography. Its popularity in the artistic community at the time grew to the point where, as significant evidence now suggests. Many famous painters in the past actually used the camera obscura to project images of nature or people from outside, which were then traced in detail onto the opposite wall in the room.

카메라 옵스큐라

카메라 옵스큐라는 '암실'이라는 뜻의 라틴어 용어로, 대개 아주 작은 구멍으로 미세한 빛만을 통과하게 하는 어두운 방을 말한다. 햇빛이 극소의 구멍을 통과할 때, 방의 반대쪽 벽에 상이 맺힌다. 그 상은 방 밖에 있는 것의 장면이지만, 이 상은 벽에 위아래가 바뀌어 반영된다. 카메라 옵스큐라의 본래 개념은 기원전 400년으로 거슬러 올라가며, 중국의 철학자 Mozi가 작은 구멍을 통해 들어오는 빛을 발견한 후, 최초로 카메라의 기본 과학적 원리를 언급했다. 이후에 그리스 철학자 Aristotle에 의해 쓰인 문서는 빛의 상실 과정에서 빛이 작은 구멍을 통과하여 방 안으로 들어오는 것을 설명하며 그가 어떻게 이 현상을 인지했는지를 상술한다. 후기 르네상스 시대에는 바깥으로부터 밝은 이미지들이 벽에 반사될 때 보이는 이 현상을 대중들도 경험할 수 있게 하려고 특별한 방이 고안되었다. 16세기 말에 이탈리아 예술가들은 이러한 방식을 더욱 발전시켜 관람에 사용된 방을 들고 다닐 수 있는 상자로 축소하고 작은 구멍을 렌즈로 대체하였다.

그러나 카메라 옵스큐라는 후기 르네상스 예술가들이 새로운 원근법과 세부 양식들로 그림과 예술작품을 만들기 위해 이를 사용하기 시작한 16세기가 되어서야 귀중한 도구가 되었다. 이 시기 예술가들은 걸작으로 여겨지게 될 작품들을 만들기 위해 카메라 옵스큐라의 사용을 개선하기 시작하면서 이것의 더 큰 발전이 현대 카메라 및 사진술의 기초와 근간으로 이어지게 되었다. 그 당시 예술계에서 카메라 옵스큐라의 인기는 현재 상당한 증거가 보여주는 정도까지 커졌다. 과거의 많은 유명한 화가들은 카메라 옵스큐라를 바깥의 자연 또는 사람의 이미지를 비추는 데 사용하였으며, 이는 방의 반대편 벽에 세밀하게 그려졌다.

One such famous seventeenth century Dutch painter who is thought to have employed such techniques is Johannes Vermeer. Critics from as early as the 1800s have long suspected that Vermeer used some kind of mechanical device, complete with either a mirror or a lens, in creating his paintings. After decades of debate, some art historians firmly believe this device was none other than the camera obscura. Q06 Q07 Although there is no tangible historical evidence that he did in fact use the camera obscura, several renowned art historians have pointed to irregularities of compositional elements in his work, Q11-1 one such historian being Charles Seymour, who was the first to actually test out the theory that Vermeer used the camera obscura in his work. He did this by observing objects that commonly appear in Vermeer's paintings through the camera obscura, using similar lighting conditions to those of the paintings, and noticed that the resulting images were practically identical to the images in Vermeer's paintings.

A Q08 Q11-2 However, the most prominent art historian to push forward the claim that artists like Vermeer used the camera obscura is David Hockney. B Q10 He postulated that artists, starting in the Renaissance period of the fifteenth century, traced optical images projected onto a wall and that these images would form the basis of the realistic qualities of paintings at that time. C Q13 Hockney's main critique of paintings from this period is that the paintings are extremely, almost perfectly accurate in their depiction of people and objects, a feat that would have been practically impossible to accomplish using only the naked eye. D **He argued that it was the camera obscura that helped create those paintings.** Q12 The camera obscura was useful for artists like Vermeer to frame a scene with a complex three-dimensional space into a two-dimensional image. He further pointed out that the accurate portrayal of three-dimensional space through perspective in Vermeer's work does not necessarily coincide with the knowledge of perspective that most artists at the time possessed, and such technique would have been hard to achieve even if Vermeer had acquired a superior knowledge of perspective over time. As a result, he concludes that Vermeer would have employed the camera obscura to achieve his almost mathematically precise accuracy in perspective, as evident in his work. Q09 Ultimately, since it is impossible to scientifically test whether all the paintings from the late Renaissance period did in fact use the camera obscura or other mechanical devices during the process of the artwork creation, the possibility of its use in art is still hotly debated among art historians today.

---

01 지문의 luminous와 의미상 가장 가까운 것은?

(A) 밝은
(B) 상당한
(C) 아름다운
(D) 쪼그라든

해설 | Vocabulary   "… he noticed light entering a room through …"의 문장에서 밑줄 친 부분으로 보아 luminous는 '밝은'이라는 의미임을 유추할 수 있다.

02 단락 1에서 언급되지 않은 것은?

(A) 카메라 옵스큐라에 의해 만들어진 반사된 이미지는 위아래가 바뀐 것이다.
(B) 르네상스 시기에 대중들은 방 안에서 카메라 옵스큐라의 이미지를 보았다.
(C) 후기 르네상스 이탈리아 예술가들은 가지고 다닐 수 있는 카메라 옵스큐라 버전을 개발했다.
(D) Aristotle은 카메라 옵스큐라라는 용어를 처음 만들어낸 과학자였다.

해설 | Negative Fact   단락 1에서 카메라 옵스큐라의 본래 개념은 중국의 철학자인 Mozi가 제일 처음 언급하였고, 이후 그리스 철학자 Aristotle이 이것을 설명했다고 하였다.

03 지문의 invaluable과 의미상 가장 가까운 것은?
(A) 현대의
(B) 귀중한
(C) 감당할 수 있는
(D) 무가치한

해설 | Vocabulary invaluable은 precious의 의미가 있다.

04 다음 중 지문에서 표시된 문장의 주요 정보를 가장 잘 나타낸 문장은? 정답 외의 보기들은 중요한 의미가 바뀌거나 주요 정보가 빠져 있다.
(A) 현대 카메라의 발전은 르네상스 시대의 걸작이라고 여겨지는 작품의 구성을 완벽하게 하는 것에 초점을 맞추면서 가능해졌다.
(B) 이 시기의 예술가들은 작품의 질을 걸작의 수준으로 높이기 위해 카메라 옵스큐라를 사용하는 데 능통했다.
(C) 이 시기에 예술가들은 위대한 예술 작품을 위해 카메라 옵스큐라의 사용을 향상시켰으며, 이는 후에 현대 사진술의 개념에 기여했다.
(D) 이 시기 동안 카메라 옵스큐라의 사용은 우수한 예술 작품이라고 여겨지는 것을 만들어내기 위해 필수였다.

해설 | Sentence Simplification ① 예술가들은 작품을 만드는 데 카메라 옵스큐라를 사용하기 시작했다. ② 이것은 사진술의 기초와 근간이 되었다. 표시된 문장을 가장 잘 옮긴 것은 (C)이다.

05 지문의 project와 의미상 가장 가까운 것은?
(A) 보여주다
(B) 그리다
(C) 묘사하다
(D) 이야기하다

해설 | Vocabulary project는 display의 의미가 있다.

06 지문의 tangible과 의미상 가장 가까운 것은?
(A) 중요한
(B) 명확한
(C) 주장할 수 있는
(D) 널리 퍼진

해설 | Vocabulary tangible은 concrete의 의미이다.

07 단락 3에서 Vermeer와 미술사가에 대해 언급된 내용은?
(A) Charles Seymour는 Vermeer의 그림에 카메라 옵스큐라가 사용되었다는 것을 증명한다.
(B) 미술사가들은 Vermeer가 카메라 옵스큐라를 사용한 것이 그의 걸작을 가능하게 했다고 믿는다.
(C) 미술사가들은 Charles Seymour에 의해 주장된 이론을 받아들이지 않는다.
(D) Vermeer가 카메라 옵스큐라를 사용했다는 것을 뒷받침하는 정확한 증거는 없다.

해설 | Factual Information 단락 3에서는 Vermeer가 실제로 카메라 옵스큐라를 사용했는지에 대한 명백한 역사적 증거는 없지만, 몇몇 미술사가들은 그가 옵스큐라를 사용했을 것으로 추정한다는 내용이다.

08 지문의 postulated와 의미상 가장 가까운 것은?
(A) 반박했다
(B) 인정했다
(C) 예상했다
(D) 말했다

해설 | Vocabulary 단어의 의미는 앞 문장 "… art historian to push forward the claim …" 중 밑줄 친 부분에서 힌트를 얻을 수 있다. postulated는 '주장하다, 말하다'의 의미이다.

09 지문에서 its가 가리키는 것은?
(A) 후기 르네상스 시기
(B) 카메라 옵스큐라
(C) 기계적 도구
(D) 예술작품 창작

해설 | Reference 단락 4에서 Vermeer가 카메라 옵스큐라를 실제로 사용했는지는 정확히 알 수 없으며, 예술작품에서 이것의(its) 사용 가능성은 오늘날 미술사가들 사이에서 뜨거운 논쟁거리라고 하였으므로 its가 가리키는 것은 '카메라 옵스큐라'임을 알 수 있다.

10 단락 4에 따르면, Hockney 이론에 관한 내용 중 옳은 것은?

(A) 카메라 옵스큐라는 르네상스 시기에만 사용되었다.
(B) 카메라 옵스큐라를 사용했다고 할지라도 사실적으로 정확한 예술작품을 만드는 것은 불가능하다.
(C) 르네상스 예술가들은 사실적인 이미지를 만들기 위해 시각적인 이미지들을 베껴 그리는 데 의존했다.
(D) Vermeer는 벽에 투영된 시각적 이미지들을 베껴 그리는 데 전문가였다.

해설 | **Factual Information** Hockney는 르네상스 시기의 예술가들이 사실적인 이미지를 만들기 위해 벽에 투영된 이미지들을 베꼈을 것이라고 주장했다.

11 단락 4는 이전에 논의된 Vermeer에 대한 미술사가들의 주장과 어떻게 관련되어 있는가?

(A) Vermeer가 자신의 그림에 카메라 옵스큐라를 사용한 이유를 설명한다.
(B) Vermeer가 카메라 옵스큐라를 사용했다고 지지하는 다른 관점을 제공한다.
(C) Vermeer와 같은 기법을 사용한 다른 예술가들을 열거하며 그들의 주장을 지지한다.
(D) 미술사가들에 의한 다양한 주장들의 개요를 설명한다.

해설 | **Rhetorical Purpose** 단락 3에서는 Vermeer가 카메라 옵스큐라를 사용했다고 말하는 미술사가인 Charles Seymour를 언급하고 있으며, 이어 단락 4에서는 다른 미술사가인 David Hockney 역시 이 주장을 지지하고 있음을 보여준다.

12 단락 4의 정보에 따르면, 르네상스 예술가들에 대해 추론할 수 있는 것은?

(A) 카메라 옵스큐라는 3D에 대한 완전한 이해 없이도 그들이 정확한 원근법을 묘사할 수 있게 도움을 주었다.
(B) 작품을 완벽하게 하려고 고급 수학 개념들을 공부했다.
(C) Vermeer와 같이 오직 소수만이 원근법에 대한 고급 지식을 사용한 것으로 유명했다.
(D) 3D 원근법의 부정확한 묘사로 비난받았다.

해설 | **Inference** 카메라 옵스큐라는 그 당시(르네상스) 예술가들이 3D 공간을 그릴 때 유용했으며, 이것은 고급 원근법 지식 없이도 가능했다고 설명하고 있다.

13 다음 문장이 지문에 들어갈 곳을 나타내는 네 개의 사각형(■)을 보시오.

> 그는 그러한 그림들을 그릴 수 있게 도운 것은 카메라 옵스큐라라고 주장했다.

이 문장이 들어갈 가장 적절한 위치는?

(A) A (B) B (C) C (D) D

해설 | **Sentence Insertion** 삽입 문장의 those paintings는 (D)의 앞 문장의 "… the paintings are extremely, almost perfectly accurate in their depiction of people and objects, a feat that would have been practically impossible to accomplish …"에서 밑줄을 가리킨다. 삽입 문장이 들어갈 적절한 위치는 (D)이다.

14 지문을 간략히 요약하기 위한 도입 문장이 아래 제시되어 있다. 지문에서 가장 중요한 내용을 표현한 세 개의 문장을 골라 요약문을 완성하시오. 일부 문장은 지문에 나오지 않았거나 중요하지 않은 내용이기 때문에 요약문에 포함되지 않는다. *이 문제는 2점이다.*

> 카메라 옵스큐라는 사진술과 사진 카메라로 이끈 시각적 도구이다.

(A) Vermeer는 자신의 그림에 사용한 수학적 원근법의 고급 지식을 가지고 있었다.
(B) 르네상스 시기 동안, 예술가들은 매우 세밀한 작품을 만들기 위해 카메라 옵스큐라를 발전시키고 사용했다.
(C) 현대 사진술은 카메라 옵스큐라가 발전한 르네상스 시기로 거슬러 올라갈 수 있다.
(D) 미술사가인 Charles Seymour는 Vermeer가 자신의 그림에 카메라 옵스큐라를 사용했다는 이론을 시험해 보았다.
(E) 카메라 옵스큐라는 이탈리아 예술가들에 의해 더욱 발달하여 대중들이 그것의 더 작은 버전을 가지고 다닐 수 있었다.
(F) 미술사가인 David Hockney는 Vermeer가 자신의 작품에 우수한 원근법을 적용하고자 카메라 옵스큐라를 사용했다고 주장했다.

해설 | **Summary** (B)는 단락 2를, (D)는 단락 3을, (F)는 단락 4를 요약한 것이다.

어휘 | **term** 용어　**refer to** ~을 말하다, 나타내다　**pinhole** 작은 구멍　**miniscule** 극소의　**upside down** 위아래가 반대로　**philosopher** 철학자　**principle** 원리, 원칙　**subsequent** 이후의　**phenomenon** 현상, 사상　**eclipse** 빛의 사라짐, (해, 달의) 식　**shrink** 줄어들게 하다, 줄어들다　**portable** 들고 다닐 수 있는, 휴대의　**invaluable** 귀중한　**perspective** 원근(법)　**masterpiece** 걸작　**photography** 사진술, 사진 촬영　**project** 비추다, 투영하다　**employ** 사용하다, 이용하다　**mechanical** 기계의, 도구의　**tangible** 명백한, 만져 알 수 있는　**renowned** 저명한, 유명한　**irregularity** 불규칙성　**compositional** 구성의　**postulate** 주장하다, 말하다　**trace** 베끼다, 그리다　**critique** 비평　**depiction** 묘사, 서술　**naked eye** 육안　**frame** 그리다, 구상하다　**mathematically** 수학적으로, 매우 정확히　**possibility** 가능성

Passage 2　　　　　　　　　　　　　　　　　　　　　　　　　　　　　　p.214

15 (C)　**16** (A)　**17** (A)　**18** (C)　**19** (C)　**20** (B)　**21** (D)　**22** (B)　**23** (B)　**24** (B)　**25** (D)　**26** (A)
27 (A)　**28** (A), (C), (F)

MARSUPIALS IN AUSTRALIA

Unique among mammals is the subclass known as metatheria, more commonly called marsupials. This group of mammals consists of animals such as the kangaroo and the opossum. Marsupials differ from other mammals in one essential way: unlike other mammals, their young do not fully develop inside the womb. Q16 Instead, they are born without being fully developed, and complete their development outside of the mother's body. They are able to do this partly because of a protective pouch that most adult marsupials possess. After being born, the tiny marsupials instinctively crawl into this pouch, where they safely feed and rest until fully grown. There are over 250 species of marsupials worldwide, but the vast majority of them inhabit the island continent of Australia, as well as surrounding islands such as New Zealand and New Guinea. The reasons for this uneven distribution are varied and complex.

Common marsupials like kangaroos and koala bears are readily associated with Australia, and factor prominently into Australian culture. It might seem perfectly logical that such a unique type of mammal would develop on an island, in total seclusion from other species, but surprisingly, Q17 marsupials did not originate in the South Pacific region. In fact, their journey to their final home in this region was a long and complicated one spanning many millions of years. Q19 The first known marsupials actually appeared in the Americas about 99 million years ago. Although the first fossil evidence was discovered in North America, it is more likely that South America was their place of origin, as a small number of marsupial species still inhabit this region. How marsupials reached Australia in such large numbers is still a debatable topic among scientists. Q18 Q21 To begin to answer this question, one must consider the geography of the planet as it looked millions of years ago, when marsupials were making their way to Australia.

20(B) At this time, the Earth was divided into two major supercontinents: Laurasia in the northern hemisphere and Gondwana in the southern. A These two giant land masses were combined forms of the seven continents we know today. Q27 Laurasia included what would later become North America and much of Asia. B Q20(A) Gondwana, on the other hand, was composed of what would become South America, Antarctica, India, and Africa. C Q20(D) Marsupials and other mammals evolved together on the same supercontinent, Gondwana. D Then, about 65 million years ago, as these supercontinents were slowly breaking apart, Q20(C) a giant piece of Antarctica

호주의 유대목 동물

포유류의 특이한 종류 중 하나는 후수류로 알려진 하위 분류인데, 이는 유대류라고 더 잘 알려져 있다. 이런 종류의 포유류에 속하는 동물에는 캥거루와 주머니쥐가 있다. 유대류가 다른 포유동물과 다른 중요한 한 가지는 바로 새끼가 태내에서 완전히 발육하지 않는다는 것이다. 대신, 새끼들은 발육이 완전히 되지 않은 상태에서 태어나 어미의 몸 밖에서 완전히 발육한다. 새끼들이 이렇게 자랄 수 있는 이유 중 하나는 대부분의 유대목 동물이 가지고 있다. 새끼를 보호해주는 육아 주머니 덕분인데, 이것은 태어난 후 새끼 유대 동물은 본능적으로 이 주머니로 들어가는데, 이곳에서 완전히 자랄 때까지 안전하게 모유를 먹으며 쉰다. 세계적으로 250종류 이상의 유대류가 있는데 대부분은 호주 대륙과 뉴질랜드와 뉴기니 같은 인근 섬나라에서 서식한다. 이렇게 고르지 않게 분포하는 이유는 다양하고 복잡하다.

캥거루와 코알라 같은 대표적 유대목 동물은 호주 하면 쉽게 연상되는 동물이고, 호주 문화의 중요 요소이다. 이런 특별한 포유동물이 다른 동물로부터 완전히 고립된 섬에서 진화했을 거라는 가정은 딱 들어맞는 것처럼 보이지만, 놀랍게도 유대류는 남태평양 지역에서 기원하지 않았다. 사실 그들의 마지막 종착점이 된 이 지역 까지의 여행은 수백만 년에 걸친 길고 복잡한 여행이었다. 처음으로 알려진 유대목 동물이 출현한 것은 9천 9백만 년 전 아메리카 대륙에서였다. 유대류의 첫 화석은 북아메리카에서 발견되었지만, 남아메리카 지역에 적은 숫자의 유대류가 아직도 서식하고 있다는 사실을 보면 남아메리카가 원산지일 가능성이 더 크다. 어떻게 유대류가 그렇게 대규모로 호주에 건너가게 되었는지는 아직 과학자들 사이에서 논란이 되는 주제이다. 이 문제에 답하기 위해서는 유대류가 호주로 향했던 수백만 년 전 지구의 지형을 고려해야 한다.

이 당시 지구는 두 개의 주요 초대륙 즉, 북반구의 로라시아 대륙과 남반구의 곤드와나 대륙으로 나누어져 있었다. A 이 두 개의 초대륙은 오늘날 우리가 알고 있는 7대륙이 합쳐진 것이다. 로라시아 대륙에는 북아메리카와 아시아의 많은 지역이 속했다. B 반면에 곤드와나는 남아메리카와 남극, 인도, 아프리카 대륙이 될 지역으로 구성되어 있었다. C 유대류는 다른 포유동물과 함께 동일한 초대륙 곤드와나에서 진화했다. D 그리고 약 6천 5백만 년 전에 이 초대륙들은 서서히 나누어지면서, 남극 대륙의 큰 부분이 떨어져 나와 호주가 되었다.

separated from the mass to become the island of Australia. Q22 Scientists believe that by the time this happened, several species of marsupials had already migrated to Australia by way of land connections that led them from their birthplace in the Americas, across Antarctica, and finally to the land mass that would become Australia. As the continent of Australia drifted northward from the supercontinent of Gondwana, these prehistoric marsupials became isolated and evolved into a vast array of different species. Today, about 200 different species of marsupials remain on the continent, greatly outnumbering native species of placental mammals. Why marsupials survived in such great numbers in Australia and not elsewhere is another topic of debate. ① Some scientists believe it was because Australia, due to its gradual movement toward ever-warmer climates, ② was spared some of the consequences of the severe climate change that occurred over the next several million years in most other parts of the world. Therefore, its wildlife had a better chance of surviving the threat of extinction.

Despite the long separation of marsupials from most other mammals, the two groups still share a number of striking similarities. Q25 This is a prime example of convergent evolution, when two different species in comparable geographical locations adapt to their environments in similar ways. Q26 For example, the flying squirrel found in the West can be compared to the flying opossum of Australia. In each instance, the animal is one that is especially vulnerable to predators on the ground, and thus has a short lifespan in the wild because it is routinely preyed upon by snakes and other predators. Q24 In order to elude common predators on the ground, both animals developed a way to take advantage of their woodland environment to increase their safety. Each developed a webbing of skin between their front and hind limbs that allows them to glide through the air from tree to tree, decreasing the amount of time they spend on the ground. Though they are separated by thousands of miles, the similar living conditions caused the two animals to evolve the same defense mechanism.

과학자들은 이 현상이 일어났을 때쯤에는 이미 여러 종의 유대류가 연결된 땅을 통해서 자신들의 고향인 아메리카 대륙에서 남극 대륙을 거쳐 나중에 호주가 된 대륙으로 거주지를 이동했을 것이라고 생각한다. 호주 대륙이 곤드와나 초대륙에서 분리되어 북쪽으로 표류하면서, 이 선사 시대의 유대목 동물들이 고립되었고 여러 다른 종으로 진화하게 되었다. 오늘날 200여 종의 유대류가 대륙에 남아 있으며, 이들은 태반이 있는 토착 포유동물보다 수적으로 훨씬 우세하다. 왜 이렇게 유대류가 다른 지역이 아닌 호주에서 대규모로 살아남을 수 있었는지에 대한 문제는 또 다른 논쟁의 주제이다. 일부 과학자들은 호주가 점차 더 따뜻한 기후대로 움직임에 따라, 수백만 년 동안 지구 대부분의 다른 지역에서 일어난 급격한 기후 변화의 몇 가지 영향에서 벗어날 수 있었다고 믿는다. 그 결과 호주의 야생 동물이 멸종의 위협으로부터 살아남을 가능성이 높아진 것이다.

유대류는 다른 포유동물과 지역적으로 멀리 떨어져 있었지만, 이 두 동물군은 놀라울 정도로 비슷한 특징을 가지고 있다. 이것은 바로 수렴 진화의 대표적 사례인데 그것은 유사한 지리적 환경에 있는 두 종의 동물이 비슷한 방법으로 환경에 적응하는 것이다. 그 예로 서양에서 발견되는 날다람쥐와 호주의 주머니 날다람쥐를 비교할 수 있다. 각 동물은 땅의 육식동물에게 특히 취약하여 일상적으로 뱀이나 다른 포식자들의 먹이가 되는데, 이 때문에 야생에서의 수명이 짧다. 땅에 있는 포식자들을 피하기 위해 이 두 동물 모두 안전을 높이기 위해 삼림 환경의 장점을 살릴 수 있는 방향으로 진화하였다. 각각의 동물은 앞뒤 팔다리 사이에 익막이 있어 나무와 나무 사이를 활공함으로써, 땅에서 보내는 시간을 줄였다. 지역적으로 수천 마일이나 떨어져 있지만 비슷한 환경으로 인해 두 동물은 같은 방어기제를 발달시키게 되었다.

---

15 지문의 instinctively 와 의미상 가장 가까운 것은?

(A) 규칙적으로
(B) 힘들이지 않고
(C) 자연적으로
(D) 신속히

해설 | Vocabulary instinctively 는 '본능적으로, 직관적으로, 자연적으로'의 의미이다. 이 의미와 가장 가까운 단어는 (C)이다.

16 단락 1에 따르면, 유대류에 대해 추론할 수 있는 것은?

(A) 유대류의 주머니는 새끼의 생존에 필수적이다.
(B) 유대류는 한 번에 많은 새끼를 낳는다.
(C) 모든 유대류는 주머니를 가지고 있다.
(D) 유대류는 호주, 뉴질랜드, 뉴기니에 고르게 분포되어 있다.

해설 | Inference 어미의 주머니는 완전히 발육하지 않은 채로 태어난 새끼가 완전히 발육할 때까지 안전하게 보호해 주는 역할을 한다.

17 지문에서 this region 이 가리키는 것은?

(A) 남태평양 지역
(B) 호주
(C) 섬
(D) 아메리카

해설 | Reference 바로 앞 문장에 the South Pacific region이 언급되어 있다.

18 지문의 debatable 과 의미상 가장 가까운 것은?

(A) 흥미로운
(B) 안정된
(C) 논란이 되는
(D) 평범한

해설 | Vocabulary   debatable의 의미는 "To begin to answer this question …"에서 힌트를 얻을 수 있다. 즉, 대규모의 유대류가 어떻게 호주에 건너가게 되었는지는 아직도 논란이 되는 주제이고, 이 문제에 답하기 위해서는 유대류가 호주로 건너갔던 수백만 년 전 지구의 지형을 고려해야 한다.

19 단락 2에 따르면, 초기 유대류의 첫 화석이 발견된 곳은?

(A) 아프리카
(B) 호주
(C) 북아메리카
(D) 남아메리카

해설 | Factual Information   단락 2에서 유대류의 첫 화석은 북아메리카에서 발견되었다고 설명한다.

20 단락 3에 따르면, 곤드와나 대륙에 관한 내용으로 옳지 않은 것은?

(A) 남아메리카와 남극은 곤드와나 대륙의 부분이었다.
(B) 곤드와나 대륙은 더 큰 로라시아 대륙의 일부였다.
(C) 현재의 호주는 곤드와나 대륙의 일부였다.
(D) 유대류는 곤드와나 대륙이 나누어지기 오래 전에 거기에 서식하였다.

해설 | Negative Fact   곤드와나와 로라시아는 별개의 대륙이었으므로 (B)는 틀린 내용이다.

21 필자가 지문에서 초대륙 을 언급하는 이유는?

(A) 선사 시대의 지구가 확연히 다른 곳이었다는 것을 알려주기 위해
(B) 호주의 여러 다른 선사 유대류를 설명하기 위해
(C) 유대류와 다른 포유류가 어떻게 함께 진화했는지 논의하기 위해
(D) 유대류가 어떻게 호주로 이주하여 고립되었는지 설명하기 위해

해설 | Rhetorical Purpose   단락 2의 마지막에서 필자는 유대류가 어떻게 호주로 오게 되었는지 알기 위해서는 수백만 년 전의 지구의 지리적 모습을 알아야 한다고 말하고 있다.

22 지문의 migrated 와 의미상 가장 가까운 것은?

(A) 펼치다
(B) 이동하다
(C) 달아나다
(D) 추방하다

해설 | Vocabulary   migrated는 "… several species of marsupials had already migrated to Australia by way of land connections"의 문장에서 밑줄 친 부분을 통해 '이동하다'의 의미임을 알 수 있다.

23 다음 중 지문에서 표시된 문장의 주요 정보를 가장 잘 나타낸 문장은? 정답 외의 보기들은 중요한 의미가 바뀌거나 주요 정보가 빠져 있다.

(A) 과학자들은 유대류가 호주에서 살아남게 된 이유가 다른 지역보다 더 고립되었기 때문인지 아니면 더 나은 환경에 있었기 때문인지에 대해 논쟁한다.
(B) 유대류는 호주에서 급격한 기후 변화의 어려움에서 어느 정도 자유로웠기 때문에 번성했으리라 믿어진다.
(C) 많은 수의 유대류가 호주에서 살아남게 된 이유는 급격한 기후 변화로 인해 다른 경쟁 포유류가 멸종되었기 때문이다.
(D) 유대류가 호주의 다른 포유류보다 수가 많은 이유는 그 섬이 남극에서 더 추운 기후로 밀려왔기 때문이다.

해설 | Sentence Simplification   표시된 문장 "Some scientists believe it was because …"에서 밑줄 친 it은 앞 문장에 언급된 유대류가 호주에서 서식하는 사실을 가리킨다. ①일부 과학자들은 유대류가 호주에서 서식할 수 있었던 이유는 호주에 있다고 믿는다. ②호주는 급격한 기후 변화의 몇 가지 영향에서 벗어났다. 원문의 내용을 가장 잘 옮긴 것은 (B)이다.

24 지문의 elude 와 의미상 가장 가까운 것은?

(A) 겁주다
(B) 피하다
(C) 방해하다
(D) 간신히 해내다

해설 | Vocabulary   "In order to elude common predators on the ground, both animals developed a way to take advantage of their woodland environment to increase their safety"에서 동물들은 땅의 포식자를 '피하기' 위해 안전을 높일수 있는 방향으로 진화하였다.

25 단락 5에 따르면, 수렴 진화가 일어나는 때는?

(A) 동물은 자신의 환경에 가장 적합하게 진화한다.
(B) 다른 동물에게서 고립된 종은 비슷한 특징을 갖도록 진화한다.
(C) 함께 진화하는 종은 다른 동물과 다르게 진화한다.
(D) 비슷한 환경의 다른 장소에서 진화하는 동물은 동일한 특징을 발달시킨다.

해설 | Factual Information 수렴 진화는 종이 다른 두 동물이 유사한 지리적 환경에서 비슷한 방식으로 주변 환경에 적응하는 과정을 가리킨다.

26 단락 5에 따르면, 날다람쥐와 주머니 날다람쥐의 진화에 영향을 준 요인은?

(A) 땅 위에서는 너무 쉽게 먹이가 된다.
(B) 먹이 대부분이 나무에 있다.
(C) 기후 변화에 적응할 수밖에 없었다.
(D) 서식지인 삼림이 사라져버렸다.

해설 | Factual Information 날다람쥐와 주머니 날다람쥐 모두 땅 위에서는 포식자에게 쉽게 잡아 먹혀 삼림 환경의 장점을 살려 진화해 나갔다.

27 다음 문장이 지문에 들어갈 곳을 나타내는 네 개의 사각형[■]을 보시오.

> 이 두 개의 초대륙은 오늘날 우리가 알고 있는 7대륙이 합쳐진 것이다.

이 문장이 들어갈 가장 적절한 위치는?

(A) A (B) B (C) C (D) D

해설 | Sentence Insertion 삽입 문장 중 These two giant land masses는 단락 3의 첫 문장에서 언급된 로라시아와 곤드와나를 가리키는 지시어이다. 삽입 문장에서 이 두 개의 대륙이 오늘날의 7대륙을 합쳐 놓은 것이라고 설명한 내용은 바로 뒤인 A에 로라시아와 곤드와나가 어떤 대륙으로 구성되어 있는지를 설명하는 것과 자연스럽게 이어질 수 있다.

28 지문을 간략히 요약하기 위한 도입 문장이 아래 제시되어 있다. 지문에서 가장 중요한 내용을 표현한 세 개의 문장을 골라 요약문을 완성하시오. 일부 문장은 지문에 나오지 않았거나 중요하지 않은 내용이기 때문에 요약문에 포함되지 않는다. *이 문제는 2점이다.*

> 과학자들은 호주에 유대목 동물이 많은 이유에 대해 여전히 논쟁하고 있지만, 이들의 고립은 수백만 년 전 초대륙의 이동과 관계가 있는 듯하다.

(A) 유대류는 두 개의 초대륙의 하나였던 곤드와나에서 진화하면서 남아메리카와 남극, 호주의 이어진 지역을 통해서 호주에 왔다.
(B) 수백만 년 동안 유대류는 곤드와나 초대륙에서 다른 종들과 함께 거주했다.
(C) 곤드와나가 여러 개의 땅덩어리로 분리되고 호주가 더 따뜻한 지역으로 이동하면서, 유대류는 오늘날까지 살아남을 수 있었다.
(D) 로라시아에는 유대류가 살지 않았기 때문에, 이전에 로라시아 일부를 형성했던 북아메리카에서는 유대류가 발견되지 않는다.
(E) 호주와 함께 초대륙을 구성했던 남아메리카 지역에는 아직도 몇몇 종의 유대목 동물이 서식하고 있다.
(F) 분리되어 있었지만, 몇몇 유대류 종은 다른 대륙의 포유류와 생김새가 비슷하게 진화했는데, 이것은 그 동물들이 비슷한 환경적 곤경에 노출되었기 때문이다.

해설 | Summary 지문은 유대류가 유독 호주와 그 인근 지역에 많이 서식하게 된 이유를 수백만 년 전 지구에서 일어났던 지각의 이동과 관계시켜 설명하고 있다. 그리고 지문 마지막 단락에서 유대류가 다른 지역 포유류와 고립되어 살아도, 비슷한 환경에 노출되면 비슷한 방식으로 진화할 수 있다는 것을 설명하고 있다. 지문의 중요한 내용을 정리한 것은 (A), (C), (F)이다.

어휘 | **marsupial** 유대목 동물, 유대류 **metatheria** 후수류 ([생물] 태반이 없는 동물) **opossum** 주머니쥐 **pouch** 주머니 **distribution** 분포 **be associated with** ~이 연상되다 **factor** ~의 한 요소로 포함되다 **originate** 시작하다, 유래하다 **make one's way to** ~로 향하다 **supercontinent** 초대륙 **hemisphere** (지구의) 반구 **evolve** 진화하다 **drift** 표류하다 **prehistoric** 선사 시대의 **outnumber** 수적으로 우세하다 **placental** 태반이 있는 **consequence** 영향, 결과 **threat** 위협 **extinction** 멸종 **convergent** 수렴하는 **comparable** 유사한 **geographical** 지리적인 **vulnerable** 취약한, 공격받기 쉬운 **lifespan** 수명 **routinely** 일상적으로 **prey upon** ~을 먹이로 삼다 **webbing** 익막, 물갈퀴의 막 **limb** 팔다리 **glide** 활공하다, 미끄러지듯 나아가다

Passage 3   p.218

29 (C) 30 (C) 31 (D) 32 (D) 33 (A) 34 (B) 35 (B) 36 (D) 37 (C) 38 (B) 39 (D) 40 (B)
41 (D) 42 [New England – (A), (B), (G)], [The Southern Colonies – (C), (E)]

COLONIAL AMERICAN FARMING

By the mid-seventeenth century, English colonial settlement in North America stretched from New England in the north to the Carolinas in the south. Early colonial American society was agricultural, with the vast majority of colonists making their living off their land in one form or another. However, considering the breadth of the geographic areas occupied by the colonists, it should not be surprising that the practice of agriculture took different forms in various colonies, and that these different agricultural practices led to the formation of distinct modes of living. This is particularly true when the southern colonies are compared to those of the north.

In the New England colonies, which can roughly be defined as stretching from what is now New York to Maine, agriculture was marginal at best, and farmers' lives involved tough and constant labor. Q29 Q31(A) The land was heavily wooded and rocky, so colonists first had to clear areas for planting, literally creating the fields they intended to farm. Most of this work had to be done by hand, Q31(C) as horses and oxen were perpetually in short supply. Even when the laborious task of preparing the fields for planting was completed, New England farmers could expect a sparse harvest. Q30 Q31(B) Q32 New England soil was poor, and the cold weather meant the growing season was brief. In short, farming in New England was a very humble occupation.

Q40-1 Q42(A) Because of the harsh conditions that prevailed, the most that Northern farmers could hope for was mere subsistence. Given the marginal nature of agriculture in the New England area, there was little sense in acquiring more land than was necessary to support one's family, and Q42(G) farms tended to be small family plots. Q33 The difficulties of New England farming also encouraged a high degree of cooperation among neighboring farmers, and it was common for them to trade with one another for necessary supplies, loan each other expensive or hard-to-find equipment such as plows and oxen, and pool their labor when large structures, such as barns, needed to be built. Q34 The result was a close-knit, Q42(B) egalitarian society in which the basic social unit was the small town or village.

Farmers in the southern colonies, especially those in Virginia and the Carolinas, faced a very different situation. Q40-2 Q35 In these areas, agriculture was easier and potentially far more profitable. The soil was rich and fertile, and the climate was much more conducive to farming. Furthermore, the difference in climate and soil composition made it possible to grow different kinds of crops than those grown in New England. Q36 Q42(C) Whereas New England farmers simply farmed to live, primarily growing staples such as corn and wheat which they needed to survive, farmers in the southern colonies focused predominately on cash crops such as tobacco, and later, cotton.

The difference was an immensely important one. **A** In growing crops for sale rather than for their own personal use, Q37 Q42(E) southern farmers had every inducement to acquire vast tracts of land, since more land for more crops would result in greater profits. **B** The commercial nature of southern farming meant that significant gaps in wealth quickly arose, with a small minority of successful farmers acquiring ever more land and growing ever richer. **C** Q41 As a result, a plantation system arose in which a small southern aristocracy of wealthy farmers owned much of the best land, while poorer farmers had to make do with small plots in less-fertile areas. **D** Southern society was thus more hierarchical than its New England counterpart.

Q39 Moreover, the existence of large plantations meant that the southern population was more dispersed, and southern politics centered around counties covering large areas rather than the small towns and villages of New England. A further consequence of the focus on cash crops and the rise of the plantation system was that southern plantation owners were perpetually short of labor. ① Whereas New England farmers were able to tend to their relatively small fields using only the labor of their family members and occasionally relying on the help of their neighbors, ② this was entirely impractical on a southern plantation that might easily cover several hundred acres. It was for this reason that southern colonies made much greater use of slave labor than did farmers in New England.

29 지문에서 this work 가 가리키는 것은?

(A) 작물을 수확하는 것
(B) 농경지에서 일하는 것
(C) 나무와 바위를 없애는 것
(D) 말과 황소를 모는 것

30 지문의 sparse 와 의미상 가장 가까운 것은?

(A) 기쁨이 없는
(B) 풍부한
(C) 빈약한
(D) 덜 익은

31 단락 2에 따르면, 뉴잉글랜드의 농사짓기에 열악했던 환경을 만든 원인으로 옳지 않은 것은?

(A) 토지가 농사에 부적합했다.
(B) 추운 날씨 때문에 재배 기간이 짧았다.
(C) 말이나 황소의 이용이 제한되었다.
(D) 뉴잉글랜드의 농부들은 노동력이 부족했다.

32 지문의 harsh 와 의미상 가장 가까운 것은?

(A) 예측할 수 없는
(B) 일관된
(C) 호의적인
(D) 가혹한

이러한 차이는 굉장히 중요한 것이었다. **A** 개인적 사용이 목적이 아닌 판매를 위한 농작물을 경작하다 보니, 더 많은 작물을 기를 수 있는 더 넓은 땅은 결과적으로 더 큰 이윤을 창출할 것이므로 남부 지역 농부들은 경작지를 차지하려는 동기가 충분했다. **B** 남부 농업의 상업적 성격으로 인해 소수의 성공적인 농부들이 더 많은 땅을 차지하게 되고 그로 인해 더 많은 부를 쌓게 되면서 부에 있어 상당한 격차가 빠르게 생겨났다. **C** 그 결과, 플랜테이션 제도가 생겨났고 그 안에서 남부 지역의 소수 부유한 상류계급이 최상의 토지를 대규모로 소유했지만, 가난한 농부들은 덜 비옥한 지역에서 좁은 땅으로 변통해야 했다. **D** 이와 같이 남부 사회는 뉴잉글랜드 사회보다 서열적 성격이 더 강했다.

또한 대규모 플랜테이션 농장의 존재는 남부 지역의 인구가 더욱 널리 퍼져 있음을 의미했고, 남부의 정치는 뉴잉글랜드의 소규모 도시나 마을 단위와는 다르게 넓은 지역을 낀 군 단위 중심으로 발전해 나갔다. 판매용 작물에 대한 집중과 플랜테이션 제도 발생의 결과로 또 들 수 있는 것은 남부 플랜테이션 농장주들이 늘 노동력 부족에 시달렸다는 점이다. 뉴잉글랜드 농부들이 가족 구성원들의 노동력과 때로는 인근 이웃 주민들의 도움을 받아 비교적 작은 농경지를 꾸려나갈 수 있던 것과는 달리, 족히 수백 에이커에 다다르는 남부 플랜테이션 농장에서는 그런 방식이 전적으로 비현실적이었다. 이런 이유에서 남부 식민지 지역에서는 뉴잉글랜드의 경우보다 노예의 노동력을 훨씬 더 많이 활용했다.

해설 | Reference this work 가 가리키는 것은 바로 앞 문장에 있다. 뉴잉글랜드의 토지에는 숲이 무성하고 바위가 많아 경작지를 만들기 위해 그것들을 없애고 땅을 개간해야 했다고 설명한다.

해설 | Vocabulary sparse 의 의미는 단락 2의 마지막 두 문장에서 추론할 수 있다. 토지가 척박하고, 추운 날씨로 재배 기간이 짧아 수확량이 많지 않다는 것에서 '빈약한'의 의미임을 알 수 있다.

해설 | Negative Fact 단락 2에서 뉴잉글랜드의 토지는 바위와 나무가 많고 척박했으며, 추운 날씨 때문에 재배 기간이 짧았고, 말이나 황소도 부족해 농사짓기가 열악했다고 한다.

해설 | Vocabulary harsh conditions는 앞 문장에서 언급된 척박한 토지와 추운 날씨를 말한다. 이러한 사실로부터 harsh 는 '가혹한'의 의미임을 알 수 있다.

33 지문에서 their 가 가리키는 것은?
(A) 농부
(B) 물자
(C) 헛간
(D) 황소

해설 | Reference 뉴잉글랜드 농부들은 협동하여 서로를 돕고 공동작업을 했다고 한다. 헛간 등의 대규모 시설을 지어야 할 때 필요한 노동력은 농부들의 노동력이다.

34 단락 3에 따르면, 뉴잉글랜드 사회의 기본 사회 단위는?
(A) 가족
(B) 마을
(C) 농장
(D) 주

해설 | Factual Information 단락 3의 마지막 문장에서 뉴잉글랜드의 기본적인 사회 단위는 작은 도시나 마을이었다고 설명한다.

35 지문의 conducive to 와 의미상 가장 가까운 것은?
(A) 필요한
(B) 적합한
(C) 익숙해진
(D) 순종하는

해설 | Vocabulary conducive to 의 의미는 앞 문장 전후에서 농사에 유리한 자연적 환경에 대해 나열해 놓은 것을 고려하여 '적합한'의 의미임을 추론할 수 있다.

36 지문의 predominately 와 의미상 가장 가까운 것은?
(A) 함께
(B) 천천히
(C) 진지하게
(D) 주로

해설 | Vocabulary 동의어 단서를 찾을 수 있는 문제이다. "… primarily growing staples such as corn and wheat which they needed to survive, farmers in the southern colonies focused predominately …"의 밑줄 친 primarily에서 정답의 단서를 얻을 수 있다.

37 지문의 inducement 와 의미상 가장 가까운 것은?
(A) 자산
(B) 방식
(C) 동기
(D) 가치

해설 | Vocabulary "… southern farmers had every inducement to acquire vast tracts of land, since more land for more crops would result in greater profits"에서 inducement 의 의미는 밑줄 친 부분으로부터 추론할 수 있다. 땅을 많이 소유할수록 이익이 더 많이 남는다는 사실에서 땅을 많이 소유해야 할 동기가 충분하다는 것을 알 수 있다.

38 다음 중 지문에서 표시된 문장의 주요 정보를 가장 잘 나타낸 문장은? 정답 외의 보기들은 중요한 의미가 바뀌거나 주요 정보가 빠져 있다.
(A) 남부 지역 농부들과 뉴잉글랜드 농부들은 농경지를 재배하기 위해 다른 사람의 노동력에 상당 부분을 의지했다.
(B) 남부 플랜테이션은 뉴잉글랜드의 경우처럼 한가족이나 이웃들의 힘으로 경작하기에는 너무 넓었다.
(C) 뉴잉글랜드 농장주들은 더 실용적으로 땅을 유지할 수 있도록 부지를 소규모로 유지하려 했다.
(D) 주변 이웃이 없었기 때문에 남부 플랜테이션 농장주들은 그들의 수백만 에이커에 달하는 농지를 재배할 수 없는 경우가 많았다.

해설 | Sentence Simplification 표시된 문장은 크게 두 의미로 나뉠 수 있다. ①뉴잉글랜드 농부들은 가족 구성원의 노동력과 때로는 인근 이웃 주민의 도움을 받아 비교적 작은 농경지를 꾸려나갈 수 있었다. ②이것은 족히 수백 에이커에 달하는 남부 플랜테이션 농장에서는 실질적으로 불가능했다.

39 단락 6에 따르면, 플랜테이션 제도가 정부에 미친 영향은?
(A) 작은 도시나 마을 단위로 지역화되었다.
(B) 많은 땅과 돈을 가진 사람들에 의해 운영되었다.
(C) 시골 지역에서는 실행되지 않는 경우가 많았다.
(D) 넓은 지역에 걸쳐 큰 군들을 포함했다.

해설 | Factual Information 단락 6의 첫 부분에서 대규모의 플랜테이션이 생겨나면서 인구 분포가 넓어지고, 정부도 그것에 맞게 넓은 지역을 포괄하는 군 단위 중심으로 발전하였다고 설명한다.

40 지문에 따르면, 북부와 남부 지역 농부들에 대해 추론할 수 있는 것은?

(A) 노력을 했음에도 불구하고 남부 지역의 농부들은 주식 경작에 성공할 수 없었다.
(B) 남부 지역의 농부들과 달리 북부 지역의 농부들은 농업으로 부유해지기 힘들었다.
(C) 남부와 북부 지역의 농부들 모두 많은 자연적 장애물을 극복해야 했다.
(D) 북부 지역의 농부들은 남부 지역의 농부들과는 달리 정부로부터 많은 재정 지원을 받았다.

해설 | Inference 북부 지역의 토지는 척박하고 수확량은 기껏해야 가족들이 먹을 정도였던 반면, 남부 지역은 여러 면에서 농사짓기에 유리한 환경에서 대규모 플랜테이션을 중심으로 부유한 농장주들이 생겼다. 여기에서 북부 지역의 농부들은 남부 지역의 농부에 비해 농사로 부유해지기 힘들었다는 것을 추론할 수 있다.

41 다음 문장이 지문에 들어갈 곳을 나타내는 네 개의 사각형[■]을 보시오.

> 이와 같이 남부 사회는 뉴잉글랜드 사회보다 서열적 성격이 더 강했다.

이 문장이 들어갈 가장 적절한 위치는?
(A) A   (B) B   (C) C   (D) D

해설 | Sentence Insertion 삽입 문장은 연결어 thus로부터 앞에서 언급된 내용을 바탕으로 도출된 결론 성격의 문장임을 알 수 있다. 남부 사회가 뉴잉글랜드 사회보다 서열적 성격이 더 강했다는 내용은 단락 5의 마지막 부분에서 부농과 빈농의 차이가 생겨나고, 부농은 비옥한 토지를 더 많이 소유하고, 빈농은 규모가 작은 척박한 토지로 생계를 유지해야 했다는 내용으로부터 도출될 수 있는 결론이므로 문단 마지막에 위치해야 자연스럽다.

42 보기에서 적절한 문구를 골라 관련된 식민지 사회와 연결하시오. 보기 중 2개는 사용되지 않는다. *이 문제는 3점이다.*

	뉴잉글랜드
(A) 대부분 생존을 위해 경작했다.	• (A)
(B) 비교적 평등한 사회를 구성했다.	• (B)
(C) 판매 가능한 작물 재배에 의존했다.	• (G)
(D) 부자들만을 위해 경작했다.	**남부 식민지 지역**
(E) 더 큰 이윤을 위해 더 많은 땅을 추구했다.	• (C)
(F) 노예의 이용을 금지했다.	• (E)
(G) 가족이나 이웃이 도와주는 경우가 흔했다.	

해설 | Fill in a Table 뉴잉글랜드는 농토나 기후 조건 등 여러 면에서 농사에 불리하고 수확량이 많지 않아, 농산물은 주로 가족을 위한 식량으로 쓰였다. 열악한 농사 환경을 극복하기 위해 가족과 이웃이 서로 협동하여, 이웃 간의 유대감이 강한 평등한 사회로 발전하였다. 반면 남부 지역은 농사짓기가 매우 유리하고 수확량도 많아, 이익을 많이 내기 위해 담배와 면화 같은 상품 작물에 주력하였다. 수확량이 많다 보니 소유한 농토가 많으면 많을수록 이윤도 더 많이 창출되었다.

어휘 | **stretch** 펼쳐지다, 이르다　**breadth** 규모, 넓이　**marginal** 생산성이 적은[낮은]　**literally** 말 그대로　**perpetually** 늘　**laborious** 고된, 힘든　**humble** 영세한, 초라한　**prevail** 만연하다　**mere** 단순한, 순진한　**subsistence** 생계, 생활　**close-knit** 굳게 단결된　**egalitarian** 평등한　**potentially** 잠재적으로　**profitable** 수익성이 있는, 이익이 되는　**fertile** 비옥한　**composition** 구성　**staple** 주식　**cash crop** 판매용 작물　**immensely** 굉장히, 매우　**inducement** 동기, 장려책　**commercial** 상업적인　**aristocracy** 상류계급　**existence** 출현, 존재　**disperse** 퍼뜨리다, 흩어지게 하다　**county** 군, 주　**impractical** 비현실적인　**slave** 노예

Actual Test 2

Passage 1
01 (B) 02 (C) 03 (D) 04 (D) 05 (A) 06 (C) 07 (B) 08 (D) 09 (B) 10 (D) 11 (A) 12 (D)
13 (D) 14 [Pottery – (C), (E)], [Stone Tools – (B)], [Metal Artifacts – (A), (F)]

Passage 2
15 (B) 16 (D) 17 (B) 18 (C) 19 (C) 20 (B) 21 (B) 22 (B) 23 (D) 24 (C) 25 (B) 26 (B)
27 (C) 28 (B), (D), (E)

Passage 3
29 (B) 30 (B) 31 (D) 32 (C) 33 (C) 34 (D) 35 (C) 36 (B) 37 (A) 38 (B) 39 (A) 40 (C)
41 (D) 42 [Shale Oil – (C), (F)], [Oil Sands – (B), (D), (G), (I)], [Both – (A)]

Passage 1

01 (B) 02 (C) 03 (D) 04 (D) 05 (A) 06 (C) 07 (B) 08 (D) 09 (B) 10 (D) 11 (A) 12 (D)
13 (D) 14 [Pottery – (C), (E)], [Stone Tools – (B)], [Metal Artifacts – (A), (F)]

POST-EXCAVATION ANALYSIS

Although one of the main tasks of archaeology is to collect ancient artifacts to piece together how civilizations lived, the analysis and care of these artifacts, once collected, is also of importance. The method of studying objects that have been unearthed via archaeological excavation is referred to as post-excavation analysis. Often there is a need for a distinction between those who excavate artifacts and those who assess and analyze the materials that have been recovered from those sites. Q02 In effect, this post-excavation analysis is crucial for archaeologists to record not only discoveries made on site, but to also provide a record that will be available for future research. Q12-1 These records are important for archaeologists to refer to as they try to make objective inferences about their discoveries. Over the past few decades, the archaeological community has witnessed several considerable improvements in scientific technology, allowing archaeologists more accuracy when analyzing and dating objects. For the most part, the initial steps of this post-excavation analysis are carried out in general laboratories, while methods that call for more thorough precision take place in specialized labs. These methods have become indispensable for the analysis of inorganic materials that are collected, namely pottery, stone tools, and metals.

Pottery is of particular interest to archaeologists, since Q06(D) Q12-2 it provides clues as to how a civilization's economy and social infrastructure would have functioned, Q06(C) as pottery was used by almost everyone in a civilization. A Q6(B) It is considered an extremely valuable artifact, as it is able to withstand most environmental conditions and is therefore usually well preserved, even after hundreds of years. B Q03 There are several common systems and techniques that researchers use to classify pieces or shards of pottery. C Q06(A) Q13 Q14(E) For example, in order to classify pieces of pottery by color, researchers

발굴 후 분석

고고학의 주요 과제 중 하나는 고대 유물을 수집하여 그 문명들이 어떻게 생활했는지 종합하는 것이지만, 일단 수집되면, 이 유물들을 분석하고 관리하는 것 또한 중요하다. 고고학 발굴을 통해 발굴된 것들을 연구하는 방법은 발굴 후 분석(post-excavation analysis)이라고 불린다. 유물을 발굴해낸 사람들과 그 유적지에서 소생시킨 자료를 평가하고 분석하는 사람들을 구분할 필요가 종종 있다. 사실상, 이 발굴 후 분석은 고고학자들이 현장에서 발견한 것들을 기록하는 것뿐만 아니라, 미래의 연구에 사용될 기록을 제공하기 위해서도 중요하다. 이 기록들은 고고학자들이 참고하는 데에 중요한데 왜냐하면 이들은 그들의 발견에 대해서 객관적인 추정을 하기 위해 노력하기 때문이다. 지난 몇 십 년 동안 고고학계는 여러 중요한 과학 기술 향상을 목격해왔는데, 이는 고고학자들이 유물을 분석하고 연대를 추정할 때 좀 더 정확하게 할 수 있도록 만들어주었다. 대개 이 발굴 후 분석의 초기 단계들은 일반적인 연구실에서 진행되고, 좀 더 완전한 정확성을 요구하는 방법들은 특수화된 연구실에서 진행된다. 이 방법들은 도자기, 석기, 금속과 같이 수집된 무기물을 분석하는 데 필수적이다.

도자기는 고고학자들이 특별히 관심을 보이는데, 왜냐하면 도자기는 한 문명 내의 거의 모든 사람이 사용했기 때문에, 그 문명의 경제와 사회 구조가 어떻게 기능했는지에 대한 단서를 제공하기 때문이다. A 도자기는 대부분의 환경 조건을 견뎌낼 수 있어 보통 수백 년이 지난 후에도 잘 보존되기 때문에 매우 귀중한 유물로 여겨진다. B 도자기 조각들을 분류하기 위해 연구원들이 사용하는 일반적인 시스템과 기술이 여러 가지 있다. C 예를 들어, 색깔로 도자기 조각을 분류하기 위해서 연구원들은 먼셀 표색계라는 시스템을 사용한다. D 이 시스템은 도자기 조각이 발견된 토양의 색, 밝기, 색 순도에 대해 매우 세부적인 정보를 제공한다. 이는 특정한 보관 조건에서 도자기가 이차적인 착색을 거칠 수 있으므로 중요하다. 연구원들은 또한 먼셀 표색계를 사용하여 조각의 표면, 외부층,

use a system called the Munsell color system. **D** **This system provides extremely detailed information on the hue, lightness, and color purity of the soil the pottery pieces are found in.** This is important because under certain storage conditions, pottery can undergo secondary coloration. Researchers also make use of the Munsell color system to distinguish colors of the surface, outer layers, and the core of the shard, all of which can have their color affected by the environment over an extended period of time. As well as the Munsell color chart, Q14(C) researchers make use of petrology, which is the study of the characteristics of rocks that influence the degree of hardness and strength of the pottery material. By examining these characteristics with great scrutiny, Q12-3 researchers can provide a more precise location for the origin of the pottery.

The second most popular area of post-excavation analysis of inorganic remains is that of stone tools. Q12-4 For the vast majority of prehistoric sites, stone tools are a significant indicator of how early humans went about their daily lives. ①Although archaeologists are tasked with studying the physical qualities of finished tools, ② Q14(B) they must also direct a fair amount of focus on the rock material that prehistoric peoples used to craft their stone tools. Q08 Q12-5 By studying the surfaces of finished tools as well as rock material, archaeologists can make inferences as to how the tools were manufactured. Based on how the tools are manufactured, archaeologists can then classify the tools into specific categories according to their size, shape, usage, color, and material.

Q11-1 The third most common post-excavation method of analysis of inorganic material used by archaeologists is the domain of metallurgical analysis. When metal objects are found, Q10 archaeologists first need to implement scrupulous cleaning methods to prevent them from further deteriorating, followed by refurbishing the metal artifact. Q11-2 Q14(A) The first method used to carry this out is called electrolysis, which is necessary for archaeologists to give the metal artifact preliminary treatment before undergoing more intense scrutiny. For example, if scientists discover a metal artifact underground, the artifact may have accumulated an encrustation of soil and sediment around it, which can erode the surface of the metal. Q11-3 After the metal artifact has been carefully and thoroughly cleaned, archaeologists can then study in detail its composition, as well as any evident peculiarities of its manufacturing. Q11-4 Q12-6 Q14(F) In certain situations, the metal artifact can be placed in a special kind of scanning electron microscope, which is useful for studying the details of the manufacture of such items like jewelry and weapons.

중심부의 색을 구별하기도 하는데, 이는 이들 모두가 장기간에 걸쳐 환경에 영향을 받을 수 있기 때문이다. 연구원들은 먼셀 색조표 뿐만 아니라, 암석학도 사용하는데, 이는 도자기 재료의 내구성과 단단함에 영향을 주는 암석의 특징을 연구하는 것이다. 매우 철저한 조사를 통해 이 특징을 연구함으로써, 연구원들은 도자기의 기원에 대해 좀 더 정확한 위치를 제공할 수 있다.

무기물 유물의 발굴 후 분석에서 두 번째로 대중적인 분야는 석기의 분석이다. 대부분의 선사시대 유적지의 경우, 석기는 초기 인류의 일상생활 방식을 추정하는 데 중요한 지표이다. 고고학자들이 완성된 석기의 물리적 특성을 연구하는 업무를 수행하지만, 그들은 또한 선사시대 사람들이 석기를 만드는 데 사용한 암석 물질에도 상당한 초점을 두어야 한다. 암석 재료와 더불어 완성된 석기의 표면을 연구함으로써, 고고학자들은 석기가 어떻게 제작되었는지 추정할 수 있다. 석기가 만들어진 방법에 기초하여 고고학자들은 그 석기들을 크기, 모양, 활용도, 색깔, 재료에 따른 세부적인 범주로 분류할 수 있다.

고고학자들이 사용하는 무기물 유물의 세 번째로 일반적인 발굴 후 분석 방법은 야금학 분석 분야이다. 금속 유물이 발견되면, 고고학자들은 우선 더 악화하지 않도록 세심한 세척법을 사용해야 하고, 이후 금속 유물을 다시 닦는다. 이를 위해 사용하는 첫 번째 방법은 전기 분해 방법인데, 이는 좀 더 철저한 조사를 진행하기 전에 고고학자들이 금속 유물에 예비 처리를 하는 데 필요하다. 예를 들어, 만약 과학자가 지하에서 금속 유물을 발견하면, 그 유물은 토양이나 침전물 외피를 유물 주변에 축적했을 수 있는데, 이는 금속의 표면을 부식시킬 수 있다. 금속 유물을 세심하고 철저하게 세척하고 나서야 고고학자들은 제조와 관련된 눈에 띄는 특징들과 구성물을 세부적으로 연구할 수 있다. 특정 상황에서는 금속 유물을 특수한 종류의 주사형 전자 현미경에 놓을 수 있는데, 이는 보석이나 무기와 같은 것들의 제조 관련 세부 사항을 연구하는 데 유용하다.

01 지문의 thorough 와 의미상 가장 가까운 것은?

(A) 중요한
(B) 완전한
(C) 조직적인
(D) 광범위한

해설 | Vocabulary   thorough 는 '완전한, 철저한'이라는 의미이다.

02 단락 1에 따르면, 발굴 후 분석이 중요한 이유는?
(A) 발굴된 물건을 연구하는 과정을 용이하게 한다.
(B) 고대 문명의 일상생활과 풍습에 대해 결정적인 통찰을 제공한다.
(C) 고고학자들이 현장에서 발견된 것들을 기록하고 이후 연구를 위해 그 기록을 보관할 수 있게 한다.
(D) 발굴에 사용되는 기술을 더욱 향상시킨다.

해설 | Factual Information 단락 1에서 발굴 후 분석은 유물의 기록뿐만 아니라 미래의 연구를 위한 기록 제공의 기능이 있다고 말하고 있다.

03 필자가 지문에서 먼셀 표색계 를 언급하는 이유는?
(A) 색에 의한 분류법이 믿을 만하지 못하다는 것을 보여주기 위해
(B) 도자기의 물리적 특징에 대한 세부적인 분석이 필요하다는 것을 강조하기 위해
(C) 색에 따라 도자기를 분류하는 것이 어렵다는 것을 시사하기 위해
(D) 도자기 조각의 분류 방법의 한 예를 들기 위해

해설 | Rhetorical Purpose 먼셀 표색계를 언급하기 이전 문장은 "There are several common systems and techniques that researchers use to classify pieces or shards of pottery"였고, 그다음 문장에 "For example"이라는 표현을 사용하였으므로 도자기 조각의 여러 분류 방법 중 한 가지 예시를 들기 위함임을 알 수 있다.

04 지문의 As well as 와 의미상 가장 가까운 것은?
(A) ~때문에
(B) ~와 비슷하게
(C) ~에 관해 말하면
(D) ~뿐만 아니라

해설 | Vocabulary As well as 와 In addition to는 모두 '~뿐만 아니라'라는 의미이다.

05 지문의 scrutiny 와 의미상 가장 가까운 것은?
(A) 조사
(B) 기초
(C) 통제
(D) 신중함

해설 | Vocabulary 이것을 통해 특징을 연구함으로써 도자기의 기원에 대해 좀 더 정확한 위치를 알 수 있다고 한 것으로 보아 scrutiny 는 '조사'의 의미임을 알 수 있다.

06 단락 2에서 언급되지 않은 것은?
(A) 도자기의 특징은 먼셀 표색계를 사용하여 분류된다.
(B) 도자기는 일반적으로 오랜 기간 후에도 잘 보존된다.
(C) 도자기는 부의 상징으로서 상류층 시민들에 의해 사용되었다.
(D) 도자기 발견은 사회의 경제와 구조가 어떻게 작동했는지를 나타낸다.

해설 | Negative Fact (A), (B), (D)는 단락 2에서 언급되었고, 도자기는 거의 모든 사람이 사용했다는 언급이 있으므로 (C)는 잘못된 내용이다.

07 다음 중 지문에서 표시된 문장의 주요 정보를 가장 잘 나타낸 문장은? 정답 외의 보기들은 중요한 의미가 바뀌거나 주요 정보가 빠져 있다.
(A) 석기의 암석 물질이 가장 중요한 물리적 특성이기 때문에 고고학자들은 대부분 시간을 그것을 연구하는 데 몰두한다.
(B) 고고학자들은 제련된 도구의 물리적 특징뿐만 아니라, 석기를 만드는 데 사용된 암석 물질에도 초점을 두어야 한다.
(C) 석기 연구를 위해 필요한 여러 물리적 특성에도 불구하고, 고고학자들은 암석 물질에 초점을 두는 것을 선호한다.
(D) 고고학자들은 암석 물질의 물리적 특성을 이해하기 위해 암석 물질을 연구하는 데 많은 시간을 보낸다.

해설 | Sentence Simplification 표시된 문장은 크게 두 의미로 나뉠 수 있다. ①고고학자는 완성된 석기의 물리적 특성을 연구한다. ②그들은 암석 물질에도 초점을 두어야 한다.

08 단락 3에 따르면, 석기의 발굴 후 분석에 관한 내용 중 옳은 것은?
(A) 석기는 선사 시대의 일상생활에 대해 도자기보다 더 많은 정보를 제공한다.
(B) 연구원들은 석기의 암석 물질에 기초하여 초기 사회에 관한 사실을 발견한다.
(C) 석기의 분석은 항상 모든 선사 유적지에 대한 확실한 지표가 된다.
(D) 암석 물질은 석기 제조와 관련된 사실을 보여주는 요인이다.

해설 | Factual Information 지문에 따르면 암석 재료를 연구함으로써 고고학자들은 석기가 어떻게 제작되었는지 추정할 수 있다고 한다.

09 지문의 erode와 의미상 가장 가까운 것은?

(A) 부수다
(B) 닳게 하다
(C) 강화하다
(D) 고치다

해설 | Vocabulary   erode는 '부식시키다'라는 의미가 있으므로 '닳게 하다, 마모시키다'라는 의미의 wear away와 유의어이다.

10 단락 4에 따르면, 고고학자들이 금속 유물을 분석하기 전에 필수적으로 해야 하는 것은?

(A) 발굴된 토류 금속 유물에 대한 예비 분석을 해야 한다.
(B) 석기 분석에서 쓰인 것과 비슷한 세척 기술을 사용해야 한다.
(C) 발굴된 금속 유물 표면에 쌓인 외피를 제거해야 한다.
(D) 그들이 사용하는 세척 방식이 유물을 더 손상하지 않도록 해야 한다.

해설 | Factual Information   지문에 따르면 고고학자들은 금속 유물을 발견하고 나서 분석하기 전에 유물의 상태가 더 악화하지 않도록 세심한 세척법을 사용해야 한다고 한다.

11 단락 4의 구성 방식을 가장 잘 설명한 것은?

(A) 금속 유물을 분석하는 데 필요한 단계들의 묘사
(B) 금속 유물을 분석하는 데 사용되는 방식들의 비교
(C) 고고학자들이 금속 유물을 분석하면서 여러 어려움을 겪는 이유
(D) 금속 유물을 다시 씻는 것의 장단점 분석

해설 | Rhetorical Purpose   단락 4는 고고학자들이 금속 유물을 분석하는 데 필요한 단계인 야금학 분석, 세척법, 전기 분해 방법 등을 설명하고 있다.

12 지문에서 추론할 수 있는 것은?

(A) 발굴 후 분석으로부터 도출될 수 있는 결과들은 다소 부정확하고 추후에 더 논의 될 수 있다.
(B) 발굴 후 분석은 고고학에서의 커지는 중요성으로 인해 유망한 직종이 되었다.
(C) 불충분한 기술 자원은 발굴 후 분석의 주요한 장애 요인이다.
(D) 발굴 후 분석과 연구로 인해 고대 문명에 대한 지식이 증가하였다.

해설 | Inference   지문에 따르면, 발굴 후 분석을 통해 도자기를 분석함으로써 문명의 경제와 사회 구조에 대해 알 수 있고, 도자기의 기원을 알아냄으로써 문명의 정확한 위치도 알 수 있다. 또한 석기를 연구함으로써 초기 인류의 일상생활 방식을 추정할 수 있고, 석기가 어떻게 제작되었는지도 추정할 수 있다. 즉, 발굴 후 분석과 연구로 인해 고대 문명에 대한 지식이 증가하였다는 결론을 내릴 수 있다.

13 다음 문장이 지문에 들어갈 곳을 나타내는 네 개의 사각형[■]을 보시오.

> 이 시스템은 도자기 조각이 발견된 토양의 색, 밝기, 색 순도에 대해 매우 세부적인 정보를 제공한다.

이 문장이 들어갈 가장 적절한 위치는?

(A) A   (B) B   (C) C   (D) D

해설 | Sentence Insertion   삽입 문장의 This system은 이전 문장의 Munsell color system을 가리키는 것임을 알 수 있다. 따라서 삽입 문장은 D에 위치하는 것이 가장 자연스럽다.

14 보기에서 적절한 문구를 골라 관련된 유물의 종류와 연결하시오. 보기 중 2개는 사용되지 않는다. 이 문제는 3점이다.

보기	유물 종류
(A) 유물을 씻는 데 전기 분해 방법을 사용한다. (B) 제조 과정에서 사용된 암석 물질을 연구한다. (C) 분류를 위해 암석학을 사용한다. (D) 발굴하기 위해 매우 발달한 장치가 필요하다. (E) 분류를 위해 표색계가 필요하다. (F) 특별한 상황에서 세부적인 연구를 위해 정밀 검사 장치를 사용할 수 있다. (G) 유물 분석의 현장 실행을 구현한다.	도자기 • (C) • (E) 석기 • (B) 금속 유물 • (A) • (F)

해설 | Fill in a Table   지문에 따르면, 도자기 범주 분류를 위해 암석학 및 표색계를 사용하고, 석기를 연구할 때에는 제조 과정에서 사용된 암석 물질을 연구한다. 또한 금속 유물을 씻는 데에는 전기 분해 방법을 사용하고, 세부적인 연구를 위해서는 주사형 전자 현미경이라는 정밀 검사 장치를 사용할 수 있다.

어휘 | **archaeology** 고고학   **artifact** 유물, 공예품   **piece together** ~를 종합하다   **post-excavation analysis** 발굴 후 분석   **witness** 입증하다, 목격하다   **thorough** 완전한, 철저한   **precision** 정확성   **indispensable** 필수적인, 없어서는 안 될   **pottery** 도자기   **stone tool** 석기   **infrastructure** 구조, 토대   **shard** 조각   **Munsell color system** 먼셀 표색계   **petrology** 암석학   **indicator** 지표   **domain** 분야, 영역   **metallurgical** 야금(학·술)의   **scrupulous** 세심한, 꼼꼼한   **deteriorate** 악화하다   **refurbish** 다시 닦다, 재단장하다   **electrolysis** 전기 분해 방법   **preliminary** 예비의   **encrustation** 외피 (형성)   **sediment** 침전물, 퇴적물   **erode** 부식시키다, 침식시키다   **peculiarity** 특징   **scanning electron microscope** 주사형 전자 현미경

Passage 2

p.226

| 15 (B) | 16 (D) | 17 (B) | 18 (C) | 19 (C) | 20 (B) | 21 (B) | 22 (B) | 23 (D) | 24 (C) | 25 (B) | 26 (B) |
| 27 (C) | 28 (B), (D), (E) |

ICE AGE EXTINCTION EVENT

The end of the last Ice Age brought many dramatic changes to planet Earth. Among them was the sudden mass extinction of countless animal species throughout the world. Some well-known examples include the woolly mammoth, the saber-tooth tiger, and the giant sloth. Because of their enormous size, these animals are referred to as megafauna. Though a few species of megafauna survive today, like the elephant and the rhinoceros, most of them were wiped out during this Ice Age extinction event. The reasons for such a wide-ranging extinction of megafauna are still unclear to scientists. Two major theories have been proposed to explain it, though each theory has its limitations.

One theory states that early humans had an active role in the extinction of megafauna through hunting. Q16 As the climate warmed and the ice sheets retreated, humans began migrating to new areas of the world, such as the Americas and the northern regions of Europe and Asia, which were previously uninhabited. Animals in these new lands were not adapted to living with humans, who were already proficient predators. Unaware of the threat humans posed, they did not know to flee them. They were also not equipped with the defenses they needed to avoid or fight off human attacks, and as a result these animals were hunted to extinction. Q17 Evidence supporting this theory comes from the fact that mass extinctions of megafauna occurred far more often in lands where human migrations took place, as opposed to areas where animals and humans evolved alongside one another. ① Very few surviving ancestors of megafauna remain in the Western Hemisphere, for example, whereas ② certain megafauna still exist in great numbers in Africa and South Asia, two regions where humans evolved alongside large mammals.

While the arrival of humans does coincide with the beginning of the extinction event, this does not constitute definitive proof for some scientists. These scientists claim that Q19 there is no evidence that any species of megafauna was regularly hunted by humans. The major exception to this is, of course, the woolly mammoth, the skeletons of which frequently display evidence of wounds inflicted by man-made weapons. Q20 Fossils from other megafauna have yet to yield such evidence, however, casting doubt on the idea that humans hunted megafauna to extinction. A further cause for skepticism is that some heavily hunted animals thrived during this period and even survive today. One example is the bison, an animal that is much hunted and whose ancestors have roamed the earth for tens of thousands of years. If the bison could be so heavily hunted and still survive this extinction event, some scientists reason that most megafauna should have survived human interference as well.

빙하기의 멸종 사건

지난 빙하기의 종료는 지구에 여러 가지 극적인 변화를 가져왔다. 그중의 하나는 세계의 수많은 종의 동물들이 갑작스럽게 집단으로 멸종한 것이다. 잘 알려진 몇 가지 동물에는 울리 매머드와 검치호랑이, 거대 나무늘보 등이 있다. 이 동물들은 거대한 크기로 인해 '거대 동물군'이라 불린다. 코끼리나 코뿔소 같은 거대 동물군의 몇몇 종은 오늘날까지 살아남았으나 대부분은 이 빙하기 멸종 사건동안 없어져 버렸다. 거대 동물군의 이러한 대대적인 멸종 사건이 생긴 이유는 아직 과학자들도 잘 모른다. 이를 설명하기 위해 두 가지의 중요한 이론이 제시되었는데, 각 이론에는 한계가 있다.

한 가지 이론은 초기 인류가 사냥함으로써 거대 동물군의 멸종에 큰 역할을 했다는 것이다. 기후가 따뜻해지고 대륙빙하가 감소하면서 인류는 아메리카 대륙과 유럽과 아시아의 북쪽 지역 등 인류가 거주한 적이 없던 새로운 지역으로 이동하였다. 이 새로운 지역의 동물들은 이미 능숙한 사냥꾼이었던 인간과 공존하는 데 익숙하지 않았다. 인간의 위험을 모르는 동물들은 도망쳐야 한다는 것을 몰랐다. 그들은 인간의 공격을 피하거나 대항할 수 있는 방어수단도 갖추지 못하였고 결국 멸종될 때까지 사냥되었다. 이 이론을 지지하는 증거는 바로 거대 동물군의 집단 멸종이 인간과 동물이 함께 진화한 지역이 아닌, 인간이 이주해간 지역에서 훨씬 많이 일어났다는 사실이다. 예를 들어, 서반구에는 아주 적은 숫자의 거대 동물군이 생존하여 남아 있지만, 인간과 거대 포유동물이 함께 진화한 두 지역인 아프리카와 남아시아에는 아직도 많은 거대 동물군이 생존하고 있다.

인간의 이주와 멸종 사건의 시작이 동시에 일어난 것은 아니지만, 몇몇 과학자들에게 이것은 결정적인 증거가 되지 못한다. 이 과학자들은 거대 동물군 중 어느 종도 실질적으로 인간에게 사냥을 당했다는 증거가 없다고 주장한다. 물론 이것의 대표적 예외는 울리 매머드인데, 발견된 그것의 뼈에서 때때로 사람이 만든 무기에 피해를 입은 상처의 흔적이 보인다. 하지만 다른 거대 동물군의 화석에서는 아직 이런 증거를 찾지 못하여서, 인간이 거대 동물군을 멸종될 때까지 사냥했다는 주장을 의심하게 된다. 또 다른 회의적인 이유는 많은 사냥의 대상이 된 동물 일부가 이 시기에 번성했고, 또 오늘날까지도 살아 있다는 것이다. 이 한 예는 들소인데, 이 동물은 많이 사냥 되어왔으나 이들의 조상으로 부터 몇 만 년 동안 지구에서 살아왔다. 만약 들소가 그렇게 많이 사냥 되어오면서도 멸종 사건을 넘기고 여전히 현존한다면 대부분의 거대 동물군이 인간과의 접촉이 있었더라도 살아남았어야 한다고 과학자들은 주장한다.

A Q27 Besides the hunting theory, Q21 there is another prominent theory set forth to explain the Ice Age extinction event. **B** This one is concerned primarily with climate. **C** **The major catalyst in this theory is temperature.** After all, it was a sharp rise in temperature that melted the frozen earth and brought about the end of the Ice Age. **D** Higher temperatures introduced several challenges to the prehistoric climate. Q22 Q24(A) Land that was once covered by forests became prairies and grasslands. This ecological change could have had any number of negative effects on megafauna. Q23 For one, it would have robbed some species of the shelter and safety provided by forests. In the forest, giant mammals could obscure themselves from smaller but faster predators. Roaming the open grasslands, however, made them far more vulnerable to predators. The biggest impact of this change would have been the change in food supply. Q24(B) Higher temperatures led to irregular rainfall. Q24(D) As a result, only those plants well adapted to the new weather patterns survived. This further changed the kinds of plants that were available to megafauna. Different plants meant that many herbivores could not get their usual vital nutrients, and many suffered because of this.

However, this theory has a few problems of its own. One observation is that large herbivores had survived previous periods of climate change. Extinction events of this severity had not occurred during other periods of similar change. Q26 Other scientists argue that the transformation from woodlands to grasslands would have provided more food for giant herbivores, and should actually have aided in their survival. Some evidence even shows that grazing animals had a lower rate of extinction than animals with mixed diets. While neither theory holds up on its own, many scientists can agree that some combination of these two theories can probably explain the Ice Age extinction event.

A 사냥과 관련된 이론 말고도 빙하기의 멸종 사건을 설명하기 위해서 제안된 다른 한 가지 두드러진 가설이 있다. **B** 이는 주로 기후와 관련이 있다. **C** 이 이론에서 가장 중요한 촉매제는 바로 기온이다. 결국에는 기온의 급격한 상승은 빙하로 덮여 있던 지구를 녹여 빙하기의 끝을 불러왔다. **D** 더 높은 기온은 선사시대의 기후에 몇몇 문제점을 가져왔다. 숲으로 덮여 있었던 땅은 대초원이나 목초지로 변하였다. 이러한 생태계의 변화는 거대 동물군에게 나쁜 영향을 주었을 것이다. 예를 들어, 숲이 제공하는 동물의 주거지와 안전성이 없어졌을 수 있다. 거대한 포유동물은 숲에서 더 작고 더 민첩한 포식자들로부터 그들 자신을 숨길 수 있었다. 훤히 트인 목초지를 돌아다니는 것은 그들이 포식자 사냥감이 될 수 있는 위험성을 높이는 일이었을 것이다. 이 변화의 가장 큰 영향은 식량 공급의 변화였을 것이다. 기온의 상승은 불규칙한 강우를 동반했다. 결과적으로 새로운 기후에 적응할 수 있었던 식물만이 살아남았다. 이는 더 나아가 거대 동물군이 먹는 초목의 종류를 바꿔놨다. 식물의 변화는 많은 초식동물이 평상시의 필수 영양분을 섭취할 수 없게 된 것을 의미하는데, 이로 인해 많은 초식 동물들이 고통을 겪었다.

하지만 이 가설에도 몇 가지 문제점이 있다. 한 가지는 많은 초식동물이 그 전에 있었던 기후 변화에서 생존했다는 사실이다. 이러한 가혹한 멸종 사건은 비슷한 변화가 있었던 다른 기간에는 생긴 적이 없었다. 다른 과학자들은 삼림지가 초목으로 변화함으로써 거대 초식동물에게 더욱 많은 식물을 제공해 오히려 생존에 도움을 주었을 거라고 주장한다. 몇몇 증거들은 방목 동물이 잡식 동물보다 멸종률이 적다는 것을 보여주기도 한다. 어떤 가설도 완벽하지는 않지만, 많은 과학자들은 이 두 이론이 어느 정도 결합해 빙하기의 멸종 사건을 설명할 수 있다는 데에는 동의한다.

15 다음 중 지문에서 표시된 문장의 주요 정보를 가장 잘 나타낸 문장은? 정답 외의 보기들은 중요한 의미가 바뀌거나 주요 정보가 빠져 있다.

(A) 거대 동물군 중 몇 종은 서반구에서 살아남았지만, 초기 인류가 있던 지역에서는 잘 살아가지 못했다.
(B) 인간이 나중에 이주한 지역보다 인간과 함께 진화한 지역에 더 많은 거대 동물군이 존재한다.
(C) 서반구로 이주한 거대 동물군은 인간의 사냥으로 멸종에 더 취약해졌다.
(D) 초기 인류는 아프리카와 아시아에서 거대 동물군을 멸종에 이르기까지 사냥했지만, 서부에서는 거대 동물군과 같이 진화했다.

해설 | Sentence Simplification 표시된 문장은 크게 두 의미로 나뉠 수 있다. ① 서반구에는 거대 동물군이 거의 남아있지 않다. ② 인간과 거대 포유동물이 함께 진화한 지역에는 아직도 많은 거대 동물군이 남아있다.

16 단락 2에 따르면, 인간이 새로운 지역으로 이주한 이유는?

(A) 악화되는 기후 조건
(B) 거대 동물군의 개체 수 증가
(C) 이전 거주 지역의 식량 부족
(D) 기온 상승으로 인한 빙하 해빙

해설 | Factual Information 인간은 기온이 따뜻해지고 빙하가 녹으면서 새로운 지역으로 이주하였다.

17 단락 2에 따르면, 인간의 공격으로부터 살아남은 거대 동물군에 대해 추론할 수 있는 것은?

(A) 그들은 매우 위험해서 인간이 피해 다녀야 했다.
(B) 그들은 인간의 공격으로부터 자신들을 보호하는 방식으로 진화했다.
(C) 그들의 개체 수가 매우 많아 인간의 사냥은 생존에 별다른 영향을 미치지 않았다.
(D) 그들은 인간에게 별로 필요하지 않았기 때문에 인간은 사냥할 필요성을 느끼지 못했다.

해설 | Inference 단락 2에서 인간의 사냥 때문에 거대 동물군이 멸종했다는 증거로 이전에 인간을 접하지 못한 동물은 인간이 위험한 존재라는 사실을 몰랐기 때문에 인간의 공격에 그대로 노출되어 멸종됐지만, 예전부터 인간과 함께 공존하면서 진화한 동물은 지금까지 살아남았다는 사실을 추론할 수 있다.

18 지문의 coincide with 와 의미상 가장 가까운 것은?
(A) 관련이 없다
(B) 방해하다
(C) 동시에 발생하다
(D) 설명하다

해설 | Vocabulary   coincide with 는 '동시에 일어나다, 일치하다'라는 의미이다.

19 지문에서 this 가 가리키는 것은?
(A) 대부분의 거대 동물군이 지금은 생존하지 않는다는 사실
(B) 거대 동물군의 멸종이 사냥에 의한 것이라는 이론
(C) 인간이 거대 동물군을 사냥했다는 직접적인 증거의 부족
(D) 거대 동물군이 인간에게 적응하지 못했다는 생각

해설 | Reference   this 의 앞 문장 "… there is no evidence that any species of megafauna was regularly hunted by humans"를 가장 잘 정리한 것은 (C)이다.

20 필자가 지문에서 들소 를 언급하는 이유는?
(A) 멸종 위기에 놓일 정도로 사냥 되었던 동물의 예를 들기 위해
(B) 인간의 사냥이 멸종 사건을 초래했다는 이론을 반박하기 위해
(C) 초기 인류가 거대 동물군을 사냥했다는 주장을 부정하기 위해
(D) 인간이 거대 동물군의 멸종을 초래했다는 이론을 뒷받침하기 위해

해설 | Rhetorical Purpose   들소 는 바로 앞 문장 "A further cause for skepticism is that some heavily hunted animals thrived during this period and even survive today"를 뒷받침하는 예시로 언급되었다.

21 지문의 prominent 와 의미상 가장 가까운 것은?
(A) 효과적인
(B) 두드러진
(C) 실현 가능한
(D) 상반되는

해설 | Vocabulary   빙하기의 멸종 사건을 설명하기 위해서 제안된 가설이므로 prominent 는 '두드러진, 중요한'이라는 의미로 사용되었음을 알 수 있다.

22 지문의 challenges 와 의미상 가장 가까운 것은?
(A) 이점
(B) 문제점
(C) 변화
(D) 영향

해설 | Vocabulary   제시된 단어 뒤에 "Land that was once covered by forests became prairies and grasslands"라는 내용이 있으므로 challenges 는 생태계 변화로 인해 거대 동물군이 겪은 '문제점'이라는 것을 알 수 있다.

23 지문의 obscure 와 의미상 가장 가까운 것은?
(A) 제어하다
(B) 보호하다
(C) 예방하다
(D) 숨기다

해설 | Vocabulary   obscure 의 의미는 앞 문장에서 숲이 거대 동물군에게 해 주었던 역할을 나타낸 "… the shelter and safety provided by forests"로부터 '숨기다'의 의미를 지녔음을 알 수 있다.

24 단락 4에 따르면, 기후 이론을 주장하는 과학자들이 믿는 기온 상승으로 인한 결과로 옳지 않은 것은?
(A) 삼림 지대의 소멸
(B) 강우량의 차이
(C) 새 거대 동물군의 출현
(D) 고유 식물의 변화

해설 | Negative Fact   기온 상승으로 숲이 대평원으로 변하고 강우가 불규칙해짐에 따라, 이 새로운 기후 패턴에 적응할 수 있는 식물만이 살아남을 수 있다고 설명한다. (C)에 관한 내용은 언급되지 않았다.

25 지문의 transformation 과 의미상 가장 가까운 것은?
(A) 발전
(B) 변화
(C) 파괴
(D) 다양성

해설 | Vocabulary   transformation 은 '변화, 바뀜'의 의미이다.

26 단락 5에 따르면, 일부 과학자들이 목초지 증가에 대해 사실이라고 믿는 것은?

(A) 새 환경에 적응하려는 인간의 능력을 방해했다.
(B) 거대 동물군에게 더 많은 식량을 제공할 수 있었을 것이다.
(C) 거대 초식동물군 멸종의 원인이다.
(D) 거대 동물군의 사냥을 증가시켰을 것이다.

해설 | Factual Information 단락 5의 중간 부분에서 일부 학자들은 숲이 목초지로 변화한 것은 오히려 거대 동물군에게 더 많은 먹을거리를 제공해 주었을 것이라고 주장한다고 설명한다.

27 다음 문장이 지문에 들어갈 곳을 나타내는 네 개의 사각형[■]을 보시오.

> 이 이론에서 가장 중요한 촉매제는 바로 기온이다.

이 문장이 들어갈 가장 적절한 위치는?

(A) **A**   (B) **B**   (C) **C**   (D) **D**

해설 | Sentence Insertion 삽입 문장의 this theory는 **A**에서 언급된 "another prominent theory"이며, **C**에서 기온의 급격한 상승이 가져오는 영향에 관해 설명하고 있으므로 삽입 문장은 **C**에 들어가야 자연스럽다.

28 지문을 간략히 요약하기 위한 도입 문장이 아래 제시되어 있다. 지문에서 가장 중요한 내용을 표현한 세 개의 문장을 골라 요약문을 완성하시오. 일부 문장은 지문에 나오지 않았거나 중요하지 않은 내용이기 때문에 요약문에 포함되지 않는다. *이 문제는 2점이다.*

> 마지막 빙하기가 끝나며 거대 동물군이 멸종한 이유를 설명하는 대표적 이론에는 두 가지가 있다.

(A) 거대 동물군이 멸종한 이유는 오랫동안 과학자들에게 수수께끼로 남아 있었다.
(B) 초기 인류의 지나친 사냥 때문에 거대 동물군이 멸종하기에 이르렀다는 주장이 있다.
(C) 빙하기가 끝나기 이전에는 아메리카 대륙과 북부 유럽에 인간이나 거대 동물군이 살지 않았다.
(D) 어떤 과학자들은 기온 상승으로 일어난 생태계의 변화 때문에 거대 동물군이 멸종했다고 주장한다.
(E) 두 가지 이론 다 결함이 있지만, 두 이론을 종합한 것은 빙하기의 멸종 사건을 더 잘 이해할 수 있도록 해줄 것이다.
(F) 들소는 거대 동물군이 인간의 사냥에서도 살아남을 수 있다는 것을 보여주는 한 가지 예이다.

해설 | Summary 지문은 빙하기가 끝나자 이와 함께 거대 동물군이 사라진 이유를 설명하는 두 가지 이론과 그 문제점에 대해 각각 설명하고 있다. (B)는 거대 동물군이 인간의 사냥 때문에 멸종되었다는 이론에 대한 단락 2의 내용을, (D)는 기후 변화로 인해 거대 동물군이 멸종되었다는 단락 4의 내용을, (E)는 두 가지 이론을 반박한 단락 3과 5를 요약한 문장이다.

어휘 | **dramatic** 극적인 **woolly mammoth** 울리 매머드(매머드의 한 종류) **saber-tooth tiger** 검치호랑이 **sloth** 나무늘보 **enormous** 거대한 **megafauna** 거대 동물군 **rhinoceros** 코뿔소 **wipe out** 없애 버리다, 완전히 파괴하다 **limitation** 한계 **ice sheet** 대륙빙하 **retreat** 감소하다 **uninhabited** (사람이) 거주하지 않는 **be adapted to** ~에 적응하다 **unaware of** ~을 모르는 **flee** 도망치다 **be equipped with** ~을 갖추다 **defense** 방어수단 **migration** 이주, 이동 **evolve** 진화하다 **mammal** 포유류 **coincide with** ~와 동시에 일어나다 **constitute** ~가 되다 **definitive** 결정적인 **wound** 상처 **inflict** (피해를) 입히다 **cast doubt on** ~에 의문을 제기하다 **skepticism** 회의, 의심 **bison** 들소 **set forth** 제안하다 **concerned** 관련 있는 **catalyst** 촉매제 **sharp** 급격한 **prairie** 대초원 **grassland** 목초지, 초원 **ecological** 생태계의 **irregular** 불규칙한 **herbivore** 초식동물 **vital** 필수인 **severity** 가혹함 **transformation** 변화 **woodland** 삼림지 **grazing** 방목

Passage 3

p.230

| 29 (B) | 30 (B) | 31 (D) | 32 (C) | 33 (C) | 34 (D) | 35 (C) | 36 (B) | 37 (A) | 38 (B) | 39 (A) | 40 (C) |
| 41 (D) | 42 [Shale Oil – (C), (F)], [Oil Sands – (B), (D), (G), (I)], [Both – (A)] |

SHALE OIL AND OIL SANDS

Crude oil has become a fixture in modern lifestyles all over the world. Without it, there would be no fuel for cars, no asphalt for our roads or buildings, and no raw material from which to make the plastics and other oil that are essential to modern life. The world consumes over 80 million barrels of oil each day, and the number continues to grow. Unfortunately, oil is a limited resource, and although demand for this valuable resource rapidly increases, many experts claim that Q29 the world supply has already passed its summit and is on the decline. For this reason, petroleum companies are exploring new sources of crude oil, namely shale oil and oil sands.

Shale oil is produced from a substance known as oil shale, which is a type of rock that contains all the basic elements of petroleum. Q30 Q32(A) Oil shale consists mainly of kerogen, the decayed organic matter found in sedimentary rock that precedes the formation of crude oil. This substance can be extracted from the rock in which it is trapped and refined into a usable form of petroleum. Q32(B) Q42(C) Oil shale was used in prehistoric times as a source of fire, as the chemicals in it make it readily flammable. Q32(C) Even today, some countries still use unrefined oil shale as fuel for power plants. The most notable of these is Estonia, where domestic oil shale is a cheaper option than crude oil. Q32(D) The largest deposits of oil shale in the world can be found in the western United States, in an area known as the Green River basin. Along with giant deposits in Russia and Brazil, these reserves make up over 85 percent of the world's supply of oil shale.

In most parts of the world, however, oil shale is mined for the purpose of being processed into crude oil. Many people believe that shale oil may one day help to meet the world's growing demand for petroleum, and perhaps extend the world's supply of crude oil for a while. Q34 However, it has yet to overcome a few important drawbacks. Q42(F) Oil shale mining can be very destructive to the environment, as it involves clearing land of trees and digging up large amounts of earth to uncover the oil shale. Another obstacle is in processing the raw materials. Q33 The most common method of processing oil shale is by heating it in a vacuum, causing it to release kerogen in the form of a vapor, which can then be trapped and distilled, creating a kind of synthetic crude oil. Q35 All this additional processing takes time and comes at a cost. At present, the process of mining and refining oil shale is very expensive, more so than that of producing traditional crude oil. As refining technology becomes more advanced, it will be cheaper to produce oil from these rocks, hopefully making shale oil as widely used as traditional oil.

Another nontraditional source of petroleum is oil sands. ①Oil sands occur when crude oil bubbles to the surface of the earth and ②mixes with water, dirt, and various bacteria ③which, over time, work to break the oil down into a very thick tar-like substance. Its thickness is so great that it cannot flow unless strongly heated.

혈암유(頁岩油)와 유사(油砂)

원유는 전 세계적으로 현대 생활 양식에서 없어서는 안 될 정착물이 되었다. 원유가 없으면, 현대인의 삶에 필수적인 자동차의 연료나 도로와 빌딩에 사용되는 아스팔트, 플라스틱이나 다른 석유 제품을 만드는 원자재도 없을 것이다. 매일 세계적으로 8천만 배럴의 석유가 소비되고, 이 소비량은 계속해서 늘어나고 있다. 불행히도 석유는 한정된 자원이고, 이 귀중한 자원의 수요가 급격히 상승하지만, 많은 전문가들은 세계의 석유 공급이 이미 최고점을 지나 이제 줄고 있다고 주장한다. 이런 이유로, 석유회사들은 원유를 공급할 새 자원 즉, 혈암유와 유사를 탐구하는 중이다.

혈암유는 석유의 기본 요소를 모두 갖추고 있는 유혈암이라는 물질에서 생산된다. 유혈암의 주성분은 유모(油母)인데 이는 원유보다 이전 단계인 퇴적암에서 발견되는 부식된 유기물이다. 이 물질은 이것이 함유된 암석에서 추출되어 사용 가능한 석유 형태로 정제될 수 있다. 유혈암은 쉽게 불에 타게 만드는 화학 요소를 포함하고 있어 선사시대부터 불을 피우는 원료로 쓰였다. 오늘날에도 몇몇 국가에서는 정제되지 않은 유혈암을 발전소의 연료로 사용하고 있다. 이 중에서 주목할만한 국가는 에스토니아인데, 거기에서는 자국산 유혈암이 원유보다 더 저렴하다. 세계에서 가장 큰 유혈암 매장층은 미국 서부 지역으로 그린리버 유역으로 알려져 있다. 이곳은 러시아, 브라질의 대규모 매장량과 함께 유혈암 세계 공급량의 85% 이상을 차지한다.

그러나 세계 대부분 지역에서 유혈암은 원유로 가공될 목적으로 채굴된다. 많은 이들은 증가하는 석유 수요를 충족하는 데 혈암유가 도움을 주고 원유의 세계 공급을 좀 더 연장할 수 있을 거로 생각한다. 그러나 아직 극복되어야 할 몇 가지 중요한 단점이 있다. 유혈암 채굴은 채굴을 위해 나무를 베고 땅을 많이 파야 하므로 환경을 크게 파괴시킬 수 있다. 또 다른 장애물은 원재료를 가공하는 과정에 있다. 유혈암을 가공하는 가장 일반적인 방법은 진공 상태에서 열을 가해 유모를 증기 형태로 추출하는 것이다. 그 후 모아지고 증류된 일종의 인조 원유를 만들어 낸다. 이러한 추가적 가공 과정 모두는 시간이 걸릴 뿐만 아니라 비용도 많이 든다. 현재 유혈암을 채굴하고 정제하는 과정에 드는 비용은 매우 비싸서 전통적인 원유 생산에 드는 비용보다 크다. 정제 기술이 더욱 발달함에 따라 이들 암석에서 석유를 생산하는 것이 더 저렴해질 것이고 바라건대 전통적인 석유만큼 혈암유가 널리 사용될 것이다.

예전과 다른 또 하나의 석유 공급원은 유사다. 유사는 원유 거품이 지면으로 올라와 물과 흙, 여러 박테리아와 혼합되고, 이 박테리아가 시간이 지나면서 석유를 점도 높은 타르와 비슷한 물질로 분해할 때 발생한다. 유사의 점도는 아주 높아 강하게 가열하지 않는 이상 흐르지 않는다. 그러나 이것의 묵직하고 끈적한 성질로 인해 아스팔트의 원료로 도로 포장에 쓰기 좋다. 오늘날 유사의 최대 공급

Q42(G) However, its heavy, sticky nature makes it handy for paving roads as a component of asphalt. Q42(D) Today, the largest supply of oil sands can be found in Canada and Venezuela. Q42(B) Presently, oil sand reserves account for two-thirds of the world's entire supply of petroleum.

Today, the only nation with a large-scale, commercially exploited oil sands industry is Canada. Oil sands account for nearly half of Canada's total oil production; production is so great, in fact, that Canada has become the number one supplier of oil to the United States, surpassing even Middle Eastern oil-producing nations. A Q42(I) Because oil sands are too thick to flow like regular crude oil, they do not pool into the kind of pressurized wells from which traditional oil is often pumped. B However, wells can be artificially created by injecting hot steam into large reserves of oil sands, simultaneously heating and diluting them so that they flow more like crude oil. C Q41 Q42(A) Only then can the oil sands be extracted; and as with shale oil, this mining process can be quite expensive and use a great deal of energy. D Adding to the expense is the cost of shipping oil sands, as they are too thick to flow through traditional pipelines. Q39 Q40 Experts continue to look for cheaper and more efficient methods of mining and processing oil sands, as their abundance could have a major impact on the world's falling supply of oil in the near future.

국은 캐나다와 베네수엘라이다. 현재 유사 매장량은 세계 전체 석유 공급의 3분의 2를 차지한다.

오늘날 대규모 상업적 목적으로 유사 개발 산업을 갖추고 있는 유일한 나라는 캐나다이다. 유사는 캐나다의 전체 석유 생산의 절반 정도를 차지하며 생산량이 뛰어나서 사실상 캐나다는 중동의 석유 생산 국가들을 앞지르고 미국의 최대 석유 공급자가 되었다. A 유사는 점도가 너무 높아 원유처럼 흐르지 않기 때문에 전통적인 석유를 퍼내는 데 사용하는 가압 유정에 들어가지 않는다. B 하지만 유사 매장지에 뜨거운 증기를 주입하고 동시에 열을 가하고 희석하면, 원유처럼 흐르게 되어 인공적으로 유정을 만들어낼 수 있다. C 그래야만 유사가 추출되는데, 혈암유와 마찬가지로 채굴 과정이 상당히 비싸고 많은 에너지를 소모한다. D 운반 비용은 생산비를 높이는 데 한몫을 하는데, 이는 유사의 점도가 너무 높아서 전통적인 송유관을 통해 흐르지 않기 때문이다. 전문가들은 유사를 좀 더 저렴하고 좀 더 효율적인 방법으로 채굴하고 생산할 방법을 계속 찾고 있는데, 이는 그것들의 풍부한 매장량이 가까운 미래 세계 석유의 감소하는 공급량에 주요한 영향을 미칠 수 있기 때문이다.

29 지문의 summit 과 의미상 가장 가까운 것은?
 (A) 최하점
 (B) 최고점
 (C) 평균
 (D) 한계

해설 | Vocabulary   지문에서 세계의 석유 공급이 이미 summit 을 지나 이제 줄고 있다고 하였으므로, summit 이 '최고점'의 의미임을 추측할 수 있다.

30 지문에서 This substance 가 가리키는 것은?
 (A) 혈암유
 (B) 유모
 (C) 석유
 (D) 원유

해설 | Reference   문장에서 This substance 는 암석에서 추출된다고 했는데 바로 앞 문장 "… kerogen, the decayed organic matter found in sedimentary rock …"으로부터 This substance 는 kerogen이라는 것을 알 수 있다.

31 지문의 readily 와 의미상 가장 가까운 것은?
 (A) 효율적으로
 (B) 천천히
 (C) 빠르게
 (D) 쉽게

해설 | Vocabulary   readily 는 '손쉽게'라는 의미이다.

32 단락 2에 따르면, 혈암유에 관한 내용으로 옳지 않은 것은?
 (A) 유기물로부터 생성된다.
 (B) 정제되지 않아도 화력원으로 쓰일 수 있다.
 (C) 아직 실용화될 준비가 되지 않았다.
 (D) 미국, 러시아, 브라질에 매장량이 많다.

해설 | Negative Fact   혈암유는 부식된 유기물인 유모라는 물질을 가공한 것이며, 가공하지 않아도 화력원으로 사용할 수 있고, 일부 국가는 오늘날에도 혈암유를 가공하지 않은 채 사용하고 있다고 한다. 또한 혈암유는 미국, 러시아, 브라질에 매장량이 많다. (C)는 본문의 내용과 정반대의 내용이다.

33 지문의 synthetic 과 의미상 가장 가까운 것은?
 (A) 원시적인
 (B) 실용적인
 (C) 인공적인
 (D) 비실용적인

해설 | Vocabulary   synthetic 은 인위적으로 유혈암을 가공하는 과정이 나오는 문장의 앞부분에서 단어의 의미를 추정할 수 있다. "… heating it in a vacuum, causing it to release kerogen in the form of a vapor, which can then be trapped and distilled …"는 원유를 생산하기 위해 인위적으로 가공하는 과정이다. 여기에서 synthetic 은 '인공적인'의 의미를 알 수 있다.

34 단락 3에서 필자가 유혈암을 채굴하는 과정에 대해 자세히 언급하는 이유는?

(A) 원유의 채굴 과정과 비교하기 위해
(B) 유혈암이 원유보다 더 싼 연료 원임을 주장하기 위해
(C) 유혈암이 대체 연료원이 될 수 있다는 주장을 반박하기 위해
(D) 유혈암 개발에 있어서 문제점을 보여주기 위해

해설 | Rhetorical Purpose 단락 3에서 필자는 "However, it has yet to overcome a few important drawbacks"를 통해 유혈암 개발 과정에 문제점이 있음을 시사하고 있다. 뒤이어 유혈암 채굴 과정을 보여주면서, 채굴 과정에서 환경 파괴가 일어난다는 사실을 언급하여 유혈암 개발의 문제점을 시사하고 있다.

35 단락 3에 따르면, 유혈암 가공에 대해 추론할 수 있는 것은?

(A) 예부터 따라온 관행이다.
(B) 환경에 해롭다.
(C) 매우 제한적으로 사용되고 있다.
(D) 실용화되기엔 비용이 너무 많이 든다.

해설 | Inference 단락 3의 마지막 부분에서 유혈암을 가공하는 과정은 시간이 오래 걸리고 비용도 많이 든다고 설명한다. 또 단락의 마지막 문장에서 가공 기술이 발달함에 따라 유혈암의 생산비가 저렴해져서 앞으로는 혈암유가 더욱 널리 보급되리라 전망하는 대목에서 현재는 아직 널리 사용되지 않고 그 사용이 제한적임을 알 수 있다.

36 다음 중 지문에서 표시된 문장의 주요 정보를 가장 잘 나타낸 문장은? 정답 외의 보기들은 중요한 의미가 바뀌거나 주요 정보가 빠져 있다.

(A) 원유 거품이 지면으로 솟아오르면 박테리아와 물에 의해 유사라는 점도가 높은 물질로 변하게 된다.
(B) 유사는 지면으로 올라온 석유의 매장물이 오랫동안 물과 흙, 박테리아에 노출되면서 생기는 타르와 비슷한 물질이다.
(C) 원유는 유사의 거품이 지면으로 올라 수년에 걸쳐 물, 흙과 함께 섞이면서 생기는 물질이다.
(D) 물과 흙, 박테리아는 원유와 섞여 유사라는 타르 성분으로 변해 거품 형태로 지면에 나오게 된다.

해설 | Sentence Simplification 표시된 문장은 크게 세 의미로 나뉠 수 있다. ①유사는 원유 거품이 지면으로 올라오며 생성된다. ②원유 거품이 물과 흙, 박테리아와 섞인다. ③시간이 지나며 석유를 점도 높은 타르와 같은 물질로 분해한다.

37 지문의 exploited 와 의미상 가장 가까운 것은?

(A) 개발하다
(B) 얻다
(C) 바꾸다
(D) 저장하다

해설 | Vocabulary exploited 는 '(자원 등을) 개발하다'의 의미이다.

38 지문의 simultaneously 와 의미상 가장 가까운 것은?

(A) 극도로
(B) 동시에
(C) 각각
(D) 제때에

해설 | Vocabulary simultaneously 는 '동시에'의 의미이다.

39 지문에서 their 가 가리키는 것은?

(A) 유사
(B) 매장량
(C) 방법
(D) 전문가

해설 | Reference 전문가들은 좀 더 효율적인 유사 채굴 방법을 연구 중이라고 하였고, "… their abundance could have a major impact on the world's falling supply of oil in the near future"에서 their 는 세계 석유 공급량과 직접적인 관계가 있는 대상임을 알 수 있다.

40 단락 5에 따르면, 혈암유와 유사가 중요한 이유는?

(A) 가정에 더 저렴한 에너지를 제공한다.
(B) 청정 연료로 만들어질 수 있다.
(C) 줄어드는 석유 공급률을 채워줄 수 있다.
(D) 머지않아 소모될 가능성이 있다.

해설 | Factual Information 단락 5의 마지막 문장에서 혈암유와 유사는 가까운 미래에 세계 석유 공급에 주요한 영향을 미칠 수 있다고 설명한다.

41 다음 문장이 지문에 들어갈 곳을 나타내는 네 개의 사각형[■]을 보시오.

> 운반 비용은 생산비를 높이는 데 한몫을 하는데, 이는 유사의 점도가 너무 높아서 전통적인 송유관을 통해 흐르지 않기 때문이다.

이 문장이 들어갈 가장 적절한 위치는?

(A) A (B) B (C) C (D) D

해설 | Sentence Insertion 삽입 문장은 유사 운반 비용에 대해 언급하고 있다. 그런데 Adding to the expense로부터 삽입 문장 앞에도 유사에 들어가는 비용에 관한 내용이 나와야 함을 알 수 있다. 따라서 삽입 문장은 "… this mining process can be quite expensive and use a great deal of energy" 뒤에 위치해야 가장 자연스럽다.

42 보기에서 적절한 문구를 골라 관련된 석유의 종류와 연결하시오. 보기 중 2개는 사용되지 않는다. *이 문제는 4점이다.*

보기	석유의 종류
(A) 채굴 과정에서 비용이 많이 든다. (B) 세계 석유 공급의 2/3를 차지한다. (C) 선사시대 사람들이 불을 피우는 데 사용했다. (D) 베네수엘라에 대량의 매장물이 있다. (E) 석유와는 다르게 재생 가능 에너지원이다. (F) 환경을 훼손시키는 채굴 기술을 사용한다. (G) 예전부터 아스팔트의 재료로 쓰였다. (H) 원유보다 청정 연료가 될 가능성이 있다. (I) 매우 걸쭉하고 점성이 높으므로 복잡한 가공 과정을 거친다.	혈암유 • (C) • (F) 유사 • (B) • (D) • (G) • (I) 둘 다 • (A)

해설 | Fill in a Table 지문은 혈암유와 유사를 비교하고 있다. 혈암유는 선사시대 때부터 불을 피우는 원료로 사용되었고, 채굴 과정에서 환경을 파괴하고 가공 과정에서 비용과 시간이 많이 든다. 유사는 걸쭉하고 점성이 높은 성질 때문에 아스팔트의 원료로 쓰이고, 캐나다와 베네수엘라에 매장량이 풍부하고 전체 석유 공급량의 2/3를 차지한다. 점성이 매우 높으므로 이것을 연료로 이용하려면 복잡한 가공 과정을 거쳐야 하며 채굴 과정에서 비용이 많이 들고 복잡한 처리 과정을 거쳐야 한다.

어휘 | **crude oil** 원유 **fixture** 정착물 **raw material** 원자재 **valuable** 귀중한 **petroleum** 석유 **shale oil** 혈암유(頁岩油) **oil sand** 유사(油砂) **oil shale** 유혈암 **kerogen** 유모(油母) **decay** 부식하다 **sedimentary** 퇴적물의 **precede** ~에 앞서다 **refine** 정제하다 **usable** 사용할 수 있는 **flammable** 인화성의 **unrefined** 정제되지 않은 **notable** 주목할 만한 **domestic** 자국의 **deposit** 매장층, 보증금 **basin** 분지, 하천 유역 **reserves** 매장량 **mine** 채굴하다 **process** 가공하다 **demand** 수요 **extend** 늘리다, 확장하다 **overcome** 극복하다 **destructive** 파괴적인 **distill** 증류하다 **hopefully** 바라건대 **nontraditional** 예전과 다른 **tar** 타르 **thickness** 점도, 농도 **account for** ~을 이루다 **commercially** 상업적으로 **exploit** (자원을) 개발하다 **surpass** ~를 앞지르다 **well** 유정(油井) **inject** ~를 주입하다 **simultaneously** 동시에 **dilute** (맑게) 희석하다 **pipeline** 송유관 **abundance** 풍부함

MEMO

MEMO